Volumes in This Series

Reports

1. *A Survey of Sardis and the Major Monuments Outside the City Walls,* by George M. A. Hanfmann and Jane C. Waldbaum (1975)

Monographs

1. *Byzantine Coins,* by George E. Bates (1971)
2. *Ancient Literary Sources on Sardis,* by John G. Pedley (1972)
3. *Neue epichorische Schriftzeugnisse aus Sardis,* by Roberto Gusmani (1975)
4. *Byzantine and Turkish Sardis,* by Clive Foss (1976)

ARCHAEOLOGICAL EXPLORATION
OF SARDIS

General Editors

Fogg Art Museum of Harvard University
Cornell University
Corning Museum of Glass
Sponsored by the American Schools
of Oriental Research

George M. A. Hanfmann and
Stephen W. Jacobs

Report 1

A SURVEY OF SARDIS AND THE MAJOR MONUMENTS OUTSIDE THE CITY WALLS

*George M. A. Hanfmann
and Jane C. Waldbaum*

with contributions by
*David Van Zanten, Stuart L. Carter,
Clive Foss, Ruth S. Thomas,
Kenneth J. Frazer,
Crawford H. Greenewalt, Jr.*

*Harvard University Press
Cambridge, Massachusetts
and London, England*   1975

Library of Congress Cataloging in Publication Data

Archaeological Exploration of Sardis.
   A survey of Sardis and the major monuments outside the
city walls.

   (Report—Archaeological Exploration of Sardis ; 1)
   Includes indexes.
   1. Sardis—Antiquities. I. Hanfmann, George Maxim Anossov,
1911–   II. Waldbaum, Jane C., 1940–   III. Title.
IV. Series: Archaeological Exploration of Sardis. Report—
Archaeological Exploration of Sardis.
DS156.S3A8 1975   939.2'2   75-17973
ISBN 0-674-85751-8

CONTENTS

PREFACE

This is the first of the final reports on the work of the Archaeological Exploration of Sardis from 1958 to 1973.[1] The Archaeological Exploration of Sardis had its inception in 1955, when the Bollingen Foundation of New York agreed to consider a proposal by George M. A. Hanfmann, then Professor of Fine Arts, Harvard University, to resume excavations at Sardis in 1958 on behalf of the Fogg Art Museum of Harvard University. Cornell University joined the endeavor upon the initiative of Albert Henry Detweiler, then President of the American Schools of Oriental Research and Professor of Architecture at Cornell. Previously, the American Society for the Excavation of Sardis had sent an expedition from 1910 to 1914 under Howard Crosby Butler of Princeton University, and again under T. L. Shear in 1922. The new Sardis program was sponsored by the American Schools of Oriental Research, which consented to act as recipients from 1958-1968 of Bollingen and Old Dominion Foundation grants.[2]

Since 1957 G. M. A. Hanfmann has guided the project, first as Field Director and later as Director. A. H. Detweiler was Field Advisor (1958), then Associate Director (1959-1970) of the Sardis project. With Detweiler's untimely death in 1970, Stephen W. Jacobs assumed the duties of Associate Director. At Harvard the Fogg Art Museum is responsible for the project and at Cornell the College of Architecture (later College of Architecture, Art, and Planning) is the principal interested division. Crawford H. Greenewalt, Jr., University of California, Berkeley, and David G. Mitten,

Harvard University, served as Assistant Directors; Greenewalt also served as Field Director in 1973 and 1974. Gustavus F. Swift, Jr., University of Chicago, acted as Administrative Financial Officer (1960-1968). In the field, Kenneth J. Frazer (1963-1972) was first Administrative Assistant, then General Manager (as well as architect), and Gülerçan Ugurluer was Administrative Assistant from 1972 to 1974. As recorder and informal supervisor of the camp, Ilse Hanfmann made an essential contribution to the organization of the project (1958-1971). Through 1974, 145 American specialists and students as well as 65 Turkish scholars, students, and assistants and 14 participants from other countries have taken part in the excavations. An informal account of the development of the project from 1957-1971 is found in *Letters from Sardis* (1972) where a complete list of participants is given.

A special research facility at Harvard was established in 1968 with Jane A. Scott as supervisor; architectural records are maintained at the College of Architecture at Cornell under the guidance of S. W. Jacobs.

From 1960 to 1972 the Corning Museum of Glass was a participant, providing annual grants. Axel von Saldern, then Curator (1960, 1968), R. H. Brill, Administrator of Scientific Research (1962, 1964), and Paul Perrot (1964), then Director, worked at Sardis on the ancient and Byzantine glass. The Massachusetts Institute of Technology participated from 1962 to 1964 in a project carried on by David Greenewalt, who investigated the application of geophysics to archaeological problems.

Our greatest debt is to our host country, whose historical heritage we are privileged to study. In

---

1. Contrary to an earlier announcement (*Sardis* Ml [1971] v) these comprehensive reports will be referred to as *Sardis* R1, R2, and so on, rather than *Sardis* 21.

2. In 1969 a policy change terminated all direct sponsorship of field work by the Schools.

1957 the Council of Ministers of the Republic of Turkey issued the permit for the Harvard-Cornell excavations at Sardis. The Sardis program then prospered under the administrative care of the Department of Antiquities and Museums of the Ministry of National Education (until 1970), thereafter under the Ministry of the Prime Minister, and since 1974 under the Ministry of Culture. We are grateful to the Department of Antiquities and Museums who shared some of the initial costs for camp construction and to the Special Trust Commission for administering grants from the Department of Antiquities and Museums used in restoring the Roman Gymnasium complex (1965–1973). We are greatly indebted to the successive Directors General and Associate and Assistant Directors of the Department and their staff for their help and understanding. The present Director General Hikmet Gürçay has been a valued friend of the project for many years.

The Director of the Manisa Museum, Kemal Ziya Polatkan, aided the expedition from its beginnings in many ways. He served as Government Representative (Commissioner) from 1958 to 1965. We are also greatly indebted to his successors as Government Representatives, Musa Baran, Osman Aksoy, Güldem Yüğrüm, and Attila Tulga for their unfailing help.

In Ankara the Institute for Palaeoanthropology, first under Muzaffer Şenyürek (1958–1960; died 1960), then Enver Bostancı (1962–1971) was responsible for study and conservation of human skeletal material. The Veterinary Faculty of the University of Ankara, with Professor Sabri Doğuer leading a team of six experts, undertook the study of animal bones found from 1958 to 1965. In 1962 and 1963 M. Saydamer of the Institute for Mineral Research, Ankara, shared with us the results of his study of the alluvia of the Pactolus.

Other Turkish collaborating institutions from 1968 to 1970 have included the Geological Department of Ege University (E. İzdar, R. Ardos, H. Bremer, O. Kaya), the Nuclear Research Center, Çekmece (1968, Sait Akpınar, Director, Talât Erben, Chemistry Department, Sevim Okar, Ayfer Aydın), and the Mineral Research Institute (MTA), Ankara, Sadrettin Alpan, Director, and Nilüfer Bayçın, Head of the Technical Laboratory.

Throughout the work of the expedition, the several Consuls and Consuls General of the United States Consulate in Izmir and their staffs were of great assistance to the expedition. The United States Embassy in Ankara was always helpful, especially in connection with administration of the grant made by the Department of State under Public Law 480 (No. SCC 29 543) from 1962 to 1966.

The expedition was started with grants by private foundations and contributions by individual donors. Grants have been received from the Bollingen Foundation (1959–1965), Old Dominion Foundation (1966–1968), Loeb Classical Library Foundation (1965–1970), Memorial Foundation for Jewish Culture (made in 1966), Wenner-Gren Foundation for Anthropological Research (1967), the Billy Rose Foundation (1970–1974), and the Charles E. Merrill Trust (1973). Cornell University contributed university funds from 1958 to 1967. The Ford Foundation gave a grant for the training of students (1968–1972) through Cornell University. Several private donations were received through the American Schools of Oriental Research. The major continuing support has come from an informal group known as the Supporters of Sardis, which includes individuals and many smaller foundations. The faith of our leading supporters, notably Mrs. George C. Keiser, Nanette B. Rodney, Mrs. J. W. Totten, Alice Tully, J. B. Elliott, T. B. Lemann, and Norbert Schimmel, has encouraged us to meet many challenges during these years.

We take this opportunity to express the gratitude of the Sardis program to the successive Presidents and Deans of Harvard and Cornell Universities and to the Presidents and officers of the several foundations for their furtherance of our work. For sustained personal interest in Sardis we are especially grateful to John D. Barrett and Ernest J. Brooks of the Bollingen and Old Dominion Foundations and to James R. Cherry of the Billy Rose Foundation.

Assistance from the United States Government first became a major factor with a grant in Turkish currency (No. SCC 29 543) made by the Department of State for the period 1962 to 1965 to the President and Fellows of Harvard College, under the Mutual Educational and Cultural Act, Public Law 87–256, and Agricultural Trade Development and Assistance Act, Public Law 480 as amended. A series of grants from the National Endowment for the Humanities, made through Harvard University, has been of great importance for continuation of the project from 1967 on (Grant Nos. H67–0–56, H68–0–61, H69–0–23, RO–111–70–3966, RO–4999–71–171, RO–6435–72–264, RO–8359–73–217, RO–10405–74–319). Most of the work for this volume was performed with the aid of these grants. We acknowledge gratefully the vital role of the Endowment in pioneering effective federal support of cultural undertakings.

The first version of this volume was put together by J. C. Waldbaum and subsequently revised by G. M. A. Hanfmann with the assistance of Julia Mansfield and Hetty Joyce. Final preparation of the manuscript for publication was carried out by Electra D. Yorsz in collaboration with Jane A. Scott. The index was prepared by Electra D. Yorsz.

We would like to thank Ilse Hanfmann for identifying Hellenistic relief ware mentioned in this volume, James Wrabetz for identifying the sigillate wares, and Jane A. Scott for help with the lamps and early travelers. We were able to draw on preliminary versions of coin catalogs of Greek and Roman coins by A. E. M. Johnston and T. V. Buttrey. L. J. Majewski advised us on questions concerning wall paintings and interior decoration; Fikret K. Yegül and Andrew R. Seager gave important suggestions for the architectural analysis of Bath CG. R. Lindley Vann advised on the unexcavated buildings, which will be published in a forthcoming volume.

Many architects, draftsmen, and photographers have contributed their work to this publication: Richard H. Penner, Fikret K. Yegül, Margaretta J. Darnell, Stuart L. Carter, David Van Zanten, Kenneth J. Frazer, Leon Satkowski, Robert P. Lewis, R. Lindley Vann, Edward D. Russell, K. Paul Zygas, Martha Hoppin, and Elizabeth Gombosi. Stuart L. Carter, Elizabeth Wahle, and Elizabeth Gombosi prepared the final version of the illustrations. All illustrations are provided by the Archaeological Exploration of Sardis unless otherwise indicated.

This, the first in the series of comprehensive final excavation reports, contains introductory chapters on the ecology and history of the urban areas of Sardis and the Sardis region, a description of the Late Roman city walls, and accounts of two major excavation areas located outside the walls: the region in the Pactolus Valley around the Artemis sanctuary, and the Roman-Byzantine Bath CG, east of the city area. The chapters on the Artemis sanctuary present the first detailed description of the entire precinct and record the results of new investigations of the temple and its altars. They include material ranging from Lydian to Byzantine times. Adjacent to the precinct is the excavation in the Northeast Wadi which yielded interesting Lydian remains. The situation described is in general that of 1972 but we have added the most important results of the 1973 campaign to the description of the Artemis Precinct.

The pottery and other objects found at these sectors are treated more extensively in other volumes of the series. The finds mentioned in this volume were selected for their chronological significance to the sector in which they were excavated. Most objects found by the expedition are currently stored in the depots of the Sardis Expedition at Sardis; some are in the Archaeological Museum at Manisa where most of the finds will eventually be permanently housed.

Our thanks go to all staff members in Turkey, the United States, and several European countries for their dedicated work, and especially to archaeologists Donald P. Hansen, Baki Öğün, K. J. Frazer, and C. H. Greenewalt, Jr., who excavated the Artemis Precinct region, and to Sherman E. Johnson, Marion Dean Ross, Mario Del Chiaro, and Duane W. Roller who had a major share in the excavations at Bath CG.

The publication of this volume has been made possible by a generous subvention from the James Morton Paton Memorial Fund of the Department of the Classics, Harvard University, and by the Sardis Publication Fund of the Fogg Art Museum, Harvard University.

George M. A. Hanfmann
Stephen W. Jacobs
Jane C. Waldbaum

Technical Abbreviations

a.s.l.	above sea level	mm.	millimeters
b	bottom	Munsell	Soil color charts produced
bw	bottom of wall		by Munsell Color Company,
C (preceding numeral)	coin		Inc. (Baltimore, Md. 1971),
ca.	circa		for color abbreviations and
cent.	century		equivalents
cm.	centimeters	N	north
D.	depth	obv.	obverse
diam.	diameter	P (preceding numeral)	pottery
E	east	P. diam.	preserved diameter
est.	estimated	P.H.	preserved height
ext.	exterior	P.L.	preserved length
G (preceding numeral)	glass	P.W.	preserved width
g.	gram	r.	right
H.	height	rev.	reverse
illeg.	illegible	S	south
IN (preceding numeral)	inscription	S (preceding numeral)	sculpture
inscr.	inscribed	SAS	Sardis Area Survey of 1962
int.	interior	T (preceding numeral)	terracotta
km.	kilometer	*t*	top
L (preceding numeral)	lamp	Th.	thickness
L.	length	*tw*	top of wall
l.	left	W	west
M (preceding numeral)	metal	W.	width
m.	meters	WP (preceding numeral)	wall painting
max.	maximum	Wt.	weight
mg.	milligram	* (preceding numeral)	level (e.g. *98.00)

A SURVEY OF
SARDIS
AND THE
MAJOR MONUMENTS
OUTSIDE THE
CITY WALLS

I A SURVEY AND SECTOR INDEX OF SARDIS

George M. A. Hanfmann
Stuart L. Carter
Jane C. Waldbaum

The general location and the name of Sardis have never been lost.[1] When in 1369 the patriarch of Constantinople transferred the archbishopric from Sardis to Philadelphia, he was entirely certain of the location of Sardis, even if he did describe it as a "field of desolation."[2] The Italian merchant who was the host of Cyriacus of Ancona in 1446 unhesitatingly led him from Foça to "the capital of Croesus." Here the founding father of Greek epigraphy measured the columns of the temple and tried to pan gold in the Pactolus. Cyriacus was perfectly sure that he was at Sardis and did not hesitate to identify Sart Çay as the Pactolus;[3] he also copied some inscriptions.[4] Thus the study of the ruins of Sardis by European scholars began as early as that of the ruins of Greece.[5]

Excavations

Treasure hunting and clandestine digging have been going on at Sardis probably since the time of Croesus. Already Lydians may have dug up the tombs of their ancestors. We have found definite evidence of Roman and medieval digging at Bin Tepe.[6] Modern scientific excavation began with H. Spiegelthal, who was Prussian Consul in Smyrna in the 1850s. In 1853 he established a camp on the royal cemetery of Bin Tepe, tunneled into the Mound of Alyattes, and found the chamber (or "a chamber"). Spiegelthal's work at the Alyattes Mound was remarkably well observed, illustrated, and reported. It is a pity that no similar account exists of his other efforts. It seems possible that he tried the Gyges Mound as well.[7]

George Dennis, at one time British Consul in Smyrna, is famed for his classic account of *Cities and Cemeteries of Etruria.* While he himself never published his researches, drawings and descriptions of some of the chamber tombs in the royal cemetery of Bin Tepe, which he researched in 1882, were published by Auguste Choisy,[8] and two reliefs discovered by Dennis are in the British Museum.[9] In the city area of Sardis Dennis dug a trench through the Artemis Temple in 1882, finding a colossal head of the Empress Faustina, now in the British Museum.[10] Choisy made interesting but schematized drawings of Buildings B, C, and D and raised the controversial issue of the use of pendentives in the Central Hall of the Gymnasium (now Building B).[11]

"Sardis impatiently awaits my spade . . ." There is no telling what Heinrich Schliemann, discoverer of Aegean Mycenae and prehistoric Troy, might have found at Sardis had he been able to realize his plan to dig there, a plan to which he repeatedly alluded in his letters in 1879 and 1880.[12] As it was, it fell to a remarkable American archaeologist to conduct the first large-scale excavations at Sardis.

Howard Crosby Butler

According to his biographer, H. F. Osborn, Howard Crosby Butler had been invited by the Turkish government to excavate at Sardis;[13] Butler himself says nothing about it. His expedition was planned with sweep and imagination. It was remarkably strong on engineering, architecture, and epigraphy, architecture having been Butler's main interest during his previous work in Syria.[14]

Butler himself has given in *Sardis* I (1922) a concise, eloquent summary of the historical significance of Sardis, of the character of the site and its archaeological promises and obstacles, and of the five campaigns, 1910–1914, which he conducted at Sardis. He had planned a long-term effort, but the outbreak of World War I in 1914 caught the expedition by surprise; some of the material was destroyed and the expedition house ruined. Butler died on his way back from Turkey in 1921. His lieutenant, Theodore Leslie Shear, made a valiant comeback in the midst of the Turkish-Greek war in 1922 but had to leave. After a stint of digging at Corinth, he was entrusted with the giant task of conducting the excavations of the Agora in Athens and never returned to Sardis.

Princeton University has maintained a Sardis archive with Butler's and Shear's records and photographs (glass plates, many of which have deteriorated). In 1953, before the present Harvard-Cornell Expedition began, G. M. A. Hanfmann discussed the possibilities of a joint Princeton enterprise at Sardis with Erik Sjöquist of Princeton, who, however, had already made plans for a Princeton excavation at Morgantina in Sicily.

The character and scope of Butler's work was determined by his decision to excavate the colossal Temple of Artemis. Proceeding with admirable technical ingenuity and using a railway crane and up to three hundred workers, he accomplished this goal in five seasons. Fortunately for his successors he lived to complete at least the draft of his publication, which was published posthumously by the epigrapher W. H. Buckler and the architect C. N. Read.[15] The treatment of the temple was thorough

and penetrating. It also contained a brief account of Church M attached to the temple. Other buildings and monuments of the Artemis Precinct were only cursorily mapped on the precinct plan and described in the general account of the excavations.

Butler's second major effort was the opening of more than 1,100 Lydian graves. This too was published only in summary form. G. H. Chase, who came out in 1914 to study the pottery, made a list of the graves and of their contents. He listed 1104 as his last number.[16] Only some seventy, however, had yielded any objects and only two appeared to have been untouched by earlier diggers. The great majority of these graves were cut into the precipitous cliffs of the western cemetery hills. Butler's excellent topographer Lloyd T. Emory had done a general contour map of the area in 1913 but to survey these precipices for a detailed map is a risky enterprise. Thus the graves opened were never located on a map; only a few drawings and photographs of chamber tombs published in *Sardis* I (1922) are identifiable with Chase's (unpublished) numbers.

The pottery, metal objects, jewelry, and seals from these graves, although not closely datable, gave the first reliable indications of the material culture of the Lydians. Architectural terracottas were published by T. L. Shear; jewelry and seals were published as a monograph by C. Densmore Curtis. Pottery, metal objects, sculpture, lamps, and glass became known only through summary references and a limited number of illustrations in *Sardis* I (1922).[17]

A column of the Artemis Temple, some sculptures, about sixty vases, and other objects were brought to the Metropolitan Museum in New York in 1916; and after T. L. Shear's campaign more were added, including the famous pot of gold, a small lydion with gold staters of Croesus.[18] A small selection of objects went to Princeton. The Istanbul Museum eventually received all of the jewelry, apparently almost all of the coins, and a number of other objects, as well as the most important sculptures. Some pots, inscriptions, and sculptures came to the museum in Izmir and a few to the museum in Manisa.

As to the Lydian city, first Butler (1914) then Shear came upon Lydian house walls in the so-called Northeast Wadi.[19] No detailed reports were published. A terrace across the Pactolus from the temple may have had a Lydian house; many architectural terracottas were found reused in later graves.[20] T. L. Shear had dug at Bin Tepe in 1914, and in 1922 he made some soundings on the Acropolis. He had no time to record them in drawings and the results were inconclusive.[21] Butler himself remained in doubt whether the Lydian city was confined to the Pactolus Valley or extended along the east-west highway in the Hermus Valley as well. The Hellenistic, Roman and Early Byzantine ruins visible above ground were entered on Emory's survey, as was the City Wall. Butler mentioned them in his brief, masterly account of Sardis in the introductory pages of *Sardis* I, but he knew that nothing certain could be said about most of them without excavations. Apart from a few stray finds of sculpture and inscriptions nothing substantial was added in the field to our knowledge of Sardis after 1922.

Careful reading of H. C. Butler's own statement (*Sardis* I [1922] ix, x), inquiries made since 1938, and knowledge of local conditions leads us to believe that the following were lost in the destruction and pilfering of the Princeton expedition house in 1921: (1) a number of complete vases left in the excavation house. As most vases mentioned by Butler and Chase are accounted for by vases now in New York, Istanbul, and Izmir, they were not very numerous. (2) Lamps. (3) Glass. These were apparently simply smashed into the ground. Not much seems to be known about the fate of several sculptures. The major Lydian monument, that of Nannas, is accounted for by pieces in Istanbul and New York. Some other pieces are in Istanbul and Manisa. The horsehead in Baltimore is still the only large object which was removed.[22] But some sculptures reproduced in *Sardis* I (1922) do not seem to exist anywhere. As to metal objects, some have been emerging in the Istanbul Museum.[23] One of a set of four golden lions, apparently concealed by workmen during excavation, is in the Ashmolean Museum.[24]

The Harvard-Cornell Archaeological Exploration of Sardis

Preliminary reports published in the *Bulletin of the American Schools of Oriental Research* (*BASOR*) and in the *Dergi* of the Department of Antiquities of the Turkish Republic constitute a chronological account of the development of the activities of the Harvard-Cornell Expedition.[25] An informal book of *Letters from Sardis* unfolds the same story from a somewhat different viewpoint.[26] We do not propose to give yet another chronological account; instead, a brief survey of the areas worked will be followed by a chapter on the regional topography of Sardis and the development of the city as far as it may be ascertained with the help of the results of our expedition.

In order to permit the reader to orient himself, we give in the following pages a brief summary of major areas excavated between 1958 and 1973 with reference to the site plan (Fig. 1) and the regional map (Fig. 2). A discussion of topographic survey and the grid system is given by S. L. Carter;[27] detailed data on various excavated sectors and unexcavated ancient surface remains are given by S. L. Carter and J. C. Waldbaum in the Sector Index, *infra*.

City Area of Sardis

East of the Sart Çay (Pactolus) Bridge we have excavated and partly restored the area of the Roman Gymnasium-Bath, Synagogue, and Main Avenue (Fig. 1 Nos. 1–3). Apart from the front of a Hellenistic structure, the buildings were largely Roman and Late Antique (Early Byzantine). Immediately south of the Gymnasium area lies the House of Bronzes (HoB) area (Fig. 1 No. 4). It includes the Lydian Market (Lydian Trench), ranging from ca. 1400 B.C. to A.D. 616 with exposures of Lydian strata of the seventh and sixth centuries B.C. most important. It borders eastward on the Roman Building R (Fig. 1 No. 59) and northward on the House of Bronzes proper, a Late Roman-Early Byzantine structure of the fifth and sixth centuries A.D. (Fig. 1 No. 4). Excavations at a Late Roman colonnaded street and two trenches with Byzantine structures (Middle Terrace and Upper Terrace; Fig. 1 Nos. 58, 5, 5a, 5b) are southward extensions of the same area. A Late Hellenistic and Early Roman cemetery (second century B.C. to second century A.D.?) are at the north edge of the entire HoB area.

Three major sectors are on the eastern bank of the Sart Çay (Pactolus) Valley. Proceeding from north to south they are the Pactolus North (PN), the Pactolus Cliff (PC), and the Artemis Precinct (AT) areas. The Pactolus North area (Fig. 1 No. 10) has the Pactolus Industrial Area (PIA) to the north (Fig. 1 No. 7); the Early Christian Basilica EA and the Middle Byzantine Church E to the east (Fig. 1 No. 11) are attached to PN. The Lydian, Persian, and Early Hellenistic levels (seventh century to 213 B.C.) have yielded the best evidence for urban architecture and a precinct for purification of gold (ca. 600 to 560 B.C.). These strata are overlaid in part by Roman, Byzantine, and Turkish constructions, the latter still continuing in the modern village houses.

Pactolus Cliff (Fig. 1 No. 13) has revealed a sequence from Lydian (seventh century B.C.) to Byzantine (sixth century A.D.) with Hellenistic and Roman chamber tombs superseding Lydian habitations.

The Artemis Precinct proper (Fig. 1 No. 17) was already excavated to a considerable extent by H. C. Butler but we have made soundings in the temple and precinct which have confirmed the existence of a Lydian-Persian altar and have clarified the sequences of Hellenistic, Roman, and Byzantine monuments. We have also cleaned and repaired the Early Byzantine Church M attached to the temple (Fig. 1 No. 18). Connected with the Artemis Precinct in antiquity, the Northeast Wadi (torrent bed; NEW, Fig. 1 No. 16) yielded Lydian structures of the sixth century B.C.

Work on the Acropolis included testing the three major areas surviving at the top of the citadel (AcN, AcT, AcS, north, top, and south; Fig. 1 Nos. 20.1–20.3). There, Lydian masonry terraces from a monumental building (AcN) and a Lydian floor and pits (AcT), both presumably of the sixth century B.C., were the only definite remnants earlier than the fortress, settlement, and cemeteries of the Byzantine and Turkish periods (possibly A.D. 616 to

1425). A short stretch of a powerful defensive wall, either Lydian or Persian (AcS-PH 1, 2, 3; Fig. 1 No. 52), was found on the south slope. A tunnel of uncertain date, winding up through north slopes of the Acropolis, was explored (TU, Fig. 1 No. 21).

In a gorge on the western flank of the Acropolis the Lydian-Persian (?) sixth century B.C.(?) structure known as the Pyramid Tomb was re-excavated (PyT, Fig. 1 No. 14). Far out to the northeast in the plain, beyond the Roman City Wall, the Roman-Early Byzantine Bath CG was partially excavated (Fig. 1 No. 28).

Soundings of the Late Roman city wall (Fig. 1 No. 9) were made northeast of the Gymnasium, in the stretch south of the House of Bronzes (Fig. 1 No. 9.30) and adjacent to the bridge across the Pactolus, which was investigated also (PBr, Fig. 1 No. 6). The exact date remains controversial but must fall within the period between A.D. 250 and 450.[28]

An attempt was made by the architects of the expedition to describe and record major ruins still visible at the urban site. Their results are incorporated in the Sector Index, *infra,* and in the site plan (Fig. 1).

It will be evident that the Harvard-Cornell excavations have been limited to the Acropolis and the western part of the urban site. Apart from Bath CG, the central and the eastern part of the site have remained unexcavated. Depending on the period in the life of the city one is considering and on the assumptions one makes about the area the city encompassed, estimates of area excavated by the expedition have varied from one percent to six percent. The chart below provides the best available guesses:

Lydian city and citadel, A. Ramage's est. (Fig. 7)	1,400,000 sq. m.	ca. 350 acres
Area enclosed by Late Roman city wall, including the citadel, D. Van Zanten's est. (Fig. 11)	1,560,000	ca. 390–400
Maximum possible extension in Late Roman and Early Byzantine times,		

G. M. A. Hanf-		
mann's est.	2,500,000	ca. 625
Total of all excavated areas, 1958–1972 (except Gygean Lake area)	54,730	ca. 13.52

Prehistoric Settlements on the Gygean Lake and the Royal Cemetery of Bin Tepe

To give scientific foundation to scattered, unreliable reports of prehistoric finds on the Gygean Lake, D. G. Mitten carried out a partial survey, mapping several sites, and conducted a small scale excavation of prehistoric sites along the shores of the Gygean Lake primarily at Ahlatlı Tepecik and Eski Balıkhane from 1967 to 1969 (Fig. 2). Early Bronze Age jars, burials, and cist graves were found, furnished with pottery and finds characteristic of third millennium Western Anatolian agriculturalists; objects of gold, silver, and copper were also found.[29] A Lydian complex (farm?) was partly excavated at Ahlatlı Tepecik. The search for the Temple of Artemis of Koloë was unsuccessful, but possible location of an important sanctuary of a *Meter Theon Lydias* was indicated by the find of a dedication at Saz Köy at the northern end of the lake.[30]

Originally, more comprehensive survey coverage was planned, which was to include all possible settlement sites between the lake and the Hermus River. Far more extensive excavations even at known sites would be needed to obtain data on chronological continuity and cultural density of these early settlements which may have lasted from as early as the sixth millennium through the second millennium B.C.

Lydian Royal Mounds and Chamber Tombs

Exploration of the Lydian mounds and cemetery began in 1962 with experimental application of geophysical location techniques near the Tomb of Alyattes (ca. 600 B.C.), father of Croesus. The marble chamber discovered by Spiegelthal was reentered, measured, and photographed. In 1966 other chamber tombs were studied at Duman Tepe to the east and, in 1963, near the Gyges Mound (Fig. 2). These studies give a more precise idea of

their construction, though the dating is still very general (sixth to fifth centuries B.C.). All graves had been robbed several times.

Digging then tunneling (1963–1966) into the huge mound in the center of the cemetery, plausibly identified as that of King Gyges, was the most complicated enterprise attempted by the expedition. The royal burial chamber was not found, but a circular monumental supporting wall for an inner mound, with what may be the royal monogram (*GuGu*), was discovered. Since Gyges fell in 645 B.C. while battling the Kimmerians, both the architecture and the writing may be very early. The sophisticated workmanship of the wall establishes the Lydians as excellent masons and stoneworkers. It becomes clear why the Persian kings Cyrus and Darius brought Lydian masons along with Ionian Greeks to do the stone work on their residences in Pasargadae, Susa, and Persepolis.

Establishment of Stratified Sequences from Prehistoric through Turkish Ages

This major objective was to be carried out with special emphasis on the Late Bronze and Early Iron Age in order to elucidate the origins and development of historical Lydian culture. We have succeeded in establishing partial sequences but no complete continuum has been attained. Early Bronze Age sites on the Gygean Lake (Eski Balıkhane, Ahlatı Tepecik) excavated by D. G. Mitten and G. Yüğrüm (1967–1969)[31] may span the third millennium B.C. The next continuous sequence begins in the city area with the hut shelter and cremation burial of the Late Bronze or possibly Middle Bronze Age (1400 B.C. or earlier) at the Lydian Market (House of Bronzes; HoB) area, where it is carried forward until the destruction of Sardis in 213 B.C. No detailed stratified sequence has come to light for the Late Hellenistic and Early Roman periods (213 B.C. to A.D. 17) or for the time of the Roman Empire (A.D. 17 to A.D. 395) but some data may be derived from the Artemis Precinct (Building L) and at sector Pactolus North (PN). The Early Byzantine period (A.D. 395–616) is well represented; for later phases of Byzantine and Turkish settlement some broad divisions may be established by stratification on the Acropolis and at PN (tenth to eighteenth centuries). The bearing of these data on stratification for the various phases of urban development is discussed in the next chapter.

Chronological Terminology

Early Bronze Age	ca. 3000–2000? B.C.
Middle Bronze Age	ca. 2000–1400 B.C.
Late Bronze Age	ca. 1400–1100 B.C.
Lydian	ca. 1100?–547 B.C.
Persian	547–334 B.C.
Early Hellenistic	334–213 B.C.
Late Hellenistic	213 B.C.–A.D. 17
Early Imperial	A.D. 17–280
Late Roman	280–395 (400)
(Late Antique)	(284–616)
Early Byzantine	395 (400)–616
"Dark Ages"	616–ca. 800
Middle Byzantine	ca. 800–1204
Late Byzantine	1204–1453
Turkish (at Sardis)	ca. 1300–present

History of Sardis

ca. 2500–2000 B.C.	Early Bronze Age settlements on the south shore of the Gygean Lake
ca. 1500–1300 B.C.	Urn with cremation burial and circular hut found in House of Bronzes (Lydian Trench) sector in Sardis city area
ca. 1300–1200 B.C.	Imported Mycenaean pottery found in Lydian Trench
ca. 1185 B.C.	Traditional date for establishment of dynasty of Herakleidai ("Sons of Herakles") at Sardis after the Trojan War
ca. 1200–900 B.C.	Imported and local imitations of Mycenaean, Submycenaean, and Protogeometric pottery found in Lydian Trench
ca. 1000 B.C.	Earliest Lydian painted pottery begins
ca. 680 B.C.	Founding of Mermnad Dynasty by Gyges; delegation to Assurbanipal of Assyria
ca. 660–645 B.C.	Invasions of Kimmerian nomads
645 B.C.	Death of Gyges in battle against Kimmerians; Royal Mound of Gyges at Bin Tepe
645–561 B.C.	Reigns of Kings Ardys, Alyattes; invention of coinage
561–547 B.C.	Reign of Croesus; expansion of Lydian kingdom from Dardanelles to Sangarios River to south coast; invention of bimetallic coinage; gold refinery on banks of Pactolus (sector PN)
547 B.C.	Capture of Sardis by King Cyrus of Persia
547–334 B.C.	Sardis capital of Satrapy of Sfarda (Biblical Sepharad) under Persians; Pyramid Tomb
499 B.C.	Attack and burning of Sardis by Ionian Greeks
401 B.C.	Xenophon and the Ten Thousand at Sardis; mention of Altar of Artemis (Xenophon, *Anabasis* 1.6.6–7)
334 B.C.	Capture of Sardis by Alexander the Great
ca. 300 B.C.	Sardians attack Sacred Embassy from Artemis of Ephesus
ca. 300 B.C.–A.D. 17	Hellenistic period at Sardis; Lydian language abandoned; building of Theater, Stadium, Gymnasia; adoption of Greek city constitution
270–ca. 190 B.C.	Sardis capital of Seleucid kingdom
215–213 B.C.	Antiochus III besieges his uncle Achaeus in citadel of Sardis, murders him, destroys the city; permits reorganization (*synoikismos*) supervised by viceroy Zeuxis
188 B.C.	Defeat of Antiochus III by Romans
188–133 B.C.	Sardis under kings of Pergamon
46–28 B.C.	Roman decrees concerning Jewish community at Sardis
A.D. 17	Sardis leveled by earthquake; Emperors Tiberius and Claudius help to rebuild it
ca. A.D. 50	Claudius gives aqueduct to Sardis
20–200	Urban renewal under Romans; Sardis reaches greatest area and largest population (possibly over 100,000)
ca. 50–60	Church of Sardis addressed in the *Revelation* (1.11; 3.1–6)
166	Visit of Emperor Lucius Verus; commemorated by inscription found in the Gymnasium
211–212	Marble Court of the Gymnasium dedicated
284–305	Reign of Diocletian; Sardis becomes provincial capital and site of Imperial weapons factory
ca. 350–400	Early Christian Basilica EA built
ca. 400–616	Great building activity at Sardis, as in other cities of the Empire; churches at Artemis Temple and at east edge of city (Church D)
616	Sardis destroyed probably by Persian attack under Chosroes II
ca. 660	Acropolis fortified and main highway reconstructed
717	Sardis captured by Arabs

787–803	Euthymius bishop of Sardis, great leader of opposition to iconoclasm
10th–12th centuries	Period of recovery at Sardis
ca. 1090–1098	Sardis taken by Turks, then retaken by Byzantines
ca. 1200	Church E built at Pactolus North
1211–1261	Prosperity of Sardis under Empire of Nicaea
1253	Byzantine Emperor and Seljuk Sultan meet at Sardis
Late 13th century	Turkish attacks begin
1304	Acropolis temporarily divided between Byzantines and Turks
ca. 1310	Sardis taken by Turks of Saruhan
1369	Ecclesiastical metropolis of Sardis abolished; Patriarch of Constantinople transfers Archbishopric from Sardis to Philadelphia
1390	Sardis taken by Ottoman Sultan Yıldırım Bayazit
1402–1425	Sardis ruled by Cüneyd of Aydın
1425	Sardis incorporated into Ottoman Empire
1446	Visit of Cyriacus of Ancona
15th century	Acropolis fortification abandoned; Sardis declines to village, but remains *kaza*, administrative center of region until 1867
1595	Sardis leveled by earthquake
17th–19th centuries	Period of decline and gradual abandonment of Sardis by all but nomads
1867	Administrative center transferred to Salihli
1872?	Railroad reaches Sardis

GMAH

AN EXPLANATION OF THE TOPOGRAPHIC PLANS, GRIDS, AND LEVELS

Sardis Topography

The site of ancient Sardis lies at the foothills of the Tmolus Mountains, just to the south of the present day Sart Mahmut railroad station which is at latitude N 38°29'55", longitude E 28°02'32". The altitude varies from ca. *95.00 meters a.s.l. at Bath CG to over *410.00 meters a.s.l. on the Acropolis. Administratively, the villages of Sart Mahmut, Sart Mustafa, and Çaltılıköy belong to the district and township (Kaza=İlce) of Salihli.

The region of Sardis and the cemetery of Bin Tepe fall within sheet Manisa 87–2 (1946) of the geographic survey used in official Turkish maps on 1:100,000 scale (Harıta Genel Müdürlüğü Basimevi and T. C. Maden Tetkik ve Arama Enstitüsü Genel Direktörlüğü).

Survey of 1913. In 1912–1913, Lloyd J. Emory undertook an admirable topographic survey of the region. This survey was drawn at 1:16,000 scale and published in *Sardis* I as Plate I (Fig. 3). It has contour intervals of 25 meters, from 100 to 400, and takes in an area from the Izmir-Manisa-Turgutlu-Salihli railroad (Sart-Mahmut station) up to 5.7 kilometers southward, well into the foothills of Tmolus in the vicinity of Sart Çamur Hamamları, the resort with sulfur springs.

Eastward, the survey indicates the Dabbagh Tchai (Tabak Çay), so named by Butler (*Sardis* I [1922] 21), in the valley next to that of Sardis for a distance a little over 2 kilometers, but contour detail is given only to 200–400 meters east of the Acropolis. Westward the great Necropolis, an area filled with precipitous cliffs and deep ravines, is plotted to a point approximately 2.2 kilometers west of the railroad station. In reading the map, we must keep in mind the peculiarity that south, rather than north, is at the top.

A very great merit is the indication of the course of the ancient aqueduct, beginning ca. 900 meters south from the southern foot of the Acropolis and continuing to ca. 2.2 kilometers into the mountain. Other noteworthy items include the indication of portions of the City Wall preserved in 1913; subsequently one part was destroyed between 1948 and 1953. Another important feature is the indication of the road system prior to modern highway development in 1953, and the change in the road to the station in 1959.

The contour interval of 25 meters is too large for the city area in the plain, and as a result none of the topographic detail is shown for that portion of the city. It is also clear that in a region with much erosion and frequent earthquakes, the contours may have become unreliable in the forty-four years which elapsed between the making of the survey and the beginning of the work of the Harvard-Cornell Expedition in 1958.

It was hoped to base our maps and plans on Emory's survey, and for this reason work from

1958–1960 was carried on with makeshift adaptation of this survey and the maps derived from it and published by H. C. Butler, *Sardis* I (1922), ill. 18 (Fig. 3, which includes Butler's designations of ancient buildings). *BASOR* 157, figure 1; 162, figure 1; and the series of sector sketch plans, *BASOR* 166, figure 1, and later volumes derive from it with adjustments. The attempt to make further use of this map was discouraged when researches of our colleagues at Princeton failed to reveal the original survey data. Without this data accurate adaptations and corrections for erosion were not possible.

Survey of 1962 – Sardis Area Survey. Realizing that a more accurate topographic survey was needed, A. H. Detweiler arranged in 1962 for the services of Ali Sait Tükün, a surveyor with the Board of Waterworks, Salihli. Tükün and his assistants plotted a new survey of the Sardis area based on primary triangulation points numbered 1 through 13, of which number 4 occupied the focal point on top of the Acropolis. One hundred and ten secondary points were established, and all points were marked by numbered concrete survey posts sunk approximately one meter into the ground. The surveyed area extended 2.8 kilometers west-east, and up to 2.2 kilometers north-south. Contour intervals were given at 5 meters, and all levels were based on mean sea level datum.

This topographic survey, entitled the Sardis Area Survey (SAS), was plotted at a scale of 1:2,000. In the north-south direction it covers the terrain from a line ca. 300 meters south of the Artemis Temple and ca. 50 meters south of the citadel (AcS) to a line about 100 meters north of the northern line of the Byzantine city wall, running through a point just to the west of the modern bridge on T.C. 68 highway. In the west-east direction the survey reaches from the foothills of the Necropolis ca. 600 meters west of the Artemis Temple to ca. 100 meters east of Bath CG. (Figure 1 is derived from the SAS, but does not extend as far in the east, west, or south directions.)

The surveyed area does not include a large part of the Lydian cemeteries. It may exclude one part of the Lydian city, if the city extended to the north and northwest beyond the Byzantine wall,

and such outlying districts as may have existed to the northeast. Not surveyed in detail are the precipitous, broken-up landslides and cliffs on the southeastern side of the Acropolis.

For the purpose of referring to the triangulation markers, the surveyor-in-charge superimposed a grid orientated in a true north direction with an arbitrary zero reference point located 4 kilometers southwest of the Sardis area. The zero reference point was arbitrary due to military security regulations. Though the grid numbering was arbitrary, the true north orientation presented the opportunity to convert from other grid orientation systems in use at the time to a uniform true north grid. This matter is presented in more detail in the discussion of the B grid system, *infra*.

The primary importance of the SAS survey is that it provided the expedition with a current, accurate topographic survey of Sardis, complete with numerous triangulation points from which the location of the various sectors and ancient monuments could be plotted with precision.

Sardis Grids

The requirement for precisely plotting finds from various strata leads most archaeologists eventually to establish some form of grid reference system superimposed upon the architectural plans. The methods of establishing and plotting grids are numerous, each having advantages and drawbacks.

Butler used a grid system in the Artemis Temple Precinct which proved impossible to re-establish in later years for reasons discussed below. When full-scale archaeological exploration was resumed at Sardis in 1958 by Harvard and Cornell, architectural recording commenced under the direction of A. Henry Detweiler and Thomas H. Canfield. Separate local grid systems were established at the Building B Gymnasium, Bath CG, and the Acropolis, because these were widely separated locations. Though the number of sectors excavated has increased substantially since that time, these three grid systems remain the basis for architectural recording at Sardis. The grid system in use at each sector is noted in the Sector Index following this section.

Butler Grid. Butler's excavations were concentrated on the Artemis Temple Precinct, for which his surveyor set up a grid system of lines approximately, but not exactly, parallel and perpendicular to the longitudinal axis of the temple. Grid lines were 2 meters apart. The lines parallel to the axis were orientated approximately west-east and were given letter designations starting with A just to the north of the temple and proceeding alphabetically to the south, with B, C, etc. For lines further north than A he assigned the designations N–1, N–2, N–3, etc. Grid lines perpendicular to the temple axis were orientated in an approximate north-south direction and were numbered with the numbers indicating the actual distance in meters, starting from an arbitrary zero point just west of the temple and proceeding eastward. The east end of the temple was located close to the grid line numbered 130.

Several factors have made it impossible to establish a precise conversion formula from Butler's grid to ours. His base lines A and zero appear to have been established arbitrarily, and no survey description remains from which they might be reestablished. A close approximation of the grid could have been obtained by measuring its location to scale on the architectural plan, were it not for an error in the labeling of Butler's plan of the "Temple Area before Excavation." The plan grid lines were drawn with intervals which scaled 20 meters apart. However the east-west lines were lettered as though they were only 16 meters apart, and grid base line A was not shown. One might have guessed the cause of the error and then made corrections accordingly, but a grid system established on such an assumption would not have been a satisfactory basis for all future work.

B Grid. In the great Gymnasium complex, the southeastern corner of Building B (the central building of the Gymnasium) was designated as grid zero for the B grid (Fig. 1). The north-south axis of the grid was established as the face of the eastern wall of Building B, a direction that in 1958 was ca. 26° 20′ east of magnetic north. The west-east axis, perpendicular to the north-south, was approximately the southern face of Building B which is also the north wall of the Byzantine

Shops. This grid system has several advantages, the foremost of which is its permanence: Building B is of such immense size and substantial construction that the architects could be assured that it would be intact for centuries to come. Further, in the nearly two thousand years of its existence one could assume that the soil under the structure had been thoroughly compacted by the building's weight and that further settlement and movement of the reference point would be negligible. Finally, the fact that the grid and Building B with its surrounding structures (Marble Court, Synagogue, Byzantine Shops, and Main Avenue) were in the same alignment meant that walls generally paralleled grid lines and that excavation trenches also followed grid lines—a considerable convenience in both plotting and referring to the locations of items. This B grid was initially used also in the House of Bronzes sector south of the Gymnasium complex.

By the 1960 season, excavations had been commenced at the Pactolus North area and substantially extended in the other sectors. It was acknowledged that grids were now needed in each sector for the recording of the increasing number of finds. At the same time it was realized that separate and unrelated grid systems for each sector could become confusing, whereas a single system extended to all sectors would not only be simpler but would facilitate relating the structures within different sectors to each other. The B grid, with its advantages already in existence, was chosen as the one to be extended. By 1961 it was used in all sectors within the ancient city area except Bath CG and the Acropolis, both of which were remote from the other sectors and, in the case of the Acropolis, separated by precipitous cliffs. These two sectors were to continue for all future seasons under the systems already in use.

The 1962 Sardis Area Survey, with its triangulation marker reference grid based on true north, offered the possibility of changing the Sardis grid system to a true north alignment. Already the SAS topographic survey had been adopted as the new base contour map as previously mentioned, and in order to locate sector buildings accurately on that map the conversion formula for changing triangulation marker coordinates in the B grid reference to coordinates in the SAS grid reference was calculated in 1963 (and later refined in 1968).

An extensive study of the proposed change to an SAS true north grid was carried on into the 1964 season, and plans were produced with this grid to test its feasibility. It was realized that not the least of the problems involved in using the SAS grid would be to convert seven seasons of recording, both architectural and archaeological, to the new system. The conclusions of this study indicated a strong advantage in retaining the B grid, and all subsequent work was done in the B grid system, with the exceptions of Bath CG and the Acropolis. The SAS triangulation markers were not without use, however, for the conversion formulas that had been calculated in 1968 for determining their B grid coordinates enabled their use in further survey work.[32]

Bath CG Grid. At Bath CG an independent but similar reference grid was established with grid zero on the exterior face of the eastern portion of the southern wall (Fig. 335). The west-east axis was the exterior face of the southern wall. The north-south axis was perpendicular to the west-east axis at a point approximately 1.10 meters east of the western face of pier SE, and was approximately parallel to the main east wall of the building. The north-south axis is at a bearing of approximately 37°24′ west of the B grid north-south axis. The B grid coordinates for the Bath CG grid zero point have been calculated at 251.27 N and 1460.65 E.

Acropolis Grid. On the Acropolis, a 1960 triangulation marker D was selected as grid zero (Fig. 4). Marker D is located approximately 3.6 meters north from the northern (inner) face of the fortification wall on a perpendicular to an alignment of said face at a point 7 meters east of the northeastern corner of the Main Gate. The Acropolis grid was plotted on drawing AC–3 "Acropolis Top, Byzantine Wall Trenches," scale 1:100, with the north-south grid line located by measuring an angle 101°19′ clockwise from triangulation line AD, and placing the west-east grid line perpendicular to the north-south through marker D. The Acropolis grid north-south axis is approximately 3°50′ east of the B grid north-

south axis. This grid was extended to the Acropolis North in 1971, replacing a previously little-used local grid in which grid zero was a point 0.3 meters west of the northwestern corner of Lydian wall 1 in alignment with the northern face of the wall. The north-south axis of the discontinued grid was parallel to the western face of the wall.

Sardis Levels

A datum system for referencing the exact level at which buildings and archaeological finds occur is essential for the recording and analysis of information. Any known point may be assumed as a reference level, and subsequent finds may be related to it by surveying techniques, but it obviously would be desirable to have a system relating to the same known constant throughout an entire area. For this purpose the generally accepted surveying datum is mean sea level, from which measurements are taken "above" (a.s.l.) or "below" (b.s.l.).

In addition to the mean sea level datum, other level systems were used at Sardis for reasons discussed below. These systems were the B datum, the Artemis Temple datum, and the Bath CG datum. The system in use at each sector is noted in the Sector Index following this section, and the information for converting from levels in one system to those in another is contained in Table 1.

B Datum. No mean sea level reference datum existed at the Sardis site in 1958 when excavations began; therefore a concrete marker B was positioned in the wall of the north apse of Building B and was assumed to have an arbitrary elevation of *100.00 meters. The B datum system was extended from Building B to the Synagogue, Road Trench, House of Bronzes, Middle Terrace, and

Table 1. Datum system conversion chart

To convert levels from these datum systems	Into these datum systems			
	B	Artemis	CG	Mean sea level (a.s.l.)
B	—	−23.27	+15.75	+15.11
Artemis	+23.27	—	+39.02	+38.38
CG	−15.75	−39.02	—	−00.64
Mean sea level (a.s.l.)	−15.11	−38.38	+00.64	—

Upper Terrace. The actual elevation of marker B was calculated as *115.11 meters a.s.l. on August 19, 1958, by the Salihli surveyors, but all of the areas listed have continued to use reference markers based on the originally assumed elevation of *100.00 meters.

Artemis Temple Datum. In Butler's *Sardis* II (1925), *Architecture,* Part I: *The Temple of Artemis,* he describes the system by which levels were noted on the "Plan of the Actual State" as printed in the Atlas of Plates. The pteroma level was assumed as zero, and the first course above the pteroma was indicated as +1, the second course +2, etc. The first course below the pteroma was indicated as –1, the second course below as –2, etc. For points on the plan not represented by individual blocks of stone, single plus or minus measurements indicated the actual distance in meters above or below the pteroma.

In Butler's *Sardis* I (1922) he includes plans of the "Temple Area before Excavation" and the "Temple Area in June 1914" that contain numbered contours and spot elevations. It is assumed that Butler's reference datum of *100.00 meters on these plans was again taken as the pteroma. In 1958 the level of the south pteroma of the temple was determined by the Salihli surveyors to be *138.38 meters a.s.l. The note on Butler's plan of the "Temple Area before Excavation" states that "datum=35 meters above sea level"; however it may be assumed that the note was either based on incomplete survey information or that it is a mistake similar to the previously described error in labeling of the grid on the same drawing.

For purposes of continuity with Butler's work in the Artemis Precinct, all levels in this area have been referenced to the south pteroma datum which in 1958 was assigned a level of *100.00 meters. In 1959 and 1960, this system of levels was extended north to Pactolus Cliffs and Pactolus North; in 1969 it was extended to the Northeast Wadi. All levels for these sectors have been based on the Artemis Temple datum. It is noted that the Artemis Temple datum *100.00 is 23.27 meters higher than the Building B datum *100.00.

Bath CG Datum. In the 1958 season, Bath CG datum *100.00 was assumed at the top of the

impost course (spring profile) on the east face of the structure CGE. In 1969 the datum *100.00 was determined to equal *99.36 a.s.l.; it is 15.75 m. below the Building B datum. Triangulation marker A, the highest point of CGE, is at *106.42 m. in the Bath CG datum system.[33]

Mean Sea Level Datum. In general, for sectors other than those already mentioned, the datum was taken as mean sea level. These areas benefited from the fact that accurate survey benchmarks measured to mean sea level existed prior to the start of excavation in the sectors, or were easily established from known reference points in nearby areas. The Kâgirlik Tepe soundings in 1958 used an assumed datum of *0.00 at the top of the highest trench scarp, and levels were indicated by numbers representing the distance in meters below the datum line. The datum line was determined in 1958 to be at *188.99 meters a.s.l., and the levels in this volume are given in a.s.l.

On the Acropolis top, triangulation marker D (Acropolis grid zero) was determined to be at *400.20 a.s.l. by the Salihli surveyors in 1960. They also determined the elevation of markers A, B, and C, and from these markers, the mean sea level datum was extended to the Acropolis North area.

The unexcavated buildings including the Theater, Stadium, Hillside Chambers, Stadium Arch, Byzantine Fortress, and Buildings A, C, and D were related to the mean sea level datum through the use of triangulation markers set during the 1962 Sardis Area Survey.

Bin Tepe

Bin Tepe lies approximately 11 kilometers from the ancient city, and would not appear on the site plan even with a scale as small as 1:2,000. It represents a separate site (Fig. 2). Therefore it was deemed unrealistic to expend the great amount of time and manpower on extending the B grid to the mounds, when in fact the relationships between city and mounds would not be apparent on the site plan. In this region, the relationships of mounds and significant features were established by triangulation. Where required, local grids were plotted appropriate to the needs of the excavation.

In 1963, Karnıyarık Tepe (Mound 63.1) was explored, and a radial grid was plotted using marker A on top of the mound as the reference zero point (Fig. 5). The north axis (radius) from this point was established as magnetic north, and radii were plotted in a clockwise direction from 0° to 360°. Concentric circle grid lines were plotted with marker A as the center, their distance shown in meters measured from marker A in a horizontal plane. Distances along the 0° radius were labeled N, along the 90° radius E, along the 180° radius S, and along the 270° radius W. It was noted that marker A was not the geometric center of the mound; that point falls approximately 4 meters west of marker A.

Excavation at Ahlatlı Tepecik on the shore of the Gygean Lake commenced in 1967 at which time a local grid was established. Grid zero was assumed approximately at the northwestern corner formed by the intersection of a north-south and a west-east trench in Ahlatlı Tepecik (Fig. 6). This placed the marker approximately 20 meters south of the lake shore. The angle of the north-south axis was approximately 32° 30′ east of magnetic north. Grid zero was established within the triangle formed by triangulation markers A, B, and C. It is 4.61 meters north and 80.72 meters west of triangulation marker K in the grid system. The grid was extended in 1968 and includes Ahlatlı Tepecik, South Cemetery, Lydian House, and Lake Trench.

Levels at Bin Tepe. In the Bin Tepe region, levels were taken from known mean sea level benchmarks. Marker A atop Karnıyarık Tepe is set at *227.72 meters a.s.l. and marker O atop Alyattes Tepe is at *183.93 meters a.s.l. Burial mounds excavated in 1966 were assigned arbitrary zero reference datum planes as follows: BT 66.1 zero equals *109.92 a.s.l.; BT 66.3 zero equals *102.54 a.s.l.; BT 66.4 zero equals *103.07 a.s.l.; BT 66.5 zero equals *103.12 a.s.l.; BT 66.6 zero equals *103.87 a.s.l.

Başlıoğlu Köy

During the 1971 season, excavation was carried out on Lydian Chamber Tomb BK 71.1 located in the vicinity of Başlıoğlu Köy, a village about three kilometers southwest of Sardis. A local grid was established with grid 0 located at the southwest corner of the inner chamber and the grid east-west line sighted from grid 0 to the southeast corner of the inner chamber. An arbitrary level datum of *100.00 was assumed on the top of the chamber wall blocks at the southwest corner. The lintel block which originally rested upon this point had been removed by earlier grave robbers.

SLC

Sector Index

Number and Location on Fig. 1	Sector	Abbreviation	Years Excavated, Surveyed	Grid	Datum	Sardis Publications	Periods, Description
1 E 125–W 55/N 123–S 30	Gymnasium complex	B	1958–62, 64, 65, 67, 68	B	B	BASOR 154, 13; 157, 35; 162, 40; 177, 21; 186, 47; 199, 42	2nd century A.D.–616
1 (part of B complex) E 15–34/N 82–40	Marble Court	MC	1960–63, restoration 1964–72	B	B	BASOR 162 to present	2nd century A.D.–616
2 E 33–125/N 0–20	Synagogue	Syn	1962–72	B	B	BASOR 1963 to present; AJA 76 (1972)	2nd–4th centuries A.D.
3 (part of B complex)	Road Trench Main Avenue (Marble Road)	RT MRd	1961, 62, 70	B	B	BASOR 166, 40	Roman, Byzantine, Ottoman
3 E 116–W 80/S 0–6	Byzantine Shops	BS	1963, 64, 67, 68, 69, 71, 72	B	B	BASOR 154, 16; 157, 32; 177, 19; 191, 16; 199, 44	Early Byzantine
4 E 4–29/S 50–90	House of Bronzes	HoB	1958–59, 62	B	B	BASOR 154, 22; 170, 13	Early Byzantine house
4 W 43–E 30/S 50–130	House of Bronzes Lydian Trench	HoB	1959–68, 70	B	B	BASOR 154, 27; 157, 30; 162, 9; 166, 5; 170, 4; 174, 5; 182, 8; 186, 31; 199, 28	Lydian, Hellenistic, Roman, Middle Byzantine, Late Byzantine
5a E 75–35/S 123–165	Middle Terrace East	MTE	1964	B	B	BASOR 177, 14	Late Hellenistic, Late Roman
5b E 0–W 22/S 167–217	Middle Terrace West	MTW	1964	B	B	BASOR 177, 14	Late Roman–Early Byzantine
5 E 70–85/S 165–210	Upper Terrace	UT	1959, 67	B	B	BASOR 157, 19; 177, 111	Late Roman–4th century
6 W 315–285/S 19–42	Pactolus Bridge	PBr	1967	B	Artemis	Infra, Chapter III	ca. A.D. 400–1952
7 W 310–325/S 175–270	Pactolus Industrial Area	PIA	1967, 68	B	Artemis	BASOR 191, 38	Late Hellenistic–Early Roman, Late Roman, Early Byzantine
8 W 82/S 223	Southwest Gate	SWG	1966, 70	B	B	BASOR 186, 37	Early Byzantine

* Areas listed with starred a.s.l. datum were never completely surveyed to establish a level datum. An approximate a.s.l. level may be obtained by referring to the contour lines on Fig. 1.

Sector Index (continued)

Number and Location on Fig. 1	Sector	Abbreviation	Years Excavated, Surveyed	Grid	Datum	Sardis Publications	Periods, Description
9	passim (numbered 9.1–9.34)	City Wall	CW	1969–72	B	a.s.l.	*Infra*, Chapter III	Early Byzantine
10	W 202–310/S 315–392	Pactolus North	PN	1960–65, 67, 68, 70, 73	B	Artemis	*BASOR* 162, 24; 166, 15; 170, 13; 174, 14; 177, 3; 182, 18; 191, 10; 199, 16	Lydian–Turkish
11	W 202–250/S 360–392	Churches E and EA	E, EA	1962, 63, 72, 73	B	Artemis	*BASOR* 170, 15; 174, 14	13th century, and 4th–5th century A.D.
12	W 251/S 448	Peacock Tomb	PT	1961, 68	B	Artemis	*BASOR* 166, 30	Early Byzantine
13	W 242–225/S 600–615	Pactolus Cliff	PC	1959–61, 68	B	Artemis	*BASOR* 157, 12; 162, 17; 166, 33	Lydian, Hellenistic, Roman, Byzantine
14	E 6–15/S 810–819	Pyramid Tomb	PyT	1960, 61, 69	B	a.s.l.	*BASOR* 162, 31; 166, 28	6th century B.C.
16	W 120–107/S 1112–1120	Northeast Wadi	NEW	1969	B	Artemis	*Infra*, Chapter VIII	Lydian habitation
17	W 200–100/S 1120–1320	Artemis Temple and Precinct	AT	1960, 61, 68–72	B	Artemis	*Infra*, Chapters IV, V	Hellenistic, Roman, Byzantine
17	(part of AT complex) W 198–210/S 1226–1247	Lydian Altar	LA	1969, 70, 72	B	Artemis	*Infra*, Chapter VI	Archaic, Persian, Hellenistic
17	(part of AT complex) W 190–174/S 1275–1284	Trench South of Artemis Temple	Trench S	1958, 68	B	Artemis	*Infra*, Chapter VII	Lydian–modern
17	(part of AT complex) W 200–166/S 1295–1315	Building L	L	1958, 68	B	Artemis	*Infra*, Chapter VII	Roman building; Archaic Lydian–Hellenistic strata
18	W 100–85/S 1240–1255	Church M	M	1960, 69, 70	B	Artemis	*BASOR* 166, 49–54; 199, 33–35	Early Byzantine
19	E 38–50/S 1071–1082	Kâğirlik Tepe Cemetery	KG	1958	B	a.s.l.	*Infra*, Chapter VIII	2nd–4th centuries A.D.
20.1	E 990–1100/S 1010–1100	Acropolis Top	AcT	1961, 62, 68, 71	Acropolis	a.s.l.	*BASOR* 162, 32; 166, 3; 170, 31; 206, 15	Lydian, Byzantine walls, Byzantine graves
20.2	E 885–990/S 950–1020	Acropolis North	AcN	1960, 71, 73, 74	Acropolis	a.s.l.	*BASOR* 162, 37; 206, 16	Lydian, Persian, Byzantine walls
20.3	E 1100–1160/S 1110–1140	Acropolis South	AcS	1960, 61	Acropolis	a.s.l.	*BASOR* 162, 32; 166, 5	Byzantine wall and barracks
21	E 865–915/S 775–820	Acropolis Tunnels	TU	1962, 64	Acropolis	a.s.l.	*BASOR* 170, 35; 177, 8; *ILN* 3/9/63, 342	Byzantine
22	E 616–632/S 923–941	Western Ridge Fortification (Flying Towers)	—	1968, 71	B	a.s.l.	*Infra*, Chapter III; *BASOR* 203, 12	Byzantine fortification
23	E 660–710/S 330–380	Byzantine Fortress	—	1970, 71, 72	B	a.s.l.	—	Byzantine
24	E 640–770/S 25–75	Roman Civic Center	Bldg A	1970, 71, 72	B	a.s.l.	—	Late Roman, Byzantine
25	E 820–1050/S 180–260	Stadium, Stadium Arch	—	1970, 71	B	a.s.l.	—	Roman, late 1st century A.D.–?
26	E 920–1060/S 260–350	Theater	—	1970, 71, 72	B	a.s.l.	—	Hellenistic with Roman rebuilding
27	E 1144–1190/S 210–242	Hillside Chambers	Rooms 1–7	1970, 71, 72	B	a.s.l.	—	Roman, late 1st century A.D.
28	E 1405–1485/N 330–200	Bath CG	CG	1958–60, 68, 69	CG	CG	*Infra*, Chapter X	Roman, Byzantine
29	E 830–880/N 65–100	Church D	Bldg D	1970, 72	B	a.s.l.	—	6th century A.D.–616

No.	Coordinates	Name	Bldg/Walls	Year	Type	a.s.l.	Reference	Description / Date
30	E 640–715/N 270–320	Roman Basilica	Bldg C	1970, 71, 72	B	a.s.l.	—	2nd century A.D. ?
31	E 845–875/N 165–180	Mill	—	1970	B	a.s.l.	—	19th century A.D. mill
32.1	W 558/S 60	Claudia Antonia Sabina Tomb	—	1972	B	a.s.l.*	*Sardis* I (1922) 170–174; *Sardis* V (1924)	Roman
32.2	W 500/N 0 (approx.) Across Road and NE of Claudia Antonia Sabina Tomb (now disappeared)	Painted Tomb	—	1972	B	a.s.l.*	*Sardis* I (1922) ill. 18, pp. 174, 181–183, pls. 4, 5	Early Byzantine
33	W 270/S 480–500 South of and on same scarp as Peacock Tomb	Pactolus Scarp: Brick Vaulted Tombs	—	1972	B	a.s.l.*	—	Roman?
34	W 16/S 1094	Roman Chamber Tomb	—	1972	B	a.s.l.*	Shear, *AJA* 26 (1922) 405 f.; 31 (1927) 19 f.	Roman
35	E 850/N 170	Road under Mill	—	1972	B	a.s.l.	—	Roman? Blocks of marble paving running EW under mill
36	E 600/S 350	Road near Byzantine Fortress	—	1972	B	a.s.l.	—	Road leads to fortress
37	E 576–603/S 66–79	Vaulted substructure west of Building A	—	1972	B	a.s.l.	—	Four vaulted rooms open to N?
38	E 301–481/S 75–142	Roman Agora	Walls 1, 2, 3, 4, 5	1972	B	a.s.l.	—	Five wall fragments representing three or four buildings of different date
39	E 187–192/N 52–77	Rubble walls east of Palaestra	—	1972	B	a.s.l.*	—	Roman?
40	E 1420/S 220	Odeum Area	—	1972	B	a.s.l.	—	Walls just below City Wall
41	E 750/S 340	Foundations below Byzantine Fortress	—	1972	B	a.s.l.	—	Walls and foundations in paving E of fortress
42	W 225–230/S 825–850	Hypocaust Building	—	1972	B	a.s.l.*	—	Late Roman remains of building with hypocaust
43	W 250–282/S 1275–1285	Marble foundation in Pactolus riverbed	—	1972	B	a.s.l.*	—	Marble blocks in Pactolus bed ca. 60 m. SE of LA
44	W 17–37/S 1024–1037	Minor Roman building (Fountain House)	—	1972	B	a.s.l.*	Shear, *AJA* 26 (1922) 407, fig. 15	Late Roman
45	W 250/S 865–890	Rubble wall in Pactolus bed	—	1972	B	a.s.l.*	—	—
46	E 70–95/S 870–880	Wall SE of PyT	—	1972	B	a.s.l.	—	—
47	W 40/S 964	Brick vaulted tomb	—	1972	B	a.s.l.*	—	Roman
48	W 468–497/S 309–378	Walls on west bank of Pactolus	—	1972	B	a.s.l.*	—	13th century A.D.?
49	E 100/S 1190	Butler's house	—	1972	B	a.s.l.*	*Sardis* I (1922) 57 f.	1910
50	E 135/S 1015	Shear's Stoa	—	1972	B	a.s.l.*	—	—

(*continued*)

Sector Index (continued)

Number and Location on Fig. 1	Sector	Abbreviation	Years Excavated, Surveyed	Grid	Datum	Sardis Publications	Periods, Description
51 E 888–895/S 957–976	Lydian Walls	AcN Walls 1, 2, 3	1960, 71, 74	Acropolis	a.s.l.	*BASOR* 206, 16–20	Persian/Lydian
52 E 1150–1160/S 1145–1155	Pre-Hellenistic Walls	AcS–PH 1, 2, 3	1973	Acropolis	a.s.l.	—	Lydian
53 E 925–970/S 1015–1035	Holes in Acropolis scarp	—	1971	Acropolis	a.s.l.	*BASOR* 206, 15	Byzantine
54 W 125/S 760	Şeytan Dere Cemetery	—	1966	B	a.s.l.	*BASOR* 186, 37	Hellenistic
55 E 84–92/S 0–3	Hellenistic Steps	—	1963	B	B	*BASOR* 174, 47–50	Hellenistic steps below Byzantine Shops: E14, E15, E17
56 W 5– E 15/S 50–63	Hellenistic tombs	—	1959	B	B	*BASOR* 157, 28	Hellenistic, Roman
57 W 255–220/S 360–390	Street of Pipes	—	1961, 62	B	Artemis	*BASOR* 170, 20–22	Roman water pipes in PN sector
58 W 20– E 55/S 125–180	HoB Colonnaded Street	—	1964	B	B	*BASOR* 177, 14–17	Roman
59 E 10–63/S 90–130	Bldg. R and Tetrapylon?	R	1960, 62–64, 70	B	B	*BASOR* 162, 17; 166, 5; 174, 8; 177, 17; 203, 11	Roman, Early Byzantine
60 E 125–130/N 0–20	East Road	E Road	1966, 68, 70	B	B	*BASOR* 187, 50–52; 203, 12–14	Roman
61 W 59–73/S 5–N 10	West Road	W Road	1966, 68	B	B	*BASOR* 186, 28–31	Roman, Byzantine
62 E 190–540/N 50–360	Conjectured ancient road	—	—	B	a.s.l.	—	Modern dirt road follows apparent early alignment
Not on Fig. 1. 850 m. West of PN 490 m. South of Salihli Highway	Hacı Oğlan Tombs	T61.3, 61.4	1961	—	local	*BASOR* 166, 30	3rd–2nd centuries B.C.
See Regional Map, Fig. 2	Indere Cemetery	T61.1, 61.2	1961	—	local	*BASOR* 166, 24	Lydian
See Regional Map, Fig. 2	Bin Tepe Cemetery	BT	1962–66	Local	a.s.l.	*BASOR* 170, 51; 174, 52; 177, 27; 186, 38	Lydian tombs
See Regional Map, Fig. 2	Karnıyarık Tepe	BT63.1	1963–66	Local	a.s.l.	*BASOR* 174, 53; 177, 27; 182, 27; 186, 38	Lydian
See Regional Map, Fig. 2	Duman Tepe	DU	1969	Local	a.s.l.	*BASOR* 186, 47	Lydian tomb
See Regional Map, Fig. 2	Eski Balıkhane	EB	1966	Local	a.s.l.	*BASOR* 199, 12	Lydian, Roman habitation, Early Byzantine
See Regional Map, Fig. 2	Ahlatlı Tepecik	AhT	1967–69	Local	a.s.l.	*BASOR* 177, 35; 186, 40; 191, 7; 199, 12	Lydian, Roman habitation, Early Byzantine
See Regional Map, Fig. 2	Başlıoğlu Köy	BK	1971	Local	local	*BASOR* 206, 11	Lydian chamber tomb(s)

II REGIONAL SETTING AND URBAN DEVELOPMENT

Clive Foss
George M. A. Hanfmann

THE ECOLOGY OF SARDIS AND MODERN RESEARCH SOURCES

The ecology of Sardis presents a broad range of challenges to the modern multidisciplinary approach but the evidence so far available is unevenly distributed among the various fields. In his account of Sardis H. C. Butler gave a good description of the general location of Sardis, and the geologist Warfield a brief useful report according to the geological criteria current before World War I.[1] Considerable data on the geology of the region have been collected by the Mineral Research and Exploration Institute, Ankara (MTA).[2] Basic data on climate, precipitation, agriculture, husbandry, and population are assembled each year by the State Institute of Statistics in Ankara. Additional data on forestation, water supply, and other subjects are collected by other ministries. As these statistics are not released for units smaller than provinces (vilayets) we were unable to secure specific statistics for the district of Salihli, which roughly corresponds to the region of ancient Sardis. We were able, however, to utilize official data for the vilayet Manisa, which covers much of ancient Lydia including the region of Sardis, and these are used in our discussion of climate, population, and agriculture.

On a subject of great interest for the resources of Sardis region—the occurrence of gold — geologist

Mustafa Saydamer, working for MTA on mineral contents of alluvia from the Tmolus range in 1963 collaborated with the expedition and wrote a brief summary of his findings.[3] The MTA has done important work to trace and assess the present gold deposits in geological strata as well as the occurrence of alluvia.[4]

Work with geophysical equipment making electrical resistivity measurements was undertaken by David Greenewalt, then of the Massachusetts Institute of Technology, in relation to locating structures underground (1962–1963).[5] More general problems of soil properties in Sardis and their relation to cultural developments in the region were broached in 1970 in the field work and subsequent publications by G. W. Olson, Department of Agronomy, Cornell University.[6] A matter of major importance for the development of the classical city was an investigation of the great marble quarries in the Mağara Deresi Gorge, in the mountain range south of the Artemis Temple, which was undertaken in 1972 by a team of Italian geologists led by Dario Monna, of the National Research Council, Rome. Their final analytical results will appear in the context of a large comparative study of the marbles of Western Asia Minor used in antiquity. Although the Harvard-Cornell Expedition was unable to undertake new comprehensive geological work or organize methodical research on palaeobotanical and hydrographic aspects of the region, it seems nonetheless useful to provide, on the basis of the scientific and historical information available, an assessment of the urban development of Sardis against a background of regional ecology.

Location of Sardis

The location of Sardis on and below a steep hill overlooking the plain of the Hermus was largely determined by geographical conditions (Fig. 8). Cities, unlike villages, do not depend solely on the availability of adequate and fertile land for agriculture: since one of their primary functions is that of a market, cities have grown up in sites favorable for trade. This is especially evident in Asia Minor, where the greatest cities have always been situated on a few natural routes and where the important locations provided by places where these routes branch or cross have offered sites for centers of commerce. It was at just such a junction that Sardis was founded. To appreciate the strategic nature of its location it is first necessary to consider the general geographic conditions of the area.

Routes and Roads (see Fig. 8)

Four valleys have always provided routes between Central Anatolia and the Aegean: they are the valleys of the Caicus (Bakır Çay), the Hermus (Gediz), the Cogamus (Alaşehir Çay), and the Maeander (Menderes) rivers. Modern highways and railways follow them as inevitably as did the primitive paths of the earliest inhabitants of the country. Of these, the Maeander Valley has been the site of the earliest and historically most important route across the peninsula, since it connects the countries of the Near East with the Aegean via the Cilician Gates and the flat southern rim of the central plateau. In the west, this route passes through Apamea-Celaenae (Dinar) and Laodicea (Denizli) to the Maeander which it follows to the coast at Miletus or Ephesus. From Laodicea, a branch of the Maeander route led to the northwest across the eastern ridges of Mount Tmolus to the valley of the Cogamus. It followed that river to its confluence with the Hermus, then continued northwest to the headwaters of the Caicus; there the route descended the

Caicus Valley to the coast near Pergamon. By this route, the interior was connected with the Dardanelles or Cyzicus and the Sea of Marmara.

The most central of these natural routes followed the northern rim of the plateau to descend through the mountains west of Acroenus (Afyon) into the upper Hermus Valley and the fertile volcanic lands of Maeonia. From there it followed the valley to reach the coast directly at Phocaea or to branch over an easy pass to Smyrna or over another to Ephesus.

Sardis was founded at the junction of the routes from Laodicea and Acroenus, near the confluence of the Cogamus and the Hermus. In this area, the massive range of Tmolus is bordered by a ridge of low foothills which provide sites for settlement and offer protection both from attack and from the flooding which commonly took place in the plains. The ridge, composed of fairly soft conglomerate, is not smooth and continuous but fragmented and broken up into isolated and sometimes quite spectacular hills. One of these, which presents a precipitous face to the plain and is bounded by small rivers on the east and west and by the mass of Tmolus on the south, offers a natural site for a city, combining convenience and defense with a readily available supply of fresh water. Hills suitable for settlement are uncommon in the area; the nearest are those on which the cities of Magnesia and Philadelphia were eventually established.

Sardis was built on and around this hill (Figs. 2, 3, 4, 14, 15), which was fortified and maintained as the Acropolis of the city in every phase of its existence (Figs. 4, 7, 65). When a strong central government offered settled conditions, Sardis, like the other cities of the region, expanded out into the plain; but in periods of anarchy and invasion it retreated back to the hilltops.

Sardis lay along ancient main routes between the interior and the Aegean. The antiquity of the Hermus route is attested by carvings of the Hittite period along it, one at the pass of Karabel which leads to Ephesus, the other near Magnesia. In the early stages of Sardian history, the city was within three days' journey of the major Greek settlements of Ionia: Phocaea, Smyrna, Ephesus, and Miletus.

Under the Romans Sardis became the center of a network of highways which connected it with all other parts of the province.

Under the Persians the famous Royal Road led down from the plateau to terminate at Sardis; it was later extended from there to Ephesus. The highway which led from the upper Maeander to the Dardanelles was also important in the period: it was the route followed by Xerxes in his campaign against the Greeks,[7] and parts of it were followed by Xenophon and his ten thousand Greeks in their expedition against Persia. It continued to be a main highway under the Romans.

In the Hellenistic period, the southern highway was the axis of communications for the Seleucids in Asia Minor; their cities of Nysa, Antioch, Laodicea, and Apamea were established along its course. The main highway of the Pergamene kingdom passed through Sardis, linking Pergamon with the Attalid foundations of Apollonis, Attalea, and Philadelphia.[8] In the Roman period this became the main military road which connected Europe and the Dardanelles with central and southern Asia Minor. Passing from Philadelphia through Sardis to Thyateira, it followed in the immediate region of Sardis a course from Mermere through a rocky defile of Kanboğaz at the west end of the lake to cross the Hermus by a stone bridge about 10 km. northwest of the city (Fig. 2). Within the city, it provided the main east-west thoroughfare, then proceeded eastwards along the southern edge of the plains of the Hermus and Cogamus.[9]

In addition to these major highways, Roman roads led from Sardis across the plain to Daldis, directly through the hills to Apollonis and Pergamon, and across Mount Tmolus to Hypaepa and Ephesus in the Cayster Valley. There was also a highway which connected Thyateira and Philadelphia directly, bypassing Sardis by running north of the lake and crossing the Hermus at Satala (Fig. 2).[10]

This system of natural routes imparted a strategic importance to the location of Sardis, which in addition benefited from its position in the middle of the rich district of Lydia. Lydia, at one time a country, later a province, forms a natural geographic division of the country between the plateau and the Aegean coast. It consists essentially of the valleys and plains of the Hermus, those of its tributaries the Hyllus, Cogamus, and those of the Cayster, along with the surrounding mountainous districts. The whole area is cut off from the neighboring regions of Ionia, Mysia, Phrygia, and Caria by mountains, through which the river valleys and natural routes afford relatively easy communication.

Territory of Sardis

Lydia has been recognized as a division of Asia Minor since it was first established as a kingdom.[11] It retained its identity, though incorporated into larger administrative districts, in the Hellenistic, Roman, and Byzantine periods. In late antiquity, the province had a separate existence, as it has had since the Turkish conquest. The Diocletianic province of Lydia, as well as the Seljuk emirate of Saruhan and the modern vilayet of Manisa, correspond to a remarkable degree, showing the continuity of regional division in a country fragmented by nature.

When it first came to the attention of the Greeks in the archaic period, Lydia was already noted for its wealth. Under the Romans, it was part of the richest province of Asia Minor and has subsequently never failed to prosper from its important location and great resources. Sardis was similarly renowned as a center of opulence in the ancient world, a reputation based largely on the fertility and extensive mineral deposits of the territory around it.

Under the Romans, and earlier, Sardis was the political and economic center of a territory — an area which the city government administered and from which it could gather products to ensure a certain degree of self-sufficiency. This territory was large and fertile, but its exact limits are difficult to determine. It stretched presumably from the range of Tmolus northwards, across the plain of the Hermus, which was known in antiquity as the Sardis plain. Probably it reached as far as the Gygean Lake, for the tumuli in the range of hills on the south shore of the lake formed the royal necropolis of Sardis.

Besides these imprecise indications, it is possible further to estimate the area of the territory of Sardis by considering the locations of the nearest cities (Fig. 2). Each of these would have had a territory of its own, which would necessarily mark the limits of the Sardian lands. The sites of Tmolus-Aureliopolis near Gökkaya, 15 km. to the west, of an unidentified city at Mermere northwest of the lake, of Daldis, 25 km. to the north in the hills above the Hermus plain, and of Satala, which preserves its name in the town of Adala, 20 km. to the northeast at the point where the Hermus issues into the plain, suggest that the whole broad plain of the central course of the Hermus — all of it easily surveyed from the Acropolis of Sardis — was included in the territory of the city. On the east most of the Cogamus Valley was included in the territory of Philadelphia, but the lands of Sardis could have stretched some 30 km. in that direction. Behind Sardis rose the great range of Tmolus, which is composed of parallel east-west ridges which enclose small but fertile plateaus. Since no known city was established in the range—the nearest was Hypaepa in the Cayster Valley—it is probable that some of the range was included in the territory of Sardis. It is primarily with this territory that the following discussions will be concerned.[12]

Agriculture

In antiquity, the products of the land were fundamental for the prosperity of a city. Sardis was particularly well-endowed with them. The Sardian plain, renowned for its fertility, was described by Strabo (13.4.5–6) as the "best of all plains" (Fig. 9). The agricultural resources of the region provided not only a great supply of foodstuffs of all kinds but also various products useful for industry.

The chief product of the plain was grain—wheat and barley—supplemented by vegetables of all kinds. Grapes grew all along the hills at the southern edge of the valley. As early as archaic times the Lydian god of wine, Baki, was associated with this region; the wine of Tmolus was famous in the Roman empire. Olives, used for soap and lighting as well as food, covered the nearby plains of Nymphaeum and the Cayster. Sardis also gained great

advantage from its location at the foot of Mount Tmolus. The cool mountain valleys provided apples, fruits, and nuts which do not grow in the hot plains, and offered pasturage in the summer for local flocks of sheep.[13] Timber for building was also to be found in the mountain; most of the forests of Tmolus have disappeared in recent times, but pine, cedar, and oak were abundant a century ago. In recent years a program of reforestation has once again covered the slopes of Tmolus around Sardis with extensive stands of pine. Agricultural products useful in industry were also abundant; the most common of these is kermes-oak, which produces a valuable red dye. The bark of pomegranates, could have been used for medicine and tanning. The region north of the Hermus is covered with valonia-oak, whose acorn is a source of tannic acid, a product essential for the tanning of leather.[14]

Modern statistics for the Hermus plain from Demir Köprü to Emiralem, which corresponds approximately to the heartland of Lydia, show the newcomers, tobacco and cotton, occupying some of the land formerly given to wheat and grapes. Statistics for Salihli list fruits, cotton, tobacco, grapes, melons, and vegetables as major products.

Table 2. Agricultural products and planted areas, Salihli region (1963–64)[15]

	Hectares	Acres
Wheat	91,588	228,970
Barley	65,621	164,052.5
Cotton	48,150	120,375
Tobacco	44,164	110,410
Grapes (raisins)	42,310	105,775
Olives	1,491	3,727.5

The territory of Sardis also provided extensive pasture lands for sheep, whose wool was used in the famous Sardian purple rugs and gold-woven textiles; and the renowned Lydian cavalry could only arise because of favorable conditions for the breeding of horses.[16] Ancient and modern husbandry in the region may be compared by means of statistics of animal bones found in the excavations, dating from ca. 1400 B.C. to A.D. 1800 and those for animals raised in 1966 in the Manisa Vilayet.

Table 3. Comparison of animal populations in ancient and modern times

	Manisa Vilayet, 1966[17]		Veterinary survey of animal bones, Sardis, 1958-1963[18]	
	Number	%	Number	%
sheep and goats	866,170	76.82	3,185	49.07
cattle	151,262	13.41	1,676	25.83
donkeys	59,551	5.26	26	0.40
horses	40,007	3.55	1,021	15.73
water buffaloes	6,207	0.55	47	0.73
camels	983	0.09	19	0.29
mules	2,240	0.10	—	—
pigs	—	—	516	7.93

Mineral Resources

Such agricultural wealth would have been ample for self-sufficiency or even prosperity, but the neighborhood of Sardis also possessed great mineral resources. The most famous of these was the gold which the Pactolus stream brought down to the city from the mountain; other deposits of gold were available in the regions of Magnesia and Nymphaeum, both within a day's journey of Sardis. Iron could be found around Magnesia, a major source of magnetite, the richest of the iron ores, and at Metropolis in Ionia on the road to Ephesus. Mount Tmolus was rich in minerals of all kinds: silver, copper, arsenic (used for pigments), and antimony (valuable as a medicine and cosmetic) were available there. Of these, silver and arsenic were to be found at the hot springs immediately south of Sardis.[19]

Cinnabar, a red ore of mercury, could be found in Tmolus within 20 km. of Sardis, and the finest quality came from the Cilbian plain, in the eastern part of the Cayster Valley. The ore was used for dyeing and the mercury for silvering mirrors. Yellow ochre, for pigments, and sulphur, valuable for softening wool, repairing glass, and making putty, were available in the immediate vicinity of Sardis.[20]

Veins of marble run through the whole Tmolus range; several quarries were worked in antiquity about an hour (4 km.) south of the city. Substantial deposits also existed in the hills northwest of the Gygean Lake. Among miscellaneous minerals known in antiquity were two more products of Mount Tmolus: touchstone, used to test the genuineness of gold, and a gemstone called sard, a kind of chalcedony much favored in antiquity, which may have taken its name from the city.[21]

All of these products were at hand within two days' journey of Sardis—most of them were to be found in the territory of the city—and they naturally influenced the kinds of industry which developed at Sardis. The variety of dyestuffs encouraged the development of textile manufacturing, and the availability of metals made the city a center of production of gold and iron. The sources do not describe every industry that existed at Sardis in antiquity but do give an indication of the variety and importance of its manufacture.[22]

Industry

With such resources Sardis naturally became a center of trade and industry in the ancient world. The famous textile industry of the city was so ancient that its origins were set in a mythical age. According to legend, Arachne did such beautiful weaving that she attracted the jealousy of the goddess Athena, who turned her into a spider. She had lived in Lydian Hypaepa, a town across the Tmolus range from Sardis. Arachne was credited with the invention of linen and nets, both products of Sardis in Roman times, and her son Closter ("Spindle") with the introduction of spindles in wool manufacture. The art of dyeing wool was supposed to have been invented at Sardis; Sardian dye was famous in antiquity. Among the numerous products of the Sardian textile industry carpets, couch covers, cushions covered with tapestry, blankets, embroidery, and chitons are specifically mentioned. The city apparently produced high quality luxury goods, appropriate for export, as well as normal articles of clothing.[23]

The art of working leather was almost as ancient as the textile industry. Homer may mention the leather workers of Sardis, but in the classical period other centers of this craft seem to have become more important in Lydia. The gold of Sardis was proverbial. The first gold and electrum coins were struck there, and a gold refinery has recently been discovered which dates to the Lydian period. The iron industry was of considerable importance, at least in the late period, and the perfume of Sardis was widely known.[24] Less is known about trade, but the very fact that so many Sardian products were esteemed in the ancient world gives an indication of their wide circulation.

Regional Settlement Pattern: Prehistoric, Lydian, Hellenistic (3000 B.C.–213 B.C.)

Although a systematic survey has yet to be made, the two soundings carried out at Ahlatlı Tepecik and Eski Balıkhane and observations of a number of other sites suggest that already during the third millennium B.C. parts of the Sardian plain were quite densely populated.[25] Individual units may have been small hamlets and villages, often not more than a mile apart; very probably, they resembled in size other villages of Yortan-type culture known to north and east.[26] We have almost no evidence for the second millennium B.C., the Middle and Late Bronze Age. Sardis was inhabited not much later than 1500 B.C. and there may be some Late Bronze Age material from Ahlatlı Tepecik. The nearest safely datable place is Gâvur Tepe at Philadelphia, where Mycenaean sherds have been found.[27] There is more to go on for the period of Lydian culture, from ca. 1100/1000 to 547 B.C. and for the Persian period, 547–334 B.C.

Villages in Anatolia tend to keep their positions through the ages because they are usually situated in places where water is readily available, and unless earthquakes and other catastrophes intervene, this remains an overriding consideration. If we accept the hypothesis that the country was divided into areas ruled by landowning aristocratic families, then more indications of the location of Lydian settlements may be derived from the distribution of groups of mounds in the vicinity of Sardis. This hypothesis is made attractive by the striking regularity with which groups of such mounds appear along the modern Turgutlu-Salihli highway. They have been plotted by A. and N. Ramage whose discussion should be consulted for more detailed information.[28]

The first group of mounds occurs some 12–14 kms. from Sardis at Ahmetli (Fig. 2). Southward

there are cemeteries in the Pactolus Valley which for one km. or so may still belong to Sardis, even though they include isolated mounds. The discovery in 1971 of a group of at least five mounds at the hamlet of Keskinler in the district of Başlıoğlu Köy[29] ca. 4.5 km. southwest of the Artemis Temple seems to indicate a separate settlement.

To the east, the pattern is less clear. The first large tumuli occur on the road to Alaşehir (Philadelphia) ca. 36 km. from Sardis and on the northeast road up the Hermus to Demir Köprü, ca. 20 km. east of Sardis (Durasallı Group).

We know very little about the actual settlement forms in Lydian times. Presumably, the wealthy aristocracy owned much of the land, but we do not know what relation they had to the farming population. It is probable that informally organized cluster or ribbon-plan villages served as nuclei in the plain. A. Ramage has suggested that a rather substantial structure, partially excavated at Ahlatlı Tepecik on the Gygean Lake, might have been a Lydian farmhouse.[30] Scattered walls on the nearby beach and inland showed that it was part of a settlement.

It is not unlikely that the great Hellenistic estate of Mnesimachus perpetuated features of large Lydian and Persian estates. According to the Mnesimachus inscription of the third century B.C., this estate contained "the village (kome) of Tobalmoura in the Sardian plain on the hill of Ilos . . . villages of Tandos and Kombdilipia . . . Periasasostra in the water of Morstas . . . Nagrioa; village of Ilos in Attoudda."[31] It had at Tobalmoura a squire's house (aule), and outside the house were houses (oikiai) of serfs (laōn) and slaves and two gardens requiring fifteen artabas of seed and slaves dwelling at that place: four slaves are named for Tobalmoura. In addition to revenues payable in gold staters, wine vessels are mentioned as revenue payable in kind.

The size of these ancient villages in the plain remains uncertain. The modern villages of the Salihli district range from 25 to 2,450 inhabitants, with 49 villages having populations between 200 and 1,000, 9 below 200, and 19 above 1,000.[32] The present population of the Salihli district was 28,328 in 1927, of whom 21,137 lived in the country. In 1965, it was 87,766, of whom 58,857 lived in the country. With a world capital as its center, instead of merely a district capital, the Lydian population of the Sardian plain may have been of about the same size as the population in 1965. The ratio of urban to rural population in 1927 was ca. 1:3, and in 1965 ca. 1:2.[33] If we assume that ancient Sardis had between 20,000 and 50,000 people in the Lydian period, the rural population of the Sardis region may have been between 20,000 (as in 1927) and 30,000, hardly more than that without the benefits of intensive agriculture. The total for the Sardis region under Croesus may have numbered from 40,000 to 80,000.

Settlement Pattern: Roman, Byzantine, and Turkish Periods

The pattern of settlement in the Sardis region is relatively well known for the Roman period. In that age, when peace and a developed network of highways provided the conditions in which trade and industry could flourish, a high standard of living prevailed. Even small towns were able to erect substantial stone buildings, and individuals could afford to set up dedicatory monuments and memorials in marble. Since many material remains of the period have survived and since the region has been relatively well explored, it is possible to gain an idea of the pattern of settlement and density of population, two aspects in which Roman and modern Lydia seem to have resembled one another.

Most of the settlements were located on the north and south sides of the Sardian plain, along the foothills of the mountains and around the Gygean Lake (Fig. 2). Remains have not been discovered in the middle of the plain, near the Hermus, for that area would have been subject to the constant danger of floods.[34] The district immediately adjacent to Sardis and that around the lake have been explored to some extent, but other parts of the territory are less well known. There are doubtless many sites as yet undiscovered and many more which will have disappeared altogether, for remains are constantly being destroyed as the local population and the demand for building materials increases. The following discussion, therefore, does not pretend to completeness.

Central Lydia in Roman times, as at the present, contained a few cities or towns and numerous villages. Of the cities, the greatest by far was Sardis, but Magnesia and Philadelphia were also places of some size and importance. The other "cities" of the area—as defined not by their size but by the possession of a territory and municipal rights, including in most cases that of striking their own coins—were probably large market towns, roughly comparable to their modern successors Ahmetli, Mermere, and Adala. These cities, as mentioned above, were Tmolus-Aureliopolis, an unidentified site at Mermere, Daldis, and Satala.[35]

The great majority of remains which have been discovered belong to village settlements. Most of them cannot now be identified, since the ancient sources rarely have occasion to mention individual villages and since few inscriptions have been found naming them. In the immediate vicinity of Sardis there were at least five villages within an hour of the city (Fig. 2): at Mersindere on the highway to the west, Metallon in the Pactolus Valley, Üç Tepeler on the hill south of the Temple of Artemis, Çaltılı on the eastern slopes of the Acropolis hill, and Sart Çamur Hamamları, the hot spring about an hour southeast of the Acropolis. The latter may have contained a shrine of the nymphs.[36]

Along the south side of the Sardian plain traces of settlements have been found in the hills to the east at Allahdiyen, where remains of Roman buildings survive, at Tatar İslâmköy in the plain, where the ruins have suggested the presence of a large estate, and at Yeşilkavak in the western part of the Cogamus Valley, where a village called Mylos has been identified.[37] Several other sites stood in the plain east of Salihli, near the confluence of the Hermus and Cogamus. Numerous Lydian burial mounds around the village of Durasallı and a Lydian inscription found not far away at Hacılı suggest that the Lydian town of Thymbrara was located in the neighborhood. That town is mentioned only in sources which deal with the Persian period; it apparently lost its importance in later ages and declined to a village.[38]

On the north side of the plain, a site at Çapaklı

has been identified as the center of a group of villages called Trikomia, while other settlements have been located between there and the lake. In one of these, Poyrazdamları, an inscription was found which commemorated the construction of a sacred precinct. Numerous settlements occupied the fertile lands around the Gygean Lake, where fish and waterfowl as well as an abundant supply of fresh water were available. Considerable remains, dating from prehistoric times through the Byzantine period, have been found all around the lake, as well as several inscriptions.[39]

The mountainous areas of the Sardis region also supported village life, as they continue to do (Fig. 2). There was a sizeable town at Gürice northwest of the lake and another at Lübbey Yaylası in a valley of Mount Tmolus about five hours south of Sardis. In the same region, pottery and small artifacts have been discovered at the resort town of Bozdağ, below the summit of the mountain.[40] Further exploration of these districts, which were quite likely included in the territory of Sardis, would probably reveal many more remains.

For the Byzantine period, not much is known of the roads or the settlement pattern, though there is at least evidence to show that the highway system remained substantially unchanged. The disasters of Persian and Arab invasions in the seventh century, which reduced Sardis from a flourishing city to a small town with a fortress, disrupted the communication system and caused widespread depopulation. The highway up the Hermus was only rebuilt forty years after the destruction of Sardis in 616, a fact which gives some idea of the wretched conditions of the times. Later, casual mentions in sources of the twelfth century show that the highway from Thyateira through Sardis to Philadelphia was in use—it was followed by the Third Crusade—and that the route along the Hermus Valley and that over the Tmolus were still functioning.[41]

In the Byzantine era the period of greatest prosperity for the Sardis region was that of the Nicene Empire (1204–1261), when the political and economic center of the state was in Lydia, at Magnesia, and the emperor's favorite residence nearby at Nymphaeum. In this time Philadelphia was the major frontier fortress of the region and Sardis was thus in a strategic location on the main highway of the kingdom.

The location of settlements in the Byzantine age remains uncertain, but the general pattern of a few towns and many villages seems to have been unchanged. The sources mention only a few villages, none of which has been certainly identified, but Byzantine remains have been noted on several of the sites which were inhabited in the Roman period, in the vicinity of Sardis, at the eastern edge of the plain, and around the lake.[42] The Roman pattern of dense village settlement probably prevailed through late antiquity, as indicated by the remains, but sharp decline of population followed the troubles of the seventh century. Recovery was gradual in this and other regions; old sites grew or were reoccupied in the eleventh and twelfth centuries, but stability did not return until the Empire of Nicaea and its successor state, the Emirate of Saruhan, were established.

Under the Turkish state of Saruhan (1313–1410), which comprised most of Lydia and had its capital at Manisa, the main centers remained those which had been important under the Romans, with only minor changes.[43] The administrative centers of the region were at Sardis, Ilıca (near Tmolus-Aureliopolis), Mermere, and Adala. Of these the latter was the most important. In documents of the time, names of several villages are mentioned, many of them on ancient sites. Modern village names are already mentioned, and illustrate the continuity from that time to the present.

The obscurity of the Middle Ages finally yields to more detailed knowledge after the establishment of Ottoman control in Lydia in the fifteenth century. The Ottoman government carried out surveys of the countryside for tax purposes; many of them have survived though few have been published. Documents from the seventeenth century show that the modern pattern of dense village settlement with a few large market towns was established by then and has undergone relatively little change except that occasioned by growth of population and alteration of trade routes.[44]

The Ottoman highway system, known from records of Turkish and western travelers, clearly illustrates the diminished importance of Sardis, then hardly more than a village. The main highway from Akhisar to Alaşehir passed through Adala, not Sardis, but accounts of travelers anxious to visit the ancient ruins of the city show that routes from Akhisar, Gördes, and the Cayster Valley were still practicable.[45] With the growth of the caravan trade from Izmir to the interior in the seventeenth century, the Hermus highway once again assumed importance, as illustrated by the increasing number of travelers visiting Sardis by that route.[46]

The greatest changes have taken place in the last century. In 1873, the railway from Izmir to Kasaba was extended via Sardis to Alaşehir. Sardis, however, remained a village and a whistle-stop on the line, for the center of the region had become established at the nearby town of Salihli, already a place of some importance in the early eighteenth century. Salihli is now the major market town of the district and has, since the construction of the railroad, replaced Adala as the administrative center.[47] The prosperity of the whole area has been increased and the accessibility of Sardis furthered by the recent construction of the highway from Izmir to Ankara, which follows roughly the route of the Persian Royal Road and passes through the ruins of the Lydian capital.

Precipitation and Floods

For the Mediterranean climate, Sardis with its annual precipitation of 51.3 centimeters is a well-watered region. Vital is the long run-off from the Tmolus range, which retains its snow cap into July. Precipitation is concentrated in violent downpours from late October into March; it rarely rains in July and August. The driest month with the lowest water table in terms of water supply underground is September.[48]

There is a drastic difference between the winter rains, which often lead to flooding, and the dry summer and early autumn months. Measurements taken at the Hermus gorges east of Sardis prior to construction of Demir Köprü Dam indicated that forty times more water passed through the gorge in winter than in summer. These water conditions had constructive and destructive aspects reflected in the archaeological record.

The destructive aspects are erosion and flooding.

	Monthly Average Temperatures in Centigrade (Manisa)	Total Monthly Rainfall in Millimeters (Salihli)
December	8.2°	83.3
January	6.8°	95.8
February	7.9°	79.2
Winter	7.6°	258.3
March	10.2°	54.5
April	15.0°	45.9
May	20.0°	32.7
Spring	15.0°	133.1
June	24.8°	15.2
July	27.7°	6.4
August	27.3°	8.1
Summer	26.6°	29.7
September	24.0°	6.2
October	17.6°	35.0
November	12.3°	50.7
Autumn	17.6°	91.9
Annual average	16.7°	Annual total 513.0

A typical phenomenon of the region is the torrent coming down through the narrow gorge or valley from the Tmolus range and then spreading a wide alluvial fan of stones and gravels into the plain.[49] Higher up there are smaller, narrower torrents, *wadis* dry most of the year, marked by alluvial deposits. It takes little to start such a *wadi*. When, during excavations at the top of the Acropolis, we dumped over the western edge of the central area, we found the next year that a clearly marked torrent of alluvium carried down during the winter had formed in the valley below. In many torrent beds sudden rains produce near flash-floods which can deposit very substantial amounts of detritus in a short time. Our excavations at the Southwest Gate in 1966 (*infra*, Ch. III) and in the Northeast Wadi in 1968 (*infra*, Ch. VIII) were completely covered with alluvium after one winter. Such floods sometimes produced major disruptions in the settled areas of the city. The following areas show evidence of alluvial deposits and flooding.

Artemis Precinct. Trench S and pits in front of Building L (Figs. 96, 220, 273) revealed a torrent bed dating from the eighth (?) to fifth century

B.C. The depth of deposits was 2–3 m.[50] The entire temple area rests on these deposits.

Flooding by the northeast torrents on the north and east sides of the temple apparently occurred in the first and second centuries A.D., making the ground rise all around the temple.[51] Another cycle followed the great earthquake of the seventh and eighth centuries and was observed near the top of Church M.[52] These floods were characteristic of the action of the steep, fast-flowing seasonal torrents coming down from the Acropolis as tributaries of the Pactolus.[53]

Pactolus Cliff and Pactolus North. At sector PC, excavation of a water channel showed that the bed of the Pactolus itself is now about 2.5 m. higher than in Roman times.[54] The Pactolus flooded PN in the fifth and fourth centuries B.C., and again after the Hellenistic age. This sector lies at the area where the Pactolus Valley begins to widen (Fig. 1 No. 10, PN; No. 13, PC).

House of Bronzes. The House of Bronzes sector (Fig. 1 No. 4) is a riverine flood plain exhibiting a wide variation of deposits, from cobblestone size to fine sand or silt. Here, the sequence of periodic flooding is very deep (from *100.0–*89.9), reaching back into the second millennium B.C.[55] This flooding was originally uncontrolled and was only partially controlled when the Lydians built their structures in the market area in the seventh and sixth centuries B.C.[56] The flood deposits, interspersed with strata showing traces of human activity, were 10 m. deep and still continued downward when excavation stopped at *89.9. They represented a time span of seven centuries (ca. 1300?–600 B.C.).

Area CG. If the House of Bronzes–Lydian Market area showed what may have been seasonal flooding or flooding of regular occurrence, the CG area (Fig. 1 No. 28) is a clear illustration of deposits by a stream out of control. Here, more than 5 m. of alluvium (ca. *100.0–*95.0) were deposited between the seventh and the tenth centuries A.D.[57] Because the flood deposits are deeper in hollows and shallower on wide inclines, the ancient city is buried at unpredictable depths.

Literary tradition hints that King Gyges tried to control the waters of the Hermus, leading them into the Gygean Lake.[58] We have found no clear evidence for structures connected with flood con-

trol, but obviously effective measures were taken in Hellenistic and Roman times to prevent the flooding of the city. It is possible, however, that on exceptional occasions the city was briefly flooded; this may have happened after an earthquake in the fourth century A.D., necessitating the "ananeosis" or renovation of the wall paintings, revetments, and other decorative elements in the Synagogue and Gymnasium. Fierce floods in A.D. 399 prevented an attack on Sardis by the Goths.[59]

The decay of water and flood control after A.D. 616 was undoubtedly a major factor in the rapid decline of the city. From the seventh through the nineteenth centuries most of the Hermus (Gediz Çay) plain was a marshy, swampy area. Thus, in 1828 Boissier observed: "Tout le terrain est marécageux, couvert des hautes herbes abritant les troupeaux des Turcomans,"[60] and Fellows, in 1838, commented on the negative effects of flooding: "The country over which [Sardis] looks is now almost deserted and the valley is become a swamp. Its little rivers of clear water, after turning a mill or two, serve only to flood instead of draining and beautifying the country."[61]

Water Supply

Location and slant of water-impermeable strata and the supply of water determine the water table. The depth at which water-bearing strata are found varies, generally increasing toward the Hermus Valley. Our own camp well, in the Pactolus bed near the camp (Fig. 1 No. 15), reached a strong flow of water at only 2.50 m. below the river bed (ca. *130 a.s.l.). A Lydian–Persian well at PN went down ca. 8 m.[62] but a well of the same period in the HoB–Lydian Market area went down better than 18 m. (*99.66–*80.80, ca. *95.0 a.s.l.) to the water.[63]

Change of water table has occurred since antiquity in the vicinity of CG. The lower story of the structure (presumably around *90.0), which must have been accessible in antiquity, is now under water, a difference of at least 2–3 m. This condition may be due, however, to the presence of poorly controlled flow from a stream or brook still used to irrigate the fields around CG.[64]

Constructive use of the water for irrigation and

drinking was practiced early by making cisterns and wells. In addition to seasonally variable streams and torrents, there are known to be at least two major springs in the Sardis area. One comes out in a cave in the west flank of the Acropolis rock. It was described by Butler as a Lydian reservoir; the other is the spring south of CG. Major providers of water are the Pactolus (Sart Çay) and the Tabak Çay, west and east of the Acropolis ridge. To this day, the peasants practice a system of irrigation by which the waters of the Pactolus are diverted in channels on specified days to specified fields; this is likely to go far back in time, possibly to the early agriculturalists of the Bronze Age.

Concrete evidence for Lydian water management is given by several wells dug in the sectors PN and HoB. An elaborate system of stone-built channels was in use around the industrial installation at PN, apparently both to supply water for industrial operations and to drain it.[65] The placing of wells, some of which seem to be located in public lanes, suggests a planned system which may have been further improved in the Persian era. The two peculiar apsidal structures in the PN sector may have served as public fountain houses.[66] Whether an underground cave for a spring in the western flank of the Acropolis was really made or used by Lydians must remain uncertain; similarly, though found with Lydian sherds, the terracotta pipes under the Artemis Temple are probably of a later age.[67]

Among the hollows and caves within the Acropolis[68] there may be some which go back to the Lydian age, but we cannot prove this. It remains equally uncertain whether the tunnels which descend through the north side of the Acropolis (Fig. 1 No. 21) were Lydian and led eventually to a water supply.[69] If they were Lydian and did lead to water, Lydian water engineering would fit into the context of Late Bronze Age Mycenaean castles and Near Eastern fortified cities with subterranean water installations and, according to recent research, with Phrygian (Midas City) and Paphlagonian settlements.[70]

During the destruction of 213 B.C., all wells of the western area of the city were stuffed up.[71] Consequently, other water sources must have been used for the reconstructed Hellenistic city. We have no evidence concerning this Hellenistic system.

A new era in the Sardian water supply began with the construction of the aqueduct which brought water down from the Tmolus and was a present from the Emperor Claudius (A.D. 53 or 54?). Water was undoubtedly distributed through intermediate tanks, and it is noteworthy that several torrent beds on the west flank of the Acropolis have long terracotta pipelines, some perhaps leading down from such tanks.[72]

The system of water pipes and drains found around the Artemis Temple, at PN, along the Main Avenue, and in the Gymnasium area (Fig. 1 Nos. 17, 10, 3, 1) reflects wide public and private distribution and consumption in the Roman period. This archaeological evidence is confirmed by an inscription listing public fountains and their output.[73] While the interpretation of quantities is controversial, the number listed in just this one fragment of the list is impressive; there must have been many more.

The fountain in the forecourt of the Synagogue,[74] of which the output was calculated at 42 litres per second, and the fountain with the bronze snakes reset by the prefect Basiliskos[75] are but chance survivors of these many fountains. A monument surrounded by flowing water was apparently functioning in the Artemis Precinct.[76] The elaborate installation in the House of Bronzes[77] may stand as an example of water supply in a private house, while the cooling tanks in two of the Byzantine Shops show how commercial establishments were served.[78]

The truly immense amounts of water consumed by the Imperial-type Gymnasium-Bath, with its big swimming pool and its various tubs and toilets (Fig. 1 No. 1), were supplied by the public system of the aqueduct. A small bath at PN was served from a reservoir on the Pactolus. This seems to have been an important distribution point, as the many pipelines near the Street of Pipes attest.[79] Bath CG, however, was probably serviced by controlled waters of the same stream which later flooded the area.

Our investigations at Pactolus North (Street of Pipes) and the Synagogue (Fig. 1 No. 2) seem to indicate that the urban water system was expanded and reconstructed between A.D. 350 and 400.[80] Retrenchment from public water supply to a

private tank system was observed in the Synagogue. After 616 the aqueduct was apparently
knocked out and most of the city system abandoned, along with the "downtown" area of the
Gymnasium. This was a death blow to the city, as
both quantity and quality of water declined. Di-
seases were apt to increase once water sources became accessible to cattle and drainage ran in the
open.[81]

One curious exception to the progressive decline must be recorded. Apparently in the
ninth century the Byzantines built a large cistern
into the Artemis Temple and very elaborate pipelines led in and out of it. This represents a respecta-
ble attempt at water conservation and distribution.[82]

A large vaulted cistern of brick—perhaps built
in Roman times—small wells, and, just possibly,
some cisterns cut into the rock were used to sus-
tain life on the Acropolis.[83] Uncontrolled and
undirected, the mountain waters which had supplied the huge baths and ample city fountains were
wasted or helped to flood the countryside and
turn the trough of the Hermus plain into swamp.

Only in the mid-twentieth century was large-
scale water planning introduced into the area again.
Gradual expansion of village fountains and storage
basins, some of which re-trapped the springs used
by the ancients, supplemented the large-scale drainage and irrigation schemes carried out after the
construction of the Demir Köprü Dam at the
gorges of the Hermus. With an extensive system of
irrigation channels almost the entire plain is now
under cultivation (Fig. 9). The marshlands in the
trough of the valley, suitable for breeding horses and
cattle, have become cotton fields and vineyards,
and the royal cemetery of Bin Tepe, which a short
time ago was not cultivated, has wheat, barley, and
sesame fields extending over it, with many mounds
being ploughed over or used for farm buildings.
Finally, in 1972 drinking water was brought down
from the Tmolus as in the time of Claudius.

URBAN DEVELOPMENT OF SARDIS

We have considered previously the evidence for
the settlement pattern in the Sardis region. In the
following discussion, we present briefly such data

as have emerged for the development of the city of
Sardis and for its subsequent decline and reversion
to village pattern.

Prehistoric and Bronze Age Settlement: 1400?–1000 B.C.

We have as yet little insight into the prehistoric
period. At Sardis itself, we know only a cremation
grave and a hut of ca. 1400 B.C., found amidst
gravel deposits on the eastern bank of the Pactolus
in the House of Bronzes sector (Fig. 1 No. 4).[84]
The arrival of Mycenaean warriors who may have
seized power around 1200 B.C. would suggest
greater organization of the site, presumably around
the citadel and a palace, but architectural docu-
mentation is confined to one wall and is in the same
HoB–Lydian Market area, in the flood deposits of
the eastern bank of the Pactolus. Strabo's reference[85]
would imply that the citadel was already occupied
before the fall of Troy, but we have not found any
Bronze Age material on the Acropolis.

Lydian-Persian: 1000–334 B.C.

For the Lydian period our excavations have
proved that the built-up areas extended into the
Pactolus Valley as far as the Artemis Temple
(Northeast Wadi houses) and as far north as the
Gymnasium. The Acropolis was occupied, according to pottery finds, not later than the mid-seventh
century B.C.[86] Beyond that, the limits of the Lydian city become a matter of conjecture, especially
as we do not know the positions of the Pactolus
torrent which during the various ages of antiquity
have repeatedly changed (Fig. 1).

The literary notices speak of the Acropolis as
Hyde (Strabo 13.4.6) and imply that the civic
center (agora) of the Lydian city was astride the
Pactolus in 499 B.C. (Herodotus 5.101). The account of the battle of Sardis in 395 B.C. by Xenophon, a contemporary well acquainted with Sardis,
seems to imply that an area west of the Pactolus
was not built up, since the Persians pitched their
camp there (*Hellenica* 3.4.20–25), but how close
this was to the city we do not know.

A. Ramage assumed that the city was essentially
in a funnel, spilling out into the plain where the
Pactolus leaves its narrow valley (Fig. 7). Hanf-

mann assumes that the city went up the lower northern slopes, that the road to the Artemis Temple area may have been a "ribbon" development, and that the east-west road was at least as important as the north-south road and was perhaps a major axis for built-up areas (Fig. 7).

There is considerable liklihood that a diagonal road, later replaced by the Street of Pipes, went from the Pactolus to the Royal Road and perhaps all the way to the northeastern corner of the city. Some indications of the limits of the city are given by Lydian tombs which presumably were outside the residential area; but consistent application of this principle results in some strange configurations.[87]

Excavations at Pactolus North have produced enough evidence to suggest that the residential quarters were densely built up, the houses separated by irregular lanes and small open spaces.[88] Their fieldstone foundations and mud pisé walls are somewhat less rustic in appearance than the houses of reeds which Herodotus (5.101) says constituted the majority of dwellings at Sardis in 499 B.C.

The Younger Cyrus (407–401 B.C.) designed a royal park famous for its regular planning. We have no archaeological evidence for its location, but together with the gardens of Tisaphernes, which were devastated by Agesilaus in 395–394 B.C.,[89] it was probably in the plain adjoining the city area to the north or west. There are, in the ancient authors, some other indications that parks and gardens in and around the city continued to be a feature of the Sardian urban area.[90]

Early Hellenistic: 334–213 B.C.

Sardis became a Hellenized city during the 120 years between the arrival of Alexander the Great in 334 and the destruction and rebuilding by Antiochus III in 213 B.C.[91] It is clear that certain major changes took place after the city came under Seleucid rule in 282 B.C. By combining archaeological and epigraphical evidence it is possible to prove that the Theater and the Stadium were added on to the area of the Lydian city, possibly at its periphery (Fig. 1), and that a city wall was built (unless it existed in Persian times) prior to 215

B.C., since the soldiers of Antiochus climbed over it into the Theater. Undoubtedly, a council house and gerousia were in existence; the latter is specifically said to have been the converted palace of Croesus.[92] South of the urban area the huge Temple of Artemis was built, at least in part, prior to 213 B.C.[93] In general, however, it is arguable that the area and haphazard plan of the Lydian city remained much the same. There is no clear evidence that any kind of oriented grid plan was used. Lydian houses in PN were in use until 213 B.C. A slight retrenchment is suggested in the Pactolus Valley by the appearance of Hellenistic chamber tombs over Lydian houses at the Pactolus Cliff sector.[94]

We must probably envisage the area from the Pactolus to the Theater as a large agglomeration of native houses interrupted here and there by complexes in modern Hellenistic marble style. These must have included the agora—possibly the same as the Lydian—at least one gymnasium, and the Metroon, of which we have some stones from the *parastades* inscribed with letters and decrees in 213 B.C. and hence earlier than that date. They were found reused in the Synagogue.[95] The Temple to Zeus, built by Alexander the Great (334–323 B.C.) may have been on the Acropolis.[96]

Architectural evidence from our excavations for the Early Hellenistic period is limited to possible Hellenistic use of Lydian terraces on the north slope of the Acropolis,[97] to the Hellenistic phase of the Artemis Temple, Altar, and Precinct, the Early Hellenistic chamber tombs at Pactolus Cliff,[98] and an industrial (?) oblong structure in the Lydian Market area.[99] Among the unexcavated buildings, the Theater contains Early Hellenistic parts. The discovery of the Early Hellenistic stele of Matis confirms that funerary monuments extended westward along the highway for at least 1 km. west of the Pactolus.[100]

Late Hellenistic: 213 B.C.–A.D. 17

No historic source suggests that Sardis had suffered any grave destruction between 499 and 213 B.C. The new epigraphic material leaves no doubt, however, that the city was punished after the siege of 215–213 B.C. to an extent which warranted a *synoikismos*. According to L. Robert, the term need not mean more than "re-population." The letter of Antiochus III, which puts his Viceroy Zeuxis in charge, remits punitive tax, permits use of the Gymnasium (which therefore must have existed before), and also allows inhabitants to use royal woods for reconstruction. The transfer of Jewish veterans from Mesopotamia to Lydia and Phrygia may have included a garrison for Sardis.[101]

Excavations at Pactolus North and the Lydian Market (HoB) area show that after 213 B.C. buildings were razed and all wells in this western part of the city were made unusable. The western area of the city, along the eastern bank of the Pactolus and along part of the east-west highway, became an extra-urban area of cemeteries and industrial installations (kilns).[102]

A Hellenistic mausoleum, of which only the front steps are preserved, was found north of the east-west highway, ca. 3 m. below the Roman level. Several Late Hellenistic vaulted chamber tombs were found south of the highway in the HoB area (Fig. 1).[103] Thus cemeteries lined the main east-west artery for at least 400 m. eastward from the Pactolus crossing, a clear indication that this region lay outside the inhabited Hellenistic urban area. This, in turn, suggests that in the refounding of 213 B.C. the entire city was moved eastward, away from the Pactolus. Its eastern boundary, however, may have stayed at the City Wall connected with the Theater, which is mentioned in the accounts of the siege of 215–213 B.C.[104]

The orientation of the Hellenistic mausoleum, eight degrees north of the later Roman alignment, suggests that the main Hellenistic east-west road (which has not been excavated) followed a somewhat different orientation from the Roman. It is natural to assume that the far-reaching refounding of 213 B.C. brought a more regular Hellenistic plan with straighter, wider streets. This need not have been a regular checkerboard grid. A bent-axis plan[105] might have been followed (Figs. 7, 10).[106] Although it may have had a Lydian predecessor, the Street of Pipes is first attested archaeologically for this period; again it is a Late Hellenistic mausoleum which provides a safe datum.[107] The street went northeast from the Pactolus, and its direction,

roughly diagonal in relation to the great east-west highway, was probably continued by the so-called Colonnaded Street, known to us only in its Late Roman form.[108] This diagonal direction may have been continued by the so-called Old Izmir Road, still visible as a hollow with a country road between major buried Roman structures.[109]

It is difficult to decide which, if any, of the alignments of later Roman buildings preserved the layout of the Late Hellenistic city (Fig. 10). If the orientation of the Theater and Stadium are assumed to go back to the Early Hellenistic (334–213 B.C.) period, then the divergent orientation attested by the Roman Complex A (possibly the Hellenistic-Roman agora), the Roman Basilica C, and the Byzantine Cathedral D, which appears to have succeeded a major Roman temple, would be the strongest candidates.

We have no excavation data to decide the issue. It may only be noted that the move away from the Pactolus clearly necessitated a transfer of the agora which in Lydian-Persian times (499 B.C.) was traversed by the Pactolus (Herodotus 5.101). The "A" area remains a possibility by virtue of its general central location, slightly elevated over the highway (Fig. 10 No. 24).

By all historical indications, the Late Hellenistic period was the period during which Sardis was transformed into a Hellenistic city similar to Pergamon, or (in housing) Priene, with many monumental buildings. Literary sources and inscriptions attest the continued use of the Theater, at least two gymnasia, one of which had a "hall of elders" (*presbeutikon*), which also served as a hall of honor, and a number of temples as well as a synagogue.[110] Unfortunately, after the disastrous earthquake of A.D. 17, much of the site was re-terraced and re-leveled,[111] burying the Hellenistic structures; and probably much of the building material was recut and reused.[112] We have neither found nor excavated any large public or residential Hellenistic buildings, but one valuable indication concerning the house types in use came from a nest of small Doric capitals which were perhaps to be burned for lime; they clearly belonged to a Hellenistic house with small peristyle of the type known in Delos and elsewhere.[113]

Roman and Late Antique: A.D. 17–616

In A.D. 17 a tremendous earthquake struck Sardis; the passage in Tacitus (*Ann* 2.47) suggests that chasms and landslides changed the aspect of the site. Helped by an Imperial grant and remission of taxes, a special commissioner, ex-praetor Marcus Ateius, went to administer relief and review the situation. It seems very possible that he had city planners and architects at hand, for the reconstruction plan in the Gymnasium area has a strikingly Roman Imperial character. Vast terracing and earth movements were undertaken and the direction of the Main Avenue as a modern colonnaded axial thoroughfare was laid down. From inscriptions we have some sidelights on the reconstruction: the restoration of a shrine or temple to Hera, for instance,[114] or the building of the great aqueduct.[115] As a result of this Roman "urban renewal" Sardis achieved its greatest extent and prosperity.

The rebuilding of the city after the earthquake of A.D. 17 led to re-occupation of the western area of the city which had been abandoned in Hellenistic times. Roman villas abound in the Pactolus Valley, and Roman habitation certainly reached farther up the north and east slopes of the Acropolis. Flung far out into the plain were such suburban public buildings as Bath CG (Fig. 1 No. 28).

We have traced parts of the colonnaded Main Avenue, the perpendicular East Road, and the Colonnaded Street in HoB. In addition, a marble-paved east-west street existed just west of the mill (Fig. 1 No. 31).[116] A serpentine ancient road with house walls preserved to ca. 1.50 m. is said to go up to the top of the Byzantine Fort (Fig. 1 No. 23) by the owner of the vineyard located in that area.[117] Other streets and buildings are known from inscriptions; thus the fragment of an informative inventory of city fountains[118] mentions the Agora Descent Road (*kathodos Agoras*), the Odeum, the Confraternity Building of Attis, the Menogeneion, and the precincts of Zeus and Mên. We know the Gerousia (Senate), Boule (Council), Gymnasium of the Elders, and Temple of Augustus and Gaius Caesar from this and other inscriptions and from ancient authors.[119] A *platia Sardianorum* is mentioned in a late Latin inscription,[120] a "Hypaepa Street" and a Tetrapylon appear in a Byzantine inscription.[121]

Public buildings—the Gymnasium, the baths, the colonnades of the Main Avenue—were richly supplied with marble-revetted walls and mosaics, both on the walls and vaults, and on the floors. As to housing, a sophisticated urban residential culture is revealed by the imposing House of Bronzes with basements, servants' quarters, marble-floored reception rooms, and rich furnishings of marble, bronzes, and glass, or by the suite of gorgeous mosaic rooms attached to the probably private bath at Pactolus North (ca. A.D. 400–450?). These structures seem to resemble the Roman *domus* type, large residences of important families.

We have not excavated completely any house or dwelling plan from the Late Antique era. The incomplete units found south of HoB entail rather loose sequences of terraced units and small courts going up the slope; the site afforded the desirable north exposure and marvelous views. The continuous terraced build-up recalls the irregular but richly furnished and skillfully terraced multistoried "Häuser am Hang" in Ephesus with their multiple apartments.[122]

Intermediate between public and private buildings were halls and structures which housed the various civic and religious associations. Some of these complexes were in the nature of club houses. An interesting inscription of the second century A.D. speaks of the tribe Dionysias (*Phyle*). It built for itself out of its own funds the stoa and the exedra and a two-story storage unit, as well as another underground storage unit in the adjoining garden.[123] The mention of gardens suggests that an unspecified percentage of the urban area was given over to "green plots," gardens, and possibly orchards. Presumably, other Sardian phylai had similar club houses and gardens; a "confraternity of Domitia" and "confraternity hall of Attis" are mentioned in the fountain's inscription.[124] The Menogeneion, too, named after a famous citizen of Sardis, may have been a stoa.

Commercial and industrial life must have flourished. From literary sources we learn about a great Imperial arms factory located at Sardis since the time of Diocletian.[125] This may have been an enterprise with several hundred workmen. Ancient writers infer, too, the persistence of the old luxury goods industries—textiles and perfumes; inscriptions from the Synagogue speak of goldsmiths. The gilding of the ornaments of the Severan Marble Court (A.D. 200–211) and of the Hall with Gold Ceiling mentioned in the inscriptions from the Marble Court shows that something of the "Golden Sardis" tradition lived on. All trades associated with building must have flourished—builders and stone masons, carpenters, mosaic workers, and wall painters. The famous Builders' Union inscription of A.D. 459 indirectly testifies to vigorous private and public building.[126] The very existence of such an extensive shopping center as the Byzantine Shops with its row of twenty-nine shops indicates a surprisingly centralized, efficient, and diversified economic life.

Agriculture must have contributed to the commercial life; the reverence in which the goddess of harvests, Kore, and her children Abundance and Good Growth continued to be held speaks eloquently for the importance of agricultural wealth. A new testimony was brought by an inscription found in 1972 (IN72.1, A.D. 211). That the city possessed grain mills is indicated by the inscription of a watermill mechanic.[127]

As to production and distribution, it is interesting that some of the economy was semi-domestic. From the finds in the basements of the House of Bronzes it seems that olive oil was probably made and wool dyed right in the servants' quarter. The Byzantine Shops seem to have been fairly specialized; there are indications of iron-mongers, glass sellers, paint sellers, and jewelers, who may have worked at smaller jobs in metal, gems, and glass.[128] The highly sophisticated bronzes, such as the lion lamp, tripod with dolphin, incense shovel, wine flagons, and samovars (*authepsae*) may have been locally made.[129]

Finally, in the area of public utilities and hygiene, we have already mentioned the fundamental contribution of the Sardian water supply system. As in other Hellenistic and Roman towns, it was supplemented by an elaborate system of drains to dispose of waste water.[130] Two interesting examples of hygiene services are known: the well-arranged

double latrine with marble seats for the visitors of the Byzantine shopping center (400 A.D.) and the hospital, mentioned in an inscription of Justinian (ca. 539 A.D.).[131]

It is arguable that the city covered an area of over 600 acres in the fourth, fifth, and sixth centuries A.D. It is also arguable that the time between A.D. 395 and 616 was the time of greatest expansion of the city area. Hanfmann believes, however, that the Roman city of the period between A.D. 200 and 395 was equally extensive and possibly more populous.

Signs of the decline of urban living, however, began already in the fourth and fifth centuries. The unsafe conditions of transportation, for one, had begun to affect industries requiring major outlay in roads and animal power. Such investment was needed to transport marble sarcophagi which weighed many tons, or even plain marble columns. The inability to perform these feats may have led to the re-employment of earlier pieces, as in the Synagogue and the Byzantine Shops and, most prominent, in the Byzantine Acropolis wall. Instead, brick and masonry piers, hastily slammed together with cement, were relied upon; and to obtain lime, marble buildings began to be stripped of their decorations and revetments. Still, an enormous amount of marble revetments was used during the *ananeosis* in the fifth century and a number of vast opus sectile marble floors was laid in the sixth.[132] The important Christian Basilica at PN and its surrounding complex also reused earlier marbles.[133]

Deurbanization[134]

When the City Wall was breached, possibly at the northwest corner, in the fall of A.D. 616[135] and the lower city devastated, a new era in the ecology of Sardis began. The splendid city of antiquity, with its numerous public buildings and extensive public services, disappeared, to be replaced by a town of very different character. Medieval Sardis was no longer a great metropolis but rather a group of small settlements resembling villages dominated by a castle on the Acropolis, which itself contained a settlement.

Although vast stretches of the City Wall remained standing, no attempt was made to restore the defenses of the city as a whole, for much of the area contained within them had been abandoned. Instead, Sardis relied for its defenses on a hilltop fortress, a situation typical of the whole Mediterranean world in the Middle Ages. This fortification was built in the mid-seventh century, apparently at the same time as the Hermus Valley highway, formerly the main street of the city, was reconstructed after some forty years of abandonment.

It is difficult to trace the development of Sardis in the centuries after the destruction of A.D. 616 by the Sassanian Persians.[136] The sources are few and uninformative, while datable archaeological evidence only begins to appear in the ninth century. When information is finally available, the pattern of a few settlements dominated by a castle is clear.

The settlement at the Temple of Artemis must have been sizable. The ability to transform the interior of the temple into a vast reservoir, supplied by orderly rain-fed cisterns and feeding in turn a number of watermains, is alone a testimony that the population in this area was considerable. Remains of the village which grew up around the temple and flourished there between the ninth and fifteenth centuries are described in detail in Chapter IV on the Artemis Precinct (Fig. 65).

Other settlements were scattered over the former area of the city. That at PN eventually became the most important, for it was there that the only major construction of the Middle Byzantine period, Church E (thirteenth century) was built. It was constructed within the ruins of a much larger Early Christian Church EA (Fig. 1 No. 11).[137] Inhabited areas were also built into the ruins: the so-called West Building may have been first a mill, and then a fortified medieval agglomeration of houses, and Building A, which seems to have medieval embrasures, may also have contained a village (Fig. 1 No. 24). To the east, another village-type settlement existed at CG, where some industrial acitivity, either smelting of iron or glazing of pottery, was taking place in the tenth to thirteenth centuries.

The most important and best known settlement was on the Acropolis behind the immensely powerful wall constructed of the ruins of the ancient city in the seventh century. There were the tightly built rubble, brick, and stone houses, quite like those of present old Turkish hill towns. Squeezed in between them were graves and a cistern; more graves were found in the rock-cut chapel beneath the summit of the hill, which perhaps replaced a Lydian cistern. Excavations of this settlement have revealed several stages of building dating from the seventh through the fourteenth centuries (Fig. 4).

All these settlements were discrete. Although together, they probably constituted medieval Sardis, with whichever of them contained the cathedral being presumably the most important, the city never grew again to be a unified whole. To the present day, it has not recovered from the disaster of A.D. 616 and has remained an agglomeration of separate villages.

The decline of the city after 616 was dramatically swift and the reduction of the population also rapid. To judge by the remains of the periods before and after the Persian attack, the inhabited area, and presumably the population, were reduced by as much as ninety percent. Although the destruction caused by the Persian and later Arab attacks was severe, the upset of man's regular constructive activities and the unleashing of the destructive forces of nature were probably the major causes of the rapid transition from an urban to a rural state.

Once the aqueducts were cut or abandoned and the state no longer had the organization or the resources to rebuild them, water, the major need for man's sustenance, was bound to fail. That was a severe problem in the dry season, but the surviving inhabitants had to face quite an opposite danger in the rainy season and in the spring, when floods could overwhelm large parts of the city area if measures to control them were no longer taken.[138] The floods, however, were less disastrous for the abandoned buildings of Sardis than earthquakes. The history of seismic phenomena at Sardis has yet to be written, but it would appear that a disturbance in the seventh century or somewhat later was sufficiently severe to split off large pieces of the Acropolis and bury the Temple of Artemis. In the eleventh or twelfth century, another quake overthrew the Marble Court; in the Ottoman period, perhaps as a result of the earthquake of 1595, which leveled Sardis and other towns in the Hermus Valley, the domes of the Middle Byzantine Church E were toppled and flung about.[139]

The Turkish conquest and Seljuk domination (ca. 1310–1425) saw no major change in this pattern of settlement. The fortress on the Acropolis and the village it contained continued to be occupied, as did the villages at the Temple of Artemis and at PN. In the latter, Church E became a workshop in a village which remained on the site until modern times (Fig. 1).

A great ecological shift occurred when the Acropolis ceased to function as a fortress, probably at the time when Ottoman power was firmly established in the area (ca. 1425). The last dated evidence from the citadel is from ca. 1415, when some of the houses on the central platform were still occupied. The ancient Mediterranean form of acropolis as refuge castle with a populace living around it *kata komas*, was now replaced by a scattering of agricultural villages. The first European travelers note the "miserable huts" of Sardian villagers, especially in romantic contrast to the past riches of Croesus, but they also mention fertile fields and gardens. The description of Evliya Çelebi, the late seventeenth century Turkish traveler, shows that the fortress was abandoned but that Sardis was still a market town of some importance, with three "quarters" and 700 houses with earth roofs. During that period, and indeed until 1867, it was the center of an administrative district (*kaza*), though its retention of this distinction long after the town had shrunk to a mere village was probably due to the conservatism of bureaucracy.

The narratives of European travelers clearly show that Sardis was in great decline from the sixteenth into the nineteenth centuries. Ravaged by earthquakes, untamed nomad tribesmen, and the popular revolts which convulsed Anatolia in the early seventeenth century, Sardis shrank to a mere village. In that period another major ecological change had occurred with the establishment of nomads in the region, people who were naturally more interested in grazing grounds for their flocks and herds than in settled agriculture. For the Turkish writer Katip Çelebi (seventeenth century), Sardis is only important as a stop on the road which led to the summer pastures on Mount Tmolus. Similarly, the travelers make frequent mention of Turcoman nomads at Sardis and show that the settled population was small, if it existed at all.

There must have been a sufficient concentration of population to warrant the appointment of Sart as a *kaza* in the eighteenth century, and by the late nineteenth century most of the nomads had been settled on the land. The transfer of the administrative center to Salihli in 1867, however, finally demoted Sart to complete village status. The building of the railway in 1873, on which Sart was only a whistle-stop, completed the demotion. Curiously, it is the modern successor to the Royal Road, the highway from Izmir to Ankara built in 1951–52, which is reversing the trend and putting Sardis back on the map. Another novel development is the creation in 1971 of an automobile road up the west bank of the Pactolus Valley into the Tmolus range. The village has been moving from the railway station toward the highway, and the excavations—first those of the American Society for the Excavation of Sardis, and now those of the Archaeological Exploration of Sardis—have made Sart-Sardis world-famous and have transformed Croesus' old capital into that curious ecological manifestation of the twentieth century, the archaeological touristic site, where past and present mingle for the sake of Wanderlust and Knowledge, and pilgrims come from near and far, by bus and car, as Herodotus would have put it, *theories heineken*, "to see and learn."

CF, GMAH

III THE CITY WALLS

David Van Zanten
Ruth S. Thomas
George M. A. Hanfmann

Literary sources contain several references to defenses of Sardis. They indicate that fortifications of various kinds existed from archaic times on. According to Herodotus (1.84) the Acropolis was fortified by the semi-legendary King Meles; this would have occurred in the late eighth century B.C., if we accept Naster's dating of Meles.[1] The Herodotean account makes Croesus rely implicitly on the impregnability of the citadel during the siege of Sardis (547 B.C.); no attempt was made to defend the lower city.[2] Archaic Sardis would thus emerge as a settlement of the "Acropolis-Refuge Castle" type, in which a fortified citadel rises over an unfortified urban area.[3] A problem for this assumption is posed, however, by Xenophon's account in the *Cyropaedia* (7.2.2–4) of the capture of Sardis by Cyrus, in which he seems to distinguish the walls of the city from those of the citadel;[4] but since this version occurs in a highly imaginative, embroidered account of an admittedly novelistic work, it can hardly be considered reliable.

Whether or not the lower city was fortified under the Persians (547–334 B.C.) also remains uncertain. Herodotus' description (5.100–102) of the Ionian capture of Sardis in 499 B.C. is devoid of any reference to city walls, and Xenophon's account of the Battle of Sardis in 395 B.C. (*Agesilaus* 1.29–33) which took place near the banks of the Pactolus, likewise omits any mention of city walls.

The Acropolis, on the other hand, was strongly fortified with a triple wall when Alexander the Great captured Sardis in 334 B.C.[5] (For possible extent of the city area in archaic and classical times see Fig. 7.)

Because the configuration of the Acropolis hill has undergone great changes through earthquakes, landslides, and erosion, archaeological evidence for the archaic and classical periods is scanty and no plausible conjectures can be made about the lines of defenses. The earliest artifacts found on the Acropolis are not earlier than ca. 700 B.C.[6] The archaic limestone and sandstone walls discovered in sector Acropolis North were at first thought to be part of the Hellenistic defenses but are more plausibly interpreted as supporting terraces of a palace, since the limestone wall shows the traces of an outside staircase.[7] A short stretch of a strong fortification wall of smaller limestone masonry with rubble filling was found in 1973 near the top of the south slope (AcS–PH 1, 2, 3; Fig. 1 No. 52). It is pre-Hellenistic, either Lydian or Persian. It may belong to one of the three defense lines seen by Alexander.[8]

In late classical and Hellenistic times, the changing character of warfare led to the enclosure of vast areas within city walls, a fashion well represented in Asia Minor by changes of site in Kolophon and eventual changes at Smyrna and

Ephesus (Early Hellenistic).[9] At Sardis, such a change could have occurred under the Persians (Polybius' "Persian Gate" probably means the "gate toward Persia" or the gate of the Persian residential quarter),[10] but the initial period of the Seleucid rule (ca. 280–250 B.C.) would seem a more logical time.

By 215 B.C. an enclosure wall, protecting the lower city, did in fact exist. In his account of the siege of Sardis by Antiochus III, Polybius clearly states that the wall along the ridge called the "Saw" connected the citadel (akra) with the city (polis). An elite force scaled the cliff by ladder and 15 men climbed over the walls to break open the gate from within while 30 attacked it from without, thus permitting 2,000 troops to enter and occupy the upper edge of the Theater, from which they could attack garrisons of both the city and the citadel. Meanwhile, Antiochus, reviewing his troops in the hippodrome (which was presumably in a flat part of the plain) was able to enter the city through the Persian Gate "on the other side of town" (tas epi thatera pylas keimenas, Persidas de prosagoreuomenas) and also to seize the "neighboring gates" (Polybius, 7.15–17).

Polybius' description suggests that the "Saw" (prion) was near a gate and this, in turn, near the Theater. The sharp ridge descending toward the Theater (Figs. 1, 15, grid ca. E 1100–950/S 800–400) is presumably the survivor of the "Saw." This location would bring the course of the Hellenistic wall more westward than the Late Roman–Byzantine wall. It is impossible to ascertain from Polybius the exact location of the Persian Gate, but the northeast corner of the city would fit both the account and the geography—far from the "Saw" and toward the east, in the flat plain. It might be conjectured that the Hellenistic wall ran northward following the scarp (ca. E 1500/S 100 to E 900/N 200 in Fig. 11). The gate beneath the cliff was perhaps a minor one, and not the gate on the predecessor of the modern east-west highway.

It is impossible to determine with certainty how far the wall extended westward, although it can be argued that the Hellenistic city retrenched eastward from the Pactolus in the Pactolus North area

(Fig. 1 No. 10), and that perhaps even the House of Bronzes/Lydian Trench area (Fig. 1 No. 4) remained outside the early Seleucid city, as suggested by the presence of a Late Hellenistic cemetery in the HoB area. Whether the Pactolus crossing was at that time protected is not known.

The reconstruction of Sardis under Antiochus III (213 B.C.) may have involved a complete replanning, as synoikismos implies repopulation. This is indicated by Antiochus' inscriptions (letters) found reused in the Synagogue.[11]

The city walls were sure to have suffered heavily in the earthquake of A.D. 17. We do not know whether they were restored thereafter. There was no evident need for them until the threat of invasion from the Goths in the third century A.D. Nicaea and several other cities of Asia Minor hastily built up-to-date city walls during and after the first Gothic incursions in A.D. 253.[12] A city wall, however, was considered a distinctive feature of an important city, even in peacetime,[13] and positive evidence for its existence might be argued from the representation of a fortress on a coin of Caracalla (A.D. 211–217).[14] After the Gothic invasions of the mid-third century a possible cause for swift building of a defensive wall occurred when another group of Goths narrowly failed to despoil Sardis in 398.[15] The present City Wall most probably dates to the late third or fourth century.[16] Clive Foss has suggested that a reference to the Southwest Gate occurs in the "Tetrapylon Inscription," which may belong to the later fifth or sixth century.[17]

There are no explicit historical or epigraphic references to the destruction of the city or of the City Wall by the Persians in A.D. 616. Numismatic and archaeological evidence, however, leave no doubt about the fact and date of the destruction.[18] Parts of the wall must have been breached and destroyed at that time, but at the Southwest Gate and in the area of Building A, there is evidence from coins and archaeology of continued use of parts of the circuit.

Foss conjectures that the rebuilding of the citadel wall on the Acropolis, of which parts survive, may have occurred around the middle of the seventh century, when the troops of Constantius II were also busy repairing the main highway.[19]

The latest evidence for use of the Southwest Gate is the hoard of coins of John III Dukas Vatatzes (1222–1254) which was found at the foot of a slight wall built against the City Wall just east of the gate.[20] This, then, is the spotty and inconclusive literary and epigraphic evidence for the city walls of Sardis.

GMAH, RST

Topographical Description[21]

The Sardis City Wall can be traced for a distance of 4,100 m. and would seem to enclose about 1,560,000 sq. m. It is entirely of the same Late Roman mortared rubble construction except for a scattering of alterations (Pactolus Bridge and Southwest Gate) and Byzantine repairs (Tower T4 and sections 33–34; Fig. 11). Built to embrace both the precipitous cliffs of the Acropolis and the flat ground where the Roman city lay on the southern edge of the Hermus plain, it necessarily passes over a variety of topographical features and is adapted to take advantage of them. The topography and the man-made defenses are partners in the system of fortification, sometimes combined, sometimes one or the other playing the major role.

Proceeding from east to west (Table 4; Fig. 11), the first traces of man-made defenses (section 0) are on the eastern-most ridge extending north from the Acropolis into the plain, beginning where this ridge ceases to be a steep cliff (Fig. 16). The wall follows this ridge-top with slight, irregular zigzags, and perhaps traces of two towers on two small knolls, until it ends in the Hermus plain along the present road to Sart Çamur Hamamları and Ödemiş, after some 450 m. (sections 1–7; Figs. 11, 14). It then runs northward for 420 m. along the east face of a low terrace until reaching the present Izmir road (sections 8 and 9). It then apparently jogs to the west about 200 m. before continuing northward for another 420 m. (sections 10–14; Figs. 11, 335). These five sections of the City Wall, north of the Izmir road, are so deeply buried in the alluvial deposits encountered in the excavations of Bath CG that the nature of the topography at their base is unascertainable.

At about grid E 1009/N 435 all traces of the wall disappear. It has been suggested by G. M. A.

Hanfmann that three low hills in an east-west line from this point, flanked by the old Izmir road, may indicate its general course, the walls perhaps curving along the northern edge of these hillocks, just north of the road.

About 20 m. north of the present junction of the old Izmir road and a small north-south track stands a terrace some 2 m. high, with a 17 m. stretch of crumbled rubble walling in the middle of its north face (section 15), perhaps a bastion protecting a gate near the crossing of these two roads. Twenty m. south of the face of this bastion a terrace of earth and fill, up to 20 m. high at its center, runs westward to a point slightly west of the corner of Building B and 60 m. south of it. There are abundant vestiges of the City Wall in its northern face, ranging from a series of fragments of rubble masonry at the east (section 16) to a continuous stretch, 240 m. long and up to 5 m. high (sections 17–21a; see also Figs. 17, 18) with two towers (T1 and T2). The wall turns north-south to link with Building B (section 21b) at the westernmost tower, T2. The solid ashlar masonry of the north wall of Building B, measuring 150 m., would seem to have been made to serve as the fortification between section 21 and 22a (See Table 4). At its northwestern corner a spur of ashlar masonry turns north at right angles (section 22a), apparently linking with the mortared rubble City Wall which reappears running northwest-southeast for 75 m., then becomes the north face of a low terrace running west to a bank of the Pactolus River (sections 22b–26; see also Fig. 19). A tower (T3) stands in the middle of section 24.

Of the three towers surviving between sections 19 and 24, two (T2, T3) are semi-circular and one (T1) square, while all are approximately 7 m. wide on the exterior (Figs. 12, 20). Towers T1 and T3 are placed at slight angles in the City Wall, but only T2 buttresses an exposed right-angle turn. All three towers consist of a hollow cavity defined by walls averaging 1.30 m. thick, bonded into the stronger City Wall at both ends. There are nowhere traces of a glacis or other reinforcement in front of them, although tower T2 does rest on an unusually solid platform.[22]

The City Wall reappears on the Pactolus bank

and at a right angle to it about 400 m. to the south (section 29). There are traces of walling (sections 27, 28) along the eastern bank of the Pactolus between sections 26 and 29; while it was common to build retaining walls along water courses in built up areas, it would be logical that here these walls were also a link in the fortification system. Approximately in the middle of this stretch of wall are traces of a bridge abutment bonded into the retaining wall which curves into the river, then turns at right angles to form a trapezoidal bastion (Fig. 57). Several wall fragments would seem to define two small guard rooms to the north of the abutment. A solid bench of masonry and spoils stands in the water course 6 m. in front of the abutment, either as a breakwater or as a support for the superstructure. This is the precise spot where the Izmir road has crossed the Pactolus, since ancient times.

At section 29, the line of the City Wall leaves the Pactolus bank and cuts east-west for some 200 m. across flat ground, then ascends a distance of some 250 m. to an earlier man-made terrace (the Upper Terrace, wall section 30; see also Fig. 21). On the slope up to the Upper Terrace the line of the wall suddenly zigzags, taking three almost right-angle turns over a distance of approximately 110 m. This creates an indentation in the line of the wall. At the corner at the very back of this indentation, a gate is located, the Southwest Gate, the approaches to which from the outside lie thus across a triangle of ground dominated by the City Wall on two sides (Figs. 43, 49). A small guard room stands just inside the gate, on the northwest of the portal. There are no traces of defensive towers either at the gate, or at the two exposed corners of the City Wall flanking it.

Just east of section 30 the City Wall seems to have turned southward at right angles and ascended a ridge connecting with the Acropolis (sections 31–34; Figs. 11, 21, 22). Approximately 80 m. south of this turn stands a tower (T4) of later, Byzantine date, on the western crest of this ridge and apparently on the original wall line. It is larger than the other, earlier towers, measuring approximately 8 m. square, and more solidly built with walls 1.40 m. to 1.90 m. thick, a solid masonry base 6 m. high, and a glacis facing down the slope to the

west. Spoils were very extensively used in its construction (Figs. 12, 22, 23).[23]

The original City Wall continued along the ridge for some 525 m., running just to the west (outside) of the crest, as it had on the eastern side of the city (section 0–6). Also as on the east, the wall becomes narrower towards the Acropolis and would apparently have finally terminated where the ridge became a spur of the conglomerate cliffs with a precipitous face towards the west (outside).

Further up, southeast and halfway between the last preserved traces of the City Wall (section 34) and the Acropolis fortress, this spur bears the Western Ridge Fortification (Flying Towers), isolated fragments of fortification of a later date in the form of two towers and a bit of wall (Figs. 11, 24).[24]

Although unexcavated and in some places quite fragmentary, enough survives of the Sardis City Wall to reconstruct its line with a good deal of precision and to analyze the close cooperation between man-made and natural elements. The fact that the wall can be traced at both ends up to where it encounters the conglomerate cliffs would indicate that its two terminations have been located; it would have been linked to the Acropolis by these cliffs, which may well have been scarped to insure security. There may also have been isolated forts along the cliffs, like the Western Ridge Fortification. Between these two ends the line of the wall can be traced from fragment to fragment, except for the 500 m. gap between sections 14 and 15, where it surely followed a roughly straight east-west line.

Besides linking the City Wall to the Acropolis defenses, topography was made to serve a variety of other defensive roles. At the east and west ends where the wall follows a ridgeline, it stands a few meters outside the crest (east of the crest on the east, west of the crest on the west) and, in the case of section 0, stands on a bench cut into the conglomerate bedrock (Fig. 16). By this arrangement, the top of the wall was easily accessible to the defenders on the inside, but crowned the steepest part of the slope on a solid foundation facing the attackers outside. Apparently in recognition of the topographical advantage the wall narrowed to only one meter near the eastern termination.

Out in the Hermus plain a similar effort was made to run the wall along the outside face of rises or built-up terraces. Sections 17–21b (Figs. 17–18) support a terrace which is 8 m. high against the wall as now preserved. As a result, only where it crossed the mouth of the Pactolus Valley (sections 29 and 30; see also Figs. 13, 21), and perhaps at the northeast (sections 10–14, today deeply buried), was the City Wall a free-standing structure. At its two extremities and along most of its north side it was, to a great extent, a facing for natural or man-made earthworks.

One detail relating to the line of the City Wall should be noted before leaving the subject: it is broken into segments from 5 to 50 m. long, set at irregular angles to each other (varying from 10 to 90 degrees) which would have stiffened it against lateral pressure (exerted either by the earth terraces behind or the enemy in front). This zigzagging does not seem well-adapted for enfilading fire (in fact, it creates blind spots from the towers, as in section 19) and seems too ubiquitous to have been determined by property lines. Its only advantage would seem to have been structural. Apparently in appreciation of the stiffening quality of this feature, the wall width varied with the frequency of the zigzags; the long straight segment of wall section 3 is 2.10 m. thick, while the segment making four angles at short intervals is only 1.25 m. thick.

Construction

City Wall section 30, a stretch some 30 m. long and 7 m. high, standing on the Upper Terrace northwest of the Acropolis, was studied in 1971 as a typical structural sample of the fortification (Fig. 13). A trench run up against its north side by D. P. Hansen in 1959 was partially reopened (Fig. 25) and a second pit, 2 m. square, was dug corresponding to the first on the south side (Fig. 13, 26). Both pits were taken below the level of the foundation bottom.[25] The wall was found to rest on a foundation 2.90 m. wide, 2.79 m. high on the north and 2.65 m. high on the south. This was composed of rubble masonry in large amounts of white lime mortar with no faces. Large slabs, a meter long and

0.20 to 0.30 m. thick, made up the lowest course. Above, the concrete-like masonry seems to divide into four layers (0.80, 0.70, 0.55, and 0.75 m. high, reading from the bottom) with rough leveling courses of flat stones on the top of each. The top of the foundation mass is roughly finished with small flat stones in large amounts of lime mortar. The sides of the foundation masonry bear no traces of formwork; the surface, mostly masses of lime mortar, are irregular and pitted as if they had congealed against the earthen sides of the foundation trench. In 1971 no evidence was found of a wider foundation trench, confirming the observation made in 1959 that the foundation trench exceeded the width of the masonry very little, if at all.

On the north face two stretches of foundation top can be seen, the easternmost one m. higher than the other, stepping up the hill, at a slight angle both to the other segment of the foundation and to the wall (Fig. 13).

The City Wall proper, 1.90 m. wide at both bottom and top, stands directly upon the foundation top, set back 0.80 m. from the south (outside) foundation edge, and up to 0.20 m. from the irregular north (inside) foundation edge. The wall is constructed of layers of unfinished fieldstones in rubble masonry with white lime mortar varying from 0.45 m. to 0.60 m. in height, faced with a course of large stones (mostly 0.30 m. in diameter) below one or more courses of small stones (about 0.15 m. in diameter), topped by a leveling course of one or two layers of small flat stones (Figs. 13, 21, 25). The degree of cohesion between successive layers seems to be a problem; a clear line of separation is often evident where the wall surface is broken and in places tumbled sections of walling (Fig. 17) have broken into wafer-like sheets along these lines of cleavage. Yet the wall has weathered into column-like shafts in several places (Fig. 27) without any evidence of structural unsoundness. Perhaps it is a matter of weight and friction rather than of adhesion.

The north and south faces of wall section 30 were pointed with a gray stucco bearing horizontal gouges made with a mason's trowel handle (Fig. 26). In the case of the north side of wall section 24, the stucco originally covered the wall surface completely and was scored with vertical and horizontal grooves at roughly 0.50 m. intervals—apparently a decorative imitation of ashlar masonry (Fig. 20). This stucco seems to have been used on all surfaces of the City Wall, even those backing up against earthen terraces. It was probably meant to protect the more fragile lime mortar of the interior masonry from weathering.

Holes about 0.15 m. wide and 0.20 m. high extend into, and often entirely through, the wall; they are firmly clamped between layers of flat stones above and below (Fig. 13; see also Fig. 20). These appear regularly above every second leveling course (that is, approximately every meter vertically), commencing about 2.50 m. above the foundation. They are irregularly placed at 2 to 3 m. intervals horizontally.[26] They apparently are putlog holes in which squared timbers would have been set during construction to support horizontal scaffolding boards against both faces of the wall. The smoothness of the wall faces and the manner in which the mortar between the stones spreads out against this face would indicate that some sort of formwork also was used in construction. The strength of the facing masonry, however, would indicate that it, rather than the formwork, held the concrete interior of the wall in place. Large planks perhaps were set on their sides upon the putlogs against which the facing masonry would have been laid by hand, after which the planks would have been removed and the core poured. Whether these timbers continued to serve some purpose after the completion of the wall is difficult to determine, although it would be tempting to assume that they supported some sort of walkway for the defenders, supplementing the narrow width of the wall itself. The total lack of vertical alignment among the holes would seem to indicate that they did not directly support wooden stair structures.

Near the middle of wall section 30 the masonry courses between levels 127 and 130 are unaligned (Figs. 13, 21, 25), although they are aligned above and below this point. The masonry is carefully keyed together, however. This would appear to indicate a horizontal break in construction, perhaps the demarcation between the production of two different work crews.

A terracotta drain, 0.25 m. in diameter, passes through the wall at the point where the two trenches were dug in 1971. It slopes 0.30 m. from south to north (that is, downhill), its south end being 0.25 m. above the foundation top, roughly at the level of the ancient ground line as determined by the excavations. No other pipes or other structure connect with the drain's two ends. It would thus seem to have been intended to channel ground water down the hill through the wall to prevent weakening or undermining.

There is no evidence of a leveled top surface or of a parapet to protect the defenders on wall section 30. There is a small fragment of finished top surface on wall section 3 (Fig. 27), but this is simply a rough leveling course of flat stones with, again, no trace of a parapet.

It might be concluded from this examination of the construction technique that the wall was erected thus: a foundation trench was dug 3 m. wide and 3 m. deep; the bottom of this was covered with large slabs, then the rest filled with rubble masonry in masses of lime mortar, forming 0.70 m. layers, with no facing, the earthern sides of the trench serving as formwork.[27] The foundation was then topped off with a rough leveling course of flat stones and the wall proper erected; the interior was filled with concrete-like lime and rubble masonry, and each layer was finished with a leveling course of flat stones. Up to a height of about 2.50 m. the masons would have worked from earthen platforms banked against the wall or from low trestles resting on the ground; above this point they would have stood on scaffolding or horizontal boards resting on putlogs set into the masonry at one-meter intervals as the wall rose. Finally, the masonry completed, the wall would have been stuccoed on its two faces, the stucco pointed with the mason's trowel handle or ornamented with imitation masonry patterns, and a greater or lesser amount of earth piled up against its inside face, depending upon the terracing at any particular point. In general, therefore, this would seem to have been an intelligent and efficient system, one which recognized the weakness of Anatolian lime-and-rubble construction in its use of solid stuccoed facing masonry and utilized a method of erection requiring a minimum of temporary scaffolding and formwork.

Faruk Akça, expedition architect in 1971, has calculated the approximate time necessary to construct such a wall.[28] For a segment 2 m. wide and 9 m. high, resting on a foundation 3 m. square, 390 man-hours would have been required per linear meter, exclusive of haulage of materials. Assuming that the wall was erected by crews of 5 men (one master-mason and 4 assistants) in ten-meter segments (as indicated by breaks in the coursing), it would require 39 ten-hour days for two teams of masons to complete one segment of the wall. If all parts of the wall were erected simultaneously—requiring 4,100 workmen, plus teamsters, waterboys, and the like—it could have been completed in as little as 5½ weeks. If fewer workmen were employed, the time required for completion would have increased in proportion, 2,000 workmen requiring 11 weeks, and so on. All existing segments of the wall, however, bond together as if it was everywhere brought to completion at the same time.

We have restricted this discussion of construction technique to wall section 30 for the most part. There are very few variations from this norm along the length of the Sardis City Wall, the most significant being the narrowing of the wall at its two ends where topography takes over the primary defensive role, and, in the case of section 0, where the bedrock is scarped to provide a foundation (Fig. 16). Otherwise the essential elements of the wall vary only in detail; the lime mortar is whiter or redder depending on whether and how much brick dust has been added (this may vary from one course to another in the same wall segment); the finishing stucco may be whiter or redder for the same reason; the masonry courses vary in width from 0.45 m. to 0.70 m.; the stones constituting the face differ in size and squareness (although the largest rarely exceed 0.40 m. in diameter); a very restricted use of brick appears in the interior leveling course of wall sections 13, 22b, 23, 33. The only striking peculiarity appears in the outside face of wall section 32 where there is a rectangular depression 0.20 m. deep, 0.50 m. wide, and one meter high above ground level. Its function is not evident.

Analysis and Parallels: Philadelphia

The Sardis City Wall is precisely the same in masonry technique as the shorter enceinte of Philadelphia (modern Alaşehir) 36 kilometers to the east in the Cogamus Valley.[29] This Philadelphia city wall is better preserved today and more is known about it from nineteenth century sources. It shows several features which cannot be found in the existing Sardis wall; whether these features were originally present in the Sardis enceinte or whether the Philadelphia fortification was simply more elaborate and sophisticated is unclear.

Several basic features are common to both city walls. Masonry technique has been mentioned. Both are 2 meters wide and 8 meters high. The wall trace at Philadelphia is irregular with frequent re-entrant angles, although the straight sections are longer than at Sardis and there are few oblique angles. The towers along both city walls are irregularly placed and are both square and semicircular in plan; the tower at the northeastern corner of the Philadelphia enceinte precisely repeats the arrangement of T2 at Sardis. Neither city wall bears any trace of a parapet on top.

The Philadelphia city wall, however, differs from that at Sardis in that there are traces of access stairways to the wall top, more extensive remains of gates, and there is also one stretch with a double curtain wall and a more complete system of towers.

A gate near the northeastern corner of the Philadelphia fortification survives in good condition today. It consists of a barrel-vaulted passage through the mortared rubble masonry of the city wall which is faced on the west (inside) side with a brick arch. Two square towers flank this gate and a ramp leads down from the terrace behind the wall to the plain. This sturdy arrangement, however, is weakened by the fact that the city wall steps back behind the northern tower, leaving its north side open to assault. E. Curtius, writing in 1872, describes two other gates then fully preserved at Philadelphia as having monolithic jambs supporting lintels 2.50 m. to 3.00 m. in span, below stone relieving arches of three voussoirs. The only trace of these other gates today is two semicircular re-entrants defining the emplacement of that in the southwestern wall section. There is no trace of flanking towers here.

Near the northeastern gate in the Philadelphia city wall are traces of two stairways built into the west (inside) side of the structures, descending parallel to the face. Three stone steps, 0.60 m. wide, survive *in situ* in one instance. Both stairways are in the same wall section, some 50 m. apart. Both only survive in the upper part of the wall, suggesting that they were linked to the ground by ladders 3 or 4 m. high.

At its southeastern corner the Philadelphia wall extends far out eastwards on a low projection of the Acropolis plateau. Here there is a 13 m. side terrace in front of it, 2 m. higher than the ground level beyond, faced by an outer curtain wall, fragments of which are at least 1.50 m. thick. (This suggests that the "bastion" at Sardis wall section 15 may be a similar fragment of double curtain.)

There are traces of at least twelve towers along the Philadelphia wall, but almost all are on the north and east, only a third of its preserved length. (Two of the towers on the north are of later, Byzantine date.) There is only one tower along the west, at an exposed corner. All these three sides face the flat ground of the Cogamus plain; why the northeast should have been so solidly defended is unclear. On that sector, however, they are placed at quite regular intervals of about 75 m., the canonical two bowshots.

That there are no traces of a parapet in either fortification would suggest that the wall was unguarded—merely a barrier in front of which bodies of troops maneuvered, as along the limes. F. E. Winter has recently remarked, however, upon the frequency of parapetless walls among Hellenic and Hellenistic fortifications and concluded that breastworks must frequently have been of brick or timber which would have decayed without a trace.[30] Then, too, access stairs like those surviving at Philadelphia, which seem only to descend partway to the ground, could have disappeared with the crumbling of the wall tops. The piling of the earth behind the Sardis wall along the north and the reduction of the wall to a narrow breastwork cut into the conglomerate ridge at its two southern ends would have reduced the need for access stairs.

Nor would a great many access stairs have been necessary if the wall were manned by a light force of one man every 2 meters, as Thucydides seems to describe in the case of Athens during the Peloponnesian War.[31] The 4,100 m. length of the Sardis wall would have required only 2,050 defenders.

Arising from the question of whether and how the Sardis wall was actually manned is the problem of whether some specific tactical system can be identified in the trace of the wall, for if it were manned, lines of fire might to some extent determine its plan. The Hellenistic writer, Philo of Byzantium, provides what we know of theoretical tactical systems.[32] He outlines five types of trace, four of which are complex and specialized. And, in fact, the peculiar in-and-out line of Sardis wall sections 17 to 24 resembles Philo's maeander trace while the zigzags around the Southwest Gate parallel his "sawtooth" trace. The apparent inconsistency in types of wall trace utilized might be conveniently explained by Philo's assertion that different traces should be used in different parts of a single enceinte, corresponding to different types of topography. Yet these two areas of the Sardis wall are the only ones which show anything which by any stretch of the imagination resembles Philo's tactical types. Furthermore, the maeander in sections 17–24 may be too large in scale to have been effective, while the zigzag in sections 29–31 is explained by the presence of the gate. The most extraordinary and omnipresent feature of the Sardis wall trace, its continual slight angling, is neither advocated by Philo nor of any immediately obvious military—as opposed to structural—advantage. In spite of two possible parallels to Philo's types, then, the Sardis City Wall trace would seem to have been determined by topography and structure, as we have earlier concluded, rather than by subtleties of defensive tactics.

The Sardis City Wall, seen in the broader context of Late Roman military engineering in Asia Minor, seems to be only of local significance. It is a quick, stop-gap thing, chiefly interesting for demonstrating how much military advantage could be taken of surprisingly little construction. It gives no hint of the developments which led to the magnificent defensive system of the Theodosian Land Walls at Constantinople in 412,[33] the brick and stone walls of Nicaea (between 258 and 269),[34] or the arrangement of moat, curtain, and towers of Singara[35] and Amida,[36] both apparently built in the fourth century. Nor does the Sardis wall even possess such minor refinements as the solid cladding of finished blocks and spoils seen in the walls of Smyrna (between 395 and 408?),[37] which in the contemporary walls of Aphrodisias is combined with a regular system of access stairways.[38] Instead the simplicity of the Sardis wall's construction, its irregularity, its paucity of towers, and its dependence upon topographical advantages make it reminiscent of the limes or of early medieval walls in the west, where likewise the essential problem was how to get by with the least possible construction.[39]

DVZ

Detailed Description of Towers

Of the known towers in the Sardis City Wall, three (T1 to T3) are in the weakest, northern side toward the plain; the fourth (T4) holds a strong position in the southwest part of the wall as it begins to ascend the Acropolis (Fig. 11). Following are descriptions of these four towers.

T1. At the western end of section 19, E 189–191/N 202.5–209.5. External L. 6.05 m. E-W; external W. 6.70 m. N-S; P.H. 4.15 m. Th. east wall 1.35 m.; interior space between east and west walls 3.35 m.; Th. west wall 1.35 m.; Th. south wall 1.90 m.; Th. north wall 1.30 m. (Fig. 12). Construction is mortared rubble. Two putlogs are in the north face of the south wall, one near each corner. Cleaning showed that this tower was rectangular, projecting from the City Wall into which the east and west walls bond. Conceivably it might have flanked a gate. On the other hand, there are no traces of a road leading north from this area into the plain below the tower.

T2. At the western end of section 21, E 96–103/N 186–193. L. ca. 5.80 m. E-W; W. ca. 6.15 m. N-S. P.H. ca. 5.70 m. Th. east wall 1.05 m.; Th. west wall 1/10 m.; interior of chamber recedes 0.77 m. southward from the face of the City Wall in section 21. Both east and west walls go straight north for 3 m., then curve (L. curve 7.50 m.) making the tower semicircular (Fig. 12). Internal dimensions: 3.65 m. E-W, ca. 4 m. N-S. The platform of the tower was constructed in the same way as the wall to a height of ca. 3 m. (2.70 m. above the village road), making a solid bastion, not easily undermined. There is a blocked putlog hole in the east wall. The tower projected northward from the wall at the place where it turned 90° southward toward the Gymnasium platform (Fig. 1). This tower may have defended an approach from the plain upward.

T3. Near the western end of section 25, W 117–125/N

202–210. L. 7.10 m. E-W; W. 7.90 m. N-S including the south wall. P.H. at tower to rubble at middle of south wall, 5.00 m.; Th. east wall 1.50 m.; Th. west wall 1.50 m.; P.L. east wall 1.40 m.; P.L. west wall 6.90 m.; P.H. east wall 3.00 m.; P.H. west wall 2.80 m.; both measured from ground level outside east wall (Figs. 12, 20). The semicircular tower is not in a straight line with the excellently preserved section 24 (Fig. 19), nor with the poorly preserved section 25. The wall is regularly built with courses of flat riverstones alternating with courses of larger stones laid in cement. Putlog holes in the eastern and southern walls suggest a floor at ca. 1 m. above the present surface, a second story at ca. 2.50 m., and possibly a third at ca. 4.30 m. On the interior are traces of stucco. Impressed in the stucco on the base of the external west, east, and adjacent north face of City Wall section 24 are rectangular dado course panels of heights varying between 0.37 m. and 0.47 m. The panels are probably intended to imitate ashlar masonry (Fig. 20). This tower was clearly designed to defend the weakest location of the wall in a swampy part of the plain near the presumed northeast exit, which may have occurred between sections 25 and 26 at the modern road.

T4. Section 31 of the wall, E 80–89/S 313–322. L. above footing 7.85 m. N-S; L. footing (incomplete) 8.80 m.; W. E-W not certain; P.H. 8.35 m. including H. of tower; 6.45 m. to bottom; 1.90 m. from bottom of tower to present bottom of footing; H. of footing above ground 0.55 m.–0.80 m. (Figs. 12, 22, 23). The eastern part of the tower merges into the earth cover over the continuation of the wall northward and southward. At approximately the present surface and 1.10 m. below the top of the west wall as preserved is a possible floor level of a chamber, high up in the tower. Possible inner space: 4.85 m. N-S by ca. 4.75 m. E-W (Figs. 22, 28). Built into the inside of the west wall in this top section are four double half-column shafts (Fig. 22). Three are in the northern half, placed horizontally at right angles to the wall; the fourth is askew semi-vertically. From south: *a:* purple veined, L. 0.56 m., W. 0.36 m.; P.H. 0.68 m. *b:* orange, as in Marble Court columns. L. 0.47 m.; W. 0.40 m.; P.H. 0.52 m. *c:* yellow, L. 0.57 m., D. 0.41 m.; P.H. 0.52 m. *d:* purple-veined, L. 0.57 m.; D. 0.41 m.; P.H. 0.52 m.

A modern rubble platform intervenes between the tower and the ancient footing (plan, Fig. 12). As preserved, this footing projects 1.40 m. beyond the north wall, 1.45 m. beyond the west wall, and 1.43 m. beyond the south wall (Fig. 22). The footing consists of ashlar spoils at the northwest corner and smaller masonry spoils and riverstones. Several large spoils also appear in the facing of the tower on the north and west sides (Fig. 23). Most of the facing of the north and west sides, and all on the south side is lost. The core consists of nearly horizontal courses of bricks and rubble mixed with large, broken-up marble spoils set in slightly pink, very pebbly, lime mortar. Where the core is exposed on the north and west sides it seems homogeneous; it is split down the middle of the west side. There are four putlog holes in a vertical row on the north side, ca. 3.30 m. in from the west face; two or three on the west face.

Several spoils built into the tower seem to have come from one structure with an Ionic architrave, pulvinated acanthus frieze, possibly Corinthian capitals, and part of an unfinished Ionic entablature with a false lion-head spout projecting from the sima (Fig. 23 upside down). Ionic architrave: H. 0.52 m.; L. 0.60 m. Top of Ionic entablature with dentils: H. 0.34 m.; W. 0.34 m.; D. 0.58 m. Part of

Corinthian capital 0.50 m. by 0.67 m. Part of Ionic entablature with false lion-head spout, unfinished: L. 0.60 m.; W. on top 0.60 m. bottom 0.44 m.; H. 0.52 m. Lion head on sima: H. 0.10 m.; W. head 0.21 m. (Fig. 23). Ionic epistyle block: H. 0.45 m.; W. 0.55 m. North side center: pulvinated frieze (torus) with acanthus, broken at side and top: L. 0.60 m.; H. 0.20 m. The construction is less chaotic than it seems at first sight. This tower is most likely a homogeneous addition of the sixth century, different in size and plan from the other three towers.

Stratigraphic Soundings at Section 30

The pits dug near wall section 30 provided the only concrete stratigraphic evidence for dating of the wall. Trench I in the Upper Terrace, excavated in 1959, showed alternating strata of burned matter and debris slanting downward toward the City Wall to a depth of ca. 9 m. below the present surface (*124.00–*115.00). D. P. Hansen, who excavated it, considered the entire deposit to be a one-time deposition, dated by the latest coins found in the fill to late fourth or early fifth century (Theodosius I, 379–395; Honorius II, 393–423; near surface, Theodosius II, 408–450).[40]

Trench II in the Upper Terrace was dug further down the slope. In it were exposed Roman structures of the first or early second centuries A.D.[41]

Trench III, dug against the north face of wall section 30, from surface at *126.20 to *121.50, revealed only mixed fill for about 0.40 m. below the wall footing of the same type as in Trench I. Sherds ranged from first to second century A.D. Roman to sixth century B.C. Lydian. Below ca. *123.00–*122.60 were natural gravels with worn sherds.

In 1971 Trench III (then called North Pit) was reopened and recleaned to a depth of *122.60 (Fig. 13). The South Pit was also opened against the south face of section 30 from a surface of *127.10 to *123.35. Findings in the South Pit from ca. *126.00 to *123.50 show homogeneous deposits up to a little below the bottom of the wall. The range of pottery in the fill is late second century B.C. to first century A.D. It is possible that the material deposited as fill comes principally from houses destroyed during the earthquake of A.D. 17.

The results of the soundings are inconclusive for dating the construction of the City Wall. Any date after A.D. 100–150 is possible in this section.

Finds: Upper Terrace Trenches

Trench I

Coins
C59.294. E 90/S 210, *124.00–*122.00. Theodosius I, A.D. 379–395.
C59.348. E 80/S 170, *115.80. Arcadius, A.D. 395–408. Constantinople.
C59.142. E 80/S 200, surface to 40 cm. below. Theodosius II, A.D. 425–450. Nicomedia.

Pottery
P59.401:1940. Small bowl, almost complete. E 100/S 210, *121.70–*120.80. Diam. rim 0.07 m.; diam. base 0.05 m.; H. 0.043 m. Eastern sigillate B, 1st phase (Samian B). Potter's stamp ΕΡΜΟΓ/ΕΝΟΥΣ on inner base does not occur elsewhere. Foot type resembles those from Priene. Cf. Hayes, p. 10, 10 B.C.–A.D. 75; Robinson, *Agora* V, Group G, pp. 24, 55, 30 B.C. to probably A.D. 50, p. 40, late first–early second centuries A.D.;[42] F. Oswald and T. Pryce, *An Introduction to the Study of Terra Sigillata* (London 1920) pl. XL, shape. (Figs. 29, 30.)

Trench III
Pottery
P59.404:1944. Fragment of base. E 50/S 240, *126.11–*124.71. Diam. base 0.05 m.; H. 0.025 m.; Th. 0.006 m. Eastern sigillate B, 2nd phase. Cf. Hayes, 10, A.D. 75–150; Robinson, *Agora* V, 25, Late Augustan or Early Tiberian to mid-second century A.D. (Groups M 31–33, H 30, G 167–171, 174, 176, 213). (Fig. 31.)
P59.423:1973. Two fragments of mended plate. E 50/S 230, *124.50–*124.20. Diam. rim 0.16 m.; diam. base 0.12 m.; H. 0.03 m.; Th. 0.004 m. Eastern sigillate B, 1st phase (Samian B). For shape cf. H. Comfort, *BASOR* 160, 16 f. figs. 1, 2, 3; Hayes and Robinson dates, *supra* P59.401:1940. (Figs. 32, 33).
P59.424:1974. Small fragment of very fine orange slipped plate with flaring rim and flat floor. E 50/S 230–235, *124.50–*124.20. P.H. 0.23 m.; diam. rim 0.28 m.; diam. base 0.14 m.; Th. 0.005 m. According to J. Wrabetz, African red ware, 2–3 century A.D. As other African red ware sherds were found outside the area of the trench, this sherd may be intrusive.
P59.425:1975. Fragment of base. E 50/S 230–235, *124.30–124.20. Diam. base 0.06 m.; P.H. 0.016 m. Th. 0.005 m. Eastern sigillate B, 1st phase (Samian B). Hayes and Robinson dates *supra* P59.401:1940. (Fig. 34.)
P59.426:1976 (IN59.56). Fragment of black-glaze ware (base) with potter's mark: ΗΛΙΟΔ/ΩΡΟΥ. E 60/S 230–235, *124.50–*124.20. Diam. base 0.07 m.; Th. 0.005 m. Probably eastern sigillate B, 1st phase (Samian B). Hayes and Robinson dates *supra* cf. P59.401:1940. (Fig. 35.)
P59.447:2022. Complete, plain, red, ribbed, piriform unguentarium. Flat bottom. E 50/S 230–235, *123.50. Diam. rim 0.04 m.; diam. base 0.05 m.; H. 0.15 m. Cf. Robinson, *Agora* V, pl. 5, G 98; 18, M6, M7. First century A.D. (Fig. 36.)
P59.491:2075. Hellenistic relief ware fragment. E 50/S 230–235, *123.70. Preserved dimensions: 0.075 m. × 0.069 m. Th. 0.006 m. "Pergamene" Cf. *Tarsus* I, 177, figs. 138, 139, nos. 305–309 for pattern. Ca. 150–50/25 B.C. (Fig. 37.)

North Pit
Pottery
P71.18:8152. Fragment of bowl. E 39–40/S 235, *126.20–*124.00. Diam. rim 0.27 m.; H. 0.045 m.; Th. 0.007 m. Possibly eastern sigillate B, 2nd phase (Samian A). Hayes and Robinson dates *supra* P59.404:1944. (Fig. 38.)

South Pit
Lamp
L71.2:8149. Late Hellenistic lamp fragment; E 38–43/S 237, *126.25–*125.00. Diam. discus 0.04 m.; P.L. 0.05 m. Ca. 125 B.C.–A.D. 25. Cf. Schäfer, 146, taf. 69 no. T2. (Fig. 39.)

Pottery
P71.7:8140. Fragment of shallow bowl. E 38–43/S 237, *123.60–*123.35. Diam. rim 0.10 m.; H. 0.015 m. Eastern sigillate B, 1st phase. Like P59.423. Hayes and Robinson dates *supra* P59.401:1940. (Fig. 40.)

P71.11:8144 (IN71.17). Base of plate with potter's stamp. E 38–43/S 237, *123.75–*123.35. Diam. foot 0.03 m.; Th. 0.003 m. Probably eastern sigillate B, 2nd phase. Hayes and Robinson dates *supra* P59.404:1944.

P71.13:8146. Ledge rim of Hellenistic (?) crater. E 38–43/S 237, *123.75. Diam. rim 0.39 m.; W. ledge 0.035 m.; P.H. 0.06 m.; Th. 0.007 m.

P71.17:8151 (IN71.12). Fragment of bowl with potter's stamp: ΙΑΤΡΟ/ΚΛΕΟΥΣ. E 38–43/S 237, *123.75. Diam. base 0.055 m.; P.H. 0.02 m.; Th. 0.003 m.–0.004 m. Eastern sigillate B, 1st phase. Hayes and Robinson dates *supra* P59.401:1940. (Figs. 41, 42.)

Evidence for Dating

At this point, it may be well to consider all available evidence for the dating of the extant City Wall. Stratigraphic data from pits in section 30 indicate only that this section of the wall was built after the second century A.D. According to J. Wrabetz, with the exception of the African red ware sherd (P59.424:1974), the pottery excavated from Trenches II, III, and the South Pit predates the last half of the second century A.D.

The use of third century architectural pieces as spoils in the Pactolus Bridge water-breakers, in the Southwest Gate, and elsewhere (*infra*) permits a late third or fourth century date. The comparisons of layout, design, and construction with other city walls, made by D. Van Zanten, allow a wide chronological range. Perhaps the most useful indicator is the resemblance of construction technique to the technique of other rubble and concrete constructions at Sardis. It would still leave a span from the second through the fourth century A.D. for possible date.

No datable inscriptions, such as were found at the gates of Nicaea, determine the date of the Sardian wall. If its rapid construction was connected with an emergency, either the Gothic invasion of the mid-third century or the uncertain conditions around 400 present plausible occasions; but it could have been constructed because of general uncertainty at any time between A.D. 250 and 400. None of the coins found in section 30 or in the bridge area was in a completely reliable findspot; their range, from Constantius II (337–363) through Arcadius (393–405), would favor construction between 350 and 400.

GMAH

SPECIAL FEATURES OF THE DEFENSES

While only one section of the City Wall was tested by excavation, two integral features of the defense system, the Southwest Gate and the Pactolus Bridge, were objects of special investigations. The results attained are reported in the following sections.

The Southwest Gate

In winter 1966 K. Z. Polatkan dug a trench along the village road which runs from PN to east of the HoB area, more or less along the western part of the City Wall. This road is known to coincide for considerable stretches with the ancient colonnaded road, a section of which, dating from ca. A.D. 400, has been excavated at ca. W 10–20/S 165–185 (Fig. 10 No. 58, Fig. 11). The opening of the trench, originally intended to divert the winter floods, revealed a piece of marble entablature decorated with acanthus and cavetto leaves and indicating the possible presence of a gate. To investigate this possibility, a sounding was undertaken in 1966[43] and re-opened and slightly deepened in 1970 (Figs. 43, 48). The trench extended from W 76–87/S 214–226 on the B grid; levels were taken from the B datum (Fig. 1 No. 8).[44]

Location
The gate consists of two piers (P 1, P 2), which represent the terminals of two stretches of the

City Wall meeting at right angles, stretch P 1 pointing eastward, P 2 northward. Adjoining the gate to the east was a marble-paved street or open piazza, at least 5 meters wide. The paving was traced for 6 meters northward (Figs. 43, 47–49).

The Southwest Gate aligns fairly well with the Street of Pipes, in sector Pactolus North, and it was undoubtedly from this direction that a street entered the city here. On the other hand, the axis of the gate does not align with the Colonnaded Street in HoB, Middle Terrace, although it is possible that this street, which makes several bends, made yet another bend toward the gate (site plan, Fig. 1 Nos. 5a, 5b, 58; see also Fig. 10 No. 58).

Inscription IN68.19, found at HoB, mentions a gate: "The *embolos* was built from the Tetrapylon as far as the *embolos* of Hypaepa, with the gate being cut out . . . "[45] Clive Foss suggests that this might refer to the Southwest Gate through which a road from the Tetrapylon to the road to Hypaepa may well have passed.

The City Wall sections adjoining the gate (Fig. 11, sections 29, 30) are cemented rubble as in the other stretches and were preserved to a height of ca. 2 m. above the level of the paved road in the stretch adjoining pier 1 (*tw* *112.20) and over 2 m. on the stretch adjoining pier 2. The gate was clearly planned together with the City Wall. The use of similar spoils in the bridge suggests that they were constructed around the same date.[46]

Construction and Use

Overall dimensions of the gate between piers were 3.43 m. N-S and 2.0 m. E-W. A clear width of 2.45 m. is indicated by two rectangular cuttings made, according to A. H. Detweiler, for metal plates placed under the door posts (Fig. 50). The dimensions of these cuttings were 0.27 m. by 0.27 m.; D. 0.05 m.; diam. of round corner holes 0.02 m. Pier 1 is 2.40 m. E-W by 2.30 m. N-S; pier 2 is 2.30 m. N-S. It is probable that a barrel vault spanned the full width of 3.43 m. between the two piers.

The passage through the gate showed clear traces of cart tracks 1.47 m. apart. Flanking the immediate approach to the gate on the north and used as facing were spoils, the most spectacular

of which is part of a Hellenistic pediment placed on its side (H. 0.52 m.) with a shield-like device in the center (Fig. 49).[47] Other very fine marble blocks from the same structure (0.55 m. square with fine drafted edge) were used in pier 1.

H. A. Thompson observes that the marble bench along the NW wall was the underpinning for a massive door jamb which would have been carried around in an L-shape to give coverage to the pivot of the door. Small vertical holes in the threshold (Figs. 43, 50) were for vertical bars to secure the door.

Pier 1 and the barrel vault for a side passage which it carried were overthrown by an earthquake in an easterly direction. As shown in Figure 46, its height can be calculated from the large reused marble pieces: (1) acanthus-cavetto frieze, used upside down as footing profile, is 0.56 m. high, L 1.13 m., W. 0.95 m. present top, 0.73 m. bottom; two rows of alternating acanthus leaves, deeply drilled; 13 cavetto leaves (Fig. 51), ca. 3rd century A.D. (?), similar block (Fig. 58) in wall *lb 3* at bridge (Fig. 54) (2) marble block, Hellenistic, H. 0.55 m.; rough-hewn top profile which is convex, between two fasciae, 0.22 m.; (3) Hellenistic block, H. 0.80 m.; (4) Hellenistic block, H. 0.55 m. Total pier H. above bench level, 2.68 m. There is no profile for the springing of the vault which was faced on the southern side with small limestone voussoirs and backed by marble blocks and rubble. Typical voussoir dimensions: face W. 0.10 m., H. 0.55 m., D. 0.45 m.[48] The vault must have been between 2.00 and 2.25 m. wide N-S; its length E-W is unknown. It is tentatively designated as "Passage" in plan (Fig. 47).

A door jamb block (Fig. 44) found north of pier 1 (ca. W 85/S 218, *112) is probably too small for a doorway with a span of over 2 meters: max L. top, 1.00 m.; max. L. bottom, 0.70 m.; H. 0.24 m.; W. top, 0.48 m.; W. bottom, 0.41 m. Back and one side broken. Profiled in front (from top: fascia, concave profile, concave profile, convex profile, fascia). It belongs to the type of door frame known from the Gymnasium. It is possible, as A. R. Seager suggests, that this piece belongs to the door under the vault which sprang from pier 1.

A rubble wall L (Fig. 43) projects southward. A lower bedding of stone and bricks and an upper bedding of cement (H. 0.25 m., 0.10 m.) extend for nearly 2 m. under the vault and in front of it. Some large white tesserae indicate that the space under the vault may have had a coarse mosaic. Immediately outside the vault alignment, however, a blue flat paving stone (t *110.45) lies over the cemented bedding (*110.45) showing that space RV was probably a paved outside area, possibly a street or court (Fig. 43).

Wall L seems to divide into a pier (tw *110.83) and a possible threshold support (*110.58). This rubble wall is 0.65 m. wide. The pentagonal limestone block B is carved in such a fashion as to suggest possible insertion of a door post between it and the large rounded marble block A which certainly belongs to the original foundation of pier 1.

Space Gu was possibly a guard room (Fig. 47). Either there was a late floor at ca. *100.80–*110.70 or one stepped down to ca. *100.25, the deepest level reached by our excavation and below the paved street level of *111.00. The reason for assuming this lower level is that the fall of rubble from the City Wall which destroyed the unit seems to go on uninterrupted to this depth—a higher floor would have stopped it.

It is noteworthy that all finds from this space Gu, below the *111.00 level were Early Byzantine or earlier. Either they antedate the construction or the room was already out of commission by the Middle Byzantine era.

Coins
C70.15. W 84/S 218.5, *110.5, south of wall L. Probably Justinianic.
No number; 5th century monogram (disintegrated). W 84/S 218.5, *110.5, south of wall L.

Pottery
P70.33:8120. Pilgrim Flask. W 83.5/S 218; *110.62. Cross on both sides. H. ca. 0.05 m.; W. ca. 0.04 m. (Figs. 52, 53.)

Metal
Two lead tokens, smooth, without design. W 84/S 219; *110.65. Lower floor of Gu. D. ca. 0.008 m.; Wt. 0.4–0.5 g.

Byzantine Occupation
The low, poorly-built rubble and brick wall K ran E-W and joined the City Wall at W 78/S 224; its preserved top was at *111.20. In unpaved earth at its southeast end, apparently in the corner of the space or room formed by K and the City Wall, a hoard of 14 Byzantine scyphate coins was found, 13 of John III, 1222–1254, Magnesia, 1 Latin imitation from Constantinople, ca. 1204–1261.[49] The use of the area in the thirteenth century and Middle Byzantine period is confirmed by findings of fragments of Byzantine sgraffito wares between the surface and *111.00, W 80/S 219.

Evidence for Early Byzantine occupation is much more abundant; the bulk of pottery finds and glass fragments closely parallel those of the Byzantine Shops. A pentanummium of Justin II (565–578), W 78/S 223, *111.15, is the best numismatic item,[50] although others have also been found around *110.50 in room Gu. The pilgrim flask P70.33 was found under the marble jamb B of the same room. It is possible that the gate ceased functioning as a full-scale vehicular entrance in A.D. 616 and was reconditioned in a more desultory fashion sometime thereafter.

GMAH

Pactolus Bridge

The ancient and medieval bridge across the Pactolus was in use with a wooden span until 1951. It was briefly mentioned by Butler and its position indicated on a small scale map (Fig. 3).[51] In 1951, when the concrete bridge for the modern highway was built slightly to the north (Figs. 54, 55), a Lydian lion was found at a depth of seven meters.[52]

In 1967 and 1969, the walls in the eastern bank, adjacent to the bridge, were cleaned (Fig. 55), as were the wall fragments within the present Pactolus bed (Figs. 54, 56, 57). This eastern bank was much overgrown and a modern water channel was running at a higher level than the Pactolus bed. On the western bank, now occupied by a gazino (restaurant), an area 16 m. long N-S was excavated in the river scarp, but only broken-up concrete rubble pieces were found. The coordinates of the bridge are on the B system; the levels are taken from the Artemis Temple datum.[53]

Location
Cleaning showed that the bridge was an integral part of the City Wall defenses described above, built in the same technique and in the same general

period. It undoubtedly served the main east-west highway, which was identical with the Main Avenue in Roman and Late Antique (Early Byzantine) times. As the general plan shows (Fig. 54; see also Fig. 10), the avenue must have veered slightly southward to make the bridge crossing. From the north, the bridge defense system was joined by an embankment which constituted section 28 of the City Wall. From the south, it was joined by the long section 28a preserved up to 3 m., which ran for 120 m. southward (Fig. 11).[54]

The Bridge Structures

There are three major groupings of walls: the trapezoidal east pier of the bridge, here called "East Bridge Abutment" (Fig. 54), with three walls projecting westward (walls II, III, IV in Fig. 54); the embankment (I), with adjacent walls V–VII; and on a lower level, in the present torrent bed, an alignment of walls (*lb 1, 2, 3*), distinguished by the reuse of large marble spoils (Fig. 58).

The walls north of the abutment may be interpreted as constituting two guard rooms, one pentagonal (walls I, VII, V), the other oblong (walls V, VI, VIII). It is not known whether any similar rooms existed on the south side, now under a village orchard. Walls *lb 1–3* in the Pactolus bed may have been breakwaters to protect the eastern pier and may have provided footing for additional supports (Fig. 58). We interpret them as a continuous embankment.

The top of the platform of the east pier was at approximately *81.78; by projecting it across to the western bank, the length of the bridge was determined at ca. 22 m.; its width was 9–10 m.

What emerges is a gate crossing, tied skillfully, if asymmetrically, into the City Wall and protected by special guard rooms, though not apparently by regular, symmetrical, flanking towers. There is no indication that the bridge went across on vaulted arches. Perhaps, like its pre-1952 successor, it was a wooden bridge, or even a draw-bridge.

Excepting walls *lb 1–3*, the walls were built of carefully selected flattish river stones, set with gray cement. The technique is the same as in other parts of the City Wall. Wall III had a stuccoed face preserved on its southern side; it showed brown scoring of the kind encountered in other Late

Roman structures at Sardis such as the Palaestra of the Gymnasium.

Walls *lb 1–3* (Fig. 54), which were perhaps breakwaters, show large masonry pieces in the lowest and sometimes in the second course (Fig. 58), with cemented rubble on top. Reused masonry pieces 0.40 m., 0.60 m., and 0.85 m. wide occurred in *lb 1*. A gigantic third century A.D. block, perhaps from an anta, with cavetto, acanthus, and palmette (Fig. 58) was used in *lb 3* (cf. Fig. 51, SWG).

Descriptive Notes

The wall complex of the guard rooms (Fig. 56) with walls V–VIII was apparently designed in relation to wall I (which is part of the City Wall system) rather than the bridge itself. It constitutes a kind of bastion. Wall I runs for a stretch of 16.75 m. northwest. It is preserved for a height of over 3 m. The corner it once formed with the East Bridge Abutment has cleaved apart, opening the cleavage space *x* (Figs. 54, 55). Here, in the hollow interior space (W 292/S 27–29, *78), were found some 70 sherds, Roman and Early Byzantine, but none was closely datable.

The original dimensions of the east pier were about 10 by 7 m. Its top is about 5 m. above the present Pactolus bed. Walls II and III were clearly advancing to support the bridge. Wall III did bond but now has cracked near the line of bonding. Wall IV has a window-like opening (Fig. 57). A rubble wall led obliquely from wall *lb 3* back to the east bank (Fig. 58). Perhaps the entire *lb* alignment constituted one lower level embankment designed to protect the lower part of the bridge pier. The bridge pier structures undoubtedly linked with the City Wall to the south, which at present, however, first appears some 9 m. south of the East Bridge Abutment.

Dating

The most reliable find spot was that of a coin of Constantius II (A.D. 337–364) found on top of wall II. A coin of Arcadius (393–405) on top of wall VI, near the surface, was less reliable. Somewhat more trust may be put in coins of Theodosius I, Arcadius, and Honorius (383–395) found in the rubble on top of the great marble block of wall *lb 3*.

Taken at face value, the coins prove that the bridge and the *lb 3* "embankment" with its reused spoils are contemporaneous and were completed between A.D. 395 and 400.

The use of spoils in the *lb* walls recalls their use in the Southwest Gate, and, indeed, the cavetto-acanthus blocks of the bridge wall *lb 3* and of the gate (Figs. 51, 58) might come from the same building. None of the other objects found contributed any conclusive argument for or against the dating suggested by the coins. To advocate an earlier dating, one would have to assume that the bridge

defenses were either added to an earlier City Wall, or were constructed earlier and only rebuilt under Theodosius.

Coins
C67.751. Constantius II (337–364). Top of wall II.
C67.543. Arcadius (395–408), Constantinople. Top of wall VI, near surface.
C67.805. Theodosius I, Arcadius, Honorius. (383–395), Cyzicus. Rubble on top of marble block of wall *lb 3*.

Pottery
P67.145:7583. Ringfoot of bowl. Eastern sigillate B (1st phase or Samian B). Incomplete rectangular stamp, illegible. Cf. Hayes, 10, 10 B.C.–A.D. 75.

GMAH

Table 4. City Wall sections.

Construction: All wall sections, except 22a, consist of *coursed rubble masonry in lime mortar*. Additional observed features are listed below.

Wall section	Dimensions in meters			Grid location Figure 11	Topography	
	Length	Height	Width			
0a	Traces of fallen rubble masonry			S 442–499 E 1311–1284	On steep east side of north–south ridge, 2.00 m. east of ridge crest.	No face surviving.
0b	8.00	2.00	1.00		"	Foundation visible: apparently resting on a bench cut into the conglomerate ridge. Wall face left at bottom. Pink mortar.
0c	7.00	2.00	1.00		"	No face surviving.
0d	3.40	0.50	2.80		Covers top of small knoll, apparently in two concentric squares. Tower?	No face surviving.
0e	Traces of fallen rubble masonry				On north–south ridge, just east of ridge crest.	No face surviving.
1	5.00	3.70	1.25	S 369–374 E 1391–1397	"	No face surviving. Marble chunks in mortar. Stucco patches. Putlog hole.
2	10.10	4.50	1.25	S 350–359 E 1411–1420	"	No face surviving. Putlog holes.
3a	9.20	2.00	1.25	S 293–324 E 1424–1432	"	West face well preserved. Putlog holes.
3b	8.40	6.45	1.25		"	West face well preserved. Putlog holes.
3c	25.00	6.50	2.10		"	East and west face well preserved. Foundation visible: 2 steps bonded into wall, 0.35 m. wide, 1.50 m. above ground, the lower 2.00 m. long and 0.80 m. below upper, on east wall face. Small section of wall top preserved: roughly levelled with small slabs and mortar, 2 sections stepping up 0.70 m. Stucco patches. Putlog holes.
3d	Traces of fallen rubble masonry 23.00				"	No face surviving.
4	11.00	4.90	1.40+	S 260–274 E 1435–1440	Cuts north–south across broad slope falling towards north.	No face surviving. Putlog holes.
5	Traces of fallen rubble masonry			S 248–252 E 1427–1430	Covers top of low knoll. Tower?	No face surviving.
6	11.60	3.50	2.20+	S 216–229 E 1447–1453	Cuts north–south across slope falling towards the north.	East and west face preserved. Possible foundation stones at bottom of west face. Traces of a wall spur on west face, perhaps a buttress.
7	3.60	1.60	2.20	S 103–107 E 1491	Passing north–south across flat ground.	No face visible.
8	Traces of fallen rubble masonry			S 20–22 E 1478–1479	Passing north–south across flat ground forming east face of 3.0 m. earth bank.	No face surviving.
9	Traces of fallen rubble masonry			N 99–102 E 1230–1233	Passing north–south across flat ground. Deeply buried.	No face surviving.
10	Traces of fallen rubble masonry			N 200 E 1180	"	No face surviving.
11	87.00	3.00	1.70	N 261–345 E 1120–1149	"	Bits of face visible. Putlog holes.

No.				Coordinates	Position	Notes
12	27.00	2.50	1.70	N 345–351 E 1094–1123	Passing east–west across flat ground. Deeply buried.	Bits of face visible on south side.
13	60.00	0.50	Faces uncertain	N 359–379 E 1012–1069	"	No face surviving. Tiles on inside of topmost levelling course. Brick used.
14	50.00	3.50	2.20+	N 394–435 E 509–527	Passing north–south across flat ground. Deeply buried.	Large stretch of face on east side. Putlog holes.
15	18.00	1.40	Inner face not visible	N 358–368 E 509–527	North face of a low bank, north of sections 16–21, flanking north–south road. Bastion?	No face surviving.
16a	4.00	1.50	0.90+	N 271–275 E 382–414	North face of a large banked-up terrace, ca. 10.0 m. high at peak.	No face surviving.
16b	Traces of fallen rubble masonry					No face surviving.
16c	3.00	0.25	Faces uncertain		"	Small trace of north face.
16d	Traces of fallen rubble masonry				"	No face surviving.
17	11.00	5.00	2.00	N 203–206 E 293–303	"	Sections of north and south faces visible. Putlog holes.
18	70.00	5.00	2.00	N 194–199 E 221–288	"	No face surviving. At east an extensive use of brick and tile with pink mortar in upper parts of wall; less so lower. Topmost course a later repair. Brick used. Stucco patches. Putlog holes.
19a	8.50	5.00	Inner face uncertain	N 202–209 E 183–221	"	East face well preserved. Putlog holes.
19b	37.00	5.00	1.70		"	North face well preserved. Tower (T 1) at west end. Stucco patches. Putlog holes.
20	21.00	4.00	Inner face uncertain	N 190–202 E 144–154	"	North face well preserved. Spoils included. Stucco patches. Putlog holes.
21a	32.00	4.00	1.80	N 186–194 E 97–128	"	North face well preserved. Tower (T 2) at west corner. Wall narrows to 1.50 m. behind tower. Spoils included. Putlog holes.
21b	3.00	1.50	Faces uncertain	N 144–147 E 100	West face of terrace, apparently linking T 3 and Bldg. B.	No face visible.
22a	3.70	1.50	1.50	N 120–127 W 51	Passing north–south across flat ground from NW corner Bldg. B.	Three courses of cut marble blocks with Pi-clamps. No evidence of superstructure. Opening 3.50 m. wide in north wall of Bldg. B, bricked-up.
22b	10.00	Traces of fallen rubble masonry		N 126–164 W 51–68	Passing northwest–southeast across flat ground.	Some brick inside. No face visible.
23	13.00	4.40	2.20	N 164–176 W 68–73	"	No face visible. Very restricted use of brick for interior levelling courses. Putlog holes.
24	33.50	6.85	2.20	N 199–204 W 93–129	Passing east–west across north face of low bank.	North and south faces well preserved. Tower (T 3) at west end. Stucco on north face scored in block pattern. Putlog holes.
25	Masses of fallen rubble masonry			N 205–210 W 129–170	"	No face visible. Perhaps a platform for a bastion or city gate.
26	7.90	2.20	2.50	N 198–208 W 190–200	Forms east bank of Pactolus River.	No face visible.

(continued)

Table 4. City Wall sections (continued)

Construction: All wall sections, except 22a, consist of *coursed rubble masonry in lime mortar*. Additional observed features are listed below.

Wall section	Dimensions in meters			Grid location Figure 11	Topography	Construction
	Length	Height	Width			
27	20.00	1.00	0.90+	N 16–46 W 260–268	"	No face visible.
28a	7.00	3.00	1.00	N 12–S 150 W 266–314	"	Good face preserved on west. Putlog holes.
28b	23.00	2.00	1.50+		"	Foundation visible: finished marble blocks and spoils form a projecting bench at the base of the wall. No face surviving above foundation. Spoils included.
28c	5.00	1.50	Faces uncertain		"	No face visible.
28d	Traces of rubble masonry				"	No face visible.
29	105.00	6.50	1.80	S 190–254 W 138–216	Passing northwest–southeast across flat ground.	North and south faces well preserved. Tower (T 5) on south face near east end. Stucco patches. Putlog holes.
Southwest Gate	32.00 E–W 12.00 N–S	2.00	2.20	S 222–240 W 64–92	On terrace rising gently to southeast.	Foundation visible: finished marble blocks (spoils) under gate abutments. Fragments of face preserved. Putlog holes. Spoils included.
30	30.00	7.00	1.90	S 232–239 E 37–71	Running east–west along northern edge of terrace, flat to south, sloping down to north.	Foundation visible: rough rubble masonry in lime mortar laid in 4 courses, 2.70 m. deep, 2.80 m. wide, projecting 0.10 m. on north, 0.80 m. on south. North and south wall faces well preserved. Terracotta drain through wall, 0.25 m. diameter, sloping 0.30 m. south to north, 0.25 m. above foundation on south. Brick used. Stucco patches. Putlog holes.
31	8.80	8.35	8.80	S 312–322 E 80–89	On wide place on north–south ridge ascending towards south.	Foundation-like bench extending 1.00 m. to 1.50 m. in front of west and north faces, mortared rubble faced with blocks, spoils. Extensive use of bricks and tiles in interior (but not on faces), extensive use of spoils in wall construction. Putlog holes.
32	20.00	6.65	2.20	S 368–388 E 119–121	On steep west side of north–south ridge.	Restricted use of brick on interior, squared blocks low in face. Rectangular depression in west face: 0.20 m. deep, 0.50 m. wide, 1.00 m. high. Spoils included. Stucco patches. Putlog holes.
33a	Traces of fallen rubble masonry			S 645–670 E 220–254	"	Foundation-like bench extending in front of face; mortared rubble faced with blocks and one spoil. Fragments of wall face visible. Spoils included.
33b	1.00	1.00	Masonry fragment		"	No face visible.
33c	Traces of rubble masonry				"	No face visible. Restricted use of brick.
33d	Traces of rubble masonry				"	No face visible. Bricks and tiles in one levelling course. Spoils included.
34	3.00	1.00	Inner face uncertain	S 688–690 E 270–272	"	No face surviving.

IV THE ARTEMIS PRECINCT

George M. A. Hanfmann
Kenneth J. Frazer

Since 1914 the configuration of the ground within the Artemis Precinct has changed. The Harvard-Cornell Expedition camp was constructed in a terraced design in 1958–1959 with a central building planned by the Department of Antiquities in 1958 and other structures subsequently added. Its enclosure runs along grid lines ca. S 1106–1110 on the north, S 1162–1163 on the south, jutting in to S 1153–1155, and from W 203–269, jutting out from W 190–203. The large parking area, built in 1959 west of the camp and northwest of the temple, has filled in much of the Pactolus riverbed of 1914. Conversely, since 1967 the torrent has been furiously undermining the area just west of the temple (Figs. 1, 59, 60). In 1972, with the aid of the Ministry of Waterworks, breakwaters were installed above (south) of the Artemis Precinct and a new banked channel dug within the Pactolus bed in order to divert the torrent from the precinct. On the opposite bank, at the foot of the Necropolis across the Pactolus a road for vehicles was built in 1971.

Topography

In *Sardis* I (1922) Butler gave a fairly detailed account of his excavation of the Artemis Temple and Precinct as indicated in his Plan II, "Temple Area Before Excavation" at 1:1000, contour intervals of 0.50 m. based on a datum of a.s.l. 35. For reasons stated above by S. L. Carter[1] Butler's grid of 2 m. squares could not be reconstructed. Our basic plan of the precinct (Fig. 59) was initially based on Butler's Plan III; parts were resurveyed in 1969 and 1970 and a complete revision was made in 1971. Butler designated noteworthy features with Arabic numerals 1–15 which have been retained; we have added 16–21 and designated other features with capital (Q, U) and lower case italic letters. Conditions described are, in general, as of 1969–1970. A major cleaning was undertaken in 1973 (*infra* Chapter VII).

Extent of Area Known

The approach to the Hellenistic temple was apparently from the west or very slightly southwest. Since no indications of a bridge across the Pactolus are preserved, it is most likely that a sacred road entered the precinct through a propylon from the north. We have no knowledge of a precinct wall. The visitor would then turn at approximately a right angle eastward to face the altar and the temple (Figs. 59, 60).

The westernmost monument known within the precinct is a base at ca. W 226.5 (if one considers Building Q and adjoining houses as a later development). This suggests that the precinct extended to at least W 240 westward. On the east side Butler dug some 50 m. beyond the temple. It seems that the steep landslide slope existed already in Late Hellenistic times but it is unlikely that the present boundary, at ca. W 72 indicated by Monument 10, was original.

On the north side the North Central Terrace and the associated North Building extended the range of the precinct from S 1138.5 to 1200. The Northeast Stoa may have been part of the uphill complex, possibly bounded by an E-W street (W 70–110/S 1110–1130). Just beyond it was the densely populated region of NEW (Northeast Wadi).[2]

On the south, the torrent coming down from the Acropolis probably constituted a natural boundary, although its position then need not have been the same as now. Building L and scattered monuments to the east indicate a slightly narrowing terrace between S 1280 and 1320. Known overall dimensions of the Artemis Precinct are thus ca. 210 m. N-S (S 1110–1320) and ca. 200 m. E-W (W 50–250).

Orientations

The axis of the Artemis Temple is oriented 293°20′ (N 360 Mag; 23°20′ N of west). The structure LA 1 (Lydian Altar), which antedates the extant temple, conforms exactly to this orientation (293°46′; cf. K. J. Frazer, *infra,* Ch. VI, "Orientation"). The structures and monuments along the southern and eastern sides and in the northeast corner conform in a general way but imprecisely. Indeed, one might argue that the southern and northern sides of the precinct may have been intended to converge slightly, thereby exaggerating the effect of axial perspective of the temple.[3] The North Street (N-S street), which we assume was at W 200/S 1150–1180 and which may have served as an entrance to the sanctuary, would also conform (Figs. 61–63).

Two marked divergencies from this orientation may be observed. The two rows of stelai bases (NSB and SSB in Fig. 59) are both at angles of ca. 8° to the south off the temple axis. This oblique approach is also seen in the area in front of Building U and may be a Late Roman practice (Figs. 61, 63).

On the other hand, uphill to the northeast, the North Terrace, North Building, Northeast Stoa, and the street behind the Northeast Stoa all form a co-

herent system which diverges from the temple orientation by ca. 14° (Figs. 59, 66). As the walls of the Lydian archaic houses in NEW conform to this orientation and as the archaic sanctuary may have been located uphill and in this direction, one wonders whether the system may not antedate the Hellenistic temple.

Levels

All soundings made by us as well as those made by Butler have run into torrent-laid deposits. Under Tomb 2 they started at *96.05 and were datable to before the Late Hellenistic–Early Roman period. During the sounding of the east cella image base in the temple water laid deposits were observed from *99.75 to *96.80 (Fig. 59 No. 17). In various trenches around LA (Figs. 181, 182) they started at *99.40 and went to *95.67; at the bottom of the LA perimeter wall (S) at *96.98; in Trench S from *97.64 to *95.40 (Figs. 59, 219, 220); in Building L from *98.90 to *96.70 (North Trench); and in pits within Building L *98.20 to *96.70 (Figs. 257, 258).

Two observations need to be made: only in Trench 2 in the Artemis Temple, in Trench S, and in the trench east of LA was the sterile hardpan underneath the deposits reached (at *95.40 in S).[4] Clearly, there was an earlier (pre-Hellenistic) and a later (second to third century A.D.) series of deposits. W. Warfield, geologist of the Princeton Expedition, commented on the buildup of the later series.[5] He alleged that by the third century A.D. the deposits of a torrent north of the temple had reached a height of 1.20 m. above the temple platform (*101.20). Deposits under the North Building reach *103.00 and those under NE Terrace, *104.00. All of these precede the last reordering of the precinct. Traces of flowing streams at the tops of the north and east walls of Church M show that in the tenth century and later the deposits rose to *105.00 and higher.

The situation is complicated along the east side which Butler had excavated in 1913.[6] According to Butler, "less than thirty meters from the east facade of the temple" (i.e., ca. W 82/S 1200 in our grid) "rose a precipitous mass of hard packed earth about 12 meters high covered with a lighter deposit

5 meters deep. The lower levels were very tough and difficult to excavate (ill. 149)." Warfield "found that the hard mass was a great fragment of the Acropolis . . . which had fallen, had been shaped into a great slope directly east of the temple . . . and had become quite as hard as the original substance of the Acropolis . . . "[7] Butler had wavered between the earthquake of A.D. 17 and "a similar catastrophe within a century earlier" but Warfield[8] firmly assigns the fall of the west end of the Acropolis hill to A.D. 17. He believed that "the Acropolis debris fell against a spur . . . which culminated in an elongated cone." This cone may have been moved some distance down the slope "but still projects from the surface," looking amazingly like a mound burial. It was tested by G. W. Olson in 1970 and found to be of natural formation (Test site #48: E 200/S 1200). "This sample was collected from the conical mound above the Temple of Artemis. Analyses are expected to shed light upon the uncertainty regarding the origin of the mound. Its symmetrical conical shape strongly suggests that it has at least been partially shaped by man" (Test site #49: E 200/S 1200). "These samples were collected from the south side of the conical mound above the Temple of Artemis. They will provide additional data to supplement those gained from Site #48. The soil profile at Site #49 does not show evidence of disturbance by man and does not contain artifacts." Soil samples Nos. 95, 96, 106, 107 from the test sites indicate that "this mound probably has been shaped by man, but not disturbed—it has been cut away but not built up."

Olson also tested the slope east of the temple (Site #5, E 0/S 1200, Samples 12–15) and reports that "after construction in the third century B.C., the temple site experienced several earthquakes and was partly covered with alluvial and colluvial material from upslope. By the ninth century A.D. a landslide covered the ruins . . . " Referring to the ravine south of the Artemis Temple, Olson adds: "Most of the lower part of the profile consists of landslide materials which covered much of the temple by the ninth century A.D." On top of this is a "thin layer of gravelly, loamy sand . . . deposited by more recent rapidly flowing water. The six inch

layer at the top of the soil profile is probably mostly wind-deposited" (field report 1970).

As far as levels are concerned, the configuration has been changed by Butler's digging and terracing.[9] Two facts are important: Butler's deep[10] (more than 2 m. below surface around the temple, at *98.00–*97.00) trenches below the foot of the presumed Acropolis landslide and east of the eastern temple facade brought forth many "fragments of Lydian pottery of early date and one jug of the sixth century B.C. or earlier, which was found directly in front of the temple." On the other hand, structures built *on* the presumed fallen mass, in two terraces, such as our Monument 10, which is shown by Butler during excavation,[11] and a "row of small chambers with walls at the rear and sides which had been open toward the temple," had thousands of fragments of pottery . . . none earlier than the first century A.D." This would confirm the dating of the landslide to A.D. 17, but our findings at Monument 10 throw doubt on Butler's chronological interpretation of this pottery.

Precinct Floors

Butler believed that he had encountered a Byzantine level and underneath it a Hellenistic and a Lydian level closely superposed.[12] He took the general precinct level he had excavated to be that of the Hellenistic precinct which continued in use in Roman times.

The safest indication of the earliest precinct floor known is given by the lowest step and paving blocks of LA (perimeter). A floor level of ca. *96.90 is indicated for the Hellenistic phase (Fig. 59). The floor level that goes with the earlier altar of limestone is not significantly different, being ca. *97.14. The placing of Lydian and Greek stelai bases (Fig. 59, NSB, SSB) which took place when an attempt was made to free the sanctuary from flood deposits and rearrange it (second or third century A.D.) indicates a floor level at ca. *97.30. To judge by the entrance to Building U (Fig. 59 No. 3; ca. *97.30), this level still held in Early Byzantine times, at least for part of the area. At the same time the level of the southern colonnade had risen to ca. *101.50 in front (west) of Church M (Fig. 59).

Apart from the Northwest Quarter, where the levels may have remained the same as in Roman times (Fig. 61), the only indications concerning Middle Byzantine levels come from the use of the platform of an extended form of LA 2 at *98.20 and the reuse of Building L with floors at ca. *100.20–100.40.

Byzantine Occupation

As Butler discovered, the Northwest Quarter of the precinct had been at one time part of a residential quarter (ca. W 190–250/S 1150–1220; Figs. 59, 60, 61, 65), probably in Early (ca. A.D. 400–616), Middle (A.D. 616–1204) and Late (1204–1300) Byzantine periods.[13] To this settlement belonged the Byzantine cistern within the temple, dated by coins of the ninth century or later on or near the bottom of the cistern; two levels of lime-kilns south of the temple, one Early Byzantine, the other Middle Byzantine with scyphate coins (tenth to thirteenth centuries);[14] and Church M with a cemetery extending from south of M to north of Building L (ca. W 80–200/S 1260–1300). This redistribution of a sacral area into sacral (churches), funerary (cemetery), residential, and functional (water supply) sections probably occurred when the temple was abandoned, i.e., after A.D. 400 (Figs. 59, 65). The houses of the Northwest Quarter and Building L were still in use from the tenth to the thirteenth century.[15]

The Northern and Northeast Quarter and the eastern high embankment (Fig. 66, W 60–200/S 1100–1200, W 40–80/S 1200–1280) do not seem to have become Byzantine residential areas. The only high wall left in the Northeast Quarter is the wall at W 116/S 1195–1200, marked *tw* *106.30 in Fig. 66, at the southeast corner of North Building. Its level is so high above the floor of the North Building that it probably belongs to the Turkish village transferred by Butler.[16]

Chronological Summary of Precinct Use

In essence, the recent geological findings confirm the general sequence of events hitherto assumed by the Harvard-Cornell Expedition, although some of the earlier statements of Warfield are superseded. The geological record and archaeological evidence suggest the following chronological summary for the use of the precinct area:

Archaic period	Alluvial deposits (see *infra,* "Temple Soundings," 1960, 1972). Trench S, Level IIb.
ca. 600 B.C. on	Sporadic Lydian remains among gravel (Corinthianizing, ca. 580–550; Fig. 151).
sixth or fifth century B.C.	Altar of Artemis(?). Floor and deposit H in front of Building L. Butler's finds at east end of temple in 1913(?)
Archaic temple of Croesus' era(?) ca. 550 B.C.	No clear excavated evidence. Other arguments: cf. *infra.*
ca. 270–220 B.C.	Building of Early Hellenistic Temple of Artemis. Enlargement of Altar (LA 2) possibly already in fourth century B.C.
ca. 220?–190? B.C.	Later Hellenistic temple structure; double cella temple.
213 B.C.	Burned level under Building L.
A.D. 17	Landslide reaching up to (and into?) eastern end of temple. Late Hellenistic Monument 10 and other structures built on eastern scarp of this side.
A.D. 17–200?	Accumulation of alluvia (described by Warfield) to above level of temple (*101.20 or higher). Roman restoration ca. A.D. 20–160. Burials (Tombs No. 2, 13?, 14?) made during first-second centuries A.D.
A.D. 140–300	Temple dug out of alluvia and reconstructed for Antoninus and Faustina but never finished. Artemis Precinct rearranged with stelai reset. Late buildings (North Building) on terraces of alluvium.
A.D. 300–868?	Gradual accumulation of alluvia.
ca. A.D. 400	Church M built.
Before A.D. 868?	Landslide covers temple and lower story of Church M.
ca. A.D. 1000–1300	Reuse of Building L and possibly of Altar LA 2 at levels of *100.20 and *98.25 respectively.
ca. A.D. 1300	Additional, lesser landslides and alluvial deposition.

DESCRIPTION OF FEATURES AND MONUMENTS

The Northwest Quarter

The Northwest Quarter extends from ca. W 190–250/S 1150–1220 (Figs. 59, 61). In general, all major walls excavated from 1910–1914 by Butler were still extant in 1969. Since Butler did not describe any of the structures in detail, we have thought it worthwhile to do so now before they disappear.

The major features of the Northwest Quarter are North Street (Fig. 62), a N-S street running uphill between Units NW and NS; two or three complexes of rectangular rooms (Fig. 61) *d, g, h, k, n* 1–5; and two monumental units—U perhaps originally a mausoleum and later a chapel(?), and Q, possibly an assembly room.

Unit NW

NW is an apparently rectangular unit of which only the southeast corner is preserved at the southeast corner of the expedition camp (Figs. 59, 61, 62). Only parts of two walls of NW can be discerned between coordinates W 201–205/S 1151–1164. Wall *a*, traceable for ca. 17.30 m., runs north-south, disappearing under the south wall of the expedition camp. It can be traced inside the camp up to the rectangular cistern on the second terrace of the camp. It is joined at a right angle by wall *a1*, which is part of a longer alignment (?) running east-west for 24 m. The south side preserved part of a rectangular room. The remains of two buttresses and piers project southward. Approximate width of Unit NW is 4.10 m.; the thickness of the mortared rubble walls, ca. 1.00 m.; internal width is ca. 2.70–2.80 m. Present level at top of foundation of southeast corner is *99.42.

Unit NS

Structure NS was a long, narrow unit built of mortared rubble walls *b* (N), *b 1* (W), *c* (E), and *g 1* (S) and lying between coordinates W 190–197/S 1159–1179. The level on top of wall *b* was *101.60, measured at the corner of *b* and *b 1* (Figs. 59, 61, 62). Northern wall *b* was 4.80 m. long. The western wall *b 1* ran south for 20.40 m. to the southwest

corner of the terracing wall *g 1*. Wall *b 1* had good stucco on its western face. P.H. 1.10 m.; W. 1.18 m. The long eastern wall *c* ran south for 20.70 m. This wall was disrupted by Butler's railway trench and only fragments of its southern part remain. The hypothetical south wall would measure 5.30 m. The building was slightly irregular in plan, rising from ca. *100.00 (Fig. 61, W 195.5/S 1179) to *101.60. The levels suggest a stepped terracing substructure, perhaps rising northward uphill in one or several steps.

North Street

This street, 4.90 m. wide, entered the precinct area from the north going downhill between structures NW and NS and passing between North Terrace and the southeast corner of Unit H. It lies between coordinates ca. W 195.5–201.5/S 1155–1180. The respective corners of wall *g1* (North Terrace at W 195.6/S 1179.4 in Figs. 59, 61, 62) and *g* (in Unit H) are preserved. The street sloped rather steeply between S 1159 at *102 and S 1180 at *97.50, a difference of 4.5 m. within its length of ca. 25 m.

Units X, Y

Units X and Y are rectangular units built against the south side of wall *a1*, apparently as foundation or basement rooms. They are situated between coordinates W 209–225.5/S 1163–1170 (Figs. 59, 61). Walls *a1* and *d* appear to have constituted the northern and southern limits of a sequence of rooms west of North Street. A niche-like projection at the eastern end of *a1* suggests one room; another to the west may be inferred. The north-south walls of Y and X are sufficiently preserved to have recognizable dimensions, which are virtually identical: 4.80 m. E-W and 5.60 m. N-S. Room Y has a door at the southeast corner, in the south wall.

Unit H

Trapezoidal Unit H consists of three rooms: *h*, which may have been an entrance porch, possibly with kitchen, and two back rooms, *k* and *k 1*. A curious stone platform and a stub wall seem to belong to the furnishings in *h*. The unit is at grid squares W 201.5–215.5/S 1176–1186 (Figs. 59, 61).

Lanes oo and o

Unit H was entered from Lane *oo* which then turned sharply east to continue into space *p* (Fig. 61). At one time Lane *oo* was blocked (hatched wall in Fig. 61). From the juncture of Lane *oo* and space *p*, Lane *o* took off southward between Unit N on the west and Building U on the east. It may have continued to Lane *ss* at S 1208. It wound up in the open area of a little "piazza" south of Building U. Lane *o*, too, may have been blocked up at one time. These lanes vary between 1.00 and 1.75 m. in width.

Unit N, Lane nn

Bounded by Lanes *oo* on the north and *nn* on the south, the very long Unit N makes the impression of a well-planned, official building, perhaps a storage or office structure. It lies at W 208–248/S 1187–1195. Rooms *n 1–4* are of equal width (5.0 m., external dimensions N-S) but of varying lengths (14.0 m., *n 1;* 4.5 m., *n 2;* 6 m., *n 3;* 8.25 m., *n 4*). Room *n 5* adjoins *n 4* on the north. The structure is built with more ambitious masonry, including spoils. Room *n 4* shows a towerlike effect from the south (Figs. 61, 67).

Building U

Building U clearly was built to incorporate Roman Tomb 2, set in an odd position near, but not quite in, the northwest corner of the structure. The date of structure U is still uncertain. If, as will be argued below, the great ordering of the sanctuary lasted through the second half of the third century A.D.,[17] structure U may have been built as a Roman mausoleum. The pronaos plus cella temple-like plan is common enough (Figs. 59, 61, 68).[18] It is, however, equally possible that the structure either was converted after the Peace of the Church or was built from the beginning as a martyrion or chapel, for it continued to function into Middle Byzantine times.[19] That ancient stelai, like that of Timarchos, were set up in front of it need not surprise: to cite venerable antiquity by using spoils was not uncommon in Byzantine architecture.[20]

Building U is bounded on the north by space *p* and on the west by Lane *o* (between W 195.5–207/S 1187–1200). It stands on a platform, ca. 1.30 m. high.[21] Adjoining U to the south is an area bounded by wall *r* on the east and Stelai Base 6 on the west (W 195–208.5/S 1200–1206). From this area, entrance to U was gained by a flight of six steps (Figs. 68, 69; only five are shown on our plan, Fig. 68) with levels from *97.74–*98.48.

The outside dimensions of the structure are 10.10 m. to 10.50 m. E-W and 12.10 to 12.40 m. N-S. The platform and lower walls consist of coarse, cemented rubble with marble and limestone spoils and larger boulders used especially for external (Figs. 69, 70) and sometimes internal (Fig. 68) facing. The walls are consistently 1.06 m. thick.[22] The southwest corner has partly slid down and the northwest corner has collapsed; the western wall between porch and main room has been robbed.

North Wall. The interstice between the vaulted Tomb 2 and the south face is filled with rubble, max. P.H. ca. *99.17. Along its south face, the wall has a recognizable footing, ca. 0.15 m. wide, marked with level *99.05 in Fig. 68. Allowing for marble slabs (*sectile*) or for mosaic with appropriate mortar beddings, the floor at ca. *99.40 would have lain over the footing and just level with the top of Tomb 2 (*99.385 without original stucco). A reused marble ashlar block with traces of Pi-clamp and inscription IN70.6 (Figs. 68, 70), *AR* left to right, is set into the wall in line with the opening into the tomb.

South Wall. It is divided into three parts, 2.75 m., 4.60 m., and 2.75 m. In the top row are several reused marble blocks, among them the one bearing the Lydian inscription, *a. rul,* used upside down (Figs. 68, 71).[23]

Staircase 3 (Figs. 59, 69). The staircase retains Butler's number 3 in our plan. Its condition as found is shown in *Sardis* I (1922), ill. 141. It had six steps, the two lowest projecting southward beyond the south wall of U. The highest step was inside the porch, top at *98.48, indicating a floor level of ca. *98.48. P.W. 3.65 m. In 1969–1970 the lowest step was lost; the marble pieces marked *98.74 and *98.93 on our plan (Fig. 68) are perhaps parts of it. The top and the fifth step were reset in 1969. The original width of the staircase was ca. 4.50–4.75 m. Counting from the top, the heights of the four steps in position are 0.16, 0.21, 0.18, and 0.18 m. The width of the tread is ca. 0.40 m. It should be noted that the steps consist of reused marble and limestone pieces of varying lengths and widths. Thus in the top step lengths are 1.00, 0.95, 0.70, 0.95 m. and the widths are 0.47, 0.65, 0.47, 0.60 m. In 1969 a piece of rough-picked gray marble (L. 0.67 m., W. 1.04 m., H. 0.43 m.) was reset on top of the southwest corner of the staircase. In addition, a fine masonry block was set south of the southwest corner where it seems to have been set in antiquity. The piece is of gray polished marble with two dowel holes on top. L. 0.83 m. (E-W); H. 0.42 m.

Tomb 2 (Figs. 59, 72, 69, 73). The tomb lies between coordinates W 202–206/S 1188–1191. In *Sardis* I (1922) Butler provided a good brief description of the tomb, which is shown in his Plan III. Curiously, he missed the wall paintings. In 1969 L. J. Majewski and G. M. A. Hanfmann recognized the paintings. The tomb was cleaned and partly excavated; the exterior was cleaned and remeasured in 1970.

The manner in which the painted stucco curved inward at the foot of the painted wall indicates the position of the earth floor, ca. 1.73–1.85 m. below the crown of the internal vault (Fig. 74). Except for the southeast third, the tomb was dug to ca. *97.00, 0.15–0.20 m. below the floor in 1970. There was a layer of earth immediately below the floor; then river gravel appeared. Levels: external top of vault *99.38; interior top *99.05; exterior floor (Lane *o*) *97.80; interior floor ca. *97.20. The following finds made just below the floor indicate a date for the tomb in the early first century A.D.

Coin
C69.229. 0.50 m. east of west wall of tomb; 0.99 m. south of north wall. Sardis, autonomous, bronze. Obv. Head of Apollo Laur. r. Rev. Club in oak wreath. 133 B.C. to Augustus.

Lamp
Uncatalogued. Small fragment of Hellenistic-Roman black clay lamp. First or early second century A.D.

Pottery
P69.25:7956. Fragment of base of red sigillate footless flat-floored plate with a slightly curved vertical wall. P.W. 0.08 m. Incised concentric circles on interior. Found with coin. Roman. Eastern sigillate B; Wrabetz Form 11, ca. 30 B.C.–A.D. 30. Probably local. Cf. R. Zahn "Thongeschirr" in T. Wiegand and H. Schrader, *Priene* (Berlin 1904) 431–2, fig. 550; P. Hellström, *Labraunda* II.1 (Lund 1965) 68, fig. 13, 35.
P69.26:7957. Fragment of red sigillate cup with vertical rim.

Found with coin (C69.229). H. 0.05 m. Roman. Eastern sigillate B; Wrabetz Form 17D, ca. 30 B.C.–A.D. 30. Probably local.

The tomb was set into carefully cemented rubble. The entire corner between its north wall and the north wall of Building U was filled out with rubble, possibly to ca. *99.40, i.e., level with a floor in U which, for other reasons, may be assumed near that level. If the footing at *99.05 had been overlaid by a bedding and a marble floor, its level might have become *99.25 or higher. In that event, the crown of the tomb at *99.38 would still have risen slightly above the floor. It is more likely, however, that the top of the vault was stuccoed and perhaps a small altar stood over it.

The original construction was that of a typical Roman vaulted tomb accessible through a trap door on the east and covered by a stone lid. The outside dimensions are overall L. 3.55 m., of which 2.67 is vault, 0.60 is trap door, and 0.35 m. brick border. The inner dimensions are 2.92 m. E-W by 2.12 m. N-S, H. ca. 1.85 m. The height of the lunette is 0.95 m.

The outer western wall was exposed and cleaned. It was seen quite clearly that the western wall of U had been built up to the sides and vault of a pre-existing tomb (Figs. 68, 73). On the other hand, the rough rubble filling in the wall below the lunette and the rough brick filling in the lunette indicate that this wall was originally not exposed, since it was underground. The exterior width of the vault is 2.35 m.; the finished interior width 1.84 m.; the exposed height from top to present level in Lane *o* is ca. 1.80 m. The jambs are made of bluish riverstones. The vault proper is ca. 0.85 m. high. It consists of 39 brick voussoirs, with joins of 0.04–0.05 m. filled with carefully smoothed lime plaster which contains many crushed brick particles. The bricks are normally 0.33 m. square, and ca. 0.035–0.045 m. thick.

The vault starts on the east and west sides with whole and half bricks in alternate courses. A pattern of seven half bricks alternates with eight whole bricks, resulting in normal alternation of joins (Figs. 72, 73).

The stone lid which covered the trap door is gone; two projecting steps, however, leading down into the tomb are recognizable (Fig. 72). The tomb was plastered and stuccoed on all four walls and on the ceiling. The western lunette, 0.95 m. high, shows the pattern of a wide (6–8 cm.) red band frame, then a zone of background ivory (4–5 cm.), and then a thin purple to black band (2 cm. wide). A bird drawn in black is seen walking left and pecking at a garland. It floats on the background. The head of the bird is lost (restored by L. J. Majewski in Fig. 72). Its wings are drawn as scales. Similar frames are recognizable on the side walls, at least on the lower side. The eastern wall and the lunette were essentially the same (in frame at least) as the western, but were partly destroyed by the steps inserted in the wall. There are preliminary incisions in wet plaster still noticeable as straight lines within a frame on the western wall.[24]

Butler uncovered similar graves on the southern side of the Artemis Precinct (Fig. 59, Nos. 12, 13, 14).[25] Also related are the mausoleum found at PN in 1967 (Grave 67.3), the small vaulted tomb under Room 16 in the House of Bronzes, and the mausolea LVC and SVC in Pactolus Cliff.[26] These date from the second to the fourth centuries A.D. The outlining of major parts of the vault and chamber with thin purple bands recalls tombs of the second and third century A.D. at Isola Sacra and elsewhere in Italy.[27] Judging by the finds made under its floor, Tomb 2 of the Artemis Precinct may be the earliest brick-vaulted Roman chamber tomb hitherto known at Sardis.[28]

The level of Tomb 2, which was intended as an underground structure, presupposes a surface level of ca. *99.50. The burial was made at the time when the high flood deposits which support the North Terrace extended further west than they do now. When the precinct was re-excavated by the Romans, the level was lowered to ca. *97.50. Lane o was driven through (at ca. *97.80) exposing the back wall of the tomb.

Area South of Building U

In front of the eastern part of the south wall of U a red sandstone slab, 2.25 m. long, forms a platform which adjoins the rubble wall r, 4.95 m. long, 0.70 m. thick, top level *97.76. The latter is clearly

an enclosure wall. The coordinates of the area are: W 195–208/S 1200–1206 (Fig. 68).

Stelai Base 6. Termed "Stelae No. 6" on Butler's Plan III and just "6" on ours (Figs. 59, 68), the western wall of the base slants at ca. 100° westward from the alignment of the west wall of U (Figs. 68, 69). It consists of reused pieces backed on west and south by rubble. The north-south length is 3.50 m. Owing to the larger width of base M and of the rubble where it adjoins Building U, the base tapers southward from a width of 1.55 to ca. 1.00 m. (Fig. 69).

The northernmost piece, M, is of marble. A fine reused masonry block x had fallen from it and was reset in 1969. Block x was of finished marble with transport and lifting bosses at the ends. It had been cut for the insertion of a stele in the top surface (cutting 0.37 m. by 0.22 m.), then the cutting was roughly expanded at the back for wedging of the stele (larger cutting 0.40 m. by 0.45 m.). Overall dimensions: L. 1.16 m.; W. 0.85 m.; H. 0.50 m.

L 1 is a limestone piece (0.80 m. N-S by 0.75 m. E-W) with a rectangular depression 0.32 m. square, with smoothed border ca. 0.20 m. L 2 is set into rubble, lozenge fashion; it measures 0.40 m. by 0.40 m. by 0.75 m. by 0.60 m. on the sides.

This stelai base represents a late (third century A.D.? or Early Byzantine?) attempt to give prominence to U by creating oblique walls as arms or boundaries of an approach area and by setting up "ancient" stelai. The inscribed stele for Timarchos (Fig. 75) may have stood on the southern end of this stelai base.[29]

Area AR

A careful study, without excavation, of the remaining walls suggests that AR was a piazza of medieval type, with Lanes o, nn, and ss coming in at varying angles from north and east, while the main approach was presumably from the south (Fig. 59). Its coordinates are W 195–209/S 1200–1215. The row of bases No. 6 was not the only pretense to decoration with ancient monuments. Another such base with reused masonry blocks, running north-south for some 6.20 m., adjoined the eastern wall of structure T (W 209.5/S 1210–

1216). The piazza, shorter on the east than on the west, was approximately 15 m. by 17 m. (Figs. 61, 63, 69).

Unit S

This unit was a slightly irregular oblong (W 210.5–223/S 1197–1208.5). It seems to have had a courtyard *ct* on the east and three rooms, *s 1–3*, on the west. It fronts on Area AR, but the entrance was probably through the courtyard. This resembles a type of rural house still to be seen at Sardis. Its southwest corner touches but does not bond with Building Q (Fig. 59; see also Figs. 63, 67).

Building Q

Butler in *Sardis* I (1922) 127 described the construction of Q as being "almost polygonal in appearance," but he did not claim that it was actually archaic. On the outside, indeed, a determined attempt had been made to create a fair approximation to ashlar masonry by recutting marble spoils, but on the inside they are backed with less regular pieces as well as with rubble and brick. An anta may be discerned at the northeast corner and a door jamb and part of a threshold are recognizable near the northwest corner in the north wall. The date is perhaps Late Roman (A.D. 280–400) rather than Early Byzantine. Coordinates are W 221–241/S 1207–1220 (Figs. 59, 76).

The original floor level is visible at the east and west walls because of the footings (ledges). The level of the floor was approximately 1.05 m. below the southwest corner, hence at *96.20. A large terracotta storage jar (Fig. 59 in Q, and Fig. 61) was set into the floor adjacent to the southern wall.

Deeply graven signs, which are probably Lydian, appear on the southern face of the southwest corner block, now placed upside down (Fig. 76).[30] On top of the same block is a later sign, *E*, ca. 0.115 m. high.

A building the size of Q, 9.50 m. wide N-S and 15.50 m. long E-W (19.00 m. with Q 1) must have been some sort of public building, but apart from the storage jar, perhaps for water, there are no indications as to its function.

Unit T

One-room Unit T is somewhat irregular in plan (Figs. 59, 61, 63) and might have been a shop (coordinates W 210–218/S 1210–1216). Its southern wall continues as an enclosure (?) wall of Area AR, which has a footing on its north face. About 10 m. east of Unit T lies the newly exposed stele base No. 1 (W 196–198/S 1211–1214, *97.71). Neatly fitted together out of limestone blocks, the base may be a work of the Late Roman period (Fig. 59; cf. Fig. 181 No. 1 and No. 35 and Fig. 114 for its possible counterpart at SSB with a third century A.D. coin).

Walls z, 1, 2, 3

The walls adjacent to wall *r* and southeast of Building U are not easily interpreted. The manner in which wall *z* bends, its height, and apparent buttresses or platforms suggest that a terrace with top level of *100 may have occupied most of the empty space just east of Building U, approximately the area within W 170–195/S 1197–1206 (Figs. 59, 61).

Evaluation

The oldest feature of the Northwest Quarter of the Artemis Precinct may be the North Street which led down into the sanctuary. When the area was covered by water-laid deposits and the temple was barely accessible (first to second century A.D.), Tomb 2 was dug into the gravel. The construction of a mausoleum above it blocked the North Street. The reuse of monuments suggests that Building U should perhaps be assigned to the Late Roman (third to fourth century A.D.) rather than to the Early Byzantine (fifth to sixth century A.D.) period. It is the personal opinion of G. M. A. Hanfmann that it became a martyrion church and that the Area AR was created to provide an approach space south of this focal point of the quarter. Building Q may also be Late Roman; it is impinged upon by Unit S. It is possible, but not probable, that Units X, Y, and N, connected with long terracing alignments, might also belong to the great Late Roman rebuilding of the sanctuary. A very medieval character is introduced by the irregular dwellings H, S, and T, and the layout of the precinct as Butler excavated it is Early Byzantine, although his finds and ours (sgraffito ware in Building U) indicate that the quarter continued in use through the Byzantine period (Fig. 61; see also Fig. 65, Reconstruction of Byzantine buildings).

The North Terrace

The North Terrace lies between coordinates ca. W 125–192/S 1160–1190 at levels ca. *100–102 (Figs. 59, 66). Its lower part steps uphill in three steps with heights of 0.50 m., 0.70 m., 0.60 m. A cemented rubble wall running for ca. 66.0 m. supports the terrace on the south (Figs. 67, 77). It is ca. 1.0–1.50 m. high, but probably not all of it was exposed. The terrace, which slants westward, is bounded on the west side by Unit NS and on the east side by the North Building. A modern deep ditch made by Butler's excavation cuts through the wall and curves westward, distorting the ancient shape. Hanfmann believes that originally a street went across the terrace to the center of North Building and then uphill (Figs. 65, 66).

Lion-Eagle-Nannas Bakivalis Monument

This monument is at the western edge of Butler's cut (Fig. 59 No. 1; ca. W 153/S 1180). As uncovered in 1913 it consisted of three bases, each in two parts, two lions, and an eagle. On one of the bases was written the famous Lydian-Greek bilingual: *Nannas Bakivalis Artimul: Nannas Dionysikleos.*[31] Butler saw that the sculptures were archaic, the bases were intended for bronze statuary, and the Nannas inscription dated probably from the later fourth century B.C. The sculpture will be discussed in detail in the forthcoming volume on sculpture. Here it is sufficient to say that the attempt to synthesize various "venerable" Lydian monuments into one group was probably made during the Late Roman reordering of the sanctuary after the floods in the late second and early third century A.D., when they were set up on the post-A.D. 17 North Terrace. Their original location is unknown. The condition of the monument in 1970 is shown in Figure 78.

North Building

The North Building stood ca. 3 m. above the level of the temple colonnade, only 10 m. distant on the south (Figs. 59, 66). The exedra NW(N) adjoined it to the west; the small appendage LW to the east. Together they formed a long southern front toward the temple; the front was buttressed. Perhaps here, as to the west, the builders were afraid that the recent flood (and slide?) deposit would move. That considerable pressure was expected (from a two storied building?) is also proved by the long western wall *wt*. Its buttresses are the most conspicuous feature of the structure (Figs. 64, 66, 79). The building itself lies between coordinates ca. W 100–140/S 1130–1200. It measures ca. 67 m. N-S (assuming that it reached to the Northeast Stoa). Its internal width was ca. 11.5 m. at the south end but as much as 13.5 m. at the north end.

Toward the west, the North Terrace was on an only slightly lower level rising gradually eastward (from *101.00 to *103.00, Figs. 77, 78), toward the probable gate in the western wall of North Building (Figs. 66, 78). On the south, Unit NS(N) was probably filled with earth to a level of *104.50. The stucco on the wall above that level clearly indicates where the floor lay; it also proved that this part was roofed. About the middle of the building, Units NM 1 and NM 2, possibly guard houses, seem to have flanked an entrance ca. 4.30 m. wide. Their floors were about a meter lower than that of Unit NN. The latter contained a well. One may conjecture that this part was not roofed.

An outlying nook, *LW* (Fig. 66), at the southeast corner of the North Building seems a later accretion. Its western wall is of the same construction as the outer eastern wall of the North Building. It is only 1.40 m. high, poorly constructed of crumbly red cement, and sits on clay (mud). Its width is 0.90 m., levels *106.30–*105.10.

East Wall. Now preserved for ca. 14 m., the wall is only 1.25 m. high and is poorly constructed of crumbly, red cement. Its outer side sits on clay at ca. *104.26. On the inside, however, the original large eastern wall of North Building reaches down to *103.22, where it is based on gravel. Thus the bottom of the outer part was 1.0 m. or higher than that of the inner. The total width of the east wall is 2.40 m. The eastern (outer) part is 0.90 m. wide.

South Wall. In the center of the wall is a patch

or repair, ca. 2.50 m. wide. There is no clear reason for this repair. Buttress *b 1* (Fig. 66) bonds with the south wall and projects to the west by 1.20 m.; it does not bond with its westward continuation, which is the southern wall of Unit NW(N) (Fig. 78).

Unit NW(N)

This is a wing of the North Building and must have been either a room or exedra, as its high double wall would make no sense otherwise. Including walls, it measures ca. 6.0 m. N-S. The buttress *b 2,* 1.20 m. long, plus the extension in poorer rubble westward for 18.40 m. constitute its northern boundary (total preserved 19.60 m.). It may have been a rectangular exedra opening to the south (Figs. 66, 77, 78).

West wall wt is preserved for ca. 60 m. (southern stretch, 26 m.; "gate" 3.30 m. wide and northern stretch 30.5 m.). It has a chance break at 13.5–14.4 m. north of the southwest corner (Figs. 64, 77–79). Farther north, there was a gate or entrance, 3.30 m. wide N-S (Fig. 79). The damaged southern jamb, just above *b 6,* is ca. 26 m. north of the southwest corner of Room NS (N). The more recognizable, northern gate jamb, which is buttress *b 7,* is 30.5 m. south of the place where the wall goes into the scarp. The gate was apparently flanked by two small rooms, NM 1 and NM 2. Room NM 2 has a south wall, 4.95 m. E-W. It turns the corner northward for about 1.5 m. Two columns (unfinished) are lying in the "gate" (Fig. 80). They may have been placed there by Butler who had dug a downhill trench through the opening.[32]

Further north, a platform, ca. 2.45 m. wide E-W, consisting of buttresses *b 8* and *b 9* and an infill of cemented rubble, projects westward from the west wall, to which, however, it does not bond. Perhaps it caught a thrust from structure NN. It is ca. 1.50 m. above the present surface to the west (Fig. 62). Probably NN was a narrow (5 m.) structure going north and uphill for some 20 or more meters.

The south room, NS(N), of North Building seems to have been bounded on the north side by a wall, part of which formed the south wall of NM 1; beyond that point it was disintegrated. The N-S length of 18 m. would make this unit a long one;

its width would be ca. 11.50 m. The thickness of its three walls may indicate two stories: W. south wall 1.15 m.; east wall 1.00 m.; west wall 1.06 m. The upper story floor level of North Building is clearly shown by the wall stucco which covers the top 80 cm. of the western wall of Building N, then stops at *104.50 (Fig. 83).

Unit NN

This unit is ca. 7 m. north of the northern jamb (28 m. on the west wall), i.e., 33 m. north of the southwest corner of North Building. Its south wall (*xu*), apparently a "late" wall in technique, is traceable 5 m. eastward to a corner. The wall then turns northward and suggests a unit which includes the well (*w*) (Fig. 66). It may be that there are two N-S walls: a western, ca. 0.60 m., and an eastern ca. 1.50 m. wide. The difference in ground level south of the south wall and north of the south wall of NN is ca. 1.00 m. to 1.10 m. (north of wall *104.67). Thus Unit NN is clearly a unit on a terrace one step (1 m.) higher than that of the Units NM 1 and 2.

The well *w* now has a curb at *104.17. It is ca. 3.0 m. deep, constructed of riverstones and ca. 0.75 to 0.80 m. wide at the mouth; its bottom is filled with stones and debris.

Architectural pieces near buttress *b 9:* (1) from a small building, a very fine Doric corner of pediment cornice (*sima*) with flaming palmette at corner and 18 *guttae* per *mutule.* Drilled in the center of each *gutta* is a hole 0.003 m. in diameter by 0.004 m. deep. H. 0.40 m. at higher end, 0.24 m. at corner; L. 1.05 m.; W. 0.62 m. Dimensions of *mutules* are 0.135 m. wide by 0.285 m. long; *viae* 0.06 m. wide; *guttae* 0.018 m. in diameter. Its style is classicistic; H. A. Thompson considers second century B.C. possible. (2) a facetted Doric column shaft piece: diam. 0.455 m.; L. 1.23 m.; 20 facets (flutes); distance between arises 0.07 m. It might belong to the same building as the cornice (Figs. 64, 81, 82).

General Conclusions About Siting of the North Building

In the view from the west, it is obvious that as a buttressed terrace, North Building towered high above the temple. It does not seem likely that this was only a terrace for a street: indications are that it had a roofed interior at the south end. The most probable use is as a terrace with buildings accompanying a street to the northeast where the building ran up against the platform or terrace on which Northeast Stoa (Fig. 66) stood, unless there was a lane separating the north end of the North Building and the south wall of Northeast Stoa. The reconstruction (Fig. 65) assumes that the North Building was a long, one-storied building.

A street probably came eastward on North Terrace then turned northeast along the west side of the North Building. At present, the west wall of the North Building runs into a high embankment. The preserved level of the wall is ca. *105.00 at top; the earth beyond it rises to *107.00–*109.00.

Unfortunately, it is not clear whether the North Building joined the Northeast Stoa at a right angle (as a supporting or buttressing element as drawn in Fig. 66)[33] or was separated by a lane or street. The eastern wall of North Building does align with the eastern wall of Northeast Stoa. The western wall of North Building, however, is definitely farther west than the west wall of Northeast Stoa. There is a sizeable difference of levels, the approximate floor of Northeast Stoa now being at ca. *109.00 (top of stone base *109.61), whereas the floor of the North Building may have been at *105.00 in the northern part. In any case, the third century A.D. replanning seems to have resulted in a dramatic terraced composition up this slope.

Northeast Terrace

A marked scarp of stratified gravel forms a gently rising terrace with a level of ca. *104.00, 4 m. above the colonnade level of the temple (Figs. 59, 66, 84). In the upper part of the terrace are two pre-Roman monuments, Nos. 21 and 20. Above them is another terrace, starting from a level of ca. *109.00. The question arises, are all of these "gravelly" deposits third century A.D.—as one must assume of the deposits of the terrace on which the North Building stands—or are they due to the landslide of A.D. 17 or even earlier? If the Northeast Terrace slope deposits are of the third century A.D. or A.D. 17, then Monuments 20 and 21 are Roman; otherwise, like the lion monument of Nan-

nas Bakivalis, they were reset in Late Roman times on higher terraces.

The solution may well be that only in the southern-most parts of the slopes are the "recent" (third century A.D.) deposits of very great height and that the higher slopes had much less of recent accumulated material. This is confirmed by the situation in the sector NEW where the floor of the Roman Northeast Stoa (second century A.D.) is only over a meter above the Lydian buildings of the sixth century B.C. (*108.50 against *107.34).[34]

Base No. 21

At ca. W 75–77/S 1182–1185 there are traces of a statue base of bluish schist stones. As far as can be seen, the base measures 3.20 m. N-S and 1.25 m. E-W. It continues northward into a base of river stones, now covered with earth. The top of the second course is at *107.58. The monument seems pre-Roman (Figs. 66, 85, 86).

Monument No. 20

Ca. 2.30 m. north of Base No. 21 is a powerful base of calcareous sandstone (Figs. 66, 85–87). Its masonry and stepped effect recall the masonry of the archaic Artemis Altar (LA 1). Its location on high ground toward the northeast with a top level of *108.68 and the way in which later rubble walls run up against it support the conjecture that it may belong to the archaic or Persian era. The base measures 3.5 m. N-S and 3.70 m. E-W at the base. The two major courses are each 0.48 m. high. There may have been an intermediate step of smaller stones, one of which is in place (0.33 m. wide, 0.21 m. high). Otherwise the lower, south side step is 0.52 m. wide, but the western one only 0.15 m. One of the two stones of the southern (frontal) side is a huge monolith, 2.15 by 0.65 m. and 0.45–0.48 m. high. Like the Pyramid Tomb, the stones are not clamped together, but there are prising holes, as in the temple (Fig. 85).

The north and east sides of the platform have raised, rounded edges, ca. 0.12 m. high (Fig. 87). They border channels for water (or sacrificial liquids?) nearly triangular in section and 0.10 m. wide. The northern channel emptied westward through an opening 0.15 m. wide; the eastern channel emptied southward. Unlike the base of Monument 10, the red and green sandstone base of Monument 20 shows no profiling (Figs. 85, 86).

The Eastern Side of the Artemis Precinct

Monument No. 10

Monument No. 10 lies about 11 m. east of Church M, about 26 m. east of the edge of the eastern temple colonnade, and about 5 m. above the floor level of the colonnade (top of limestone base *104.90; floor of colonnade, *100.00). Its coordinates are W 63–73/S 1251–1267 (Figs. 88, 89).

The structure was described and illustrated by Butler,[35] who underpinned the foundation with brick and cemented riverstones (Fig. 89). More was preserved in Butler's time, but he showed only one oblong rectangular room, ca. 15 m. N-S and 5.25 m. E-W, with an exedra (our 10 D) attached at the northwest end. We found the southern end destroyed, but were able to ascertain that the alignment had at least three rooms, 10 A, 10 B, 10 C, and that it continued northward beyond the exedra 10 D. The preserved length of the north-south wall is 14.60 m. A rubble tower (*TF*), 2 m. by 2 m., projects eastward from the west wall. An oblique wall, 0.90 m. wide, at W 69–70/S 1253.20–1256.45, is superposed upon the original wall (1.06 m. wide) and is a later addition. It was preserved to a greater length (ca. 7 m.) in Butler's time. One would assume that the floors of the chambers 10 A-C were on a somewhat higher level than the exedra and marble base 10 D (Figs. 88, 90).

As seen in Figure 89 the marble plinth *mb 10* had been dislodged since 1913, one part lying near its limestone base, the other just east of Church M. They were put together in the drawing (Fig. 88), then reunited *in situ* in 1973.

After cleaning, the exedra 10 D is seen to consist of three rubble walls, a stucco floor, and a projecting base. The walls formed originally a room 4.60 m. N-S by ca. 2.20 m. E-W. A footing for revetments, ca. 0.20 m. high, runs around the base of the exedra walls (*105.20 in plan; Figs. 88–90) which were stuccoed and revetted. A fragment of Hellenistic relief ware (Fig. 92) was found on top of the footing in the stucco of the back wall. It was

placed there before the revetment was put up.

Three very fine superposed ivory white stucco floors were found one above the other at *104.80, *104.90, and *104.97. Three footprints were observed on the plaster in the northeast corner (Fig. 90). A coin hoard came from the earth bedding under the lowest floor at the north side of the base. Its location and level (*104.80) are indicated in Figure 88.

According to L. J. Majewski, the presence of stucco and two water pipe lines (ca. 0.20 m. in diam.) projecting from the east wall onto the floor suggests that water may have streamed over the floor and cascaded down the base. One might think of a ship's beak or some aquatic mythological figure as the statue. H. A. Thompson (by letter) suggests a water clock. The preserved lengths of the pipes are 0.43 m. and 0.64 m., northern and southern respectively; they were both cut in later times (Figs. 88, 90).

The lower part of the base, which projects 1 m. west beyond the north and south walls, is 2.20 m. N-S by 1.74 m. on the lower step. It consists of two simply profiled courses of gray limestone under which are two modern courses of brick and rubble (Fig. 91).[36] The upper limestone course steps back by 0.20 to 0.25 m. Each step is 0.31 m. high. The plan of the top limestone course as exposed in 1970 is shown in the small-scale overall plan of Monument 10 in Figure 88. The position of the marble plinth (*mb 10*) reunited in 1973 is indicated by a dotted rectangle. On the top limestone course two cuttings with channels for lead are clearly seen. Two blocks were carefully clamped together by two round-headed swallow-tail clamps (Figs. 93, 94); L. of clamp cutting 0.35 m.; W. at end 0.06 m.; D. at clamp hole 0.03–0.04 m. The type seems earlier than the straight bridge clamps used in the marble base. Half of the northern clamp cutting is lost; it was filled in with cement.

The marble plinth, its two blocks carefully clamped together, measures 1.47 m. N-S by 1.15 m. E-W; H. 0.18 m. A photograph, profile, and elevation of the marble plinth as reunited appear in Figure 88 c-e. It has elegant classicistic (?) profiles. The two simple bridge clamps are 0.22 m. long.

Four rectangular (dowel?) cuttings, all with channels, indicate an additional marble course (Figs. 88, 94). H. A. Thompson (by letter) considered the piece Hellenistic.

The following objects were found at Monument No. 10:

Coins
Eight bronze coins were found on the step. Size and shape suggest Hellenistic types. All were badly corroded. Only four and a half survived cleaning; only two show any recognizable traits. P. Franke (1970) discerned a quiver and thought it might have been a posthumous Alexander. A. E. M. Johnston agrees. She considers the coins (all Alexanders) as probably imported and points out that they have a striking time range from ca. 330 or 320 until ca. 170 B.C.[37]

Pottery
P69.94:8059. Bowl fragment of red Hellenistic relief ware. W. 0.03 m.; H. 0.02 m. In stucco of back wall at ca. *105.20, ca. 0.20 m. above the floor; stuck on purpose on top of footing of wall before the stucco was applied. Vine with tendrils, tall many-leafed palmette. "Pergamene," second century B.C. Kraus, p. 15, fig. 9:11. (Fig. 92.)

Not catalogued: a foot with grapes. Late Hellenistic relief ware, *105.00–*104.50. In mixed context with predominantly red and brown plain wares; yellow-white slip Hellenistic, two sigillate sherds; and Late Hellenistic bowl rims, as well as a black Hellenistic relief sherd.

The bulk of the material in and under the monument is Late Hellenistic. The presence of two small, indistinctive sigillate sherds may, but need not, indicate that the fill under the monument was laid down just after A.D. 17. This entails the assumption that the bronze Alexanders still circulated into the first century A.D., some 200 years after the latest were struck. It is also peculiar that no coins later than pseudo-Alexanders were found. It would be perfectly tenable to advocate a Late Hellenistic date, before the earthquake, for Monument 10.

The South Side of the Artemis Precinct

A number of large architectural pieces are lying east-west in the southwest corner of the precinct; perhaps a dozen more are scattered along the south side (Figs. 59, 95).

As shown in Butler's plan,[38] there seems to have been a Late Roman projecting rubble terrace in the western part of the south flank of the temple. It is traceable for 30 m. On the west, it projects 4.70 m. southward from the south edge of column base No. 64 (Figs. 59, 96, 97).[39] It contains, south of column base No. 42, an east-west row of gray marble slabs.[40] The marble blocks are 2.65 m.–2.95 m. from the south edge of the column bases and 1.50 m. from the south edge of the rubble terrace.

The inner rubble platform, only 0.50 m. south of the column bases, extends, in varying form, along the entire length of the temple. There is, however, no lower outer platform in the eastern part, east of column base No. 42 (*100.46). The top of the marble blocks varies from *99.99–*100.10 (*100.04, Butler); top of rubble is at ca. *100.00. The bottoms of two terracotta pipes (*d 4, d 3*) south of base No. 46 are at *97.97 and *98.27 respectively (Figs. 59, 96). This inner platform is a real wall, 1.60–1.80 m. wide and at least 2.20 m. high above the present surface of the precinct along the south side.

An area ca. 6 m. south of Church M, and level with the floor of the temple at *100.00 (Figs. 59, 95) has water long into summer; this area turns into a swamp in fall and spring. It descends from the terrace in the southeast corner of the precinct and is marked by greener vegetation. K. J. Frazer tested it in July 1972 but found no spring. The colossal head of Zeus,[41] originally located in the cella of the temple, was found by us lying in this southeast area.

East of Building L, there is at present an embankment with several walls and vaulted tombs, Nos. 11–14; behind it the ground rises steadily eastward (Fig. 59). These structures were originally underground, as was Tomb 2 on the north side of the precinct. The ground must then have risen quite steeply, by about 2 m. between the eastern end of Building L and Tombs 13 and 14 (Figs. 59, 98). The ground level may be calculated from the height of the vault of Tomb 14 to ca. *103.00 (*102.90). If the tombs are correctly dated to Early Byzantine (rather than Roman Imperial) times, then they formed a higher, southern part of that Early Christian cemetery which stretched from Church M westward all the way to the western end of Building L.[42]

Tomb No. 13
The tomb was built of mixed rubble and brick; its single brick lacing course and at least two layers

of ivory stucco are still recognizable. It lies at
W 157–162/S 1290–1293.5; its orientation is approximately east-west. Interior dimensions are
2.92 m. long, 2.50 m. wide. Wall thicknesses are
0.40 m.–0.50 m. The east side is preserved to a
height of ca. 1.0 m. (Fig. 99). Like Tomb 2, on
the north side (Figs. 61, 72, 73), the tomb was
entered from above by individual stone steps inserted into the east wall,[43] of which one survives
(Fig. 98). Entrance of the tomb from above proves
that it was originally underground. A wall of large
rubble, ca. *101.00, takes off northwest and continues to a length of 3.10 m.; it may have been part
of a cemetery enclosure.

Tomb No. 14

The north wall of this tomb is ca. 2.40 m. south
of the southeast corner of Tomb No. 13 (W 156.5–
160.5/S 1296–1299). The tomb is oriented east-
west like the temple; its external face is rough and
unfinished. Interior dimensions are L. (E-W) 2.74 m.
north, 2.80 m. south; W. (N-S) 2.08 m. (Figs. 59,
98, 100).

Walls of rubble and single brick bonded courses
were covered on the inside by heavy yellow painted
stucco. The highest preserved point is at the southwest corner, 0.95 m. above the inner floor at
*101.29.

The southern wall at *100.90 ca. 0.75 m. above
the present surface shows the spring of a barrel
vault. The liberal application of cement speaks for
an Early Byzantine date. The cement is hard and
gray and includes pot sherds.

Lydian Sarcophagus

Just south of a heap of large stones, perhaps a
base (?) intentionally set (top at *101.79), lies about
one half of an oval Lydian-Hellenistic sarcophagus
(Figs. 59, No. 7, 101). Int. D. 0.40 m.; ext. D.
0.50 m.; W. at end 0.90 m.; L. 2.20 m. The limestone was picked with a large point.[44] K. J. Frazer
conjectures that the sarcophagus came from a Lydian burial nearby; he would interpret wall *w* (Fig.
59) as the remnant of a dromos.

Tomb No. 12

The tomb has become a formless heap. The level
is *101.83 at the bottom of the north side. There
is just a short stretch of aligned wall of the south
side visible. Its coordinates are W 120–124/S 1288–
1292 (Fig. 59).

Wall w

Wall *w* is southeast of Tomb 12 at W 111–122/S
1295. It is ca. 2.30 m. from the aligned preserved
piece of the south wall of Tomb 12 (Fig. 59). The
wall was constructed of large (0.50 by 0.50 m. and
larger) river stones. It reaches widths of 1.35 m.
and 1.50 m. at the top. This speaks for terracing
or fortification, rather than a building. The wall
runs NW-ESE in relation to the temple. Its north
face is clearly traceable for 11.20 m. and continues
into the earth. The bottom is *102.00 at the northwest end; preserved height, ca. 2.00 m. The level
at the top is *103.20. Perhaps this was part of a
Middle Byzantine precinct wall or cemetery.

Wall wt East of Tomb 12

About 10 m. east and slightly north of wall *w,*
lower *wt* comes out at an angle slightly more north
from that of wall *w* (W 102–105/S 1287–1289). Its
construction is similar to that of wall *w* but somewhat more regular. L. 8.00 m. (Fig. 59). The lower
part, 3 m. long, is preserved up to four courses; H.
ca. 0.80 m. (bottom *102.42; top *103.22). The
lower wall seems to serve as footing or terracing
for the upper which runs at a more westerly angle
and is traceable for a length of 2 m. The level of
upper wall *wt* is *104.67 on the north face of the
mid-wall; the top is ca. *105.10.

Nothing was visible in 1970 of Tomb 11, which
may be concealed under a flat earth platform ca. 4
m. north of the east end of wall *wt* at a level of ca.
*104.00.

Brick and other walls emerge from the steep
slope east of the east end of upper *wt:* 6 m. east, a
brick wall, N-S direction, ca. *105.00–*106.00, W.
1.65 m.; 11 m. east, a high rubble wall, N-S direction, ca. *107.00

Western Side of the Artemis Precinct

The area south of the Northwest Quarter (Fig.
59) is now an open space. On its east side is the
Altar of Artemis which in its late phase was immediately attached to the west side of the temple.
The three major groups of monuments are the row

of stelai designated NSB, the altar with various stelai and bases attached, and the alignment of bases designated SSB. It is located at ca. W 196–230/S 1218–1257 (Figs. 59, 181, detailed plan).

The area was originally, at least, 34 m. E-W and 39 m. N-S. In the following description, the bases for stelai and other monuments have been numbered 1–45, going in general from north to south.

North Stelai Bases (NSB)

In 1910, while pursuing his Level II at the southwest corner of the temple, Butler came upon two rows of bases for stelai and statues. Similar stelai were found around the Altar LA, especially along the north side.[45] In 1911 he came upon the row of stelai ca. 8 m. north of LA extending toward the west, and a row of bases on the opposite side. In front of one of these was a complete stele of well-dressed crystalline marble with a long Lydian inscription.[46] The "half marble" base, broken in half and described below under No. 11 A, with a height of 0.67 m., might belong to this stele (Figs. 102, 106).

One might suppose that the carefully set and aligned stelai Nos. 5 and 8–11 are in their original positions. This is clearly not the case, however, with Nos. 6, 7, and 12–14, which consist of recut blocks and pieces. It seems more probable that during the reordering of the sanctuary in the late second or third century A.D. an attempt was made to set up the stelai in the manner considered traditional. The setting of the Nannas Bakivalis inscription and the Lion-Eagle monument on a later terrace (Fig. 78) and the setting of the Timarchos stele in a poorly cut secondary base (Fig. 75) afford clear examples of this procedure.[47]

As Butler did not give an enumeration of the platforms and bases, it seems advisable to do so. The first precise plan of the lowest course still *in situ,* drawn by D. Van Zanten, appears on Figure 181. Numbers refer to this plan, which shows, however, only pieces *in situ* in 1970 and not pieces displaced since 1914.

The following is a descriptive catalog of surviving pieces.

No. 1. This interesting platform lies in line with the Roman rubble platform of the northern temple colonnade. It also lies in the hypothetical line of the western frontal columns of the temple. The possibility was suggested that this was a buttress, either for the platform or of a column base. Otherwise, it might be an unusually large monument. Like its counterpart on the south (Fig. 181 No. 35), it is certainly a Late Roman effort. In its later life, it may have served as the corner of the small Early Byzantine piazza in front of Building U.

Preserved is a lower, rough-trimmed "base" course composed of 18 reused stones, marbles, limestones, and sandstones, both green and purple. The base course has very irregular edges; L. (N-S) ca. 3.10–3.15 m.; W. (E-W) ca. 2.15 m. Three stones of a second (top) course are preserved at the northwest corner. They are set back from the edge of the base course ca. 0.16 m. Their own surface shows another step-back by 0.06 m. Thus the base was stepped for at least three courses, more suitable for a monument than a buttress. The height of the course is 0.30 m. The southwest corner marble stone (second course) has a leading channel 0.09 m. wide and a dowel hole, 0.065 by 0.07 m. The stone is very roughly cut to fit its neighbor to the east.

No. 2. A fine torus from a temple column.[48] Diam. 2.1 m. Not shown on plan (Fig. 181).

No. 3. Ashlar marble block, not *in situ.* 1.20 m. × 0.64 m. × 0.60 m. Not shown on plan (Fig. 181).

No. 4. Roughly globular, rough shaped stone. Diam. 0.70 m. Not *in situ.* Not shown in plan (Fig. 181).

No. 5. A single marble block lying E-W seems to have been intended as a base, its rough-punched lower part meant to be underground. Front parts show drove or flat chisel work over claw chisel. Top: anathyrosis on front and sides surrounds a rectangular claw-chiseled area to hold a higher course. W. 0.80 m. N-S; H. of rough part 0.18 m.; H. of finished part 0.15 m. Front anathyrosis band 0.10 m.; sides 0.16 m. Rectangular area on top 1.00 m. × 0.70 m. Level *97.20 (Fig. 102).

No. 5 A. The block which fits this area is lying just to the southeast. W. 0.69 m.; L. 0.97 m.; H. 0.41 m. (Fig. 102).

No. 6. Two rough-punched limestone or half marble blocks cut to make together a N-S platform. The rectangular block had originally two square dowel holes with leading channels. 1.22 m. N-S; 0.63 m. E-W; H. 0.14 m. (Fig. 102).

No. 7. A platform of reused yellowish marble slabs. 0.75 m. N-S; 0.95 m. E-W; H. 0.18 m. above ground (Figs. 102, 105).

No. 7 A. On it, shoved southward, is a stele base with boss on front. Careful claw chisel work on front and sides, large punch work at back. On three sides of top a raised border. Top, carefully smoothed, has cutting for stele. Dimensions of base: 0.45 m. N-S, 0.83 m. E-W, H. 0.467 m. Dimensions of top cutting: 0.14 m. N-S, 0.33 m. E-W, D. 0.11 m. (Fig. 102).

No. 8. Adjoining No. 7 on the west is a large rectangular marble base, its top at a somewhat higher level than the bases Nos. 9–11, to which it may belong—*t* *97.28, versus *96.81 (Fig. 105). W. 1.20 m. N-S; L. 1.42 m. E-W; H. fully exposed 0.21 m. Well-preserved second block of marble with cutting for stele: W. 0.95 m. N-S; L. 1.25 m. E-W.; H. 0.29 m. Anathyrosis band: 0.15 m., same workmanship as No. 7 A with fine claw chisel. Dimensions of cutting: 0.27 m. N-S, 0.54 m. E-W; D. 0.12 m. (Figs. 102, 105).

No. 8 A. The large base now on top of No. 8 is profiled

on three sides. Because it fits no cutting, it cannot belong to either No. 10 or No. 11. At the bottom is a concave profile, lower part 0.05 m.; concave part 0.04 m.; top fascia 0.015 m. One corner begins to curve for the upper profile. On top is a rectangular roughened area, 0.22 m. by 0.50 m., with two round dowel holes, probably the bottom of a cutting for a stele. Overall dimensions: L. 0.78 m.; W. 0.73 m.; H. 0.33 m. (Figs. 102, 104–106).

No. 9. A foundation platform of half marble which has on top, near its front, a sundial engraved by the first Sardis expedition. Roughly trimmed (punched) on the north side. L. 1.42 m. E-W; W. 0.65 m. N-S; plus three limestone fragments. (Figs. 105, 106).

No. 9 A. A marble block (from the temple?) is set up on the north side. Three dowel holes with pouring channels are preserved, of which two are recut. W. 0.56 m. N-S; L. 1.52 m. E-W; H. 0.30 m. (Figs. 105, 106).

No. 10. A finely worked marble base, very similar to No. 11, but smaller. Back not fully exposed. Dimensions of platform: W. 1.30 m. N-S; L. 1.50 m. E-W; level *97.15. Dimensions of base: 1.245 m. N-S; 1.14 m. E-W; H. 0.22 m.; anathyrosis band on top 0.16 m. (Figs. 102, 106).

No. 10 A. On top of No. 10, displaced. Good marble base. W. 0.63 m. N-S; L. 0.105 m. E-W; H. 0.30 m. Original cutting for a stele 0.33 m. by 0.135 m.; D. 0.10 m. (Fig. 106).

No. 11. Very carefully worked marble base on marble platform which seems to have been made for it and is *in situ.* Top block has two large rectangular dowel holes with pouring channels and a central dowel hole. Very fine anathyrosis around the edge. The lower base and the roughened area of top block show very fine claw chisel work over short point strokes. Dimensions lower base platform: W. 1.45 m. N-S; L. 1.58 m. E-W; H. 0.175 m. Top block: W. 1.10 m. N-S; L. 1.25 m. E-W; H. 0.275 m. Anathyrosis and weathering show that the monument (pillar?) was 0.90 m. N-S and 1.00 m. E-W. Dowel holes 0.08 m. by 0.08 m.; D. 0.05 m. Anathyrosis strip 0.13 m. wide (Fig. 106).

No. 11 A. Broken in half, one part of half marble stele base lies in front (south) of No. 11. P.W. 0.35 m.; P.L. 0.58 m.; P.H. 0.67 m. Careful cutting on top: L. 0.35 m.; W. 0.17 m.; D. 0.10 m. Would fit on top of No. 11 (1.00 by 0.90 m. roughened area). This may be the socket for the Lydian inscription No. 22 found by Butler[49] (Fig. 106).

No. 12. A platform base of marble, crudely fitted. 1.40 m. N-S; 1.40 m. E-W; level *96.94. Possibly from marble blocks of temple (Fig. 181; see also Fig. 102).

No. 12 A. A marble block lies on No. 12; it has anathyrosis, dowel hole, and an unarchaic letter B. L. 0.77 m.; W. 0.59 m.; H. 0.24 m.; H. of letter 0.05 m. Very careful work.

No. 12 B. Perhaps out of place. Porous limestone, resembling CG material. Lower part intended to be underground, rough: H. 0.25 m.; upper part, 0.12 m., is well smoothed. W. 0.65 m. N-S; L. 1.27 m. E-W; H. 0.35 m. Cutting: W. 0.28 m. N-S; L. 0.77 m. E-W; D. 0.08 m. Top *97.34. Probably Lydian (Fig. 102).

No. 13. Platform base of eight pieces. Mostly sandstone. Veering northeast of other alignment. Added to it are three slabs forming a V. Top level with ground *96.89 (Fig. 181).

No. 14. Three sandstone voussoirs lying on the ground; central keystone larger. Level of top *97.05. D. Van Zanten thinks it is a wall. Dimensions: 0.25 m., 0.35 m., 0.30 m. E-W; 0.45 m., 0.45 m., 0.35 m. N-S; H. 0.45 m., 0.65 m., 0.45 m. (Fig. 102).

No. 14 A. Lying on top of No. 14. Stele base of white-gray marble. Displaced and askew. Three faces and top finished by abrasion. Top rough-hewn with pointed chisel. Careful rectangular cutting for stele: top ca. 0.74 by 0.67 m.; H. 0.45 m.; cutting 0.24 m. by 0.175 m., D. 0.08 m. (Fig. 102).

Stelai Bases Around Altar LA 2 (Nos. 15–33)

No. 15. Large rectangular platform and stele base at corner of LA 2. The limestone base of several closely fitted stones is set against the finest top level of plaster and rests on earth. L. 1.10 m. N-S; W. 0.97 m. E-W; H. 0.25 m.–0.30 m. varying at bottom. Marble base on top: L. 0.835 m. N-S; W. 0.49 m. E-W; H. 0.29 m. Cutting for stele: 0.335 m. N-S; 0.185 m. E-W; D. 0.11 m. Leading channel 0.19 m. long, now turned east to front (instead of west to back?). Front and back of stele reversed(?) (Fig. 103).

Between No. 15 and Nos. 16–24, which are set up along the north side of LA 2, is a rubble wall, ca. 1 m. wide E-W. The distance from it to the (restored) backing wall of the northwest steps of the Artemis Temple is 2.95 m. It is preserved to the top of LA 2 wall at *98.43. The wall was partly demolished by Butler (Fig. 103). Also along the north side is a set of poor flat stones and bricks, partly placed there by Butler. The levels of these vary but are generally ca. *96.85 at the bottom, *97.15 at the top (Fig. 107).

No. 16. Two irregular masonry marble blocks lying N-S and a third, perhaps a step, on top of them, E-W. Bottom: 0.53, 0.51 m. E-W by 0.96 m. N-S. Top block: 1.38 m. E-W by 0.37 m. N-S; H. 0.24 m. One blunt-headed clamp cutting N-S near eastern end; another N-S in western end (Figs. 103, 107).

No. 17. Three marble blocks are cut on top to receive two other marble blocks. The hollowed recess is set back 0.12 m. from the north edge. Lower course: 1.13 m. N-S; 0.51 m., 0.42 m., 0.45 m. E-W; H. 0.16 m., 0.17 m., 0.17 m. Upper course: 0.42 m., 0.48 m. N-S; 1.19 m., 1.18 m. E-W; H. 0.27 m. The northernmost block shows a small (0.03 by 0.04 m.) dowel hole with leading duct; at eastern edge, part of a clamp cutting indicating reuse (Fig. 107).

No. 18. Four limestone pieces of friable splintering local limestone, very roughly trimmed, two lying N-S *en echelon,* two E-W. Overall dimensions of base: 0.98 m. N-S., 1.10 m. E-W., H. 0.40 m. Dowel hole on the southernmost of the two E-W blocks, 0.065 m. by 0.04 m. possibly a statuary dowel? The entire arrangement is secondary, with reused blocks (Figs. 103, 107).

No. 19. Lower course a marble and limestone piece; upper course a marble stele base. Squared marble piece, lying N-S, perhaps a reused step(?): 0.96 m. N-S, 0.385 m. E-W, H. 0.17 m. Dowel hole 0.045 by 0.06 m., D. 0.02 m. near north edge. Limestone piece broken at north edge. Extends ca. 0.25 m. west under the stone of No. 20. Max. L. 1.00 m. E-W, broken at north edge. Upper course: front line visible, fine punch work south of it, smoothed for a band of 0.20 m. north of it. Set up 0.09 m. off stucco on north wall of LA 2. Cutting for stele: 0.28 m. N-S, 0.26 m. E-W, D. 0.135 m. Prising hole behind, dowel hole just north of cutting (0.04 m. by 0.04 m., D. 0.02 m.). Overall dimensions of base: 0.65 m. N-S, 0.97 m. E-W; H. 0.28 m. (Figs. 103, 107).

No. 20. Wedged in between Nos. 19 and 21. Bottom at

*96.86 rests on rubble. Lower course: limestone piece partly cut to fit over the limestone block of No. 19; limestone "bridge" piece cut out to east, 0.25 m. by 0.06 m. for remaining stone. Otherwise, 0.78 m. N-S, 0.77 m. E-W, H. 0.28 m. Upper course: marble stele base, 0.13 m. off the stucco of north wall of LA 2. 0.50 m. N-S; 0.73 m. E-W; H. 0.41 m. Smoothed on top. Claw chisel on frontal (north) side. Very rough punched back (south) side. Cutting for stele: 0.21 m. N-S, 0.42 m. E-W, D. 0.10 m. (Figs. 103, 107).

No. 21. Lowest course: two dense, white limestone pieces, one lying E-W, the other N-S, both projecting 0.16 m. north beyond the second course. Second course: two marble pieces, one N-S, the other E-W. They project 0.12 m. beyond the third course. Third course: a long marble stele base lying E-W. Level *97.71 (top). The top of the second course is level with the top of the lower course of No. 20. The N-S block of the lowest course is not exactly measurable: ca. 0.86 m.? E-W stone 0.98 m.; N-S stone 0.34 m. in E-W direction; H. ca. 0.20 m. Second course: E-W stone 0.54 m. N-S, 0.83 m. E-W; N-S stone 0.50 m. N-S, 0.37 m. E-W; H. 0.31 m. and 0.29 m. Top course: 0.37 m. N-S, 1.02 m. E-W, H. 0.29 m. Cutting: 0.13 m. N-S, 0.39 m. E-W, D. 0.09 m. Half-clamp cuttings at south and west sides; L. 0.08 m.; rectangular hole for Pi-clamp 0.02 m. square. The stele was ca. 0.62 m. by 0.17 m. at base. On the west side of the cutting a depressed area, 0.19 m. E-W by 0.17 m. N-S for the bottom of the stele. Fine punch work. Prising hole and dowel ca. 0.04 m. by 0.035 m. These holes show that the stele was set asymmetrically to center, perhaps because the monument continued to right. That it did continue is proved by the clamp cutting on the west side. The back is rough chiseled. That another block joined on the west is proved by anathyrosis bands near the top (0.09 m. wide) and at front (north), 0.10 m. wide. The stele block was also fastened at the back, as evidenced by the southern clamp cutting. On the other hand, this appears to have been originally intended as a stele base, although for another, longer monument (Figs. 103, 107).

No. 22. This base has an unusually profiled top part. As L. S. Meritt suggested, the piece is a reused pier or anta capital of the second half of the sixth century B.C. Unfinished at the back and set upside down for use as a stele base. Lower course: two large limestone blocks, one N-S, the other E-W: 0.64 m. N-S, 0.39 m. E-W; 0.38 m. N-S, 0.70 m. E-W; H. 0.39 m. Upper course: profiled marble stele base, profiled on three sides and around southwest corner for 0.15 m. along the back side. The back is rough-trimmed and broken behind the stele cutting where it should have joined the wall. Apparently it was never used in actual construction. Overall dimensions: bottom, 0.615 m. N-S by 1.04 m. E-W; top, 0.545 m. N-S, 1.00 m. E-W at front. The original profiles at present upside down: crowning fascia, 0.07 m.; cyma reversa, 0.18 m. (0.14 m. to innermost point); astragal, 0.02 m.; lower fascia, 0.105. The original bottom has a rectangular cutting 0.16 m. wide, 0.56 m. long, 0.09 m. deep, located 0.225 m. in from the front face and 0.22 m. in from each side. In its present upside down position, a cutting 0.05 m. deep can be discerned in the original top, located 0.10 m. in from the front face, but no further measurements are possible. The profiled piece is not in the original position and hangs over backwards. Nos. 19–22 must have presented an imposing array of four vertical stelai (Figs. 104, 107, 108).

No. 23. Large marble block on two limestone blocks,

one E-W, the other N-S. Lower course: 0.56 m. N-S, 0.725 m. E-W; 0.56 m. N-S, 0.36 m. E-W; H. not clearly measurable, ca. 0.17 m.? Upper course: 0.56 m. N-S, 0.95 m. E-W; H. 0.31–0.32 m. Fine claw chisel on top. Monument is set directly against stucco of north wall of LA 2 and might be the only one of all north bases in original position (Figs. 107, 108).

No. 24. Set curiously just off northwest corner on poor rubble and stone. Seems possibly constructed by H. C. Butler. Lower course: a N-S block backed by another small block and E-W block of limestone. The E-W block is cut back on the west side. The result looks more like a footing profile of a base than a cutting for a step as in the image base of Artemis. NW stone: 0.53 m. N-S, 0.34 m. E-W, H. 0.33 m. E-W stone: 0.72 m. N-S, 0.69 m. E-W (bottom), 0.64 m. (top), H. 0.29 m. The profiled part is 0.17 m. high. Upper course: 0.61 m. N-S, 0.86 m. E-W, H. 0.27 m. Its west side shows a dowel hole 0.08 m. by 0.06 m., D. 0.04 m., and two half-cuttings for large Pi-clamps, L. 0.11 m.; hole: 0.002 m. by 0.02 m., D. 0.04 m. The piece, then, was originally a vertical block with the present west side on top and hence reused (Figs. 107, 110).

No. 25. The block of its third course was found fallen in 1969 revealing on its back the rough-punched Lydian(?) inscription IN69.25 (Fig. 109).[50] The monument is seen in *Sardis* I (1922) 41, ill. 27. It was set up in the same way in 1970. Level ca. *98.10 (top). Top: very rough hewn battered marble block with anathyrosis; 0.80 m. N-S, 0.54 m. E-W, H. 0.29 m. Third course (second from top): fine claw-chiseled marble block with boss on west side largely worked off. Curiously, it is the rough-punched back (east) side which has the Lydian(?) inscription. It looks as if this rough punching was done after the original block had been made. (The three other sides are fine claw chisel and flat chisel work.) 0.76 m. N-S, 0.47 m. E-W, H. 0.41 m. Second course: similar but larger block with bosses on three sides (north, south, west), fine chisel work; 0.84 m. N-S, 0.85 m. E-W, H. 0.33 m. Lowest course: set about 0.20 m. off (west) from the west wall. The base has been cut on the south side to fit the projecting west steps of LA 2 (hence is later than the steps). Stone is rough-punched on the west side as if to receive a step or pavement. East stone: 0.89–1.00 m. N-S, 0.49–0.65 m. E-W, H. 0.34 m. West stone: 1.10 m. N-S, 0.33 m. E-W (Figs. 109, 110).

No. 26. Reproduced in *Sardis* I (1922) 41 f., ill. 27–28. Lowest course: three limestone pieces, rough picked, set against the west steps; 1.46 m. N-S, 1.29 m. E-W, H. 0.16 m. (incomplete). Second course: two marble blocks N-S, set back on the west side by 0.11 m.; 1.23 m. N-S, 0.57 plus 0.58 m. E-W, H. 0.34 m. Third course: tall stele base, set back 0.17 m. Bosses on north and south sides. Cutting 0.43 m. N-S, 0.18 m. E-W. Overall: 1.10 m. N-S, 0.92 m. E-W, H. 0.53 m. Fourth course: small, well-worked marble blocks. Set up on bricks in 1970 to show the disregard of ancient users for the stele cutting in the third course which was solidly covered up by this block. 0.81 m. N-S; 0.625 m. E-W; H. 0.255 m. On top, along west side and part of south side, finely incised setting line, 0.045 m. from west, 0.073 m. from south side. Fine point work within the setting line; claw chisel outside (Fig. 110).

T 1 and T 2. * Two marble foundations immediately to

*The description of the situation along the western side of LA and of the bases and monuments *T 1, T 2,* and stelai bases 27 through 33 is by K. J. Frazer.

the west of the LA 2 steps (W 209.00–211.15/S 1235.75–1238.80, top level *96.80; Fig. 111). Centers of dowel holes with pour channels are 9.35 m. and 9.30 m. from northwest and southwest corners of LA 2 respectively. The midpoint between them lies virtually on the LA 2 axis. Markings on the foundations' upper chiseled surfaces suggest each originally supported a rectangular block or pier, presumably marble, whose lower dimensions would have been 1.10 m. E-W and 0.41 m. N-S and their centers 2.31 m. apart. An offering table may have stood at this spot; its general proportions and appearance may have been echoed later by those of the marble table set before the Synagogue apse.[51] The doweling on these two stones would indicate a date from the Late Persian period on, but more likely in the Hellenistic or Early Roman period (Fig. 111).

A shallow clearance to the west at the south end of the LA 2 steps, W 210.85–215.00/S 1244.75–1246.75, revealed a pavement (?) foundation of ca. 8 sq. m. The stones are of the very friable gray or green sandstone and are very irregular in shape; some of them appear to be set in mud mortar. They bear no setting marks on their upper surfaces. Their upper level is uniform enough at ca. *96.85. This may be the pavement foundation for a marble pavement of the precinct.

No. 27. A nondescript marble block, its edges extensively chiseled away, ca. 1.50 by 0.85 by 0.24 m. high, lies just to the west of T 1 and T 2. In its upper dressed surface are three lewis holes 0.08 m. by 0.025 m. by 0.08 m. deep (Fig. 111).

No. 28. Reproduced in *Sardis* I (1922) 41, ill. 26. Three limestone blocks make up a base of 1.08 m. N-S by 0.88 E-W and 0.26 m. high. The largest (1.08 m. by 0.64 m.) has a step in its east edge and the two smaller blocks (0.60 m. by 0.24 m. and 0.48 m. by 0.24 m.) are fixed to it, each by a Pi-clamp. Inset from the northwest and southeast corners are square dowel holes with pour-channels. Tooling on upper surface of base indicates that a block 0.93 m. N-S and 0.61 m. E-W originally stood centrally on this base and set back 0.17 m. from its west edge. Top level of base *97.13 (Fig. 112).

No. 29. Reproduced in *Sardis* I (1922) 41, ill. 26 (with stone balls on top). Three marble blocks set one atop the other. The lowest course, 1.42 m. by 0.82 m. and 0.29 m. high, set against the west edge of the lower marble step of LA 2, appears to consist of three separate blocks. The block at the northwest corner, set upside-down in its reuse, has a very fine drafted edge (now against the ground) 3 cm. wide, divided into two equal fasciae of 1.5 cm. Two upper blocks (1.25 m. N-S by 0.73 m. E-W; H. 0.405 m. and 1.06 m. N-S by 0.645 m. E-W; H. 0.425 m.) have been set back from the west edge of the block below by 0.035 m. and 0.07 m. (top) respectively. The uppermost block has a channel 0.145 m. wide and 0.07 m. deep cut centrally along its N-S axis; the west edge of the channel has been roughly chamfered. A roughly finished length of limestone column lies alongside the bottom of this structure; lower diam. 0.365 m., L. 0.91 m.; upper diam. (broken off here) 0.345 m., with a circular cavity ca. 0.10 m. diam. cut 0.06 m. into its base. This piece matches a complete column, broken into two fitting parts, which lies to the south of the southeast anta of the Artemis Temple; the length of this column (rejoined) is 2.315 m.; lower diam. 0.365 m.; upper diam. 0.32 m. Another fragment lying ca. 45 m. south of the expedition house southwest corner may belong (Fig. 112).

No. 30. Marble base, 1.255 m. N-S consisting of two blocks 0.51 m. (outer) and 0.42 m. E-W respectively. Two

missing Pi-clamps once held together the two blocks which have now fallen a few centimeters apart. The upper surface has dowel-holes with pour channels set in from the north side and the southwest corner. Finished borders indicate that another block once lay on it, inset 0.18 m. from the north and south edges and 0.22 m. from the west edge (Fig. 112).

No. 31. Rough foundation of two reused marble blocks, 0.50 m. by 0.38 m. and 0.54 m. by 0.44 m. on its west side, and two rougher limestone blocks on its east side, 0.45 m. by 0.34 m. and 0.50 m. by 0.33 m. The limestone block in the northeast corner and perhaps the one at the southeast corner, is of the same vesicular limestone (tufa) as the LA 1 structure. Top level, *96.60 (Fig. 112).

Nos. 32 and 33. Two stele foundations, not included in the NSB and SSB groups, approach the southwest corner of LA (Fig. 181). Their levels at *97.14 and *97.10 would have them antedate the bases and foundations in the neighboring SSB with the exception of No. 35. Nos. 33 and 35 might have been associated with LA 1 or the first period of LA 2; No. 32, because of its dowel holes with pour-channels, could only have been associated with LA 2 or possibly the Late Persian period (*infra*). Other bases and foundations of the earlier periods must exist in the NSB area, but on the north side there is a finer bracket between their levels and the later Roman levels; the foundations of all monuments on this side lie between *96.85 and *96.95. The earlier foundations are probably only recognizable by their lying askew within NSB or lying out of its general alignment (e.g., the surviving corner of a foundation lying at an angle and contiguous with No. 13). Some earlier foundations may also lie in and aligned with NSB but may have been reused for later Roman stele or statue bases.

The axis of the avenue between NSB and SSB, at 286°, inclines ca. 7°50′ towards the south from the orientation of the AT/LA axis at 293°49′. This indirect approach to the altar, in its later LA 2 period, may have been laid out to conform to the direction of the route of the customary sacred pilgrimage from Ephesus,[52] or it simply may have been an indirect approach from the southwest of a causeway for the marble quarried for the late (peristyle) construction period of the Artemis Temple. This might provide yet another reason for the orientation and re-ordering of the stelai and statues as a screen for construction ramps to keep the frontal approach to the altar and to the northwest steps of the temple clear and presentable for the extended duration of the rebuilding project.

South Stelai Bases (SSB Nos. 34–45)

The entire SSB alignment is ca. 17.5 m. E-W, between coordinates W 196–213/S 1252.5–1258; levels at floor *97.33 to *97.16 (Figs. 113, 114, 181). It backs on a carefully aligned rubble and masonry wall (*rb 1*) described below (Figs. 113, 117). In its present shape, the western part of *rb 1* is of poor construction, with earth rather than cement as binding medium. *Rb 1* clearly takes its alignment from the venerable looking monument No. 40 (Fig. 113), which has carefully aligned green sandstone masonry blocks behind it. The alignment, therefore, may have existed before the present wall against which most of the bases and monuments are set up on bricks and rubble, but, except for Nos. 41–45, these supports seem post-antique. The bases now found upon them might have been set up by Butler after his excavations.

K. J. Frazer thought at one time that the two rubble walls, *rb 1* and *rb 2* might have contained a ramp for temple construction. If we remember, however, that a rubble wall linked Altar LA 2 to the row of stelai and probably the wall *rb 1* behind them (Fig. 181), then it becomes probable that the entire area with its *cul de sac* effect had some aesthetic function in the Late Roman arranging of the entire precinct. The finding of a coin imitating those of Claudius Gothicus in the "channel" of base or platform No. 35 makes it likely that the row of stelai bases was set up during the second half of the third century A.D. (possibly shortly after the wall *rb 1* was built?).

Coin. C70.3a. W 197/S 1253.5, in plastered channel of base No. 35. AE 0.3/0/2 11 mm. Bearded head radiate to right. Rev. altar with flames. According to T. V. Buttrey, the coin is an imitation of posthumous type first struck under Quintillus, brother of Claudius Gothicus. Coin may be dated ca. A.D. 270–295. Cf. H. Mattingly and E. A. Sydenham, eds., *Roman Imperial Coinage* V. 1 (London 1927) 233, no. 261 (Figs. 115, 116).

Following is a descriptive catalogue of the surviving pieces:

Walls rb 1 and rb 2. During cleaning operations at SSB, two stone and mud-mortar walls, *rb 1* and *rb 2*, were noted. Wall *rb 1* (east end at W 197.75–199/S 1254–1256; west end at W 205–211.25/S 1256–1257.15; top level *98.20) provides a backing wall on the south side of SSB. The shorter wall, *rb 2*, lies parallel with SSB and *rb 1*, ca. 2.50 m. further south. Wall *rb 1* was cleared down to its foundations at *97.07; *rb 2* was recorded as it stands. Beyond a 3.50 m. unexcavated area, the east end of *rb 1* reappears with a further 1.40 m. run, overlaps the southwest corner of SSB No. 35 by a few centimeters, and comes to a square-dressed end. Its southeast corner overruns by 0.40 m. the northwest corner of AT peristyle column base No. 64 (Figs. 117, 181).

Mass ca. Further cleaning immediately to the south of the eastern end of *rb 1* brought to light a concreted mass of water-worn stones and marble fragments laid against the west side of column base No. 64 at *97.54 (top). The mass, now known as *ca* (Fig. 117), was thought to have been part of the stone and lime-mortar consolidation set around the majority of the Artemis Temple peristyle column bases. On closer inspection, however, it was found to consist of two widths, 0.90 and 1.00 m., and part of a third, apparently wider, section laid parallel and contiguous with each other. Their orientation is nearer to that of the Artemis Temple peristyle than to that of *rb 1* and *rb 2* (Figs. 113, 181).

No. 34. Rectangular marble block set up on 0.27 m.

high rubble and spoils, the rubble overlapping the platform No. 35 by 0.08 m. Top smoothed in front for ca. 0.20 m., for 0.08 m. on sides. Then a zone of fine claw chisel; then toward back for 0.49 m. medium punch work. A narrow fine band at back, 0.015 m. The back is split off in layers. The west side is claw chisel work with anathyrosis; the east side is broken at bottom. Bottom in general irregular; perhaps euthynteria or base for steps (KJF): 0.80 m. N-S, 0.98 m. E-W; H. 0.52 m. E, 0.43 m. SE corner (Fig 114).

No. 35. Situated the nearest to LA, about 5.10 m. from its south wall. The angle of its alignment is ca. 8° south of the temple axis (Fig. 114). It is a platform or substructure for a base consisting of seven blocks of rather fine, hard limestone (*a, b, c, d, e, f, k*), two of poorer limestone, similar to LA 1 (*g, i*), and a marble (?), *h*. Overall dimensions: 1.64 m. N-S, 1.89 m. E-W; H. of one block visible is 0.36 m. below the level of *97.33. All limestone blocks are medium punched. Six may have come from one structure; the second block on the north side had a channel 0.40 m. distant from east and west edges. Coin C70.3a was found in it. The third block westward had a circular dowel-hole near the northern edge, within anathyrosis, with much lead still in it (anathyrosis 0.06 m.; diam. 0.04 m.), probably for bronze or iron pin.

a: 0.87 m. N-S, 0.34 m. E-W, ashlar
b: 0.74 m. N-S, 0.60 m. E-W, coin findspot
c: 0.74 m. N-S, 0.60 m. E-W, broken off southeast corner
d: 0.65 m. N-S, 0.46 m. E-W, flat chiseled, may be from another monument
e: 0.61 m. N-S, ca. 0.50 m. E-W, ashlar
f: 0.36 m. N-S, 0.85 m. E-W, ashlar with L-shaped channel at eastern part
g: 0.28 m. N-S, 0.06–0.08 m. E-W, fill-in block, rough limestone like LA 1.
h: 0.28 m. N-S, 0.13 m. E-W, riverstone or marble (?), rounded corners
i: 0.24 m. N-S, 0.69 m. E-W, irregularly cut, rough limestone like LA 1
k: 0.67 m. N-S, 0.57 m. E-W, irregular limestone block; round dowel hole in center started crack through entire stone (Fig. 114)

No. 36. Simple, well-worked marble block. Anathyrosis in front 0.08 m. Sides and front fine claw chisel. Back rough-punched. Its back is only 0.02 to 0.03 m. distant from rubble wall (*rb 1*). 0.58 m. N-S, 1.06 m. E-W; H. 0.33 m. (Figs. 114, 117, 118).

No. 36 a. Lies to the north of No. 36. Marble base for large stele. Broken off at back, from cutting on. Front and sides fine claw chisel. Top has at front anathyrosis, 0.04 m. Back very rough, almost quarry trim, hence the base was intended to be set against a wall. Cutting: 0.04 m. N-S, 0.74 m. E-W; 0.12 m. deep. Overall dimensions: 0.51 m. N-S, 0.90 m. E-W; H. 0.52–0.53 m. (Figs. 114, 118).

No. 37. Large marble block. Back very roughly done. Sides and front fine claw chisel. (Back punching probably not original.) Lowest part of front rough, uneven for ca. 0.13–0.14 m., hence intended to set into ground, invisible. Top has claw chisel over gouge. Anathyrosis, ca. 0.10 m. in front, 0.05 m. on sides of the top (Figs. 114, 118).

No. 37 a. Profiled marble base, may have fallen from No. 37. Elegant profiles at top and bottom. Top has fine, thin drafted band, 0.01–0.015 m. Inside it, fine point picked area. 0.62 m. top; 0.60 m. bottom N-S; 0.76 m. top and bottom E-W; H. 0.048 m. Top profile 0.11 m.; intermediate vertical 0.27 m.; lower profile 0.10 m. Must have had another marble slab on top, 0.50 m. N-S, 0.74 m. E-W (Figs. 114, 118).

No. 38. Large marble slab base set up higher than No. 37 on a rubble base 0.24 m. Back has very rough punching; front and sides fine claw chisel. No clear anathyrosis on top. Cutting shows flat chisel work to fit stele into edge of cutting: 0.54 m. E-W, 0.24 m. N-S, 0.14 m. deep. Overall dimensions: 0.72 m. N-S, 1.08 m. E-W, H. 0.51 m. (uneven) (Figs. 114, 118).

Nos. 39 a, b, c. Two courses. Two ashlars of very hard, fine-grained limestone set up lower than No. 38 but on similarly deep support of 0.24 m. high bricks and rubble. Both broken at back and No. 39 b also in front. Both had projecting footing or profile but that of No. 39 b is broken. No. 39 a: 0.84 m. N-S, 0.46 m. E-W; H. 0.33 m.; projection 0.11 m.; H. 0.10 m.; overall H. 0.40 m. No. 39 b: 0.65 m. N-S, 0.46 m. E-W; projection, 0.05 m., broken off. No. 39 c: lying in front of Nos. 39 a, b, probably originally from top; ashlar, same hard limestone; 0.46 m. N-S, 0.92 m. E-W, H. 0.29 m. (Fig. 114).

No. 40. This most venerable looking and possibly original monument (i.e., in its original position?) consists of backing of very hard limestone blocks, A, B, C, as foundation for a basis of several limestone and sandstone blocks (a-f). Similar stones now lying south of the wall *rb 1* may belong to the rubble construction of *rb 1,* since they are carefully aligned. If so, then the base was there first, then the wall. Also, No. 40 is sitting by ca. 0.10 m. lower than the big stone backing in wall *rb 1* which is behind the base. No. 40 sits directly on pebbles—this again speaks for its being earlier than wall *rb 1* which sits on loose earth over gravel. Backing stone A: 0.50 m. N-S, 0.30 m. E-W, H. 0.45 m.; B: 0.68 m. N-S, L. 1.66 m. E-W, H. 0.45 m.; C: 0.35 m. N-S, 0.50 m. E-W, H. 0.25 m. Overall dimensions: 1.00 m. N-S, 1.65 m. E-W; level *97.45 (on e). Bound only with earth. May have been repaired with riverstones. Some are rounded pieces of greenish limestone, others (e, f) shelly limestone (Fig. 119).

No. 41. Five fallen pieces of marble are lying on top of No. 41 and between Nos. 40 and 41. The longest of the pieces could have fit only on No. 40 but not on No. 41; L. 1.25 m.; W. 0.43 m.; H. 0.18 m. It had two clamp holes, two dowel holes on top, and two neatly cut dowel holes at bottom. Another piece measures L. 1.15 m.; W. 0.43 m.; H. 0.27 m. It also has clamp and dowel holes. A third piece is lying broken, L. 0.63 m.; W. 0.57 m.; H. 0.40 m. A fourth piece is fallen on wall *rb 1,* broken on all sides except top, L. 1.10 m., W. 0.55 m., H. 0.30 m. No. 41 is set up on flat stones and bricks, 0.25 m. high. Lower part roughened, same on sides, 0.14 m. high. Back rough punched. This is the first base which veers away from alignment with wall *rb 1* by 0.15–0.25 m. (apparently so set by Butler). 0.85 m. N-S, 1.17 m. E-W, H. 0.37 m. (Fig. 119).

No. 42. Set up on the same base of flat stones and bricks as No. 41 (by Butler). Lower part, large marble base, 0.88 m. N-S, 0.99 m. E-W; H. 0.36 m. Roughened for underground setting in the lower part for a height up to 0.25 m. Left (east) side has fine anathyrosis at top, 0.025 m. wide. The rest, very fine claw chisel work down to rough-punched zone. Top: similar claw chisel over medium dotted punch work. Upper set up by Butler. There are earth and stones between the lower and upper. Upper blocks: stele base with bosses on front (north) and left (east) sides. Back very rough-punched, even. Cutting: 0.21 m. N-S, 0.33 m. E-W, 0.12 m. deep. Overall: top 0.61 m. N-S, 0.59 m. E-W; H. 0.45 m. There follows a break of 1.45 m. in the low base

(Butler's 7, of brick and flat stones). In it a marble piece; all sides rough-picked, 0.89 m. by 0.48 m.; H. 0.29 m. (Fig. 119).

Nos. 43 and 44. The last two bases sit on Butler-prepared bases of flat marble, rubble, and bricks, 0.80 m. N-S, 2.50 m. E-W; 0.27–0.33 m. high. Set 0.45 m. off from wall *rb 1* (Fig. 114). The two bases are dissimilar: No. 43, marble, has smooth bands of ca. 0.10 m. around a rough-picked rectangle on the north side; the same bands are on three sides of the south side, where there are two large dowel holes at top. The east side is quite smooth, the west quite rough. The top is claw-chiseled, not very fine. This is either a masonry piece from the temple or a very large base, which originally continued on the south side. 0.74 m. (above profile), 0.77 m. (below profile, N-S), 1.17 m. E-W, 0.28 m. high. Dowel holes 0.04 m. by 0.04 m.; D. 0.04 m. No. 44: Marble block but without drafted bands. Top claw-chiseled in fan patterns over an irregularly shaped area; the part toward the front (north) and west side smoothed over. On the east and west sides similar claw-chisel work. Back and bottom very rough and bottom unevenly broken. 0.78 m. N-S, 1.12 m. E-W; H. 0.30 m. at front, back up to 0.36 m. (Figs. 113, 114).

No. 43 a. Belongs to No. 43. Rough (back) side now turned north. Very fine, small drafted edge on top. 0.63 m. N-S, 0.81 m. E-W; H. 0.27 m. (Fig. 114).

No. 44 a. Belongs on top of No. 44. Has rough bosses on the east and west (short) sides. 0.65 m. N-S, 0.86 m. E-W, H. 0.29 m. (Fig. 114).

No. 45. The last in the row is a peculiar fragment of marble set at ground level. Its setting might be ancient as it is out of alignment with Butler's brick flat stone bases for Nos. 43 and 44. Its direction aligns with wall *rb 1.* Rough-picked on top. 0.78 m. N-S, 0.35 m. on north side (E-W), 0.75 m. on south side (E-W); H. 0.18 m. (Fig. 113).

Conclusions

Practically all monuments appear to be reset or reused. Doubtful exceptions are No. 23 along the north side, which would then be Hellenistic, and No. 40 of SSB. Apart from the peculiar archaic capital reused as base No. 22, there is remarkable homogeneity of workmanship and considerable coincidence in size of both overall dimensions and cuttings in most of the gray local marble solid-block bases and stelai bases. Fine claw-chisel work, anathyrosis, and careful fitting seem to show that these stelai bases mostly belonged to the Persian or Early Hellenistic periods (as was assumed for the Lydian inscriptions of the stelai shafts by Butler and Buckler). Those of SSB may have been set against a wall first built in the first or early second century A.D. (wall *rb 1* contained sigillate sherds), but the entire setting operation seems to be the outcome of reordering of the precinct in the late second and/or third century A.D.

GMAH, KJF

V THE ARTEMIS TEMPLE: NEW SOUNDINGS

George M. A. Hanfmann
Kenneth J. Frazer

The best known landmark of ancient Sardis is the enormous Temple of Artemis, with its two standing columns. Located at the western foot of the Acropolis and overlooking the Pactolus and a large necropolis of rock-cut Lydian tombs to the west, the temple has stood visible, at least in part, throughout the centuries. Even when most of the temple and its precinct were covered by debris from successive floods, earthquakes, and landslides, the standing columns still revealed the location of the temple.[1]

The earliest attempt to clear any part of the temple was made by Robert "Palmyra" Wood, who, some time before 1750, excavated one of the standing columns.[2] In 1882 George Dennis, British Consul in Smyrna, made a trench and two test pits and discovered a colossal female head which he thought belonged to the goddess Cybele, but which Butler correctly identified with Faustina the Elder (second century A.D.).[3] In 1904, Gustave Mendel, working for the Imperial Ottoman Museum in Constantinople, made several test pits around the column bases in order to estimate the cost of a complete excavation of the temple.[4] His descriptions were published, but the excavation was not continued for lack of sufficient funds.

From 1910–1914, H. C. Butler and the Princeton Expedition accomplished the excavation of the great Artemis Temple. A report on excavations of the Artemis Temple area was given in *Sardis* I (1922) and the publication of the temple itself in *Sardis* II (1925). Butler's clear account of the activities of the season of 1914 and his illustrations[5] show that the condition of the temple, lying between "spacious terraces" (created by Butler's method of excavating with a railroad and building up terraced dumps), appeared to be essentially the same in 1914 as in 1958. The only substantial difference is that in Butler's time, the part of the site to the north and east was still covered by several village houses.[6] Their place is now partly occupied by the Harvard-Cornell Expedition camp (Figs. 59, 60). The Princeton Expedition house was wrecked in 1920 or 1921 by villagers, who pulled out wood and carried off tools. The picturesque ruin was demolished by local authority after the earthquake of March 1969.

As excavated by Butler, the temple and its environs cover an area of ca. 230 m. by 200 m. or 46,000 sq. m. Butler's Plan II is a good survey of the area before the excavations of 1910–1914 and Plan III of the same area after.[7] The plan shown in Figure 59 differs from Butler's Plan III only in that the 1958–1961 and 1970 excavations have been added, our B grid has been superposed, and the area has been resurveyed and the plan corrected for monuments presently extant.[8]

Butler had made a trench immediately along

the south side of the temple, and he had excavated within, especially around the earlier statue base. In his publication he introduced a useful system of numbering the columns which we have continued to employ (Fig. 120).[9]

State of Research

Butler assumed that an archaic temple of the time of Croesus (ca. 550 B.C.) existed in the location of the present temple and that at least the base of the east cella and a number of red sandstone blocks came from this structure. He believed that the two strange columns (Fig. 120 Nos. 11, 12; Figs. 121, 122) on unfinished bases might have belonged to a fifth century B.C. structure, especially since one of them had a Lydian inscription on its foot.[10] He envisaged the present temple as built essentially under the Persians, during the fourth century B.C. He assigned to the Roman period a final great rebuilding, reflected in his plan and restoration.[11] He also thought that the entire structure attached at the west might be archaic Lydian, possibly an altar.[12]

After Butler's publication, there was some criticism of details of his reconstruction, notably by W. B. Dinsmoor, who thought that the eastern and western porches had remained unroofed and that the entablature had a frieze similar to that of the Temple of Apollo at Didyma.[13] No one challenged the basic sequence of dating proposed by Butler; the debate about the dating of the temple cella revolved around the date of the Mnesimachos inscription cut on the inside of the northern wall of the west cella and the dating of the coin "hoard" found within the base. The low date of the hoard (ca. 190–188 B.C.) suggested by Franke has been opposed by H. Seyrig, who proposes ca. 220–200 B.C.[14]

After the first season of excavations in 1959, G. M. A. Hanfmann argued that no archaic structure had existed on the site.[15] His view was that the temple was begun after the battle of Kyropedion in 281 B.C. by the Seleucids, as a two-cella temple, with the joint cult of Artemis (facing west) and Zeus (facing east) as protectors of Necropolis and Acropolis respectively. Because the fragment of a colossal Hellenistic statue of Zeus (Fig. 148)

seemed to resemble coins of Achaeus, he dated the installation of the two images to the reign of Achaeus (ca. 220–215 B.C.). He believed that the pseudo-dipteral plan had been invented prior to Hermogenes and hence might go back to ca. 270 B.C. He suggested that the Roman reconstruction began immediately after the earthquake of A.D. 17 (possibly to accommodate the images of Tiberius and Livia, the great benefactors after the earthquake) and continued until the Second Neocorate, awarded Sardis under Antoninus Pius.[16]

In October 1961, G. Gruben, without contacting the Sardis Expedition, worked for several days at Sardis.[17] He then published an important re-examination of the Artemis Temple. Gruben distinguished three phases (Fig. 123). The first was Early Hellenistic, ca. 270–200 B.C., of which only the cella with a deep, square pronaos and a short opisthodomos with two columns *in antis* were built. The plan intended was dipteral with two rows of columns all around. The second phase, after Pergamene kings took over in Sardis (after 188 B.C.), followed a revised plan in keeping with the "pseudo-dipteral" plan popularized by the architect Hermogenes. The third, the Roman phase, was undertaken under Antoninus Pius. The two-cella plan was now introduced to accommodate the cult statues of Antoninus Pius and Faustina (ca. A.D. 140–160).[18]

From 1962 on, regular seminars were held at Sardis on the temple and its history, including a consideration of Gruben's proposals and observations. A special study was made by K. J. Frazer, architect of the expedition. Following up partly Butler's, partly Gruben's observations, he proposed the following hypothesis:

1. In the very beginning, the focal point of the area was the image base (Figs. 59 No. 17, 120, 127–130, 139). Either a small shrine or the earliest altar may have existed here.

2. An archaic temple of dipteral plan, closely resembling that of the Artemision in Ephesus, was built in the time of Croesus, ca. 550 B.C. The Altar LA 1, in its earliest form, may belong to such an archaic temple (tentative reconstruction Figs. 124, 125). He thought some columns of such a temple may have been erected.

3. An Early Hellenistic temple closely followed the archaic, and like the temple at Ephesus, was built on the archaic foundations.

4. A major Hellenistic revision led to replanning and changes of floor levels in the western end, and, as was seen in 1972, the opening of the eastern door and change to a two-cella plan. The pseudo-dipteral plan was also adopted.

5. The situation during the Roman phase was investigated by Frazer jointly with D. Van Zanten, and their work led to the partial reconstruction of the western end of the temple, presented in Figure 126. In this reconstruction of the situation after A.D. 17, it is assumed that the western end of the temple was never completed. The two unfinished bases, identified by K. J. Frazer as counterparts of the two unfinished bases in the eastern colonnade (Fig. 120 Nos. 11–12; Fig. 122), were apparently erected (Fig. 120, Butler's Nos. 53, 54), but it is not clear whether the entablatures and roof over the porch were ever put in place. D. Van Zanten had, indeed, thought that the double shrine had only an emergency roof over the double cella but evidence for marble paving of the southern colonnade (*infra*) calls for roofing of that part as well.

Field Activities Undertaken by Harvard-Cornell Expedition

The original plan of the Harvard-Cornell Expedition was to ascertain whether a clearly defined archaic level still existed in the precinct. Stratigraphic investigations in Trench S and Building L (*infra*) seemed to negate this possibility. The next proposal was to proceed with re-excavation of the interior of the temple as a preliminary step towards putting the temple in an orderly condition. We had planned to start with the eastern cella and then proceed to units west of it. Partial cleaning of the east cella and the sounding at the image base in 1960 and 1961 were to serve this purpose; the sounding also permitted a recheck of Butler's account of building conditions and stratification. Heavy commitments of funds and equipment for Bin Tepe tunneling and for the restoration program at the Gymnasium ended this project.

Collapse of the northwest steps at the temple

in 1968 led to resumption of activities, since the steps had to be repaired and reset. From 1969–1973, a program of cleaning and pre-publication recording was undertaken for the entire precinct. Upon K. J. Frazer's initiative, excavations were undertaken around Altar LA and a series of soundings were made within the temple in 1972 to clarify specific points of importance for Frazer's hypothesis.

It should be clearly stated what was *not* done. Contrary to the 1960 plan, we did not carry out a complete re-excavation of the temple. It is still possible to urge, as Frazer does, that additional study of foundations and strata with Lydian sherds might reveal some archaic material. On the other hand, Hanfmann is satisfied that enough tests were made within the temple and precinct to prove that no substantial archaic structures existed in the precinct area around the present temple or within the temple, although they may have existed on higher ground to the northeast. It is also perfectly clear that no rich archaic level comparable to deposits around the Artemis altar at Ephesus[19] existed either around the image base or around Altar LA.

Finally, the clearing and partial reconstruction of the temple remain a challenging but expensive task. The Harvard-Cornell Expedition has taken the most necessary measures to protect the temple and precinct,[20] but a satisfactory solution would entail large-scale earth moving, digging away the insignificant Byzantine remains, and undertaking careful study of all marble parts of the temple still extant prior to actual restoration of walls and columns. The landscaping, too, would require considerable work.

Investigation and Repair of the Image Base in the East Cella

The structure which Butler regarded as the basis for an archaic cult statue consisted of two courses of what he described as "purple sandstone" masonry in the east cella. He based his (tentative) conclusion for the date on a single coin of Croesus found in the base.[21] It is quite clear, however, that this single coin, which supposedly appeared near the center of the base, cannot prevail against the finding of 127 silver and bronze coins, virtually all of which date to the Hellenistic period predating the year 200 B.C. The 54 Hellenistic silver coins were found along the east side of the basis, the 72 Hellenistic bronze coins along the north side.[22] P. R. Franke has analyzed the coins and correctly concluded that the basis must have been built in Hellenistic times, as he thought, shortly after 200 B.C. The position of coins is shown in a general way in Bell, *Sardis* XI (1916) v (Fig. 128), and adjusted to the general basis plan in Butler, *Sardis* I (1922) ill. 71 (Fig. 127).

Compelled to abandon his excavations on short notice in 1914, Butler left helter-skelter the sandstone masonry extracted from the basis and a gaping hollow in the center of the eastern cella. Initially, the Harvard-Cornell Expedition proposed no more than putting the chaos of stones into some semblance of order and filling the hole in the east cella. It was decided, however, to take advantage of the removal of stones and recheck Butler's sounding under the Image "Basis."[23]

In July 1960 work began in moving sandstone blocks which had been left lying in heaps in the western part of the east cella. Equipment used for these operations included a Thern Dorin Gear Winch, a Yale and Towne hoist (donated by the Yale and Towne Company), and a tripod loaned by the Reynolds Construction Company. During the 1960 campaign, the eastern cella was cleaned and excavated in its northeast corner; two blocks of the north wall of the cella were replaced, and the blocks left lying by the Princeton Expedition were arranged in order (Figs. 129, 130).

In 1961, partial reconstruction of the basis was begun. Each block moved was numbered (e.g. 61.1, 61.2, etc.), and recorded on a plan (Fig. 133). Blocks 61.103–61.110 were numbered in 1970; of these 61.103–61.105 were neither moved by Butler nor by us in 1961. Forty-six blocks were placed in the first course, with 21 blocks already in position along the south and west sides of the cella. Fifty-five additional blocks were available (61.47–61.102), many of which were only broken pieces, but there were not enough blocks extant to finish the second course. The blocks were placed along the periphery of the basis (with their tops

at ca. *101.40 as shown in Figs. 135, 136). No cement was used in the reconstruction in order to allow future alteration of the arrangement. All stone fragments too small to be used in the second course were collected and piled along the south wall of the temple. Small rubble stones were cleaned up and piled along the north wall opposite pier 71.

In 1970, a review of the evidence was made by G. M. A. Hanfmann. Part of the image base was recleaned, new measurements and photographs taken, and the drawings revised. Finally, in 1973, T. Yalçinkaya, C. H. Greenewalt, Jr., and J. L. Miller collaborated in evacuating from the east cella all marble blocks which had been left stranded in 1914. Only the fragments of the jambs of the great eastern door were set up on bases Nos. 65 and 66 (Figs. 131, 132).

Masonry Pattern

Upon investigation, it was seen that a number of stones on the southern and eastern side of the base had not been moved by Butler. They are shown without numbers in Figure 133. There is not enough preserved to reconstitute a complete pattern of positioning. Oblongs running east-west may have changed into a pattern of north-south oriented stones under the actual image. Butler's drawing of the stones in plan, presumably of the top course, was too small and inexact to permit identification of individual stones (Fig. 127).[24] The reconstitution of the base made in 1960–1961, therefore, had to adopt an arbitrary pattern (Fig. 133). The numbering of stones (61.1–61.110) should permit ready identification of those moved.

Butler described the masonry as "irregularly quadrated blocks of purple sandstone in two courses (each) 42 cm. thick. Some of these were held together by iron clamps of Pi shape with short legs. The basis extended from the column foundations of one side to those on the other. Its irregular outline suggests that its outer edges had been broken when the new column foundations were put in, or in the clearing out of the cella at the time of its conversion into a cistern."[25] Butler's drawing in *Sardis* II (1925) Atlas, (scale 1:200) shows a very irregular array of blocks reaching to the edges of column bases 69 and 71 on the north and 70 on the south, and not reaching column base 72. In fact, our findings showed undisturbed stones near column 72 which had not been drawn by Butler. Butler's draftsman gave no indication of clamps or other cuttings. A freehand, but more detailed sketch of the basis, with findspots of the two coin hoards (Fig. 127),[26] also renders the masonry very irregularly, again without clamps or cuttings.

Material

The basis contained both the "purplish sandstone" blocks and the "greenish sandstone" blocks, so designated by their surface appearance. (Both are used in the external wall of Altar LA 2). According to E. İzdar, Department of Geology, Ege University, Izmir, the red-brown ("purple") rock is a mica-bearing sandstone of the upper miocene period; the greenish rock is a younger coarse-grained sandstone with fine micaceous cement, and more iron impurities.

Sizes and Dimensions

One hundred and two blocks were measured and numbered in 1961. If we disregard the broken and odd-shaped blocks, recurrent sizes fall into groups of ashlars in approximate multiples of 2 feet (ca. 0.60 m.), 2½ (0.72–0.75 m.), 3 (0.90–0.96 m.), and 3½ feet (1.05 m.) for length, and 1½ feet (0.45 m.), 2 (0.55–0.60 m., mostly 0.58 m.), 2½ (0.75 m.), and possibly 2¼ feet (0.55 m.) for width, with frequent height of 0.42–0.45 m. (1½ feet); several large square blocks measure 3 by 3 feet (0.90 by 0.90 m.). There are also two heights involved: one is 0.42–0.45 m., postulated by Butler for both courses, and another, apparently intentional, is 0.48–0.50 m.

A number of stones, now set up along the east

Tabe 5. Sizes of ashlar blocks in the east cella base in m.

	Stone No.	Length	Width	Height
Oblong	61.16	1.05	0.60	0.55
	61.36	0.60	0.45	0.45
Squared	61.12	0.90	0.90	0.43
L-Shaped	61.93	1.10	0.55	0.50
	61.95	0.95	0.60	0.45

Table 6. Dimensions of cut-back blocks in m.

Stone No.	Length of cutback	Total length	Width	Height	Height of cutting
61.104*	0.55	1.05	0.60	0.60–0.50	0.07
61.72*	0.55	1.05	0.50	0.49–0.50	0.07
61.105*	0.30	0.70	0.60	0.085	
61.106*	0.21	0.70	0.68	0.070	
61.107**	0.12	0.67		0.420	0.12

*Greenish stones
**Purple stone

edge of the second course of the basis (Figs. 133, 134) are cut to receive steps (lower part indicated by hatching in plan). The cut-back stones may represent three different sizes of steps; two of these are used in the tentative reconstruction (Fig. 134; see also Fig. 136).

Working

Remains of tool marks give evidence for working and dressing of the stones:

1. Very rough quarry trimming with quarry hammer. In some cases this may represent secondary retrimming (Fig. 136).

2. Sharp, large cutting tool (large chisel) obliquely used; diagonal or cross strokes, vertical face of 61.51 (Figs. 137, 138).

3. Pointed chisel, with near vertical strokes.

4. Flat chisel, finishing and polishing with abrasive.

A fragment shows one part rough-trimmed, the other polished and finished (Fig. 139 blocks 61.17, 61.16, 61.16A, 61.16B). No traces of multiple toothed tool were observed.

Clamps, Dowels, Prising Holes, and Other Cuttings

Butler speaks as if he had seen masonry linked by short-legged Pi-shaped iron clamps.[27] We saw none in place. Only a half-dozen examples of clamp cuttings were recorded among ca. one hundred stones:

61.16B. A fine cutting for a swallow-tail clamp (Figs. 140, 141). L. of half cutting 0.15 m.; W. at end 0.07 m., at edge 0.03 m., at spread 0.035 m.; D. 0.03 m. for shallow, small iron clamp (slight hollow at end). 61.16A (south of 61.16B). Has a typical, rather rough cutting for a rectangular Pi-clamp. L. 0.19 m.; W. at end 0.095 m.; L. to cutting 0.115 m.; D. cutting 0.04 m.

In block 61.11, 17, 25, 45, and unnumbered stone *x* south of 61.22 (Fig. 142) such clamp cuttings occur near the center of the long sides without corresponding cuttings in the next stone. Thus, the clamp cuttings suggest that the stones in the base were taken from other, earlier structures. The diversity of masonry sizes bears this out.

Prising Holes. Sharp, narrow cuttings to insert metal bars for moving the stones occur in a number of blocks, e.g. 61.18: L. 0.10 m.; W. 0.04 m. at top, 0.005 m. at bottom.

End Dowel. A rectangular cutting 0.25 m. wide, 0.33 m. high, was recorded at the end of block 61.14. As K. J. Frazer points out, it is the upper part of a dowel hole placed at a join.

In general, the blocks do not give clear indications of their age, but lack of multiple tooth work and sparing use of clamping favor a stage of construction techniques earlier than that of Altar LA 1, where clamps were used regularly. It does not seem at all certain that these blocks all came from an earlier image base or indeed from one structure. They could have come from substructures, terracing walls, and the like.

Additional Features of Image Base Area

Several features not clearly recorded in Butler exist at present. One is the linking wall *t* (Figs. 133, 135); three ashlar blocks of the same yellowish, greatly weathered stone as Altar LA have been cut somewhat obliquely and wedged in between column bases 69 and 70.

Another feature is Quadrangle LI (Figs. 133, 144), which consists of rough-picked, reused marble slabs from the temple and one green sandstone block joined with cement and rubble. Quadrangle LI runs south roughly from the center of the present east side of the image base for 3.75 m., turns north for 6 m., and comes back to base 70 for 2.25 m. It also overlies, on its east side, the column base pier 67. This proves that the marble slabs were placed at a time when the column bases no longer carried columns, as their present level of *101.20 is 0.35 m. below the original height of the tops of the column base piers.[28] At the northward turn of the marble rectangle LI is a block with large Lydian letters (*u, r,* or possibly a contracted *u-ar*).[29] The south edge is broken; L. 1.23 m., W. 0.85 m., H. ca. 0.40 m. The block also has an incised cross, presumably intended as a setting mark for the present alignment of LI and hence not Lydian. The marble slabs forming the rectangle LI were used apparently to support some sort of rectangular wall or platform attached to the image

base at a late date (more likely Late Roman than Christian, as there is no evidence that the Christians ever tried to repair anything in the temple).

Conclusions Concerning the Image Base

The location and distribution of silver and bronze coins (Fig. 127) make it certain that the part of the basis structure found by Butler was built in Hellenistic times and was not rebuilt in Roman times. Apart from the Croesus coin, the 54 silver coins could not have stayed in place during a Roman rebuilding. They were found in the vertical joins of the upper course.[30] The base was built either by ca. 215 B.C.—the Zeus image on it dating from the time of Achaeus[31] —or at latest it was complete by ca. 200 B.C.

The cement layer on which the lower of the two preserved courses was laid (ca. *100.45) was Hellenistic. The excavator (W. C. B. Young) stated that the Roman rubble wall went under the base at the point of contact with pier 71, but not under the pier, and argued from this and from the presence of brick fragments in the fill and the lime-plaster setting of the base that the base was reset in Roman times. The cemented rubble under the base, however, seemed a result of an attempt by Roman builders to tie in under the pre-existing structure; disturbance by Butler and the Roman pier builders accounts for the brick fragments and Roman pottery found in the upper level.

Because different types of clamps occur in nonfunctional position, it follows that the stones of the base were taken, at least in part, from earlier buildings, archaic and/or Persian in period.

The top of the second course of the basis was approximately level with column bases as now preserved, *101.30–101.40. This is below the floor level of the cella (*101.54) in the corner, *101.574 on the wall just west of the basis. As suggested by D. Van Zanten, there was probably at least a third course, possibly of the same kind of stone, on the image platform (Fig. 134). He assumes a fourth course of marble. If the temple builders used the sandstone purely as convenient foundation material, then the third course might already have been of marble. If they aimed for venerable and archaic bichrome effect, an edge of the present base might have been visible. The occurrence of 0.50 m. high stones might prove that the third course was higher than the first two courses.

Steps and a platform of marble, were seated on at least two, and possibly three, sandstone steps. This arrangement may belong to the original Hellenistic phase. (The tentative reconstruction in Fig. 134 shows only one step; cf. Fig. 136).

According to D. Van Zanten, the base of the image of Athena at Priene shows a similar way of cutting steps into the substructure stones after the blocks have been set. Other resemblances are the use of rough limestone and similar cutting and clamping. It is, therefore, legitimate to assume that at Sardis, as in Priene, a marble course formed the top of the platform. While the temple of Priene was designed and built by Pytheos and dedicated by Alexander the Great in 334 B.C., the image was not set up until the mid-second century B.C., when Orophernes of Cappadocia, the donor "hid some coins bearing his portrait in the statue's pedestal as a kind of donation record," thereby firmly dating the base and the image which was an imitation of the Athena Parthenos.[32]

The strange, rough-trimmed marble slab quadrangle LI (Fig. 129) may have been part of the Roman changes required for the installation of the colossus of Antoninus Pius.

We have found no cogent evidence of cuttings, dowels, etc., which would show what went on top of the preserved sandstone blocks. A colossus of the size and weight of Zeus would require a fairly large base to spread the load (P.H. 1.10 m.; est. H. if seated, over 5 m., if standing, over 7 m.; est. weight over 30 tons if the entire image were of marble); Antoninus Pius (P.H. 1.05 m.) would not have been much smaller. Technically, it would be feasible to have two colossi (Zeus and Antoninus Pius) on such a base, but there is no evidence to decide between this and the assumption of only one colossal image.

The Romans did tie the entire width (N-S) of the base to the cross wall by building the cemented rubble wall r, top *100.96, bottom *99.43 (Figs. 129, 130, 133, 134, 143, 145). The height of wall r virtually proves the existence of an additional course of ca. 0.50 m. in height above the present top of the basis at *100.40–100.30.

Column base piers 69 and 71 are shallowly founded (Fig. 130) at ca. *100.00. The excavators noted fragments of brick, possibly from the time when the piers were being constructed. Butler believed these piers to have been set or reset in Roman times.

To sum up, the base was constructed of partly reused materials. There is no clear indication whether it ever faced west, as demanded by Gruben's and Frazer's reconstructions of the Early Hellenistic phase. As preserved, it faced east. It seems to date either to ca. 220–215 B.C. or ca. 200–190 B.C. It conforms to known forms of Hellenistic image bases. Perhaps one has to assume that it was finished only in time to serve the second, later Hellenistic, two-cella phase when Zeus and Artemis shared the temple, a phase which Hanfmann and Frazer now date to ca. 220 or 200 B.C. In this case, the first image to occupy the base was probably the Zeus colossus (Fig. 148).

The Romans tied the base more securely to the cross wall, perhaps because the base was to carry a heavier load. Hanfmann suggests that when the temple received the honor of Imperial cult, Zeus was not evicted. Rather, the Imperial colossus of Antoninus Pius, probably seated, joined the colossus of Zeus as *paredros*. It is for this reason that head fragments of both colossi who sat in the east cella have been found nearby.[33] The weight of the two images increased the stresses on the base. One would expect, in this case, that Artemis remained enthroned next to the empress Faustina; a colossal female head, found by Butler, now in Istanbul, may, indeed, be part of such an Artemis statue.[34]

Numismatists often assume that an ancient Anatolian image of a goddess with ears of corn and pomegranate shown as official city goddess of Sardis on coins from the first to the third century A.D. is the image of Artemis-Kore worshipped in the big Artemis temple.[35] The size of the image is not known; it is also not certain whether this was an archaic image or a Roman imitation. It does not seem likely, however, that it required a large base; and its archaic facial type would not agree with the colossal fragment cited above which follows a classical fifth century Artemis type.

Stratigraphic Sounding in the East Cella, 1960

In 1960 a trench was begun in the eastern cella running about 10 m. eastward from the west wall of the cella and south from Roman rubble wall *r* (Figs. 129, 145). The trench was dug in four steps to a depth of ca. 4 m., down to *96.80 (Fig. 130).

The top of the level of the first course of the image base was at *100.92 north of column base 72. At *100.48 the cement bedding of the sandstone platform appeared, laid on pebbly earth. From ca. *100.92–*99.43 was rubble wall *r*, the top of which comes up to the top of the sandstone platform. This wall did not go under pier 72, but around its northwest corner. Wall *r* at bottom, *99.43, rests on sandy earth (Figs. 130, 145).

From *99.75–*99.45 the trench contained Lydian and Hellenistic pottery and fragments of terracotta water pipe. At around *99.34, the soil in the trench became less pebbly, but water-laid (torrent) deposits continued to the bottom at *96.80 (Fig. 145). At *98.77 the trench was filled with brown earth and rubble, obviously turned over previously and also including brick fragments.

The first level, ca. 0.50 m. below the lower course of the image base, reaching from *99.90–*99.80, contained large amounts of Roman household ware and some Hellenistic and Lydian sherds. The second level, *99.75–*99.00, produced about 50 percent later Lydian and 40 percent unidentifiable worn, plain wares. A piece of Lydian tile and a fragment with Lydian grafitto as well as a fragment of Corinthianizing vase with siren's wings (Fig. 151) were found in an earthy layer. The level from *99.00–*98.00 contained only fifteen Lydian sherds, from *98.00–*96.80 (Fig. 130) only two Lydian sherds.

No significant architectural traces were found below the present basis and temple. The builders of the temple constructed the piers directly into torrent deposits and filled the interstices with river stones and pebbles. They founded the basis of the image on a layer of (water impermeable?) gray cement (ca. *100.40).

The scanty finds below the first level were probably carried down by torrents from above. They do not contradict an early Hellenistic date for the temple; they also leave open the possibility that (as observed at Building L) some sort of activity from the sixth to the fourth century B.C. in between flood seasons is reflected in the relatively abundant pottery. The Corinthianizing sherd found in the second level and datable to ca. 580–550 B.C. provided the only more precise chronological clue. We may recall that Butler found a Lydian pot at the east end of the temple.

Finds

Statue Fragments
Colossal neck and chin of Antoninus Pius. Butler, *Sardis* I (1922) ill. 57; *BASOR* 166, 34; *Dergi* 11 (1961) 44, fig. 18; A Giuliano, *Rivista dell'Instituto Nazionale d'Archeologia e Storia dell'Arte* 8 (1959) 188; Inan, Rosenbaum, 74, no. 40, pl. 26:1 with refs. (Figs. 146, 147.)
Hellenistic Zeus. Found by Butler in east cella. Rediscovered lying below the south wall of the east part of the temple. P.H. 1.10 m. *Sardis* I (1922) ill. 61; *BASOR* 166, 34, fig. 27. (Fig. 148.)

Pottery
P60.102:2370. Lydian black on red bowl rim sherd. Wavy metopal lines. East cella, south of bases 71, 69; *100.80–*99.80. Diam. 0.28 m.; P.H. 0.0215 m.; Th. 0.005 m. (Fig. 149.)
P60.112:2380. Lydian cup base. Exterior: black streaked on white burnish; interior: plain. East cella, south of bases 71, 69; *100.66–*99.00. Diam. base 0.02 m.; P.H. 0.033 m.; Th. 0.007 m. (Fig. 150.)
P60.114:2382. Corinthianizing sherd with part of siren's wing. East cella, south of bases 71, 69, *100.66–*99.00. P.W. 0.064 m.; P.H. 0.033 m.; Th. 0.005 m. According to J. A. Schaeffer, probably local or East Greek imitation of Corinthian or Attic, ca. 580–550 B.C. (Fig. 151.)
P61.60:3256. Neck of Lydian lekythos. 3 m. north of base 72; 3.5 m. east of cella wall; *100.70. Diam. 0.03 m.; P.H. 0.023 m.; diam. neck 0.018 m.; Th. 0.004 m.

Terracotta
T60.6:2381. Spindle whorl. East cella, south of bases 71, 69; *100.66–*99.00. Diam. 0.03 m.; H. 0.017 m. (Fig. 152.)

Stone
S61.24:3486. Roman cuirass torso. 3.85 m. west, 2.0 m. south of pier 78; *98.94. P.H. 0.66 m., W. 0.46 m., Th. 0.24 m. *BASOR* 166, 34. C. C. Vermeule, *Berytus* XV (1964) 97, no. 1a, pl. XVII.II; *Berytus* XVI (1966) 59.

Soundings in the Artemis Temple in 1972

In 1972 an attempt was made to find evidence for foundations of an archaic temple which might have remained undetected by Butler and to determine whether remains of an earlier, dipteral plan might be detected on the north flank of the temple. It was Frazer's suggestion that one or two such columns, or their bases only, may have been put in before the pseudo-dipteral plan of the present temple was carried out (Figs. 123, 124).[36] A total of ten trenches or soundings was dug. The following is a brief description with indications of objectives and results. The locations of Trenches 1–10 are shown in the plan in Figure 120.

Trench 1. 2.20 m. by 4.70 m. running N-S. Objective: to locate the remains of any column base foundations which may have existed as next in line to column No. 7[37] in a partly executed dipteral plan. The trench went through completely sterile levels at *100.20 to *98.22. No trace of column base foundation lying in line west of column No. 7 was found, nor was there anything to indicate that any structure had existed at this place at an early date which had subsequently been removed (Fig. 157).[38]

Trench 2. 2.00 m. by 5.40 m. running N-S (Figs. 156, 158, 159). Objective: to locate any remains of a column base foundation of a column *in antis,* in line with columns Nos. 4 and 11. From a level of *99.70 onwards, marble fragments and chips appeared. A total of 52 worked marble fragments was taken, among them six large ones, 22 of these between the levels of *99.70–*98.60. Among fragments of rectangular blocks, most had dowel and Pi-clamp cavities and prise holes. Of interest were four blocks or fragments with ca. 0.045 m. diameter circular dowel holes with pour-channels, which are at variance with the usual square and rectangular dowel hole generally used in the Artemis Temple construction. One damaged block bore incised letters Κ ϫ (Figs. 160, 161).

At *99.11 appeared part of a marble volute from a Hellenistic Ionic capital of the temple (Figs. 162–164) and five other smaller fragments. Among the other marble fragments were ten pieces from a marble tiled roof of a building of considerably smaller scale than the temple. One triangular marble fragment bears an incised inscription in uncertain, but non-Lydian, script. Half of the front of an antefix of terracotta of the Perso-Lydian era (fifth to fourth century B.C.) was the earliest, a coin of Constantine II (A.D. 324–330) was the latest among the finds.

The wide range of periods of the artifacts recovered from Trench 2 makes it appear that this area had been excavated on a number of occasions.

The bottom of the trench, at *98.44, was in clean, solid clay.

In view of the size, tooling, and general appearance of the rough and pick-dressed masonry recovered in the trench, K. J. Frazer believes that marble foundation blocks from the pair of columns *in antis* were dismantled and their marble foundation blocks recovered. G. M. A. Hanfmann is of the opinion that the marble fragments come from the dismantling of the temple itself in the Constantinian age.

Trench 3. 1.00 m. by 2.00 m. N-S, against the threshold of the east door of the temple (Figs. 120, 153–155, 165). Objective: to check the strength of the wall foundations under the door space in order to find out whether they were designed to carry a solid east wall. Results: the foundations for the east wall of the temple cella were found to consist of the euthynteria and three lower courses, all in all, 1.78 m. deep, some 0.24 m. deeper than the euthynteria and the four small courses at the north end of the same wall in Trench 3 A (Figs. 158, 166). Below the marble blocks of the euthynteria, the blocks were of different material: green or gray sandstone, limestone, and conglomerate, heavy well-cut blocks set on their clay bed. From a comparison with the two successive west walls in Trenches 7 and 8 (*infra*) where the foundations under the door space are noticeably lighter and less well laid than those under the solid walls, it becomes obvious that the east wall was originally designed to be doorless.[39] Notable among the small finds was a solid lead plumb-bob (Fig. 177) weighing 1,340 grams, which was found on top of the second course below the euthynteria, ca. 0.30 m. south of the central axis of the door space above.

Trench 3 A. 2.00 m. by 1.50 m. (Figs. 120, 153, 154, 158, 166). Objective: to expose the foundations of the east wall of the temple and of the south side of the northeast anta and to compare them with the east wall foundations under the east door threshold. The depth of the four foundation courses including the euthynteria was only 1.65 m. against 1.78 m. under the door. As at the east door, the foundation blocks consisted of different types of stone. The marble blocks, four in number, as with the peculiarly chiseled marble block in Trench 2, may have originally belonged to another structure. Their dressed surfaces indicate that they were above ground and visible. Their chiseling seems again to indicate a cautious and perhaps early approach to anathyrosis (Figs. 167, 168).

Trench 4. 3.80 m. by 2.00 m., and 9.50 m. by 1.80 m. A T-shaped trench. Objective: to locate the remains of foundations of a great flight of steps from the pronaos level (*100.04) down to LA ground level (LA 1, *97.21; LA 2, *97.32); to locate the remains of the base foundations of the south column of the westernmost pair of the *in antis* columns of the pronaos. Since this was an area of great rebuilding in Hellenistic and Roman times, nothing remains (Fig. 120).

Trench 5. 2.00 m. by 5.50 m. N-S. Objective: to study the stratification in order to locate the builders' foundation trench of the south wall of the temple. Just below the ground level, which is also the level of the upper edge of the euthynteria (of the outside, south wall, *100.04), large, square Roman bricks, some 0.335 m. square, were cleared. They were presumably bedding material for the now disappeared Roman marble (?) paving blocks for the south pteroma. They were set in weak lime-mortar, only a centimeter or two thick, which in turn lay on a clay stratum of ca. 0.22 m. in depth.

Immediately below the level of the bricks, at *99.67, and lying roughly parallel with the temple foundations, at 1.95 m. from the edge of the euthynteria, was a terracotta pipeline of six sections, each averaging 0.345 m. The joints were sealed with mortar or cement bond. Diameter was 0.14 m. Sherds at this level consisted of Hellenistic relief and Roman wares with a large number of Lydian pieces.

From *99.67 down, the fill in the southern part of the trench was gravel and sand, with some stones, as if laid by river flooding. Devoid of finds, this was undoubtedly the original ground into which the trench for the temple foundations was sunk. In Trench S, some 20 m. south and 30 m. west, the comparable Level III lay at *96.20 (see *infra*).

At a level of *98.13 (Figs. 169, 170) lay a second, lower, terracotta pipeline. It rested on a plinth of clay and small clay chips (H. 0.10 m.). It is protected by a small riverstone wall bedded on the same plinth. The cavity between the pipe and the side walls was filled with clay, and the top covered with flat marble chips, some of which showed pick-dressing. The top level on the cover-stone is at *98.43. Frazer thinks that two pipe-lines crossing Trench 5 were most likely used to carry water away from the east end of the temple to the Pactolus Valley.[40] Frazer also hypothesized that a verdant, often wet area near the southeast corner of the temple was a spring or water concentration to be led away from the temple, but Trench 10 failed to bring proof (see *infra*).

Terracotta pipe sections from flared to flanged end: L. 0.38 m., 0.445 m., plus tapered end for insertion into next section, L. 0.04 m.–0.065 m. Each section had a distinct bulge at the midriff. No cement or gypsum was found at the joints (Fig. 171). The pipes compare in length with HoB Roman pipes, which were, however, fixed at the joints with white cement.

In the 1960 trench in the temple, between bases of columns 69–71, a pipe was found running at *99.75 and *99.45 along with Hellenistic and Lydian pottery. In Trench S (1958), one pipe (*d 1*) at *97.65 had a flow toward the temple, the other (*d 2*), at *97.57, away from the temple (Figs. 96, 221, 222); both ran N-S.

The pattern in Butler's Plan III suggests that these pipe lines were not concentrating on the Byzantine reservoir of the ninth century;[41] that they were found 2 m. below the floors of the temple (in 1960, floor ca. *101.50; pipe ca. *99.50; in 1972, ca. *100.00, *98.10) would suggest that many were laid either during the original building in Hellenistic times or, more probably, during Roman rebuilding after Claudius built the new aqueduct for Sardis (ca. A.D. 50).

Trench 6. L-shaped, 2.00 m. by 1.50 m. N-S, and 2.65 m. by 3.60 m. E-W. Objective: to locate the remains of column base foundations which may have existed next in line to column No. 2 in a partly dipteral plan (Fig. 120). Part of a rectangular marble block was found at the correct level (top at *98.65) for the column foundation, but was out of any useful alignment (Fig. 172).

The block was rock dressed on two sides; 1.24 m. by 0.47 m. by 0.37 m. It had a rectangular slot, 0.30 m. by 0.20 m. by 0.12 m. in its rough side; the opposite, dressed side shows no clamp, dowel, or prising holes. Frazer concluded that both Trenches 1 and 6 were in all likelihood excavated in antiquity. "The base west of column No. 2 was possibly built, while that west of column No. 7 is very doubtful" (Frazer, field report). A good reason for thinking that the area involved was excavated in Roman antiquity is provided by the stone and lime mortar consolidation masses at the northeast corner in Trenches 6 and 6 A. They were apparently taken from within the area we excavated.

Trench 7. 1.50 m. by 8.25 m. N-S. Objective: to inspect the wall foundations under the threshold space and under the solid wall foundations for comparison with the east wall foundations in Trenches 3 and 3 A. Results: (Figs. 120, 145–155, 173) the trench dug to *97.428 (depth ca. 2.00 m.) amply demonstrated the greater strength of actual wall foundations compared to the foundations under the door thresholds.

The west wall foundations rest on deep river gravel and sand and river-worn stones. Those carrying solid wall are comprised of pick-dressed rectangular marble blocks, measuring as much as 2.33 m. in length and 0.51 m. in height. Their width is concealed in the foundation. The depth of solid wall foundations, including the euthynteria, is 2.03 m. The foundations under the now missing euthynteria are 1.77 m. deep and consist of limestone, gray or green sandstone, conglomerate, and purple sandstone. No marble was used. The blocks are often very roughly dressed; the stones of the lowest course should be described as fairly large boulders.

A purple sandstone block in the second to bottom course of these doorway foundations has been roughly pick-finished and is cut with a shallow step 0.18 m. wide and 0.07 m. high. This is typical of the upper course blocks along the east side of the sandstone cult basis foundations in the east cella of the temple (Figs. 134, 136).[42]

The mixture of Lydian, Hellenistic, and Roman sherds was completely disturbed by demolition of the wall to middle foundations in Late Hellenistic

or Early Roman period and by modern intrusions down to *98.37.

Trenches 8 and 8 A. 8.75 m. by 1.00 m. N-S. Objective: to inspect the wall foundations under the later threshold space and under the rest of the wall for comparison with the east and "original" west wall foundations in Trenches 3, 3 A, and 7. Results: (Figs. 120, 153–155, 174) this foundation was exposed by Butler, except for 2–3 m. at its south end. The previously unexcavated section contained a bridge of small marble blocks bedded on a 0.10 m. thick layer of mortar extending between the south wall foundations and the column foundations of the western pronaos columns of the second phase (Fig. 124; cf. Figs. 153, 174). These were in the third phase incorporated in the foundations of the cross wall. For the comparatively weak door foundations, another bridge was constructed, this one consisting of stone and mortar mass, only 0.82 m. deep, resting on a bed of mortar 0.12 m. thick. Butler mistook the remains of the bridge of small marble blocks between the main north wall foundations and the north column base foundations for the remains of an earlier structure and did not recognize the column base foundations of the second phase as such.

Trench 9. 0.60 m. by 3.20 m. E-W (Figs. 153, 158, 175). Objective: to ascertain whether the steps toward the east door were in this situation in the original executed plan of the Artemis Temple. As in Trench 3, a sandwich of smallish stones (0.20 m.) set in lime mortar, the same stones set in clay bonding (0.55–0.60 m.), and another layer of small stones in lime mortar were laid over solid clay fill. This is unlike the regular temple foundations which were bedded in gravel and sand. The foundation of the steps and this bedding mass were laid on top of solid clay which may have been natural. One wonders, however, to what extent wet, solid clay may have been used as a stabilizing mass around the temple foundations at the east side of the temple.

The lower dressed marble course of the steps foundation at its west end does not bond into the wall; it is merely notched to rest on the small ledge formed by the upper edge of the east wall euthynteria and the slightly set-back face of the ashlar course immediately above (Fig. 153). What appear at first to be straight Pi-clamp cavities on the steps' foundation blocks show traces of having been extended and recut slightly to take a swallow-tail type of clamp (Fig. 175).

We further tested under the inner (west) side of the great east doorway (opposite Trench 3, not shown on plan Fig. 120). It too was bedded in a stone and mortar mass which extends for several meters out into the east cella (Figs. 154–155, section B-B).

Trench 10. 1.50 m. by 4.50 m. N-S (location on Fig. 120). Objective: to locate a source of fresh water seepage noticeable in the southeast foundations. Results: area of green grass some 8 m. SSE of Church M, with surface at *101.29 did not produce evidence of water bearing strata. The trench went to 2.80 m. (*98.45), equivalent to level of the lower pipe in Trench 5, through topsoil and alternating clays and sand/gravel layers. Possibly the trench should have been put farther to the north.

Finds

Trenches 1, 9, and 10 produced no finds; Trenches 2, 4, 6, 7, and 8 were all disturbed. Only Trench 5 produced any stratified contexts.

Trench 5 (Sherd stratification according to K. J. Frazer)

*99.95–99.78. In ratio of 3 Roman : 1 Hellenistic : 1 Lydian (including 5 pieces of sigillate ware)

*99.78–99.35. In ratio of 2 Roman : 1 Hellenistic : 1 Lydian (including five pieces of Hellenistic-Roman relief ware)

*99.67–99.08. 35–40 pieces; only 6 recognizable, of which 4 were Hellenistic, 2 Lydian

*99.45–98.80. In ratio of 1 Roman : 2 Lydian : 2 indeterminate

*98.75–98.55. 70 pieces; all Lydian, including "bread tray" fragments and terracotta pipe fragments

*98.55–98.05. 80 pieces; all Lydian

*98.55–98.30. Terracotta part of semicircular cover tile; all Lydian sherds

*98.37–98.12. Flanged terracotta pipe in rubble wall without mortar (virgin soil here?)

Trench 2

Terracotta
T72.1:8192. Half of front face of a terracotta antefix. *98.73. One half preserved. No traces of paint. Raised frame. In relief, 3 petals of a 5-petalled palmette on stem. At bottom right a double spiral. H. at middle 0.072 m., at

edge 0.042 m.; P.W. 0.072 m.; Th. 0.018 m. According to A. Ramage (letter January 1974) it belongs to his category II, probably 5-4 century B.C. Similar fragments were thrown into a well at PN in 213 B.C. (*BASOR* 182, 23). (Fig. 176.)

Stone
Capital H Fragments. Fragments of a volute from Ionic capital of the Hellenistic temple. Found with fragments of ashlar marble blocks, 2.75 m. from the southeast corner of the northeast anta, *98.76. A bronze coin of Constantine II (A.D. 324–330) was found 0.33 m. away from the eye of the volute. The major piece consists of about two thirds of a volute and about 0.20 m. of the bolster. The bolster is decorated with a flaming half-palmette of four petals and a spiral. As K. J. Frazer observed, there is a secondary rectangular cutting in the eye area. Diam. eye 0.13 m.; cutting at top 0.06 m., 0.07 m., 0.025 m.; at bottom 0.025 m. by 0.025 m. Depth of cutting 0.06 m. Below the palmette, the bolster shows somewhat rougher surface because of less regular treatment with a multiple tooth chisel. The palmette area is more finely finished. The leaves are strongly raised (0.025 m.–0.035 m.) above background (Figs. 162–164).

The closest parallel is Butler, *Sardis* II (1925) cols. 11, 12, Atlas pl. XI. These had quadripartite torus with half-palmettes in external compartments. Next in Atlas pl. XVI, Capital E, also with quadripartite torus, but the palmette is not flaming (this supposedly now on base 22 near the southeast corner of the temple). The workmanship of the new fragment seems definitely Hellenistic, not Roman.

Other fragments, 1.25 m. from south side of northeast anta at *98.57:

A: fragment of double coil. Seems larger than those of external volute; possibly from double coil separating the compartments of the torus. P.L. 0.25 m.; P.W. 0.07 m.; P.H. 0.125 m.; W. of coils 0.065 m. and 0.055 m. At *98.32.

B: Fragment of double coil of outer edge of volute with adjacent parts of interior and exterior. P.H. 0.16 m.; P.L. 0.17 m.; P.W. 0.10 m. Same findspot as A.

C: Fragment of double coil of volute from external edge. P.H. 0.09 m.; P.L. 0.19 m.; P.W. 0.11 m. Same findspot.

D: Fragment of double coil volute with part of exterior. P.H. 0.075 m.; P.L. 0.13 m.; P.W. 0.115 m. Same findspot.

E: Small fragment of volute. P.H. 0.05 m.; P.L. 0.085 m.; P.W. 0.05 m. Same findspot.

IN72.6. Marble fragment of stele or tile (?). Found with fragment from Trench 2 at ca. *98.50, during washing. One surface dressed with multiple tooth tool. Others broken. Back was treated with large point. Slab was thickest (0.0475) at this surface and tapered from it. If a stele, then the inscription was written secondarily, upside down in relation to bottom. However, the *ductus* of inscriptions with the deepest part on top, getting shallower toward bottom of signs, shows that C. Foss's reading with dressed area on top is probably correct. As R. Gusmani declared the inscription to be non-Lydian, some alternative, possibly Semitic script, must be considered. K. J. Frazer suggested this was of Arabic date. G. M. A. Hanfmann considers the slab classical or Hellenistic and the inscription secondary. Four signs: ʔλЧl . H. 0.020–0.028 m.; P.H. 0.129 m.; P.L. 0.165 m.; Th. 0.045 m. bottom, 0.035 m. top. Note: when the piece stands on the wide, worked side it leans forward; this might fit a tile or a piece attached to a cornice at bottom?

Trench 3

Metal

M72.1:8178. Plumb bob or weight of lead with remains of iron ring let in hoop on top. Found under the threshold of the great east door, on top of the third foundation course under the euthynteria (W 121/S 1234, *98.78). Cylindrical with flat bottom slightly rounded toward the sides. H. 0.074 m.; W. 0.062 m.; P.H. iron ring 0.017 m. W. ring 0.014 m.; Wt. 1,340 grams. Not closely datable but must be contemporary with the laying of Hellenistic foundations. Too heavy for usual plumb bob, but perhaps used for large masonry alignment over great height? Not many sherds in trench in association. (Fig. 177.)

Trench 7

Pottery

Sherd of marbled Lydian skyphos. W 166/S 1240, 1.85 m. east of column base no. 78, *98.39. In fill at north end of trench, below euthynteria, next to three sandstone boulders . . . with gray and black ware sherds. P.H. 0.035 m.; P.W. 0.02 m.; Th. 0.004 m. According to C. H. Greenewalt, Jr. this form appears through the sixth century.

Glass

Fragment of so-called Arab bracelet. Byzantine black and red glass ring. Ca. 1.25 m. south of temple axis and 0.90 m. west outside the original west wall. W 166/S 1240, *97.75. P.L. 0.038 m.; Th. 0.006 m. Probably Byzantine, twelfth century. A cogent proof for mixed up stratification in this trench.

Blue and green glass ring bezel, probably Roman. W 166/S 1232, *99.67; according to K. J. Frazer, found in a rubbish heap of recently deposited artifacts, some as recent as the 1960s. No engraving on underside. So-called glass paste. Not closely datable. H. 0.006 m.; L. 0.016 m.; W. 0.013 m.

Conclusions

Stratification in Trench 5 indicated that there was a level or layer attesting use of the area in archaic and probably in Persian times. It occurred at *98.75–*98.00, 1.25 m. to 2.00 m. below the floor of the colonnade. Comparable finds were made at a somewhat higher level in the pit near the image base.

The situation observed at and under Building L is more complex because the ground was sloping unevenly (cf. *infra,* Ch. VII). At Building L, Room A had a late classical–Early Hellenistic level at ca. *98.40–*97.00. Under Room B it was at *98.40–98.20, and in the pit north of A and B it lay at *97.20 (Figs. 247, 248, 249). An earlier pre-Hellenistic archaic level was observed under Room A at *98.30–*97.40. The levels suggest that the area slanted south and west. These pre-Hellenistic remnants are all of the same character: islands of clay floors between deposits of gravel, often only clay patches. A possible mud-brick wall remnant

was noted only in the pit north of A and B (Fig. 273).

Apparently, there was some sporadic use of the sanctuary area from ca. 600 B.C. on at a level of ca. *99.35–98.00 under the temple and *98.00–*97.00 in the area south of the temple. Below these levels were torrent deposits and hard clays, untouched by man (as high as *98.34 at the northeast corner of the temple in Trench 1).

Archaic Altar and Temple

The data observed from 1961 and 1972 soundings are consistent with the interpretation advanced by G. M. A. Hanfmann in 1958: the site of the temple was largely a flooded area with only intermittent occupation until ca. 550–500 B.C. Something was done in the Persian era to control the flooding, and the building first of an archaic (or early Persian) Altar LA 1, followed by the enlarged form LA 2, preceded the construction of a major temple (cf. *infra,* Ch. VI). On this hypothesis, the archaic temple of Artemis was elsewhere, possibly higher up to the northeast. No clearly identifiable archaic building parts were found and no large level of archaic dedications has come to light.

Conversely, K. J. Frazer believes that the sandstone image basis contains reused marginal blocks of a more ancient structure, possibly an early archaic naiskos housing the statue: "The lower course of the present base would be the now disarranged surviving center of the foundation of the ancient structure.[43] It is clear from clamp holes that some stones of the present basis are reused (Frazer, field report).

Observations on the Persian and Hellenistic Phases

Like Gruben, Frazer assumed two phases of Hellenistic building.[44] His Trench 8 conclusively proved the existence on the west of the two earlier *in antis* column bases overbuilt by the cross wall. They are shown in this position on Gruben's plans of phases I and II (Fig. 123). In Frazer's view, the earliest temples had a dipteral plan, like the archaic Artemision in Ephesus. He had hoped that traces of their bases might remain, but was unable to substantiate this conjecture in Trenches 1 and 6 (Fig. 124). Like Gruben, Frazer had conjectured the existence of two columns *in antis* at the east end. Here also, the not inconsiderable remains of heavy limestone foundation blocks were not perhaps sufficient evidence for the northernmost column base (Trench 2).

By comparative study of foundations under the east door and the west door and the present platform for stairs, he obtained proof that the Early Hellenistic temple was planned without an east door. He also made observations which show that the change to a second door occurred in the second Hellenistic period. The reasons are as follows. (1) The ashlar course which would have been visible if the door had not been built was begun but not completed; it was then concealed by the steps. Hence the change occurred fairly quickly. (2) The marble steps of Hellenistic workmanship showed traces of earlier Pi-clamp cavities recut to take the swallow-tail clamps. Frazer proposed that they were perhaps the early Hellenistic western steps, transferred east during the time of the demolition of the original west wall and portal.

According to Frazer's theory, a new start was made on the temple and an east door opened either under Achaeus (220–215 B.C.) or Antiochus III (213–190 B.C.). He believes that the Early Hellenistic temple had gone up quite high, and that its east wall was dismantled down to and including the course immediately below the present threshold blocks when this door was opened.[45] The opening of the east door is strong indication that the temple became a two-cella temple at this stage. Hanfmann has argued that the colossal image of Achaeus-like Zeus (Fig. 148) was installed at this time. This assumption entails a major change in the chronology and function of the middle period of the temple. Previously, Gruben had suggested that the division into a two-cella temple had occurred as late as the second century under Antoninus Pius (ca. A.D. 140–160).

Important for the Roman phase was the existence of bedding tiles for a marble pavement observed in the southern colonnade (Trench 5). Hitherto, because of numerous unfinished parts, we had considered that after the earthquake of A.D. 17 perhaps only the inner shrine with an emergency roof had been completed under the Romans (Fig. 126). Now it appears likely that the roofing over the colonnades had also been completed during the Roman repairs.

GMAH, KJF

VI THE ARTEMIS ALTARS LA 1 AND LA 2

Kenneth J. Frazer
George M. A. Hanfmann

In 1910 H. C. Butler, in excavating toward the Artemis Temple, came across a row of stelai.[1] As Butler's plan (Fig. 178) and photos (*Sardis* I [1922] ills. 25–26) make clear, these were the bases at the northwest and southwest corner of the basis structure LA (Fig. 181 Nos. 21–26, 28–31). He also found, directly behind a large marble base, a short section of stuccoed wall, ca. 1.75 m. high, running N-S, with a flight of six steps adjoining it to the north (*Sardis* II [1925] 3 f.). From his plans (Fig. 178), his descriptions, and an important photograph in *Sardis* II (1925) ill. 2, it is clear that he had uncovered an oblong platform, in general proportion of two to one (E-W), about 20 m. long and 10 m. wide. On the west side it had a staircase of seven steps, or six, not counting the step to the precinct floor level (Fig. 185). On the north and south, the stair was flanked by a "perimeter wall" (term coined in 1969); the same wall encompassed the structure on the north, east, and south sides. The north-south width of the seven steps on the west side was about 14.5 m. Their top was level with a stone platform of what Butler called "red sandstone" masonry, nearly square in plan (approximately 6.10–6.80 m. on the sides). The level of the platform was 1.62 m. below the level of the stylobate of the temple, which corresponds to *98.38 in our system. The walls, especially on the eastern side,

rose to as much as 0.89 m. (*99.3) above the platform.[2] The exteriors of the northern, eastern, and southern perimeter walls were all covered by hard white plaster (stucco). The entire structure was joined to late and poor walls which yet ran in front of the line of the temple facade (Figs. 178, 181). Butler partly observed, partly assumed, that the perimeter walls were built of red sandstone masonry of the same kind as the central platform.[3]

Because he believed the red sandstone (actually calcareous tufa; see *infra*) to be distinctive of Lydian archaic structures and because he believed that he was at this point following a Lydian-Hellenistic level characterized by Lydian stelai set up around the structure, Butler thought that the entire structure was an archaic Lydian building.

At first he interpreted the structure as an oblong stoa, but the broad flight of steps eventually made him change his opinion. In his reconstructed plan of the temple (Fig. 179) he inferred that at least in the last stage the building served as a staircase and platform to enter the temple. To compensate for the fact that the temple colonnade floor was higher than that of the platform by 1.62 m., he introduced side staircases; to explain the importance given to the central platform, he projected a strange kind of podium from the temple front along the east-west axis (Fig. 179).

By the time he was completing the Artemis

Temple volume, Butler had, in fact, accepted the interpretation of the Lydian Building as an altar. It is clearly so understood in the elevation and section in *Sardis* II (1925) ill. 97, even though Butler there seems to envisage a later platform and altar high above the original LA (Fig. 180).[4]

Butler stated that he had practically no finds. The peculiar exceptions were cups with metal implements, egg shells, and coins, several of which were found behind the stelai bases along the northern perimeter side (Fig. 181, Nos. 16–23). Of the identifiable coins, one was a Late Hellenistic coin of Smyrna, the other a coin of the time of Trajan.[5]

Butler did not excavate the structure completely, nor did he report all of his activities. It is not known whether it was he or free-lancing treasure hunters who made a dent into the north side going all the way down to the soil on which the structure was built (Fig. 183).

From 1914–1969 the structure remained in overgrown and chaotic state. In the meantime H. Schleif, and following him H. Hoffmann, pointed out that the structure resembled the oblong type of archaic Greek "stepped" altars developed in East Greece.[6] They are best known from the pre-Rhoikos and Rhoikos (ca. 550 B.C.) altars at the Heraion of Samos and the sixth century B.C. altar of Cape Monodendri near Miletus. A connection with Sardis seemed the more plausible because the same great artist-architect who was an associate of Rhoikos at Samos, Theodoros of Samos, had also done work for Croesus.[7]

In 1959 G. M. A. Hanfmann conjectured that the altar might have been built in the fifth century B.C. and might be identical with the altar of Artemis at which Cyrus the Younger and Orontas swore their oaths of friendship between 407 and 401 B.C. G. Gruben repeated the conjecture and more confidently dated the altar to the late fifth century B.C.[8]

A number of problems remained unresolved, however. Was there one structure or two? What were their dates or date? And what was their relation to the temple during the various periods of development?

Under the general direction of K. J. Frazer, a week of clearing and excavation took place in 1969.[9] A number of dislodged stones were removed to the area west of the structure and trenches were dug on the north and south sides of the inner platform. These trenches were designated *a* and *b* in our plans and sections. In 1970, these two trenches were enlarged and additional trenches dug, designated *c* through *g* (Figs. 181–184, 186, 190, 191, 197, 198).

The inner platform, LA 1, and the outer perimeter structure, LA 2, were recognized as distinct entities. Numbering and removal of limestone blocks from the top of LA 1 was continued at the beginning of the 1970 season (Figs. 184, 186),[10] and the structures were positioned in our B grid. The relative orientations of the Artemis Temple, LA 1, LA 2, and their adjacent monuments and the axial relationships of these structures were established with transit. Plane tabling and leveling of the LA complex and of nearby salient features of the Artemis Temple were carried out[11] (Fig. 181).

ALTAR LA 1

Trenches and Stratification

Trenches *a* along the north side and *b* along the south side of the inner structure LA 1 cleared the steps of the archaic structure down to sub-foundation bedding at *96.48 (Figs. 181, 182). By breaking through the east wall of structure LA 2 (Figs. 186–189, 197, 198, 200, 202), the northeast and southeast corners of the archaic structure LA 1 were freed. Thus it was proved that LA 1 was originally an independent structure. These two trenches also served to investigate the composition of the east wall of the later structure LA 2 and its substructures, the lowest level of which was at *97.14.

Trench *c*, running ca. 10 m. along the east side, reached the bottom of the wall of LA 2 at *96.95 and of the limestone blocks of LA 1 at *96.70. It produced important evidence that the eastern euthynteria of archaic structure LA 1 had originally extended farther east (Fig. 190).

Trenches *d* and *e*, going from the east wall of LA 1 to the west wall of the temple, were taken to a depth of *95.54 but failed to pick up any further traces of original eastward extension of structure LA 1 (Figs. 190, 197).

Trenches g and f (Figs. 181, 182) aimed at outlining structure LA 2. Trench f along the south wall of LA 2 (Fig. 191) reached the bottom of wall plaster (stucco) at *97.25 and the bottom of boulder foundation stones at *96.94. Underneath, to *96.73, were waterlaid sand and gravel.

Trench g (Figs. 181, 182) was dug at the northeast corner of structure LA 2, which had been reported by Butler as being linked by a wall to the six marble steps (Figs. 178–181) at the northwest corner of the Artemis Temple. In his restoration,[12] he also showed a return of the northwest marble steps of the temple as meeting the north flank of LA 2, yet Trench g went to *95.67 without encountering any sign of either the wall or the steps' foundations.

Trenches dug outside the structure LA (c, e, f, g; Figs. 103, 181, 182) encountered fine sand (e, *95.92–95.54) and water laid gravels (g, *95.67; f, *96.73; d, *96.41; b, *96.51; a, *97.0). Finds were very scarce. A small concentration of sherds was found at the southern end of Trench e at *96.89.

The bottom of limestone structure LA 1 was founded directly on this water laid gravel at ca. *96.70 (bottom of euthynteria course; *96.69 on the north, *96.71 on the south side; see Fig. 103).

Material relevant to the dating of structure LA 1 was found within the perimeter of structure LA 2 in Trench b (Fig. 184) in 1969. The fragment of a Lydian lamp was found at *96.3, at a level below the bottom of the foundation but at some distance south of it.

Finds

L69.10:8036. W 200.5/S 1240.5–1242.0, *96.3. Fragment. H. 0.019 m.; W. rim 0.01. Nozzle fragment of Lydian lamp. Resembling Broneer Type I (sixth century B.C.) and III (fifth century). BASOR 199, 31 n. 26. (Fig. 192.)

P69.77:8033 (=IN69.27). W 202.0/S 1246 (in Butler's dump), *97.9. Lydian sherd with graffito. Fragment of central section of plate ("fruitstand"). Red on white slip. At right angle to wheelmarks, an incised ⫪ below it are tops of two triangular signs. R. Gusmani (by letter February 1974) notes that the cross stroke is not oblique as in Lydian; "Carian is but one of the possibilities." He does not include it among Carian inscriptions in Sardis M3 (1974). L. 0.065 m.; W. 0.065 m.; Th. 0.005 m. BASOR 199, 31 n. 26, sixth or fifth century B.C. (Fig. 193.)

P69.79:8037. W 200.5–202.5/S 1240.5–1245, *96.47–

*96.24. Below base of LA 1. Lydian black on red ring foot fragment. H. 0.026 m.; diam. foot 0.103 m.; Th. 0.008 m. (Fig. 194.)

P69.81:8039. W 200.5–202.6/S 1240.5–1242.5, *95.69–*95.40. Below base of LA 1. Base of Lydian plain ware pot. P.H. 0.029 m.; diam. base 0.059 m.; diam. foot 0.079 m.; Th. 0.005 m.; H. foot 0.022 m. (Fig. 195.)

A few more sherds relevant to LA 1 were found in 1970:
Rim, body, part of horizontal loop handle of Lydian skyphos. Between top and bottom of east euthynteria of LA 1, ca. *96.5–*95.3. Local clay and red "glaze" except for red band below exterior lip. H. 0.03 m.; W. 0.038 m. The piece is of interest for dating of LA 1. This standard type of Lydian skyphos can occur in the sixth and probably into the fifth century B.C. (Fig. 215 c.)

Piece of East Greek? Geometric Cup or Cotyle. W 197.4–198.5/S 1237–1242, *96.5–95.3. Originally yellowish-white slip on exterior, greenish-black glaze on interior, exterior, vertical metopal lines. H. 0.04 m.; W. 0.038 m. Hardly later than the seventh century. (Fig. 215 d.)

Concerning the finds from outside Trenches d, e, and g, the excavator (C. H. Greenewalt, Jr.) considered them not "sealed" and hence not conclusive: "most of the pottery belonged to types conventionally dated to seventh through fifth centuries B.C."

Finds (Uncatalogued)

Trench c, at euthynteria level of LA 1 and below to *96.41. Two "streakily glazed" skyphos fragments; a rim fragment of an Ionian cup type with offset rim; a small fragment of palmette glazed bowl.

Trench e to *96.89. Fragments of "streakily glazed" skyphoi; a column crater rim plus handle; an Orientalizing dish painted on the outside with dark voided rays and red narrow bands; a bichrome dish with straight and zigzag bands.

Trench g, at *96.40–*96.00. P70.29:8105. Ionian cup type rim; Lydian vessel with multiple pendant hooks, *95.25–*95.00.

The finds help to circumscribe a rather wide range for structure LA 1, permitting a dating in the sixth or fifth century B.C. for the first construction of the structure. Its independent existence ended when the perimeter structure LA 2 was built partly over the steps of LA 1, probably in the late fourth or early third century B.C.

Description of LA 1: Present Condition

As exposed in 1970, the structure LA 1 is a nearly rectangular structure of limestone masonry, 8.82 m. E-W by 8.14 m. N-S on top of the euthynteria course and 6.80 m. E-W by 6.10 m. N-S on the top course (plan, Fig. 181). It consists of a foundation course (euthynteria) and three upper courses or steps. It is a stepped pyramid on the north, west, and south sides, but on the east side it misses one step as the second and third courses from bottom are cut to one vertical face (Fig. 182, Section D–D; Fig. 189). As seen in the same plan, both its northwest corner and its southwest corner were exposed, but otherwise most of the west side remains concealed under the later steps of structure LA 2 (Fig. 185). As mentioned in the introduction, the north side was considerably damaged by a previous attempt to reach the bottom of the structure (Figs. 184, 183). L-shaped setting marks 0.06–0.08 m. long on top of the highest preserved course (0.28 m. in from the northeast and northwest corners; Fig. 196) prove that there was originally a fifth course. Stones from it were reused in the facing of the walls of the later structure LA 2.

Orientation

Magnetic bearings were obtained in 1970 for all four sides of LA 1, using the second and third course upper edges only; the fourth (present top) course is incomplete and the first course (euthynteria) too irregularly laid. The following figures include bearings perpendicular to (90° from) the readings for the east and west walls, giving a better average magnetic bearing for the E-W axis of the altar.

		Magnetic Bearing	*E-W Magnetic Bearing*
North side:	course 2:	294°14′	294°14′
	course 3:	293°41′	293°41′
South side:	course 2:	291°42′	Askew - not included in average E-W bearing
	course 3:	291°20′	
East side:	course 2:	23°40′	293°40′ (adjusted)
	course 3:	23°40′	293°40′ (adjusted)
West side:	course 2:	23°14′	293°14′ (adjusted)
	course 3:	24°05′	294°05′ (adjusted)
Average magnetic bearing, E-W axis:		293°46′	

The south side of the "rectangle" is slightly askew, with an average variation of 2°26′ from the average bearing of the north side; instead of being a right angle, the southeast angle is slightly obtuse and the southwest angle is slightly acute.

The average of east, west, and north side bearings yields a bearing from magnetic north of just under 293°46′ for the axis of LA 1, which is very near the orientation of the axis of the Artemis Temple, whose bearing was determined to be 293°20′. Sighting along the axis of the temple to midpoint between the north and south outer surfaces of the north and south walls of LA 1, the midpoint of LA 1 was found to be only 0.06 m. south of the temple axis. Thus, the Artemis Temple and LA 1 are virtually co-axial.

Design and Construction

In the following discussion, the courses will be referred to as courses 1 to 4, with the bottom course (euthynteria) being the first. The top of the foundation course is remarkably level (*97.14; Fig. 181), but the individual blocks vary in depth between 0.39 and 0.46 m. and are sunk into the bedding material accordingly (Figs. 189–191). The outer edge is fairly regular on the north, jagged on the south. The eastern side presents a number of peculiarities. While it projects only 0.05 m. beyond the higher courses at its northern end, it displays a curious curve southward, coming out to as much as 0.52 from the wall (Figs. 190, 197). Two headers (Fig. 198) project beyond the line of the curve; one (projecting 0.36 m.) shows a chisel-cut line 0.10 m. deep (Fig. 199). Apparently an attempt was made to cut it level with the wall. This was given up and instead the eastern parts of this and the other header were crudely broken off by battering. The northernmost block of the euthynteria, 0.63 m. from the northeast corner (Fig. 200), shows on its upper surface one half of a Pi-clamp cutting and its vertical pinhole. This indicates that another block, with the other half of the clamp, lay alongside and to the east. The width of the euthynteria on north and south sides varies from 8.82 to 8.87 m. It may be assumed that its top was flush with the ground level around the structure (ca. *97.14).

Although the actual width of the upgoing steps varies from 0.30 m. to 0.35 m., it was apparently intended that the tread should be half the width (0.60 m.) of a stairblock. The height diminishes upward, from 0.43 m. at the lowest step, through

0.41 m. at the second; 0.39–0.40 m. at the third; and 0.36–0.37 m. at the present top course.

Course 2 is ca. 0.30 m. wide on the tread and 0.41 m. high on the riser. The only peculiarity occurs again on the east side. Instead of stepping back, the second and third courses have been sliced from top to bottom in an irregular but generally outward curving face, its bottom edge some 0.08 m. to 0.10 m. out from its top. In several places, vertical chisel lines run unbroken across the face of both courses (Figs. 187–189, 197, 199). Course 3 on the north and south sides is 0.30 m. wide and 0.40 m. high. As may be seen in plans (Figs. 181, 203) and photographs (Figs. 183, 186, 201), almost half of the fourth course is missing. The damage extends over the western half except for the northwest corner. The block now set up at the southwest corner may not be correctly placed. The height of the course is ca. 0.39–0.40 m. Setting marks (Fig. 196) prove that the fifth course was set back approximately the same distance as other courses. The present height from the top of the euthynteria to the top of the fourth course is 1.178 m. (*97.14–*98.318); with the addition of a fifth course of 0.35 m. to 0.36 m., the structure would have risen to ca. 1.54 m. (ca. *98.66). There is no evidence to show whether a sixth course existed. It is certain that LA 1 was partly reduced, probably by taking down the upper course or courses, when LA 2 was built. As K. J. Frazer observed, ashlars from LA 1 are used in the east wall of LA 2.

Masonry: Material, Tooling, Coursing, Clamping

The same kind of stone is used throughout. Erol İzdar, Ege University, Izmir, described it as a calcareous tufa, probably deposited by action of sulphurous waters running through fissures of calcareous rocks (*Karste*). G. W. Olson added that it displays cavities and smooth channels formed by organic materials trapped in the mass when it was laid down, but long since disintegrated. Unweathered, the stone is yellowish-gray to gray in color, even though Butler described it as red.

The largest among the blocks measured were 1.70 m. by 0.60 m. by 0.40 m., with a cubic measurement of 0.408 cbm. and an estimated weight of over a ton.[13] The smallest block was 1.10 m. by 0.45 m. by 0.40 m. Average measurements were 1.30 m. by 0.60 m. by 0.40 m.

Tooling and chiseling marks could barely be detected on the blocks because of weathering. Perceptible marks were made, perhaps at the quarries, by the heavy pointed chisel and by the heavy toothed (trimming) hammer. This lack of finished tooling indicates that the blocks were originally faced with finer, probably marble slabs. The blocks are not always true rectangles, but if any block has been cut with an angled side, its neighboring block has been cut also at an angle so that the two fit together with an admirably fine joint (Fig. 200). It will be noted that the join lines sometimes run in slight curves (Figs. 201, 203).

No certain example of marble facing has survived. One would assume that these casing blocks were wide enough to be clamped (clamps and cavities would be concealed under the next higher marble casing block) and would sit firmly in position without the necessity of pins to hold them to the vertical faces of the core structure behind, as would have been the case with thin marble revetments.

Each course is relatively consistently laid in one direction, with one or more tie courses. On the top (fourth) course all the stones are in north-south rows, except for an edge row laid east-west along the northern edge and a series laid side-by-side as a tie through the western part of the platform (Figs. 183, 203). In course 3 the blocks generally lie in east-west rows, counteracting the north-south arrangement of the top course. In course 2 the blocks are also in east-west rows, with ties consisting of two stones set north-south, appearing on the southern edge and a row of stones orientated north-south and set side-by-side through the center of the platform. In course 1 (euthynteria) the blocks are rowed north-south as on the top course, with two ties of blocks set east-west appearing on the east edge and in the center break. Not all the masonry adheres to this system—especially in course 3 where the whole of the northeastern corner is rowed north-south and the western side is a confusion of different orientations.

There are no dowel holes cut in any of the upper

surfaces exposed to view, nor is there anything resembling lifting bosses or lewis holes. There are
prising slots, but very few.

At the northeast and northwest corners of
course 4, inset from the edges at the appropriate
distances (0.28 m.) to indicate a setting back of
the next highest but no longer existing course,
are L-shaped setting marks. They are cut to a depth
of slightly under 0.005 m. and their arms are 0.06
m.–0.08 m. long (Fig. 196). In the southeast corner
there is a lot of weathered pitting on the limestone
surface at the point where a setting mark might be
located. The lone block at the southwest corner
of course 4 is suspect, being noticeably out of
alignment and, apart from one other block also on
the south side of the top course, it has no clamp
cavities, nor does it sport an L-shaped setting mark.

Thirteen clamps, still embedded in their original
lead, have been found *in situ* in the stonework of
LA 1 (Figs. 203, 204). Of these, three have been
lifted for study purposes. In addition, many more
clamp cavities, already robbed, have been cleaned
and studied, including some in the blocks which
were removed from the altar in earlier times and
which are now laid out to the west of the LA complex. All clamps and cavities belong to the Pi-type
(Figs. 205–207).

The following rhythm of clamping in the upper
surface of all four courses seems to have been used
by the ancient builders: in the top course only,
practically every marginal block was clamped to its
neighbor; in the three lower courses, where the
marginal blocks were laid with their long sides outward, practically every block was clamped to its
neighbor; again, in the three lower courses, where
the marginal blocks were laid side-by-side with
their short sides outward, the clamping sometimes
missed every other joint, sometimes two joints in
succession.

The positioning of the clamps varies, but the
great majority of them lie between 0.24 m. and
0.40 m. in from the edge of their step, and all are
parallel with it. One clamp, on the south side of
course 3, is as much as 0.85 m. from the edge.

It has been noted that no dowels appear to
have been used in the structure. The builders relied
on the precise cutting and fitting of blocks in their

horizontal and vertical dimensions and the extensive clamping mentioned above. The rough texture
of the limestone itself in LA 1 would have prevented, to a great degree, lateral movement of
upper courses where dowels would be required
with smoother finished surfaces.

The clamp cavities vary in length from ca. 0.21
m. to ca. 0.32 m., with an average length of 0.26 m.
The length of the clamp itself would be ca. 0.02 m.
shorter. The width of the cavities is between 0.02
m. and 0.03 m. at the centers and tends to widen
at each end; the channels are ca. 0.02 m. to 0.025
m. deep (Fig. 204).

It appears that three or four different masons
may have been employed in cutting the clamp cavities in LA 1, the individual characteristics of their
work being revealed principally by the way in
which they cut the holes for the vertical arms of
the iron clamps. One made a distinct 'T' slot up to
0.05 m. wide at each end of the channel to allow
him maneuvering room with his chisel to sink the
vertical hole neatly enough at the junction of the
bars of the 'T' (Figs. 204, 207); another gained
maneuvering room for his chisel by widening each
end of the cavity into a funnel-like shape with a
shallow pin-hole at its vortex—a lazy man's way;
a third and more painstaking method was an attempt by the mason to keep his channel straight
from end to end but to sink the vertical holes about
0.015 m. in from the end of the cavity. One or two
cavities were T-shaped at one end and straight at
the other.

The clamps themselves, of wrought iron, were
most likely made before the cavities were cut in
their different lengths, with a uniform cross-section
throughout, ca. 0.015 m. by 0.006 m. Their vertical
prongs were ca. 0.035 m. to 0.04 m. deep from the
top of the bar, sometimes ending in the same dimensions as their horizontal shaft, sometimes
tapering slightly to a blunt point and sometimes
flattened a little.

When the lead was poured around the iron clamp
to fill the cavity and its vertical holes, it spread out
where the channels were unintentionally widened
during their cutting, generally at the ends (Figs.
205, 206). This sometimes gave the finished product a deceptively flared or butterfly (or dovetail)

appearance (Fig. 206). The porous nature of the limestone blocks also tended to distort the shapes of the cavities. Sometimes when the lead was still warm and very malleable, a number of punch marks was made with a pointed chisel to force it deeper into the cavity around the clamp (Figs. 205, 206).

In his "Clamps and Chronology,"[14] C. Nylander would appear to place the LA 1 type of clamp in the latter part of the sixth century B.C., attributing its introduction in Iran to Greek and Lydian influence. R. Martin[15] would also place this type of clamp ("crampon à griffes") towards the end of the sixth century, since it is in the later stages of its development from a butterfly (or dovetail; Fr. "queue d'aronde") to a true rectangular shape.

Decorative Pieces

As suggested above, the LA 1 structure is what remains of the core of the original monument. The casing would have consisted of marble blocks of considerable thickness, of ca. 0.25 m. to 0.30 m., and of the same height as the successive courses of the core structure. They would have stood on their own; there are no signs of fixing pins or their holes in the vertical face of the core blocks.

None of the marble casing blocks remain; they would have been stripped from the monument at the time when LA 2 was built and put to use elsewhere. The same applies to most of the architectural ornamentation. We must remember that such pieces could come from either the platform structure or the altar that presumably stood on it (cf. the reconstruction, Fig. 125).

H. C. Butler had already found several marble pieces which might belong to the altar.[16] One of them is a fragment showing on each of its faces a double reversed scroll crowned with a palmette, which G. M. A. Hanfmann likens to the decoration of the sixth century altar at Monodendri,[17] and another is a fragment which Butler says might be part of an antefix of an earlier temple: "the design is almost precisely like that of a fragment of ornament from the top of a stele from Dorylaion."[18]

In the 1969 excavations an interesting marble corner piece with an egg-and-dart motif of archaic appearance was found in the southern part of the robbed gap in LA 1, at a level below the foundations where it possibly fell during the robbing operations (S69.13:8040; Fig. 208).

A very fine fragment of lotus-palmette ornament (S69.12:8034; Fig. 209), found unstratified in the upper level of LA 2, might come from a lotus-palmette frieze, but not enough is preserved to be sure. Again, the fragment dates ca. 525–500 B.C.[19]

A new, tantalizing possibility emerged in 1973 with the discovery in unstratified context, some 50 m. northwest of LA 1, of the first archaic Ionic profiled architectural part of limestone found in the Artemis Precinct (Figs. 210, 211). Although the limestone may not be the same as the limestone of the altar steps, the style would fit the general date of LA 1. Lydian-Ephesian in style, the piece, which is probably part of a crowning element, dates ca. 550–530 B.C. Undoubtedly painted in its original state, it may qualify as an ornament of the wall surrounding the top of the altar platform.

Finds

AT/H 73.1, architectural fragment August 7, 1973. Found fallen from the wall of modern house AT/H, shown on Butler's map, *Sardis* I (1922) Plan III, "House"; ca. W 247/S 1217, *98.17. Covered by Butler's dump, the house became a mound, partly excavated in 1973; it is designated Platform "H" on our plan (Fig. 59). Limestone with marble-like veins. Egg and dart with bead and reel below. P.H. 0.28 m.; W. face 0.26 m.; Th. 0.18–19 m. Only front and back have original surfaces. The large egg and cushion-like beads resemble those of the Artemision of Ephesus (ca. 560–550 B.C.); cf. D. H. Hogarth, *Excavations at Ephesus, The Archaic Artemisia* (1908) Atlas, pl. V, d, e, f, g, and of Sardian terracotta simae, *Sardis* X (1926) fig. 9, pl. VIII. The size of ornament (egg H. 0.105 m.) would be suitable for an enclosure wall at the top of the altar. The small depth (thickness) of 0.18 m. shows that the piece was backed by another block. Possibly a crowning element *(epicranitis)*. (Figs. 210, 211.)

Design and Date of LA 1

Taking into account the data gained concerning a possible eastward extension and making use of the reconstruction of the altars at Monodendri and Ephesus,[20] K. J. Frazer has presented a tentative reconstruction of the archaic Lydian Altar LA 1 (Fig. 125). He assumes that, like Monodendri, it was entered from the side. The celebrant would first ascend a lower platform, then turn toward the west, toward the great cemetery in the cliffs west of the Pactolus, which Artemis was protecting.[21] He would ascend the higher platform, where the actual altar was presumably located. Apart from some uncertain marble fragments (*supra*), we have found no pieces of this altar, but it would have been located on the top course, which is now lost. Its shape is conjectural.[22] Frazer has assumed that the marble facing would be iso-domic ashlar with drafted margins as at Cape Monodendri.[23]

As regards the relationship between the LA structures and the Artemis Temple, Butler, in referring to the LA complex as "Lydian Building" found "difficulty in harmonizing this building in its present position, with the temple which stood directly to the east of it; for its solid, unbroken rear wall [of LA 2] would have stood directly opposite to the west end of the temple. One solution is to make the Lydian Building an altar; but there is some objection to it, unless we admit that the temple faced westward . . . " Now that we know that not only the Artemis Temple of Sardis, but also those of Ephesus and Magnesia faced westward,[24] Butler's difficulty is obviated.

Frazer assumes that there was an archaic temple and that it had almost the exact appearance and proportions of the archaic sixth century B.C. temple of Ephesus, but on a slightly reduced scale (Fig. 124).[25] The existence of an archaic temple is a hypothetical assumption (see *supra*, Ch. V) but the existence of a westward oriented archaic altar is highly probable. The cult of Artemis at Sardis was supposedly derived from Ephesus; in Frazer's view, temple and altar might best fit the Croesus era; but the archaeological evidence is not sufficiently precise to permit exact dating. If one considers the evidence of clamp forms and possible relevance of archaic limestone (Fig. 210) and marble fragments, a date in the later sixth century is more plausible than one in the fifth.[26] Since there are no certain traces of fire associated with the building, no definite connection can be established with the burning of Sardis by the Ionians in 499 B.C. The *terminus ante quem* is constituted by the construction of the structure LA 2, which seems to have occurred either in the fourth century B.C. or in the Early Hellenistic age. The marble corner acroterion, used by G. Gruben to date the

altar to ca. 400 B.C., may have belonged to the later structure, or to a renovation of the archaic altar.[27]

Even in its incomplete state, the archaic Altar LA 1 is an important witness for Lydian skill in masonry construction. In the developmental sequence of masonry structures at Sardis, it takes its place after the wall in the Gyges Mound (650 B.C.?), after the terracing walls on the Acropolis (600–550? B.C.), after the Pyramid Tomb (547 B.C.?), all of which do not have clamps. It may be close in time to the chamber tomb in Bin Tepe which uses clamps of early shape,[28] and it is certainly earlier than the great Hellenistic temple.

ALTAR LA 2

Plan

In plan LA 2 is nearly a true rectangle (Figs. 103, 181, 183, 186) with its average N-S length of 21.22 m. almost double its E-W axial measurement of 10.74 m., i.e. to the line of the outer edge of the lowest marble step on its west side.[29] The distance from its northeast corner to the ancient masons' setting marks, which indicate where the northwest anta of the Artemis Temple once stood, is 15.57 m. At its approximate geographical center lies the pyramidal-shaped LA 1, of which the north edge (course 3) is parallel with the north outer face of LA 2 at a distance of 7.35 m. The south edge of the same course of LA 1 is, however, not parallel with the south outer face of LA 2, at distances of 7.45 m. at their east ends and 7.07 m. at their west ends. This correction was deliberately applied by the builders of the later structure so as not to repeat in its south wall the 2° 46′ northeast-southwest deviation on that side of LA 1. The east wall of LA 2 meets and passes over the east side of LA 1, with its outer edge coinciding with that of LA 1 as it does so (W 198.75–199/S 1233.30–1240.70).

In 1969 and 1970 the tops and inner surfaces of the north, east, and south perimeter walls were cleared (Figs. 103, 183, 186). Some of these inner surfaces bear remains of plaster, probably Late Roman/Byzantine, up to 0.02 m. thick. The upper parts of the walls show signs of rebuilding during later ages with inferior materials (Fig. 201) and are distinguished by the inclusion in their substance of Roman (or Byzantine) bricks and Byzantine and Ottoman glazed sherds. Even Butler added sundry relics and also applied some cement plaster to help preserve the walls.

The walls have an average width of 1.00 m. (Figs. 200–202) and enclose a roughly level platform of over 140 sq. m., of which just under one third is taken up by the top fourth course (platform) of LA 1 (ca. 41.5 sq. m.) and the balance by a gravel and sand fill overlaid with stones set in a mud mortar. The outer surfaces of the perimeter walls were laid bare to their foundations in Trenches c, f, and g.

Design and Construction

On the north, east, and south sides of LA 2 the perimeter walls vary in their surviving levels from ca. *98.40 to *99.20 (Fig. 182). Their foundation stones, for the greater part consisting of heavy, smooth boulders (Figs. 189–191, 213) stand on deep deposits of stratified small stones, gravel, and sand at ca. *96.95. This is only ca. 0.25 m. higher than the bottom of the euthynteria course of LA 1 (*96.70). From the original outer ground level, at ca. *97.30 therefore, the walls of LA 2 survive to as high as 1.90 m. The maximum height of wall preserved above the platform of LA 1 (*98.32) is ca. 0.90 m.

All three walls, east, north, and south as well as the steps are essentially from one period. Perhaps the more irregular construction of the south wall (Fig. 191) might be interpreted as signs of rebuilding, but the materials and construction of facing are of the same kind as in the east and north walls.

The walls consist of an outer shell of large masonry, ca. 0.60 m. in width (also width of the original wall), and a later brick and rubble wall inside it, bringing the total average width to 1.00 m. Already in the original construction large river stones were piled from inside against the lowest course to strengthen the foundation.

The top surfaces within the perimeter walls of LA 2, on either side of the top platform of LA 1, were cleared down to an ancient prepared level of average to small sized boulders set in a mud mortar at ca. *98.30. In the area south of the LA 1 plat-

form, these stones have for the most part disappeared but survive in narrow widths along the inner surfaces of the east and south walls (Fig. 181). This stone and mud layer, together with the LA 1 platform, probably formed the bedding level of the LA 2 pavement visible in Figures 186, 201, 213, 214. The idea is made more positive by the survival of a number of small areas of lime mortar which overlie and run down between the bedding stones and the presence of a smooth, flat, and originally nicely squared marble slab of 0.905 by 0.795 by 0.127 m. dimensions.

This bedding is original. It consists of three to five courses of large, flattish, rounded riverstones (averaging 0.20 m. in L. and 0.10 m. in H.) laid on clay and mud and varies in depth from *98.30 to *97.80 to *97.50, being 0.50 to 0.80 m. deep. It reaches approximately the same level as the present top of LA 1, *98.32 (Figs. 182, 183, 186, 189). If this represents the Early Hellenistic period, the stucco facing need not be of the same time. It could have been put on after A.D. 17. The poorly built interiors of upper walls in which brick parts are mixed with small stones (Figs. 201, 202) are quite clearly later. Their latest stage was Middle Byzantine but they may embody Roman, Late Roman, and Early Byzantine parts. Depending on preservation of the original facing they vary in width from 0.30–0.40 m. on the east side to 0.50–0.60 m. on the north side and almost two-thirds of wall-thickness on the south side (0.80 m.). These interior rubble and brick walls are preserved to only 0.30 m. height in the north wall, 0.50–0.90 m. on the east wall, and up to 0.70 m. on the south wall, above the approximate level of the platform (*98.10–20; floor bedding). There is no doubt that the upper part of the south wall is the latest, as it displays a disorderly mixture of bricks and little stones. (The east wall with flat stones and little brick seems the earliest.)

The marble pavement is probably attested by a surviving paving stone which lies at W 205/S 1230, *98.28 on the stone and mud mortar surface (Figs. 185–186). If the original lime mortar was laid over these bedding stones to a depth of 0.10 m. (the familiar bedding technique for mosaic and marble pavements), the marble blocks would then have been laid on it in both the north and the south parts of the LA 2 surface area. In the same operation, with the same lime mortar setting, they would also have been laid over the (present) top of the LA 1 platform itself, which stands at *98.32. This would have given the whole area, between the inner surfaces of the LA 2 perimeter walls and the top of the steps on the west side, a marble paved surface area of ca. 145 sq. m. and a height of ca. *98.53.

For comparative purposes, levels were taken of the top surfaces of the bedding blocks for the pavements in the Artemis Temple cella and pronaos (*101.565 and *99.98 respectively). Allowing for 0.125 m. paving slabs, which would have rested on them and on a stone/rubble (?) fill level with them over the whole floor bedding surface, we would come up with paved levels for the cella and for the pronaos of *101.69 and *100.105 respectively. These levels would have been 3.16 m. and 1.575 m. respectively higher than the restored pavement level of LA 2. It is interesting to note that the difference in level of 1.575 m. between the Artemis Temple pronaos pavement and the LA 2 pavement would have been the same as the difference in level between the cella pavement and the pronaos pavement, observed as 1.585 m. (Fig. 182; cf. Fig. 180).

West Steps of LA 2

The rough, mainly sandstone, bedding stones of the LA 2 west steps overlie the stepped limestone courses of the west side of LA 1 on a fill of river-worn stones and gravel (Figs. 112, 185, 199, 213). They were uncovered by Butler in 1910–1911 and again overlaid with a protective earth layer, probably at the end of his last season of operations at the Artemis Temple. We cleared them again in 1970, and from a study of the photographs in *Sardis* I (1922) and *Sardis* II (1925) they appear to have undergone little or no change in these last fifty-six years. The marble steps are still in position for short runs in the lowest two courses, at both the north and the south ends (Figs. 110, 112). Measuring up from these two steps, and using the ancient masons' setting marks on the marble surfaces and the setting ledges cut into some of the sandstone blocks, it is possible to establish that

the original six marble steps had risers, starting from *96.88 (i.e. probable ground level on the west side of LA 2) of 0.24 m. for the first five, 0.22 m. for the sixth, and a seventh of ca. 0.22 m. which would have been the height of the pavement itself, calculated as having stood at ca. *98.53. The treads, measured on the first two marble steps (*in situ*), averaged 0.36 m.

The bedding stones for the west steps of LA 2 are again of sandstone, mostly rough-cut, in regular steplike proportions; undressed smaller stones fill spaces between irregularly laid larger ones (Figs. 111, 185). Sometimes the blocks have been cut back to provide setting ledges for the marble steps which were once laid on them. There are no reused LA 1 limestone blocks and relatively little of the purplish sandstone among the west steps bedding blocks. They consist, in the main, of the more friable sandstone.

Orientation and Axial Relationship

Sightings with transit were taken along the outer faces of the four walls of LA 2. In the readings which follow, bearings perpendicular to (90° from) the readings for the east and west walls were included in order to give a better average magnetic bearing for the E-W axis of the altar as a whole:

	Magnetic Bearing	E-W Magnetic Bearing
North wall:	293°08′	293°08′
South wall:	293°37′	293°37′
East wall:	23°40′	293°40′ (adjusted)
West (W. step):	24°52′	294°52′ (adjusted)
Average magnetic bearing, E-W axis:		293°49′

It has been noted above that the magnetic bearing of the E-W axis of the Artemis Temple was 293°20′. The 29′ difference in orientation, indicated by the above observations and calculations, is slight, considering the roughness of the stone wall surfaces of LA 2. Despite the use of string stretched from corner to corner, there was some difficulty in obtaining accurate sightings along the walls. We calculated the magnetic bearing of LA 1 to be ca. 293°46′, which to all intents and purposes, is matched by LA 2's orientation of 293°49′.

The distance between the outer faces of the north and south walls of LA 2 was measured along the same line as LA 1 and its midpoint located. It almost exactly coincided with the midpoint of LA 1 on this line. As this midpoint of LA 1 was only 0.06 m. north of the projection of the Artemis Temple axis, the midpoint of LA 2 must also lie almost exactly on the westward projection of the axis of the Artemis Temple. Thus, the Artemis Temple and LA 2 are virtually on the same orientation and are virtually co-axial with LA 1.

Masonry, Coursing, Plaster

The outer thickness of the perimeter walls of LA 2 is constructed from reused and roughly dressed masonry, laid without any kind of mortar. Generally, the coursing is random throughout the whole structure. The masonry and the overall appearance of the north wall (Fig. 107) and the part of the east wall which lies to the north of the intervening LA 1 east wall (Figs. 186, 200) differ considerably from the appearance of the perimeter walls lying to the south of LA 1 (Figs. 186, 189). Presumably, the northern sections of the perimeter wall were built first, containing as they do a much larger proportion of reused and other roughly dressed masonry; they include some fifteen or so blocks which have obviously come from LA 1, probably from its one (or more) now completely missing upper course(s). They are of the same pitted and vesicular limestone (tufa). Interspersed with these blocks are many purplish sandstone blocks, also mostly rough-dressed. According to E. İzdar, Geology Department, Ege University, this is a mica-bearing sandstone of the Upper Miocene period which occurs in the northern Tmolus range around Bozdağ. A number of gray and greenish, more friable sandstone blocks are also used. According to İzdar, these are from the same lithological area as the red sandstone but from younger deposits. The components of the rock are metamorphic and the matrix contains mica and some quartz. The rock is a coarse-grained sandstone with fine micaceous cement.[30]

The southern sections of the perimeter wall of LA 2 do not appear to contain any of the reused limestone blocks from LA 1; the dressed blocks generally are fewer and smaller. The purplish sandstone still predominates, but in less regular shaped blocks. More of the friable sandstone blocks and

the occasional quartz or marble small boulders also appear on this side of LA 1.

The stone thickness of the outer LA 2 perimeter walls is anything up to 0.65 m. and the inner thickness is composed of smaller, irregular-shaped stones, mostly water worn, which are cemented together and to the backs of the outer stones with a tough mud mortar (supra, Trenches a and b). Together the two thicknesses make up the ca. 1.00 m. width of the LA 2 perimeter walls (Figs. 103, 200–202).

Considerable areas of the north, east, and south outer faces of the LA 2 perimeter wall still carry the original (?) lime plaster (Figs. 103, 108, 189–191, 212), which varies from ca. 0.05 m. to 0.11 m. in thickness and curves out at the bottom to form a lip on top of the foundation stones. This lip (Figs. 187, 190) at about *97.25 to *97.30 gives us the original ground level on these three sides of the structure. The plaster has been laid in five applications, of which the inner two are the thickest (Fig. 214). The second and third layers from the inside are "frogged," or scored, with a chevron pattern to help the next outer layer to adhere (Fig. 190). The outermost, sometimes only ca. 0.003 m. thick, is the thinnest and at the same time the hardest layer. L. J. Majewski says that the lime plaster is highly calcareous and is an external type of plaster. All layers would have been applied in one series of operations and do not represent a number of renewals of the plaster surface over the years. Several small pieces of extremely hard and nicely polished white plaster were found in the vicinity of the perimeter walls, but it is not known whether this was from yet one more outer layer or whether it was from an interior surface. Wherever it came from, it would have given the effect of a fine marble revetment.[31] It was 0.0125 m. thick.

There are no signs of any clamping or doweling in any of the visible stonework of LA 2.

Stratification Under Foundations

In 1969 and 1970 trenches were dug to levels below the foundations of both LA 1 and LA 2. The lowest levels reached were *95.54 and *95.67 in Trenches e and g respectively (Figs. 181, 182). In the trenches lying outside the LA 2 complex, stratified layers of small water-worn stones and gravel were found (Fig. 191). The fill within the LA 2 perimeter walls, on either side of LA 1, also consisted of similar, apparently naturally stratified material (Figs. 183, 198). Both in and outside LA 2 the stratification was horizontal, which would indicate that it was created by repeated but slow flooding.

The presence of this same stratified material up to about *98.00 *within* the LA 2 perimeter walls, on which the pavement bedding stones are laid, poses a problem. G. M. A. Hanfmann considered the possibility of a deep series of flood-laid deposits which surrounded up to this level and, to a great extent, covered LA 1 when it stood alone. When the later builders came to erect LA 2 they could have completely cleared the area all around these deposits and merely isolated what are now these two high-standing stratified floor levels. They would have then enclosed them with the perimeter walls, whose foundations go down to ca. *96.95 on the north, east, and south sides, and with the steps on the west side. There is a major objection to this, however: considering the evidence of the reverence in which this original altar was held by the Lydian people, in all probability from their sovereign period and certainly through the Persian and Hellenistic periods (e.g. the stelai and other monuments), it is unlikely that many years of flood deposits would have been allowed to accumulate and to surround and partly bury it to the extent of over a meter.

Another solution may perhaps lie in the fact, also appreciated by the ancient builders in Sardis, that these deep deposits of river stone, gravel, and sand form a stable bedding for building foundations provided they are used in their natural water-stratified condition. Ramming a fill of this material, as one would ram a fill of earth or clay, would be ineffective in binding it together. If therefore, LA 1 and its surrounding area, monuments, etc., were still standing clear when LA 2 was built, the empty spaces between its perimeter walls, the west steps, and the LA 1 platform would have been filled by manual labor. By carefully leveling each shallow layer of stones, gravel, and sand (probably using a larger than natural proportion of sand), covering it with sufficient water to consolidate it

before laying the next lot, and then repeating the leveling and watering, eventually a deep, firm deposit would have been built up on which to lay the bedding stones, mortar, and pavement of the later altar. This patient and undoubtedly laborious method was probably the one used (G. M. A. Hanfmann now agrees). It would have served to provide us with our stratified floor fill above the original ground level.

In Trenches *e* and *g* from *95.90 and *95.74 respectively, a deep, unmixed layer of fine sand extended downward for 0.35 m. in the case of *e,* and in *g* the trench stopped at *95.67 before the bottom of the sand stratum was reached. This phenomenon has been noted in the 1961 trench below the cult-statue base in the Artemis Temple and again in Trench S, to the south of the temple. This stratum must have been laid down by a particularly heavy flooding as it shows no bands of other stratified material or small finds.

Stratification: The Finds

C. H. Greenewalt, Jr., who excavated to gain stratified data in 1970, noted that since LA 2 had been previously exposed by H. C. Butler, none of the artifacts discovered in earthy debris heaped against the outside walls and on top of LA 2 can be considered to be in reliable findspots. Indeed, such modern indicators as a coin of Murad V (1876) show the unreliability of most of the contexts. On the other hand, the finds do indicate the approximate range of use. Over the step beddings on the west side, fragments ranged from Late Roman and Early Byzantine lamps through Byzantine and Turkish glazed wares. Fragments of Byzantine glass and Byzantine and possibly Turkish sgraffito wares were found in debris heaped against the south wall at the top of Trench *f* (Figs. 181, 182). They illustrate the types of objects in use during the period when the Byzantines transformed the temple into a cistern and probably built some ungainly structure into LA (cf. the reconstruction of the Byzantine state of the temple precinct; Fig. 65). The accumulation of Hellenistic and Early Roman sherds in some less exposed loci near the western steps at least confirms the date of LA 2 inferred on other grounds.

For the actual date of the first building of LA 2, evidence was obtained at the west ends of Trenches *a* and *b*. "Here above the western steps of LA 1, but below the bedding stones of LA 2, were recovered fragments of a 'streakily-glazed' skyphos and of 'Achaemenid-Ionian' type bowls. If the context may be considered 'sealed' between the LA 1 and LA 2 structures, the pottery would suggest that LA 2 was constructed before the advanced Hellenistic period" (Greenewalt, field notes; cf. Figs. 183, 185, 186).

Finds (Uncatalogued)

Achaemenid bowl. W 206.5–208/S 1240–1242, *98.12. Southwest corner of LA 1 as it steps under later step foundation of west perimeter of LA 2. Fragment of rim and body of "Achaemenid bowl," a species of Ionian bowl. Brown clay, grayish core, streaky, reddish-brown "poor glaze" interior and exterior. H. 0.026 m.; W. 0.056 m. Thin, soft fabric, perhaps not local. At Sardis, these bowls may have continued to 213 B.C. (Figs. 215 b, 216.)

Thick hydria rim. On upper steps of LA 1 where overlapped by LA 2, northeast corner; W 200.5–201.3/S 1232–1235, *98.76–*97.14. Rounded, everted rim with thin black glaze, except for reserved band on inner lip. Thick oblique stroke on left, perhaps from Lydian? graffito. L. 0.047 m.; H. 0.042 m.; Th. rim 0.013 m. (Fig. 215 a.)

Part of lower wall of Late Lydian painted vase. Northeast corner of LA 2, behind east outer stones of perimeter *in situ*. W 200.5–201.5/S 1232–1234, *98.76–*97.14, northeast corner of LA 1, third and fourth step. Exterior: part of dark brown spiral and leaf? on yellow slip; interior: yellow slip. Late fourth or third century B.C. (Fig. 218 e.)

Rim of Late Lydian plate or bowl. Northeast corner of LA 2 within perimeter, W 200.5–201.5/S 1232–1234.5, *98.76–*97.14. Breach in plaster covering the outer, east face of perimeter wall, around northeast corner of LA 1 at third or fourth step. Inverted rim, orangy slip, purple stripes on interior, red slip on exterior. L. 0.075 m.; H. 0.036 m. (Fig. 218 a.)

Ionian-type cup. W 206.75–208.00/S 1232–1235.50, ca. *98.11. Northwest corner of LA 1 as it steps under later step foundations of west perimeter of LA 2. Thin walled; brown-red glaze inside and out.

Rim of brown "poor glaze" bowl. Trench *f*, along south face, W 204–209/S 1248–1249, *96.95–*96.65. Vertical wall, rim. Typical soft, local brick clay originally covered with reddish-brown early (still Lydian) "poor glaze." Fourth century B.C., hardly later than early third. L. 0.08 m.; H. 0.022 m. (Fig. 218 d.)

Rim of red-slip fish plate. East outer side of east LA 2 long wall, W 197.5–198.5/S 1237–1241, *96.90–*96.42. Local soft clay, very thin red worn "poor glaze" inside and out. L. 0.06 m.; W. 0.064 m.; H. 0.04 m.; Th. 0.011 m. Later fourth or third century B.C. (Fig. 218 c.)

Rim of Late Lydian painted vase. Trench *c*, W 197.5–198.5/S 1232–1236, *96.64–*96.34 (going down outside foundations of LA 1). Thickish everted ledge rim; streaky black-brown paint on exterior, thin stripe below lip, interior, light yellow slip. (Fig. 218 b.)

Fragment of Lydian jug. W 197.5–198.5/S 1232–1236, *96.64–*96.34. Exterior: thin streaky paint put on while vase rotated. A thin, white horizontal band. Interior plain. (Fig. 215 e.)

Fragment of fourth century or Hellenistic "poor glaze" jar. In trench at right angle to perimeter LA 2. W 195–198/S 1235–1237, *97.15. Grooved top of rim. (Fig. 215 f.)

P70.29:8105. Ionian cup fragment, rim and part of body. W 200–204.5/S 1224.7–1225.7, *96.40–*96.00, in gravel below bases along north side of LA 2. Heavy, early rim form. Orange local clay. Exterior: thin purple paint, except for reserved strip at bottom of lip. Interior: reserved rim, then typical glossy Lydian red "glaze." H. 0.031 m.; W. 0.055 m.; diam. ca. 0.14 m. Context not closely dated but sherd confirms use of area in sixth-fifth century. (Fig. 217.)

Design

Even before it was understood that Altar LA 2 was a later structure than LA 1, scholars had noticed that it belonged to a well known type of East Greek altar which had steps along the entire entrance side and a parapet or wall around the other three sides,[32] with projecting, anta-like side walls flanking the imposing staircase. First introduced in archaic times, when the huge Rhoikos altar at Samos (ca. 550 B.C.) also introduced an approximation to the 2:1 ratio of length to width,[33] this type of altar is attested for late classical–Early Hellenistic Ionia by the later altar at Ephesus (after 356 B.C.).[34] Its popularity for later Hellenistic architecture is proved by the altars at Priene and Magnesia (mid-second century B.C.).[35]

Like these great Ionian altars, Altar LA 2 was intended to be aligned axially with the temple. It is, however, totally abnormal in being so close to the temple structure; the rule was that the distance from the temple approximately equalled the long dimension of the altar.[36] At Sardis the altar would have abutted the western colonnade, if the colonnade were ever built (Figs. 123, 124, 126, 181).

K. J. Frazer observes that the crowding was probably foreseen in the planning stage and was unavoidable because of the restricted east-west length of the building site. He suggests that perhaps LA 2 was intended initially to be a temporary building to be used only until the western porch was finished and the architectural union of altar and temple was completed. It is controversial whether this union ever came about. Despite diligent search, we have not found the least trace of the foundations for the porch or the four porch columns that should have been there (Fig. 181).[37] Apparently, the western end of the temple was never completed. The fact that the entire eastern side of LA 2, the side turned toward the temple, had well preserved external type plaster (Figs. 103, 186, 190, 214) is strong evidence that LA continued to its very end as a free-standing structure.[38] Traces of use in Late Roman and Byzantine times refute Butler's assumption that LA 2 was completely buried under a great staircase and temple platform in Roman times.[39]

The heavy construction of the north, south, and east perimeter walls (with walls still preserved up to 0.90 m.) argues that the walls may well have stood over two meters above the pavement. The steps of the staircases and the pavement were probably of marble; Frazer suggests that entablatures and balustrades would have been of marble also. It would not be improbable that the interior was originally revetted with marble. Unless we accept Gruben's attribution of a piece that may have belonged to the altar itself[40] rather than its precinct wall, no decorative pieces have been identified. One would like to assume articulation of the upper walls above the platform by pilasters or half-columns, but the evidence is missing.

On the outside, the platform walls of the altar were finished with fine, hard, white plaster, which would have given them a marble-like appearance. Hanfmann considers it very unlikely that such plaster could survive the earthquake of A.D. 17, which heavily damaged the temple. He suggests that this plaster coat may have been put on as late as the second or third century A.D., when the sanctuary was re-ordered and the monuments along the structure LA 2 put into their present position.[41]

Development and Date of LA 2

While the stratigraphic finds reported above rule out any date earlier than the fourth century, they do not provide close dating; Lydian and Persian period types of pottery lingered at Sardis until the destruction of 213 B.C. That the Hellenistic Artemis Temple was related to the altar is again not wholly conclusive for chronology; on the assumption that the plans for the two were designed simultaneously, K. J. Frazer endorses a date between 290 and 280 B.C. If one were to consider the temple a Seleucid creation, the date would have to be after the battle of Kyropedion (281 B.C.).

As one studies the upper parts of the walls of LA 2, it becomes clear that the internal rubble parts have certainly been restored and repaired, probably several times (Figs. 181, 182, 186, 187, 191, 197, 200–202). On the other hand, one has the distinct impression that the masonry parts of the eastern (Figs. 197, 198, 200) and northern walls (Fig. 107) are quite carefully laid. Presumably, they date from the original Hellenistic construction. Nothing very definite was observed concerning the dating of the repairs. The latest may be as late as the Middle and Late Byzantine (A.D. 616–1300) period.

From the coins and other finds made behind the stelai bases and monuments along the east, north, and west sides, it is clear that these monuments were placed during the great re-ordering of the sanctuary, perhaps after a series of floods, in the second and third centuries A.D. (cf. *supra*, Ch. IV, "Conclusions"). This happened after the structure LA 2 had received its plaster coat (Figs. 103, 107–112, 181, 212).

Two strikingly placed marble foundations, T 1 and T 2, are interpreted by Frazer as marking the place for an offering table, possibly of the Hellenistic or Early Roman period (Figs. 111, 181).

Although special efforts were made to ascertain the origin and date of the arrangement, it is still uncertain when the structure LA 2 was linked to the marble northwest staircase (Northwest Steps; Fig. 181) of the temple. Our evidence favors Frazer's assumption (Fig. 124; "third building phase") that this happened not before the Late Hellenistic phase against Gruben's assumption of symmetrical staircases in the Early Hellenistic stage (Fig. 123).

There is no blinking the fact that the interpretation of the stucco on the eastern wall of LA 2 as stucco suitable for an external wall brings about a head-on collision with the evidence of the north-west staircase (Figs. 59, 181). If we accept both as-sertions, we obtain the peculiar result that a person going up the western end of these steps would only do so to precipitate himself some five feet into the empty corridor separating structure LA 2 from the present western edge of the temple platform![42] Frazer made the interesting suggestion that the steps originally served the western entrance to the cella and were only transferred to the north side as an emergency measure, when the western pro-naos began to be built in his second (Hellenistic) phase (Fig. 124 center). This may well explain their origin, but it does not explain what happened at their western corner.

Butler had given much thought and accurate study to these peculiar steps and had already sug-gested that they might have belonged to a tetra-style porch, but eventually he found the notion of continuing them across and above the temple as the only appealing solution (Figs. 179, 180). Gruben makes two symmetrical flights of steps come up to a platform, obviously not believing that the altar ever stood free (Fig. 123). A. Bammer (orally) had considered whether these steps might not be the remnant of an earlier north-south ori-ented temple. Perhaps the most plausible solution is to assume that (a) the staircase was put in posi-tion only after the altar stucco had been applied, (b) that temporary walls were built to link the steps with the altar, as Butler maintained he had found in his excavation, and (c) that only an earth platform (which would not have damaged the plaster) was put in between LA and the present temple front, pending the construction of the three columns which should have been built there (cf. Fig. 126).

The difficulty even with this architecturally quite satisfactory assumption is that the stairs seem very nicely and carefully set and clamped and are apparently Hellenistic work, as Frazer has em-phasized, while Butler's linking walls appear to be of poor, Late Roman concrete. They thus refer the linking of stair and LA 2 to the second or third century A.D.[43] The even less satisfactory alterna-tive is to assume that the temple continued un-finished with the big deep corridor gash separating the altar and the western edge of the platform.

In the discussion of the monuments of the Arte-mis Precinct, we have observed that a rubble wall, running southward, linked the structure LA 2 to the row of stelai and the wall *rb 1* (Fig. 181; cf. Fig. 178). This wall was apparently erected in the late third century A.D. Perhaps the strange rubble chamber in the west side of the temple, across from the northeast corner of LA 2, dates from the same time.

As we have pointed out in the description of the Artemis Precinct, the creation of a special oblique approach in the two series of converging stelai and monuments, the north and south bases NSB and SSB (Figs. 102, 113, 114, 181), may have taken place between A.D. 280 and 300 (*supra,* Ch. IV, "Extent of Area Known").

It is not certain when the altar began to be covered up with earth. By A.D. 400, the temple was being quarried and the level in the southern colon-nade had risen by a meter. It is probable that earth banks had begun to form around the structure LA as well. In his description of his excavation of LA 2, Butler indicates that he had observed one Late Roman–Early Byzantine level with coins ranging from Constantine (306–337) to Heraklios (610–641) and "above these, a meter or more below the surface, numerous concave Late Byzantine copper coins (scyphates) . . . Upon the same general levels were found fragments of glazed bowls and dishes of various shapes and colors, showing crude designs, some geometrical or floral, and some pictorial" (sgraffito wares). He also speaks of the terracotta pipes, and his Plan III shows at least two pipelines within LA (*Sardis* I [1922] 44, ills. 31, 32). Simi-lar objects, though upheaved, including pipe frag-ments, were observed in our excavations, and a couple of sgraffito fragments at least were found so much within the inner (eastern) wall of LA 2 as to suggest that they had survived Butler's digging.

The reconstruction of the Byzantine settlement (Fig. 65) seeks to recapture something of the situ-ation of LA 2 during the time that the great cistern was functioning (ca. 900–1400; see *supra,* Ch. IV, n. 13).[44] It assumes that the upper walls of LA were still visible, but that the earth around it had already risen. It had buried the building to a depth of one to two meters by the time Butler began his excavations in 1910.

Conclusions

H. C. Butler considered the structures LA 1 and LA 2 to be an archaic building subsequently buried; G. Gruben considered them a building of the Persian era closely attached to the temple. We have proved that there are two buildings. The archaic Altar LA 1 belongs most likely to the sixth century B.C., to the great series of Samian, Ephesian, and Milesian altars with fine Ionic decoration.

Conversely, Butler thought that the structure LA 2 had been concealed and incorporated into a vast and implausible staircase platform of the temple. Although K. J. Frazer indicates the west front of the temple as completed and abutting the altar, our findings are actually that the LA 2 structure continued to stand free and that the western porch was never really completed. This seems almost unthinkable in view of the careful setting of the steps of the northwest staircase (Figs. 178 m, 181) but that is the evidence.

There is much merit in Frazer's suggestion that LA 2 was built as a temporary structure. It might even have been built as such a temporary accommodation for worship when the construction of the great Hellenistic temple was first begun (after 281 B.C.); then, with means lacking even to complete the temple, it survived. The mixture of marble and stucco may be explained as due to economy, though in Hanfmann's view this economy may be the result of a later Roman repair, not of original Hellenistic construction. Even so, gleaming in the sun in front of the colossal temple, this essentially Hellenistic altar must have presented an impressive sight.

The problem posed by A. Bammer for the Artemis Temple—how the worshipper could see the goddess and vice versa—has been considered by Frazer, who rightly points out that the high enclosure walls would have prevented the celebrant from viewing the image. About the possibility that the image was shown in the pediment, one can say very little, as we are not even certain that the western facade and pediment of the Roman restoration were ever completed.

KJF, GMAH

VII EXCAVATIONS ON THE SOUTH SIDE OF THE ARTEMIS TEMPLE

George M. A. Hanfmann
Jane C. Waldbaum

TRENCH S

The small Trench S, the first to be made by the Harvard-Cornell Expedition in 1958, was designed to test the possibility of an earlier archaic level in the Artemis Temple Precinct, the existence of which had been suggested in the account of Butler's campaigns[1] (Figs. 59, 96, 219). The trench was located just outside the 10 m. strip along the southern flank of the temple previously sounded by Butler.[2]

The trench measured approximately 9 m. N-S and 15 m. E-W, W 173.4-190/S 1274.5-1284.4.[3] Its northern surface was at *98.01-97.55. Its southern part was a higher strip, part of Butler's terrace, at *99.04-98.76. (Figs. 95, 96, 221).

The east side of the trench was approximately in line with the southwest corner of column base No. 44[4] (Fig. 120)—actually a point ca. 0.20 m. west of the west edge of the base. The distance from the southwest corner of the column to the northeast corner of the trench was 15.40 m.; the distance from the north edge of the trench to the face of the Roman rubble wall platform which supported the stylobate of the south side of the temple was 10.30-10.50 m.

The west edge of the trench was approximately in line with the west edge of column base No. 56. The distance from the southwest corner of that column base to the northwest corner of the trench was 15.40 m., 10.30 m. from the Roman rubble wall of the external south colonnade platform (Fig. 96).

The trench, including a curving ramp on the west, was originally given a "local" grid numbered from grid zero at the northeast corner. Coordinates in the E-W direction were designated by numbers corresponding to the actual number of meters (from 0 to 15) west of grid zero. Coordinates in the N-S direction were designated by the letters A through J, starting with A 1.0 m. south of grid zero and continuing with each subsequent letter being 1.0 m. further south (J = 10 m. south). Of these A to F were on the lower surface level of the temple precinct (ca. *97.60); G, H, I were on the higher terrace slopes of Butler's camp (*98.76-99.04). Stones and boulders lying in the southeast corner at W 175-177/S 1279-1280, *98.35-97.75 did not add up to any real architecture (Figs. 96, 219). Four main levels were distinguished in the trench when it was opened in 1958 and were reconfirmed in 1968 when the trench was re-examined (Figs. 219, 220).

Level I, *99.04-97.64: Surface to Late Roman

Level I was a mixed surface level including some of the ancient, possibly Late Roman (third to fourth century A.D.) "floor" of the temple precinct in its lower part. Its higher southern part included in part Butler's terracing dump (*99.04–97.70); the ancient precinct level lay at ca. *97.72–97.65.

This level was preserved primarily in the southern part of the trench (trench extension; Figs. 96, 219, 220). Most of it was dug away by Butler when he leveled the area. Level I rises from south to north but little was found in the north edge of the trench. No clear indication of architectural context and no clearly defined substrata were detected within this level. Several large boulders appeared, but not enough of this level was preserved to determine whether the boulders belonged to any occupation.

Lying within Level I were two terracotta pipes (Figs. 59, 96). The larger (in diameter), d 1, found near the southeast corner (Fig. 221), ran N-S (W 174/S 1278–1282) and was made of red micaceous clay with walls 0.02 m. thick; ext. diam. ca. 0.29 m.; int. diam. ca. 0.235 m.; top (at W 174/S 1282) *97.85; bottom (at S 1278) *97.65. The sections measured 0.33 to 0.35 m. joint-to-joint giving a length of 0.68 m. for two sections together. The joints were filled with white (lime?) mortar. Finger grooves were noticeable on the inner surface. The inner flange of this pipe pointed towards the temple. Nine sections of pipe were visible in W 175–176/S 1278–1281 with the last joint just south of S 1281. There was some evidence in the form of extra fragments of pipe for a connection beyond this point. The southern end of this pipe was cut by Butler's excavations. There were openings of two pipes still visible in the concrete of the temple stylobate support column No. 46 (Figs. 59, 96). Their levels, however, (Fig. 96; eastern pipe d 4: ext. top, *97.27, int. bottom, *97.76; western d 3: ext. top, *98.27 int. bottom, *97.99) are higher by 20–30 cm. than d 1. The approximate static capacity of pipe d 1 was 240.32 cc. It was probably associated with the water supply system of the Byzantine reservoir established during the seventh century in the temple.[5]

The smaller pipe d 2 was preserved for a length of 14.35 m. in forty-eight sections cutting diagonally across the trench (Fig. 222), entering it on the north at W 180/S 1275 and leaving it on the south side of the ramp at W 192/S 1284. The level was *97.66 at the north side of the trench at W 180/S 1275 but *97.57 on the south side, suggesting that this pipe was a feeding line from the reservoir in the temple and that its flow was from north to south. It might have had some function in connection with Building L (Fig. 96). The gradient was 1:150 (0.10 m. in 15 m.). The pipe was made of red clay covered with whitish slip. Each section was ca. 0.295–0.30 m. long; the joints were sealed with white lime mortar. Two joined sections averaged 0.59 m. in length. The ext. diam. was ca. 0.14 m., the int. diam. ca. 0.11 m; 0.09 m. at the joint. There was no outer lip of any prominence at the joints. The pipe was completely filled with earth and pebbles; the inner flange was towards the temple. Its static capacity was 197.16 cc. for one section (Fig. 223).[6]

Finds

Since they were found near the surface, pottery and objects from Level I were generally mixed, ranging from Byzantine to Early Lydian. Among the fragments were bits of Greek black glaze and West Slope ware sherds. A Roman sigillate rim and a Roman coin of the third century A.D. may belong to the Late Roman–Early Byzantine precinct level.

Coin
C58.1. W 179/S 1281, *97.90. According to T. V. Buttrey, imitation of Roman coin, ca. A.D. 270–295. Obv. Radiate (bearded) head to right. Rev. Man holding spear in r., branch in l. hands; garment around lower body. (Figs. 224, 225.)

Pottery
P58.35:38. W 182–186/S 1279–1282, *99.30–97.90. Ring foot of bowl. Diam. of foot 0.09 m. Hard, micaceous clay. Dark green, white, and lighter green glaze with decoration inside. Outside white. Middle Byzantine. (Fig. 226.)
P58.36:39. W 182–186/S 1279–1282, *99.30–97.90. Two fragments of deep plate. Flat base and small piece of rim. Outside gray and white with wide bands. Inside white glazed with dark green painted designs. Middle Byzantine. (Fig. 227.)
P58.1:1. W 175–189/S 1274.5–1283, *99.10–98.25. Several fragments, including base of mastos. H. 0.04 m. Black glazed. Imported Greek Hellenistic. Other sections, P58.56, found lower down; W 178–181/S 1279–1283, *98.90–97.70. (Fig. 228.)
P58.42:45. W 182–186/S 1279–1282, *99.30–97.90. Fragment of skyphos rim. Black glazed inside and out with white horizontal bands. Diam. 0.26 m. Lydian. (Fig. 229.)

P58.60:64. W 178–181/S 1279–1283, *98.90–97.70. Fragment of neck. H. 0.055 m.; W. 0.05 m. Three horizontal black bands above black wavy line on buff ground. Lydian bichrome ware. (Fig. 230.)

Level II A, *97.64–97.05: Roman/Early Byzantine; Hellenistic and possibly Persian Period

Below Level I, which consisted of surface deposits, the situation became more complex. In 1958 it was thought that there were only three levels (II, III, IV) in a rather straightforward sequence, with III possibly broken in two phases.[7] It appeared at that time that both Levels II and III were water-laid deposits while IV was hardpan (Fig. 219).

In 1968 the stratigraphy was rechecked by clearing a two meter strip in the north side of the trench at W 177.5–179.5/S 1275–1279 (Fig. 220). Level II A was then confirmed as a mixed deposit of material underlying the present surface of the sanctuary and laid down during much of classical antiquity (Persian? to Early Byzantine), perhaps from the fifth century B.C. on. The top 0.45 to 0.50 m. were recent wind and water-laid deposits immediately under the present surface of the sanctuary. A Lydian graffito (P58.110) and two early lamps (L58.1, 2: 111, 125) were found near the top of this level at *97.45, providing the earliest datable objects although the level as a whole is not stratigraphically dependable.

A patch of stones appeared under the sanctuary surface (W 175–177/S 1275–1276, ca. *97.50–97.20) at the northeast corner of the trench. A line of stones and boulders, somewhat varying in level (from *97.15–96.50), was lying along the southeast corner (W 175–178/S 1275–1282) in an approximate rectangle (Fig. 219). The Lydian graffito and lamp were lying on top of these stones (Figs. 234, 236). Other stones and boulders were lying in a line parallel to the southern edge of the trench. There seems to be no reason to think them anything but river boulders remaining from a torrent bed.

Much of this level seems to have been water-laid and contains layers of sand separated by layers of gravel. Concentrations of small stones were found in some sections of the gravel.

Finds

Pottery
P58.87:106. W 175–176/S 1275–1276, *97.60–97.10. Relief ware fragment. Palmette and hare. Hellenistic. Late 2nd to early 1st cent. B.C. Cf. Goldman, *Tarsus* I, 236, fig. 140 D. (Fig. 232.)
P58.93:104. W 175–192/S 1281–1283, *97.60–97.40. Neck of black-glazed jug with raised horizontal ridges on outside. Inside red clay with red painted band. Ancient repair hole. Hellenistic. (Fig. 233.)
P58.110:124 (=IN 58.14). W 178/S 1282, *97.35 (on top of large stones). Fragment of jug shoulder with graffito. W. 0.056 m. Black paint on buff ground. Incised inscription. Lydian. 5th to 4th cent. B.C. Cf., *BASOR* 154, 9; 158 (1960), 6 f. Gusmani, *LW* 268, no. 57, r̥lam; *Sardis* M3, A II 6, x̥lam. (Fig. 234.)

Lamps
L58.1:111. W 175–189/S 1281–1282–1283, *97.60–97.40. Nozzle and part of reservoir. Max. diam. 0.05 m. Wheelmarks preserved. Red brick color. Lydian, second quarter of 6th century to end 6th century B.C. Cf., Howland, *Agora* IV, 14–16, pl. 30. (Fig. 235.)
L58.2:125. W 178/S 1284, *97.35. Found with P58.110. Lamp fragment. Max. diam. 0.06 m. Brick red color. Half of nozzle preserved. Lydian, middle 6th cent. B.C. to early 5th cent. B.C. Howland, *Agora* IV, 17–18, pls. 30–31, Types 6B, 7. (Fig. 236.)

Level II B, ca. *97.00–96.20: Seventh to Sixth Century B.C.

Level II B was found to consist not of a single layer of mixed flood debris but to be made up of several subphases, distinguished by occupational debris. There were four such subphases, each ca. 0.20 m. deep and separated by gravel and thin clay (Fig. 220). The recognition of these as occupation deposits was based on analogy with occupational deposits of known habitation layers such as those in the Lydian Trench at the House of Bronzes and at Pactolus North.[8]

This level could be dated primarily to the later seventh and sixth centuries B.C. by finds of East Greek and Lydian pottery in 1958.[9] Approximately 30 sherds from the 1968 excavation also fit in with the general Lydian-Greek designation of this level, although none was very distinctive in itself. The outside limits of Level II B fall perhaps from ca. mid-seventh to fifth centuries B.C.

Finds

Pottery
P58.129:146. W 185–189/S 1277–1279, *97.40–96.00. Two fragments of horizontal loop handle from cup. Outside: black metopal bands on buff; inside: red paint. Lydian imitation of Rhodian. (Fig. 237.)

P58.152:209. W 183–189/S 1275–1276, *97.10–96.50.
Small fragment. Black concentric circles on reddish buff
ground. Lydian or Greek Protogeometric. (Fig. 238.)
P58.104:118. W 190–193/S 1281–1282, *96.75–96.55.
Cup fragment with rim and horizontal loop handle. Diam.
0.10 m. Outside: three red bands below handle, black
around rim and handle. Ionian or Lydian Geometric. (Fig.
239.)

Lamp
L58.3:185. W 180–186/S 1282, *97.00–96.50. Open shape.
Cf., Howland, *Agora* IV, pl. 2:32–33 Type 5. Probably
Lydian, late 6th cent. B.C. (Fig. 240.)

Stone Object
S58.1:151. W 185–189/S 1277–1279, *97.40–96.60. Sling
bullet. Round granular stone. Diam. 0.035 m. (Fig. 241.)

Level III, *96.20–95.40: Eighth Century B.C. or Earlier and Seventh Century B.C.

This level had first a band of gravel and small
stones, ca. *96.20 to ca. 95.80, then more loose
sand to *95.40. Sherds were primarily Lydian and
were extremely scarce, showing up between *96.00
and *95.70. There were also a few bits of brick, a
fragment of mudbrick, and one or two pieces of
broken worked marble. A few sherds were possibly
Greek Protogeometric and Geometric, suggesting a
date in the eighth century and earlier.

This level was sharply divided from II B and was
apparently formed by water-laid deposits with
greater preponderance of gravel and pebbles than
II B. The gravel and sand were extremely loose.
Level III was a thick stratum over the entire area
of the trench. The top of the stratum was fairly
level throughout. In some areas there was a greater
concentration of sand and in others large pebbles
and stones. At the bottom of Level III, just above
Level IV, a terracotta die was found.

Finds

Pottery
P58.200:310. W 176–178/S 1279–1280, *96.20–95.40.
Fragment of early ware. Outside plain. Inside: black con-
centric circles on red-buff. Lydian. (Fig. 242.)
P58.150A:205. W 179–182/S 1275–1276, *97.00–95.80.
Fragment of juglet. Black concentric bands on reddish-gray.
Lydian. (Fig. 243.)
P58.199:309. W 180–182/S 1275–1279, *96.20–95.40.
Vase fragment. Red ray-like bands and black horizontal
bands on brick-buff. Lydian. (Fig. 244.)

Terracotta
T58.5:216. W 179/S 1277, *95.40. Die. Complete. Worn
surface. 0.025 m. X 0.025 m. Pattern of dots: 1 opp. 6;
2 opp. 3; 4 opp. 5. Lydian. *BASOR* 154, 9. (Fig. 245.)

Level IV, *95.60–93.50

Level IV was observed in a small test pit 2.5 m.
X 3.0 m. dug in the northeast corner of the trench
(Figs. 96, 219, 246). In 1958 it was taken down
from *95.40 to 93.60, and re-examined in 1968
to a depth of *95.00. It consisted of virgin soil;
hard, moist, compact, aerated sand of a brownish-
green color (according to Gerald W. Olson, soils
specialist) and devoid of sherds. At the top of the
level the compacted sand stood up in large roundish
boulder-like formations with pockets of large damp
gravel in the interstices perhaps formed by water.

Level IV was immediately under III and probably represents the bottom of the stream bed which
coursed through the precinct area. The soil was
devoid of finds down to the point where digging
left off.

Summary

The sounding in Trench S proved that this area
was a torrent bed, perhaps occupied or at least
walked upon intermittently in some parts before
the Hellenistic Temple of Artemis was constructed.
There was no cogent evidence for a precinct level
earlier than Butler's Hellenistic-Lydian (actually
also Roman) level, but then Level I of the trench
was thoroughly disturbed by Butler's digging. Finds
made in and between the water-laid deposits of
Levels II–III suggest that the stream flowed through
the area from the eighth or seventh century B.C.
on; no Bronze Age objects were found.

                                        GMAH, JCW

BUILDING L

Building L, initially called Lydian Building by
the Harvard-Cornell Expedition, is on the southern
side of the Artemis Precinct. It was drawn by
Butler's architects, but Butler does not seem to
have commented on it in his publication of the
area.[10] The building was excavated in 1958 by
the Harvard-Cornell Expedition and re-examined
in 1968 when it was incorporated in the B grid,
W 166–199/S 1297–1315 (Figs. 96, 247).[11]

Site

The building seems to have been an important
element of a rise along the south side of the temple

precinct (Figs. 59, 95), with its later floor levels about one meter higher than the level of the sanctuary. The distance from the southern edge of the southern peristyle of the temple to the north wall of Building L is about 38 m. (Fig. 96); the north wall is not precisely parallel to the long side of the temple, and a survey showed that the layout of the building as a whole was imprecise. The long east-west walls were not strictly parallel and the eastern wall did not form a right angle with the north wall (Figs. 96, 247; cf. Fig. 266).

The western side of the building and much of the southern side were severely flooded and torn away by the action of the Pactolus, whose bed in 1910–1914 was somewhat to the east of its present bed.[12] The action of the torrent on the southern side of the sanctuary, coming down from the hollow leading to the Acropolis, probably also contributed to the destruction of the building.[13] A large part of Room A in the northwest corner of the building was torn away as were parts of Rooms G, F, H, I, and J in the southern part of the building, at least on the surface and immediately below (Fig. 247).[14] The room south of A is gone completely. We do not know whether the building ended with Rooms H, I, J on the south, nor do we know how far it might have extended to the west. The structure stood several meters higher than the present torrent bed south of it.

Description

The building was monumental in conception. Its incomplete length (E-W) is 30 m. along the north wall; the incomplete width (N-S) is 18 m. As now constituted, it shows three rows of rooms running east-west. The northern row consists of Rooms A, B, C, D; the middle Rooms F, E, G; and the southern and least complete, Rooms H, I, and possibly J (Fig. 247). The major walls would have been capable of bearing a second story. The fact that there were substantial differences of floor levels which rose markedly from west to east (A: *98.15– *98.30 early, *98.50 later; B: *98.30 early, *99.15, later; C: *99.40 early, *100.00 later; D: *99.70 early, *100.00, later) suggests that the building was terraced like the stoa at Assos,[15] with two or more stories in the western and southern

parts and possibly a basement space leaning against the hill slope (Fig. 248).

As the northern frontage of the rooms increases from east to west, one might assume that the building was symmetrical around Room B as the central unit. Ratios of room dimensions from east to west are approximately 3:4:6.5, or 15.3:20.3:32.5 feet, assuming a foot of ca. 0.30 m. (D: 4.60 m.; C: 6.10 m.; B: 9.75m.). The N-S dimensions of the northern rooms vary from 8.30 to 8.50 m.[16] The middle rooms (F, E, G) were considerably narrower in the N-S direction: 3.50 m. for Room G, 4.55 m. for Room E. The very uniform walls may be based on 2.5 feet; their most frequent thickness is ca. 0.75 to 0.80 m. Rooms B and D have footings (ledges) inside and outside, presumably indicating beginning of foundation.

There were apparently doors from the north into units B and C and from the east into D; at least B and C as well as C and D communicated with each other. There was a door from the east into G, and B and F communicated north-south, as did E and I. Fragments of window glass, probably Late Roman, were found on the Roman–Early Byzantine floor of Room B (*98.30), but nothing further is known about the fenestration.

Function

It has been suggested that the building might have been a stoa, although excavation north of Rooms A and B and surface cleaning in front of Room D showed no evidence of a colonnade located north of Building L. The division of rooms might be appropriate for a storage building, but nothing in the contents suggests storage. Some sort of dwelling for priestesses is a possibility. In any case, the size of the rooms seems large and would be more suitable for semi-public functions such as dining halls and meeting rooms.

Construction and Date

The structure was built of cemented rubble consisting of local riverstones (Figs. 265, 266), except for part of wall c between units E and G, W 173– 175/S 1309–1315, which is in rubble alternating with a bonding course of brick (3 courses). This may be a later addition. The northeast corner of the entire structure is fashioned like a pier with two squared ashlar blocks and large boulders aiming at ashlar effect (Figs. 247, 266). A similar pier may have been part of the original structure at the end of wall d at S 1307. In the rubble, two courses of 0.08 m. each often alternated with one course of stones ca. 0.15–0.16 m. high (½ foot?). The rubble of the lower parts of the walls is set in grayish white cement. This cement lasts well underground but breaks up when exposed to air. Foundation parts of the walls are faced with thick (up to 0.04 m.), coarse brick and mortar. This external facing was pressed even by boards.

Three major phases may be distinguished. On the evidence of other Sardian buildings (Stadium, Hillside Chambers, foundations under the Gymnasium, filling of Theater, and filling between columns of the Artemis Temple), cemented rubble came into prominent use in the rebuilding of Sardis after A.D. 17. A date in the first century A.D. would fit indications of finds associated with the early floors where pottery of Late Hellenistic character and an Augustan lamp (Fig. 271) were found.

These earlier floors are partly extant and proved by traces at the bottom of walls in C and E which have stucco plaster. Fragments of earlier plaster in white were also found under the later, higher floor in E.

A repair around A.D. 400 is attested by alteration of several rooms and by use of poor red cement plaster on the walls of some rooms. Tiles used as wall facing (in C and E) and the tile box put into the floor in C are probably from this time. Many finds and some coins (Anthemius, A.D. 467–472; Justin II, A.D. 572–577,[17] Room B) prove the continuous use of the structure which may have lasted to A.D. 616. "High" earth-floors around *100.00–99.90 probably belong to this phase.

A careful review of building and records shows that there were at least three major series of floors:

1. The thick lime-plaster floors, almost lost in A at ca. *99.60–99.00 (Fig. 249); B (Fig. 257), high at *99.15 on the east, down to ca. *99.00 on the south; C and D at ca. *100.00; E at *100.31. These floors were at first taken for Early Byzantine, but they lay over roof tiles (e.g. in A and B) which presupposes a destruction. Perhaps the destruction is

that of A.D. 400 rather than 616. Coins attest a squatter occupation from the tenth to thirteenth centuries, but only bits of walls in F, E, and possibly G can be assigned to it.[18]

2. The (later) Roman floors, indicated in part by position of footing (ledges) at *98.85 in Room B, *99.90 in Room D (Fig. 247). As these footings are an integral part of construction, the floors must be original. In Rooms C (*99.40) and E (*99.85) these are also determined by fine white stucco reaching to the floor line. Room A had a floor with fine stucco fragments at *98.65.

3. The earlier floors, which antedate the building, were connected with the burned level in A (*98.30–*98.15; Fig. 249), B (*98.30–*98.20; Fig. 257), and the North Trench outside of Rooms A and B (stone level *98.23; Fig. 273). A coin of the second century A.D. (C58.210) was allegedly found below the burned level and "ashy floor" of Room A, but the rest of the material included fourth and fifth century B.C. as well as Hellenistic sherds and is possibly related to the destruction of 213 B.C., which may be represented by the burned level.

4. The lowest "floor," an island of compacted earth among gravel, appeared in the corner of North Trench, outside Rooms A-B at *97.20 (Figs. 247, 273). It contained some collapsed mud brick and abundant sherds, charcoal, and bones. Traces of at least ephemeral architecture are present. The Lydian pottery found is not closely datable and may well extend from fifth century to 213 B.C., through the later Lydian-Persian and Early Hellenistic periods.

Room A

The preserved dimensions of Room A are 6.9 m. E-W by 5.6 m. N-S to the break at the south end of the east wall (W 193–199.9/S 1300.1–1305.7; Fig. 247). The north wall is preserved to full length, the east and west walls only in part. By analogy with the other rooms in the series A-D, the original N-S dimension was perhaps 8.6 m., the original E-W dimension was ca. 6.10 m. The width of the north wall is 0.75 m. and that of the north-south wall between A and B is 0.80 m. The walls are now preserved to a height of 2.20 m. characterized by courses of small flat stones alternating with courses of larger round ones. The foundation level of the east wall goes down to *97.20. The first (Roman) floor level associated with the wall is at *98.65. The lower part of the north wall at the west end (W 198–199.5) was restored in 1968. The western and southern walls of Room A were entirely destroyed by the course of the torrent.

Numerous fragments of painted plaster (WP58.1) recovered in the room at levels *99.70 to *99.60—red, green, black, and white, as well as some blue, red, and pink, and one with a light blue design—indicate that the room at one time was probably decorated with brightly colored frescoes.

Finds

Finds in Room A from surface to first floor level at *98.65 include several fragments of Hellenistic or Roman relief ware. This general context, however, was mixed and contained examples of Byzantine and Lydian wares, as well as the Hellenistic-Roman majority. The mixture could perhaps be attributed to flood disturbance as well as to later Byzantine reuse of the building.

At the western side of Room A at ca. *98.80 below the stones which marked the fall over the Roman floor, the finds were late classical and Early Hellenistic (see "Finds: Room A, stratigraphic pit," *infra*).

Coin
C58.210. W 194/S 1302, *97.90, below stucco floor. Macedon. Alexander with figure on horseback. Range 330–170 B.C.

Lamp
L58.33:735. Among stones. *98.60. Part of body and spout. P.L. 0.076. P.H. 0.025. Wheelmade, nozzle added; possible scar for handle; flat rim, had wide opening. No later than third century B.C. Howland, *Agora* IV, 46, type 21B.

Pottery
P58.451:726. South extension of Room A, *99.15. Tiny fragment of relief ware. Interior once black, possibly also exterior. Part of petal in relief. W. 0.02 m. Probably second century B.C. Cf. F. Courby, *Les vases grecs à reliefs* (Paris 1922), 388, fig. 81.5. (Fig. 250.)
P58.436:699. Northeast corner of room, *99.00. Fragment of relief ware. Paint worn. L. 0.029 m. Egg and dart on upper part. Mid-2nd to mid-1st century B.C. Cf. Goldman, *Tarsus* I, 172 f., fig. 129, 153.
P58.372:661. *98.60–*98.30 below stones. Part of kantharos handle. L. 0.042. Horizontal; one side flat; red paint on red-buff fabric. 4th century B.C. (Fig. 251.)
P58.369:658. *98.60–*98.30 below stones. Fragment of shallow dish. Everted rim. Diam. 0.12 m. Thin, fine, black glaze. Attic, 4th century B.C.

Stratigraphic Sounding in Room A

In 1958 a test pit, 2.5 m. N-S X 1.8 m. E-W (W 192.5–195/S 1300–1303), was opened in the northeast corner of Room A to a depth of *96.90. In 1968 this pit was reopened to a depth of *96.00 (Fig. 249). It was re-examined in 1970.

The section along the south side next to the east wall of Room A revealed evidence of recent flooding near the surface. Below earth and roof tiles and fallen stones, collapse of roof and upper walls extended from *98.65 to *98.45. Just under this bedding was a layer of gravel and under that at ca. *98.40 to *98.15 was a burned ashy layer slanting westward and characterized by pieces of reddish clay from mud brick or pisé and larger than usual bits of charcoal. This ashy layer is even more clearly attested in Room B (*infra*). The pottery in this level was Lydian-Hellenistic. Under this upper burning was an ashy white-clay floor running from *98.30 (east) to *98.15.

Beneath the ash layer were alternating bands of gravel and stones to ca. *97.60 and under this was a light silt layer and earth interspersed with sand and gravel bands to ca. *96.75. At the southeast corner of the trench was a small pit (top, *97.97; bottom, *97.55) lined with lime and filled with silt. The bottom of the Roman wall was found at ca. *97.20. From about *96.70 down to the bottom of the sounding was a river deposit of sand, gravel, and stones almost devoid of artifacts. The pottery found *beneath* the burned ash level was pre-Hellenistic and contained a large proportion of archaic (sixth century B.C.) Lydian and imported Greek wares. This seems to reflect the same kind of deposits as the Levels II B and III in Trench S (*supra*) made before the construction of Building L and of the Hellenistic Artemis sanctuary.

Finds: Room A, stratigraphic pit

Pottery
P58.409:685. *98.30–*98.15. Burned ash layer. Three fragments of heavy buff ware with worn tan paint, two joining. Plate rim. Diam. 0.30 m. Hellenistic. (Fig. 252.)
P58.412:688. *98.30–*98.15. Burned ash layer. Fragment of grooved fish-plate rim. Diam. 0.24 m. Hellenistic.
P58.407:683. *98.30–*98.15, in ashy layer. Small fragment of Protogeometric red ware. W. 0.025. Interior red-buff; exterior red with parts of four concentric circles in black. Lydian. (Fig. 253.)

P58.391:679. *97.60–*96.60. Part of foot and body of bowl. W. foot 0.052 m. Interior: brown paint on buff fabric; exterior: brown and white paint. Lydian, possibly 6th cent. (Fig. 254.)

P58.388:676. *97.60–*96.90. Rim fragments of red ledge-rim crater. Diam. 0.24 m. Interior: plain red with horizontal incised groove at base. Lydian. 6th cent. B.C. (Fig. 255.)

P58.501:856. Just below north wall of room, from *97.20 down. Fragment of plate with plain exterior; interior: lines of purplish-brown. W. 0.065 m. Lydian. (Fig. 256.)

Room B

The north wall of B is located at W 182–192/S 1298.2–1300 (Fig. 247). Its height at the northeast corner was *99.70–*99.60, then it dips down to *99.04 and is destroyed 1.20 to 2.20 m. from the northeast corner. It then rises again to *99.33. Its width varies from 0.75 m. to 0.85 m.

The wall was faced with reddish stucco on the exterior and interior faces below present ground level. The exterior stucco facing is pressed flat but not otherwise finished. No traces of color were preserved.[19] At ca. *98.85 of inner (south) face was found the top of a ledge of stone projecting ca. 0.15 m. from the wall and intended as a footing for the floor at ca. *98.90. A similar footing was observed on the west wall.

The west wall a of Room B (W 191.2–192.9/S 1300–1305.7) has been exposed for a length of 5.75 m. N-S. It is preserved up to *98.97–*99.48 at the top. The south end of the wall runs into the river gravel and high earth. A late, thick, lime-plaster floor is associated with the wall at *99.07. The floor (marked *99.15 in Fig. 247) is very uneven and drops to ca. *99.00 near center.

The east wall b, (W 181.4–182.3/S 1299.1–1307.3; interior, Fig. 265) is bonded into the north wall of B and communicates with Room C by a door (S 1300.45–1301.35). A late, thick, lime floor lies just west of the door at *99.75 and is traceable along the wall to the southeast corner of the room.

There may have been a door in the south wall (W 183–184/S 1307.5) near the southeast corner. A large stone at the north side suggests a jamb foundation. A white plaster floor lies just east of this at ca. *99.15 (Fig. 257, top left).

Intruding upon the door threshold in the south wall (Fig. 247), the wall bb with its differing orientation was one of the few remnants of the Middle Byzantine squatters' phase (*100.20, top). Under the lime floor of this phase was a dense southward fall of roof tiles (pan and cover) showing that the roof had collapsed inward.

Finds

Surface finds in Room B included a range of sherds from Byzantine to Lydian and a Roman lamp of mid-third century to fifth century A.D. type. Middle Byzantine coins and glazed pottery attest an occupation in the eleventh to thirteenth centuries. The Roman and Early Byzantine pottery, glass, and coin of Justin II may belong to the Roman–Early Byzantine floor. Below the level of plaster at ca. *99.00 were Hellenistic materials.

Coins

C58.269:901. South side of room, *99.80–*99.70. Justin II, Nicomedia, Follis, A.D. 575–577. *Sardis* M1 (1971) no. 459.

C58.280:920. Middle of room, *99.20. Michael VII, Constantinople, A.D. 1071–1078. *Sardis* M1 (1971) 137, no. 1181.

C58.211:614. South side of room, *99.20–*99.00. Theodore I, Nicaea or Magnesia, A.D. 1208–1222. *Sardis* M1 (1971) 141, no. 1203.

C58.266:897. Southeast corner of room, *100.00–*99.90, Sardis, 1st cent. B.C., Head of Herakles.

Pottery

P58.405:681a. *99.00. Tiny fragment of black-glazed cup. W. 0.021 m. Attic Greek. (Fig. 259.)

P58.406:582a. *99.00. Fragment of fish-plate rim. Diam. 0.14 m. Slightly everted rim. Buff ware.

P58.503:860. Surface to *99.60. Fragment of white-glazed rim. Diam. 0.28 m. Byzantine.

P58.413:685a. W183–188/S 1305–1307, surface to *99.00. Ring foot with stem and part of bowl. Glazed ware. White slip-painted circles with dots. Byzantine. (Fig. 260.)

Glass

G58.54:683a, b. Surface to *99.00. Two bracelet fragments. In fill above higher floor with Byzantine pottery. Larger: pale green with striations along curve. Bluish tints on green. L. 0.056 m.; W. 0.004 m. Smaller: twisted band in red, silver, and black. L. 0.052 m.; W. 0.005 m. Middle Byzantine. 12th to 13th cent. A.D. Cf. Hanfmann, "Glass," 53–54 n. 19.

G58.71:866. Surface to *98.60. Several fragments including vessel fragments. Ring foot, diam. 0.045 m. Yellowish-brown with greenish light. Cf. Hanfmann, "Glass," 52 n. 8. Possibly Late Roman.

G58.88:1026. *99.40–*99.20. Large, low ring base of dark green translucent glass. W. 0.071 m. Found with C58.280. Middle Byzantine. Cf. Hanfmann, "Glass," 52 n. 8.

Stratigraphic Sounding in B

A test pit opened in the northwest corner of Room B in 1958 was enlarged in 1968 to 4.5 m. E-W × 2.5 m. N-S against the north and west walls of the room (Figs. 257, 258). In general, the stratigraphy of this pit corresponded to that of the sounding in Room A, with analogous strata at somewhat higher levels because of the slope in terrain (Fig. 249).

In the north section of the pit (Fig. 258) the top of the wall was at ca. *99.35, the footing for the floor at *98.80. The wall of cemented rubble continued down to the foundation level at *97.80, sloping off to the west to *97.55. Directly below the wall was a band of hard clay and sand, sealing off the deposit of river gravel and sand lying below to *97.25. Brown clay, interspersed with sand, lay below that to ca. *97.10 and at the bottom, from about *96.90 down, was a flood layer of gravel and sand.

The section in the east side of the pit (Fig. 257) showed the late white plaster floor associated with the wall at *99.15 to *98.95 lying over a layer of fallen roof tiles at *98.90 to *98.50. Beneath was a deposit of river borne gravel mixed with scattered tiles and cement splashes, ca. *98.50 to *98.30; here was probably a floor overlying a second layer of gravel, sand, and cement (second gravel), *98.30 to *97.85. Pottery from below the second gravel layer was datable to fourth to third century B.C. In the southeast corner (not shown in Fig. 249) under the lime floor and down to ca. *97.85 is a dense southward fall of roof tiles, showing that the roof had collapsed inward. It is adjoined on the south side by a burned layer from *98.60 to *98.20 containing Late Lydian to Hellenistic pottery, bits of fired tiles, and burned bones. This level corresponded to the burned level in Room A at *98.30 to *97.70.

In the southeast corner of the pit from *97.85 to *97.75 was a layer of brown clay, just below which was another deposit of river laid gravel, *97.75 to *97.25. Brown clay was under this from *97.25 to *97.10, higher than along the north wall. From *97.10 down was river sand and gravel. The lowest earth, sand, and gravel layers were virtually free of artifacts.

Finds

Pottery

P68.45:7660. Southwest corner, *98.20–*98.00. Bowl fragment with inverted rim. Diam. rim 0.16 m.; diam. foot 0.06 m.; H. 0.06 m.; Th. 0.005 m. Roman(?). (Fig. 261.)

P68.54:7673. East end, *97.90. Fragment of coarse, red pithos. Graffito on foot of pithos. At break (on right) one sign, cross above arrow; the other (on left) lambda-like(?). (R. Gusmani [by letter February 1974]: "meaningless scratches; not real letters.") H. 0.04 m.; W. 0.044 m. On exterior, part of graffito. Late Lydian.

P68.55:7674. *97.90. Red slip, omphalos bowl; base and foot with concave center. Part of a graffito letter? Diam. foot 0.08 m.; diam. inner base 0.05 m.; H. 0.025 m.; Th. wall 0.006 m. Hellenistic, 4th–3rd century B.C. (Fig. 262.)

Lamp

L58.30:725. *98.70. Complete nozzle (modeled) of wheel-made Hellenistic lamp. L. 0.041 m. 3rd century B.C. Schäfer, 122H4 (possibly Attic import); H5, Pergamene variant. (Fig. 263.)

Room C

The plan of Room C is completely preserved. Its dimensions east to west are 6.10 m.; N-S, along the east wall, 8.30 m.; along the west wall, 8.30 m.; W 174.2–181.5/S 1298.2–1307.2 (Figs. 247, 265). A late floor lay at ca. *100.00; several parts of it were of thick white plaster. An earlier floor, at ca. *99.30, was discerned in two places.

The north wall stands to ca. 1.00 m. above the modern surface in the eastern part (*100.51) but goes down to surface level at W 180–181.6 near the northwest corner of the room, perhaps for a door. The east wall *c* bonds into the north and south walls. It stands from 1.00 to 0.30 m. high (*99.50) in the middle to *100.30 at the south corner. One may suspect that a door existed at ca. S 1301–1302. The west wall *b* is much disrupted and only two or three low courses show above ground; its northwest corner is at *99.82. This is the one wall which had fine wall-facing stucco preserved on its east face, at S 1301.8–1302.5, 0.30 to 0.60 m. below the *100.00 floor. It seems to bend and stop for a floor level at ca. *99.40 (Fig. 264).

Traces of a door were found in the west wall *b* ca. 1.45 m. from the northwest corner (S 1300.45). A jamb-like stone on the south side and loosened threshold stones lay in the doorway. The width of the doorway is 0.90 m. N-S, the E-W depth is 0.90 m. The level of the threshold was probably below the fine stucco line at *99.40–99.35, above the cut masonry footing in the wall.

At the south end of the room was a large mass of stones, 4.60 m. to 5.0 m. E-W × 2.25 m. to 2.40 m. N-S (Figs. 247, 265), referred to as "fallen wall x"; its top was at *100.60–100.30. The heap apparently came from the collapse of the upper part of the south wall northward into the room. It lay over a thick plaster floor. A similar white lime floor lay (*100.00–99.75) next to the west face of the east wall c (W 175.2–175.4/S 1298.5–1300) corresponding to the line of the floor in the southwest corner of Room B. A rough stucco facing going down to the late white floor was found in the northeast corner of C at *100.00–99.00. Fine stucco went down to a lower floor at *99.40. The southwest corner was faced with upright tiles. In the northwest corner below the late white lime floor of the room was a "chest of tiles," 0.60 m. by 0.45 m., top at *99.60, bottom at *99.20, probably left from a late reuse of the building. It consisted of a schist slab and reused tiles.

Finds

Pottery recovered from Room C comes from mixed surface material ranging from Hellenistic to Byzantine. A few coins, also of mixed dates (Roman-Byzantine) were found in the debris.

Coins
C58.213:617. *100.80–100.70 (surface). Ephesus and Alexandria. Gordian III, A.D. 238–244.
C58.212:616. *100.70 to *100.60 (surface). Late Roman, uncertain mint, A.D. 408–423.
C58.267:899. Southwest corner of room. *100.60 (surface). Theodore I or John III, A.D. 1208–1254. *Sardis* M1 (1971) 145, no. 1229. (From period of reuse of building?).

Pottery
P58.546:918. *100.60–*99.80 (surface). Ring base fragment. Buff ware with yellow-green glaze on interior. Plain exterior. Diam. foot 0.06 m.; W. 0.077 m. Byzantine.
P58.549:927. *100.60–*99.80 (surface). Fragment of relief ware rim; Diam. 0.14 m. Bead and reel motif along lower part. "Megarian," 3rd to 2nd cent. B.C. Cf. G. M. Crawford, *Samaria Sebaste* 3 (London 1957) 276, fig. 62.4; Goldman, *Tarsus* I, 255, fig. 131 n. (Fig. 270.)
P58.550:928. *100.60–*99.80 (surface). Relief ware fragment. W. 0.041 m. Mid-2nd to mid-first cent. B.C. Cf. Goldman, *Tarsus* I, 172, 235, fig. 138 A-B, Hellenistic-Roman Unit.

Room D

Room D was the best preserved room in Building L. Its plan is completely preserved, ca. 4.60–4.85 m. E-W by 8.50 m. N-S; W 168.5–174.6/S 1297.6–1306.5 (Figs. 247, 266). A sounding made in the

northeast corner (W 170/S 1297.6) shows the construction of the walls to be two courses of flat stones alternating with a single course of squarish stones laid in rather soft cement.

Along the north wall an external footing projects northward to 0.30 m. at the northeast corner. It was made up of small cemented stones and a large blue-black corner stone. The northeast exterior corner was the only place in Building L where ashlar masonry was used. The preserved height was 1.06 m. above ground level (*101.06), the highest preserved wall in the building. The width of the wall, excluding the footing, was 0.75 m. on the top near the northwest corner. The top levels of the walls at the four corners of the room are: northeast, *101.06 m.; northwest, *100.51 m.; southwest, *100.30 m.; southeast, *100.50 m. Large masses of fallen stone and tiles were found in the room from the collapse of upper walls and roof.

The interior north wall (W 170–174.6/S 1297.6–1298) showed traces of rough backing stucco. It is interrupted for the floor line at ca. *100.00. This floor is also attested by a partial projecting footing inside the east wall d (0.10 m. wide) which starts north of a break for a possible door in the east wall (ca. W 169/S 1303). The footing rested on a hard bedding of irregular tamped stones and brick.

In the eastern wall a door was placed at S 1303.30–1304.40, south of the northeast corner. With its frame, it is 1.10 m. wide and has a threshold at *100.18. Traces of a plaster floor started at *99.95, just below the door threshold, varying from *99.95 to *99.55.

The east wall d bonds into the south E-W crosswall. The south wall had a footing of river stones, 0.20 m. wide at the base of the wall, with much white floor stucco over it at *99.90. The top level of the south wall is ca. *100.79. There are traces of thick wall stucco backing throughout.

Room E

Room E lay south of C, north of I, and between Rooms F and G. Its preserved dimensions are 6.20–6.30 m. E-W × 4.50–4.60 m. N-S; W 173.4–180.2/S 1307.3–1312.3 (Figs. 247, 265, 267). The north wall is complete in plan, and parts of the east c and west b walls are also preserved. A south wall e, 4.75

m. long, was preserved only below floor level. This wall has the remains of a door to Room I at W 173.5–174.4 (Fig. 268). The top of the wall is at *99.23, possible footing for thresholds at *99.35; its western end is at *99.04.

The level of the top of west wall *b* is at *99.70. The inside, east face had pieces of white facing stucco preserved. At one time the wall was carefully surfaced like that of Room C. Upright tiles were used as wall facing in the northwest corner of E, similar to those found in the southwest corner of C. Ivory-white stucco was also found in patches along the north wall of E.

At S 1309.5 the construction of the east wall *c* of E (Figs. 247, 267) changed from cemented rubble to brick and rubble in the alternating pattern of three courses of brick and one course of mortared rubble. The size of the bricks is 0.33 m. long by 0.33 m. wide by 0.05 m. high. The height of the mortar joint is 0.02 to 0.025 m. high. As far as excavated (S 1314.7) wall *c* continued in this technique. The sequence was apparently: eastern wall *c* in original rubble construction; addition to wall *c*, with brick bonding courses; then the southern wall *e* in poor rubble technique.

A floor of the Late Roman or Byzantine phase was found at *100.31. Under the floor were the remains of wall stucco which had probably fallen from the walls of an earlier phase and were spread evenly to provide a bedding for the later floor. An earlier floor was found at *99.85. Pottery associated with this floor included Late Hellenistic and Early Roman relief ware sherds, a few fragments of red sigillate ware, some Hellenistic "poor glaze" fragments, and Early Roman ridged ware sherds. The floor itself must date to the Early Roman period, probably shortly after the earthquake of A.D. 17.

The scarp of the excavation in the southwest corner of E (W 181–183/S 1309–1314) shows loose, burned tiles and traces of ashes slanting southward from *99.30 to *98.60. This evidence of burning lies under the collapse of walls and roof which reaches up to *100.60. Conceivably, this collapse might be associated with the destruction of A.D. 616 in which the building probably perished by fire.

Within and above this fall and burnt deposit are river-laid deposits from ca. *98.50–*101.00. The top of the trench is at *102.00, almost four meters above the top of wall *b* as it vanishes into the scarp at *98.17 (W 180/S 1314.5). The upper flood deposits are probably Early Byzantine and later.

Finds

Coins
C58.268:900. *100.40–*100.31. Roman. T. V. Buttrey: *Virtus Exercitus,* Arcadius-Honorius A.D. 395–408.
C58.271:903. *100.30–*100.00. John III, Magnesia, A.D. 1222–1254. *Sardis* M1 (1971) 144, no. 1222.
C58.272:904. *100.00. Latin imitation of Alexius III, A.D. 1204–1261. *Sardis* M1 (1971) 146, no. 1233.

Lamp
L68.20:7895. W 180/S 1312, *100.00. Triangular handle with acanthus pattern. Curved profile. H. of leaf 0.061 m.; H. back 0.075 m.; Th. 0.007 m. 2nd half of 1st century B.C.–1st half 1st century A.D. Menzel, 25, 26, no. 96. (Fig. 271.)

Pottery
P68.187:7907. Near wall *c* W 176/S 1307.5–1312, under upper floor *99.60. Black-glazed, rouletted plate fragment. High ring foot, exterior unpainted. H. 0.03 m.; W. 0.08 m.; diam. foot 0.006 m. (Fig. 272.)

Stone Object
S58.36:888. Southeast corner, *101.20–*100.50. Foot and part of basin of stone mortar. Basalt (?). Concave interior, simple rim. Approx. diam. 0.35 m.; H. foot 0.075 m.; total H. 0.11 m.; W. 0.125 m.

Glass
G58.77:922. Surface to *100.50. Fragment of ring base and part of body of cup, smooth white glass. W. 0.052 m. Cf. Hanfmann, "Glass," 52 n. 8; *AJA* 44 (1940) 314, fig. 14, no. 20. A. von Saldern: perhaps Roman Middle Imperial.
G58.93:1040a-e. *100.50–*100.31. Fragments of several bracelets. Three black and red twisted, one greenish, one yellow-green (shapeless). Cf. Hanfmann, "Glass," 53 n. 18, 54 n. 19. Middle Byzantine(?).

Room F

Only the northeast part of Room F was preserved. The north wall measures 7.4 m. E-W (W 181.1–188.5). A secondary Byzantine wall, *bb*, at ca. *100.20 (W 182.1–183.3/S 1307.5–1309.8) overlies part of the north wall and runs off at an angle to the south. The southern boundary wall was not found but the width of the room can be conjectured as ca. 4.50 m. N-S by comparison with Room E (Fig. 247).

The east wall *b* between Rooms F and E (and H

and I) has a top level of *99.70. It continues southward at a greater depth. It was excavated to (*98.90–*98.80 without reaching its bottom, showing that well-preserved parts of the building (especially foundations) may lie to the south below the flood deposits.

Stone enclosure *cc* (Fig. 247) is rectangular, ca. 1 m. N-S by 0.90 m. E-W, and ca. 0.50 m. deep (*98.53–ca. *98.00). Its stones laid in earth run up against the rough foundation facing stucco of wall *b*. There are no traces of fire nor is its construction tight enough for a well. As fragments of Hellenistic ware were found within, the enclosure may have been made during construction activities on the lower part of wall *b*, just after A.D. 17.

Finds

Pottery from Room F was recovered mostly from near the surface and was of mixed context. Some clearly belonged to Middle Byzantine occupation.

Pottery
P58.552:931. *101.00–*100.00. Small fragment of relief ware. Very worn. Raised ridges on exterior. H. 0.02 m. 2nd cent. B.C. Cf. Goldman, *Tarsus* I, 172, 235, fig. 138, 306, "Middle Level Hell.-Roman Unit"; F. O. Waagé, *Antioch-on-the-Orontes* IV:1 (Princeton 1948) fig. 15.28.

Glass
G58.81:934a-c. *101.00–*100.00. Fragments of three bracelets. Two striped red and white, one black. Cf. Hanfmann, "Glass," 54 n. 19. Byzantine, 13th cent. A.D.

Room G

Room G lay directly south of Room D and east of Room E. Its preserved dimensions were 5.1 m. E-W by 3.30–3.50 m. N-S (to wall *f*); W 167.5–173.3/S 1306.7–1310.0 (Fig. 247).

The east wall *d* originally displayed at S 1307.6 a fine piece of limestone masonry in a kind of pier. The original east wall of G continues southward. A later addition runs above and at an angle. The level of the top of wall *d* varies from *100.20 to *99.75 and its length has been traced to S 1312, ca. 6 m. from the northeast corner of G (Fig. 269). The west wall *c* is a wall common with Room E and has been described as the east wall of that unit.

In the northeast corner another N-S wall *d'* appeared, partly under wall *d* and projecting 0.25 m. to 0.30 m. further to the west. It extended north

as far as the crosswall between D and G and its west, inner face was covered with plaster which was smeared over the corner and around onto the wall between D and G. The top of this wall is at ca. *100.50.

The eastern part of the south crosswall *f* was found, S 1310, ca. 3.50 m. south of the wall between D and G (Fig. 269); it bonded into wall *d* at the east, and apparently formed a crosswall between G and Room J to the south. It was 0.60 m. wide with a top at ca. *99.58. Another, higher secondary E-W crosswall *g* was found, directly south of *f* and which crossed over *d* to the east. It was 0.45 m. to 0.50 m. wide with a top at ca. *100.17.

Finds

Finds in Room G were scanty and mixed, ranging at the surface from Hellenistic to Byzantine. A "poor-glaze" Roman or Hellenistic lamp was found in surface deposits and a Late Byzantine coin near the east wall. Three Roman Imperial coins were found unstratified.

Coins
C58.276:911. Trench along east wall, *100.50–*100.30. John III, Magnesia, A.D. 1222–1254. *Sardis* M1 (1971) 143, no. 1214.
1968, uncatalogued. West of wall *d* near possible south termination, *100.60. John III, Magnesia, A.D. 1222–1254. *Sardis* M1 (1971) 143, no. 1208.

Lamp
L58.53:999. *102.30–*101.20 (surface). Fragment of top and steep collar of an "Ephesus" lamp. Collar added on a tournette, therefore early. H. 0.025 m.; W. 0.039 m. Late 2nd or 1st cent. B.C. Cf. T. L. Shear, *AJA* 26 (1922) 401; Broneer, *Corinth* IV, 66–70 for discussion of type. (Fig. 275.)

Rooms H, I, J

Evidence for further rooms to the south of F, E, and G was uncovered in the 1968 excavation (Figs. 247, 266). As yet there are few data available on the contents and dimensions of the rooms. Certain evidence for Room I south of E and J south of G is given by E-W crosswalls *e* and *f*; N-S walls *b*, *c*, and *d* continued southward beyond them. The existence of Room H is only conjectural to conform with the general symmetry of the building (Figs. 247, 248).

Trench North of A and B (North Trench)

In 1958 a stratigraphic sounding just north of Rooms A and B was dug to test the stratigraphy of Building L and the history of the area prior to the construction of L (Figs. 96, 247). The pit was re-examined in 1968 in the area W 188–191/S 1294.5–1298.5 and again in 1970 from W 188.5–189/S 1294.5–1297.5. The east section of this pit (Fig. 273) showed earth mixed with scattered stones from *99.40–*98.90 (modern top level); a level of collapsed wall stones and a fine, flat, marble slab occurs at *98.23. From this level down were bands of gravel and earth dipping northward towards an area of "fat," wet earth: deposit H, W 188.5–189/S 1294.5–1295.7 (Fig. 274). Deposit H, down to *97.20 consisted of clayey, wet, brown earth and traces of charcoal. In it were found abundant sherds, Lydian to Early Hellenistic, and animal bones, some burned, including a pig jaw at *97.25. The densest concentration of material was at the bottom of the deposit, *97.20. In the northeast corner deposit H overlay a clay floor (or possibly a mud-brick collapse) ca. 0.40 m. thick (*97.10–*96.70) which continues briefly along the north side of the trench. At the same level in the rest of the trench are thin earth bands, probably natural deposits. Below this, at *96.70, is gravel, continuing to hardpan at *95.40, similar to that encountered in Trench S (supra).[20]

Finds

Coins
C58.265:896. Dump. Theodore I, Nicaea, A.D. 1208–1222. Sardis M1 (1971) 141, no. 1201.
C58.174:559. Middle, northwest side of trench, *98.90–*98.70. Theodore I, Nicaea, A.D. 1208–1222. Sardis M1 (1971) 141, no. 1200.

Lamps
L58.5:231. Middle of trench, *99.60–*99.40. W. 0.071 m. Open shape. Body and rim fragment. Probably 6th cent. B.C. Howland, Agora IV, Types 4–6A, pls. 1 and 2. (Fig. 276.)
L58.31:734. North side of trench. *98.50–*98.10. Fragment of rim and open reservoir. Est diam. 0.084 m.; H. 0.02 m. Late 6th to early 5th century B.C. Broneer, Corinth IV, 32, figs. 14, 17–21, Type IV, profile 17. (Fig. 277.)
L58.32:733. North side of trench. *98.10. Top half of handle. Max. P.L. 0.021 m.; W. 0.012 m. Mold made. 2nd half of 1st cent. to 1st half of 2nd cent. A.D. Perlzweig, Agora VII, 5 f., no. 176, pl. 6.

Pottery
P58.500:834. Northeast side of trench, *97.50–*97.00. Large fragment of a jug with traces of vertical band handle. W. 0.19 m. Lydian(?). (Fig. 278.)
P58.359:647. Northeast side of trench, *98.00–*97.50. Relief ware rim, red interior, egg and dart on lower part of exterior. Diam. 0.08 m. 2nd cent. B.C. Cf. R. Zahn, in Wiegand, Schrader, 407, fig. 531.42.
P58.358:646. Northwest side of trench, *98.00. Three joining fragments of red relief ware. Simple rim, diam. 0.12 m. Exterior: relief circles in horizontal band below rim; palmette and amphorae with lids (loutrophoroi?) on lower part. Mid 2nd–1st cent. B.C. Cf. Goldman Tarsus I, 172 f. Hell.-Roman unit. (Fig. 279).
P58.474a:811. Northeast corner of trench, brownish deposit, *97.70–*96.90. Fragment of black-glaze Greek ware with stamped palmettes. W. 0.061 m. (Fig. 280.)

Terracottas
T58.19:648. Northwest side of trench. *98.00. Terracotta weight; pyramidal shape with hole pierced through top at peak. Shallow hole on one side. H. 0.055 m.; base 0.037 m. (Fig. 281 a.)
T58.20:820. Northwest side of trench. *98.00–*97.50. Among stones. Terracotta weight, pyramidal shape. In upper part, two holes going almost all the way through, sides slightly concave. H. 0.055 m.; base 0.037 m. (Fig. 281 b.)

GMAH, JCW

THE CLEANING AND REORGANIZATION OF THE ARTEMIS TEMPLE PRECINCT IN 1973

In 1973, the architects T. Yalçinkaya and J. L. Miller in collaboration with archaeologist C. H. Greenewalt, Jr. undertook the following operations:

Clearance of temple colonnades. Pieces left in random positions were moved outside the south and east colonnades. They included a twenty-five ton block[21] now placed just east of the two columns from which it fell. Stones lying in irregular positions in the north colonnade were removed to the northern side of the precinct or arranged in blocks in depressions between the column foundations of the northern colonnade. A major hollow in the colonnade itself was filled in.

Clearance of east cella. Forty-seven architectural pieces were removed from the east cella; five were placed in locations on the south cella wall. The others have been placed along the northern edge of the lower precinct, in front (south of) the North Building. Parts of the two jambs of the eastern entrance portal were set up in the cella. General cleaning and leveling was undertaken in the western units. All stones moved have been marked and numbered and all movements have been recorded in field reports and special plans (Figs. 131, 132).[22]

Altar area. Lydian bases recorded by Butler as surrounding the LA 1 and LA 2 Altars (*supra,* Chapter IV "Stelai Bases Around Monument LA 2"; Fig. 181) have been cemented in place. West of LA, stones evacuated from the altar have been placed in more compact formation and a number of random stones were moved with the result that a partially unimpeded view may be had from the west.

Viewing platform at southwest corner. The mound, which had formed around a modern house, *Sardis* I (1922), Plan III, "House," was transformed into a raised viewing platform. W 243–249/S 1210–1217 *98.17. (Fig. 59, Platform "H," just west of Building Q).

GMAH

VIII THE AREA NORTHEAST OF THE ARTEMIS PRECINCT

Crawford H. Greenewalt, Jr.
Jane C. Waldbaum

NORTHEAST WADI

Sector NEW (Northeast Wadi) is located northeast of the Artemis Temple beside and in a large torrent bed (wadi) on the lower slopes of the Acropolis (Figs. 1, 59, 285). Stratified antiquities of Roman and pre-Hellenistic periods had been excavated in this region by the Butler mission in 1914, and pre-Hellenistic antiquities exposed in the torrent channel had attracted attention in subsequent years.[1] In this area Butler observed the following remains:[2] directly below the torrent bed "a solid mass of accumulated earth and, in the uppermost layers of this," artifacts and architectural remains of the Roman period, some of the latter bedded on "older foundations in connexion with which appeared wares of Hellenistic date"; six meters below were "levels" of the sixth and seventh centuries B.C. containing the remains of rubble walls and pottery; ca. 1.30 m. below these remains of the "6th-7th century level . . . another well defined stratum of pottery resembling the early sub-Mykenaian wares of the Ionian coast"; ca. one meter below this stratum, a layer of sherds, "which Professor Chase is inclined to assign to the eighth and ninth centuries."

The altitude of the torrent bed in this area was decreased as a result of Butler's excavations.[3] In 1969, a summer rainstorm revealed an ancient deposit of artifacts resting only a few centimeters below the existing surface of the torrent bed; the artifacts included pottery of pre-Hellenistic Lydian types and a spectacular fragment of a large amphora painted in a colorful Wild Goat style.[4] The promise of more pottery of this quality in the immediate environs and the opportunity to investigate stratified pre-Hellenistic antiquities with a minimum of preliminary earth removal and in an area of Sardis where pre-Hellenistic antiquities were comparatively unknown provided the incentives to excavate once again in this region.

A trench was projected to include the segment of the torrent bed which surrounded the exposed pottery deposit and an adjacent part of the south bank.[5] Ultimately, this trench embraced an area of ca. 65 sq. m. (within coordinates W 107–119/S 1113–1120);[6] the irregular outline reflects the excavators' attempts to anticipate architectural remains. The highest part of the trench, the existing upper surface of the south bank (at *113.72),[7] lay some 4.5 m. above the lowest part, the bottom of a pit in the torrent bed (at *109.30); but most of the remains uncovered in excavation were bedded at levels intermediate between these two. This trench was the principal excavational feature in Sector NEW (for plans and sections cf. Figs. 282–284).

The conservation of the pre-Hellenistic architectural remains exposed in the principal trench would have been extremely difficult, for they lay directly in the path of the torrent and below the existing surface of the torrent bed. No attempt was made to protect these remains. By June of 1970 the trench had become filled with earth and gravel to approximately the same level as the surface of the torrent before the 1969 excavations; the pre-Hellenistic architectural remains, either buried or destroyed, were no longer visible.

The Pit at the Northeast Stoa

The only other excavational feature of Sector NEW was a small pit dug against the south face of the north wall of a building which had been partially cleared in 1914, the Northeast Stoa (cf. Figs. 59, 282).[8] The lower part of the south face of this wall was constructed of ashlar masonry, with rectangular limestone blocks crowned by a string course of narrower blocks. The pit was dug for the purpose of recovering evidence which would help to date this construction. The ashlar masonry was found to terminate at ca. *114.62, just below the 1969 ground surface immediately south of the wall, and to be bedded on rubble-and-mortar construction. The pit was dug to ca. *113.63 in all parts and abandoned. Significant chronological material was not recovered. The outline of the pit (measuring 1.35–1.50 m. wide E-W by 2.50 m. long N-S, located within coordinates W 91–93.25/S 1128.80–1131.70) appears on the plan in Figure 282.

The Roman Remains in the Principal Trench

The earthy debris of the torrent channel's south bank above the level of the torrent bed yielded remains of an L-shaped wall and of a pithos containing pottery and metal artifacts.

L-shaped wall. Segment oriented SE-NW emerged into trench from south scarp; transition from SE-NW to N-S orientation effected 0.75 m. from east scarp; N-S oriented segment terminated in broken end 1.60 m. north of south scarp. Th. 0.70 m.; max P.H. 0.80 m.; top at *113.78, bottom at *112.78. Construction of small stones and tile: roughly coursed and bonded with pink-and-cream-colored mortar. (Figs. 282, 284.)

A large, irregularly shaped mass of stones and mortar bedded appreciably higher (bottom at *113.31) than the L-shaped wall and contiguous to its western face probably represents a dislodged

and fallen section of the same structure. The wall remains are the western terminal parts of the south wall of a large building which had been partially exposed in 1914 (Fig. 292).[9] Remnants of another wall oriented southwest-northeast and embedded at approximately the same level as the L-shaped remains had become partially exposed in the north bank of the torrent channel. These other remains, which are not recorded in Butler's publications, evidently belong to the same building as the L-shaped wall.[10]

The mortar and tile ingredients of the L-shaped wall and parallels in construction and level offered by the adjacent Northeast Stoa, which may be dated on the basis of context material to the Roman period, suggest that the L-shaped wall and other remains associated with it also date from Roman times.[11]

The pithos remains lay just north of the wall remains in the south side of the trench, almost contiguous to the south trench scarp and partly buried under the east scarp. The underside of the pithos was preserved intact and rested in an upright position, bedded at a level somewhat lower than the wall remains.

Pithos. Max. P.H. 0.70 m.; max. P. diam. 1.10 m.; Th. wall. 0.03 m. Bottom interior at *112.80. (Figs. 282, 286.)

The pithos contained at least 17 complete or fragmentary items: at least 13 unpainted pottery vessels (5 or more amphorae with pointed feet; 2 or more closed vessels with ring feet; 2 hemispherical bowls with straight rims and ring feet; 1 bowl with carinated rim; 2 small flasks [Fig. 287]; 1 small vessel with pointed foot); a ceramic plastic attachment in the form of a dolphin (Fig. 288); a terracotta bust of a lady (Figs. 289, 290); a terracotta head of a child (Fig. 291); and a bronze coin. The evidence of the terracotta bust and the coin suggest that this assemblage may be dated to the second half of the second and/or the early third centuries A.D.

Coin
C69.2. Greek, Trajan-Hadrian (A.D. 99–137).

Pottery
P69.13:7937. Bulbous unguentarium with ring foot. Clay gray-beige. Glaze mat, sepia over all. H. 0.105 m.; diam. body 0.073 m. (Fig. 287.)
P69.12:7936. Vase attachment in form of dolphin (han-

dle?). Carved and incised details. Clay. L. 0.098 m.; diam. base 0.02 m. X 0.03 m. (Fig. 288.)

Terracottas
T69.3:7938. Bust of lady with "melon" coiffure. Shawl around shoulders knotted over bosom; low foot support. Thin wall. Clay micaceous, reddish-brown (Munsell 2.5 YR 6/6 "light red"). Cream slip over surface. Dark deposit on head. H. 0.125 m.; max. W. 0.089 m. The coiffure ("melon" waves framing the face, large bun at the back of the head) resembles those rendered on portraits of late 2nd century A.D. empresses Faustina the Younger (Marcus Aurelius) and Lucilla (Lucius Verus); cf. H. A. Grueber, *Roman Medallions in the British Museum* (London 1874) pls. 24, 26; H. Mattingly, E. A. Sydenham, *The Roman Imperial Coinage* III (London 1930) pl. 11, nos. 237, 238; L. M. Lanckoronski, *Das römische Bildnis in Meisterwerken der Münzkunst* (Amsterdam-Basle-Antwerp 1944) XXVII; Grandjouan, *Agora* VI, 15, fig. 1, 16. (Figs. 289, 290.)
T69.4:7939. Head of child with lock of hair. Neck terminates in broken edge. Head slightly turned to proper left. Seam from two-piece molding runs through neck, ears, top of head. Clay micaceous, reddish brown (Munsell 2.5 YR 5/6 "red"). Cream slip over surface. H. 0.054 m.; Th. 0.0012–0.004 m. (Fig. 291.)

A photograph taken in 1914 (Fig. 292)[12] indicates that the wall remains exposed in 1969 already had been exposed in 1914, for the photograph illustrates what can only be the same wall remains viewed from the northwest looking southeast and surrounded by deep trenches. The depth of the trenches suggests that the pithos had also been exposed in 1914, but since the items recovered from it in 1969 clearly indicate it had not been disturbed since antiquity, Butler must not have excavated the earth in the pithos and/or in the space within the angle of the L-shaped wall.

Pre-Hellenistic Stratum

The debris excavated directly west of the L-shaped wall down to a level ca. 0.50 m. below the bedding of the wall (ca. *112.29) evidently had been deposited after 1914. This debris consisted almost entirely of gravel and sand laid in horizontal layers (Fig. 284) containing occasional chunks of stone and mortar (apparently dislodged segments of wall construction), worn pottery fragments of Lydian and fourth century B.C. types, and artifacts of the twentieth century A.D.[13] Torrents of rainwater which had run off the Acropolis slopes through the narrow trench dug by Butler between the building to which the L-shaped wall belonged and the Northeast Stoa to the south of it (Figs.

282, 292) must have been responsible for the deposit of these materials.

The excavated debris, east of and beneath the L-shaped wall remains, down to the level of the pre-Hellenistic pottery deposit (top at *112.50), consisted of soil and small stones with scattered worn pottery remains of pre-Hellenistic and nondescript later types.

In the south side of the trench where debris deposited in antiquity had not been disturbed by torrent water, the top of the uppermost pre-Hellenistic stratum lay ca. 25 to 50 centimeters below the bedding of the Roman wall remains (ca. *112.50–*112.29) and was distinguished by scattered sherds of pre-Hellenistic pottery types, the deposit of artifacts which had inspired excavation, and wall remains preserved *in situ*.

Pre-Hellenistic Walls
The wall remains preserved *in situ* in the uppermost pre-Hellenistic stratum framed small rectilinear and curvilinear spaces. The wall remains were constructed of field stones (quartz, sandstone, and schist or gneiss; maximum size 0.15 m. by 0.30 m. by 0.30–0.35 m.) roughly coursed and apparently laid dry or with mud/clay bonding. (For the location of these walls, see Fig. 283.) Wall units and segments have been designated with letters of the alphabet (lower-case italics in text and plan; upper case Roman in photographs); their features may be summarized as follows:

a circular wall. Proper face on inside only. Int. diam. 1.30–1.33 m.; P.H. 0.82 m.; Th. 0.25 m. (two stone rows). Top at *112.61; bottom at *111.80 (interior space excavated to *111.71). (Fig. 293.)

b straight wall. Orientation NNE-SSW. West face proper; east face vertically and laterally uneven. Both ends concealed beneath trench scarps. Max. P.L. 4.30 m.; max. P.H. 1.03 m.; Th. 0.80–0.95 m. Top at *112.37 to *112.50; bottom at ca. *111.18.

c straight wall. Orientation NNE-SSW. Bonds with *d, e*. Both ends concealed beneath trench scarps. Max. P.L. 5.40 m.; max. P.H. 0.61 m.; Th. 0.60 m. Top at *111.99; bottom at *111.38. (Fig. 294.)

d straight wall. Orientation WNW-ESE. Bonds with *c, f, g*. Abutted by *h, m*. Character of juncture with *b* uncertain. SE part of south face and SE end concealed beneath trench scarp. Max. P.L. 6.5 m.; max. P.H. 0.56–0.57 m. Th. 0.55 m. Top at *112.11; bottom at *111.35–*111.34. (Fig. 295.)

e straight wall. Orientation WNW-ESE. Character of juncture with *c* uncertain. WNW end broken. North side concealed beneath trench scarp. Max. P.L. 2.90 m.; max. exposed Th. 0.55 m.; ca. 1.65 m. distant from juncture with *c,* level of top surface abruptly drops ca. 0.30 m. from max. P.H. of 0.79 m. top at *111.95 to 0.48 m. top at *111.64; bottom at *111.16. (Fig. 296, 294.)

f straight wall. Orientation NNE-SSW. Bonds with *d.* Abutted by *j, k.* Proper face on east side; on west side only by doorway (see *infra*) and at NNE end. NNE end broken. Max. P.L. 3.25 m.; max. P.H. 0.21 m.; max. exposed Th. 0.50 m. Top at *111.42; bottom at *111.21. Contains doorway with cobbled schist threshold 0.36 m. wide; top at *111.11, and jamb footings, each consisting of a single block of coarse sandstone: one 0.32 m. by 0.32 m. by 0.72 m.; the other 0.27 m. by 0.52 m. by 0.58 m.; top at *111.47. (Figs. 296, 297.)

g straight wall. Orientation NNE-SSW. Bonds with *d.* NNE end broken. Max. P.L. 0.35 m.; max. P.H. 0.26 m.; Th. 0.53–0.55 m. Top at *111.47; bottom at *111.21. (Fig. 297.)

h cluster of stones one course deep. Adjacent to north face of *d.* 0.40–0.45 m. N-S by 0.55 m. E-W. Top at *111.21, more or less horizontal, and below bottom stones of *d;* bottom at *111.08. (Fig. 295.)

i straight wall. Orientation NNE-SSW. Bonds with *j.* South end thicker, constructed of larger stones, and bedded higher than north end (at north end, stones accidentally removed during excavation are indicated by dotted line on plan, Fig. 283. Max. P.L. 1.65 m.; max. P.H. 0.62 m.; Th. 0.35 m. (north end), 0.52 m. (south end). Top at ca. *111.37; bottom at *111.16 (south end), *110.75 (north end). (Fig. 297.)

j straight wall. Orientation WNW-ESE. Bonds with *i.* Abuts *f.* Proper face only on north side. Max. P.L. 1.20 m.; max. P.H. 0.66 m.; max. P.Th. 0.30 m. Top at *111.41; bottom at *110.75. (Fig. 297.)

k straight wall. Orientation E-W. Abuts *f.* Proper face only on south side. Max. P.L. 0.40–0.50 m.; max. P.H. 0.69 m.; max. P.Th. 0.30–0.35 m. Top at ca. *111.42; bottom at *110.73. (Fig. 297.)

l cluster of stones. Orientation NNE-SSW. Adjacent to S face of *e.* 0.70 m. E-W by 0.60 m. N-S. Top at ca. *111.32–*111.12, surface uneven and below bottom stones of *e;* bottom at *110.90. (Fig. 294.)

m straight wall. Orientation E-W. Abuts *f.* West end and south side concealed beneath scarps. Max. P.L. 1.10 m.; max. P.H. 0.30 m.; max. exposed Th. 0.45–0.50 m. Top at *111.66; bottom at *111.36. (Fig. 297.)

Pre-Hellenistic Deposit

The only other permanent feature within the stratum of these walls was uncovered in the southeast corner of the trench, somewhat to the east of wall *b.* There (i.e. emerging from the south and east scarps and from the balk supporting the Roman L-shaped wall remains, extending northwards to S 1118.75), bedded at an even horizontal level (ca. *111.42; top at ca. *111.55) some 0.24 m. above

the bottom of wall *b,* lay an assemblage of closely-packed stones, mud bricks, coarse pottery and "bread tray" fragments. This assemblage evidently had been subjected to intense heat, for the stones were flaky and powdery, the bricks very hard and a dark gray color, and the adjacent soil an abnormal orange-red color mixed with carbonized matter.

Hunks of mud brick and/or pisé were detected in the debris adjacent to the juncture of walls *c* and *d.*

Many of the artifacts and other remains recovered from the stratum of debris which lay between the tops and bottoms of the pre-Hellenistic walls were bedded at the same levels. In the oblong space between *b* and *c* north of the S 1117.50 coordinate line, the artifacts and other remains (whose accidental exposure had inspired excavations at NEW) rested at an even level (*112.16) just below the preserved top of *b* at *112.50 (Fig. 299). In the western part of the trench, within coordinates W 114.50–117/S 1113–1116.50, other finds totaling some 16 items rested at an even level some 0.44 m. lower down (*111.72). Of these, some were intermingled with and partly overlaid by scattered stones which evidently had fallen from *c* and/or *e* (Fig. 300); others lay near *d.*

In the northwest corner of the trench, the debris within the area delimited by the broken ends of walls *e, f, i,* and *k* from the level of the tops of these walls to ca. *110.84 was abnormally loose and contained some pottery fragments recovered from the evenly-bedded deposits higher up, at *112.16 and *111.52. The debris which lay between the preserved faces of *j* and *k* consisted largely of ashy material and was disposed in parallel strata which dipped downwards in parabolic curves between the tops of the two walls.

The debris, recovered from the space enclosed by *a* and extending from the top of *a* to a depth of 0.09 m. below the bottom (W 107.50–108.75/S 1114.95–1116.30 *112.80–112.10), contained quantities of pottery fragments. Most of these were of undistinguished coarse or ordinary Lydian types; the more distinctive included parts of a "Rhodian" sub-Geometric oinochoe, a bichrome crater, and a few vessels painted in a Wild Goat style of unusual delicacy. No more than a third of any one pot was retrieved. The debatable pottery seems to belong to the seventh century B.C.

P69.89a:8049. Shoulder fragments of "Rhodian" sub-Geometric oinochoe. Clay reddish beige (Munsell 7.5 YR 7/4 "pink") at outside surface blending to pale gray inside surface. Glaze reddish brown (Munsell 2.5 YR 4/6 "red" to 3/4 "dark reddish brown"). Decorative motives include triple stripes, zigzag fillers, cross-hatched lozenge chains, "Rhodian tree." (Fig. 301.)

P69.90:8050. Neck and upper body fragments of bichrome crater. Clay micaceous, reddish brown (Munsell 5 YR 6/6 "reddish yellow"). Inside, reddish glaze. Outside, cream slip over which decoration in reddish and dark glazes (Munsell 2.5 YR 5/6 "red" to N 3/ "very dark gray"). On rim surface, zigzag line with spaces containing outline triangles. On neck, S chain. On body, rows of concentric circles between bands. H. 0.173 m.; diam. body ca. 0.44 m. (Fig. 302.)

P69.44:7985. Fragments of skyphos-bowl preserving rim and handle stump and decorated in Orientalizing style. Clay micaceous, reddish brown (Munsell 5 YR 6/6 "reddish yellow") blending slightly to brown at core. Inside, reddish brown to sepia glaze (Munsell 2.5 YR 4/4 "reddish brown" to N 3/ "very dark gray") removed (by a stylus while the glaze still was wet?) to introduce seven narrow bands (or single spiral band of seven turns). Outside, cream-yellow slip (Munsell 10 YR 8/3 "very pale brown" to 8/6 and 7/6 "yellow") over which decoration in glaze ranging from sepia to soft brown (Munsell 10 YR 3/1 "very dark gray" to 7.5 YR 5/6 "strong brown"). Handle stump glazed, ringed with bands and row of buds. Bowl divided by plain bands into three zones. In upper zone, grazing deer, cross and dot filling ornament. In middle zone, grazing goats, cross and dot, circle and dot, pendant lotus flower filling ornament. In bottom zone, chain of lotus flowers. P.H. 0.051 m.; est. diam. rim 0.11 m.; Th. 0.0025–0.0045 m. (Fig. 303.)

P69.48:7989. Fragments of vessel with flat rim (lebes?) and Orientalizing decoration. Clay micaceous, friable, reddish brown (Munsell 5 YR 6/3 "light reddish brown"). Outside, cream slip (Munsell 10 YR 7/4 "very pale brown") over which decoration in glaze ranging from sepia to reddish brown (Munsell 10 YR 3/1 "very dark gray" to 2.5 YR 5/6 "red"). On rim, chain of lotus flowers. On body fragment (outside surface only surviving), chain of lotus flowers (whose border apparently is greater in diameter than the rim) below which a zone displaying complex geometric and floral motive, long-necked bird with head reversed, and pendant hooks and triangle, swastika filling ornament. Est. diam. rim 0.38 m.; Th. rim 0.0032–0.0058 m.; L. body fragment 0.107 m. (Fig. 304.)

P69.88:8048. Rim fragment of dish with Orientalizing decoration. Clay micaceous, reddish brown (Munsell 2.5 YR 5/6 "red"). Inside and out, beige slip (Munsell 5 YR 6/6 "reddish yellow") over which decoration in reddish brown glaze (Munsell 2.5 YR 4/6 "red") and purplish-sepia paint (Munsell 5 YR 3/1 "very dark gray"). Inside, metope stripes and crosses, lozenge motive (rim surface), bands (rim-to-bowl), rays (? - tip preserved; tondo). Outside, tongues (rim) bands (rim edge, bowl). Est. diam. 0.40 m.; P.L. 0.09 m.; Th. 0.007–0.0085 m. (Fig. 305.)

The deposit exposed between *b* and *c* and bedded at the same even level *112.16 contained remnants of at least 48 vessels. Among these some 13 different shapes were represented, including the amphora, hydria, oinochoe, jug, lekythos, lydion, column crater, casserole, skyphos, dish, omphalos phiale, stand, and "bread tray"; and several distinctive fabrics: cooking ware, and wares decorated with wavy-line, streakily-glazed, marbled, and Wild Goat style painting. Intermingled with these pottery remains were a spindle whorl, a thin rod of bronze, a corroded lump of iron, and bones of *bos, capra,* and *ovis.* Several of these bones had belonged to immature animals and exhibited cuts and breaks which indicated that the animals had been butchered. (Figs. 306, 299.)[14]

P69.71:8025. Shoulder and body fragments of large amphora ("Myrina"-type shape) with Orientalizing decoration. Clay micaceous, reddish brown (Munsell 2.5 YR 5/6 "red"). Outside, cream slip (Munsell 10 YR 8/3 "very pale brown") over which decoration in sepia-greenish brown-orange brown glaze (Munsell 7.5 YR N 3/ "very dark gray", 10 YR 4/3 "dark brown", 2.5 YR 4/6 "red") and purple brown paint (Munsell 10 R 4/1 "dark reddish gray"). Surface abraded in places (slip worn, glaze flaked). Three decorative zones. In upper, two confronted sphinxes *passant,* and swastikas, rosette, pendent, and ascendent triangles filling ornament. In middle, animal and grazing goat (two grazing goats?) confronted, sphinx *passant,* grazing goat and S-motive, lotus flower and other filling ornament. In lower, loop and tongue chain. Est. max. diam. ca. 0.68 m.; est. diam. neck at base 0.27–0.29 m.; P.H. ca. 0.36 m.; Th. 0.0125–0.015 m. (Scattered W 110.60–116.70 /S 1114.50–1116.40 *112.50–112.16). (Fig. 307.)

P69.54:8002. Lower body fragment of large closed vessel with Orientalizing decoration. Clay micaceous, reddish beige to pale gray (Munsell 5 YR 6/6 "reddish yellow" to 7.5 YR 6/2 "pinkish gray"). Outside, cream slip (Munsell 10 YR 8/2 "white") over which decoration in glaze ranging from sepia to orange yellow (Munsell 7.5 YR N 3/ "very dark gray" to 2.5 YR 4/8 "red" and 7.5 YR 7/8 "reddish yellow"). Two decorative zones and band below. In upper, hoofed animal and rosette filling ornament. In lower, spiral motive (repeated?). Max. P.L. 0.27 m.; max. P.H. 0.26 m.; Th. 0.013–0.028 m. (W 110.60–111.40 /S 1115–1116.70 *112.29–112.18).

P69.58.8006. Round-mouth oinochoe. Clay reddish brown. Inside neck and outside, streakily-applied brown-to-sepia glaze over which decoration in white paint as follows: tongues at the top of the shoulder; pairs of narrow bands on lower shoulder, belly; single band at juncture of body and foot. H. 0.216 m.; diam. body 0.33 m. (W 111.25–112.40 /S 1116.10–1117.20 *112.50–112.31). (Fig. 308.)

P69.82:8041 (partly NoEx69.19). Lydion. Clay micaceous, friable, reddish beige (Munsell 2.5 YR 6/6 "light red"). Outside, cream slip over which decoration in glaze ranging from brown to reddish brown (Munsell 5 YR 3/1 "very dark gray" and 5 YR 4/2 "dark reddish gray" to 2.5 YR 4/8 "red"). Streaky glaze inside neck, on lip and outside on neck, lower body, and foot. Narrow banding on shoulder. H. 0.191 m.; max. diam. ca. 0.15 m. (W 110.60–

111.40/S 1115.00–1116.70 *112.29–112.18). (Fig. 309).

P69.59:8007. Large ribbed lydion. Clay micaceous, tan (Munsell 5 YR 6/6 "reddish yellow"). Inside neck and outside, glaze evenly or streakily applied and ranging from sepia to orange brown (Munsell 10 YR 3/1 "very dark gray" to 2.5 YR 5/6 "red"). H. 0.191 m.; est. max. diam. 0.176 m. (W 110.60–111.40 /S 1115.00–1116.70 *112.29–112.18).

P69.56:8004. Column crater. Clay micaceous, tan (Munsell 5 YR 6/6 "reddish yellow"). Inside and outside, streakily-applied glaze ranging from sepia to orange brown (Munsell 5 YR 3/2 "dark reddish brown" to 2.5 YR 5/6 "red") over which decoration in white paint: narrow bands on rim surface and shoulder, groups of three metope stripes on rim edge, row of dots at base of neck. Est. H. 0.227 m.; est. max. diam. rim 0.283 m.; diam. mouth inside at top 0.24 m. (W 110.60–112.40 /S 1115–1117.20 *112.50–112.16). (Fig. 310.)

P69.60:8008. Column crater. Inside and outside, streakily-applied glaze ranging from sepia to reddish brown, over which decoration in white paint as follows: on neck, spaced solid rectangles; at foot of neck, row of dots; on body, more or less evenly spaced, four narrow bands; on shoulder-belly, three irregular lines. H. 0.259 m.; diam. body ca. 0.35 m. (W 110.60–112.40 /S 1115–1116.70 *112.29–112.18).

P69.57:8005. Stand. Outflaring top and bottom, cylindrical stem with ridges at top, middle, bottom. Clay orange-beige outside blending to gray-beige at core (Munsell 5 YR 6/6 "reddish yellow" to 10 YR 6/2 "light brownish gray"). Inside, except for midpoint, and outside, light reddish brown glaze (Munsell 2.5 YR 5/8 "red"). H. 0.19 m.; diam. top and bottom at upper edge 0.16 m. (W 110.60–112.40 /S 1115–1117.20 *112.50–112.16). (Fig. 311.)

The artifacts exposed near *d* and *e* and bedded at another even level (*111.72) included some eleven complete and fragmentary vessels among whose shapes were the amphora, omphalos phiale, column crater, lydion, lekythos, and flask, and whose decoration included bichrome, marbled, and Wild Goat style painting; also two open lamps, two round disks of schist (evidently amphora or pithos lids), and a saddle quern.

L69.7:7991. Open lamp with omphalos. Complete except for small chips off rim. H. 0.025 m.; Diam. 0.083 m. (W 114.90/S 1113.40–1113.50 *111.62). (Fig. 312.)

P69.28:7960. Lower shoulder and body fragments of very large closed vessel with Orientalizing decoration (from same vessel as next item?). Clay micaceous, reddish brown outside blending to gray beige at core blending to orange beige inside (Munsell 2.5 YR 5/6 "red" to 10 YR 6/3 "pale brown" to 5 YR 6/6 "reddish yellow"). Outside, cream slip (Munsell 10 YR 8/3 "very pale brown") over which decoration in orange red glaze (Munsell 10 R 5/8 "red") ranging to orange yellow where dilute. Two zones of decoration with two border bands between. In upper, hind foot of animal (leg solid glaze, foot outline and reserve with spots) and swastika filling ornament. In lower, two grazing goats (to r.) and complex lozenge-"Rhodian Tree" filling ornament. P.L. 0.17 m.; P.H. 0.29 m.; Th. 0.0085–0.0245 m. (W 114.50–114.60/S 1115–1115.20 *111.73). (Fig. 313.)

P69.55:8003. Mid-body fragments of very large closed

vessel with Orientalizing decoration (from same vessel as previous item?). Clay as in previous item. Outside, white cream slip over which decoration in glaze, mostly orange brown but in places black and dark brown or yellow brown (Munsell 2.5 YR 5/8 "red"; 2.5 YR N/2.5 "black"; 7.5 YR 3/2 "dark brown"; 5 YR 5/8 "yellowish red"). Zone of decoration (below which either another zone preserving top of animal back or uneven band?) showing grazing billy goat (to r.) and swastika and pendent and ascendent palmette filling ornament. P.L. 0.28 m.; P.H. 0.23 m.; Th. 0.012–0.023 m. (W 113.70–114/S 1114.50–1114.71 *111.72). (Fig. 314.)

P69.73:8027. Mid-body fragments of very large closed vessel with Orientalizing decoration. Clay micaceous, orange beige (Munsell 5 YR 6/6 "reddish yellow"). Outside, white cream slip over which decoration in glaze ranging from dark brown to orange brown to green sepia (Munsell 7.5 YR 3/2 "dark brown" to 2.5 YR 4/8 "red" to 2.5 Y 4/4 "olive brown"). Two zones of decoration with two border bands between. In upper, two shrubs flanked by human feet (outline and reserve) confronted. In lower, back of animal (?) and swastika filling ornament. P.L. 0.275 m.; P.H. 0.155 m.; Th. 0.0087–0.0135 m. (W 114.80–115.70 /S 1114.70–1115.90 *111.72–110.84). (Fig. 315.)

P69.76(A-K):8030. Neck and shoulder fragments of very large amphora with Orientalizing decoration. Shelf rim with inner ridge on top. Clay micaceous, reddish tan (Munsell 5 YR 6/6 "reddish yellow"). Outside, cream slip (Munsell 10 YR 8/2 "white") over which decoration in glaze ranging from black to orange brown (Munsell 5 YR 2.5/2 "dark reddish brown" to 2.5 YR 4/8 "red"). On rim edge, metope stripes. On neck, guilloche. On shoulder, zone with rosette-star in frame, bovine animal and swastika, pendent palmette, and cross-and-chevron filling ornament. H. neck ca. 0.22 m.; Th. rim edge 0.0012 m. (scattered fragments; W 114.30–117.70/S 1112.50–1115 *111.72–110.82. (Fig. 316.)

P69.47:7988. Fragment of marbled omphalos phiale. Clay slightly micaceous, reddish brown at exterior blending to gray brown at core (Munsell 2.5 YR 4/4 "reddish brown" to 7.5 YR 4/2 "dark brown"). Inside and outside, cream slip over which continuous band marbling in glaze ranging from sepia to orange (Munsell 10 YR 2.5/1 "black" to 10 R 4/8 "red"). Max. P. diam. 0.14 m.; diam. omphalos inside 0.043 m.; H. 0.027 m. (W 115.00–115.50/S 1115–1116 *111.12). (Fig. 317.)

The pottery remains which were irregularly distributed in the debris between the tops and bottoms of the pre-Hellenistic walls included a few fragments of Wild Goat style, Chiot, and Corinthian wares.

P69.53:8001. Fragment of closed vessel decorated in Orientalizing style. Clay slightly micaceous, reddish-brown (Munsell 2.5 YR 5/6 "red"). Outside, beige slip (Munsell 10 YR 7/4 "very pale brown") over which decoration in dark reddish brown glaze (Munsell 2.5 YR 3/4 "dark reddish brown"). Running goat and lobed cross, swastika, rosette (?) filling ornament; top of lower border. P.L. 0.047 m.; Th. 0.0045–0.005 m. (W 115.50–115.70/S 1113.30 *112.07). (Fig. 318.)

P69.84:8043. Bowl center fragment of Chiot chalice. Clay beige (Munsell 7.5 YR 6/4 "light brown"). Inside, sepia glaze (Munsell 5 YR 2.5/2 "dark reddish brown") over which decoration in red (Munsell 2.5 YR 4/4 "reddish brown") and white paint. Two white bands encircling rosette with alternating red and white petals. Outside, white slip over which decoration in glaze, ranging from dark brown to orange (Munsell 5 YR 2.5/2 "dark reddish brown" to 5 YR 6/6 "reddish yellow"). Max. diam. 0.035 m.; Th. 0.003–0.0065 m. (W 115–116.60/S 1112.70–1116 *110.84–110.74). (Fig. 319.)

Interpretation of Architectural Remains

The pre-Hellenistic architectural remains of Sector NEW (Figs. 283, 285, 294) have certain elements of construction and design in common with pre-Hellenistic architectural remains uncovered in sectors HoB and PN. As at HoB and PN, the lower parts of NEW walls were built of unworked or very roughly dressed fieldstones, laid in uneven courses and with proportionally large stones in the lowest courses. Hunks of mud brick and/or pisé detected in the debris near the juncture of walls c and d indicate that these materials had been employed in the upper parts of the walls, as at HoB and PN (where mud brick and pisé remains resting *in situ* on stone socles have been uncovered).[15] The circular wall a, with its solitary inside face and diameter of ca. 0.30 m. (Fig. 293), and the small rectangular wall complex f-i-j-k, with its solitary inside face penetrating to a level appreciably lower than other nearby walls (Fig. 297), each resembles one or more structures uncovered at PN.[16] The construction of these walls indicates that their surviving parts were designed to rest below ground level; their form and size suggest that they were used for storage (the considerable amount of pottery retrieved from the space surrounded by a probably arrived there as refuse; for the assemblage consisted of very improbable items, with a chronological range of 25–50 years).[17]

It is tempting to imagine that the missing segments of e and f joined and that these walls together with c and d enclosed a trapezoidal room or court (measuring ca. 3.50–4.00 m. by 4.30–4.50 m.); and that the abrupt change in the level of the top surface of wall e indicates the existence of a doorway at the lower level (Fig. 296).

Since g bonds with d and appears to have been rendered obsolete by f and j, it is conceivable that d at one time extended westward only so far as g and that g (rather than f) limited the space to the

north of d. Had this been the case, however, the subsequent extension of d ought to have joined the earlier segment in a butt joint; and such a joint was not detected in the wall remains.

The irregular disposition of stones in l (Fig. 296) and the solitary course of stones in h (Fig. 295) suggest that neither l nor h were parts of walls. Their position beneath the bottom stones of e and d suggests that their deposit antedates that of e and d. Further speculations about the relationship of the walls based solely on their remains involves too many uncertain factors to be worthwhile.

The threshold of the doorway in f and the disposition of artifacts in some of the intramural spaces attest the level and partial location of at least two occupational surfaces contemporary with the pre-Hellenistic walls. The absence of any vestige of these surfaces suggests that, as in the pre-Hellenistic settlement areas at HoB and PN, these surfaces consisted of trampled earth which would readily disintegrate without leaving a trace.

The numerous artifacts deposited at horizontal levels between b and c and near d and e (Figs. 299, 306, 309, 311) must have rested on surfaces which existed at these levels (i.e. *112.16 and *111.72); the similarity of the artifacts recovered at both levels suggests their contemporaneity and that of the surface on which they rested.

Other evidence indicates the location of surfaces at lower levels, near the bottoms of the walls.[18] The threshold of the doorway in f (cobbled surface at *111.11) indicates that a surface existed west of f near the bottom of its west face (and some 0.60 m. below the surface supporting the artifacts near walls d and e); and the deeper beddings of wall f east face and walls i, j, and k relative to that of f west face indicate that the surface of the space bounded by f-i-j-k lay appreciably lower—perhaps by as much as 0.60 m.—than the surface west of f (i.e., possibly as low as *110.73, the highest level at which any of those four walls were bedded). These two surfaces located west of f and within unit f-i-j-k, linked as they were by the doorway in f, would have been contemporary.

The assemblage of burnt brick, stones, and pottery in the southeast corner of the trench, east of b (top at ca. *111.55), was bedded at an even level (ca. *111.42), which suggests that the deposit rested on a surface. Such a surface must have preceded the construction of wall *a*, for the absence in wall *a* of an outer face indicates that the level of the outside surface contemporary with *a* was no lower than the wall top (*112.62), at least one meter above the burnt materials in the southeast corner of the trench.

At least two consecutive surfaces, then, are to be associated with the pre-Hellenistic walls: with the earlier surface or surfaces may be associated the threshold in the doorway of *f*, the hypothetical doorway in *e*, and the deposit of burnt materials in the southeast corner of the trench; with the later, the horizontally-bedded artifacts between *b* and *c* and near *d* and *e;* and perhaps wall *a*. If two consecutive surfaces only existed, they would indicate that ancient ground level in the immediate area inclined downward gently from east to west, as does the surface of the terrain at present.[19]

There is very little evidence to suggest whether the spaces between and near the walls at any one period were roofed or open to the sky. Wall *b* probably was the outer wall of a roofed building, for it is appreciably thicker than the interior walls and courtyard walls of pre-Hellenistic buildings exposed in sectors HoB and PN; which of the lateral spaces was roofed, however, and which was open is not easily determined. The narrow space between *b* and *c* might have been an outdoor cul-de-sac between two property units (which shared a common south wall, *d*),[20] or it might have been a closet-like room near the outside wall of a building. The remains exposed in NEW might belong to one or more property units.

The general character of the pottery, considered together with the quern and bones of slaughtered flock and herd animals recovered from the later pre-Hellenistic surface levels, and the total absence of objects in sets and of votive character suggest that the pre-Hellenistic complex served secular and domestic purposes rather than religious and commercial ones.[21] The shapes and decoration of the pottery suggest that the complex functioned in the latter part of the seventh and the earlier part of the sixth centuries B.C.[22]

The spaces between the pre-Hellenistic walls were excavated to levels 0.10 m. to 0.80 m. below the wall bottoms (east of *b* to *111.27; between *c* and *b* to *111.12; within the space framed by *c-d-h-i-j-k-e*, *110.43 to *110.75; within the space framed by *d-f-j-i*, ca. *110.82; west of *f*, to *111.02 to *110.92). Directly west of *c*, a small trial pit was dug to a depth of nearly two meters below the bottom of *c* in an attempt to reach the pre-seventh/ sixth century levels located in 1914 somewhat further to the east of NEW main trench (trial pit 1.50 m. by 2.00 m., located in coordinates W 112.75–115.00/S 1115.70–1117.75, *110.47 to *109.30).

Neither architectural remains nor floor surfaces were recognized in these lower depths. Pottery fragments of undistinguished appearance were recovered sporadically throughout the earthy debris as far down as the bottom of the pit. Hunks of mud brick lay higgledy-piggledy underneath *c* and *e* at their juncture (Fig. 284).

Two distinct strata were detected below the wall remains. The upper stratum was a lens of gravel and sand, recognized in the south part of the trench under *d*, *i*, and *j* (in coordinates W 114.70–116.50/S 1115.20–1117.80). From a maximum thickness of 0.45 m. bedded at ca. *110.65 at the east end, the lens narrowed and inclined to 0.10 m. bedded at *110.57 at the west. This stratum evidently was part of a water-laid torrent or flood deposit. The lower stratum was detected in the trial pit; it consisted of contiguous lenses of greenish-coloured earth, carbonized matter, and sand which inclined slightly from *110.01 at the east end to *109.87 at the west. These lenses were interrupted at the southeast corner of the pit by an intrusion consisting mainly of sand and an intermediate lens of clay (Fig. 284).

CHG

KÂGIRLIK TEPE CEMETERY

The small, flat-topped hill of Kâgirlik Tepe ("stone" or "masonry" hill) was sounded in 1958 in the hopes that early Lydian remains would be found there. Instead, a small Roman cemetery was discovered of which thirteen graves were wholly or partially excavated, here designated 58.A-M (Fig. 320).[23] Kâgirlik Tepe is located ca. 200 m. to the northeast of the Artemis Temple (E 38-50 /S 1071-1082; Fig. 1 No. 19); a benchmark on the top of the hill is at level *188.99 a.s.l. A stepped trench 13.0 × 3.5 m. was opened running down the sloping western side with its top at the western scarp of the hill (Figs. 321, 322).

The graves were of several different types: three (four?) were rectangular graves with brick linings and covered with slabs (Graves 58.A, B, H, F?); three were of tiles arranged to form a triangular shelter (D, E, G); one was placed in the earth with no built grave structure at all (C); and the others were too disturbed to determine the original type (I, J, K, L, M).

All of the tombs opened in this cemetery were disturbed by robbers and water seepage and hence yielded very scant finds. Only two datable objects were found, in Grave 58.H: a glass bottle (G58.14: 420; Fig. 328), second to fourth centuries A.D., and a Roman lamp (L58.35:784; Fig. 327), late first to second centuries A.D. The likelihood is, then, that the cemetery as a whole dates somewhere in the range from the first to fourth centuries A.D.[24]

At first, an area ca. 4 m. × 3 m. was opened, beginning with the west edge of the hill at the crest of the terrace or flat top of the hill and running eastward and downward. The first burial was encountered ca. 60 cm. below the surface in the northwest corner of the trench. The grave was very shallow with the top of the skull ca. 46 cm. below the surface.

Throughout the area of the trench were found scattered bits of "lime mortar" and small pieces of bone. At a depth of about 1.0 m. from datum (*187.99) was an extremely hard layer of earth containing a white limey substance and spreading out throughout the trench. The hard dirt layer was quite thick but did not constitute a floor or wall. Occasional small concretions of pebbles and sand were found in its makeup. The layer was quite sterile archaeologically, containing no sherds or other artifacts. The layer is believed to be a sort of hardpan formation caused by the leaching out of lime deposits in the soil through

the action of water. At the end of the season, the trench was filled in, in accordance with an agreement with the land owner.

Description of Graves

Grave 58.A. Grave 58.A was located in the northeast corner of the trench at levels *188.35-187.89 (0.64-1.10 m. below datum). Only the corner of a large flat schist stone with its edge cutting diagonally across the northeast corner of the trench was exposed. A second, smaller stone leaned against the edge of the first stone in a vertical position. A considerable number of tiny pieces of lime-like substance were found scattered through the earth associated with this grave and with Graves 58.B and 58.C. This may have been the result of break-up of the hard layer described above. No objects or pottery were found in association with this grave.

Grave 58.B. Grave 58.B was located in the southeast corner of the trench at levels *188.29-187.83 (0.70-1.16 m. below datum). It was built of bricks. As with Grave 58.A, only a large flat lid stone with its edge cutting across the southeast corner of the trench was exposed. A very small stone leaned vertically against the flat slab close to the southernmost edge of the stone. No pottery or objects were found with this grave (Fig. 323).

Grave 58.C. Grave 58.C was found at the eastern edge of the trench between Graves 58.A and 58.B at level *188.39 a.s.l. (0.60 m. below datum). It consisted of a "surface burial" with the remains of a skeleton, head to northeast, apparently put directly into the ground with no casket or specially built tomb. Some of the bones were lying on the flat stone of Grave 58.B. The skull was broken by the pick and the rest of the skeleton was incomplete. An unsuccessful attempt to lift the bones was made. No pottery or objects were found with the burial.

Grave 58.D. Grave 58.D was located on the north side of the trench at levels *188.13-187.91 a.s.l. (0.86-1.08 m. below datum). Grave 58.D was a caved-in tile grave. It was ca. 0.65 m. wide and 1.20 m. long as far as excavated. As it ran outside the excavated area its full length was not determined (Fig. 324).

Grave 58.E. Grave 58.E was on the south side of

the trench opposite Grave 58.D and about 2.15 m. from the southeast corner of the trench. It was a tile grave at levels *188.17–188.03 a.s.l. (0.82–0.98 m. below datum). Grave 58.E extended mostly beyond the excavated area. Two of its tiles were exposed, set diagonally against each other to form a little "gable" of triangular section. Fragments of a skull were found beneath the two exposed tiles of 58.E.

Grave 58.F. Grave 58.F was found on the north side of the trench west of 58.D at levels *187.99–187.39 a.s.l. (1.00 to 1.60 m. below datum). Only the corner of the grave was exposed. It was apparently constructed of bricks and cement like Grave 58.H. The top of the grave was covered with a flat stone, 0.08 m. thick. Its top was at about 1.10 m. below datum.

Grave 58.G. Grave 58.G appeared along the south edge of the trench at level *187.79–187.54 a.s.l. (1.20–1.45 m. below datum). This grave consisted of two flat pan tiles set against each other to form a "gabled" triangular shelter like Grave 58.E. The head of the tomb was covered with a third piece of tile. The end of the tomb was destroyed when the area was disturbed in antiquity. As found, its dimensions were 0.60 m. long, ca. 0.25 m. high. No bones were found when the preserved end was cleaned (Fig. 325, left).

Grave 58.H. Grave 58.H was the only one of the brick built graves which was fully excavated. It was thought at first that the grave was undisturbed, but it too proved to have been opened. It was located against the southern part of the trench at its western end at levels *187.15–186.46 a.s.l. (1.84–2.53 m. below datum). The dimensions of 58.H were 1.40 m. × 2.50 m. outside, 0.70 × 1.85 m. inside. The top of the grave was covered with small tile pieces which were most likely the remains of a later tile grave. Grave 58.H itself was covered with three large cap slabs of chlorite schist (Fig. 325). The cover slabs sealed the inner cavity and were set with lime mortar on top of the brick walls of the tomb. The tomb walls were formed of seven courses of brick, 32 × 32 cm. or 34 × 34 cm., Th, ca. 4 cm., set in thickly laid mortar (Fig. 326). The grave had been opened and filled in with drifted earth containing sherds and other objects. Other

Roman tombs of this type were found in the cemetery area west of the House of Bronzes in 1959.[25]

The skeleton was incomplete and in poor condition. Bones were powdery and impossible to clean. The earth in the tomb was full of fragments of bone. The main concentration of bone, however, was in the eastern section of the tomb.

Several objects and pieces of pottery were found in this grave, among which were a glass bottle (Fig. 328) dated to the second to fourth centuries A.D. and found at a depth of 0.32 m. from the top of the tomb.[26] Some fragments of white glass, a Roman lamp handle datable to the late first or second century A.D. (Fig. 327), and some sherds of Roman relief ware (Fig. 329) were also found inside this tomb.

Grave 58.I. Grave 58.I was in the western part of the trench just north of Grave 58.H, 6.90 m. from the eastern end. Its level was *187.05 a.s.l. (1.94 m. below datum). Several bones, a skull, and a few sherds make up the remains of this very disturbed burial. A single brick with some lime plaster adhering, 0.36 × 0.17 × 0.05 m., was found to the north of the skull, 1.50 m. below datum. Beneath the brick was one long bone, possibly also belonging to the grave. A fragment of a ledge rim from a "poor glaze" red ware crater (P58.486:788) was found associated with the skull of Grave 58.I. This would be normally dated not later than Early Hellenistic and the fragment may be intrusive.

Grave 58.J. Grave 58.J was located near the south side of the trench, west of burials 58.E and 58.K. It was found at level *187.76 (1.23 m. below datum) and consisted only of a few bones and a fragment of glass.

Grave 58.K. Grave 58.K was directly east of Grave 58.E and very close to it at level *188.04 a.s.l. (0.95 m. below datum). All that remained were some disturbed bones and a bronze finger ring with the gem missing (Fig. 330), diam. 0.019 m.

Grave 58.L. Grave 58.L appeared in plan (Fig. 321) just to the west of Grave 58.A on the north side of the trench at level *187.89–187.54 (1.10–1.45 m. below datum). It was a tile grave similar to Grave 58.E in construction.

Grave 58.M. Grave 58.M is shown in plan just

to the west of Grave 58.H on the south side of the trench (Fig. 321). It was found at level *186.81 (2.18 m. below datum). The grave was not excavated by the expedition.

Finds

The skeletal material was poorly preserved and some was lost in attempt to lift it. Bones from Graves I, J, K were shipped in 1958 to Professor M. Şenyürek, Institute of Palaeoanthropology, Ankara, but no report was received.

The following pottery and objects were found in clear association with Kâgirlik Tepe burials and are useful for dating purposes.

Lamp
L58.35:784. Inside Grave 58.H. Fragment of handle and attached fragment of rim. W. 0.023 m.; W. body 0.038 m.; H. 0.0355 m. Powdery orange clay with white slip over which was an orange slip. Flat rim with triple groove. High handle, twice grooved in front. Cf. Perlzweig, *Agora VII*, 88, no. 176, pl. 6 dated second half first to early second century A.D.; for the red on white fabric, p. 5 f. (Fig. 327.)

Glass
G58.14:420. Inside Grave H. Flask, almost complete. H. 0.115 m.; diam. rim 0.03 m.; L. neck from rim to shoulder 0.045 m. Approx. diam. of body 0.08 m. One side of body injured in excavation. A. Von Saldern (letter February 1974) dates second-third century A.D. citing D. Barag, "Glass Vessels of the Roman and Byzantine Periods in Palestine," (diss., Jerusalem 1970) pls. 4 f. Cf. Hanfmann, "Glass," 53 n. 12; *BASOR* 154, 13 n. 21; O. Vessberg, *OpusArch* 7 (1952) 131 f., pl. 7:12. (Fig. 328.)

Pottery
P58.484:786. Inside Grave H. Fragment of relief ware, L. 0.023 m. Buff fabric interior encrusted. Exterior: relief palmette and horizontal relief bar. Roman. (Fig. 329.)

Metal
M58.58:767. Grave 58.K, associated with bones. Small bronze finger ring, diam. 0.019 m. Narrow band expands upward to hollow, oval bezel. Gem missing. Cf. F. H. Marshall, *Catalogue of the Finger Rings, Greek, Etruscan, and Roman, in the Department of Antiquities, British Museum* (London 1907) pl. XXXII, nos. 1310, 1320, 1373 for shape; p. xlvi for shape in period first century B.C. to second century A.D. See also M. Almagro, *Las Necropolis de Ampurias* II (Barcelona 1955) pl. X.13 and p. 150 no. 2 for shape in gold. Late first century A.D. (Fig. 330).

JCW

IX THE ROMAN BATH CG: SITE, PLAN, AND DESCRIPTION

Jane C. Waldbaum
George M. A. Hanfmann

The building known as CG lies in the plain north of the foot of the Acropolis and east of the easternmost sections of the Byzantine city wall. It is thus the farthest to the east of the visible monuments of Sardis and the easternmost sector excavated by the Sardis Expedition (Figs. 1, 331, 335).[1]

Butler originally thought that the building was the remains of a city gate of Roman or earlier date.[2] His plan[3] shows two parallel walls and part of a third wall to the north directly in line with the Byzantine city wall. His Plan I puts it slightly to the east of the wall. He did not excavate or describe the remains of the building in detail: "Here there are considerable remains showing dressed stones and other signs of a great city gate, and it is not improbable that the old Royal Road passed out at this point. A thorough investigation here might reveal a defended gate of the Roman period or perhaps even earlier; for, as yet, we have no means of knowing if the Hellenistic and Lydian city extended thus far on this side of the Acropolis."[4]

More accurate surveying on the part of the present expedition has shown the building to be misplaced on Butler's original plan, although it was somewhat more correctly placed on his Plan I. The building was found to lie not on the line of the Byzantine city wall as shown in Butler's drawing but well outside and ca. 260 m. to the east of it. It was probably built at a time when the present

wall did not exist. Like the Pactolus North area it was maintained during the Early Byzantine era when it was extramural (Fig. 335).

In 1958, investigation of this structure was begun by the Harvard-Cornell Expedition with the purpose of testing Butler's theory. In the course of three years' initial excavation at this site (1958–1960) with some renewed activity in 1969, the building was found to have been not a gate, but rather a bath of the Roman–Early Byzantine period.[5]

Visible before excavation of structure CG in 1958 were two parallel walls of large limestone ashlar masonry of which four courses of the eastern wall were exposed to a height of 3.50 m. above the surface of the ground for a length of ca. 25 m. (Fig. 331). The distance between the two walls at that level was ca. 14 m. A brook flowed northward along the east side of the eastern wall carrying large volumes of water (except in summer) and clayey deposits, and huge masonry blocks had fallen in wild cascades along the face of the eastern wall.

Structure CG had been noted and sketched by several European travelers of the eighteenth and nineteenth centuries. A plan (Fig. 332) from de Peyssonel, pl. XI, seems to show the essential features of CG, with its parallel east and west walls as well as a circular unit and two more walls to the north. The description which accompanies the plan also seems plausible for CG: the remains of a great building which "... Mr. Smith took for the Cathedral Church, I do not know on what evidence, because I saw nothing that would be characteristic of a Christian Church ... The building is of stones of enormous size. It runs from north to south, with the door to the south. There is a great arch of enormous simplicity, entirely without architectural ornament ... A cornice runs along the building, both inside and out, and the space within the walls is filled with stones of the same size as the standing walls. This proves the walls must have been much higher. As they stand now, the walls are fifteen or sixteen feet high. Near the northern ends the side walls of the building are cut by two little oval towers, whose remains still exist. I cannot imagine for what use they were built, and I do not venture to conjecture what this old building was."[6] De Peyssonel's illustrations and description are suggestive of CG as outlined by recent excavation, although there are certain problematic features in his observations. His plan is similar to Butler's illustration 18, although de Peyssonel's inclusion of the "oval towers" indicates that more of the structure was visible in his time.

A drawing by E. Landron for the traveler Ph. Le Bas in the 1840's[7] seems to show the east side of CG somewhat better preserved than at present and crowned with a kind of attic above the piers (Fig. 333). It appears at that time submerged nearly to the top in a lake along the east side, showing that the building was at times almost entirely flooded.

Bath CG appears on the main Sardis B grid between E 1405–1485/N 330–200; the present surface level is ca. *104–105 m. a.s.l. (Figs. 1, 335). A grid relating only to CG was established in the 1959 season with the southwest corner of the eastern wall CGE as the zero point.[8] An arbitrary datum line of *100 was established at a point on the top of the impost course (spring profile) of the eastern face of CGE. Elsewhere this area varies from *99.89 to *99.98 (a.s.l. ca. *99.34).[9]

The Plan of CG

As excavated, the plan of building CG appears as a complex of large rectangular halls of varying dimensions and proportions broken on the east by a round room adjoining a narrow corridor and a smaller squarish room (Fig. 336).

Hall CGC

The main space excavated in the complex consists of the great hall CGC oriented north-south and with its massive eastern and western walls (CGE, CGW) built of large limestone masonry blocks and articulated by a system of arches and half-domes. The north and south ends of the hall were delimited by thinner screen walls pierced by arched entranceways (Figs. 337, 343, 344, 365, 371).

Walls CGE and CGW

The eastern wall of the main hall, CGE, extends from N/S 0 on the local grid to ca. N 31.5 on the west side; and from ca. E 1 to E 6.40, not counting projections of piers and profiles. It is thus 31.5 m. long and about 5.40 m. wide without piers, 6.75 m. wide with piers. At the northern end the ashlar masonry of wall CGE curves into the southwestern part of circular Hall HM bonding in with the rubble masonry of which the rest of this circular unit is constructed.

The east side of wall CGE, presumably the eastern facade of the building in its main phase, displays five piers, numbered 0–4, projecting eastward beyond the face of the wall with four arched recesses between them. The southernmost of these, TE, is in fact, a barrel-vaulted "tunnel" with a "blind" west end; three—SCE, MAE, NCE—communicate through doors with recesses SCW, MAW, NCW on the interior of the hall. On the analogous western face of CGW, the tops of five similar piers, the vaulted tunnel TW, and the upper portions of three other arches were exposed. Two large piers project to the south on the southeast and southwest corners of both CGE and CGW (Figs. 334, 336).

Not counting the projection of the corner piers, CGW extends between grid points W 15.20 and 20.30 (southern end) and W 15.40 to 20.75 (northern end), and ca. N 0 to N 28.40 in the north-south direction. Including platform N, the northern boundary of CGW is N 31.60. The wall is thus ca. 5.25 m. wide without piers, 8.05 m. wide with piers and projecting profiles, and 31.50 m. long. Its northern face aligns approximately with the limits of the southern half of circular unit HM. Northward, CGW continues into rubble wall CPW–1; southward, a wall is known to exist beyond wall SpS.

The highest masonry preserved lies between N 4 and N 11.50 on CGW, rising over that stretch from *105.07 to *105.51. Cemented rubble lies over the limestone masonry on both CGE and CGW. It is preserved from W 16.5/N 3.5–10.30. Its highest preserved point on CGW is *106.14, on CGE, *106.42.

Hall CN

North of CGC was another large rectangular hall, CN, also on a north-south axis and entered from the south through a brick archway communicating with CGC. The main walls of this hall (CNE, CNW, A) were of rubble construction. The hall was not excavated to a great enough depth to establish the existence of any other doors or special features (Figs. 336, 337).

Hall HM

Circular Hall HM projects eastward and northward from the northeast corner of CGE (Figs. 336, 337). In its interior eight arched niches were hollowed out (A 1–A 8) in an alternating pattern of rectangular and half-domed recesses. Some of these communicated with adjoining halls and rooms.[10]

Corridor CR and Room HN

South of HM was Corridor CR, making up a series of small arches, vaults and the only preserved stairway found in CG. It was divided from Room HN by brick and rubble wall w, a possible addition from a later phase (Fig. 336; this wall appears as upper case W on plan).

No completely corresponding features were excavated on the west side of the building. In place of HM is a "platform area" N, adjoining the northwest pier of CGC and the north side of CGW.[11] The north and south ends of a heavy rubble wall CNW were found, corresponding to CNE on the east, but no further units to the west were opened (Fig. 337).

Halls CP and CQ

North of CN and HN three long heavy rubble walls (A, P, Q) running east-west formed the walls of two large rectangular halls (CP, CQ) with main axes perpendicular to the main north-south axis of the building (Fig. 336). Two "blind" arches (a'1, a'3) were revealed at the east end of CP and a brick half-dome (a'2) at the west end. No arches or vaults appeared in CQ at the levels excavated.

Indications of outer units extending to the west of CP were revealed in the (narrower) extensions of wall A and the exposure of the top of what may have been the eastern half of a monumental entranceway embellished with carved marble entablatures.[12] Time and means did not permit fuller investigation of this area.

Walls a–d

Four rubble walls (a-d) running east-west were added to the eastern piers of CGE in a later building phase and indicate the existence of additional (unexcavated) units east of the eastern facade of CGE. They were apparently intended as part of the bath complex and not as water breakers as tentatively proposed in 1958.[13] The entire length of these walls and the layout of possible rooms between them were not explored, but again there were indications that the use of arches and vaults remained of prime interest to the builders or remodelers of a later period (Figs. 336, 337, 343).

Comparisons

Certain features of the plan of CG compare strikingly with portions of the plans of other Roman bath complexes in western Asia Minor.

Hierapolis. The interior of Main Hall CGC is of almost identical proportions and dimensions as a large niched hall of the great, late second century A.D. baths at Hierapolis, a day's journey to the south (Figs. 338, 339). The masonry construction of the baths at Hierapolis is likewise so similar as to suggest perhaps the same school of architects for the original phase of CG.[14]

The same interior system of half-dome, rectangular niche, half-dome, and the exterior piers to the south (on one side only at Hierapolis) applies in both cases, although there do not appear to have been communicating doorways through the niches at Hierapolis. Other surrounding halls, some with ceiling vaults preserved, show certain similarities to

CG, but the general arrangement of rooms and interior access is quite different.

Miletus: Baths of Capito. A more striking parallel in overall plan may be seen in the first century A.D. Baths of Capito at Miletus (Fig. 340).[15] There is a central Hall 2, a caldarium, with arched niches in which the pattern of rectangular niche, half-dome, rectangular niche is the reverse of that of CGC and Hierapolis. The room communicates with a circular Room 5, the laconicum, through niches on the interior of 5. The relation of the laconicum to the connecting caldarium is somewhat analogous to the relation of circular Hall HM and the Hall CGC. Room 5 of the Capito Baths also connects to Hall 3, another caldarium, in much the same way as HM links up with Hall CN. The rectangular, axial arrangement of the large rectangular niched halls is strongly reminiscent of CG, although there are also great differences.

Miletus: Baths of Faustina. Interesting similarities of plan are also to be seen in the late second century A.D. Baths of Faustina at Miletus (Figs. 341, 342).[16] Here the niched hall, frigidarium (4), has large piers on the exterior wall of one side which form part of a series of cubicles for the apodyterium (1). This is somewhat reminiscent of the east side of CGE with its piers and rubble east-west walls. It must be remembered that the full extent of the units lying to the east of CGE is not known.[17]

CGC: Exterior Treatment

The only section of CG of which we almost certainly have the exterior portions is Hall CGC. The rest of the units to the north seem to have been interior, although some, such as wall Q of Hall CQ were not excavated to a great enough depth to determine this with certainty.

The east side of CGE and west side of CGW are heavily weathered and show signs of having been exposed to the elements. Furthermore, they show no signs of having been revetted as do the unquestionably interior walls of CGE (west) and CGW (east) and the interior of HM (Figs. 343, 344).

At some later time the rubble walls *a-d* were added to the east face of CGE, possibly indicating the creation of additional units east of CGC. The fact that the walls do not bond with the piers on which they abut shows that they were something of an afterthought. We do not know their original height nor their full depth nor the distance they extended to the east (Figs. 337, 345, 346, 351).

Cornices

The arches on the eastern face of CGE spring from a profiled string course at ca. *99.90 (Figs. 412, 414). A similar profile was exposed on the southern and southwestern ends of CGW but some 20 cm. lower (*99.70) and serves as the spring point for TW, the only arch fully exposed on the west face of CGW.

The string profile on both CGE and CGW continues around the southern faces of the walls and turns northward into the hall where it continues for a length of 1.65 m. on both sides, turning down at that point for 50 cm. and terminating (Figs. 347, 348).

De Peyssonel speaks of a "cornice [running] along the building both inside and out" and the elevation which he uses shows a kind of string course or cornice above the arches on the east side. Landron's drawing (Fig. 333) shows a similar feature. As it stands now, much of the upper part of the building has been destroyed and none of this upper cornice is preserved *in situ*.[18]

South Facade and South Arch

The southern faces of CGE and CGW were each buttressed at the east and west ends by large piers, of which the two flanking the central opening between the two walls are best preserved (Figs. 334, 336, 337, 350). The remains of piers at the southwest corner of CGW and the southeast corner of CGE are only poorly preserved and do not even reach the level of the profile (Fig. 416).

The masonry of both southern faces is laid in alternating high and low courses. Two small windows or airholes, *h'1* and *h'2* (Fig. 425). 0.53 m. wide and 0.43 m. high and 0.72 m. wide and 0.37 m. high respectively, appear on wall CGE. They are asymmetrically placed in the first row of blocks above the profile and open on the interior of tunnel TE (Fig. 334). A similar hole appears in the south facade of CGW (Figs. 350, 351).

Walls CGE and CGW were once linked on the south by a massive masonry arch with a span of ca. 11.75 m. The arch itself is not preserved, but its existence is attested by the discovery of sixteen to twenty fallen voussoirs, including a keystone, lying at W 2–12/S 2–N 2, from *102.53 and below (Figs. 349, 350).

The six central voussoirs numbered A 9–14 were lying upside down in windblown brown earth. They had toppled forward with their upper edges fallen to the south and lower than their (original) lower edges. The original upper edges were at *101.36–101.25; the original lower edges at ca. *102.50–102.40. The voussoirs had presumably fallen before the final occupation of the building was discontinued, since remains of earth floors and a shepherd's (?) hearth were found near the voussoirs and on the same levels. They had definitely fallen *after* the main period of the building's use, however, as the accumulation of earth and debris under the voussoirs was well above the levels of any original floors, perhaps as much as five meters.

The preserved voussoirs were quite large. The keystone (A 10) measured H. 1.14 m., bottom W. 0.34 m., top W. 0.38 m., D. 1.30 m. The other voussoirs varied somewhat in size and some were heavily eroded making accurate measurement impossible. Measurements obtained where feasible were:

A 9: H. 1.25 m.; bottom W. 0.42 m.; top W. (eroded); D. 0.82 m.

A 11: H. 1.14 m.; bottom W. 0.33 m.; top W. 0.47 m.; D. 0.82 m.

A 14: H. 1.15 m.; bottom W. 0.35 m.; top W. 0.42 m.; D. 0.80 m.

All widths are given for the original top and bottom, not as fallen. As the original front sides of the voussoirs remained buried to the north we cannot tell if they were ever revetted or adorned with sculpture.

It is not clear where the arch sprang. C. de Peyssonel's description suggests that much of the arch was still preserved in the mid-eighteenth century.[19] His drawing, presumably of that arch, shows it preserved somewhat above the springing, but the drawing is too inaccurate in its proportions to be of much help in reconstructing the original appear-

ance. F. K. Yegül, an architect for the Sardis Expedition, suggests a springing at ca. *102, or at about the level of the third masonry course above the string profile of the southern piers of CGC (Fig. 350).

Below the arch was probably an east-west screen wall, pierced perhaps by a lower (brick?) arch to form a door or entranceway into the hall. In digging a stratigraphic pit against the east side of the southeast pier of CGW[20] the top of a marble lintel or east-west wall SpS came to light at W 12.1–13.0/S 0.50–0.25, *97.43, ca. 2.26 m. below the string course at *99.69.

The East Face

The four arched niches on the eastern face of CGE (TE, SCE, MAE, NCE) all spring from the same profile level at ca. *99.90 but form a gradually widening and heightening progression from south and north to the central arch MAE. By comparing the exposed crowns of the western arches of CGW it is probably safe to assume that a similar arrangement was carried out on the western facade (Figs. 343, 344). With the exception of TE, all the arches on the east face gave access through doorways into the Main Hall CGC in the original phase of the building.

Units SCE, MAE, and NCE are shallow, vaulted niches separated by three large piers (1, 2, 3) which project about 1.20 m. to the east. At the south, long, vaulted, narrow, 'blind' corridor or tunnel TE runs through the entire width of the wall which in turn widens at this point (Figs. 336, 351). A fourth pier (4) projects to the east at the southeastern corner of the wall (Figs. 343, 415). Perhaps the entire arrangement including piers 4, 3, the southeast corner pier of CGE, and TE should be thought of as one *large* pier penetrated by TE, with a similar arrangement in CGW with TW (Figs. 336, 371).[21]

Piers 1–4 of CGE are not of equal width (N-S) but increase from south to north, with piers 2 and 1 about equal. Their widths are: pier 4, 1.30 m.; pier 3, 2.30 m.; pier 2, 3.25 m.; pier 1, 3.25 m.; pier 0, on its face, ca. 1.50 m. All have the impost profile across the front and extending westward into the vaulted niches (Figs. 336, 343).

The later rubble walls *a-d* project eastward from

piers 1–4 and run into the scarp where they presumably continue. These walls may have been connected by rubble vaults, and at least two, *a* and *b*, had the remains of small blind arches preserved on their north and south sides (Figs. 352, 355).

The existence of a lower story was established by the discovery of the tops of arches below TE, MAE, and NCE. The arches below TE and NCE were of brick; that below MAE ("lower arch") was of masonry. SCE was not excavated to a great enough depth to prove the presence of a lower arch (Figs. 343, 345, 346, 351, 353). The levels of the tops of the lower arches were: TE, *98.89; MAE, *97.60; NCE, *97.95. The arch in TE may have been secondary. It lay diagonally from pier 4 on the south to rubble wall *c* on the north.[22] Since the water table was reached at *94.80 in 1959 (even higher in 1969, *97.70 at start of digging), most of the height of the lower arches remained under water and the associated floor levels were not exposed. This inability to explore the lower story and possible basement structures hampered the excavators in reaching firm conclusions as to date and function of the various parts.

The lower arch of MAE was better exposed than those of TE and NCE and within and below the arch were found a small furnace and certain features which may relate to the heating system of the bath (Figs. 343, 345, 354).

The arch itself is wider than the arched doorway above it (ca. 3.75 m. wide at springing). Its voussoirs are badly worn on the intrados. The crown of the arch is at *97.35, the bottom of the keystone at *96.85. The fifth voussoir southward, which makes the transition from radial to horizontal, has a narrow profile at the top which continues horizontally southward and is probably associated with the floor or platform level at *95.80 (Figs. 343, 354). The second and third voussoir to the south had been "scooped out" to permit the insertion of a half-domed brick furnace.

A poor and disrupted Byzantine brick floor was found at ca. *97.60 just above the arch. Under the keystone and upper voussoirs of the "lower arch" are about 50 cms. of brick and rubble infill ending on the south with a row of carefully laid bricks (1.35 m. below the top of the keystone, 3.25 m.

from the north wall of the vault). The furnace is fitted into the southern part of the arch (Figs. 343, 354). The width of the half-dome of the furnace is 1.10 m.; D. 0.60 m.; top *96.50; spring of furnace dome *95.80. The threshold was under water when excavated in 1959. It appeared to have had a vent or chimney going backward and out into MAW. The top part of the furnace arch had dropped into the water by 1969.

Remains of a brick heating chamber and other features associated with furnace activities were found. Terracotta pipes ran horizontally from the furnace arch to join other, vertical pipes near the south side of MAE. Heavy deposits of charcoal mixed with bones and other burned matter from *97.0–*96.4 are apparently the residue from the furnace operations (Fig. 354). A cement floor against the south pier of MAE at ca. *95.8–*95.6 seems to belong with the heating chamber of the subfurnium.[23] It rests on masonry blocks. Several small but heavy cast plaques (0.05 m. × 0.05 m.) with pegs or bosses projecting from the center of each side were found above the subfurnium floor at ca. *97.0–*96.4 (Fig. 359) and may have formed some kind of attachment on the furnace walls or doors. The furnace floor is divided by a channel ca. one meter below the floor level (*94.6). It leads straight into the opening of the furnace arch and was perhaps used for fueling the furnace (Figs. 355, 356). A brick pier in the northern part of MAE may have supported the springing of a brick arch which spanned the east end of the subfurnium.[24]

The projected interior dimensions of the heating chamber are 3.00 m. north-south by 2.20 m. east-west. The height of the heating chamber requires a ceiling at ca. *97.0 (if one were crouching), more likely at ca. *97.50 (cf. Figs. 343, 354).

The West Face

CGW has not been excavated to the same extent as its eastern counterpart. In fact, only the southern face, the tops of the arches and parts of tunnel TW have been cleared. Enough was exposed, however, to demonstrate the general similarity in plan and design to CGE (Fig. 344). Around TW and pier 3 north of the west side is well preserved to two courses above arch TW. The face is not preserved above the crowns of the other arches.[25] As with the east face of CGE there is no evidence that the external west face of CGW was revetted.

From the preserved tops of the piers on the west side we can see that the same asymmetry of width prevails as on the east side. Widths from south to north are: pier 4, 1.40 m.; pier 3, 2.10 m.; pier 2, 3.50 m.; pier 1, 2.50 m. Dimensions of the arches so far as known are shown below in Ch. X, Table 10.

Of the western arches only TW was cleared. It corresponds so closely to TE in appearance, dimensions, etc., that the symmetry of the other arches with those of the east face of CGE may be assumed. Some interesting deviations do occur, however. Arch MW, for instance, had a double ring of voussoirs on its face, of which only the lower ring is preserved. Originally there seem to have been eleven voussoirs in each ring. Curiously, this treatment is carried out on the two interior central arches MAW and ME (Figs. 368, 371), but not on MAE which corresponds in position to MW (cf. plan, Fig. 336).

Roofing of CGC

A considerable amount of cemented rubble was found on the tops of the walls CGE and CGW overlying the topmost masonry course at ca. *106 on CGE, a little lower on CGW. This suggests a barrel vault of cemented rubble construction (Figs. 343, 344, 357). Such a vault perhaps rose somewhat higher than the south masonry arch which seems to have sprung from about *102.[26]

Stratigraphy

Along the east face of CGE was stratigraphic evidence for the periodic flooding of the building (Fig. 343). In SCE down to ca. *99.25 the fill was almost entirely river sand with a few pebbles, fragments of plaster, and a little brick (Figs. 353, 422). The plaster may have fallen from the soffit of the arch, although no trace remained in place. Below *99.0 was mostly river sand. In front of MAE a heavy deposit of river pebbles goes from ca. *102.5–100.5. Under it is clean brown mud (Fig. 354).

At ca. *98.8, above the threshold of the "inner arch" was a poor and disrupted Middle Byzantine floor associated with the furnace. A red cement Roman floor appeared at *95.80 (the same level as the springing of the furnace dome). The cement floor rested on heavy limestone masonry blocks. This floor was divided by an east-west channel which led straight to the opening of the furnace (Figs. 355, 356). The bottom of the channel was at ca. *94.6, ca. one meter below the cement floor. At *94.8 the water table was reached in 1959, preventing further digging.

Finds in front of SCE and MAE show that there was a Middle Byzantine occupation of this part of the building represented by pottery fragments, glass bracelets, and at least one coin. These deposits were found in levels from ca. *101.0 to ca. *98.5. This phase was preceded in MAE by levels between ca. *98.0 and *95.5 containing coarse Roman wares.

No significant finds were discovered in either TE or NCE, nor along the west face of CGW where digging did not penetrate deeply enough to expose the occupation levels. A few finds of Byzantine pottery near the south face of CGE help to confirm the general stratigraphic conclusions for the eastern face.

Finds: East Face CG

In SCE, Middle Byzantine sherds were found from about *101.0–*99.0. Scattered finds related to the structure itself include a piece of a marble grille (from a window?) found just above the springing on the south side of the arch. Some fragments of brick and tile, some glass fragments, and a few scattered human bones were also found.

In MAE, aside from the pipes and bronze plaques associated with the furnace, a few significant finds were noted. Near the surface at ca. *103.0 was a silver Ottoman coin, C58.4. Byzantine sherds and a coin of 972–1028 A.D. were found between *100.20 and *99.0. From *97.0 to *95.5 were mostly coarse Roman wares. Also in this level were the bronze "plaques," found at *97.0–*96.4 and *97.0–*95.75 (Fig. 359), and two mosaic tesserae, one yellow, one blue at *96.80–*95.50).

Some fragments, possibly belonging to the original decoration of the building were found, mostly in the upper levels: a piece of a marble rosette in high relief from a ceiling coffer (?), ca. *99.0; the hand of a colossal marble statue, perhaps second century A.D.; and a fragment of a Greek inscription at ca. *100.0.

SCE

Pottery
P58.340:629. Ca. *100.70, under arch. Ring base of small bowl. Diam. 0.08 m. Buff ware with worn greenish glaze on interior. Middle Byzantine.
P59.394:1919. *100.0–*99.0. Fragment of plain red-ware lid with plastic rope pattern and incised grooves. 0.08 m. × 0.09 m.; Th. 0.008 m. Early Byzantine (?). (Fig. 360.)

MAE

Coin
C58.257. E 3/N 17, ca. *99.0. Constantinople, copper, follis. Basil II A.D. 972–1028 = *Sardis* M1 (1971) 130 no. 1155.

Glass
G58.41:553. Ca. *99.00. Bracelet fragment. Green with some darker and blue-green tones. Diam. 0.07 m. Byzantine. Cf. Hanfmann, "Glass," 53 n. 18.
Uncat. ca. *98.50. Blue fragment. Possibly 10th century A.D. Cf. Hanfmann, "Glass," 53 n. 18.

Pottery
P58.241:570. Ca. *99.0. Ring foot, stem, and part of bowl and everted rim of footed bowl. Plain ware. Diam. bowl 0.16 m. Byzantine. (Fig. 361.)
P58.245:558. In front of MAE. Level not recorded. Three joining fragments of a yellow glazed deep dish. Everted rim, carinated profile. Diam. 0.16 m. Middle Byzantine.
P58.439:701. North side of arch. Ca. *98.0. Fragment of rim. Red, wet-smoothed ware. Slightly flaring everted rim, hints of ridges at base of rim on exterior. Diam. 0.12 m. Roman.

Stone Objects
IN58.5:752. Just under east face of MAE. Ca. *100.0. White marble fragment. H. 0.22 m.; W. 0.22 m.; Th. 0.14 m. Greek inscription:]ς καὶ το[ ]/ ου. (Fig. 362.)
S58.27:557. East face of MAE, ca. *99.0. Marble fragment with relief of four-petalled flower. W. 0.116 m.; Th. 0.02 m.; W. flower 0.105 m. Possibly from a coffer. (Fig. 363.)
S58.29:715. North side MAE, ca. *98.10. Fragment of rough pinkish stucco with traces of molded ribs. Perhaps from wall decoration. L. 0.11 m.
S58.34:722. Joint of "inner arch." Ca. *99.0. Found as late rubble wall removed. Fine-grained marble wrist and palm of colossal statue, ca. twice life size. Thumb and fingers broken off at base. Clean break at wrist. L. 0.15 m.; W. at wrist 0.075 m.; W. across fingers 0.10 m.; Th. and wrist 0.06 m.; Roman, probably second century A.D.

Metal Objects
M59.56:1890. *97.0–*95.75. Rectangular bronze plaque with hole in center. L. 0.046 m.; W. 0.039 m.; Th. 0.007 m.; diam. hole 0.015 m. (Fig. 359.)
M59.57:1904. South side MAE. *97.0–*96.4. Six bronze plaques. Two rectangular with protruding knobs or bosses (Fig. 359); two rectangular without bosses; one round knob; one plaque with hole in middle.
a) L. 0.05 m.; W. 0.05 m.; diam. boss 0.017 m.
b) L. 0.05 m.; W. 0.045 m.; diam. boss 0.017 m.
c) L. 0.05 m.; W. 0.043 m.
d) L. 0.05 m.; W. 0.04 m.
e) Diam. knob 0.038 m.; H. 0.013 m.
f) L. 0.038 m.; W. 0.03 m.; diam. hole 0.018 m.

Finds: South Face CG

Pottery
P59.519:2125. Ca. 2.50 m. southeast of southeast pier of CGE. Bottom *98.10. Red ribbed jug ca. three quarters preserved. Walls broken in four fragments. Max. diam. 0.47 m.; P.H. 0.44 m.; Th. walls 0.0125 m. (Fig. 364.)

CG: Interior Treatment

Hall CGC

The interior of the main excavated space of Bath CG is a large rectangular hall of which CGE and CGW form the east and west long walls. The internal dimensions of the hall are 15.5 m. E-W by 31.4 m. N-S. Four piers project into the hall and the southeast, southwest, northeast, and northwest corners which were once joined by northern and southern east-west screen walls pierced by arched entrances into the hall (Figs. 336, 337, 365–368, 371).

In each of the side walls, CGE and CGW, are three arched recesses, alternately half-domed, vaulted, half-domed, which, in CGE at least, communicate with three arched recesses opening on the eastern facade. The function of these recesses on the interior is not altogether clear, but some connection with water supply and heating arrangements for the bath are likely. The interior side walls and niches were apparently covered with marble revetments and the tops of the half-domes were stuccoed and painted.

Function of Hall CGC

Most likely CGC was used either as the tepidarium or warm bath, or as the caldarium or hot bath. This was the largest and apparently most important unit in CG and it seems to have been associated as well with the appropriate heating arrangements.[27] It also connected with the (presumed) laconicum or sweat bath (HM) as Vitruvius says is necessary for tepidaria.[28] The similar Hall C at Hierapolis is thought to have been the caldarium.[29]

CGE West Face

The west face of CGE formed the eastern long wall of the interior of Hall CGC (Fig. 365). It was cut by two large half-domed niches, SCW and NCW, and by MAW in the center, a rectangular vaulted niche. These were the counterparts of the openings on the eastern exterior facade of the wall and were echoed on the other side of the interior by similar niches in wall CGW. Tunnel TE did not open on the inside, so that the southwest end of CGE forms a large pier flanking the main entrance to the hall.[30]

The sections of wall between the niches have no projecting piers but are flush with the openings of the niches (Fig. 368). The walls and voussoirs of the arches are covered with round holes, some of which contain the remains of iron pins or clamps. These are the remains of pins which held revetments to the walls. Judging from the holes, the revetments continued at least as high as the highest preserved course, presumably as high as the springing of the central vault (Fig. 366). According to L. J. Majewski, the size of the holes indicates very large pins (Figs. 417, 418) used to hold quite heavy slabs of marble to the walls.[31]

As on the east face of CGE, the levels of the crowns of the arches were not identical. The crown of half-dome SCW was at *103.30, vault MAW at *104.97, half-dome NCW at *103.96, thus emphasizing the central arch. The voussoirs of all three arches were given different treatment as well. On SCW the tops of the three central voussoirs were cut on an even horizontal line and were capped by a large horizontal ashlar block (Fig. 366). MAW had a double ring of concentric voussoirs, 21 in the lower ring, 11 in the upper ring (Fig. 367). The outer (upper) ring of voussoirs rests directly on the voussoirs of the lower ring, beginning over the seventh voussoir from the bottom. The line of the outer curve (extrados) is fairly even. The three central voussoirs of NCW projected higher than the extrados line and are cut evenly across the top. Similar but not identical treatment is seen on the opposite wall CGW (Fig. 371) where the central vaulted arch ME also has a double row of voussoirs and NE, corresponding to half-dome NCW, has a single central voussoir rising above the extrados line.

Half-Domes SCW and NCW

Neither SCW nor NCW formed a true half-dome, as the niches deviated from the semi-circular in plan by being too deep for the width and somewhat off center in axis—SCW to south, NCW to north (Fig. 351). The door in the rear of SCW (Fig. 366) is symmetrical to the arch on the west face, while that in NCW is off center to the south (Fig. 336).

The voussoirs of SCW and to a lesser extent NCW were covered with revetment pin holes. There were also regular rows of pin holes, some filled with iron, below the spring level of the dome in SCW. NCW was not excavated below the spring level and so similar evidence for revetment in that niche is lacking.

While the lower part of SCW was apparently revetted, the upper part appears to have been plastered and painted. A patch of bluish-gray paint laid on white stucco over a reddish plaster bedding was visible on the ceiling of SCW ca. 45 cm. east of the face. In both SCW and NCW were traces of secondary brickwork laid in cement, remnants of a later stage in the building's decorative history (Fig. 370). Greater amounts of such brickwork were exposed in MAW, the central niche.

Vertical cuttings, possibly for drainpipes, were found in the north and south walls of SCW and in the south wall of NCW (Fig. 369) where a large piece of terracotta pipe was still preserved. Similar pipe cuttings were observed in the Hierapolis baths and are probably to be connected with water inflow for the bathing establishment.

Niche MAW

MAW is the central, rectangular niche of the east side of CGC. It is actually a shallow barrel vault, two to three rows of voussoirs deep east-west (Figs. 351, 367). Evidence of earthquake damage was apparent on the east part of the ceiling near the face of the inner arch where the voussoirs appear to have pulled away to the west from the stones bonding in with the eastern part of the building. The vault rises 3.9 to 4.0 m. above the threshold of the inner arch. A floor was found at *98.90.

The masonry of MAW is still covered to a large extent with secondary brick and stucco facing, beginning at the level of the springing and continuing downwards to the lowest part excavated. The brick is laid in even courses evenly spaced with pinkish mortar.[32] Above the springing no regularly coursed brick remains but there are patches of mortar or stucco and irregular brick fragments especially observable in cracks and gaps in the ashlar (Fig. 370). These patches extend ca. 40 cm. to one meter above the springing. On the ceiling were other patches of reddish stucco, particularly on the keystone, and other patches with brick fragments appeared in cracks.

East Face CGW

Only the tops of the arches SE, ME, and NE of CGW were cleared by excavation so that the plans of the niches were not determined. As far as can be judged from the exposed arches, however, the pattern followed is similar (but not identical) to that of the west face of CGE (Fig. 371). As with CGE, the tops of the arches rise to different levels with the main emphasis on the highest central arch ME which has a double row of voussoirs like MAW. The crown of SE is *102.92; the highest preserved level of ME *103.61[33] and of NE *103.44. These levels are, in turn, somewhat lower than the corresponding levels on the west face of CGE, though this may be due to the settling of the western wall.[34] Further evidence of the shaken condition of CGW is seen in the fact that the large arch over ME has slid inward inside its northern jamb, and that a cascade of large masonry spilled in a northeasterly direction from levels of *105 and higher down to *101 and from N 25 to N 32. The irregular positions of stones resulting from this led to the greater difficulty in obtaining consistent measurements and data from this side of the building.

As with the west side of CGE, the masonry of the east face of CGW shows clear indications of having been revetted. Although the masonry surface is much more worn than CGE, some of the pin holes are still visible on the voussoirs of the arches and on the southeast pier.

South End of CGC: Southeast and Southwest Piers

The southeast pier of CGC (southwest pier of CGE) projects 2.25 m. westward into the hall and measures 5.40 m. across the west face. The pier is hollow as tunnel TE cuts through most of its length. On the opposite side, the southwest pier (southeast pier of CGW) projects 2.30 m. eastward into the hall and measures 5.40 m. across the east face. It too is hollow, penetrated most of its length by tunnel TW. The southwestern pier was excavated to a deeper level than the southeast pier in the course of digging a stratigraphic pit[35] but the main floor levels and the principal entrance level of the southern gate were not found (Figs. 350, 371, 374).

North End of CGC: Piers NE and NW, Spurwalls SpE, SpW

The northern end of Hall CGC was closed off by a screen wall of ashlar masonry through which a brick archway provided the means of communication between CGC and the units to the north.[36] On the east is a limestone pier, the northeast corner pier of Hall CGC. The width of the pier E-W is 2.20 m.; L. N-S, 2.90 m.; E 1.10-W 1.10/N 29.60–32.50. This is smaller than the southeast pier (Figs. 336, 337).

The northeast pier was revetted with marble over a heavy brick red grout. The marble slabs are roughly trimmed at the back and show clamp holes, some filled in, indicating that the slabs were reused.

Westward, the pier projected in a narrower spurwall SpE (Fig. 372), made partly of limestone blocks, partly of brick (on south and east faces). The bricks at the eastern end formed the springing of a brick-tile arch (now collapsed) which had formed the doorway through the wall. The original N-S depth of the arch must have been ca. 1.50 m. The arch was made up of half and whole pieces of standard tile, ca. 0.42 m. to 0.44 m. square for the whole, 0.21 m. for the half width.

The northwest pier of CGC lies at W 13.45–15.70/N 29.23–31.60. Its overall dimensions were probably intended to be square, 2.35 m. × 2.35 m., but are in fact 2.37 m. N-S × 2.25 m. E-W. Three courses are exposed with the top at *102.65. It is also constructed of limestone masonry. The topmost exposed course bonds into the "platform" (Area N).[37] The northern face of the pier served to effect a beginning for the rubble wall CNW (Fig. 336). Its top lies at *101.89 and is very carefully constructed. The interlocking of limestone masonry and rubble is somewhat farther south than it is on the eastern side of CGC. There is no clear evidence at the depth reached that there was real interlocking of masonry and rubble such as appeared in HM.[38]

The limestone masonry of spurwall SpW (Fig. 373) is only 0.64 m. wide (plus bricks on the south side) as against 1.10 m. for SpE. The brick pier for the western springing of the arch (top at *100.62) is also composed of half and whole width tiles, for a total preserved width N-S of 1.27 m. One full-sized tile is missing on the south to make up the full width of 1.50 m. known from SpE. Many pieces of tile were found scattered in the trench, probably fallen from the arch.

The arch in the north wall of CGC must have had a clear span of ca. 4.40 m. (W 4.80–8.25; Fig. 336). No threshold was found, but an approximate level of ca. *96.00 seems likely judging from the proportions of the arch. The archway opening is slightly asymmetrical to the east with respect to the northeast and northwest piers (Figs. 336, 344; cf. the reconstruction Fig. 430).

Area N

Area N (also called platform N), is a rectangular platform of solid, carefully joined ashlar masonry which forms the northern end of wall CGW and appears to have been a transitional element between CGC, CN to the north, and possible other elements to the northwest.[39] It was ca. 3.50 m. long, 5.20–5.35 m. wide E-W (W 15.40–20.75/N 28.20–31.70). The lowest level reached in this area was *100.94 on just one stone of the west face of the platform. More representative average levels were *101.94 and *101.54. Area N was bonded in with the northwest pier of Hall CGC and aligned approximately with the center line of unit HM to the east (Figs. 337, 371).

A large fall of masonry made it impossible to excavate the northwest corner of Area N (W 18.20/N 31). At the northern end of this spill of masonry (W 19–18/N 30–31; top *102.16, bottom ca. *101) lay a profiled block of the same general kind as the blocks of the profile course usually encountered at ca. *99.7 or *99.9 on the outside of CGE and

CGW.[40] Its position at such a high level suggests that it came from high up on the building. De Peyssonel, in the description assumed to be of CG,[41] mentions a cornice running inside and outside the building. This is also shown in his sketches and in Landron's drawing (Fig. 333, exterior east side). Quite possibly, such a profile served to define the springing of the interior central vault.

Building Phases of CGC

CGC was the most extensively explored unit of Bath CG, both architecturally and stratigraphically. In the course of excavation three major building phases were distinguished for the structure itself followed by several periods of occupation and industrial activity within the unit, interspersed by periodic heavy floods. Still later strata were revealed by a deep stratigraphic pit at the southwest pier of CGC and by a lesser sounding at the northwest pier which included a series of industrial hearths.

Initial Phase. CGC and at least the southern part of HM were constructed of limestone masonry, probably in the Early Roman Imperial period. No floor levels from this phase have been excavated, and its original function is uncertain but it is likely, considering its resemblance to the great baths at Hierapolis, that it was intended as a bath from the start.

Second Phase. CGE and perhaps the entire limestone structure was apparently converted to a new use by building into its arches and niches a number of rubble and brick walls and other features, primarily of rubble. Evidence of extensive remodeling and redecorating in the northern units (HM, HN, below) and the addition of elaborate revetment and fresco work probably belongs to this phase too. This phase began in Roman Imperial times and certainly continued into Early Byzantine, perhaps fifth or sixth century A.D. Sometimes after this, around the sixth or seventh century A.D., the entire CG complex was overwhelmed by floods and buried very rapidly, perhaps after the Sassanian destruction of Sardis in A.D. 616.

Third Phase. The final building phase actually consisted of several sub-phases and appeared over flooded phase II floors at the height of the upper story of the buried building (*99.0 and above). This Middle Byzantine secondary occupation was clearly seen in the east and west recesses of the Main Arch (MAE, MAW).

Several workshops or industrial establishments involving considerable firing and producing a slag, possibly resulting from the smelting of iron, flourished for a time in the upper part of the building in several locations. This activity also is dated to the tenth and eleventh centuries A.D. by coins, pottery, and glass found in associated levels. At this time too, major vandalism of the building's marble decoration may have occurred, perhaps for the voracious limekiln activity. This is evidenced by sporadic finds of very fragmentary sculpture and architectural moldings belonging to earlier periods in the upper levels of debris.[42]

Stratigraphy of the Later Phases

Because of the level of the water table, the excavators were never able to explore the foundations and earliest remains of the building. The stratigraphic pit at the southwest corner of CGC (southeast pier of CGW; cf. Fig. 336) and other, smaller test trenches revealed the later sequences of occupation and flood. In 1969 the pit was reopened at W 10–13/N 0–2 and from *101.76 to *96.7 where the water table was reached (Fig. 374).

In the top meter or so of deposit were three large stones, apparently fallen from either the central arch or the roof of the building (A 17, 18, 19; tops at *101.54, *101.96, *101.93). These were removed and rolled to the bottom of the trench at the east side of CGW. From the top of the pit there were about 4.5 m. of alternating occupation and flood debris before the top of the southern cross wall SpS was reached.[43] Below this level was another meter or more of flood deposits.

As shown in Figure 374, the sequence began with a level of top soil from surface to ca. *101.76. This was followed by a heavy ash layer sloping from east at *101.76 to west at *101.68. The level was almost 20 cm. thick and corresponds roughly with the level of the hearths at the north end of CGC.[44] Below this was a very thick layer of clay and sand with some heavier bands of sand towards the bottom from ca. *101.50 to *100.60.

Below the clay and sand layers were heavier bands of burned material alternating with thin bands of plaster. The burned deposits contained bits of brick and charcoal and extended from ca. *100.61 at the highest to *99.62 at the lowest against the east side of CGW. The plaster bands were at *100.33 (2 cm. thick) and *100.20 (7 cm. thick). Below this was a thick level of mixed debris; earth mixed with plaster, brick, and stone bits. This extended from *99.89 at W 10.5 to *99.64 at W 13.5 and continued to *99.44. Below was another, narrower band of ash, from *99.44 to *99.34, in almost a straight horizontal line. This is followed by another band of earth, brick, and plaster down to about *99.15, then an ashy band containing some brick and slag pieces from *99.15 to *99.05 which does not extend all the way across the trench but ends at about W 12.40. A layer of sand follows from *99.05 to ca. *98.86, then comes a layer of clay and sand with some bits of plaster and brick to ca. *98.60, then plain sand again to *98.50, then sand and clay with some charcoal and brick at the top, most pure river deposit to ca. *97.37, then river gravel to *97.07, clay and sand again to water table at *96.70 where digging ceased.

The history which can be read from this section shows at least two major phases of burning or industrial activity at *101.70 and *100.60 with minor ones at *99.45 and *99.15. In between these periods of activity the building appears to have been under continual assault from floods which left thick deposits and were a primary cause of the ruin of the building.

North End CGC: The Hearth Area

At the northwest pier of CGC a shallower sounding was made from W 8–13/N 26–33, *102.52 to ca. *100.89 in an attempt to elucidate the northern crosswall and doorway.[45] Here as at the southern end evidence was found for later, probably Middle Byzantine activities.[46]

A series of "hearths" was found to have been installed west of and partly within the northwest pier and the rubble wall CNW. The original tops of the hearths were at ca. *102.15, bottoms at ca. *101.90. A heavy, black deposit of burned matter containing slag and charcoal was encountered from ca. *101.70 to *101.50 and below it another deposit, red in color, appeared from *101.30 to *100.90. This was apparently dumped industrial waste, refuse from these or other furnaces or hearths in the vicinity. Several mosaic tesserae were found loose in the dump, one at W 8.3/N 30.5, *101.15; several at W 9.5/N 28–29, *100.60; another at W 10/N 30, *100.20.

Part of the northwest pier was demolished and much of the spurwall SpW (Fig. 373) disrupted by the industrial activity. The operational levels of the furnaces (floor?) were between *101.90 and *101.50 but the dumped refuse sloped down to *101.00. The general character of this "industrial" stratification from ca. *102.0 to *101.50 and below seems much the same as along the east side of CGC and in the southwest stratification pit.[47]

The first hearth, hearth I (Figs. 337, 375) was found at W 10.5–12.0/N 29.0–31.3, top ca. *102.15, bottom of firing ducts at ca. *101.90. Its superstructure was oval in shape. It was built into the northwest pier of CGC, of which one L-shaped block formed part of the south wall of the hearth. It looked as if five voussoirs of a rubble arch (as A 3–8 in HM) were taken and spaced to form the firing ducts. The bottoms of an upper set of ducts were at *101.50; those of the lower set at ca. *101.00. The upper part of the furnace platform was later excavated at N 32.95. Its length was 3.85 m.; the lower part was 2.25 m. N-S.

A second hearth, hearth II, was at W 10.0–11.4/N 27.0–28.5. The bottom of the "heating chamber" was again at *101.90. Between the two hearths and east of hearth I at W 9.5–12.0/N 27.0–28.5 was a rubble floor at ca. *101.60 (hearth III?). Burned deposits began at *100.97, ca. 0.80–1.00 m. below the present surface, and continued slanting from W 12.5 to W 7.5 as if cast broadside from a level slightly higher than the bottom of the hearths. It looks as if there was at first an accumulation of charcoal and slag around the bottom of the hearth, then a band of earth, lime, burned earth, and brick fragments, then a higher band of charcoal and ashes. Large amounts of charcoal and ashes are preserved in the firing ducts.

S. M. Goldstein, an archaeologist and conservator of the expedition, investigated the area from W 8–12/N 25.5–34.0 at the levels of the hearths and suggested that the area was a dump from the smelting of iron ore. Many lumps of iron in a spongy state with slag adhering to the top of them were found in a thick layer of loosely compacted ash. In the same fill with the porous masses of iron were found quantities of vitrified brick and slag. A completely vitrified tuyère fragment (W 9–11/N 25.5–32.0; *101.5) was also found adhering to a section of vitrified brick on which it may have rested when in use. The iron lumps are lozenge-shaped masses, somewhat thicker in the center than at the edges. They appear to be blooms of iron which were formed by reducing iron ore in a smelting furnace. These blooms would be worked in a secondary furnace and the porous slag would be broken away from the isolated collections of iron by hammering and reheating.

The furnace installations would have been quite substantial and the extreme temperatures of at least 1,500° C. would produce quantities of scoriated and vitrified brick from old furnaces. The location of slag attached to stone as well as brick suggests that the furnace complex was probably built within CG, but the exact findspot has not been located. The random stratigraphy of ash, brick, iron, and slag suggests a dump and the quantity of material indicates that a sizable industry was involved.[48] The date of this dump is most likely Middle to Late Byzantine and relates to other levels of industrial activity found throughout CG.

Stratification Near the East Side of CGC

Some digging within the western niches of wall CGE helped to confirm the later sequences of industrial activity found at the southern and northern ends of CGC (Figs. 351, 365, 368).

Half-Dome SCW

SCW was excavated to *99.00 in the northern part, *98.17 in the southern part (Fig. 366). A marked layer of burned earth and ash was found at *100.22 and a second level of black ashes at *99.50. This corresponds to the second and third burned levels found in the southern pit.[49] From *100.0 to *99.0 were found several examples of

Middle Byzantine pottery, helping to date the burned levels. Under the lower level of burning was soft gray mud with a thin band of ashes under it. River pebbles and sand continued to *98.55, remnants of the massive flooding that has already been detected elsewhere in the building. A secondary blocking wall in the door between SCW and SCE had its base at *99.00 and clearly rested on flood deposits.

Niche MAW

A similar sequence was found in clearing niche MAW (Fig. 367). A series of levels with light deposits of gray ash appeared at about *101.55 followed from about *101.20 by several heavier ash levels. Pottery in these levels was largely Byzantine.

Below the ash levels were two marked strata of charcoal, lime, and slag. The upper level at ca. *99.60 contained partially burned fragments of marble, possibly indicating the presence of a lime-kiln. The lower at ca. *99.00 contained large quantities of slag. The base of a large pithos, P58.301, was found at *99.90, just above the "lime" layer, 0.80 m. from the north side of the recess, 1.15 m. from the east wall. Fragments of glazed Middle Byzantine ware were found to *99.40.

The lower of the two "industrial" strata seemed to belong to the period of transformation when the interior of MAW was plastered over and faced with brick, the door was walled up with brick and rubble, and a slighter wall of brick and spoils was built just to the west of MAW (top *98.85; W. 0.50 m.; H. 0.40 m., running N-S). A red cement floor at *98.50 goes with the wall. This was presumably the same period when virtually all the openings in CGE and HM were blocked up with rubble and mortar (Figs. 343–345).

Half-Dome NCW

NCW was dug only to the level of the top of the doorway (Fig. 365), ca. *100.00, but again a level of ashes was found over stucco floor at *101.30 and a twelfth century A.D. coin was found in loose brown earth accumulated near the north wall at *99.92. Just south of the sixth voussoir from the center southward a stone had been removed and in the hollow was a well preserved human skull of a person aged 18–20.[50]

Finds: CGC

Coin
C60.12. W 10.70/S 0.0, *101.60, ca. 1.5 m. east of the east face of the southeast pier of CGW near fallen voussoirs. Attributed to John I, A.D. 972–1028. *Sardis* M1 (1971) 130, no. 1157, Anonymous Class A.

Pottery
P60.2:2233. W 4–9/S 3–N 2, *102.0–101.0. Between southern piers. Base of bowl. Hollow ring foot, coarse walls. Yellow and brown glaze. Incised spirals and cross pattern on inside. W. inner base 0.087 m.; diam. of foot 0.06 m.; H. 0.03 m.; Th. 0.01 m. Middle Byzantine. (Fig. 376.)
P60.3:2234. W 4–9/S 3–N 2, *102.0–101.0. Fragment of bowl rim. Straight rim. Exterior: white painted band along rim, rest plain red. Interior: yellow-green glaze with band of brown, incised guilloche design below rim. Wall thickens from rim down. L. 0.07 m.; W. 0.053 m.; max. Th. 0.009 m. Middle Byzantine. (Fig. 377.)

Stone Objects
S58.2:169. W 1.5/N 8–9, *104.50. Fragment of sculpture? Crystalline material, wavy relief pattern. L. 0.065 m.; W. 0.05 m.; H. 0.03 m. From original decoration of building?
S58.3:203. W 0–3/N 16–17. Sculptured marble fragment. Wavy relief pattern. W. 0.075 m.; H. 0.025 m.; H. relief 0.005 m. Part of original decoration of building? (Fig. 378.)
S58.4:204. No grid recorded. Fragment of marble rosette. Four petals. Perhaps from a coffer or cassette. Max. W. 0.095m. Antonine?

Metal Objects
M60.4:2244. W 10/S 5–N 2, between southern piers, *102.0. Bronze small hinge, flat object with short handle with broken round thin end. Hole in center. Main part broken off across center. Decorated with tiny punched rings in chevron pattern. L. 0.053 m.; L. handle 0.01 m.; W. 0.021 m.; W. at narrow end 0.017 m.; W. handle 0.007 m.; diam. round piece 0.015 m. (Fig. 379.)
M58.25:228. W 0–3/N 23. Fragment of lead strap used as anchor for iron clamps in stone. Two pieces restored. L. ca. 0.265 m. Th. 0.015 m. (Fig. 380.)

Finds: SCW

Pottery
P58.344:631. E 1–5/N 6–11. *101.90. Two fragments (not joining) of plate, one with rim, diam. 0.28 m. Pale yellow glaze on buff fabric. Middle Byzantine. (Fig. 381.)

Stone Objects
S58.54:1023. E 1–5/N 6–11, *99.50–*98.50. Two mosaic tesserae, 0.01 m. sq. Th. 0.005 m. One green, one yellow.

Metal Object
M58.22:224. E 1/N 9, *103.40. Iron knife. Narrow tapering blade, straight back, rounded tip, tapering tang. Overall L. 0.135 m.; L. tang 0.05 m.; W. 0.02 m. (Fig. 382.)

Finds: MAW

Pottery
P58.447:719. E 1/N 13–19.5, *101.37. Rim fragment. Flat rim; yellow glaze on buff interior; exterior plain. W 0.06 m.; diam. 0.22 m. Middle Byzantine.
P58.361:624. *99.35–*98.70. Numerous fragments of red ware with incised waves, one with a lightly incised leaf, one

with horizontal ridging. Included are three rim fragments, 0.13, 0.13, 0.18 m., two small pithos bases, one flat base, one straight handle. (Fig. 383.)

P58.663:1168. Under center of arch in west face east wall, *100.24, 2.66 m. below soffit. Base of large coarse pithos. Wet-smoothed. Contained some fragments of fiber or cloth on bottom. Diam. ca. 0.85 m.

Terracotta Objects
T58.25:887. Under center of arch. *98.60. Horse and rider figurine. Half of horse's head missing. One hind and one front leg missing, other two legs partly broken. Rider's head missing, also arm and feet. Bridle for horse added with separate piece of clay. L. horse 0.09 m.; H. from hind leg of horse to shoulder of man 0.085 m. (Fig. 384.)

Uncatalogued. Two terracotta tiles with handprints. Crude, thick tile. Handprint made when tile was wet.

Glass Objects
G58.42:554. *99.90. Two joining fragments of a handle. Black. Small nodule of glass at top of curve. L. 0.033 m. Found with green-glazed pottery. Byzantine, tenth–twelfth century.

G58.53:651. *98.90. Fragment of handle and part of body of vessel. Clear watery greenish glass. L. handle 0.027 m.; W. at base of handle 0.017 m.; L. body 0.0345 m. Byzantine, tenth–twelfth century.

Metal Object
M58.115:720. *98.50. Fragment of bronze bracelet. Wide flat band with open ends. Bottom part bent inwards. Diam. 0.06 m.; W. 0.045 m.

Finds: NCW

Coin
C69.3. E 4/N 25.2, *99.92. Found in loose, brown, wind blown earth. Bronze. John Comnenus, A.D. 1118–1143. Not in *Sardis* M1, as it was found after 1968.

Units North of CGC

North of the Main Hall CGC the situation becomes more complex. Directly north is one large hall on a north-south axis and two halls perpendicular to it on an east-west axis. None has been excavated to the same extent and depth as CGC and only their outlines and tops of some arches have been brought to light. Units in the northeast part of the building, HM, CR, and HN, have been more widely explored.

Unit CN

CN is a second large rectangular unit directly north of CGC and more or less on the same (north-south) axis (Fig. 336). It is reached on the south through the arched door in the north wall of CGC (Fig. 430) and its main walls are CNE on the east, A on the north, and CNW (mostly unexcavated) on the west.[51] No other doorways and no interior

features were found in excavation which in this area of the building did not go much below the modern surface. It is likely, however, that at one time there was a door or passageway to HM via arch A 4[52] through wall CNE (cf. Fig. 387).

The hall itself originally measured ca. 18.5 m. N-S by 12.5 m. E-W (E 1–W 13.5/N 32–50.5). Since major portions of the main walls had fallen away at the levels excavated, the unit appears somewhat larger in plan (Fig. 336). The unit was not probed stratigraphically but some of the Middle Byzantine hearth area described overlapped from the northwest end of CGC to the southwest end of CN.

Unit HM

North of NCW in CGE and bonding in with it at E 7/N 25.75–27.50 is the circular structure HM, one of the most interesting units of CG, both architecturally and for the evidence it provides on the building's history (Fig. 336). When first excavated, HM was thought to be a hemicycle, but on further exploration it was shown to have been a completely circular unit for at least part of its history.[53]

The circular shape of this unit is common for the Iaconicum or sweat bath, almost standard in Roman thermae.[54] A similar room with four niches instead of eight occurs in the Baths of Capito at Miletus and had this function (Fig. 340 No. 5).[55] Another proposal, advanced by W. Reusch during his visit to Sardis in 1969, is that the unit served as a dressing room (apodyterium).[56]

The southern part of the structure (Fig. 388)— about a quarter of it—was constructed of the same limestone masonry as CGE and CGW; the northern three fourths was of the same mortared rubble technique as the other northern units of the building: CN, CP, CQ, and HN (Fig. 387). The northernmost part of the ashlar section approximately intersected the line of the west face of CGE. The southeastern end coincided with pier 0 of the east face of CGE (Fig. 385). The masonry slabs of the southwest section were backed with roughly fitted stones inserted between NCW and HM. The highest preserved level of HM walls was at *102.15 in the ashlar section (Fig. 386).

Within the structure were eight arched niches, A 1–A 8, alternately half-domed (A 2, A 4?, A 6,

A 8) and vaulted (A 1, A 3?, A 5, A 7). Two niches, A 1, A 2, fall in the ashlar section, six (A 3–A 8) in the rubble (Fig. 387). At one time, four of these niches (A 2, A 4, A 5, A 7) went all the way through the wall of HM communicating with CGC, CN, and HN to the west and north and to undefined units to the east (A 7). None of the niches was excavated to floor level, but a floor is likely to have occurred around *96.00 or lower, judging from the height of the door lintel in A 2.

There is little evidence for how the circular room was roofed. It may have had a rubble dome which would then have entirely collapsed.[57] No spring point for a dome was identified on the walls, but it may have started higher than the preserved top. The entire circle was filled with rubble and brick mixed with earth which was not entirely cleared away; it may have contained the remains of a collapsed dome.

Later all of the niches had been blocked up with earth and/or brick and the doors of those which communicated with other parts of the building were sealed. Covering the former arches, the walls of HM at this time were revetted. A thick layer of soft pinkish grout covered much of the west wall where the rubble and ashlar join and entirely concealed arch A 3. In the surface of this grout were clear impressions of large square tiles (H. 0.48 m.; W. 0.047 m.), with vertically aligned pinholes in the seams between them (Fig. 388).

Pipes. Remains of four vertical cuttings for pipes were found on the interior walls of HM. Pipe 1 is between A 1 and A 2; W. 0.20 m.; H. 3.56 m.; D. 0.14 m.; bottom *98.81 (Figs. 387, 388). Its top is at the preserved top of the wall; it runs down through five courses of ashlar and makes a right angle at the bottom cutting the western voussoirs of A 1. A trace of cement was preserved in the cutting with which the pipe had been fastened. Pipe 2 is at the south side of A 4, partly bricked up and partly restored (incorrectly) in 1959 (Fig. 387); P.H. 1.70 m.; W. 0.20 m.; D. 0.17 m. Pipe 3 is in the rubble section between A 5 and A 6. It is bricked up; its lower part lies in the restored part of the wall. Its top is lost in destroyed wall. P.H. ca. 1.0 m.; W. ca. 0.20 m.; top missing. Pipe 4 is between A 8 and A 1, still in the rubble section.

P.H. (to ground level) ca. 2.0 m.; W. 0.14 m. (Fig. 387).

It is uncertain whether these cuttings were intended to hold drainage pipes, water induction pipes, heating pipes, or some combination of the three. Some broken remains of terracotta pipes were found in the fill of HM but their association with these cuttings is not established.

Arches. Of the eight arched niches of HM, the two masonry ones, A 1 and A 2 are most dissimilar from the rest, A 4 is probably a secondary rebuilding, and A 3, 5, 6, 7, 8 are most alike in outward appearance.[58]

A 1 was the only one of HM with regular, wedge-shaped limestone voussoirs. It was a rectangular vaulted niche which had been blocked up to the spring level (*98.65) with bricks. The interior of the vault and the back wall had been plastered and revetted with green and white marble slabs of which five fragments remain *in situ* on the underside of the vault (Figs. 387, 389)[59] together with the impressions of twenty-three long narrow tiles and some iron pins. The blocking bricks had also been covered with grout and revetted, presumably in the same period as the revetment of HM walls.

A 2 is a half-domed niche hollowed out of two huge limestone blocks balanced against each other and joined with mortar (Fig. 387). Two courses of curving masonry are below, and beneath these is a curved opening for a door. The doorway was filled with bricks up to the lintel and the bricks continued westward under the lintel. The door would probably have provided access to CGC through the northeast corner of the pier. Like A 1, it had at one time been covered with thick plaster and some faint traces of paint appeared on the southeastern wall of the niche near the doorway.

A 4 gave evidence for a major restructuring of HM, possibly at the same time that the other arches were blocked up. A 4 is the only arch of the eight to have been constructed of brick, and instead of a niche it formed a barrel-vaulted tunnel or passage, apparently leading to CN (Fig. 390). The main part of the arch face was heavily restored by the Sardis Expedition in 1960, but it appears to have been much wider than all the other arches, so wide that it intersects and interferes with the eastern voussoirs of the totally blocked up and camouflaged arch A 3 (Fig. 387). This suggests that there had originally been a rubble niche or vault in the present location of A 4, similar in appearance and proportions to A 5–A 8, which was then enlarged and remodeled when the other arches were being closed up. It does not represent the final stage of HM, however, as the interior of the vault had been filled to the top with earth and rubble in the same way as the interiors of A 5–A 8.

A 5–A 8 were all very similar on the faces but had differing interior plans and decoration. The facades of all four were made of small, narrow voussoirs set in thick mortar. In all four, the central three voussoirs were of white stones, slightly larger than the other voussoirs and were spaced with two narrower dark stones making an alternating pattern of dark and light stones emphasizing the center of the arch (Figs. 387, 391).[60] A 3 was apparently constructed in the same fashion as A 5–A 8 although only the upper voussoirs of the arch were left uncovered by later brickwork (Fig. 392).

A 5 and A 7 were vaulted niches which had doorways through the backs to other units. That in A 5 had been filled up with rubble on the interior HM side, while its counterpart opening on the exterior CR side had been given a stone backing wall making it a "blind arch."[61] A 7 was left open, forming a barrel-vaulted passage to the east.

A 6 and A 8 were semi-domed niches, neither of which apparently had doors. Only the face of A 8 was exposed; the interior was filled almost to the top with rubble.

Evidence for interior decoration was found in A 5 and A 6. A 5 was covered on the inside with at least two layers of thick pinkish plaster in which were impressions of long, narrow revetment tiles, similar to those in A 1. In A 6 the interior was plastered in at least three layers. L. J. Majewski, who examined the niche, suggested that the layered plaster was of the type used as mosaic bedding elsewhere at Sardis,[62] a suggestion substantiated by the finding of three mosaic tesserae embedded in the second layer. No tile impressions or mosaics were found in any of the other niches, although layers of plaster adhered to the upper parts of some of the niches and a few blue and green tes-

sarae were found in front of A 4 at *98.20. It is tempting to conjecture, however, that revetment alternated with mosaic where rectangular niche alternated with half-dome.

Restoration in HM. In 1960 extensive repairs were made to HM. The entire top and northeast side of A 4 had to be replaced in brick along with much of the wall above it. The eastern jamb was repaired in stone following the original stone coursing. The central part of A 5 and the wall above it was replaced in rubble as were the east and west jambs of A 5, A 6, and the north jamb of A 7. The rubble was set in heavily outlined mortar and is clearly distinguishable from the ancient masonry (Fig. 387).

Finds

HM was excavated to ca. *100.00 in the center, ca. *98.10 around the edges of the interior. No floors were reached either in the center or in any of the niches. Most of the finds, therefore, are probably from the latest fill.

Within and around HM from ca. *102 to *100 were Byzantine glazed wares and glass bracelet fragments. Some architectural fragments, a part of a marble window grille, and a small piece of molding were found and several pieces of terracotta pipes were scattered throughout the fill in the center of the structure, particularly in front of and around arch A 8. A Byzantine coin was found between *100.35 and *99.90 near the center of HM.

Coin
C58.277:912. Ca. E 5/N 34, *100.35–*99.90. Anonymous Class A, attributed to John I, A.D. 972–1028. *Sardis* M1 (1971) 128 no. 1134.

Pottery
P59.228:1586. Within and east of HM, ca. *102.50–100.80 (in fill). Four fragments (not joining) of green-yellow glazed ware. Th. wall 0.011 m. Byzantine.
P59.240:1609. Inside HM. *100.80. Small red ware flask. Small mouth and neck. Small pierced handle, flaring foot. Incised diagonal lines form pine cone pattern. H. 0.06 m.; diam. 0.03 m. Cf. the pine cone thymiaterion, Robinson, *Agora* V, 38 no. G159, pl. 43, 1st half 1st cent. A.D. Grandjouan, *Agora* VI, 69 no. 866, pl. 22, pine cone mold, 3rd cent. A.D. (Fig. 393.)
P59.253:1630. Along northeast wall of HM to *99.50. Fragment of small bowl with disk foot. Vertical black band on exterior. Graffito on under part of foot: α. H. 0.025 m.; diam. foot 0.04 m.; Th. 0.005 m. Late Roman, 3rd or 4th century A.D.? (Wrabetz). (Fig. 394.)

Stone Object
S59.8:1417. 1 m. east of HM, *101.65. Part of openwork marble grille for window. Diam. ca. 0.21 m.; P.W. 0.175 m.; H. 0.15 m.; Th. 0.05 m.

Glass Objects
G59.47:1542. Inside HM, *101. Fragment of thin blue glass bracelet. L. 0.033 m.; W. 0.005 m. Middle Byzantine. Uncatalogued fragment of spiral twisted glass bracelet. Red, white, blue. Square in section. L. 0.034 m.; W. 0.007 m. Byzantine.

Area North of HM

The area directly north of HM (Figs. 336, 397), consisting basically of Room HN and Corridor CR, was one of the most complex of the entire building. Although it was not very large as units in CG go, it was divided into several units and provided evidence both for lateral and vertical access in the building by means of a series of passageways and the only stairway uncovered in CG. The probable function of these units is unclear; however, some kind of service unit offered possible interpretation for CR; otherwise one might consider connection with heating, suggested by the discovery of several fragments of hypocaust tile in this area. HN, with its rather elaborate fresco decoration, is more of a puzzle, as it would have been suitable neither for a service or utility room nor for a bathing room. Perhaps a lounging room of some kind is more likely for HN; possibly it was an open, arcaded court, at least in its early phase.

The area as a whole is bounded on the south by the northern exterior face of HM; on the west by the east face of wall CNE; on the north by the south face of wall A; on the east by staircase St, landing L, landing K, wall F (Fig. 395). Some of these units, such as landings K and L and the area to the east of HM had connections to the east and seem to indicate the presence of further rooms and units in that direction which were not explored. The area appears to have gone through more than one period of change and renewal; the two main phases distinguished are the earlier "rubble" phase and a later "brick" phase.

Room HN

Originally there seems to have been only one large room directly north of HM. It would have been rectangular, ca. 12 m. north-south by 8 m. east-west (E 2.0–10.0/N 38.5–50.5) and was

probably entered from HM through a door in arch A 5.[63] The massive walls of this unit were of mortared rubble construction: wall CNE to west, the eastern part of A to north, and F (the southern extension of CPE) to east (Fig. 336). CNE had two arches on the eastern face, *a* to the south, *b* to the north (Fig. 397). Both were constructed of limestone rubble voussoirs like those of HM arches A 5–A 8. Arch *a* was originally open allowing communication between HN and CN to the west. Arch *b* was not excavated far enough to determine if it had a door. The two arches were not of even height or width: W. *a,* 4.30 m.; springing, *98.14; crown, *100.22; W. *b,* 3.20 m.; springing unexcavated; crown, *99.44.

On the east side of the original unit there appear to have been three arches: *c, d,* in wall F and *g* to the south, later blocked by the staircase (Fig. 397). All three arches are of brick construction with *c* and *d* resting on stone piers. One or more of these arches may have been open to the east, but none was cleared enough to establish this with certainty.

The curve of the central arch *c* was complete with the springing preserved on both north and south sides at *97.64. The springing on the north side interfered with the curve of *d* which shared a jamb with *c* (Fig. 397). It is possible that *d* was constructed later than *c*. The two arches are of different heights and shapes. W. *c,* 2.10 m.; crown, *98.63; W. *d,* 1.10 m.; crown, *98.24. Neither is symmetrical with arches *a* or *b* opposite.

Northward from the center of *d* at ca. N 47.50 the wall seems to have a pier for a door leading eastward, crowned by a limestone block at ca. *98.0. The door was apparently closed off by collapsed brick and rubble at ca. *99.44. Arch *g* is a much wider brick arch which now forms the eastern end of CR and probably made a passage through wall *a* (Fig. 397). At present, it is interrupted by the stairway and by wall *w* and is not exposed as far as the springing which was probably at ca. *97.64 with crown at ca. *98.32. Its full width was probably ca. 3.40 m. There do not seem to have been any arches in the south side of wall A, the north wall of HN.

In the second stage, the original large room was divided by the introduction of wall *w* running east-west at E 2.25–9.51/N 41.85–42.65 from the stairway to wall CNE and forming corridor CR at the south end of the unit (Fig. 395). The wall divided the faces of arches *a, c,* and *g* (Fig. 397); arch *a* was bricked up, and the northern outer face of arch A 5 in HM was blocked with stones and transformed into a blind arch. Arches *e* and *f* in wall *w* allowed communication between CR and HN while vaults *x* and *y* and the staircase occupied CR. Wall paintings were applied to the walls of HN at this time.

Characteristic of the second phase is the use of brick-tile bonding courses in rubble walls, as in wall *w* and in walls *b, c,* and platform *c* to the east of HM and CR. Wall *w* is constructed of three brick courses alternating with 0.155 m. of rubble. The top of the wall was finished with broken, horizontally laid tiles, ca. 0.50 m. wide, and had been "shaved" or cut down to ca. *99.60. At ca. *98.80 was a thin marble profile. A facing of twelve horizontal brick courses rose above the profile forming the springing for vault *y*. A similar arrangement for the opposite springing was preserved on the north wall of HM (Fig. 396). Four rectangular beam holes occur above the marble profile in wall *w* and opposite in HM (Fig. 396).

Corridor CR

Vault x was a brick barrel vault with a tile floor preserved over it at *98.75. It was located at the western end of CR, filling the corner between the western curve of HM (Fig. 397) and the south end of wall CNE and extending from E 4.7–2.3/N 38.8–41.6 (Fig. 396a). The south wall of the vault followed the curvature of the north wall of HM, the north wall was formed by wall *w*. The western end of vault *x* springs from a rubble pier with limestone quoins in HM and was sealed by a brick wall which filled arch *a*. The roof of the vault forms an upper floor or landing and cuts across and partly obscures the face of arch *a*. On this floor was found a Late Roman/Early Byzantine lamp (L 60.47; Fig. 403), fourth–sixth century A.D., which helps to date this phase of construction. Under the vault in the south wall was found the top of another brick arch *h* whose span was from east to west, top at *97.50, est. W. 2.40 m. It does not go through HM at the level excavated, nor does it correspond to any of the arches within HM.

Vault y was a second brick barrel vault, higher than *x* and directly east of it (Fig. 397). The center of the arch had fallen out leaving only the rows of tiles of the springing and shoulders on the faces of wall *w* and HM (Fig. 396). Its highest preserved course is at *99.12, springing at *98.48, W. 1.90 narrowing westward to 1.75 m. at E 5. The other side of arch A 5 in HM opened at one time into the south wall of *y*, spanning it laterally from east to west (Fig. 396a)—top at *98.32, springing, *97.64. It was originally constructed of narrow, limestone voussoirs. When the original stone arch was broken it was repaired with marble and a smaller, brick arch was inserted into the strengthened frame. Figure 396a, taken in 1960, shows the western side of this brick arch below the preserved shoulder of vault *x*. The brick had been removed and does not show up in Figure 396, taken in 1969. Barrel vault *y* was built after the stone arch was partly dismantled and its jambs rebuilt. The brick/stone arch seems to have intersected vault *y*.

The apparent means of communication between CR and HN to the north was through two brick arches *e* and *f* in wall *w*. Only the tops of these arches were exposed, crown of each at *97.70. Both were flat arches. Arch *e* was to the west, opening in the north wall of vault *x;* arch *f* to the east opened in vault *y* (Fig. 398).

The staircase area. Staircase St was a remarkably well-preserved staircase of eight steps built of brick tiles and supported on a brick half-arch (Fig. 398). The approach to the stair is from the north (Fig. 336). One or two steps lead from landing K at *100.7 down to landing L (Fig. 400). The west wall here had been pulled out, but once joined and bonded into wall *w*. Two or three tile steps led southward to the top of St. The stair descended to the south in seven steps (Fig. 399) to a small landing against the north face of HM. Then it turned 180° and continued descending northward passing through arch *f* in wall *w* to reach unit HN. The stair crosses in front of and blocks arch *g* which originally was open to the east (Fig. 398).

East of the stair are the remains of another brick arch *a*, projecting from the eastern face of HM. Tile platform *c* at ca. *100.0 and rubble walls running east from the southeast face of HM suggest that there was the floor of an upper story at approximately this level (Fig. 336). These walls *a, b, d* are of brick and rubble construction, similar to wall *w*. The side of HM appears to have been dug out to accommodate wall *a* running north, while wall *b* running east from HM was bonded into *a* and formed a right angle with it. Tile platform *c* was between *b* and *d* to the south while wall *d* projected east from the south outer wall of HM, more or less on a line with the projected line of pier 0 of the east face of CGE (Fig. 401).

The top preserved course of wall *d* was at *99.75. The brick courses had thick mortar joints, almost the thickness of the bricks; four brick courses alternated with five rubble courses. The wall was 0.60 m. wide; its length was not determined as its eastern end ran into the scarp.

This whole unit (room?) to the east would have communicated with HM through arch A 7 (Fig. 387) before it was blocked up. The brick and rubble walls are all the result of one period of construction; however, whether or not the blocking up of A 7 and A 5 took place at the same time remains a problem.

Evidence for upper story. The traces of wall paintings on wall CNE (Figs. 428, 429) were visible for a clear height of three and a half meters, showing that there was no floor between levels *98.0 and *101.5. The position of the arches (*a* and *b*) in wall CNE (Fig. 397) indicates that the painting continued downward below the lowest excavated point. The highest level of the paintings appears to make an even line along the wall at *101.5 while the wall continues to rise. In the opinion of L. J. Majewski the appearance of the wall along this line suggests a possible upper floor at this level. Two large beam holes, possibly supports for floor boards, are seen in the wall above the top line of the paintings (bottoms of holes at ca. *101.50; Figs. 395, 397, 402). The possibility is further strengthened by the discovery in the southern part of HN and the northern part of CR at ca. *99.15, of a number of hypocaust tile fragments, leading to the impression that some unit with hypocaust heating collapsed into the area. A large amount of rubble and brick found in clearing the hall is also suggestive of the collapse of a possible vaulted roof or ceiling.

Finds

Finds in HN, other than the hypocaust fragments mentioned above,[64] included fragments of marble revetments along the north face of wall *w* and the east face of CNE at ca. *99.00. A pair of marble blocks was found lying near the northwest corner of walls *w* and CNE, possibly fallen from wall *w*.

Lamp
L60.47:2857. On landing above vault *x*.*98.67. Almost complete; nozzle missing. Small body with solid vertical handle, strigilate panel. Small high disk with hole in center. Footprint in center of base. Mold-made. H. with handle 0.034 m.; without handle 0.025 m.; W. of body 0.048 m.; diam. of base 0.025 m. Late Roman, fourth to fifth cent. A.D. Cf. Menzel, 94, 98–99, no. 634, fig. 81:13. (Fig. 403.)

Pottery
P59.232:1599. Eight fragments of ring-footed bowl. Along east face of CNE, *100.75–100.50. Glazed with incised design inside. Diam. foot 0.08 m.; diam. rim 0.22 m.; H. 0.095 m.; Th. 0.01 m. Middle Byzantine. (Figs. 404–405.)

Glass
G59.48:1544. East end of wall A, ca. *100.30. Fragment of twisted spiral bracelet. Red, white, blue. Square section at end. L. 0.034 m.; W. 0.007 m. Middle Byzantine.

The Northern Units

At the extreme northern end of CG two other units were outlined by excavation. These were the large oblong "halls" CP and CQ. The two halls were of almost identical dimensions and lay parallel to each other with their main axes east-west, perpendicular to the main axis of the building as a whole. Interior dimensions of CP were: L. (east-west) 24.70 m.; W. (north-south) 11.3 m. Those of CQ were: L. ca. 26.70+ m.; W. 12.5 m. No north-south cross walls were found in CQ so that the interior length is only approximate (Fig. 336).

The main east-west walls A, P, Q are of massive mortared rubble construction. Enough of the north and south faces of each wall were exposed to determine the correct thicknesses: A, 4.1 m.; P, 4.6 m.; Q, 3.8 m. Probably these walls were intended to support barrel-vaulted roofing.

Hall CP

This unit was excavated along the north face of wall A and the south face of wall P in sufficient depth to expose the tops of two stone arches (*a′1, a′3*) and a brick half-dome (*a′2*). It was cleared at the east and west ends to disclose the top of the eastern crosswall CPE and the southern end of the western crosswall CPW, both of rubble construction. Wall CPE bonded in with wall A (but not with P) and was the same width as wall F on the south side of A. Thus the eastern end of CP is flush with that of HN (Fig. 336).

Near the eastern end of CP were two large arches $a'1$ in wall A and $a'3$ in wall P opposite. Both had long, narrow stone voussoirs. Under arch $a'1$ wall A was packed with rubble to form a "blind arch" (Figs. 406, 407). Fifteen voussoirs of $a'1$ were preserved *in situ,* three on the east, twelve on the west (Fig. 406). Their average length is 0.85 m.; width from 0.08 m. to 0.13 m. at top; 0.07 to 0.11 m. at bottom. The top of the arch had fallen away with the top of wall A. The springing was not cleared but the estimated total span of the arch is ca. 9.0 m.; depth to backing stones, 0.55 m. to 0.60 m.

Only one side (the east) of $a'3$ was excavated, so that its exact width was not determined. It appeared, however, to stand opposite $a'1$ and the two were possibly linked by a north-south cross vault. The arch was cleared to a greater depth than $a'1$, exposing twenty-seven voussoirs *in situ* on the east side, some of which were blocked by the end of wall CPE abutting on wall P (Fig. 407). The crown of this arch had also fallen out.

Near the western end of unit CP at W 10–15 was a semi-domed niche in the north face of wall A. The niche was faced with an arch constructed of a double row of bricks of which part of the lower row is now missing (Fig. 406). The arch is ca. 4.70 m. wide, top at *100.15. The interior is lined with traces of backing plaster. The excavation did not go down far enough to show whether a door to the south existed, but on the basis of proportions of the arch, a floor is possible at ca. *95.50. No similar arch was found in the south face of wall P opposite.

The western end of wall P appeared to have fallen completely away, but one would expect it to have aligned with the west face of either wall A or wall Q (which did not quite align). The southern end of crosswall CPW was found running north from the northwest end of wall A but its northern end was not picked up at wall P.

Hall CQ

No distinctive interior features were discovered in CQ. Excavation was minimal, confined to outlining enough of walls P (north side) and Q (south side) to find the face and determine the dimensions of the unit (Figs. 336, 406, 408). The entire length of wall Q was not discovered as the eastern end was not visible above ground but the western face of the wall was cleared at W 18.2/N 83.3–86.2 (Fig. 408). No traces of presumed crosswalls CQE and CQW were discovered at the levels excavated (no deeper than ca. *101.0).

Unit West of CP

Some evidence was found that further units existed to the west of CP and CN, leaving open the question of the actual original extent of Building CG. About 3.5 m. below the present surface the top of a narrow rubble wall WA was found running west from the western end of wall A (Figs. 336, 406), W 17.30–20.15/N 50.45–51.50, *99.80. In front (north) of this wall was a carved marble block c, and set at right angles to c forming a corner with it were three more marble blocks a, b, d running north along the west side of wall CPW (Figs. 336, 410, 411). Blocks a and b were clamped together with an iron clamp. The blocks were pieces of entablature, apparently reused, and having carved floral decoration, possibly dating to the first or second century A.D. (Fig. 409). According to architect F. K. Yegül, the closest parallel to this decoration at Sardis is in mid-second century blocks reused in Building D and built into the Acropolis fortress walls.[65] At the southeast corner under blocks b and c was the top of a broken Ionic capital. Two brick tiles were found *in situ* on top of b showing that the top surface had been covered.

In 1969 block b was removed by the Sardis stone crew leaving a piece at the corner of the southern end of CPW. Beneath a and b on top of CPW were exposed four marble slabs, 0.08 m. thick (Fig. 410, left), and beneath these, against the west face of wall A was found the top of a small half-dome with a north-south span, 1.25 m. wide, crown at *99.21 (Figs. 410, 411). Its construction is similar to that of the niches and half-domes in HM, close enough to suggest contemporaneity for this and HM. The interior of the dome was plastered, and in the opinion of L. J. Majewski, this may be the same kind of plaster observed in HM arch A 5, and assumed to be mosaic bedding.

The entablatures formed a left inner corner of what was possibly a monumental entranceway of some sort, backed by walls A and CPW on the west and by wall WA on the south. If so, it would most likely have had its main gate or door to the south. This would imply another major unit south of this and west of CN, and also a corresponding, symmetrical arrangement to the west to complete the entranceway. Another possibility for this configuration is an arcade or niched courtyard with the semi-domed niche in CPW as one of the flanking arches. Such a screen or court might have permitted entrance into unit CP, for which so far no certain entrance is known.

JCW, GMAH

X THE ROMAN BATH CG: CONSTRUCTION AND DECORATION

Jane C. Waldbaum
George M. A. Hanfmann

Although CG was incompletely excavated and its original plan and date of building are not certain, it provides important information about building techniques of the Late Roman/Early Byzantine period and the decorative treatment of a building of this scale. We therefore include a brief analysis of construction and decorative techniques used in CG in order to provide a clearer picture of the building as an architectural entity. Much of this material will have been described and illustrated more fully in the previous section in relation to its function and placement in the building. In the following section, the intent is to summarize and compare similar features (arches, domes, etc.) and to discuss the materials and techniques utilized by the builders.

Walls: Building Techniques and Materials

Several different construction methods and types of materials are represented at CG: ashlar masonry, rubble masonry, rubble and brick together, and brick alone. It appears that where brick and/or rubble features are found in conjunction with the ashlar construction they are mostly secondary, but where rubble is used alone for major walls, as in the northern part of the building, there exists a question as to the chronological relation to the ashlar.[1] Cemented rubble is used, however, over the ashlar on top of both CGE and CGW in

connection with a presumed cemented barrel vault which once linked these two side walls.[2]

Ashlar Masonry

Heavy limestone ashlar masonry was used in CG for the following features:

1. The two side walls of the Main Hall, CGE and CGW, including vaults and half-domes (Figs. 334, 343, 344, 365, 368).

2. The southern quarter of the circular unit HM, bonding in with CGE (Figs. 385–387).

3. The large stone arch between CGE and CGW at the south end of CGC (Fig. 349).

4. The piers and spurwalls SpE and SpW at E 1–W 13/N 29–30 (Figs. 372–373).

5. The platform found at E 5–8/N 13–16, *95.8–*95.6 in MAE (Figs. 356, 357).

The Material. A relatively unweathered sample of stone from the interior of one of the fallen voussoirs of the south arch was examined by a geologist and classified as a "fragmental limestone" or lithocalcarenite.[3] It consists of a fine matrix of white calcareous cement containing coarse-grained angular fragments of white micritic limestone and some red, yellow, and brown inclusions. A very few of the limestone particles are slightly rounded, and none is recrystallized. The angularity of the coarse limestone particles is uncommon under normal weathering conditions.[4] This sample is thought to be representative of most of the ashlar masonry used on CG.

The stone weathers gray where exposed to air, but where buried in earth or exposed only to water, it may appear pink to orange to yellow in bright light. The surface of the building has weathered and eroded badly, forming large holes and presenting a deeply pitted appearance (e.g. Figs. 334, 345, 366–368). The holes continue on a smaller scale deep within the matrix of the stone. Local informants report that similar stone is found today at Gökköy and Sart Çamur Hamamları, villages not far from Sardis, but the ancient quarry has not been identified.

Size of stone blocks. Limestone masonry blocks, other than voussoirs, range in size from 0.60 m. to 3.25 m. in length; from 0.50 m. to 1.20 m. in width; and from 0.27 m. to 0.60 m. in height. The largest known piece is a stretcher from pier 2 in CGE (Figs. 343, 345, 412), L. 3.15 m.; W. 1.10 m.; H. 0.88 m.

The stones seem to have been roughly measured to approximate some system of measurements in feet. The foot seems to have been based on the Roman foot of ca. 0.296 m. as in the better trimmed stone heights. Widths of 0.87 m. and 0.88 m. occur quite frequently, possibly as multiples of three feet.[5] It is probable that the blocks were trimmed close to several standard sizes in the quarry and then cut down as needed, with much latitude permitted in the variety of dimensions.

The most common sizes are a large "double height" block of ca. H. 0.60 m., W. either 0.90 or 1.20 m., and L. ca. 1.10 m. "Flat" stones of similar lengths and widths but in two "small" heights, 0.27–0.35 m. or 0.45–0.50 m., also occur. The same dimensions may recur as width or height or length, depending on the use of the stones as "headers" or "stretchers" (with short end or length presented to surface), or whether in horizontal position (with largest surface flat) or vertical position (with largest surface as height).

Weight of the blocks. A sample of limestone from a voussoir of the south arch was found to have a density of 2.42 grams per cubic centimeter.[6] A cubic meter of this stone would there-

Table 7. Characteristic sizes of ashlar blocks used at CG in m.

Category	Length	Width	Height
small	0.74	0.81	0.56
medium and low	1.05–1.20	0.85–0.95	0.36 m.
medium and high	1.05–1.20	0.85–0.95	0.45–0.60
long	1.40–1.90	0.65–0.95	0.45–0.55
			0.80–0.90
	2.10–2.35	0.80–0.90	0.70 m.,
			0.55–0.60
very long	2.58–3.10	0.65–1.10	0.36–1.10

fore weigh about 2,420 kg. or 2.66 tons. A large stone from the building of about 3 cu. m. would thus weigh ca. 8 tons (7,260 kg.); the "medium" size, ca. half a cubic meter, would weigh ca. 1.44 tons (1,306.3 kg.); and the majority of stones would probably fall between one half and three tons.

Coursing of masonry. Certain general schemes of coursing are obvious in the two south faces of CGW and CGE (Figs. 334, 350) and to a lesser extent on the east and west faces of CGE (Figs. 343, 365). The systems are based on alternate high and low courses, but beyond that, there are no detailed regularities. There is no regular alternation of headers and stretchers, nor of uprights and horizontals. Comparison of the south faces of CGE and CGW above the spring profiles reveals an interesting lack of correspondence (Fig. 350) with CGE starting with a high course and CGW a low course directly above the profile and proceeding to alternate upwards with no attempt to achieve correspondence. A similar system is recognizable on the eastern face of CGE with rather impressive monumental effect made by the very large stones used in piers 1–4 (Figs. 343, 345, 346).

Bonding of masonry: piers. The piers buttressing the east and south sides of CGE (and presumably the west and south sides of CGW) are bonded into the main face of the wall following only a general scheme. In general, courses above the profile level of the piers bond into the wall where structurally feasible. Thus, courses that are in front of voussoirs do not bond, while those above the vault line do. An exception is pier 1 (between MAE and NCE) where the stone in the first course above the profile on the north side of the pier is an L-shaped block carved in one piece with the lowest voussoir of the arch (Fig. 413). The profile block of pier 1 also bonds into CGE but the two courses below profile and the courses above profile on the south side of the pier do not bond but abut on the east face of CGE (Fig. 354, right). In pier 2, the course directly below profile bonds in with CGE, the second one down does not, the third does (Fig. 355). The first three courses above profile do not bond, but the fourth one does. In pier 3, the profile and the course below profile bond in, as do the third and fourth course below profile. The five courses above profile do not bond (Fig. 414). In pier 4, the two courses directly below profile are bonded into the main structure; the first two courses above profile are not. The fourth one up on the north side is an L-shaped block making a corner with the east face of CGE (Fig. 415).

Because the eastern piers of CGE do bond in with the massive back wall (as presumably do the piers on the west face of CGW) and because they are themselves so massive and well built, they may have been intended to receive a massive vault structure from the east of CGE (and west of CGW). Thus it is not unlikely that there are further structural units to the east and west such as are found at Hierapolis (Fig. 339) and the Baths of Capito at Miletus (Fig. 340) surrounding the main units of the bath.[7]

The southeast pier of CGE (Fig. 416) is only preserved to *98.70. The easternmost stone on this level and the one below it bond into the main structure and pier 4 on the east side (Fig. 343). It is evident from the appearance of the wall of CGE, however, that the next courses above *98.70 did not bond in.

Clamping and doweling. The masonry does not exhibit any systematic use of doweling or clamping, although there is some evidence that clamps were used occasionally.

A clamp was found among the fallen stones of CGE near NCW, ca. W 3/N 25, which according to the fieldbook entry "appears to be lead set in mortar" and may have been a lead anchor for an iron clamp. A lead anchor also came from W 0–3/N 23 (Fig. 380) and a lump of lead from W 0–5/N 18–19, *102.54–101.80. A rough stone block with an iron

clamp was found at the west face of CGE near NCW at ± *102.50. The "entablature" blocks *a* and *b* from the west end of wall A were linked at the upper surface with a leaded iron clamp preserved on top of block *a*.

Dowel holes and dowels seem to occur occasionally, but not systematically, as vertical bonds. In general, builders relied on weight, trimming, and fitting to hold the blocks together.

Wedging. The only device observed with some frequency was the use of iron wedges. These were found near the faces of arches, sometimes cutting across joins in the fashion of a clamp, but usually spread against the stone as if hammered in with great force. Some better preserved examples occur in the west face of arch SCW on the west side of CGE (Figs. 417, 418). These devices were explained by a local master mason as iron wedges driven in between voussoirs to tighten any loose joints after an arch or vault was constructed. Wedges, therefore, unlike clamps, are always found near the surface of the joined stones.

Lifting holes. Several blocks, *in situ* or fallen, show lewis holes for lifting the blocks into position. These appear as dove-tailed holes in the face of the stone.[8] Examples occur in the lunette of TE at the west end of the tunnel, H. 0.06 m., L. 0.15 m., *100.20; in the lunette of SCE above the lintel (Fig. 419); and in the keystone of arch NCE, under which is also visible a large hole for a pin to hold revetment or sculptural ornament in place (Fig. 346).

Tools and tooling. The limestone used in CG is a difficult material to work in that it is friable on the surface, highly subject to weathering, and takes no fine finish. The stone cutting, even where not eroded, appears to have been rough. There are no drafted margins and no anathyrosis.

The roughest treatment was done with the trimming hammer. Most of the ashlar masonry was only trimmed with a large pointed chisel, possibly in the quarry (Fig. 420). Finer surface treatment was then produced with a multiple pronged hammer or multiple toothed chisel. The marks of the latter instruments are particularly clear on the stones of the projecting string profile on the east face of CGE (Fig. 421).[9]

Use of marble. Although limestone was the chief building stone in the ashlar section of CG there are a few places where marble blocks were used. Most of the following examples may have been secondary, belonging to an Early or Middle Byzantine repair or displacement.

A marble block, apparently fallen from the pier, was found lying along the south face of CGE at E 4/S 1 (Fig. 334, bottom, left of pier; Fig. 416). Another marble block was used as a lintel at the south end of CGC, W 12–13/S 0.5–0.25, top at *97.40 (Fig. 348). Two marble blocks, obviously reused, were used as facing for the west side of pier NE in CGC. Strictly speaking, these were revetments rather than structural blocks and may have come from an Early Byzantine repair. The backs of these blocks were only roughly trimmed to fit the space and there were cuttings for clamps which were not used to hold the blocks in their present positions.

Two marble blocks were found lying in the earth in HN just north of wall *w* at E 3–4/N 43, tops at *99.58. These are probably spoils but may have come from upper levels of wall *w*. The two fine pieces of second century A.D. entablature found at the west end of wall A are also examples of obvious reuse (Figs. 409–411).

Rubble Masonry

The small, flat fieldstone or riverstone rubble laid in cement ("mortared" or "cemented" rubble) is used in the walls of the entire section of the building north of N 32.5 and in the secondary walls *a-d* running eastward from the east face of CGE.

Most of these rubble walls were quite high and thick. The rubble is laid in horizontal courses on the wall faces, several high courses alternating with a low or thin one. The mortar joints are 2–4 cms. thick, 2–4 cms. wide. For example, the northern face of wall A shows a course of thin (2–4 cm.) slabs; then courses 13, 16, 10, 18 cms. high; then another flat course. The wall faces are given an even, finished appearance while the wall cores are more haphazard in coursing (Fig. 408).

The major walls have thicknesses of 3.50–4.00 m. (wall A); 3.15–3.25 m. (wall CNE); ca. 2.50 m. for HM. Walls *a-d* show thicknesses of 1.50–2.10

m. (Fig. 336). Construction of walls *a-d* is similar in general to that of the northern walls (compare Fig. 422 with 408).

Rubble walls are combined with limestone arches consisting of relatively small and thin voussoirs.[10] Such arches appear in HM (A 5–A 8; Figs. 387, 391), wall A (*a'1;*Fig. 406), and CPW (in west face) under entablature (Fig. 410), wall P, south face (*a'3;* Fig. 407), in the east face of CNE (*a;* Figs. 395, 397). Brick arches or vaults are also sometimes found, as in arch *a'2* of wall A (Fig. 406) and A 4 in HM (Fig. 390).[11]

Rubble and Ashlar Construction

Rubble and ashlar masonry are found bonded together in two sections of CG: in the circular unit HM and in the northwest section of CGC where rubble wall CNW is fitted into masonry area N and W 13.35–15.65/N 3.165 (Fig. 336).

When HM was first excavated it was believed that the rubble portion represented a later addition to an original masonry hemicycle.[12] Closer investigation, however, has yielded some strong reasons for assigning the rubble and ashlar sections of HM to a single building period.

The strongest evidence for the contemporaneity of the two sections is the way in which the rubble is bonded in with the masonry in the area where the two come together (Figs. 385–388). On the east side of arch A 1, rubble forms the eastern jamb *under* the first masonry voussoir and runs through the arch to form the eastern part of the rear interior wall of the niche. The rest of the rear wall and a lunette of three blocks are of heavy ashlar (Fig. 423). The interior of the niche was once plastered over and revetted so that the use of two construction techniques would not have been visible.[13]

The western joint of rubble and ashlar occurs between niches A 2 and A 4 (Fig. 387). Here, under the thick grout which was partially removed, a large ashlar block was seen jutting into the rubble in such a way that half the block was surrounded on three edges by smaller rubble stones (Fig. 424). Here, too, the two techniques were intimately keyed or bonded together and did not simply abut on each other. This configuration was also covered with plaster and revetted so that it was invisible to the user of the room.

Expedition architects who have examined the structure have put forward several possible explanations for the utilization of two different forms of construction at this point in the building.[14] The most likely is that ashlar masonry was used to support major vaulting, while rubble, presumably less costly and easier to work with, was used where there were less demanding structural requirements.[15] Hence, the thrust of the northern arches NCE and NCW of CGE and the massive vault of CGC would require the use of heavy limestone as a buttress in the southern part of HM; the ashlar section of HM would therefore form a logical structural extension of CGE. This system shows up best in plan (Fig. 336), where it can be clearly seen that the east end of the ashlar section in HM aligns exactly with the east face of CGE, while the northwest end aligns with the north face of pier NE in CGC. The builders thus seem to have been more concerned with the structural integrity of the monumental Hall CGC than with that of HM.[16]

Rubble and Brick Construction

Several rubble walls which adjoin the northeast quadrant of HM (E 11–15/N 30–40) use the brick "bonding course" technique of construction.

Wall *a* (north-south) consists of three or more brick courses alternating with several stone courses and covered with white stucco (Fig. 398); wall *b* (east-west) and platform *c* which bond with *a* were of similar construction. Wall *d* (east-west) has the best preserved example of this type of coursing, with five horizontal rubble courses forming the lower part and rising up to *99.16 (Fig. 401). They are surmounted by four brick courses (preserved top *99.75); each course is 15 cm. high including joint. The joints are almost as thick as the bricks. The width of these walls is 0.45 m. for *b* and 0.60 m. for *d*.

Wall *w* which forms the northern boundary of Corridor CR (Fig. 336) consists of alternating brick and rubble courses and forms the base of vault *y*. The vault under the staircase St (Fig. 398) and the walls to the east and south are clearly all part of one system and are largely of brick.

Brick and Tile Construction

Brick was used in CG mainly for relatively minor features and not for major structural units such as whole walls. It is found primarily in the northern part of the building used in arches (A 4 in HM [Fig. 390]; arches *e, f,* and *g* in CR [Figs. 397, 398]; and in HN, arches *c* and *d* [Fig. 397]). It is found in arch *a'2* in wall A (Fig. 406) and in the arch below NCE in CGE (Figs. 343, 346), in the construction of vaults *x* and *y* in CR (Figs. 396, 397), and in the support of the staircase St in CR (Fig. 398). The large arch opening between CGC and CN was also of brick, of which only the springing remains.

Brick or tile laid flat was used in the series of landings or floors east of HM and CR/HN as well as in bonding courses in walls (Figs. 400, 401).

A secondary use of brick is in the Early Byzantine remodeling of CG when many open arches were bricked up: in HM, A 1, A 2 doorway, A 3 entire (Fig. 387), and arch *a* in the east face of wall CNE. Traces of secondary brickwork used to cover the walls of niches SCW and NCW and especially MAW are still visible (Figs. 369, 370). Some loose brick fragments were found in the stratigraphic section cut at the southwest corner of CGC (Fig. 374).

The variations in brick sizes used in different ways throughout CG are summarized in Table 8. There were apparently three main sizes chiefly used, giving rise to the possibility that features using similar sized bricks may belong together chronologically.[17] The three sizes were: 0.36 m. × 0.36 m. × 0.04 m.; 0.34 m. × 0.34 m.? × 0.04 m.; and 0.30 m. × 0.30 m.? × 0.04 m.

A few pan tiles and roof tiles were found in the center of CGC, in MAW, and along the south face of CGW. Several were very thick and had impressions of hands on the surface. Some roof tile fragments were found in the vicinity of MAE and MAW and three pieces of curved tile were found just below the top of SCE.

Beam holes and putlog holes. A number of rectangular cuttings were found in several parts of the building and were interpreted as beam or putlog holes. The best examples are in the upper parts of

Table 8. Sizes of bricks used in CG (in meters)*

Use	Location	Length	Width	Thickness
Arch voussoirs	Arch under NCE, east face CGE	0.28–0.30	–	0.04
	Springing, arch between CGC and CN	0.40	0.35	0.05
	Supporting arch of staircase St	0.36	–	0.04
	Arch g in CR	0.36	–	0.04
	Arch f in wall w	0.34	–	0.04
	Arch e in wall w	0.34	–	0.04
	Vault y in CR, springing	0.29	–	0.04
	Vault x in CR	0.32	0.32	0.04
	Arch A 4 in HM, face	0.30	–	0.04
	Arch A 4 in HM, inside, north haunch	0.28	–	0.0375
	Arch A 4 in HM, inside, ceiling	0.30	–	0.04
	Arch a'3 in unit CP	0.36	–	0.04
Bricked up stone arches	A 3 in HM	0.30	–	0.04
	Arch a, east face CNE	0.30	–	0.04
Secondary use as wall covering	MAW, S. wall, interior of arch (ca. E 3/N 14) (some marble revetment slabs used as brick in second highest course	0.32–0.34	–	0.03–0.04
	MAW, north wall, interior of arch (ca. E 3/N 19.8)	0.32–0.34	–	0.03–0.04
Floors or landings	Floor c, east of HM (ca. E 14/N 31)	0.36	0.36	0.04
	Landing L, ca. E 10–11/N 40–41	0.36	0.36	0.04
Lacing courses	Wall w, south side	0.34	–	0.05
	Wall w, north side	0.34–0.35	–	0.04
	SE pier, CGC, "bench" and pier at *97.48 against east side	0.34	0.34	–

*In many instances, it was not possible to measure the width of the bricks, as they were embedded in walls and did not expose all surfaces.

tunnels TE and TW, in arches A 2 and A 4 in HM, in the south face of wall w and north exterior face of HM, and in the upper part of wall CNE in HN. Taken together, these cuttings or holes provide the only evidence for use of wood in CG.

In TE there are six pairs of these cuttings, irregularly spaced east to west in the third course above the profile at ca. *100.65 (bottom) both on the north (Fig. 351, section A-A) and south walls. Most pairs are not quite aligned north to south though some are. Sample dimensions are: W. 0.25 m., H. 0.11 m., D. 0.23 m.; W. 0.20 m., H. 0.20 m., D. 0.33 m.; W. 0.25 m., H. 0.17 m., D. 0.25 m.; W. 0.20 m., H. 0.18 m., D. 0.23 m.; W. 0.21 m., H. 0.17 m., D. 0.24 m. Two similar cuttings were exposed in the north wall of TW, one at W 19.80, H. 0.20 m., W. 0.20 m.; the other at W 18.60, H. 0.20 m., W. 0.25 m. These were perhaps used for scaffolding.

In HM A 2, a rough cutting is seen in either side of the niche opening at *98.41 on the south side, *98.38 on the north, possibly intended to hold a marble or stone beam. Dimensions: W. 0.09 m., H. 0.22 m., D. 0.25 m. (south); W. 0.20 m., H. 0.25 m., D. 0.18 m. (north).

Two large rectangular cuttings appear close together in the upper part of wall CNE at about *101.50 (bottom) just north of wall w. These may be part of an upper floor system which is thought to have existed at this level (Fig. 402).

Above the marble profile in wall w in CR were four rectangular holes, matched by four holes in the north outer wall of HM opposite. One of the holes in w was one brick course higher than the other three. The dimensions of these holes from east to west were: W. 0.25 m., H. 0.21 m.; W. 0.22 m., H. 0.16 m.; W. 0.15 m., H. 0.16 m.; W. 0.14 m., H. 0.16 m. (Fig. 396).

Foundations and Substructures

No foundations have been reached anywhere within complex CG. It remains uncertain how the peculiar wet conditions of the site were surmounted, although certainly the water level was lower at the time of construction than at present.

Floors

A floor of red cement was observed in MAW of CGE at *98.50, and another in MAE against the south pier (2) at *95.80–*95.60 associated with the heating chamber of the furnace. A similar red cement floor was seen near the southeast corner of CGW, extending along the south face from about W 15–23/N 0-S 2, *100.00. A pebble floor lay over it at ca. *100.20. The cement floor was picked up at ca. *100.00 about 5 m. south of the south face of CGW and is probably to be associated with the Middle Byzantine industrial activity known elsewhere in CG.

Tile floors and landings were found in the northeastern part of the building over the lower arch of NCE at *98.00; over vault *x* in CR at *98.67, and east of HM and HN at ca. *100.00. A disrupted brick floor was found in MAE at *97.60 just above the lower arch and dated to the Byzantine period.

Doors

Most of the openings between units in CG are arched but three are trabeated: the doors between SCE/SCW, NCE/NCW, and the door in A 2 of HM (Figs. 346, 353).

The doors in SCE and NCE are similar in construction and appearance. Both served as passages through wall CGE into the Main Hall CGC. Both are asymmetrically placed when viewed from the east (Figs. 336, 343). Both have huge monolithic lintels and jambs of squared limestone blocks. The lintel of SCE is larger than that of NCE and is cracked, but still remains in place. Lintel dimensions, SCE: L. 2.85 m., H. 0.60 m., W. 1.00 m.; NCE: L. 2.10 m., H. 0.65 m., W. (not known). The doors are each 1.80 m. wide. Both were found blocked with rubble but only SCE was cleared by the expedition (Figs. 346, 353). The threshold of NCE was at *97.95 over the lower brick arch, the threshold of SCE was not excavated.

The doorway in half-dome A 2 in HM is curving, ca. 1.60 m. wide, and has a large monolithic curved lintel. The lintel is 1.70 m. wide, 0.72 m. high, the bottom is at *98.25. Judging from the height of this door, the floor of the recess must have been about two or more meters below or around *96.00. The doorway under the lintel had been filled with bricks which blocked the intended access, probably to unit CGC.

Arched doorways in CG included MAE/MAW in CGE, the arches at the north and south ends of CGC, arch *a* in wall CNE, and arches A 4, A 5, A 7 in HM. Their construction will be discussed below with arches.

Windows

No actual windows or window openings have been found extant in CG. A couple of marble grille fragments were found, one in the vicinity of SCE, just above the springing of the main arch and another in the fill in HM; however, these were not *in situ* and could not be placed confidently on the building. Some fragments of window glass were found in several spots: in CR under vault *y*, *98.5–*97.5; along wall CNE at *99.5; and along the north side of wall *w* at *99.5–*99.0. Bits of greenish blue glass were found on the landing above vault *x* (E 2–5/N 42, *98.67) with the Early Byzantine lamp L60.47 (Fig. 403). It would seem strange if units of the height implied by the strong walls around HN and elsewhere in the building had no fenestration, especially the staircase and landings which had particular need of light.

Two narrow airholes were let into the south wall of CGE (*h'1*, *h'2*) and one in CGW (*h'3*), allowing some light and air to penetrate the tunnels TE and

Table 9. Main communications in CG

Direction	Location	Type	Width	Depth	Height
North–South	South end CGC	Stone arch	ca. 11.80 m.	—	—
	North end CGC/CN	Brick arch	ca. 4.40 m.	ca. 1.50 m.	—
	Arch A 5 in HM	Stone arch	2.10 m.	2.40 m.	—
East–West	CGE into CGC:				
	SCE/SCW	Stone, post-and-lintel	1.80 m.	0.82 m.	—
	MAE/MAW	Stone arch	2.50 m.	1.30 m.	ca. 4.60 m.
	NCE/NCW	Stone, post-and-lintel	1.80 m.	1.00 m.	1.90 m.
	CNE arch *a* into CN	Stone arch	ca. 3.25 m.	ca. 4.20 m.	—
	HM:				
	A 2 into CGC	Stone, lintel	1.60 m.	ca. 1.25 m.	—
	A 4 into CN	Brick vault	3.30 m.	3.00 m.	—
	A 7 to tile floor *c* (to east)	Stone vault	2.40 m.	2.50 m.	—

TW (Figs. 334, 350). In TE both holes were exposed inside the vault (Fig. 425). Both were rectangular with bottom edges just above the spring profile on the exterior. They are "funneled" from south to north (outside to inside) so that the openings are wider on the interior than on the exterior. The dimensions of $h'1$ (E 1.6/S 0) are: W. 0.53 m., H. 0.43 m., top *100.33 exterior; W. 0.72 m., H. 0.37 m. interior. Those of $h'2$ (E 3.03/S 0) are: W. 0.30 m., H. 0.67 m., top *100.20 exterior; W. 0.71 m., H. 0.39 m. interior. Both are 1.45 m. deep north-south (thickness of wall). The height of the airhole in TW is 0.52 m.

Arches, Vaults, and Half-Domes

Most of the known openings in CG were arches and the passages or niches created were either vaulted or semi-domed. The voussoirs were constructed of masonry—either large, as in the ashlar section of the building, or smaller, in the rubble section—or of brick; and despite their often irregular and uneven appearance have withstood earthquake and flooding for nearly 2000 years.

Masonry Arches

Most of the arches were apparently intended to be true semicircular arches with a 2:1 ratio of span to rise. In actual practice, however, most of the arches deviate from this proportion in some degree, being generally a little wider than the norm (Tables 10–12). The "inner arch" of MAE/MAW presents another variation and is higher than usual, forming an arch that is more oval than semicircular in appearance (Table 10, Figs. 343, 365). Its spring begins one course higher than the outside arches and progresses on voussoirs varying in inner width from ca. 0.55 to 0.32 m. to a keystone of ca. 0.65 m. flanked by voussoirs of ca. 0.45 m. on the south side and 0.50 m. on the north side. The length of the voussoirs decreases upward from 1.75 m. at the spring to 0.68 m. for the keystone (Fig. 354).

Treatment of voussoirs is often irregular. On the east face of CGE, the central three or more voussoirs of all four arches, TE, SCE, MAE, NCE, are cut off evenly at the top. The haunches of all four are irregular (Fig. 343). The northern voussoirs of

TE are longer than the southern ones, requiring a triangular filling stone on the south side and the notching of the fourth voussoir from the bottom on the south to accommodate it (Fig. 343). A similar use of notched stones occurs on the south side of MAE (Fig. 345) and NCE (Fig. 346).

On the west face of CGE, arch NCW is made distinctive by elevating the tops of the three central voussoirs above the extrados line (Fig. 365). This is reflected on the opposite wall by the elevation of the (single) keystone of NE on CGW. The outer arch of MAW is given emphasis by a double row of voussoirs along the tops of the arch (Fig. 365). This treatment was repeated on both ME and MW of CGW (Figs. 344, 371).[18]

Brick Arches
Several of the arches, particularly in the northern part of the building and the lower part of CGE, are of brick. The construction is generally of the same narrow, flat bricks or tiles used elsewhere in wall construction and facing. In some cases, such as A 4 in HM, vaults x and y in CR, and arches e and f in wall w, the brick arches are secondary to the main construction of CG (Table 12).

The construction of A 4 in HM is unusual. The original form of A 4 is difficult to determine as it was badly damaged and has been heavily restored by the expedition. Enough has been preserved, however, to show that the original curve of the arch was not semicircular but rather wider and uneven in outline (Figs. 387, 390). The brick voussoirs of the arch on the north side rest on a narrow pier of flat stones; on the south, there is a flat stone impost, but the rest of the pier is brick.

Arches e and f in wall w, on the north side of Corridor CR, are the only two "flat" arches in CG (Fig. 398). The exposed inner height of arch e at the western end of w was only 0.20 m., the internal width 1.56 m. (Table 12). The arch springs from stone imposts, the western pier has rubble at the top, brick below. The tiles used are 0.32 m. square, 0.035–0.045 m. thick. The joints between the tiles are irregular in width and vary from 0.02 m. to 0.03 m. Arch f, to the east of e, shows a family resemblance to e but has fewer bricks—twenty-four in all (Fig. 398). The north side of vault x rests on arch f.

Table 10. Arches of large masonry construction

Location	No. voussoirs	Inner form	Span (W. at spring)	Rise (int. H.)	Ratio	*Bottom keystone	*Crown	*Spring	*Face above preserved
CGE, east face (Fig. 343):									
TE	11	barrel vault	2.25	0.96	+2:1	100.90	101.70	99.94	103.33
SCE	19	vault	4.10	1.94	+2:1	101.90	103.10	99.96	104.70
MAE (upper)	21	vault	6.00	2.99	+2:1	102.92	103.83	99.93	105.31
MAE (inner)	14	vault	2.60	2.00	1.25:1	102.32	102.92	ca. 100.32	105.31
MAE (lower) (incomplete)	13 (est.)	vault	ca. 3.75	ca. 1.65	+2:1	96.85	97.35	ca. 94.60	105.31
NCE (upper)	11	vault	2.10	1.35	−2:1	101.20	102.30	99.85	104.08
CGE, west face (Fig. 365):									
SCW	21	half-dome	4.90	2.45	2:1	102.13	103.30	99.68	106.26
MAW (top ring)	11	vault	—	—	—	103.76	104.97	—	104.97
MAW (lower ring)	21	vault	6.00	3.00	2:1	102.61	103.76	99.61	104.97
MAW (inner)	14	arch	2.60	2.00	ca. 1.25:1	102.32	102.92	100.16	104.97
NCW (incomplete)	19 (?)	half-dome	±4.75	±2.40	ca. 2:1	102.13	103.96	?	103.96
CGW, west face (Fig. 344):									
TW	9	barrel vault	2.00	0.88	ca. +2:1	100.50	101.30	99.62	102.84
SW	—	—	—	—	—	unexc.	unexc.	—	104.84
MW	12 (visible)	—	—	—	—	102.45	103.65	—	103.65
NW	11 (visible)	—	—	—	—	101.52	102.56	—	102.56
CGW, east face (Fig. 371):									
SE	9 (visible)	—	—	—	—	101.88	102.92	—	105.07
ME (top ring)	9 pres. orig. 14?	vault	—	—	—	missing	(103.61)	—	103.61
ME (lower ring)	14 (visible)	vault	—	—	—	102.38	(103.61)	—	103.61
NE	8 (visible)	—	—	—	—	102.12	103.44	—	104.01
South arch CGC	fallen; ca. 16 pres.	vault	±11.15	ca. 6.0	—	not pres.	not pres.	—	not pres.
HM A 1	8 (very uneven)	vault	2.65	1.20	ca. 2:1	99.87	100.47	98.67	102.15
HM A 2	2 hollowed blocks	half-dome	2.25	1.20	−2:1	99.85	—	—	102.15

Masonry Vaults

Recesses SCE, MAE, and NCE of wall CGE are actually shallow barrel vaults of masonry formed by a single ring of blocks (Figs. 414, 351). MAW on the west side of the wall was two rows deep (Fig. 351). A similar pattern probably existed in wall CGW (Fig. 336).[19] Tunnels TE and TW are longer barrel vaults. The profiled string course visible on the exterior east face of CGE runs into TE on both the north and south walls for a length of ca. 3.5 m. The system of voussoirs seen on the arch face (Fig. 343) is not followed exactly on the inner vault, and not all the "keystones" are on center.

Brick Vaults

Three brick barrel vaults are known in CG. Of vault *y* only the springing remains (Fig. 397). A 4 in HM presumably led to CN on the west (Fig. 336). The bricks on the interior were set radially on the haunches and transversely or "pitched" on the crown.[20]

Table 11. Arches of small masonry (rubble) construction

Location	No. voussoirs	Inner form	Span (W. at spring)	Rise (int. H.)	Ratio	*Bottom keystone	*Crown	*Spring	*Face above preserved
HM:									
A 3	19 (interrupted)	—	2.15	0.90	+2:1	±99.75	100.15	98.40	102.71
A 5	34	barrel vault	2.20	1.05	+2:1	99.84	100.34	98.79	102.45
A 6	34	half-dome	2.25	1.05	+2:1	99.72	100.27	98.67	102.50
A 7	37	vault	2.20	1.05	+2:1	99.85	100.45	98.80	102.40
A 8	34	half-dome	2.25	1.15	−2:1	99.66	99.71	98.51	100.45
HN:									
a	incomplete	vault?	ca. 4.5	ca. 2.25	±2:1	99.78	100.22	98.14	103.28
b	23 (visible)	—	ca. 2.80	ca. 1.50	−2:1	99.44	99.99	ca. 97.94	103.44
back side A 5 (h)	19 (visible)	vault	ca. 2.0	—	—	99.14	99.59	—	103.24
CP:									
a'1	15+	"blind"	ca. 9.0	ca. 4.5	ca. 2:1	not pres.	not pres.	not pres.	
a'3	27+	"blind"	—	—	—	—	not pres.	not pres.	

Table 12. Brick arches CG

Location	No. voussoirs	Size of bricks	Inner form	Span	Rise	Ratio	*Bottom keystone	*Crown	*Spring
CGE:									
TE (lower)	incomplete	—	vault	—	—	—	—	—	—
NCE (lower)	37+	Th. 0.04 W. 0.30	vault	ca. 2.35	ca. 1.0	+2:1	97.75	98.05	96.75
SpS	incomplete	—	arched door	—	—	—	—	—	—
SpE/SpW	incomplete	Th. 0.05 W. 0.35 X 0.40	vault						
HM:									
A 4	(restored)	Th. 0.04	vault	±3.50	±1.75	2:1	100.34	±100.69	±99.34
CR:									
x	48	Th. 0.04 W. 0.32 X 0.32	vault	1.93	0.75	ca. 2.5:1	98.34	98.66	97.67
y	incomplete	Th. 0.04 W. 0.29	vault	1.90–1.75	—	—	—	—	98.48
f	24		vault	2.40	unexc.	—	96.35	97.70	97.11
e	34	Th. 0.34	vault	1.56	0.20	7.08:1	97.36	97.70	97.16
g (under staircase)	39 visible	Th. 0.04–0.05 W. 0.30	—				not exposed	ca. 98.32	97.11
staircase support	24 visible	Th. 0.04 W. 0.36							
HN:									
c	39	—	—	1.20	1.05	+1:1	98.27	98.63	97.64
d	28			1.70	1.15	1.07:1	97.93	98.24	97.34
CP a'2	50 visible	Th. 0.07 W. 0.36	half-dome				100.10	100.15	not exposed

Vault *x* in CR is almost completely preserved (Table 12). Its maximum length extends from E 4.7–2.3/N 38.8 (southwest corner)–41.60. The south wall of the vault followed the curvature of the north wall of HM and the vault itself goes off slightly southward from alignment with wall *w* (Figs. 336, 396–397). The north wall was formed by wall *w*. The west end of the vault was sealed by the brick wall which was used to fill up arch *a* in wall CNE. The western end of the vault partly obscures arch *a* in CNE. The barrel vault arches in 48 tile courses of 0.31–0.33 m. tiles with recessed joints of ca. 0.02–0.03 m. The entire south side rests on top of arch *h*. The wall is supported on the southwest corner by a rubble pier with limestone quoins, exposed H. 1.60 m., *98.60–*97.00.

Half Domes

In the masonry section of the building SCW and NCW and presumably SE and NE are half-domes; in HM, A 2, A 6, and A 8 are half-domes (and possibly the original A 4); and beyond that, arch *a'2* in unit CP and the small niche in the west side of CPW are half-domes faced with brick.

A peculiarity of SCW and NCW is that they are slightly deeper than true half domes (plan, Fig. 336). Half-dome A 2, on the other hand, is slightly shallower than normal, while A 6 and A 8 are close to the normal 2:1 proportions of width to depth. The two brick half-domes were not cleared sufficiently to determine proportions.

Because of the deterioration of the top of wall CGE at the north end, the exterior construction of dome NCW is exposed to view (Fig. 426) showing the cutting and fitting of blocks used in the dome.

Evidence for Water Supply and Heating

Evidence found for supply of water or heat to the bathing establishment of CG consisted of a few fragments of hypocaust tiles, vertical pipe cuttings and fragments of pipes, and the furnace in MAE. Since the main floor levels were not reached, no bathing pools nor basins were exposed.

Hypocaust tiles. Some hypocaust tiles were found in HN, possibly fallen from an upper room. Two were at E 2–9/N 42–47 along wall *w*, *99.15 (diam. 0.28 m.; Th. 0.05 m.); another at *99.60–*98.40; another in the west face of *w* at *99.00,

and still another near the face of *w* north of the stairway; another in the fallen debris of wall F, ca. *99.40. Elsewhere in the building, one was found in front of NCE, *96.70 (diam. 0.28 m.; Th. 0.05 m.) and another in MAE (diam. 0.14 m.; Th. 0.045 m.).

Pipe cuttings. In wall CGE, vertical cuttings for pipes were found in SCW (north and south walls; Figs. 369, 371), in NCW (north and south walls), and in HM (*p 1, p 2, p 3, p 4;* Fig. 336). The cutting in the south side of NCW had a fragment of terracotta pipe still preserved in it. The pipes in NCW and SCW most probably were connected with the intake of water into basins for bathing which may have been housed in these niches.[21] The tops of these cuttings went up into the wall of the dome; the bottoms opened out at a level somewhat below the spring line of the dome in SCW (Figs. 369, 371).

The four cuttings in HM were also vertical. The function, however, is more ambiguous and it is thought that these pipes may have been used to carry hot water to heat the room (if it was a laconicum), rather than for intake of water for bathing.

Pipe fragments. Several lengths and pieces of pipe were found in niche MAE in CGE. A first group was found between levels *97.90–*96.90 mixed in heaps with fragments of mortar as if discarded. Others were found at levels associated with the furnace (*95.55, *95.80), and may have had to do with conduction of water to and from the furnace (or boiler) itself. One length was found partly *in situ* with top at *97.60, its bed traceable for 0.82 m., and 0.25 m. of length still in place; diam. at large end, 0.08 m.; inner diam. at narrow projection at one end, 0.046 m.

Other pipes lay over a floor in MAE at *95.55, running more or less east-west into the furnace area. The top of one, *d'1*, was at *95.80. One section length was 0.42 m.; outer diam. 0.155 m.; inner diam. 0.11 m. The outside was ribbed. Another, *d'2*, running northwest-southeast was exposed for a length of 1.90 m.; length of section was 0.445 m.; outer diam. 0.205 m.; inner diam. 0.135 m. A third length, *d'3*, ran from *d'2* to a stone basin, 0.28 m. × 0.25 m. × 0.24 m. high in the southwest corner of MAE. A stone channel or drain at *94.50 leads into the center of the furnace. Doubtless, an intricate system of pipes once fed the heating system centered in MAE.[22]

Several pieces of ribbed pipe were also found in front of NCE at ca. *95.80, below the springing of the lower brick arch. Still other pipe fragments were found in HM, but these pieces were mostly in the central debris and not in association with any of the cuttings on the walls. Enough fragments were found of one length to reconstruct the inner diameter of one section at 0.11 m. More fragments appeared in CR (not *in situ*) at ca. *97.20–*96.80 (diams. 0.12 m., 0.22 m.).

Decorative Treatment

Revetments

The presence of extensive revetment over the interior of much of the building CG is attested in several ways. Numerous holes over the masonry of unit CGC indicate revetment of the interior of that hall, while remains of fragments of actual marble slabs in niche A 1 of HM and the presence of impressions of slabs in thick grout show use of this type of decoration in HM as well.

Revetments in situ. Five fragments of finely finished marble slabs, four white, the one on the keystone dark green, were found *in situ* in HM arch A 1 on the top interior of the arch (Figs. 387, 389). Pieces of narrow marble molding were also found *in situ* at *98.50, ca. 1.55 m. below the top of the arch at the rear of the niche, probably remains of part of a string course or footing profile for the interior revetments (Fig. 423). In the revetment grout which covered the rest of the interior of the arch were impressions of all twenty-three complete narrow tiles or slabs and remains of iron pins in the joints between the impressions, ca. 0.25 m. in from the face of the niche (average diam. 0.06 m.). It was thus possible to restore the pattern of revetment in this niche (Fig. 387). The original length of the tiles was 0.65 m.; thickness, ca. 0.016 m.–0.02 m.; width, 0.18 m.–0.21 m. On the back wall of the niche were holes of revetment pins which probably held other slabs in a vertical position. These holes were in an irregular pattern suggesting an ornamental design. Revetment grout

covered not only the inner side of the voussoirs but also part of the back wall and the face of the bricks which had been used to block the niche in a later phase. This showed that at least one phase of revetment in this niche was secondary and may have been added at the same time as the revetment of the inner walls of HM.

The setting plaster was laid in two layers: below, a layer of red grout, 0.04 m. thick; on top a thin layer of white plaster, 0.02 m. thick. Majewski suggests that the white layer may have been a secondary surface for fresco. A few holes in the outer face of the voussoirs possibly indicate surface revetment. Perhaps the interior arch tiles extended ca. 0.15 m. beyond the face of the arch where they would have joined with the face revetments.

Revetment impressions. Further evidence for revetment in HM was provided by revetment impressions in heavy layers of grout. The wall of HM between arches A 2 and A 4 (covering A 3) was covered with thick grout showing a pattern of almost square tiles (0.50 m. × 0.47 m.). The grout is ca. 0.03 m. to 0.06 m. thick and contains pebble inclusions. Pin holes appear in the joints between the tile impressions (Fig. 387). In arch A 5, a vaulted niche, grout was found with a pattern of long thin tiles similar to those in A 1.

Revetment pin holes. The most extensive evidence for interior revetment in CG comes from the western face of wall CGE. Pin holes are seen along most of the surface of the arch faces SCW, MAW, NCW and on the wall face between and above the niches. These holes continued up the wall as high as it is preserved and presumably originally climbed to at least the level of the springing of the great central vault. They were also found on the interior of niches SCW and MAW below spring level.[23]

The best preserved and most intensively studied section was the face of arch SCW and the interior of that niche (Figs. 387, 417, 418). Numerous pin holes were seen on voussoirs 3–16 of the arch (Fig. 417) and were most frequent in the keystone and upper voussoirs (Fig. 417 Nos. 6–14; Fig. 418), perhaps indicating the attachment of heavy sculptured or profiled slabs. Several of the holes contain the remains of iron pins (Fig. 419).

On the interior of SCW several fairly regular horizontal rows of holes appeared on the stone courses below the level of the lintel and arch springing (ca. *99.84 and below; Fig. 369). Revetment inside the niche apparently covered only the lower walls as far as the springing of the dome where decoration continued in paint.

The average size of revetment pin holes in SCW is ca. 0.04–0.05 m. long, 0.02–0.03 m. high, originally rectangular in shape. The average horizontal distance between holes where they are placed in rows is ca. 0.15 m.–0.20 m. The average vertical distance between rows is ca. 0.50 m. (Fig. 427). There is only one row of holes on an average ashlar block running approximately across the center of the stone, although this pattern can be highly variable.

Broken remains of iron pins were also observed in some of these holes. They may well have been the same kind of hooks which were employed in the revetments of the Synagogue.[24]

The eastern face of CGW is more weathered than the west face of CGE and less completely excavated. Some possible pin holes were detected on the north face of the southeast pier and along some of the arches of the east face of the wall (NE, ME), but it is very hard to distinguish weathering patterns from possible pin holes on this wall. It is most likely that such holes do exist and that the entire interior of CGC was lavishly revetted. Analogous evidence may be seen on the walls of the main hall of the Hierapolis bath, which has been compared to CG in other respects.[25]

Elsewhere, three rows of pin holes appear on the south face of SpE at the northeast corner of CGC (Fig. 372). Those in the grout on the wall of HM have already been discussed.

Isolated fragments of probable revetment slabs were found in several locations in CG, not *in situ.* A few pieces came from between CGE and CGW around levels *102.5–*100.5; a couple of pieces of white marble slabs and a veined marble fragment come from ca. *100, north of HM; and another piece came from along the west face of CGE at the south end of the building (W 1/N 2).

Several fragments of narrow profiled moldings, similar to the footing profile in HM A 1 were also found: in SCW at *99.50–*98.50; east of HM at surface level; inside HM at *100.0; four meters west of the northeast corner of wall A at ca. *101.0; and within CR. The high levels at which both the moldings and the revetment fragments were found seem to indicate that they had fallen from high on the building at a rather late date (during the Middle Byzantine period). Perhaps the marble decorations were stripped from the walls at this time to be used in limekiln operations, of which there were a few traces in CG.[26]

Date of revetments. At least two periods of revetted decoration could be detected at CG. The first, on the interior of CGC and its niches is presumed to be part of the original decoration of the building, as exposed unrevetted masonry would have been unlikely for the interior of a major hall in such a monumental bath building. Some of the revetment in HM may have been original, particularly the interior of arch A 1; but much of it is decidedly secondary. The revetment which covered the early (original) arch A 3 and which was laid over the bricks used to block A 1 was surely later than the first phase of the building and may date to the Early Byzantine remodelling. The Middle Byzantine period may have been the time at which the revetments of both phase one and phase two were removed and destroyed.

Wall Painting

An outstanding example of fresco painting was found in HN and dated to the Early Byzantine period, and a few later traces of painted decoration appeared in various other parts of the building.

HN wall paintings WP60.1. The most important remains from the later period of unit HN were the fragments of fresco found on walls CNE and A in HN. They extended from ca. N 42.2–50.0, almost to the northeast corner of wall A, and in height from levels *98.0–*101.50.[27]

A watercolor made in 1960 by G. Bakir rendered what was recognizable at the time of excavation (Fig. 428) and shows how they were then interpreted. A newer representation by L. J. Majewski, done in 1968, gives the most recent conception of what they were once like (Fig. 429). According to Majewski, "the wall was a fine painted version of marble revetments with beautiful imitation of *opus sectile* panels."[28]

The fragments begin over the northern voussoirs of stone arch *a* on the west face of CNE but were not found on the inner brick arch. Fragments *in situ* appeared rather crude but colorful with patches of red, green, and orange on a yellowish-white background. Patterns of panels and vertical zones of green and red existed but were indistinct. Other colors observed were pink, purple/violet, dark blue, and black. The largest remaining piece of wall painting was removed by the laboratory staff in 1969, impregnated with polyvinylacetate, mounted, and partly restored in lighter tones.[29]

The paintings were dated in the Early Byzantine period on stylistic grounds. Because Early Byzantine mural paintings from secular buildings are scarce in Asia Minor the Sardis fragments are of some importance.[30]

Another example of painting comes from SCW where the half-dome was covered with at least two layers of plaster. The masonry was covered with white plaster with a straw binder, 0.02–0.04 m. thick. Over the white was a thin layer 0.005 m. thick, of bluish gray color (intended as blue, the color of the vault of heaven?).[31] Traces of paint were also found in HM arch A 2 on the left (southeast) wall, although not enough remained to suggest a reconstruction of a design. L. J. Majewski further suggested that the remains of a white plaster coating in arch A 1 at *98.57 could have been the ground for a fresco decoration.

Mosaic

Individual cubes of mosaic were found sporadically in all digging seasons. Two, one yellow, one green, were found in SCW under the arch, *99.50; one bluish iridescent cube was found in the baulk between HM and wall A at *101.0; one came from NCE at *98.30–*97.50; three came from the fill in front of NCE; two more examples were discovered in HN; six came from MAE; one from staircase St; one from in front of A 4 in HM. Individual cubes also came from the southern end of the building, e.g. a bluish glass tessera with gold leaf from W 2/N 8, *101.5 in a crack between the fallen voussoirs. Five cubes were found at W 9.5/N 28–29, just south of the northwest pier of CGC;

another with gold leaf from W 9/N 30.6, *101.6 (same area as previous five, possibly a dump); and others were found at W 8.3/N 30.5, *101.15 and W 10/N 30, *100.2; two were from W 11/N 30.5, *100.25. As with the revetment fragments, the discovery of tesserae scattered about in Middle Byzantine strata suggests that the decoration of the building was dismantled at this time.

More cogent evidence for the use of mosaic came from HM A 6, the half-domed top of which was covered with three layers of plaster, the topmost layer thin and white. L. J. Majewski observed that this type of layered plaster is commonly used as the setting bed for mosaic.[32] Some of the plaster in A 6 was removed and three mosaic cubes which had sunk into the second layer were recovered. It is tempting to think that the alternating half-domes and vaulted niches in HM had alternate mosaic and revetted decoration.

Conclusion

Building CG is incompletely excavated. We possess only an incomplete plan, no lower stories or floor levels, and the original date is uncertain. Nevertheless, its interpretation in some detail forms a genuine contribution to the history of architecture and urbanism at Sardis.

Despite its incompleteness, CG is a major structure, comparing in size, plan, and techniques of construction, and perhaps in date, with other major bath buildings of Western Asia Minor, especially those at Hierapolis and Miletus (Fig. 430). Its identity as a bath is established both on comparative grounds and by the scanty but significant remains of a heating system, hypocaust tiles, and water pipes.

Close study of the construction of CG has resulted in interesting technical information. The masonry technique employed in the main section of the building and the building stone used are unique so far at Sardis, suggesting that CG was conceived as an architectural experiment.

Enough evidence remains to show that CG in its main phases was elaborately decorated with marble revetments, mosaics, and fresco paintings. The total effect of the building when complete with its massive vaults and arches and its splendid decoration must have made it one of the most impressive buildings of Roman Sardis.

Although the original date of construction is uncertain, it is most likely that the main part of the building was erected sometime after the earthquake of A.D. 17, perhaps in the first or second century. As evidenced by the frescoes and finds such as L60.47, the building was still in active use in the Early Byzantine period when it was remodeled and perhaps added to. After its abandonment as a bath (A.D. 616?) it was rapidly buried by flood deposits to its upper stories. When in use again in the Middle Byzantine period it was apparently an industrial quarter for smiths. Its original function had been forgotten, and its decoration was used to feed the limekilns.

AREA SOUTH OF CG

In 1962, ca. 35 m. south of the main CG complex, remains of a large wall running east-west were discovered. At first it was thought that it was part of the CG complex, possibly part of a system for storing or conducting water to the bath. Further examination in 1969, however, showed that it was probably not directly related to CG.[33]

Wall S

The large wall, wall S, was exposed for a maximum length of ca. 8.5 m. (W 5–13 on the CG grid) and a maximum width of ca. 3.0 m. (in the area S 36–40), varying to 2.20 and 2.50 m. Its top was at *102.38 at the western end and *102.60 at the eastern end (Fig. 335). The lowest depth reached in excavating the wall was *100.80, for an exposed height of 1.80–1.60 m. Its actual height is unknown.

The wall makes an obtuse angle to the south at W 7.6/S 40.3, meeting a second wall, S 1. Part of the face of the wall is preserved near this point at W 7.7/S 40, and another at W 9/S 39. The preserved face is made of bricks and flat rubble in alternating courses (Fig. 431). The core of the wall is of mixed rubble and brick in a white mortar bed. "Splashes" of cement or mortar were visible in earth south of the wall, ca. 1.0–0.50 m. below the modern surface.

Wall S 1

This wall runs ca. 2.0 m. east-west, 2.10 m. north-south with its top at *102.0 (Figs. 431, 432). It bonds with wall S on the south and turns westward into the scarp at W 14. It was excavated to a depth of 1.10 m. (*100.90) at the meeting with wall S. Its construction is similar to that of S: brick and rubble set in gray mortar. The construction is irregular, but a course of four bricks bonds into the northern face of wall S.

From the corner with S 1 along the north face, wall S appears to curve 0.37 m. in a straight length of 6.30 m. Allowing for a disrupted face, the curvature may have been more marked and is suggestive of a curved enclosure of some sort (Fig. 335). The interior of the "enclosure" seems to have had a "zigzag" arrangement (Fig. 433). It is interesting to note that there was no evidence of flooding south of the wall, but abundant evidence for it north of the wall.

Function. It has been suggested that walls S and S 1 originally formed some kind of outworks or fortress. In a later period it came to be used as a cemetery with Islamic graves set directly into the top of the wall. The "sloshing" of cement observed south of the wall may have been due to several possibilities: parts fallen from wall S southward, possible preparation for graves in the top and southern half of the wall, possibly (but less likely) associated with the building of the wall itself.

The Cemetery

Five graves were found in wall S, Graves 69.1–5 (Fig. 433). They were long and narrow, made of stone and brick and lined with terracotta tiles on the bottom. The graves were plastered over on the sides with the plaster going over the bottom tiles. The bodies were laid directly on the tiles. Because of the orientation of the bodies and lack of finds, it is thought that they are relatively late burials, probably Islamic.

Grave 69.1. This was a long, narrow, tile-lined grave. It was located at W 6–7/S 40, bottom *102; top, *102.35. The western end was destroyed. P.L. 1.60 m.; W. 0.34 m. at west end, 0.28 at east end. It is composed of stone and brick on the south side, three tiles on the bottom, two of which have double ridges through the center and a rounded edge at one long end. The easternmost tile is L. 0.65 m., W. 0.32 m.; the middle tile L. 0.66 m., W. (incomplete) 0.38 m. The full width is given by the broken tile at the west end which shows raised edges at the long sides: P.L. 0.32 m., W. 0.42 m. The entire grave was plastered, the plaster overlapping the bottom tiles.

Grave 69.1 contained a femur and other parts of a skeleton; apparently a secondary burial or later intrusion removed half of the body. The age was 17, sex male, stature 176.5 cm. Orientation with head to west, prone extended.[34]

Grave 69.2. Location W 9.80–11.75/S 38.0–38.6; top *102.0; south edge *102.28. Originally covered with slabs. Bottom *101.76. Internal L. 2.05 m.; W. at east end, 0.35 m.; W. at west end, 0.45 m. The grave was completely preserved and showed marked taper to east. Two skeletons were found lying side by side (Fig. 434). The grave was apparently cut into wall S from the top and carefully lined with grayish white plaster. The bottom is lined with three grooved tiles with rounded edge to west (Fig. 435). The westernmost tile had a wavy line on it; the easternmost tile was plain. The first skeleton was male, aged 20, stature 179.5 cm.; the second was female, aged 18, stature 159.3 cm. Both were oriented with head to west, face up, prone extended. A late (Ottoman?) plain(?) pot base was found at the feet of the skeletons.

Grave 69.3. Unexcavated. Only a small portion of the grave lay within the excavated area of wall S; W 12.25–13/S 38–39; top *102.38; W. ca. 0.40 m.; L. ca. 0.45 m.

Grave 69.4. Location W 6.5–7.5/S 36.5–35.0; top *100.90. This grave was opened but the only finds were a large amount of burned ash and a few unidentifiable sherds. It is probably a cremation of

the post-Roman period. It was lined with tile, possibly indicating that it had been reused, and there was a cover slab. Some pot sherds were found in the vicinity of the grave near the north edge of wall S, but there is no evidence that they were associated with the grave. The sherds were Late Roman, Byzantine, and Early Islamic.

Grave 69.5. Location W 4.20–5.30/S 42.1–42.85; top of cover, *102.66; bottom *102.33. The grave lies somewhat higher and southeast of 69.1. It is a shallow oblong, ca. 1.10 m. east-west, 0.35 m. north-south. It does not taper eastward as do the other graves in this area. The depth is ca. 0.27 m. The grave was covered with a fragment of an inscribed marble stele instead of schist slabs (Fig. 436). The stele lay face up and was wedged in loosely by bricks and earth and loose white cement. It was only 0.55 m. below the modern surface. The stone, when removed, was found to lie on a plastered area with regularly arranged stones around it at the east end.

The skull was that of a child with small teeth, H. 0.15 m.; W. 0.16 m. Only a bit of plain red pottery was found. Below the neck the skeleton was encased in a limey white mass. Isolated brittle bones were in the uneven bottom of the grave.

IN69.14. This was the stele that covered Grave 69.5. It has obviously been reused, since it was broken off at the bottom and right side. The stone was a fine-grained white marble. There were finely drafted margins, 3.2 cm. wide on left and upper edges; letters missing on right. Parts of seventeen lines were preserved.[35] Below is a smoothly finished blank area. One simple incised line is preserved below the "frame." P.H. 1.375 m.; P.W. 0.37 m.; Th. 0.138 m.; H. of letters 0.036 m.; W. of letters 0.041 m. Approximate date: late third to early fourth century A.D.(?).

JCW, GMAH

NOTES

BIBLIOGRAPHY
AND
ABBREVIATIONS

CONCORDANCE OF FINDS

INDEX

NOTES

A complete listing of short titles appears in the Bibliography, pp. 189-193. Abbreviations of periodicals used throughout are those listed in the *American Journal of Archaeology* 74 (1970) 3-8. Abbreviations of classical authors generally follow the scheme set forth in the *Oxford Classical Dictionary*, 2nd ed. rev., N. G. L. Hammond and H. H. Scullard (Oxford 1970) ix-xxii.

CHAPTER I

1. H. C. Butler gives an outline of the rediscovery of Sardis in *Sardis* I (1922) 4 f. Cf. also the informal account in Hanfmann, *Letters*, 4-12. A detailed treatment by Jane A. Scott will be found in a forthcoming Sardis monograph.

2. Miklosich, I, cclv, 509-510.

3. Father E. W. Bodnar kindly placed at our disposal Cyriacus' account in an unpublished letter. Detailed citation in J. A. Scott (*supra,* n. 1, forthcoming).

4. O. Riemann, "Inscriptions grecques provenant du receuil de Cyriacus," *BCH* 1 (1877) 84. Republished in *Sardis* VII (1932) 58 f. nos. 41, 42; 71 no. 58; 87 no. 80.

5. Some of the seventeenth, eighteenth, and nineteenth century travelers (C. de Peyssonel, P. Le Bas, and F. Adler, for example) provided not only descriptions but also illustrations. See de Peyssonel, 336-337, and Le Bas, 4. F. Adler did architectural drawings for E. Curtius; cf. Curtius, "Beiträge," 84-88, map, pls.

6. Roman, in the Gyges Mound BT 63.1; and medieval, in the small grave BT 63.2. Cf. *BASOR* 174, 55; 177, 30.

7. J. F. M. Von Olfers, "Über die Lydischen Königsgräber bei Sardes und den Grabhügel des Allyates nach dem Bericht des Kaiserlichen Generalconsuls Spiegelthal zu Smyrna," *AbhBerl* (1858) 539-556; summary in G. Perrot

and A. Chipiez, *History of Art in Phrygia, Lydia, Caria, and Lycia* (London 1892) 258-266. Cf. *BASOR* 170, 52-59.

8. Choisy, "Tombeaux," 73-81.

9. G. Dennis in *British Dictionary of Biography; Sardis* I (1922) 10; Pryce, 99-101, figs. 164, 165 nos. B 269, B 270; G. M. A. Hanfmann and N. H. Ramage, "Catalogue of Sculpture from Sardis," (forthcoming).

10. Described in a letter by F. H. Bacon, which is published in *Sardis* I (1922) 7-8. Inan, Rosenbaum, 75, no. 41, pl. 26:2-3.

11. Choisy, *Byzantines*, 160, figs. 177-178, pl. 16:3.b.

12. H. Schliemann, *Briefwechsel* 1876-1890, ed. E. Meyer (Berlin 1958) II, 81, 110, 425 n. 84. London, to Sir A., August 22, 1879: "Ancient Sardes, which is bound to throw much light on Trojan antiquities, impatiently awaits my pick and spade;" to L. P. di Cesnola, July 24, 1879: "after Mycenae and Troy . . . it is not in Yucatan but at Sardes in Lydia where I ought to dig, because in the latter, every fragment of pottery . . . will reveal a new page of history." He made a similar statement to T. Stanton of the New York Herald on July 10, 1880. Meyer pointed out that Schliemann became interested in Sardis through the British Orientalist A. H. Sayce, who had visited Sardis ("Notes from Journeys in the Troad and Lydia," *JHS* 1 [1880] 86-87) and was a friend of Schliemann's.

13. Osborn, passim.

14. On Butler's life and works cf. V. L. Collins, ed. *Howard Crosby Butler, 1872-1922* (Princeton 1923) with bibliography by H. S. Leach.

15. Preface dated November, 1924. *Sardis* II (1925).

16. G. H. Chase (1875-1952) was John E. Hudson Professor of Archaeology at Harvard. His records are at Harvard. Cf. Hanfmann, *Letters*, 8.

17. Publications by the first Sardis expedition are listed in the general bibliography.

18. Shear, "Staters," 349-352; Shear, "Sixth Report," 396-400. Andrew Oliver, Jr., "Lydia," *BMMA* XXXVI

(1968) 197. Four of thirty-six staters are in New York, the rest in Istanbul. Metropolitan Museum nos. Lydion 26.59.6; staters 26.59.29–65.

19. Shear, "Sixth Report," 400 f.

20. It was our opinion from inspecting the riverstone walls in 1958 when they were cut by a small village road that they could well be Lydian. The enlargement of the western, left-bank road to an automobile road in 1971 has destroyed them. Cf. *Sardis* I (1922) 76–78; *Sardis* X (1926) 1.

21. Shear, "Sixth Report," 401.

22. Shear, "Horse," 215–230; Hill, 155–159, figs. 1–4.

23. Cf. Oliver, passim.

24. Chase's Tomb 75: *Sardis* XIII (1925) 34 no. 86; Ashmolean Museum 1928.323.

25. *BASOR* 154, 5–35; 157, 8–43; 162, 8–49; 166, 1–57; 170, 1–65; 174, 3–58; 177, 2–37; 182, 2–54; 186, 17–52; 187, 9–62; 191, 2–41; 199, 7–58; 203, 5–22; 206, 9–39. *Dergi* IX:1 (1959) 3–8; X.1 (1960) 3–20; XI.1 (1962) 18–22; XI.2 (1962) 40–45; XII.1 (1964) 26–33; XII.2 (1965) 8–23; XIII.2 (1965) 58–63; XIV.1 (1965) 151–154; XV.1 (1966) 75–78; XVI.2 (1967) 77–84; XVIII.1 (1969) 61–64; XIX.1 (1972) 99–119.

26. Hanfmann, *Letters.*

27. "An Explanation of the Topographic Plans, Grids, and Levels," (*infra*).

28. On general historical grounds, C. Foss favors a date shortly after the invasions of the Goths into Asia Minor (256–268); the archaeological evidence discussed by G. M. A. Hanfmann, *infra* Ch. III, is inconclusive for the City Wall but indicates a date later than Constantine for the bridge fortification. An early 5th century coin found in the trench near the bridge may still be construed to indicate a date around 400.

29. *BASOR* 186, 40–43; 191, 7–10; 199, 12–16; *Dergi* XVII.1 (1968) 125–127; Mitten, Yügrüm, "Eski Balıkhane"; Mitten, Yügrüm, "Ahlatlı Tepecik."

30. *BASOR* 177, 35–36, fig. 34.

31. Cf. *supra*, n. 29.

32. Conversion formulas for SAS and B grids and magnetic north variation data.

$$x_b \text{ (E, W)} = .88968 \, (y_{SAS}) - .45657 \, (x_{SAS}) - 2104.627$$
$$y_b \text{ (N, S)} = .88968 \, (x_{SAS}) + .45657 \, (y_{SAS}) - 6916.323$$

B grid north-south axis is 27°10′ east of SAS grid (true) north-south axis.

This angular relationship of grid axes, derived by triangulation, should be used when converting from one grid system to the other. Working with magnetic north relationships may give less precise results because not only were the magnetic bearings frequently taken with less precise instruments, resulting in differing readings, but also the value for magnetic variation from true north is uncertain. In 1967 two different values for magnetic variation were obtained from government authorities.

Harıta Genel Müdürlügüne advised that magnetic north was 1°40′ east of geographic north in 1955, and that to find the variation for subsequent years, add plus 5′ for each year after 1955.

Istanbul Kandilli Observatory on the other hand gave the following readings for a nearby area:

1910: 3°24′ W	1958: 2°14′ E	1963: 2°31′ E
1911: 3°14′ W	1959: 2°18′ E	1964: 2°32′ E
1912: 3°04′ W	1960: 2°22′ E	1965: 2°35′ E
1913: 2°54′ W	1961: 2°25′ E	1966: 2°37′ E
1914: 2°44′ W	1962: 2°28′ E	1967: 2°39′ E

Though the information from these two sources differs, it is useful in determining approximate relationships of magnetic north to true north.

33. In *Sardis* M1, p. 16 the Bath CG 100.00 datum is erroneously given as *100.47 instead of *99.36 a.s.l.

CHAPTER II

1. W. Warfield, "Report on the Geology of Sardis," in *Sardis* I (1922) App. I.

2. A map has been published: Jeoloji Hartası, 1:100,000, Manisa 87:2; the reports by Birgi and Saydamer cited below are unpublished.

3. Saydamer, passim.

4. Through the kindness of Sadrettin Alpan, Director, MTA, and C. A. Wendell, Minerals Attaché, American Embassy Ankara we were able to consult the detailed report by M. Saydamer on gold prospecting of the Alluvium between Turgutlu and Salihli (Ankara 1963) and the very important report, "Occurrences of Gold in the Sardis (Salihli) Region," by S. Birgi (Ankara 1944).

5. D. Greenewalt, *BASOR* 170, 59–60; 174, 56–58.

6. Olson, Hanfmann, 11–14; Olson, passim.

7. Royal Road: Herodotus 5.52; *Sardis* M2 (1972) no. 19. Campaign of Xerxes: Diodorus 11.2,3; Herodotus 7.32; *Sardis* M2 (1972) nos. 156–160.

8. For the geography of the region see Philippson, *Byzantinische Reich,* 134–147 and *Reisen* II, 63–76. For the routes see Magie, 49–52, and for Roman highway systems, 39–42, 799, 786 f.

9. This route appears in the *Itinerarium Antonini,* a manual of the greatest highways in the empire, compiled in the third century (published in *Itineraria Romana* I, ed. O. Cuntz [Leipzig 1929] 50), and in the Peutinger Table, a map of the fourth century. Its general course is known from the numerous milestones which have been found on the section between Thyateira and Sardis (Magie, 799, to which should be added two unpublished milestones from Kanboğaz: manuscript supplement to Sardis inscription report, 1972). For the bridge and the course of the highway around the west end of the lake see W. H. Buckler, "Monuments de Thyateira," *RevPhil* 37 (1913) 325 f. An abutment of the bridge survives on the north side of the Hermus about 2 km. west of the village of Kesterlik. It is about 10 m. long, 3 m. high and 2.5 m. wide, is built of rubble with much whitish mortar, and contains a good deal of brick. From its style of construction, it would seem to be Byzantine or even Turkish.

10. Sardis–Daldis road: Magie, 786; Sardis–Apollonis–Pergamon: Strabo 13.4.3–5; road over Tmolus: C. Foss, "Researches in Mount Tmolus," forthcoming. The direct route from Thyateira to Philadelphia is shown on the Peutinger Table. It later became a major Ottoman highway. Its existence is wrongly doubted by W. Ramsay, *Historical Geography of Asia Minor* (London 1890) 167.

11. For tentative identification with Assuwa–Asia during the second millennium cf. *Sardis* M2 (1972) nos. 11, 26; Hanfmann, "Prehistoric Sardis," 160–183.

12. Sardian plain: Strabo 13.4.5-6. Neighboring cities: Tmolus-Aureliopolis: Keil, Premerstein, I, 13 f.; Buresch, 186; Robert, *Villes*[2], 276 f.; Mermere: Buresch, 184; Keil, Premerstein, I, 61 and inscr. 126; W. H. Buckler, "Lydian Documents," *JHS* 37 (1917) 105–107; Daldis: Buresch, 192; Keil, Premerstein, I, 64–68; Satala: Robert, *Villes*[2], 280–313; Cogamus Valley: Keil, Premerstein, III, 15–48. It is not certain whether Mermere is to be identified with the city of Kerassai, which appears in Nonnus (13.464–466) and the bishops' lists and which was probably located near Mount Tmolus in the vicinity of Sardis. See the discussion of Robert, *Villes*[2], 273–278. Several ancient sites of the region have not yet been identified. Nonnus mentions Kimpsos "with fine pebbles," "craggy" Itone, and the peaks of Oanos (13.464 f., 471–474). These were probably all located in Mount Tmolus, Robert, *Villes*[2], 313–317.

13. In the discussion of agricultural and mineral resources, products farmed or mined at the present time have been included if they would have been suitable for use in antiquity, even if they are not attested in the surviving ancient texts. For a general survey of agricultural products see Magie, 36, 46. Grain and wine: Magie, 806 with references to the sources. Products of Tmolus: Theophrastus, *Hist.Plant.* 4.5.4 (hazelnuts, chestnuts, grapes, apples, pomegranates).

14. Timber: Cuinet, III, 528; reforestation: *Manisa 1967,* 121, 229 f. For 1966–68, an area of 2,500 hectares with 7,500,000 trees was reforested in the Sabuncubeli in Mount Sipylus; forest yields in 1967 were 7,299 cbm. of rough and commercial (industrial) timber and 120 tons of resin for the entire vilayet of Manisa which still has 45% of its area considered as forest (366,235 out of 738,672 hectares). The use of woods of various kinds was attested by charred beams in Lydian sectors, by charcoal found on top of the chamber tomb at Keskinler, and by the leg of a wooden couch found in one of the Bin Tepe graves (BT 63.2), *BASOR* 206, 14; 174, 55.

15. From the report of the Köy İşleri Bakanlığı.

16. Hanfmann, "Horsemen," 570–581.

17. *Manisa 1967,* 223.

18. Doğuer, et al., 56, Table I. Some of the more interesting finds of this study are: (1) that bones of the main species were distributed equally throughout the various periods; (2) 88.7% were bones of domesticated animals, and of those, 40% belonged to small ruminants; (3) that camel and buffalo bones were found only in Lydian levels, suggesting that the Lydians had domesticated these animals.

19. Mineral resources: Ryan; MTA Publication 113; Magie, 45 f. Gold: Strabo 13.1.22-23, 13.4.3-5, 14.5.27-28; for ancient workings in the Pactolus Valley south of Sardis see the report of M. Collignon in *CRAI* (1903) 75, and for the site of Metallon near the mines, C. Foss, "Researches in Mount Tmolus," forthcoming. See also Hanfmann, Waldbaum, 310 f. M. Saydamer (1963) found gold in alluvia of practically all major mountain torrents running into the Hermus plain between Turgutlu and Salihli. In the seventeenth century it was believed that gold could be found in the mountain behind Nymphaeum, where lead

and silver were being mined; Refik, 44, a letter from the Kadı of Manisa to Murat III. Iron: for magnetite of Magnesia see *RE* s.v. "Magnet" col. 473, and *Manisa Vilayeti* (a geographical, historical and economic survey of the province published in Manisa in 1932) 104, and H. Blümner, *Technologie und Terminologie der Gewerbe und Künste der Griechen und Römern* IV (Leipzig 1884) 208. Blümner notes that the absence of any mention of iron derived from magnetite in the ancient sources is probably due to chance; cf. Herodotus 1.34 for confiscation of iron arms by Croesus. For modern sources in the region see Mason, 116, and Ravndal, 142. Ryan 86; MTA Publication 113, 74; *Iron Ore Deposits of Turkey,* Mineral Research and Exploration Institute of Turkey, Publication 118 (Ankara 1964) 44. The establishment of a large factory for the manufacture of weapons at Sardis in the late third or fourth century suggests that there must have been considerable sources of iron in the vicinity. Copper: Ravndal, 141; Philippson, *Reisen* II, 68; Arsenic: Mason, II, 129; Ravndal, 155; Philippson, *Reisen* II, 68; Antimony: Ravndal, 154; Philippson, *Reisen* II, 66; IV, 43. Silver and arsenic at Sart Çamur Hamamları: Ryan 66; MTA Publication 113, 14, 88.

20. Cinnabar: Pliny, *N.H.* 33.114. The ancient workings are still visible above the village of Ayasuluk (probably to be identified with the ancient Nicaea of the Cilbiani: Keil, Premerstein, III, 57, 59) in the Cayster Valley; a modern mine may be seen on the mountain road from Sardis to Ödemiş just south of the village of Allahdiyen. Yellow ochre: Pliny, *N.H.* 33.160; sulphur: Philippson, *Reisen* II, 71 (at Allahdiyen, MTA Publication 113, 139) and 72 (in the valley of the Tabak Çay east of Sardis); the latter source is probably that of the hot springs of Sart Çamur Hamamları, an hour south of Sardis, *Sardis* I (1922) 20 f.

21. Marble: ancient quarry near Sardis, *Sardis* I (1922) 19, 176; ancient quarries at Mermere near Gygean Lake: Keil, Premerstein, I, 61–64; Philippson, *Reisen* II, 10. Touchstones: Pliny, *N.H.* 33.126; Theophrastus, *de Lapidibus,* 45–47. The touchstone was a kind of slate, cf. C. Frondel, in *Dana's System of Minerology* III (New York 1962) 225, and Hanfmann, Waldbaum, 324 n. 53; Caley, Richards, 156–158. Sard: Pliny, *N.H.* 37.105; *Sardis* M2 (1972) no. 137. Although Pliny states that the stone was named from Sardis, the name may actually be of Persian origin.

22. *Sardis* M2 (1972) nos. 128–139.

23. Textiles: Magie, 47 f. with full references, but note that the "Sardian chitons" which he cites (812 n. 77) from Pollux 7.77 were actually from Sardinia; the adjective used, *sardonikos,* applies to the island, not the city. For the textile industry at Sardis in late antiquity see C. Foss, forthcoming monograph "Byzantine and Turkish Sardis," and *Sardis* M2 (1972) no. 133.

24. Leather workers: Strabo 13.4.6, quoting an otherwise unattested variant of *Iliad* 7.221. The line refers to the leather workers of Hyde, a place mentioned in *Iliad* 20.385 as lying beneath "snowy Tmolus": Strabo 13.4.6 writes that some identify it with Sardis, others with its Acropolis. Ivory: *Iliad* 4.141; R. D. Barnett, "Early Greek and Oriental Ivories," *JHS* 68 (1948) 18 f. Gold refinery, recently discovered by the present expedition: Hanfmann, Waldbaum,

310-315. Iron work: C. Foss, "Byzantine and Turkish Sardis," forthcoming. Perfume: Athenaeus 15.690b-d; Pliny, *N.H.* 13.10, 20.197; *Sardis* M2 (1972) no. 131.

25. D. G. Mitten, *BASOR* 191, 7-10; 199, 12-15; Mitten, Yüğrüm, "Eski Balıkhane." Mitten, Yüğrüm, "Ahlatlı Tepecik."

26. Cf. the survey by D. H. French, "Prehistoric Sites in Northwest Anatolia, II. The Balikesir and Akhisar-Manisa Areas," *AnatSt* 19 (1969) 41-98. Numerous Yortan cemeteries, e.g. at Gölde, were illicitly excavated in the Lydia-Kekaumene region in recent years. For the Yortan type tripod vase at Ahlatlı Tepecik see Mitten, Yüğrüm, "Eski Balıkhane," 195, fig. 9.

27. Y. Boysal, "New Excavations in Caria," *Anatolia* 10 (1966) 46.

28. A. Ramage, N. Ramage, 141-160, fig. 1.

29. *BASOR* 206, 11 f.

30. Ramage, 73 f.

31. *Sardis* VII (1932) 3 no. 1; cf. *AJA* 16 (1912) 41-51 for a discussion of these villages and towns. Atkinson, 48-49, 69-75. Translation and discussion of economic points, E. Cavaignac, *Population et capital dans le monde Méditerranéen antique* (Strasbourg 1923) 122-128.

32. Actually, these "village" units often include several hamlets.

33. Official statistics after *Manisa 1967,* 107. The district of Salihli (map, ibid., 77) probably corresponds pretty closely to the immediate ecological area of Sardis, except that the ancient land may have extended somewhat farther westward into the present district of Turgutlu, at least along the Hermus and the southern shore of the Gygean Lake (Marmara Gölü).

34. See *infra,* "Precipitation and Floods."

35. See *supra,* "Territory of Sardis."

36. Mersindere: *Sardis* VII (1932) no. 144. Metallon and Üç Tepeler: C. Foss, "Researches in Mount Tmolus," forthcoming. Çaltılı: *Sardis* VII (1932) no. 146 and unpublished Sardis inscriptions IN58.9, IN68.11. Sart Çamur Hamamları: *Sardis* VII (1932) no. 209 and p. 97, IN60.40.

37. Allahdiyen: C. Foss, "Researches in Mount Tmolus," forthcoming. Tartar İslâmköy: Sardis inscriptions IN59.64, IN64.57; this site was apparently adjacent to the village of Tatar Dere (which has now disappeared or merged with its neighbor) where Keil, Premerstein, II, 8, saw numerous ancient and Byzantine remains. The two villages are mentioned as separate but adjacent by Arundell, *Seven Churches,* 176. Yeşilkavak (formerly called Monavak): Buresch, 186; Keil, Premerstein, II, 9 f.; there are no remains now visible, but a tumulus stands above the village.

38. Sites at and around Durasallı: Buresch, 194; Keil, Premerstein, II, 9; III, 10-14; there are no remains now to be found at Durasallı. Mounds: A. Ramage, N. Ramage, 149 f. Lydian inscription: Keil, Premerstein, III, no. 16. Thymbrara: Xenophon, *Cyr.* 6.2.111; 7.1.45; Diod. 14.80.2 (there called Thybarna); Buresch, 194.

39. Çapaklı: Buresch, 133; Keil, Premerstein, I, 67 f.; an occasional fragment is still to be found in the village; mounds stand nearby at Gebeç and Tepecik Çiftliği. North side of plain: Sardis inscription IN68.1 (Yağbasan Köy); *BASOR* 177, 36 (Kemerdamları); inscriptions of Poyraz-

damları: Buckler, *JHS* 37 (1917) 102-104. North side of lake: *BASOR* 177, 35 f. South side of lake: unspecified findspot: *Sardis* VII (1932) no. 5, 153, 160; Ahlatlı Tepecik: *BASOR* 191, 7-10; 199, 12-15; Eski Balıkhane: *Sardis* VII (1932) no. 139; Mitten, Yüğrüm, "Eski Balıkhane," 191 f. West side of lake: Keil, Premerstein, I, 64, unpublished milestones from Kanboğaz, *supra* n. 9; the remains of a large stone building stand beside the modern road and a fragmentary inscription mentioning an aqueduct is built into a local fountain.

40. Gürice: Buresch, 184; Keil, Premerstein, II, 4-8; Buckler, *JHS* 37 (1917) 108; tombs and fragmentary inscriptions are visible at the site, which seems to have been fairly considerable. On Lübbey Yaylası and Bozdağ, see C. Foss, "Researches in Mount Tmolus," forthcoming. Antiquities found at Bozdağ were made available for inspection through the courtesy of Bay Mutahhar Başoğlu of Ödemiş and Bozdağ, who is well versed in the history and archaeology of this relatively unexplored region.

41. For the route of the Third Crusade see the narratives of Ansbert and the *Historia Peregrinorum,* ed. A. Chroust, in *MGH, Scr. rer. germ.* V (Berlin 1928) 74 f., 153 f. The other routes were followed by Turkish attacks in 1110: Anna Comnena 14.1.6.

42. Late antique and Byzantine remains have been found at Gürice, Kılcanlar, Kemerdamları (unpublished), Eski Balıkhane, Bin Tepe, Tatar Dere, Durasallı, and Lübbey Yaylası; on these sites see the references *supra,* ns. 35-40, and *BASOR* 186, 47-52. Unpublished inscriptions show that the sites at Çaltılı and Sart Çamur Hamamları were inhabited in late antiquity (IN68.11, IN60.40). Villages in the neighborhood of Sardis are mentioned in the narratives of the Third Crusade, see *supra,* n. 41. To judge by its name, the village of Candaules, mentioned only in the life of some obscure martyrs of the Great Persecution, was probably in the vicinity: *Synaxarium Ecclesiae Constantinopolitanae* (Brussels 1902) 16.

43. For the administrative centers of Saruhan, see the extremely useful work of M. Çağatay Uluçay, *Saruhan Oğulları ve Eserlerine dair Vesikalar* II, 10 f., and 37-117. The latter section is a publication of archival documents of the province classified according to regional centers; the documents include the names of many villages.

44. For the towns and villages of the vilayet of Manisa in the seventeenth century see Uluçay, *supra,* n. 43, vol. I, 16 f.

45. For the Ottoman highway system see the map at the end of vol. II of Fr. Täschner, *Das anatolische Wegenetz nach osmanischen Quellen* (Leipzig 1924-1936). Relevant texts of the travelers will be published by J. A. Scott in a forthcoming monograph.

46. For the caravan trade of İzmir, see in addition to the travelers, Fr. Täschner, "Wegenetz".

47. Salihli is mentioned as a large and inhabited village by Sieur Paul Lucas, *Voyage du Sieur Paul Lucas fait par ordre du roy dans la Grèce, l'Asie Mineure, la Macedoine et l'Afrique* I (Paris 1712) 305, who passed through ca. 1705. By the time of Arundell, who visited Salihli in 1826 and 1832 (*Seven Churches,* 176; *Discoveries* I, 30 f.), it was an important market town. Thus the local story that the town

was first settled around 1790 by a camel driver named Sadık Dede may be dismissed; for that see *Manisa Vilayeti* (Manisa 1932) 302. This story is related in Türkdoğan, 11 where a brief sketch of the history and geography of the town is given. According to Türkdoğan, Salihli became the administrative center of the region in 1875.

48. From Köy İşleri Bakanlığı, chart of monthly average temperatures and rainfall.

49. As observed by geologist C. Taran and G. F. Swift, Jr. in his field report on the Lydian Trench area, 1970.

50. See *infra*, Ch. VII; *BASOR* 154, 8, 11. Torrent bed L: 3.60–4.47 m. over hardpan in Trench S; also over hardpan, *BASOR* 162, 30, n. 43 for river deposits under the temple. (They are, however, considered intentional fill by M. C. Bolgil and K. J. Frazer.)

51. See *infra*, Ch. IV "Levels". The dating of these flood deposits depends on the dating of Monument 10. If the monument is dated by the (Early Hellenistic) coins, then at least the east embankment must be Hellenistic.

52. Observed in 1969–70 on the occasion of the cleaning of Church M.

53. W. Warfield in *Sardis* I (1922) App. I.

54. *BASOR* 199, 38–39. The excavation revealed at this depth a series of Roman architectural pieces, apparently from a structure in which the pediment from the Persian era was reused.

55. Report by G. F. Swift, Jr., cf. *BASOR* 162, 3–16; 170, 14; 186, 32–36; section fig. 4; "Deposits consisted alternately of sands and gravels and beds of clay; from level *94.1 down to *89.9 lay beds consisting of coarse sand with occasional heavier gravels; only at one point, *91.4, was there a thin band of clay." Evidence of flooding begins with the Lydian era, (ca. *100.0–*99.0; *BASOR* 174, 14) and reaches down at least 10 m. (to *89.9; *BASOR* 186, 36). The modern surface was at *103.0–*102.0. As Swift observed, occupation, even in Lydian times, was only intermittent, interrupted by the floods.

56. The lowest occupational strata were conservatively considered to be of the fourteenth century B.C., (*BASOR* 162, 16), "possibly as early as 1300 B.C." (*BASOR* 185, 36). Flood deposits continued underneath.

57. For CG stratification, cf. *infra*, Ch. IX; *BASOR* 157, 43.

58. Strabo 13.4.7; *Sardis* M2 (1972) 77 no. 279.

59. Zosimus 5.13, 18. Discussed in detail by C. Foss in forthcoming monograph, "Byzantine and Turkish Sardis."

60. E. Boissier, *Flora orientalis* (Geneva 1867) 38.

61. Fellows, 289, and see Fig. 333.

62. PN well: *BASOR* 166, 20–22; top of well, *88.3; bottom with flowing water, *80.2.

63. Well in HoB: *BASOR* 174, 12; excavation from *99.66 to *80.80, the bottom was not reached because of water.

64. *Infra*, Ch. IX; *BASOR* 157, 42. In 1959, an exceptionally dry year, we reached water at *94.8 (local level); usually the water stands around *97.0.

65. *BASOR* 177, 4; 191, 12–13.

66. *BASOR* 166, 20–22.

67. K. J. Frazer, *infra*, Ch. V, "Trench 5". Archaic terracotta pipes have been found in the Athenian Agora,

but the Sardian examples seem to resemble those of the Roman period; cf. Thompson, Wycherley, *Agora* XIV, 199, fig. 51.

68. H. C. Butler, *Sardis* I (1922) 24 f. considered the cutting of cisterns one of the reasons why the Acropolis rock had often fallen off. When investigated, however, the alleged cisterns at the top turned out to have served as a church (*BASOR* 206, 15, n. 3). A chamber at the top of the tunnels in the north side resembled a cistern; cf. *infra* n. 69.

69. *BASOR* 170, 35–37, fig. 24.

70. E.g. Mycenae, Tiryns, Acropolis of Athens, Jerusalem, Hazor, Gezer, Gibeon. H. von Gall, *AA* (1967) 585–587 for the Phrygian and Paphlagonian tunnels.

71. *BASOR* 182, 23.

72. *Sardis* VII (1932) no. 10. A good, brief description of the traces of the aqueduct in *Sardis* I (1922) 35–36, Map I.

73. *Sardis* VII (1932) no. 17.

74. Fountain of the Synagogue forecourt: *BASOR* 191, 29–30. It is still not certain whether it was identical with *krene synagoges*, *Sardis* VII (1932) no. 17, line 7. There may have been a fountain in Room B, just west of the Synagogue.

75. *BASOR* 211, 22, fig. 4, IN72.26.

76. *Infra*, Ch. IV, "Monument No. 10," Figs. 86, 87.

77. The House of Bronzes had both residential and commercial uses. In addition to regular water supply pipes, a long, vaulted underground cistern provided water, but this may have been publicly accessible, *BASOR* 157, 24 (water tanks for cleaning wool?).

78. *BASOR* 157, 32–33, fig. 18.

79. *BASOR* 170, 21–22, fig. 13. The pipes slant toward the lower city.

80. *BASOR* 162, 25 n. 34; and 170, 70, fig. 13; 191, 30–1; renovation of water system dated between A.D. 350 and 400 by coins.

81. The caisson well dug by the expedition in the Pactolus bed was tested and found to have a very high percentage of colon bacilli (twenty times that regarded as permissible in Massachusetts) owing to pollution.

82. G. M. A. Hanfmann is doubtful that the sophisticated system of pipelines leading in and out of the temple belonged to the Byzantine cistern. The system may be Roman or even Late Hellenistic in origin. H. A. Thompson reminds us that G. Gruben, *AthMitt* 76 (1961) 162 n. 13, argued against the existence of a cistern.

83. *BASOR* 162, 34, Trench C; 166, 39; 170, 32; vaulted brick cistern, there dated to the seventh to tenth centuries.

84. Bronze Age grave and hut near the Pactolus: *BASOR* 170, 7 f.

85. The arrival of Mycenaeans seems to be remembered in the tradition that the rule of descendants of Heracles began 505 years before Candaules; Herodotus 1.7; cf. *Sardis* M2 (1972) no. 26; Strabo 13.4.6, cf. *Sardis* M2 (1972) nos. 17, 8 and 15; *Iliad*, 20.395.

86. Acropolis, archaic remains: *BASOR* 162, 34.

87. H. C. Butler, *Sardis* I (1922) 34–35, 137, noted that Lydian graves were found along the torrent gulches coming

down toward the Pactolus from the Acropolis. As long as these burials appeared only in the upper reaches, the eastern bank could be envisaged as fairly substantial residential area (Fig. 7). At the mouth of the Şeytan Dere torrent, however, Lydian burials have been found so close to the eastern bank of the Pactolus that there would be very little place left for any road and houses; *BASOR* 186, 37–38, fig. 17 (Fig. 1 No. 54). Yet, a couple of hundred yards to the southeast we have evidence for a built up area in NEW, *infra,* Ch. VIII, (Figs. 1, 59, 282 f.). Either there really was an interval in habitation structures strung out along the Pactolus, or, more likely, the Lydians were not too strict about proximity of graves to houses.

88. Pactolus North: *BASOR* 177, 4–8, figs. 1–2; 182, 18–25, figs. 14–15; Ramage, 21 f.

89. Xenophon, *Oec.* 4.20–25; *Sardis* M2 (1972) 287–289.

90. Parks, perhaps Lydian: Athenaeus 12.515d–f; *Sardis* M2 (1972) no. 130; Roman: *Sardis* VII (1932) no. 12.6.

91. *Sardis* M2 (1972) nos. 192–210. Inscriptions of Antiochus III: L. Robert, in D. G. Mitten, *BASOR* 174, 34, discusses these *parastades* of the Metroon with letters of Antiochus and decree of Sardis honoring Queen Laodike.

92. By Vitruvius 2.8.9–10; *Sardis* M2 (1972) no. 291, following an Early Hellenistic source (not Mucianus as is sometimes suggested).

93. For the discussion cf. *infra,* Ch. V. An approximate date is given by the inscription of Mnesimachus carved on the western part of the north cella wall. Cf. most recently Atkinson, 62–67.

94. "Tomb of the Lintel," *BASOR* 157, 16, figs. 3, 5. Hanfmann, *Letters,* 64, figs. 41–42.

95. Gymnasium: mentioned in the Antiochus III letter of 213 B.C.; cf. Polybius 31.6 = *Sardis* M2 (1972) no. 210, 164–163 B.C. Metroon: it may have existed already in the fifth century B.C.; cf. Plutarch, *Them.* 31; *Sardis* M2 (1972) no. 274. The preserved marble blocks were tentatively considered "classical" by G. Roux and possibly fourth century B.C. by A. Bammer who saw the blocks at Sardis.

96. Temple of Zeus: Arrian *Anabasis* 1.17.3–6; *Sardis* M2 (1972) no. 235.

97. Acropolis: coin of Antiochus III: *BASOR* 162, 39, n. 63; the date of the wall itself is now known to be Lydian.

98. Pactolus Cliff: see *supra,* n. 94.

99. Hellenistic Structure C in HoB area: *BASOR* 170, 10–11, fig. 2. Coins of Alexander and Antiochus III: *BASOR* 174, 14, fig. 2 (plan).

100. Matis: Hanfmann, Polatkan, Robert, 45–56, pls. 9–10; Hanfmann, *Letters,* 48, fig. 29.

101. Destruction and synoikismos of 213 B.C.: Robert, *NIS* 9–21, 58 (on Viceroy Zeuxis). For the Jewish veterans' settlement see Josephus, *AJ* 12.147–153; Hanfmann, Waldbaum, 318–319 and literature, n. 78. L. Robert (by letter, January 1974) notes that the settlement of veterans refers to the years between 211–205 B.C. and objects to its use as evidence for Sardis.

102. Cemeteries: *BASOR* 157, 28 plan fig. 9; Hellenistic Steps: *BASOR* 174, 47–49, figs. 29–30; limestone, orientation 60°15′ west of 1963 magnetic north, against Roman

orientation of 69°, ibid. 48, n. 21. Late Hellenistic Mausoleum M in Pactolus North: *BASOR* 174, 22–24, fig. 11 (plan). The Street of Pipes is there attributed to post–A.D. 17 plan. Hellenistic tile kiln: *BASOR* 177, 4. The lamp kilns in the industrial area on the Pactolus may have had a Hellenistic phase; cf. *BASOR* 191, 38. It is not clear whether the metal working establishment in the HoB area continued after 213 B.C.; cf. *BASOR* 166, 7, amphora handle ca. 250 B.C.

103. Mausolea: *BASOR* 157, 28; 174, 47–49.

104. Theater and City Wall: Polybius 7.16.6; *Sardis* M2 (1972) no. 284.

105. Bent axis: with east-west highway turning northeast through the hollow, cf. Figs. 7, 10. This type of plan is known at several places in Asia Minor and Syria; cf. Martin, *Urbanisme,* 158 f., figs. 22, 23 (Kremna, Side), 32, (Palmyra).

106. Modern road and Nos. 28, 29; bend at E 1000/N 50, in Fig. 10.

107. Late Hellenistic Mausoleum M: *BASOR* 174, 22–24, fig. 11.

108. Colonnaded Street: its somewhat hypothetical course is shown in plan, Fig. 10; *BASOR* 191, 40, fig. 36.

109. Fig. 1 (between grid squares E 200–1300/N 50–500).

110. *Sardis* VII (1932) no. 4. Cf. *Sardis* M2 (1972) nos. 210, 275, 291, and for the history, nos. 206–216.

111. It can be shown that the ground between the House of Bronzes and the Hellenistic Steps sloped much more steeply in the Hellenistic than in the Roman period. The entire Gymnasium complex was built over terraced fill of Hellenistic structures. At the Hellenistic Steps the Hellenistic level was 4 m. below the Roman (*92.62 versus *96.50), *BASOR* 174, 48. The so-called Upper Terrace is also an artificial formation, apparently started after A.D. 17, *BASOR* 157, 19 f.; 177, 14.

112. For reuse of the Metroon blocks cf. *supra,* n. 95. Many marble and limestone blocks used in construction of the Gymnasium piers make the impression of retrimmed or recut blocks. The use of cemented rubble in post–A.D. 17 building may have also promoted lime burning; cf. the lime kilns on the Pactolus, *BASOR* 191, 38.

113. Seven Doric capitals from peristyle house: *BASOR* 170, 13, fig. 12, found with Hellenistic relief ware. For Hellenistic peristyle houses cf. the Delian house, Martin, *Urbanisme,* 235–240, pl. 32.1, with 8 small columns, and fig. 47 (Priene).

114. Inscription of Iulia Lydia who "after the earthquake" (*meta ton seismon*) restored the *naos* and image originally given by her grandfather, IN63.123.

115. Aqueduct: *Sardis* VII (1932) no. 10.

116. For location of modern watermill, *Sardis* I (1922) 30, ill. 28; possible ancient forerunner, *Sardis* VII (1932) no. 169.

117. Information given by Orhan Araz, August, 1971.

118. *Sardis* VII (1932) no. 17; *BASOR* 191, 29 f.

119. Vitruvius 2.8.9–10, on Gerusia; fountain inscription: *Sardis* VII (1932) no. 17; Menogenes documents: ibid. no. 8, Temple of Augustus and Gaius Caesar, Agora, *Presbeutikon* (Hall of Elders), *Paideutikon* (Hall of the Boys), Precinct of Zeus Poleus and Artemis.

120. IN63.A1 found in 1963. On Roman column base, reused. *BASOR* 174, 46.

121. Hypaepa, tetrapylon inscription: IN68.19–20, *BASOR* 199, 29, fig. 16.

122. H. Vetters, *AnzWien* 107 (1970) 7–13, figs. 1, 3, 4, 7; Mansel, *Mélanges* 69–92.

123. *Sardis* VII (1932) 31, no. 12, pl. 5.

124. *Sardis* VII (1932) 39, no. 17.

125. *Not. Dign. or.* XI:18–39 (ed. O. Seeck, Berlin 1876). Cf. also A. H. M. Jones, *The Later Roman Empire 284-602*, 2 (Norman, Okla. 1964) 834, n. 24; and C. Foss, "Byzantine Cities of Western Asia Minor" (Ph.D. diss., Harvard University 1972) 52 f., 58 f.

126. Builders' union inscription: *Sardis* VII (1932) no. 18.

127. *Sardis* VII, no. 169, fourth or fifth century A.D.

128. Crawford, passim; *BASOR* 170, 49–51; 191, 17–22; 199, 74.

129. Cf. D. G. Mitten, "Two Bronze Objects in the McDaniel Collection," *HSCP* 69 (1965) 163–167; Crawford, "Lamp," 291–294; J. C. Waldbaum, forthcoming monograph on Sardis metalwork.

130. A detailed study of water supply of Pergamon is described by G. Garbrecht, 43–48.

131. Latrine: *BASOR* 157, 35, fig. 19; Hospital: *Sardis* VII (1932) no. 19.

132. North room, Building B: *BASOR* 177, 25; Marble Court: *BASOR* 206, 24, figs. 14–16.

133. Preliminary report, *BASOR* 215.

134. See C. Foss, *supra* n. 125, 99 f. and forthcoming monograph on Byzantine and Turkish Sardis for fuller treatment.

135. Cf. *infra*, Ch. III.

136. The dating has been determined on the basis of coin finds; see C. Foss, forthcoming monograph on Byzantine and Turkish Sardis and *BASOR* 166, 45; 186, 28 f. For a divergent interpretation, cf. P. Charanis, "A Note on the Byzantine Coin Finds in Sardis and Their Historical Significance," *Leimon, Offerings to N. B. Tomadakis* (Athens 1973 = *Epet* 39–40 (1972–1973) 175–180. Contradicted by C. Foss, "The Destruction of Sardis in 616 and the Value of Evidence," *JÖB* (forthcoming).

137. Cf. *supra*, n. 133; *infra*, n. 139.

138. Cf. *supra*, "Precipitation and Floods," and "Water Supply."

139. A. H. Detweiler, "Preliminary Report on Church E" *BASOR* 174, 14–20, figs. 8–10.

CHAPTER III

1. Mitten, 44; Naster, 3–16. Meles, a Heraklid ruler, is supposed to have carried a lion cub around the Acropolis to insure its impregnability. Assuming they were unscalable, Meles neglected the cliffs of the south side of the Acropolis in his circuit, thus leading ultimately to the fall of the Acropolis to the Persians in 547 B.C.

2. Herodotus 1.84. For other references to the siege cf. *Sardis* M2 (1972) nos. 113–123.

3. Cf. Winter, 6, 8, 54, 100–104. Winter's description of the type in Early Iron Age Greece applies verbatim to

Sardis: "The ideal site was the tip of a spur, which ran out from the flank of a mountain and was linked to the main mass only by a narrow ridge . . . the dwellings of the lower classes extending down the slopes of the hill . . . within convenient distance of the citadel above . . . and the fields below . . . " and "we shall look in vain for walls enclosing the outer city . . . " (54).

4. "When Cyrus came up to *the wall* in Sardis . . . he set up his engines as if intending to assault it and made ready his scaling ladders . . . in the course of the following night he sent some Chaldaeans and Persians to climb up what was considered the most precipitous side of the Sardian citadel . . . When it became known that the citadel [*ta akra*] was taken, all the Lydians immediately fled from *the walls* wherever they could in the city . . . " (Italics are ours). Cf. *Sardis* M2 (1972) no. 122. Xenophon's reference to a "Persian . . . who had learnt a way down to the river and the same ascent," and thus led the Persians into the citadel, does not jibe well with the topography. Both the Pactolus on the west, and even more the Hermus on the north, are quite far away from the top range of the citadel.

5. Arrian, *Anabasis* 1.17.4; *Sardis* M2 (1972) no. 235.

6. *BASOR* 162, 34–36, figs. 17, 18. For discussion of date cf. Greenewalt, passim.

7. *BASOR* 162, 37–39, figs. 21, 22. Reconsidered by C. H. Greenewalt, Jr., "The Acropolis," *BASOR* 206, 15–20, figs. 5–7. The definitive treatment of these and other walls investigated in 1971–1972 will be found in a forthcoming report in this series. It is possible, of course, that staircases and platforms were parts of a fortified palace area, as they were in the Takht complex at Pasargadae, which may have been built by Lydian masons from Sardis. Cf. Hanfmann, Waldbaum, 316–317, pl. 39.

8. Sherds found within the wall permit no dating closer than sixth and fifth centuries B.C. Preliminary reports: *BASOR* 215, *Dergi,* forthcoming.

9. Winter, 111, 115 fig. 90 (Ephesus); Colophon: L. B. Holland, "Colophon," *Hesperia* 13 (1944) 99 f., 17 f. Smyrna: Naumann, Kantar; Ephesus: Bean, 163, fig. 33. Cf. also Martin, *Urbanisme,* 41, 55, 163.

10. Polybius, *Histories* 7.15–17. *Sardis* M2 (1972) no. 203.

11. Mitten, *BiblArch* 59–61; Robert, *NIS,* 10–14, 58; D. G. Mitten, "The Synagogue," *BASOR* 174, 34. For L. Robert's views cf. *supra,* Ch. II, "Late Hellenistic: 213 B.C.–A.D. 17," and n. 91.

12. D. M. Robinson and W. H. Buckler, *Sardis* VII (1932) no. 83, thought the inscription by a governor Achollios referred to the building of the city or citadel walls, but L. Robert, *Hellenica* 4 (1948) 35, J. Keil, *JOAI* 36 (1946) 121, and Magie, II, n. 28, have seen that the inscription does not warrant this interpretation. The dating of the inscription, too, has been brought down from 250 to late fourth or early fifth century A.D.

13. In the relatively peaceful era of Trajan, Dio Chrysostomus wanted Prusa to have city walls among other projects designed to improve its status as a city, *Discourses* 45.13.

14. F. Imhoof-Blumer, *Zur griechischen und römischen Münzkunde* (Geneva 1908) 132, no. 6, pl. VI no. 6.

15. Zosimus 5.13, 18.

16. Cf. *infra,* "Evidence for Dating."

17. IN68.19–20, *BASOR* 199, 29, fig. 16.

18. *Sardis* M1 (1971) 1–2. For P. Charanis' criticism cf. *supra,* Ch. II, n. 136.

19. *Sardis* M1 (1971) 2–3, (641–664).

20. *Sardis* M1 (1971) 143 f.

21. J. B. Ward-Perkins and David Whitehouse of the British School in Rome have very kindly talked with me and criticized this analysis; to them I owe great thanks (David Van Zanten).

22. See *infra,* "Detailed Description of Towers."

23. See *infra,* "Detailed Description of Towers."

24. The Acropolis walls and "Flying Towers," now officially known as the Western Ridge Fortification, will be treated in a forthcoming volume in this series by C. H. Greenewalt, Jr. Cf. *BASOR* 203, 14, fig. 8, and "Sector Index," s.v. Western Ridge.

25. See *infra,* "Stratigraphic Soundings at Section 30."

26. Somewhat similar masonry technique in Sardis Building A was observed by R. L. Vann in his forthcoming study on the unexcavated buildings at Sardis.

27. This total lack of formwork is unusual (cf. Ward-Perkins, *Great Palace,* 62 f. on Early Byzantine construction techniques) and perhaps unwise, considering the swiftness with which Anatolian lime mortar weakens in contact with ground water.

28. Faruk Akça's calculations, made in 1971, are as follows (assuming that all materials, i.e. stones, lime, sand, water, are present at the site):

Excavation of one cubic meter: 3 hours digging; 1 hour removing dirt; 1 hour carrying dirt away; 1/6 hour grading. Total: 5 1/6 hours (add one hour per meter extra for digging deeper than two meters).

Building a rough stone wall for one cubic meter: ½ hour mixing mortar; 4 hours, master mason; 8 hours workmen. Total: 12½ hours (add 2½ hours for height 3–6 meters; 5 hours for height 6–9 meters).

"Assuming that the wall has a foundation 3 meters deep and is 2 meters wide by 9 meters high:"

Excavation for one linear meter:

first 2 meters: 2 X 2 X 1 X 12½ = 50 man-hours

additional meter: 2 X 1 X 1 X 6 1/6 = 12 1/3 man-hours

foundation: 3 X 2 X 1 X 12½ = 75 man-hours

first 3 meters: 3 X 2 X 1 X 12½ = 75 man-hours

next 3–6 meters: 3 X 2 X 1 X 15 = 90 man-hours

next 6–9 meters: 3 X 2 X 1 X 17 5/6 = 107 man-hours

Total: 409 1/3 man-hours

"Because it seems apparent that the wall was built in ten meter segments in most instances, we shall assume that two teams of five men (one master mason and four workmen) did the work. Therefore, if working a 9-hour day, they worked approximately 45 days to complete one segment."

29. See Curtius, "Philadelpheia." The Philadelphia city wall is also known from nineteenth century prints.

30. Winter, 73–77. He found the solution to the puzzle of parapetless walls in texts, especially Aeneas Tacitus' *Poliorcetics* 33. Parallels appear in the Isthmus wall of 480 B.C. (Herodotus 8.71), and in the emergency extension of the city wall at Plataia in 429 B.C. (Thucydides 2.75).

L. B. Holland explored the structural details of such a brick parapet in the context of the Hellenic walls of Athens: "The Katastegasma of the Walls at Athens," *AJA* 54 (1950) 337–356. F. K. Yegül recalls that long sections of breastworks in the earlier Hadrian's wall, England, were of timber; cf., for instance, *Vindolanda: Roman Fort and Civilian Settlement* by Robin Birley (Newcastle upon Tyne, England 1973) 36.

31. With the help of G. M. A. Hanfmann, the following calculation has been made of the average distance guarded by a single warrior, based on Perikles' appraisal of Athenian strength ca. 431 B.C., as recorded in Thucydides 2.13: 16,000 men garrisoned the city walls and forts, 14,000 of whom Winter (p. 305) proposes were stationed on the wall. The length of the walls adds up to 148 stadia (Phalerian wall, 35 stadia; circuit wall, 43 stadia; long walls, 40 stadia; Peiraeus walls, 60 stadia, but half undefended). Taking the length of the stadium as 193 m., the length of wall defended was thus approximately 28,564 km. This figure, when divided by the number of defenders, 14,000, indicates that the average defender guarded 2 m. of the wall in time of attack. At other times the defenders would be divided into watches.

The walls of fifth century Athens were extraordinarily long in relation to the population of the city—as was also true in Late Roman Sardis. The purpose of this exercise, like that of the construction calculations in n. 28 *supra,* is to demonstrate that the seemingly formidable Sardis wall was easier to construct and man than might be supposed.

32. Transcribed, translated, and analysed in H. Diels and E. Schramm, "Philons Belopoiika," *AbhBerl* (1918) no. 16; (1919) no. 12; esp. 17–21. Analysed by Winter, 116–124.

33. See F. Krischen, *Die Landmauer von Konstantinopel* I (Berlin 1938); and Schneider.

34. See Schneider, Karnapp.

35. Modern Beled Sinjar. See D. Oates, *Studies in the Ancient History of Northern Iraq* (London 1968) 97–106.

36. Modern Diyarbekir. See Gabriel. His fourth century dating of the walls, though accepted by D. Oates, *Studies in the Ancient History of Northern Iraq* (London 1968) 105–106, is controversial. Cf. D. Van Berchem, "Récherches sur la chronologie des enceintes de Syrie et de Mesopotamie," *Syria* 31 (1954) 265–267. Procopius, *Buildings* 2.3,7, states that Justinian was the builder.

37. See Walter; Naumann, Kantar; and Müller-Wiener.

38. Soc. Dilettanti, 45 f., plate ch. II.1.

39. See, for example, Lawrence; W. Schleiermacher, *Der römische Limes in Deutschland* (Berlin 1959) 13–15, 34–41; Reichs-Limeskommission, *Der obergermanisch-rätische Limes des Rommerreichs,* im Auftrage der Reichs-Limeskommission herausgegeben (Heidelberg 1894–); P. MacKendrick, *Romans on the Rhine* (New York 1970) 254–255, bibliography on the limes; Olwen Brogan, "The Limes in Germany," *ArchJ* 92 (1935) 1–41, especially 31–33, pl. IV A, the Raetian stone wall.

40. *BASOR* 157, 20.

41. *BASOR* 157, 20.

42. As with Eastern Terra Sigillata B 1 pottery, the Robinson and the Hayes chronological systems differ con-

cerning Eastern Terra Sigillata B 2 ware. Hayes ignores the first century A.D. finds of this type from the Athenian Agora.

43. Briefly published, *BASOR* 186, 27–28, fig. 1. In late August 1966 and again in 1969 the gate area was flooded. In 1969, the trench was completely covered with sand and gravel.

44. Cf. *supra*, Ch. I, "Explanation of Topographic Plans, Grids, and Levels."

45. *BASOR* 199, 29, fig. 16.

46. Cf. Fig. 55; around A.D. 400?

47. *BASOR* 186, 27, fig. 1.

48. Similar voussoirs are frequent in Bath CG, *infra*, Ch. X.

49. Cf. *Sardis* M1 (1971) nos. 1209–1225, 1232.

50. *Sardis* M1 (1971) no. 383.

51. *Sardis* I (1922) 31, ill. 18.

52. Manisa Museum, no. 303, lioness, ca. 570–550 B.C. It came to the museum June 20, 1951. Briefly mentioned by H. Gabelmann, *Studien zum frühgriechischen Löwenbild* (Berlin 1965) no. 130a, p. 91. It will be published in detail by G. M. A. Hanfmann and N. H. Ramage in the forthcoming volume on Sardis sculptures. Unfortunately, it cannot be determined whether the piece was reused in the Roman foundation or was at a Lydian level.

53. Cf. *supra*, Ch. I, "Explanation of Topographic Plans, Grids, and Levels"; *BASOR* 191, 38.

54. The section was tested in 1967. The bottom of the wall was at *79.36, well above the present Pactolus bed; the top as far as preserved was at *82.46. The old Pactolus bed may have been 4 to 5 m. below the foot of the wall. H. A. Thompson questions the possible use of surviving remains for a bridge because of absence of massive piers. Unfortunately, it is not known what was destroyed in building the new highway, nor was any record made prior to 1951 of the manner in which the medieval wooden bridge was supported at both ends.

CHAPTER IV

1. Cf. *supra*, Ch. I, "An Explanation of Topographic Plans, Grids, and Levels."

2. Cf. *infra*, Ch. VIII, "Northeast Wadi."

3. On the intentional use of this convergence device by the Romans, cf. Schlikker, 748–765.

4. Trench 2: *infra*, Ch. V, "Soundings in the Artemis Temple in 1972"; LA: *infra*, Ch. VI; see also Trench 5: *infra*, Ch. V, "Soundings in the Artemis Temple in 1972."

5. W. Warfield in *Sardis* I (1922) App. I.

6. *Sardis* I (1922) 130–134, ills. 143–150.

7. *Sardis* I (1922) 133.

8. *Sardis* I (1922) 178.

9. *Sardis* I (1922) 133 f., ills. 149 f.

10. *Sardis* I (1922) 133, ills. 149 f. From comparison of the view, ill. 145, it seems that the level from which Butler's trenches started was approximately the same as that today or slightly lower; the trench shown is about 2 m. deep. He was presumably reaching levels of *99.00–*97.00.

11. *Sardis* I (1922) 132 f., ills. 146 f.

12. *Sardis* I (1922) 134.

13. *Sardis* I (1922) 127. C. Foss, "Byzantine and Turkish Sardis," (forthcoming) distinguished "Dark Ages," A.D. 616–ca. 850, from Middle Byzantine, A.D. 850–1204. Cf. also our chart *supra*, Ch. I, "Chronological Terminology."

14. *Sardis* I (1922) 52, 63, 74; Bell, *Sardis* XI (1916) viii gives a list of post–A.D. 668 coins, but does not indicate which were found in the cistern. Unfortunately, Butler alluded to, but never explained, his grid system, used also by Bell (*Sardis* I [1922] 54). Coins listed by Bell reach from 867 to Michael VIII (1261–1282), and even John V (1341–1391). It is thus not clear when the landslide supposedly covered the temple. Warfield in *Sardis* I (1922) 179 does not seem to envisage a sudden landslide. He conjectures that the present level of the precinct was reached in the 10th century A.D. but does not say how he obtained this dating. Olson, in reviewing the situation in 1970, found evidence of landslide material lying above stratified alluvia from ca. *103.00 upward along the east side of the excavation. For doubts concerning the cistern cf. Ch. II, n. 82.

15. Practically all of the 171 Byzantine coins listed by Bell as post–A.D. 668 came from the Artemis Precinct. G. E. Bates, *Sardis* M1 (1971), lists 11 coins from Building L: no. 459 Justin II (A.D. 572–577); no. 1181, Michael VII (A.D. 1071); and skyphates of Theodore I (A.D. 1208–1222); nos. 1200–1205, John III (A.D. 1222–1254); nos. 1208, 1214, 1222, 1229, Latin Crusader Imitation (A.D. 1204–1261).

16. *Sardis* I (1922) Plans I-III show these houses and even a mosque. We came upon some of their walls when building the enclosure for our camp.

17. W. Warfield in *Sardis* I (1922) 179 and coin found in base No. 35 (*infra*).

18. Crema, figs. 636–637; J. M. C. Toynbee, *Death and Burial in the Roman World* (London 1971) 130 f.

19. The structure was not excavated by the Harvard-Cornell Expedition, but during the cleaning, Middle Byzantine sgraffito sherds were found near the north wall.

20. The Little Metropolitan Church in Athens is a notable example.

21. Assuming the precinct floor at AR to have been at ca. *97.26, and the porch floor of U at ca. *98.74.

22. Butler had the structure fairly correctly drawn in *Sardis* I (1922) Plan III, and gave a photograph of the steps, ill. 141. Curiously, he asserted that "to the north of these steps there was no building to which they might have led" (p. 126). He gave a picture of the stele of 155 B.C. with inscription honoring Timarchos (ill. 140), of which we have found only the lower part. He described Tomb 2, but erroneously stated that it had no remains of painting.

23. IN69.22. Read by Gusmani, *Sardis* M3 (1975) B I, 1, as *a.r ul;* he considers *ul* as possibly "wrote." He cautions that the inscription cannot be proven to be in Lydian script. Dimensions: L. 0.67 m.; W. 0.29 m.; H. 0.22 m.; H. of letters, 0.14 m.; W. of letters, 0.06 m. Cf. *BASOR* 199, 33 and n. 31.

24. The description is based on that by Majewski who will publish this painting as WP69.1 in his forthcoming volume in this series on wall paintings and mosaics.

25. *Sardis* I (1922) pl. III.

26. Grave 67.3, *BASOR* 191, 10. It was dug away in

1968. *BASOR* 157, 26, figs. 9, 13, Unit 16; p. 14, fig. 3, LVC, SVC.

27. Cf. G. Calza, *La necropoli del Porto di Roma nell'Isola Sacra* (Rome 1940) 140 f., Tav. 1. Judging by drawing alone, V. M. Strocka suggests a date as late as the fifth century A.D., comparing Ephesus room H2/17.

28. The Late Hellenistic chamber tombs in the House of Bronzes area and in PN had rubble vaults. *BASOR* 157, 28 f.,Tombs 59 *j, k, n; BASOR* 174, 22, Chamber Tomb Ch.

29. Butler, *Sardis* I (1922) 128 f., ill. 140, had found the stele "broken in two pieces, lying near its moulded base" west and a little south of the steps of U. His ill. 140 shows it re-erected and re-constituted. In 1969 we found only the lower part (IN69.23) overturned. We reset it on its base which had been underpinned by Butler (Fig. 69), only to find it overturned again in 1970. Cf. *Sardis* VII (1932) no. 4, pl. 3 (complete stele), text dated ca. 155 B.C. The profiled base is not original and is, indeed, one of the proofs for the Late Roman attempts to re-set earlier documents in the "correct" fashion. The remaining fragment of stele is shown in Fig. 75.

30. *Sardis* VI.2 (1924) no. 39, with drawing; block mistakenly said to be in foundations of the temple. Gusmani, *LW*, no. 39, "Mason's mark?" *tiv.*

31. After *Sardis* I (1922) 125 f., ills. 136–138; Shear, "Lion," made an important study of the monument. For the Nannas inscription see Gusmani, *LW*, no. 20. The sejant lion is in the Metropolitan Museum of Art, New York; cf. Richter, 5, no. 6, pl. IX. The couchant lion and the eagle are in the Archeological Museum, İstanbul. The Nannas inscription base is at the Sardis Expedition camp; the other bases are *in situ* (Fig. 78).

32. Drum A (eastward): L. ca. 1.90 m.; diam. 0.85 m. Somebody had begun to cut down and flatten its side. Dowel holes: 0.04 m. by 0.04 m. by 0.05 m. (deep). 0.16 m. from periphery, 0.07 m. by 0.07 m. by 0.05 m. (deep), west end. Diam. ca. 0.84 west end, 0.86? m. east end; another dowel(?) hole on side, 0.05 m. by 0.05 m. by 0.045 m. from perimeter. Drum B shows medium claw chisel trim at both ends; then larger point work; then rough quarry trim. A hollowed *belt* for transport is in center (Fig. 80). Side A has 2 dowel holes, 0.065 m. by 0.065 m. with pouring channels, 0.16 m. long, a shallow center dowel depression. Side B has 2 dowel holes, 0.04 m. by 0.04 m. without pouring channels; rough-trimmed central dowel depression. Drum A has same rectangular dowel holes but a large round rotation area on eastern end; two large (ca. 0.08 m. by 0.08 m.) rectangular dowel holes with pouring channels at western end. Diam. of exposed western end is 0.86 m.

33. In the reconstruction, Fig. 65, they are assumed not to join.

34. Cf. *infra*, Ch. VIII "Northeast Wadi"; and *BASOR* 199, 35 f.

35. *Sardis* I (1922) 132, ills. 146 f.

36. The profiles are slightly rounded; they are oversimplified in plan Fig. 88.

37. Cf. forthcoming Sardis monograph on Greek and Roman coins.

38. *Sardis* II (1925) Atlas, pl. I.

39. Numbers of columns are after the system used by Butler in *Sardis* II (1925) 19, pl. A and Atlas, pl. I.

40. Shown in *Sardis* II (1925) Atlas pl. I.

41. *Sardis* I (1922) 67, ill. 61; *BASOR* 166, 34–35, n. 63, fig. 27.

42. Grids: ca. W 80–200/S 1260–1300. For the cemetery see *Sardis* I (1922) 134, 135; *BASOR,* 154, 11; and the discussion of Byzantine settlement at Artemis Precinct, *infra.*

43. This is a standard arrangement in Roman and Early Byzantine vaulted chamber tombs at Sardis; cf. the "Peacock Tomb," *BASOR* 166, 31, fig. 26 where all three stepping stones are preserved in the east wall. In the House of Bronzes, Unit 1, a basement that may have been a tomb originally had two steps in the east wall; cf. *BASOR* 154, 22, fig. 10.

44. For similar Lydian sarcophagi see *Sardis* I (1922) 160, ill. 177, and the Early Hellenistic sarcophagi of comparable shape and size found in the region Hacı Oğlan, *BASOR* 166, 30, n. 52, fig. 25.

45. *Sardis* I (1922) 40 f.

46. *Sardis* I (1922) 66 f., ill. 60. In summer of 1973, the existing stelai bases were solidified and cemented in place on the north side, and one on the east side of LA 2. Two additional bases were found in heaps of stones and two bases shown lying on the ground in *Sardis* II (1925) 3, ill. 2, were moved somewhat westward. See also Ch. VII, "The Cleaning and Reorganization of the Artemis Temple Precinct in 1973."

47. Nannas Bakivalis: *Sardis* I (1922) 125 f., ills. 136–138. Timarchos: *Sardis* VII (1932) no. 4, pl. 3; *Sardis* I (1922) 128 f., ill. 140, Keeper of Treasury at Pergamon, later Keeper (*neokoros*) of Artemis Temple, Sardis, ca. 155 B.C. He was crowned with olive wreath in the theater of Sardis.

48. *Sardis* II (1925) 63, Atlas, pl. I.

49. *Sardis* VI.2 (1924) no. 22; *Sardis* I (1922) 66, ill. 60.

50. Gusmani, *Sardis M3* (1975) B I, 2, among "Inscriptions of Uncertain Affiliation": of the two signs the "arrow" appears in nearly all Asia Minor alphabets; the second sign "has hardly anything to do with *samekh* and remains isolated."

51. Synagogue apse table: *BASOR* 199, 50 f., fig. 41.

52. F. Eichler, "Die oesterreichischen Ausgrabungen im Jahre 1961," *AnzWien* (1962) 50–52, first publ. with transcr. D. Knibbe, "Ein religiöser Frevel und seine Sühne: Ein Todesurteil hellenistischer Zeit aus Ephesos," *JOAI* 46 (1961–1963, app. 1964) 175–182. F. Sokolowski, "A New Testimony on the Cult of Artemis of Ephesus," *HThR* 58 (1965) 427–431. J. and L. Robert, "Bulletin epigraphique," *REG* 76 (1963) 163–164, no. 211 (after Eichler); 78 (1965) 155, no. 342 (after Knibbe); 79 (1966) 422, no. 369, (after Sokolowski). R. Fleischer, 200–201, thinks as Sokolowski, that the sanctuary of Artemis of Ephesus was a different, smaller shrine.

CHAPTER V

1. See Butler, *Sardis* I (1922) 25 f. and *Sardis* II (1925) 4 f. for list of travelers who reported on various stages of the decay of the temple. A detailed treatment of the travelers will appear in a forthcoming monograph by J. A. Scott.

2. *Sardis* I (1922) 5.

3. *Sardis* I (1922) 7; İnan, Rosenbaum, 75, no. 41, pl. 26. British Museum.

4. *Sardis* I (1922) 8 n. 1.

5. *Sardis* I (1922) ill. 19, 159, overall view.

6. *Sardis* I (1922) 16, 38, Plans I and II. We came upon occasional traces of the village houses when building our camp in 1958-1960. A modern house at the western edge of the Artemis Precinct (Fig. 59, platform H just west of Building Q, ca. W 247/S 1217; *Sardis* I [1922] Plan III "House") had become a mound and was transformed into a platform for viewing the temple in 1973. The important limestone fragment of archaic Ionic architecture (AT/H 73.1), Figs. 210, 211, was found built into the wall of this house.

7. Done on a scale of 1:1000, contour intervals of 5 m., grid of 20 m. squares.

8. Cf. *supra*, Ch. I, "Explanation of Topographic Plans, Grids, and Levels."

9. *Sardis* II (1925) pl. A and Atlas, pl. I.

10. H. C. Butler, "The Elevated Columns at Sardis and the Sculptured Pedestals from Ephesus," in W. H. Buckler and W. M. Calder, eds. *Anatolian Studies Presented to Sir William Mitchell Ramsay* (Manchester, London, New York 1923) 51-57; Inscription: R. Gusmani, *LW,* no. 21. K. J. Frazer has found at least one, possibly two blocks which may have belonged to similar unfinished bases of the western end of the temple.

11. Plan and restoration: *Sardis* II (1925) pl. A and Atlas pl. I; cf. also *Sardis* I (1922) Plan III, pl. II, 110 f.

12. Cf. *infra,* Ch. VI.

13. Dinsmoor, 226-229, 275, 337 n. 1, 340, fig. 82, pl. LIII. Dinsmoor also objected to Butler's overly elaborate western stairs and thought the "Lydian Building" (altar) might have been buried during the construction of the big temple in the fourth century B.C. A. W. Lawrence, *Greek Architecture* (Baltimore 1957) 198 f., fig. 109, dated the temple around 330 B.C. Like Dinsmoor, Lawrence noted that the column spacing at the ends recalled the archaic plan of the Ephesus temple. For the roof situation, cf. Fig. 126.

14. Franke, 205; H. Seyrig, "Monnaies Héllenistiques," *RN* 6:5 (1963) 23-24 and cf. n. 19 *infra*. On the Mnesimachos inscription see Atkinson, 62-67, who proposes 205-200 B.C.

15. An inscription found at Ephesus records that the Artemis Temple at Sardis was founded from Ephesus, that an annual sacred embassy went from Ephesus to Sardis, and that for an unknown reason the embassy was attacked by Sardians, forty-five of whom were subsequently sentenced to death. There is no agreement on the exact date of the inscription; cf. D. Knibbe, "Ein reliöser Frevel und sein Sühne. Ein Todesurteil hellenistischer Zeit aus Ephesos," *JOAI* 46 (1961-63) 175-182; L. Robert, "Bulletin Épigraphique," *REG* 78 (1965) 155. Knibbe dates the inscription to the third century B.C., Robert thinks it dates ca. 340-320 B.C. R. Fleischer, 187-201, believes the sanctuary of Artemis of Ephesus was a different, smaller shrine. See also Ch. IV, n. 52, *supra*.

16. *BASOR* 154, 9, 11 f. where Hanfmann was still trying to retain Butler's dating to the Persian period; 166, 34 f., n. 62, fig. 27 where the date is changed to Seleucid. Cf. also

Figs. 146-148. Neocorates: *Sardis* VII (1932) 64, 72. Cf. also Hanfmann, *Sardis und Lydien,* 31. The very complex questions concerning the identities of various divinities designated as "Zeus"—whether the Lydian, Olympian, Polieus, or Persian Ahura Mazda ("Zeus Varadates")—and the relations of Artemis of Sardis to Artemis of Ephesus, Artemis of Koloe, Cybele, "Kore," Artemis Anahita, and Ma cannot be discussed in this framework. The inscription in honor of Isidorus, cited among the Menogenes documents, and dated ca. 2 years before the earthquake of A.D. 17 mentions the sanctuary of Zeus Polieus and Artemis in a way which makes it likely that it was identical with the sanctuary of Artemis. This suggests that the division of the temple between Zeus and Artemis already existed in the second Hellenistic structure which preceded the Roman reconstruction after A.D. 17. *Sardis* VII, 17, 23, 15, no. 8, text xii. For the possible identity of Artemis with "Kore" of Sardis, cf. Fleischer, 196-201.

17. Gruben himself notes that he took no instrument levels and did a number of dimensions by "Augenmass" (eyeballing); Gruben, 156 n. 1. His factual data must be used with caution.

18. Gruben, Beil. 82-90 (supplementary plates with photographs), pls. V, VI (reconstructed plans, wall sections). Berve, Gruben, 470-473, fig. 136, slightly different plan of last phase, pls. XXI (color), figs. 127-131, figs. 44-46 (same 1970).

19. D. G. Hogarth, *The Archaic Artemisia* (London 1908); P. Jacobsthal, "The Date of the Ephesian Foundation-Deposit," *JHS* 71 (1951) 85 f. Recent excavations: H. Vetters in M. J. Mellink, "Archaeology in Asia Minor," *AJA* 77 (1973) 186; *AnzWien* 109 (1972) 8 f., fig. 6, pls. 12, 13; F. Eichler, "Die österreichischen Ausgrabungen in Ephesos im Jahre 1967," *AnzWien* 105 (1968) 92 f., pl. 4, figs. 4-7; "Die österreichischen Ausgrabungen in Ephesos im Jahre 1966," 104 (1967) 24 f., fig. 4. For an important discussion of the fourth century and archaic temples as well as the archaic altar cf. A. Bammer, 7, 40-42. Bammer, "Recent Excavations at the Altar of Artemis in Ephesus," *Archaeology* 27 (1974) 202-204, shows clearly that the "deposit" area was quite distant from the altar.

20. For the cleaning and partial reorganization of the Artemis Temple and Precinct undertaken in 1973, see *infra,* Ch. VII, and the reports for 1973 in *BASOR* 215 and *Dergi* (forthcoming).

21. For geological definitions of "purple sandstone" see E. İzdar's analysis, *infra,* "Material." H. W. Bell, *Sardis* XI (1916) v f., "The coin of Croesus was discovered in a horizontal position between the upper and lower rows of masonry. No coins whatever were found under the basis where excavation was carried on to a depth of several meters . . . The Croesan coin was apparently deposited, or lost during the building of the existing basis." *Sardis* XI (1916) v, gives a sketch of the disposition of coins, here Fig. 128. The coin is his no. 223, Half Stater, Basis Hoard, Cat. p. 22. K. J. Frazer has proposed other reasons for existence of a Croesan temple, see *infra*.

22. Franke, 205, believed the two hoards were concealed after the defeat of Antiochus III by the Romans, ca. 190-188 B.C. G. M. A. Hanfmann, *BASOR* 166, 34 has argued that the hoard may date from the time of

Achaeus (220–213 B.C.) as originally suggested by E. T. Newell, "The Coinage of the Western Seleucid Mints," *Numismatic Studies* IV (1941) 187 n. 154. H. Seyrig, "Monnaies Hellenistiques," *RN* 6:5 (1963) 23 f. refuted Franke's date, upheld Newell and S. P. Noe, "Bibliography of Greek Coin Hoards," 2nd ed. *Numismatic Notes and Monographs* 78 (1937) no. 925, and suggested that the lower date "rend paradoxale l'absence d'Antiochus III." For a coin possibly datable to 197 B.C., cf. n. 14, *supra;* n. 26, *infra.*

23. *Sardis* I (1922) 76, "A deep excavation below the basis, carried on by means of trenches 3 m. in depth, failed to reveal any evidence of temple deposit here . . . "

24. *Sardis* I (1922) ill. 71; *Sardis* II (1925) 29, 108 f., pl. A, Atlas, pl. I.

25. *Sardis* II (1925) 29.

26. *Sardis* I (1922) 75 f., ill. 71.

27. *Sardis* I (1922) 65.

28. *Sardis* II (1925) Atlas, pl. I shows only the six central stones of LI.

29. Gusmani, *LW,* 263 no. 36; *Sardis* VI.2 (1924) no. 26.

30. Franke, 203–208.

31. Cf. *supra,* n. 16. On the coin erroneously identified as Attalus II or III by Bell, cf. U. Westermark, 14 f., who says the coin cannot be later than 197 B.C. and attributes it to Attalus I.

32. G. Gruben in Berve, Gruben, 480. In April 1870 A. O. Clarke found the five silver coins, of which two "were lying in small hollows prepared for them in the bed of the course," i.e. the lowest course, consisting at that time of only the four center stones. See Society of Dilettanti, *Antiquities of Ionia* IV (London 1881) 25. According to the architect, R. P. Pullan, who had been there in 1861, "the pavement of the cella was found entire, and at the west end the foundation of a large pedestal was uncovered, adjoining the wall of the posticum. Near this pedestal we found the foot of a colossal statue, and fragments of an arm of corresponding dimensions," *Antiquities of Ionia* IV, 29, pl. v, vi, xv. He estimated the height of the Athena statue to be 20 feet. See also Wiegand, Schrader, 84, 110–111. For coins see S. P. Noe, *Numismatic Notes and Monographs* 78 (1937) 220, no. 835.

33. *Sardis* I (1922) ill. 164. A detailed discussion, including all surviving fragments of colossal statues, will be given in the forthcoming volume of Sardis sculptures by G. M. A. Hanfmann and N. H. Ramage.

34. *Sardis* I (1922) ill. 164.

35. R. Fleischer, 187–201, pls. 77–80. M. J. Price, B. Trell, "Sardis." in "Architecture on Ancient Coins" (forthcoming). The goddess is also shown on a capital discussed by G. M. A. Hanfmann and M. S. Balmuth, "The Image of an Anatolian Goddess at Sardis," *JKF* 2 (1965) 261–269.

36. The following discussion is based on a report by K. J. Frazer, abbreviated by G. M. A. Hanfmann. For the theory that a dipteral temple preceded the pseudo-dipteral, cf. Gruben, 155–196.

37. The numbering of columns follows that proposed by Butler, *Sardis* II (1925) pl. A and Atlas, pl. I.

38. After digging Trench 10 (*infra*), K. J. Frazer reasoned that the heavy clay excavated from Tench 1 may have been deliberate fill laid down after the column foundation of a dipteral temple was excavated and removed. (Ed. note: this seems overly ingenious and can hardly be taken as convincing proof of the existence of a dipteral plan.).

39. For other data concerning the steps which led to the eastern door cf. Trench 9, *infra.*

40. The systematic recording made by Butler of the great pipes in and around the temple is shown on Plan III, *Sardis* I (1922), with dotted lines, but unfortunately without levels. Cf. *Sardis* I (1922) 44, ills. 31–33, working at levels 2 and 3, ca. 2 m. and 4–5 m. below surface respectively, "throughout both levels . . . i.e. from 0.50 m. below the surface to a level of about 1 m. above level 2, an astonishing number of Byzantine terracotta pipes were unearthed . . . running in all directions and in all parts of the excavations . . . (They) varied in diameter from 10 to 32 centimeters, had carefully fitted flanges set in the hardest cement." Ill. 32 shows a pipe crossing the Lydian Building, hence probably above *98.33, top level of LA.

41. *Sardis* I (1922) 95, ill. 97. For the discussion of cistern see Ch. II, n. 82, *supra.*

42. G. M. A. Hanfmann expresses the following reservations: Two blocks built into foundations of the Hellenistic temple are slim evidence on which to create an archaic building. For the dating of the base to Hellenistic age and a discussion of the "cutback" stones and their occurrence in Priene and other classical and Hellenistic structures, see *supra,* "Conclusions Concerning the Image Base" and Fig. 134. They are not a distinctive archaic feature, but are used at all times to support the pavement.

43. Both courses of this cult-statue basis were left undisturbed in their Late Hellenistic arrangement until 1911 (*Sardis* I [1922] 74, 76). The silver and bronze coin deposits then discovered in the vertical joints of the upper course attest to this. At the same time the Princeton excavators were of the opinion that the original foundation, of whatever structure it supported, must have been too extensive to have remained *in situ,* in its entirety, when the foundations for the Early Hellenistic column bases were being laid within the original cella of the temple. Thus, it must have been to some degree reduced in area by the builders of that period. The foundation blocks so removed, including the marginal ones with the cut-back edges, were then laid as a second course on the reduced original course in preparation of the foundation for the cult statue basis. The silver Croesus coin would have been deposited or dropped between the lower and (new) upper course of blocks in this re-arrangement of the ancient structure. (K. J. Frazer)

44. Gruben 180 f.; cf. also Akurgal, *Civilizations* 128, figs. 44–46. In a discussion of "The Historical Background" of the Mnesimachus inscription which is adversely affected by the author's failure to consult our excavation reports (especially, *BASOR* 166, 34–35), Atkinson, 62–67, suggests that the Temple of Artemis, which he confuses with the Temple of Cybele, was burned by the army of Antiochus III in 214 B.C. in punishment for the support given by the temple to the pretender Achaeus. He suggests that the temple was rebuilt between 214 and 200 B.C. and the

Mnesimachus inscription carved on the temple wall between 205 and 200 B.C. It must be stated that we have observed no traces of burning in the Hellenistic parts of the Artemis Temple; and the Temple of Cybele, the "Metroon" built in the fifth or fourth century B.C., suffered no damage in 214–213 B.C. Letters addressed by Antiochus III himself in 213 B.C. to the Sardians were inscribed on the *parastades* of the temple; we have found these inscribed blocks reused in the Roman synagogue, cf. *BASOR* 174, 34.

45. The evidence for this is the fine marginal dressing along the joins in the masonry. It occurs up to the end along the top edge of the second course below the threshold blocks and is not matched (as one might expect) by a similar band along the bottom edge of the course above. Normally, both sides of the join would be dressed in one operation. The upper course is later, having been laid to replace the dismantled courses.

CHAPTER VI

1. *Sardis* I (1922) 41–43, 104, 127 f., ills. 25–29, 100, Map III. *Sardis* II (1925) 3 f., ill. 2, Atlas, pl. I, and cf. *supra*, Ch. IV.

2. *Sardis* II (1925) Atlas, pl. I.

3. *Sardis* I (1922) 41; *Sardis* II (1925) 3 f., Atlas, pl. I.

4. *Sardis* II (1925) 87: "... it is possible to imagine the Lydian Building as an altar at the rear of the new temple; for there seems to be no doubt that the later temple faced the east though the earlier one may have faced west, and no remains of the altar were found in the 55 m. excavated at the east end. The steps in question, when restored, would descend from the pteroma level, in front of the four middle columns, to the altar; or a high altar may have been set on the Lydian basis in front of the middle intercolumniation with steps on either side of it, and in that case, the altar steps descended, as now, to the ancient level of the rows of the stele bases, where an open square would have extended to the river side. If this restoration of the Lydian Building and the side steps be accepted, it is not necessary to bury either of these features in the reconstruction of the perfected plan (plate A and ill. 97)."

5. *Sardis* I (1922) 127. For the coins: *Sardis* XI (1916) xix, nos. 208, 228.

6. Schleif, 210; Hoffmann, 195; Şahin, 60–61, fig. 12.

7. Herodotus 1.151, silver bowl in Delphi given by Croesus was the work of Theodoros.

8. *BASOR* 154, 11; 199, 31 n. 26; Xenophon, *Anabasis* 1.6, 7. Cf. *Sardis* II (1925) 87, 102, 140; Gruben, 157, 180; 76, fig. 3, pl. V, here Fig. 124.

9. Reported in *BASOR* 199, 29–32, figs. 18–20.

10. The 1969 and 1970 stones were listed on "stone plan" (Fig. 184). Those lying west of the east wall of LA 2 were numbered LA 70:1–19; those lying near the "robbed pit" of the north side were numbered LA 70:20–36. One block, no. LA 37 (Fig. 184) was wedged into correct position on the south side. All displaced blocks were moved to open ground west of LA (Fig. 186) where they were rearranged in 1973.

11. Reported in *BASOR* 203, 7, fig. 1.

12. *Sardis* I (1922) 104, pl. II. For the actual condition of the steps cf. ibid. ill. 100 (cf. Fig. 178), which does, indeed, show the steps as coming up to the alignment of the eastern wall of LA 2; for the condition in 1968 and restoration by M. T. Ergene see *BASOR* 199, 33, fig. 21.

13. The weight estimate by K. J. Frazer is based on statistics from *Türkiye Mermer Envanteri*, MTA, Publication 134 (Ankara 1966) 14, which gave weights for limestone-marble from 2.4 to 2.7 tons per cbm. A value of 2.5 was "arbitrarily used."

14. *Iranica Antiqua* 6 (1966) 136, 144; cf. also Nylander, *Ionians*, 42–45, figs. 10–11; 64–67, figs. 19–20; 79–81, Table 1, where he credits Lydians with earliest examples of "double-clamp."

15. Martin, *Manuel*, 273.

16. *Sardis* II (1925) 76–80. H. A. Thompson (by letter) expresses strong doubt that the limestone structure LA 1 could have had marble revetments which would leave no traces of attachments.

17. Gerkan, von, *Milet* I.4, pl. XXIII. It may come from the actual altar, not the platform LA 1.

18. *Sardis* II (1925) 80, ill. 94. On the Dorylaion stele cf. E. Berger, *Das Basler Arztrelief* (Basel 1970) 39, fig. 39, dating ca. 500 B.C., against Butler's far too early date of 570 B.C. K. Friis-Johansen dated it ca. 525 B.C., *The Attic Grave Reliefs* (Copenhagen 1951) 77, figs. 34a, b.

19. *BASOR* 199, 42, fig. 20. This piece will also be published in the forthcoming sculpture volume. Central and left side lotus, a bit of right lotus leaf, and a bit of palmette leaf preserved. L. 0.11 m.; W. 0.135 m.; Th. 0.03 m. LA, W 201/S 1231.4, *98.41, not stratified (in top layer of LA 2). The raised median ridge for lotus leaf occurs in the late sixth and early fifth century B.C. See E. Buschor, "Altsamische Grabstelen," *AthMitt* 58 (1933) 34 f., Beil. 14 (V:3), dated by Buschor 520–500 B.C., and the Dorylaion lotus, n. 18 *supra*.

20. Gerkan, von, *Milet* I.4, pl. XXVI; Dinsmoor, 140, fig. 51; Hoffmann, 195, pls. 55:1, 58:11–12. For Ephesus we owe much to the courtesy of A. Bammer who was always willing to inform us of the results of his excavations of the Artemis Altar. Pending final report cf. Bammer, 7 n. 28, 41, figs. 5a (archaic altar and temple), 5b, 43 (later altar and temple), and literature, 44, 69; see also H. Vetters, *AnzWien* 107 (1970) 6; A. Bammer, *AntK* 13 (1970) 114 f., *Archaeology* 27:3 (1974) 203, plan. Bammer assumes that the later altar may stand on foundations of the archaic altar; that like Monodendri and Samos, the archaic altar had a low parapet-like wall; and that "both temple and altar were each, independently, open to the west." However, in Ephesus, the priest within the altar area went on by a north-south ramp toward the image which stood in the southwest corner, as shown in plan fig. 5 and sketch, fig. 43. He would have turned toward the south during the worship. It may be noticed in passing that the Cybele altar in the Pactolus North sector at Sardis has a step on the west side which clearly shows that the celebrant turned eastward, *BASOR* 199, 17, fig. 7.

21. Artemis is invoked in Lydian inscriptions as the goddess who protects the graves and to whom fines for violation of graves must be paid.

22. Frazer bases his reconstruction on the reconstruction of the altar in Monodendri, itself conjectural. It is likely enough that the altar was an oblong and that it had egg and dart molding. It seems, however, that a double volute finial may come from the corner of such a small altar, which would then have the cap molding turned up at the corners into voluted corner acroteria like the outer enclosure at Monodendri. Dinsmoor, 140, fig. 51. Another possible shape, with projecting flanks and volutes at sides of the top, is seen in an archaic altar at Miletus reconstructed by F. Krischen, in C. Blümel, *Die archaisch-griechischen Skulpturen der Staatlichen Museen* (Berlin 1963) 60, fig. 192. For other possibilities cf. C. Yavis, *Greek Altars* (St. Louis 1949) and Hoffmann, 189 n. 5, who also mentions the archaic altar in the Delphinion at Miletus and illustrates variants of relation of altar to stepped platform, fig. 13 (Aphrodite Naukratis), fig. 18 (Delos), fig. 19 (Altar of Chians, Delphi). Cf. also Şahin, 36-58, figs. 5, 9.

23. Nylander, *Ionians,* 84-86, fig. 27, where he also cites other Greek examples. Monodendri, however, is pseudo-isodomic.

24. Akurgal, *Civilizations,* 127.

25. The latest authoritative discussion of the relation between the archaic and the younger Artemision at Ephesus in Bammer, 7-13, fig. 4, shows the archaic temple with only two (not three) rows of columns on the west side, and in contrast to earlier reconstructions, an opisthodomos closed toward the back, thus producing differences from Frazer's reconstruction based on earlier interpretations (Bammer, fig. 4, by Wilberg). Bammer believes that the third row of columns was added either in a classical, or more probably, in the fourth century B.C. reconstruction after the fire. It will be noted, that according to Frazer, (Fig. 124) in the "first building phase" the archaic colonnades were planned but not yet built.

26. For the finds, clamps, and marble fragments, cf. *supra;* the altar of Cape Monodendri is itself not well dated, but belongs to the sixth century, as does the Milesian altar reconstructed by Krischen in C. Blümel, *Die archaisch-griechischen Skulpturen der Staatlichen Museen* (Berlin 1963), fig. 192. They antedate the destruction of Miletus in 494 B.C.

27. Gruben, 180 n. 76.

28. The masonry in the Gyges Mound and on the Acropolis is much more monumental, *BASOR* 182, 27, fig. 22; 206, 15-20, figs. 5-7. The resemblance in the general design of the stepped construction and in the size of masonry is most marked with respect to the Pyramid Tomb, cf. *BASOR* 199, 38, fig. 28. The tomb with the clamps is BT 62.4, *BASOR* 170, 58, fig. 42; Nylander, *Ionians,* 66.

29. All measurements given here exclude the thickness of the exterior plaster, which has mostly disappeared from the masonry corners of the structure.

30. Communication to S. M. Goldstein, August 11, 1970. İzdar adds that the white material in one of the friable sandstone samples was probably hydrated feldspar, now existing in the form of clay and serisite. He noted that the samples contained iron impurities.

31. After renewed examination (1973), G. M. A. Hanfmann believes that an original stucco facing may have existed, rather than a marble revetment, as no marble revetment holes are preserved. In his view, the present stucco probably postdates the earthquake of A.D. 17.

32. Schleif, 210; Hoffmann, 195. Cf. Şahin, 59-61, fig. 12.

33. Hoffmann, 193, pl. 58:12. Berve, Gruben, 448, figs. 113-115; 119′ 11 7/8″ by 54′ 4 3/4″.

34. Bammer, 7-12, 41-42, figs. 5, 7b, 37, 42, 43. Bammer considers that the altar might be earlier than the post-356 B.C. Artemision. Detailed reports cited, Bammer, 69.

35. Priene and Magnesia: Berve, Gruben, 480, fig. 140. Magnesia: Akurgal, *Civilizations,* 183, fig. 61 a; A. von Gerkan, *Der Altar des Artemis Tempels in Magnesia am Maeander* (Berlin 1929). Şahin, 91-121, figs. 20-25. The Altar of Zeus in Pergamon belongs to the same general type but is far more elaborate and is not connected with a temple.

36. Bammer, 7 n. 29 with literature. This observation has been made for Priene, Magnesia, and Tegea.

37. In fact, there is no real evidence for five columns, H. C. Butler, *Sardis* I (1922) 42, ill. 35, nos. 59-63 (cf. Fig. 120). Butler's account might be construed to indicate that there were traces of column Nos. 59 and 63 in the guise of late rubble walls which he removed, ibid., 42 n. 1: "these walls were later found to have been concrete casings of column foundations which had been removed"; Gruben seems to have tried to indicate this possibility in his drawing (Fig. 123). But Butler did not come back to this suggestion and our trenches in 1969 and 1970 failed to substantiate it (Fig. 181, Trenches *g* and *f*).

38. As reported in the description, this is the expert opinion of L. J. Majewski. The dating of the plaster is a different matter. Butler opined that "the stucco was in all essentials like some of the oldest known examples of this material," *Sardis* I (1922) 41, but forbore to date it. At Sardis, we seem to have examples of Early Hellenistic stucco in the Tomb of the Lintel, Pactolus Cliff; of Late Hellenistic stucco in the chamber tombs in the House of Bronzes sector and in Monument 10 of the Artemis Precinct, *BASOR* 157, 16, 28; Ch. IV, *supra.* None of them, however, has quite the same elaborate build-up as the plaster-stucco of LA 2. G. M. A. Hanfmann believes that the LA plaster is Roman rather than Hellenistic.

39. Cf. n. 41, *infra.* Butler's attempt to create an imposing and complicated platform which would have enclosed LA 2 and buried it below a great marble facade is best seen in *Sardis* II (1925) ill. 97, and plate A, (Fig. 180). It should be noted, however, that Butler himself (ibid., p. 87) thought that a high altar could have been set up on LA, *supra,* n. 2. Dinsmoor, 227 n. 1, and Gruben, 175, rejected the attempt to bury LA.

40. Gruben, 180 n. 76; *Sardis* II (1925) 76 f., ill. 90, which he tried to date by the anthemion of the stele with the bilingual inscription of 394 B.C. The inscription stele is clearly earlier. The corner acroterion might belong to the later fourth century or even early third century B.C.

41. For the evidence on the rearrangement of the pre-

cinct, see Ch. IV, "Lion-Eagle Monument" and "Conclusions," *supra.*

42. Butler's excavation report, *Sardis* I (1922) 40–52, includes the detailed sketch, ill. 35, which shows most clearly what exactly of the walls linking LA 2, steps, and base A 64 he still found. He notes specifically that "there appeared . . . a wide passage between the rear (eastern) wall of the Lydian Building and the concrete casing of the three column foundations that stand in a row 5 m. to the east of it." This passage, in fact, separated LA from the western platform of the temple. Butler's later plans and discussion, *Sardis* II (1925) 17, ill. 9, 34–36, ill. 29, include a stone-by-stone plan of steps. He theorized that the steps turned the corner and continued southward above the buried altar; this is also illustrated in his plate A and represents his solution for the Roman period. Gruben's plan of actual conditions and three phases, Gruben, 175–178 (critique of Butler's reconstruction), 180, assigns the staircase either to the earliest or to the second period, before a colonnade was ever built.

43. Butler, *Sardis* I (1922) 42, ill. 35 is the most reliable statement: "we came upon rough walls of rubble concrete projecting to the north and south . . . they were very crudely constructed . . . I had them removed after they had been surveyed." Cf. *supra,* n. 37. Butler never revived this interpretation which would have been crucial for the existence of the missing columns of the west porch. "To our surprise the stucco walls [of the Lydian Building] ended abruptly on the line of the rubble walls which projected at either hand . . . " Cf. also Fig. 184, walls shown by dotted lines.

44. In his careful reconsideration of the history of the temple, Butler stated that (a) one cannot know whether the temple was converted into a cistern before or after the great landslide of the ninth century, and (b) that the cistern continued in use until "comparatively recent times, but certainly before the middle of the seventeenth century and presumably after the destruction of Sardis by Timour about 1400," *Sardis* II (1925) 13–14.

CHAPTER VII

1. *Sardis* I (1922) 148, 151.

2. *Sardis* I (1922) 42 f., 134, 145; *BASOR* 154, 8–9, figs. 1–2.

3. Cf. "Explanation of Topographic Plans, Grids, and Levels," *supra,* Ch. I.

4. The columns are numbered as in *Sardis* II (1925) Atlas, pl. I.

5. *Supra,* Ch. V, "Trench 5" and Ch. II, n. 82.

6. Butler mentions encountering many pipelines of this kind, *Sardis* I (1922) 44 f., 95, ills. 31–33. His complete survey of these pipes apparently was not preserved.

7. *BASOR* 154, 9.

8. HoB and PN stratigraphy will be treated by G. F. Swift, Jr. and Andrew Ramage in a future report in this series. Cf. *BASOR* 182, 8–14; 186, 32.

9. *BASOR* 154, 9, fig. 13.

10. *Sardis* I (1922) Plan III, lower left corner showing rooms B, C, D.

11. *BASOR* 154, 10–13, fig. 1; *BASOR* 199, 29 f. The preserved walls lie between W 166–200/S 1296–1315 on the site plan (B) grid.

12. *Sardis* I (1922) Plans II, III. In 1972, the Pactolus bed was led into a channel with high banks. The threat the torrent had presented to the sanctuary during its recent eastward advance was thus averted. *BASOR* 211, 32.

13. W. Warfield in *Sardis* I (1922) 179.

14. The situation in Room I with wall *b* at *98.20 preserved below the section destroyed by flood indicates that walls may have survived at a lower level in the unexcavated (southwest) part. Walls *c* and *d* also continued under the debris.

15. Akurgal, *Civilizations,* 65, fig. 22.

16. The measurements from mid-wall to mid-wall produce somewhat different ratios.

17. *BASOR* 154, 35; *Sardis* M1 (1971) no. 459.

18. For coins see *Sardis* M1 (1971) nos. 1181, 1214, 1222, 1229, 1233: Michael VII, A.D. 1071–1078, to John III, A.D. 1222–1254.

19. A sample of stucco from the exterior of Room C, 0.035 m. thick, was examined by L. J. Majewski, who noted that it had been pressed flat against the rubble masonry of the wall, the imprint of which shows on the inner face of the stucco.

20. A number of tile fragments, pottery fragments, etc. were extracted in 1970 from corner at deposit H ca. *97.25 and from the floor ca. *97.10–*97.00.

21. *Sardis* I (1922) 71, 93, ills. 65, 93; *Sardis* II (1925) 8–10, 49, ill. 44.

22. See *supra,* Ch. V, "Investigation and Repair of the Image Base in the East Cella." Cf. *Dergi* 22:1 (1975) 19, figs. 19–21 and *BASOR* 215.

CHAPTER VIII

1. Butler, 427–430; *Sardis* I (1922) 149, 154; Shear, "Sixth Report," 400–401; Hanfmann, "Horsemen," 570–579.

2. *Sardis* I (1922) 151–152.

3. In 1953, a little further up the torrent bed to the east of the NEW principal trench, G. M. A. Hanfmann observed a pottery fragment decorated in a Wild Goat style (and preserving the lower part of an animal frieze). In the same general area, as recently as 1970, remains of walls built of fieldstones and evidently of pre-Hellenistic date were to be observed (one, a line of 7 stones crossing the torrent bed diagonally, within coordinates W 88–89/S 1116–1119; top at *114.43, appears on the plan, Fig. 282).

4. On July 5, 1969, a ten-year-old boy from Sart Mustafa (Yüksel Karakoç) presented two items to the expedition: the huge amphora fragment and part of a banded lydion. These items were purchased by the expedition and inventoried respectively NoEx 69.18 (P69.71:8025) and NoEx 69.19 (P69.82:8041). For the amphora fragment as presented, *BASOR* 199, 35, fig. 24; Hanfmann, *Letters,*

225, 226, fig. 190. On July 7 the same boy brought more pottery fragments from the same deposit. Fragments from the same amphora and lydion were recovered in subsequent excavations, from the artifacts and other remains which rested between walls *b* and *c* at *112.16 (cf. Figs. 283, 299).

5. The south bank of the torrent was selected in preference to the north bank because the south bank lay lower (thus offering less earth which would have to be removed in order to reach the pre-Hellenistic deposit) and, unlike the north bank, was uncultivated. At the time of excavation the north bank included the edge of a vineyard. On the slopes of both banks there flourished at the time of excavation *vitex agnus-castus*, L., the Chaste Tree (ancient Greek ἄγνος or λύγος) a shrub sacred in antiquity to Hera of Samos and perhaps to Artemis at Sardis; see Pausanias 7.4.4, 8.23.4–5; Athenaeus 12.515 f. The shrub appears in Fig. 285.

6. Sector NEW coordinates are keyed to B grid. Cf. *supra*, Ch. I, "Explanation of Topographic Plans, Grids, and Levels."

7. NEW levels are keyed to the Artemis datum. Cf. *supra*, Ch. I, "Explanation of Topographic Plans, Grids, and Levels."

8. *Sardis* I (1922) 152–154, ill. 169, "long stoa building." The building is not certainly identified as a stoa, but the name continues to be used as a convenience.

9. *Sardis* I (1922) Plan III.

10. There appears to be some discrepancy between the plan of this building which is published in Butler, *Sardis* I, Plan III and its existing remains. The remains, however, are largely concealed by blackberry brambles and *vitex agnus-castus*, L., and were not carefully re-examined.

11. An inscribed marble pedestal recovered in the west room of the Northeast Stoa appeared to the excavators of 1914 "to be practically *in situ*," and has been dated, on the evidence of letter forms in the inscription, to the "latter half of the second or the beginning of the first century B.C.," *Sardis* I (1922) 153–154; *Sardis* VII (1932) 49, no. 24.

12. Reproduced from *Sardis* I (1922) 151 ill. 169.

13. I.e., a fragment of a black-glazed palmette-stamped bowl of 4th century B.C. type, and a segment of Decauville railroad track and a cold-cream tin of the 20th century A.D.

14. Identification and analysis by 1969 expedition anthropologist D. J. Finkel.

15. At Sector HoB in Buildings *h* and *k*; at PN in unit XXVII. For a description and analysis of mud brick and pisé in pre-Hellenistic architecture at Sardis cf. Ramage, 60–61, 62, 63, 83–84.

16. A circular structure in PN is located near unit XI, within coordinates W 280–281/S 347–350, a rectangular structure within coordinates W 235–240/S 368–370; cf. *BASOR* 199, fig. 8, a circular structure against unit XVIII.

17. A circular wall, similar in form and construction to the Sardis examples but appreciably larger, was uncovered in excavations at Old Smyrna; it may be dated to the latter

part of the 7th century B.C., and has been interpreted as a granary. See Akurgal, *Kunst Anatoliens,* 301, fig. 2.

18. At HoB and PN, ground and floor surfaces normally have appeared ca. 10 cm. above the bottoms of walls; see Ramage, 80.

19. The exposed wall remains, presumably of pre-Hellenistic date, located some 15–20 m. east of NEW principal trench (within coordinates W 88–89/S 1116–1117) with their top at *114.43 may also be indicative of the pre-Hellenistic incline (for these remains see Fig. 282).

20. Such a narrow space might have been designed to provide ventilation, as perhaps the ditches between hillslope houses which are recorded in the Astynomoi Inscription from Pergamon, *OGIS* no. 483.120–156; Günther Klaffenbach, "Die Astynomeninschrift von Pergamon," *AbhBerl,* Klasse für Sprachen, Literatur und Kunst (1953:6) (Berlin 1954) 4–7, pl. I; Martin, *Urbanisme,* 59; Cook, 193–194.

21. A. Ramage has remarked that the concentration of burnt materials in the southeast corner of the trench "is to be interpreted as domestic rather than industrial because the fired bricks are entirely 'reduced' to a blackish grey. This is much more likely to occur with the sooty fire and low temperatures of a household installation," Ramage, 8.

22. The pottery from NEW will be fully published by C. H. Greenewalt, Jr., in a forthcoming volume in this series.

23. *BASOR* 154, 13.

24. The tile graves are a common type in the Roman period, ranging from Spain to eastern Turkey in the 2nd to 5th centuries A.D. A cemetery with graves of this type dated 2nd to 4th century A.D. was excavated at Ampurias on the Mediterranean coast of Spain, M. Almagro, *Las Necropolis de Ampurias* (Barcelona 1955) II, 289–332, figs. 266, 308, pls. XII.5; XIII.1, 3, 5, 6. Similar graves dated late 3rd to 4th century called "tile tent" graves also appeared at Tarsus in eastern Turkey, Goldman, *Tarsus* I, 19 f., figs. 64–66, plans 8, 9. Cf. also late 2nd and early 3rd century graves in Britain, R. Newstead, "The Roman Cemetery in the Infirmary Field, Chester," *AnnLiv* 6 (1914) 143 no. 23, 155 no. 29, pl. XXXII, and 4th to 5th century tile graves at Ravenna, *NSc,* 5th series, 1 (1904) 177 f.

25. *BASOR* 157, 28.

26. Hanfmann, "Glass," 53 n. 12.

CHAPTER IX

1. The condition in 1913 is seen in the plan, Fig. 3.

2. *Sardis* I (1922) 30 f., ill. 18.

3. *Sardis* I (1922) 30, ill. 18.

4. *Sardis* I (1922) 30 f.

5. *BASOR* 154, 18–22; 157, 38–43; 162, 43–47; 199, 40.

6. Peyssonel, de, 348–349, plan and views pls. IX, X, XI; cf. also Butler, *Sardis* I (1922) 32, ill. 19.

7. Le Bas, 44, pls. 56–58.

8. This point has subsequently collapsed and now has only a theoretical position in mid-air over the southwest

corner of the eastern wall. Cf. *supra,* Ch. I, "Explanations of Topographic Plans, Grids, and Levels."

9. Cf. *supra,* Ch. I, "Explanation of Topographic Plans, Grids, and Levels."

10. See *infra,* Ch. X, "Doors."

11. De Peyssonel's plan of CG (Fig. 332) shows in place of Area N a round (actually oval) unit corresponding to what must be HM on the east side. His text also speaks of two "oval towers." Nevertheless, down to a level of ca. *101.0 there was no indication that a circular unit comparable to HM in CGE did exist on the west side.

12. Cf. Figs. 410–411.

13. *BASOR* 154, 21.

14. Humann, 5, figs. pp. 8, 9; *BASOR* 162, 45. An Italian expedition led by P. Verzone has been excavating at Hierapolis since 1957. Their reports are published in *Annuario della Scuola Archeologica di Atene* starting in 1961. Also relevant is Verzone, figs. 1–7, which discusses the later history of the bath when a Christian chapel was built into one of its rooms. The bath at Hierapolis is described in some detail by Krencker, 288–295 and figs. 427–434.

15. Gerkan, von, Krischen, *Milet* I.9, 24 fig. 29, 28 f.

16. Gerkan, von, Krischen, *Milet* I.9, 62 f., figs. 115, 85 (detail).

17. Other examples of Roman baths in western Asia Minor are at Alexandria-Troas (Koldewey, pls. II, II), and at Perge and Aspendos in Pamphylia (Lanckoronski, 47 f., fig. 26, 0, 0_1 for Perge; p. 97 f., figs. 69, 70 for Aspendos). Krencker, 283–295, has good, short treatments for Miletus, baths at Humeitepe (pp. 283–284), and the Faustina Baths (pp. 284–285); Ephesus, Baths of Antoninus Pius (p. 288); Hierapolis (pp. 288–295) and Aezani (p. 295). In addition he very usefully summarizes the major bath buildings of the Roman Empire in a geographical arrangement and generalizes on the essential features of the Imperial thermae. Another probable parallel is the as yet unpublished baths at Aphrodisias.

18. Cf. *infra* "South End of CGE" and "Area N."

19. Peyssonel, de, 348.

20. *Infra,* "Stratigraphy of the Later Phases"; Fig. 374.

21. At Hierapolis there are a number of such extra-large piers or towers which were hollow inside and contained stairways and windows giving access to higher stories and to the roof, possibly for repairs.

22. It is no longer exposed and could not be measured in 1969.

23. Two parallels to the subfurnium in Trier are published by Wilhelm Reusch of the Rheinisches Landesmuseum, Trier. They are (1) in the imperial summer residence in Konz near Trier: "Eine kaiserliche Sommerresidenz des 4. Jahrhunderts in Konz an der Saar," *Saarbrücker Hefte* 16 (1962) 57; "Zwei Diatretglas-Fragmente aus Konz und Trier," *Trierer Zeitschrift* 32 (1969) plan Abb. 1, section Abb. 2, p. 297; (2) in a pre-Constantinian building in the west part of the Imperial Baths at Trier. We are indebted to Reusch for providing these comparisons. For a discussion of the praefurnium in Roman baths, and in particular of the heating arrangements in the private bath complex in the villa at Boscoreale see *DarSag* V.1, 215, fig. 6874; 874,

fig. 7482. See also F. Vivanet, *NSc* (1894) 209, fig. 2; A. Mau, "Scavi de Boscoreale," *RömMitt* 9 (1894) 353 f.; *MonAnt* (1897) 446 f., figs. 43–45; *RE* 44 (1944) s.v. "praefurnium." A number of Roman bathing establishments with several rooms equipped with heating arrangements, sometimes two or three to a room, were found at Timgad in North Africa. See R. Cagnat, A. Ballu, E. Boeswillwald, *Timgad: Une Cité Africaine* (Paris 1905) 217–296.

24. *BASOR* 157, 42.

25. See *infra* Ch. X, Table 10.

26. The similar hall in the Hierapolis bath (*supra,* n. 14) had a masonry vault, but this is less likely for CGC. The position of the springing at Hierapolis is preserved quite high on the wall, giving some idea of what the proportions of the hall were like (Fig. 358).

27. *Supra,* "The East Face," Figs. 343, 355, 366 for MAE furnace which connected by a pipe or vent with MAW.

28. Vitruvius, 5.10.2 and *infra* "HM."

29. Krencker, 290.

30. *Supra,* "The East Face."

31. The entire arrangement of the hall, including revetment, is almost exactly paralleled at Hierapolis (Fig. 358); cf. Humann. A. H. Detweiler noted in 1958 that the fact that all the arches on the west face of CGE could be seen together with no projecting piers dividing them, although they were treated so unsymmetrically, suggested that none of the stonework was originally visible. His conclusion is supported by our subsequent evidence for revetments and plastering of the wall surfaces.

32. H. brick 0.04 m.; L. brick 0.32 m.; Th. mortar 0.04 m.

33. This is not the level of the crown as the voussoirs of the upper ring have fallen out.

34. *Supra,* "Cornices."

35. *Infra,* "Stratigraphy of the Later Phases."

36. The main hall of the baths at Hierapolis (*supra,* n.14) is also closed off by a thin screen wall with an arched doorway off center (Fig. 338). The door through the north wall of CGC was somewhat larger and more central.

37. *Infra,* "Area N.'

38. *Infra,* Ch. X, "Rubble and Ashlar Construction."

39. Area N stands in about the same position as one of de Peyssonel's "little oval towers" (Fig. 332). None of the Sardis Expedition's probes in this area showed any evidence that there had been an oval or circular structure here or that the platform was the remains of such a structure. It appears that de Peyssonel saw only HM, the eastern circular unit, and assumed the western one in the interests of symmetry.

40. Its height was 0.50 m. (back) to 0.57 m.; lower W. 0.53 m.; upper W. 0.68 m. of which 0.25 m. were projecting profile.

41. *Supra,* n. 6.

42. *Supra,* "MAE, Stone Objects," IN58.5; S58.27; S58.29; S58.34; *infra,* "CGC, Stone Objects," S58.2; S58.3; S58.4; S58.5; S58.25 (MAW).

43. *Supra,* "South Facade and South Arch."

44. *Infra,* "North End CGC: The Hearth Area."

45. *Supra,* "North End CGC, Piers NE and NW, Spurwalls SpE, SpW."

46. Some of this later deposit was found in CN as well as in CGC (see Fig. 337) but for convenience it will be discussed with the evidence from CGC.

47. Fig. 374, *101.76–*101.56.

48. S. M. Goldstein, Laboratory Report, 7/5/69. Goldstein does not believe that any of the "hearths" found could be the actual smelting furnaces because there is insufficient evidence for high temperatures in the hearths themselves which would correspond to the temperatures indicated by the slags and vitrified brick found in the vicinity. He points out that if such high temperatures had existed, the gray cement in the rubble found around the hearths would have calcined. Since very little of the central area between the two side walls CGW and CGE has been excavated it is entirely possible that the actual smelting furnaces were elsewhere in this area.

49. Fig. 374.

50. E 1–2/N 18–19, *101.4–*101.2. See Bostancı, "Skulls" 1967, 17–22 Tables A-M, 47–48, "Tomb no. V.20, 1958, age 18–20, sex male." Also Bostancı, "Skeletal Remains," 124, Table A, and Bostancı, "Skulls" 1969, 156, Table 12, 160 Table 14, 179 Table 26.

51. The north and south ends of rubble wall CNW were found at W 14.75–17.20/N 47.25–50.35 and W 13.40–15.70/N 31.60–32.75 respectively. The faces were not preserved and the walls were broken away in some places so that their dimensions do not appear to coincide in the east-west direction at present.

52. *Infra,* "Unit HM," Arches.

53. *BASOR* 157, 41.

54. Vitruvius 5.10.5 says the laconicum "ought, as it seems, to be circular, so that the force of the fire and heat may spread evenly from the center all around the circumference."

55. Gerkan, von, Krischen, *Milet* I.9, 32. A preserved example of a domed laconicum was also found in the baths near the forum at Pompeii; G. T. Rivoira, *Roman Architecture* (Oxford 1925) 37, figs. 38–40.

56. In the Baths of Caracalla in Rome a round room served as the caldarium. Cf. J. B. Ward-Perkins, *ERA,* 272, fig. 104. Reusch (by letter February 1974) cites for circular apodyteria the Baths of Vieil-Evreuz and the Bath of Trajan in Rome (Krencker, 255–256, figs. 385 a-b; 267–268, figs. 397–398); cf. Rudolf Hartmann, "Das Laconicum der römischen Thermen," *RömMitt* 35 (1920) 152–169; R. A. Staccioli, "Le 'rotonde' delle terme pompeiane," *ArchCl.* (1955) 75–84.

57. Vitruvius, 5.10.5, implies that a dome was common for the laconicum.

58. For dimensions and levels of arches see *infra,* Ch. X, Tables 10, 11.

59. *Infra,* Ch. X, "Revetments."

60. It is not known whether this would actually have shown up when the room was in use, or whether this section was also covered with revetment, as seems more likely.

61. *Infra,* "Vault *y.*"

62. Cf. the forthcoming volume in this series on Building B (Gymnasium).

63. *Supra,* "Unit HM," Arches.

64. See also *infra,* Ch. X, "Evidence for Water Supply and Heating."

65. R. L. Vann treats Building D in his forthcoming study of the unexcavated buildings at Sardis; the Acropolis will be published by C. H. Greenewalt, Jr., in a subsequent volume in this series.

CHAPTER X

1. *Infra,* "Rubble and Ashlar Construction."

2. *Supra,* Ch. IX, "Roofing of CGC."

3. Cf. A. V. Carozzi, *Microscopic Sedimentary Petrography* (New York and London 1960) 224 f. for description and discussion of this type of rock and its formation.

4. Carozzi (*supra,* n. 3) 228.

5. A. E. Berriman, *Historical Metrology* (London 1953) 121. And see Jones, 76 n. 8, pl. 15, the Statilius Aper monument (1st century A.D.) from which the Roman foot was ascertained.

6. Compare average densities of limestone given by R. D. Daly, *et al.,* "Density of Rocks," in S. P. Clark, Jr., ed., *Handbook of Physical Constants,* rev. ed. (Geological Society of America 1966) 24, Table 44: 2.58 g. per cm.^{3}, 2.66 g. per cm.^{3}.

7. We owe these observations to architect F. K. Yegül of the Sardis Expedition.

8. See Martin, *Manuel,* 216–219, figs. 98–102.

9. The identification of tools and tool marks was made chiefly by Chief Foreman Hasan Koramaz of the Sardis Expedition, a master mason. A. B. Tilia argued for Persepolis that the so-called multiple chisel was actually always a multiple-pronged hammer. She calls the tool the "toothed trimming hammer" or "toothed pick." This is in fact the same tool; the differences are verbal. Cf. Tilia, 70, (drawings of tools), figs. 1–2 (photographs of tool marks). Similar tools are also described and drawn in Martin, *Manuel,* 179–182, figs. 70–72, and pl. XVI.1–5 for photographs of tool marks on stone, and in Orlandos, 45–54, figs. 27–41.

10. *Infra,* Table 11, "Arches of small masonry (rubble) construction."

11. *Infra,* Table 12, "Arches of brick construction."

12. *BASOR* 157, 41 f.

13. In the Baths of Capito at Miletus, cf. Gerkan, von, Krischen, *Milet* I.9, 24 fig. 29, rubble and ashlar were used together within and around arched niches, cf. ibid. figs. 43, 44, pp. 32 f. At Miletus, however, they appear to be more regularly "interwoven" than in CG, where the two techniques are quite separate apart from the two areas of join. A similar technique to the baths at Miletus may be seen in a Roman bath at Aphrodisias south of Sardis, and at Alexandria-Troas (Koldewey, pl. III.1, 2, and Ch. IX, n. 17) where the inner core of the exterior wall is of rubble and the outer surface is faced with limestone ashlar. The interior walls were revetted over the limestone blocks (pl. III.5, 6).

14. We owe the following observations primarily to architects F. K. Yegül and A. R. Seager.

15. A similar system was used in Building B at Sardis, although there the ashlar is confined to fewer positions. (See

forthcoming volume in this series for detailed description of Building B.) A. R. Seager suggests that the CG masonry technique is more akin to Hellenistic building practices while that of Building B represents a development away from ashlar to Byzantine small masonry work.

16. For an excellent discussion of the simultaneous use of dressed masonry and "mortared rubble" in Roman and Early Byzantine buildings of western Asia Minor see Ward-Perkins, *Great Palace,* 53–104, especially 82–83, 96–101 (appendix listing examples); and pls. 26A-E; 27A-E; 28a, b, d, e; 29A, B. Ward-Perkins visited CG in 1969 and was of the opinion that the major sections of ashlar and rubble masonry were most likely one phase, probably dating sometime after the mid-first century A.D.

17. Ward-Perkins, *Great Palace,* 55–56 cautions against putting too much faith in dating by sizes of Early Byzantine bricks. He notes only a general tendency towards dimunition in size from earlier to later examples (Table p. 56) but finds considerable variation even here.

18. The voussoirs of the top row of MW had become dislodged and fallen away.

19. The extrados of the vault over ME/MW was exposed by the falling away of masonry from the top of CGW. See top plan, Fig. 337.

20. Cf. Ward-Perkins, *Great Palace,* 58 and pls. 5, 7.

21. Members of the Sardis Expedition, in a visit to Hierapolis, observed a similar niche in the bath building that had a cutting like those in CG and a piece of pipe *in situ.*

22. Bath heating systems fed by pipes were found at Timgad (R. Cagnat, *et al., Timgad: Une Cité Africaine* [Paris 1905] 255); at Boscoreale (A. Mau, "Scavi di Boscoreale," *RömMitt* 9 [1894] 353–357, figs. pp. 353, 355; *MonAnt* [1897] 451–455, fig. 45a, and cf. *DarSag* V.1, 215, fig. 6874).

23. NCW was not excavated below spring levels so no holes were found there.

24. Cf. forthcoming volume in this series on the Synagogue. The Synagogue revetment pins were 0.10 m. or more long, 0.006 m. thick, 0.18 m. wide. When revetments were placed over masonry the pins were placed in holes similar to those found in CG. In the Synagogue, the revetment grout was pinkish and varied in thickness from 0.07–

0.12 m. The marble slabs in the Synagogue varied from 0.17–0.96 m. in length. There was usually one pin in the center for shorter, two pins for longer revetment slabs. Distances between pins were often from 0.33–0.36 m. (From A. R. Seager, unpublished preliminary report, "Architecture of the Synagogue, 1968," 23 f.) The unevenness of the surface of CG masonry would require thicker grout and longer pins, 0.05 m. for the hole, at least 0.10–0.15 m. for the grout and revetment slab.

25. At Hierapolis the rows of revetment holes which cover the interior walls extend to the height of the vault springing, which is there well preserved, Fig. 358.

26. A layer of marble chips and ashes was found at W 3–4/N 29–32, *101.0 in both 1960 and 1969. Further indications of possible limekiln activity were observed by G. W. Swift, Jr. in 1960 in a pile of marble lumps at the southwest corner of CGE, W 1.5–3.0/N 1–2. By stratification both belong to Middle Byzantine period.

Collections of architectural and sculptural marble fragments were found in the second story level of MAW and MAE (ca. 30 pieces in MAW, 18 in MAE) and again seem to belong to the period of Middle Byzantine activity and may well be limekiln collections. Some of these marbles may come from CG itself; in some cases they did not, as for instance a fragment of a Roman sarcophagus.

27. *BASOR* 162, 47, fig. 29, brief description.

28. *BASOR* 199, 54.

29. *BASOR* 199, 54.

30. The paintings and their reconstruction will be described in detail by L. J. Majewski in a forthcoming volume in this series on paintings and mosaics.

31. Similar decoration can be seen in the half-domed niches of the Hierapolis bath where the upper parts of the half-domes are covered with stucco molded in the form of scallop shells and also tinted blue.

32. Vitruvius, 7.3.6–7 says plaster on walls is built up of six layers, and this in fact was the case in Sardis Building B.

33. *BASOR* 199, 40, fig. 31.

34. We owe the identification of skeletal material to physical anthropologist David Finkel.

35. The text will be published and discussed in the forthcoming volume in this series on inscriptions.

BIBLIOGRAPHY AND ABBREVIATIONS

Abbreviations of periodicals used throughout are those listed in the *American Journal of Archaeology* 74 (1970) 3–8. Abbreviations of classical authors generally follow the scheme set forth in the *Oxford Classical Dictionary,* 2nd rev. ed., N. G. L. Hammond and H. H. Scullard (Oxford 1970) ix–xxii.

All publications preceding the first Sardis expedition will be found in the prospective *Bibliography of Sardis* (available in mimeographed form). A preliminary selection appears in Hanfmann, *Letters,* 346–349. Reports of the Harvard-Cornell Expedition have appeared regularly since 1959 in the *Bulletin of the American Schools of Oriental Research* and *Türk Arkeoloji Dergisi* of the Turkish Department of Antiquities. The three monographs published by the current expedition are cited under *Sardis,* below.

The reports of the first Sardis expedition were published under the general series title of Sardis, Publications of the American Society for the Excavation of Sardis. Seventeen volumes were planned by H. C. Butler, Director of Excavations (*Sardis* I [1922] viii); of these, nine were actually published and are cited here under *Sardis.*

Akurgal, *Civilizations*   Akurgal, E. *Ancient Civilizations and Ruins of Turkey* (Istanbul 1970).

Akurgal, *Kunst Anatoliens*   Akurgal, E. *Die Kunst Anatoliens von Homer bis Alexander* (Berlin 1961).

Arundell, *Discoveries*   Arundell, F. V. J. *Discoveries in Asia Minor* (London 1834).

Arundell, *Seven Churches*   Arundell, F. V. J. *A Visit to the Seven Churches of Asia* (London 1828).

Atkinson   Atkinson, K. T. C. "A Hellenistic Land Conveyance," *Historia* 21 (1972) 45–74.

Baedeker, *Konstantinopel*   Baedeker, K. *Konstantinopel und das westliche Kleinasien* (Leipzig 1912).

Bammer   Bammer, A. *Die Architektur des jüngeren Artemision von Ephesos* (Wiesbaden 1972).

Bean   Bean, G. E. *Aegean Turkey* (New York 1966).

Berve, Gruben   Berve, H. and Gruben, G. *Greek Temples, Theaters, and Shrines* (New York 1963).

Birgi   Birgi, S. "Sart (Salihli) Civarındaki Altın Zuhurları" (Occurrences of Gold in the Sardis [Salihli] Region), Mineral Research and Exploration Institute of Turkey (Ankara 1944).

Boehringer   Boehringer, E. *Neue deutsche Ausgrabungen im Mittelmeergebiet und im Vorderen Orient* (Berlin 1959).

Boehringer, *Pergamon*   See *Pergamon.*

Boethius, Ward-Perkins   See *ERA.*

Bostancı, "Skeletal Remains"   Bostancı, E. "An Examination of Some Human Skeletal Remains from the Sardis Excavations," *Antropoloji* 1 (1963) 121–131.

Bostancı, "Skulls" 1967   Bostancı, E. "Morphological and Biometrical Examination of Some Skulls from the Sardis Excavations," *Belleten* 31 (1967) 17–22.

Bostancı, "Skulls" 1969   Bostancı, E. "Study of the Skulls from the Excavation at Sardis and the Relation with the Ancient Anatolians," *Ankara Üniversitesi Dil ve Tarih-Coğrafya Fakültesi 185, Paleoantropoloji Kürsüsü* Seri III (Ankara 1969).

Broneer, *Corinth* IV   Broneer, O. *Corinth* IV. *Terracotta Lamps* (Cambridge, Mass. 1934).

Buresch   Buresch, K. *Aus Lydien* (Leipzig 1898).

Butler   Butler, H. C. "Fifth Preliminary Report on the American Excavations at Sardes in Asia Minor," *AJA* 18 (1914) 427–430.

Caley, Richards   Caley, E. and Richards, J. *Theophrastus on Stones* (Columbus, Ohio 1956). Ohio State University Graduate School Monographs. Contributions in Physical Sciences I.

Chandler   Chandler, R. *Travels in Asia Minor* (Oxford 1775).

Chishull   Chishull, E. *Travels in Turkey and Back to England* (London 1747).

Choisy, *Byzantines*   Choisy, A. *L'art de bâtir chez les Byzantines* (Paris 1883).

Choisy, *Tombeaux* "Note sur les tombeaux Lydiens de Sardes avec planches et plusieurs figures dans le texte," *RA* 32 (1876) 73–81.

Cockerell Cockerell, C. R. *Travels in Southern Europe and the Levant 1810–1817* (London, New York 1903).

Coler, von, et al. von Coler, H., Graefinghoff, K., von Gaertringen, H. F. F., Pringsheim, H., and Regling, K. "Nysa ad Maeandrum nach Forschungen und Aufnahmen in den Jahren 1907 und 1909," *Jahrbuch des Kaiserlich Deutschen Archäologischen Instituts* Ergänzungsheft 10 (1913).

Collins Collins, V. L., ed. *Howard Crosby Butler, 1872–1922* (Princeton 1923) with bibliography by H. S. Leach.

Cook Cook, J. M. *The Greeks in Ionia and the East* (New York, Washington 1963).

Crawford Crawford, J. S. "Roman Commercial Buildings of Asia Minor" (Ph.D. diss., Harvard University 1969).

Crawford, "Lamp" Crawford, J. S. and Greaves, J. "A Brass Lamp from Sardis," *AJA* 78 (1974) 291–294.

Crema Crema, L. *L'architettura romana* in *Enciclopedia Classica* III Vol. 12.1 (Turin 1959).

Cuinet Cuinet, V. *La Turquie d'Asie* (Paris 1894).

Curtius, "Beiträge" Curtius, E. "Beiträge zur Geschichte und Topographie Kleinasiens (Ephesos, Pergamon, Smyrna, und Sardes)," *AbhBerl* (1872) 1–91.

Curtius, "Philadelpheia" Curtius. E. "Philadelpheia: Nachtrag zu den Beiträgen zur Geschichte und Topographie Kleinasiens," *AbhBerl* (1872) 93–95.

Dinsmoor Dinsmoor, W. B. *Architecture of Ancient Greece* (London 1950).

Doğuer et al. Doğuer, S., Deniz, E., Çalışlar, R., and Özgüden, T. "Osteological Investigations of the Animal Remains Recovered from the Excavations of Ancient Sardis," *Anatolia* 8 (1964) 49–65.

ERA Boethius, A. and Ward-Perkins, J. B. *Etruscan and Roman Architecture* (Baltimore 1970).

Fellows Fellows, C. *A Journal Written During an Excursion in Asia Minor* (London 1839).

Ferrero See *TCAM*.

Fleischer Fleischer, R. *Artemis von Ephesos und verwandte Kultstatuen aus Anatolien und Syrien* (Leyden 1973).

Franke Franke, P. R. "Inschriftliche und numismatische Zeugnisse für die Chronologie des Artemis-Tempels zu Sardis," *AthMitt* 76 (1961) 197–208.

Gabriel Gabriel, A. *Voyages archéologiques dans la Turquie orientale* (Paris 1940).

Garbrecht Garbrecht, G. *Pergamenische Forschungen* I, *Gesammelte Aufsätze,* Deutsches Archäologisches Institut (Berlin 1972) 43–48.

Gerkan, von, *Milet* I.4 von Gerkan, A. *Milet* I.4, *Der Poseidonaltar von Kap Monodendri* (Berlin 1915).

Gerkan, von, Krischen, *Milet* I.9 von Gerkan, A. and Krischen, F. *Milet* I.9, *Thermen und Palaestren* (Berlin 1928).

Goldman, *Tarsus* I Goldman, H. *Tarsus* I (Princeton 1950).

Grandjouan, *Agora* VI Grandjouan, C. *The Athenian Agora* VI, *Terracottas and Plastic Lamps of the Roman Period* (Princeton 1961).

Greenewalt Greenewalt, C. H., Jr. "Lydian Vases from Western Asia Minor," *California Studies in Classical Antiquity* 1 (1968) 139–154.

Gruben Gruben, G. "Beobachtungen zum Artemis-Tempel von Sardis," *AthMitt* 76 (1961) 155–196.

Gusmani, *LW* Gusmani, R. *Lydisches Wörterbuch* (Heidelberg 1964).

Hamilton Hamilton, W. J. *Researches in Asia Minor* (London 1842).

Hanfmann, "Glass" Hanfmann, G. M. A. "A Preliminary Note on the Glass Found at Sardis in 1958," *JGS* 1 (1959) 51–54.

Hanfmann, "Horsemen" Hanfmann, G. M. A. "Horsemen from Sardis," *AJA* 49 (1945) 570–581.

Hanfmann, *Letters* Hanfmann, G. M. A. *Letters From Sardis* (Cambridge, Mass. 1972).

Hanfmann, "Prehistoric Sardis" Hanfmann, G. M. A. "Prehistoric Sardis," in G. Mylonas, ed. *Studies Presented to D. M. Robinson* I (St. Louis 1951) 160–183.

Hanfmann, *Sardis und Lydien* Hanfmann, G. M. A. *Sardis und Lydien,* Akademie der Wissenschaften und Literatur, Mainz, Abhandlungen der geistes und sozialwissenschaftlichen Klasse 6 (1960) 499–536.

Hanfmann, *Studies* Mitten, D. G., Pedley, J. G., and Scott, J. A., eds. *Studies Presented to George M. A. Hanfmann* (Cambridge, Mass. 1971). Fogg Art Museum Monographs in Art and Archaeology II.

Hanfmann, Polatkan, Robert Hanfmann, G. M. A., Polatkan, K. Z., and Robert, L. "A Sepulchral Stele from Sardis," *AJA* 64 (1960) 45–56.

Hanfmann, Waldbaum Hanfmann, G. M. A. and Waldbaum, J. C. "New Excavations at Sardis and Some Problems of Western Anatolian Archaeology," in J. A. Sanders, ed. *Near Eastern Archaeology in the Twentieth Century: Essays in Honor of Nelson Glueck* (Garden City, N. Y. 1970) 307–326.

Hayes Hayes, J. W. *Late Roman Pottery* (London 1972).

Hellstrom Hellstrom, P. *Labraunda* I.1 (Lund 1965).

Hill Hill, D. K. "The Horse of Sardis Rediscovered," *ArtB* 24 (1942) 155–159.

Hoffmann Hoffmann, H. "Foreign Influence and Native Invention in Archaic Greek Altars," *AJA* 57 (1953) 189–195.

Howland, *Agora* IV Howland, R. H. *The Athenian Agora* IV, *Greek Lamps and Their Survivals* (Princeton 1958).

Humann Humann, C. "Altertümer von Hierapolis," *JdI* Ergänzungsheft 4 (1898).

İnan, Rosenbaum İnan, J. and Rosenbaum, E. *Roman and Early Byzantine Portrait Sculpture in Asia Minor* (London 1966).

Jannoray, *Delphes* II Jannoray, J. *Fouilles de Delphes* II, *Topographie et Architecture: Le Gymnase* (Paris 1953).

Jones Jones, H. S., ed. *A Catalogue of the Ancient Sculptures Preserved in the Municipal Collections of*

Rome: The Sculpture of the Museo Capitolino (Oxford 1912).

Keil   Keil, J. *Ephesos: ein Führer durch die Ruinenstätte und ihre Geschichte* (Vienna 1964).

Keil, Premerstein   Keil, J. and von Premerstein, A. "Bericht über eine Reise in Lydien ausgeführt," *DenkschrWien* 53.2 (1908). "Bericht über eine sweite Reise. . ." 54.2 (1911), "Bericht über eine dritte Reise. . ." 57.1 (1914).

Kleiner   Kleiner, G. *Die Ruinen von Milet* (Berlin 1968).

Koldewey   Koldewey, R. "Das Bad von Alexandria-Troas," *AthMitt* 9 (1884) 36–48.

Köy İşleri Bakanlığı   Köy İşleri Bakanlığı. Topraksu Genel Müdürlügü, *Gediz Ovası Toprakları Raporu* (Village Works Ministry, Soil and Water Conservation Directorate, *Report on the Soils of the Gediz Plain*) (Ankara 1968).

Kraus   Kraus, T. *Megarische Becher im Römisch-Germanischen Zentralmuseum zu Mainz,* Römisch-Germanisches Zentralmuseum zu Mainz, Katalog 14 (Mainz 1951).

Krautheimer   Krautheimer, R. *Early Christian and Byzantine Architecture* (Harmondsworth, Middlesex 1965).

Krencker   Krencker, D. *Die Trierer Kaiserthermen* I, *Trierer Grabung und Forschungen* Bd I.1 (Augsberg 1929).

Lanckoronski   Lanckoronski, Le Comte C. *Les Villes de la Pamphylie et de la Pisidie* I (Paris 1890).

Lawrence   Lawrence, A. W. "Early Medieval Fortifications Near Rome," *BSR* 32 (1964) 89–122.

Leake   Leake, W. M. *Journal of a Tour in Asia Minor* (London 1824).

Le Bas   Le Bas, P. *Voyage archéologique en Grèce et en Asie Mineure* (1842–1844) ed. S. Reinach (1888).

Magie   Magie, D. *Roman Rule in Asia Minor to the End of the Third Century after Christ* (Princeton 1950).

Manisa 1967   *Manisa Il Yıllığı 1967* (Yearbook of the Village Manisa) (Izmir 1968).

Mansel, *Mélanges*   Akurgal, E. and Bahadır Alkim U., eds. *Mélanges Mansel* (Ankara 1974).

Martin, *Manuel*   Martin, R. *Manuel d'archéologie grecque* I, *Materiaux et techniques* (Paris 1965).

Martin, *Urbanisme*   Martin, R. *L'Urbanisme dans la Grèce antique* (Paris 1956).

Mason   Mason, K., et al. *Turkey* II (B.R. 507A Geographical Handbook Series, Naval Intelligence Division 1943).

Menzel   Menzel, H. *Antike Lampen im Römisch-Germanischen Zentralmuseum zu Mainz* (Mainz 1969).

Miklosich   Miklosich, Fr. and Müller, Io. *Acta et Diplomata Graeca Medii Aevi* (Vienna 1860).

Mitten   Mitten, D. G. "A New Look at Ancient Sardis," *BiblArch* 29 (1966) 38–68.

Mitten, Yügrüm, "Ahlatlı Tepecik"   Mitten, D. G. and Yügrüm, G. "Ahlatlı Tepecik beside the Gygean Lake," *Archaeology* 27 (1974) 22–29.

Mitten, Yügrüm, "Eski Balıkhane"   Mitten, D. G. and Yügrüm, G. "The Gygean Lake, 1969: Eski Balıkhane, Preliminary Report," *HSCP* 75 (1971) 191–195.

MTA Publication 113   *Bilinen Maden Zuhurları Fihristi.* Maden Tetkik ve Arama Enstitüsü 113 (Ankara 1963).

Müller-Wiener   Müller-Wiener, W. "Die Stadtbefestigungen von Izmir, Sigacık und Çandarlı," *IstMitt* 12 (1962) 59–114.

Munsell   Munsell Color Company, Inc., Baltimore, Md., soil color charts for color abbreviations and equivalents (1971).

Naster   Naster, P. "De laatste lydische Herakliden," *Philol. Studien,* Katholiek Univ. Leuven 7 (1935–1936) 3–16.

Naumann, Kantar   Naumann, R. and Kantar, S. "Die Agora von Smyrna," *Istanbuler Forschungen* 17 (1950) 70–75.

Nylander, "Clamps"   Nylander, C. "Clamps and Chronology," *Iranica Antiqua* 6 (1966) 130–146.

Nylander, *Ionians*   Nylander, C. *Ionians in Pasargadae* (Uppsala 1970).

Olfers, von,   von Olfers, J. F. M. "Über die Lydischen Königsgräber bei Sardes und den Grabhügel des Alyattes nach dem Bericht des Kaiserlichen General-Consuls Spiegelthal zu Smyrna," *AbhBerl* (1858) 539–556.

Oliver   Oliver, A. "A Bronze Mirror from Sardis," in Hanfmann, *Studies,* 113–120.

Olson   Olson, G. W. "Some Aspects of Soils and Civilizations at Sardis, Turkey," Part of Report of Committee XIV on Environmental Soils Science to the National Technical Work Planning Conference of the Cooperative Soils Survey in Charleston, S. C., January 25–28, 1971.

Olson, Hanfmann   Olson, G. W. and Hanfmann, G. M. A. "Some Implications of Soils for Civilizations," *New York's Food and Life Sciences Quarterly* 4:4 (1971) 11–14.

Orlandos   Orlandos, A. K. *Les matériaux de construction et la technique architecturale des anciens Grecs,* Part 2 (Paris 1968).

Osborn   Osborn, H. F. "Howard Crosby Butler," in *Dictionary of American Biography* 3 (1929) 361.

Perlzweig, *Agora* VII   Perlzweig, J. *The Athenian Agora* VII, *Lamps of the Roman Period, First through Seventh Centuries after Christ* (Princeton 1971).

Pergamon   Boehringer, E., ed. *Pergamenische Forschungen* I, *Pergamon, Gesammelte Aufsatze,* Deutsches Archäologisches Institut (Berlin 1972).

Peyssonel, de   de Peyssonel, C. *Observations historiques et géographiques sur les peuples barbares; . . . suivies d'un Voyage fait à Magnésie, à Thyatire, à Sardes, etc.* (Paris 1765).

Philippson, *Byzantinische Reich*   Philippson, A. *Das byzantinische Reich als geographische Erscheinung* (Leiden 1939).

Philippson, *Reisen*   Philippson, A. *Reisen und Forschungen im westlichen Kleinasien* (Gotha 1910–1915).

Price, Trell   Price, M. J. and Trell, B. "Ancient Architecture on Coins" (forthcoming).

Prokesch, von   von Prokesch, A. *Erinnerungen aus Aegypten und Kleinasien 1825* III (Vienna 1831).

Pryce Pryce, F. N. *Catalogue of Sculpture in the British Museum* I:1 (Oxford 1928).

Ramage Ramage, A. "Studies in Lydian Domestic and Commercial Architecture at Sardis" (Ph.D. diss., Harvard University 1969).

Ramage, A., Ramage, N. Ramage, A. and Ramage, N. "The Siting of Lydian Burial Mounds," in Hanfmann, *Studies*, 143–160.

Ramsay Ramsay, W. M. *Historical Geography of Asia Minor* (London 1890).

Ravndal Ravndal, G. *Turkey, A Commercial and Industrial Handbook* (Washington, D.C. 1926).

Refik Refik, A. *Osmanlı Devrinde Türkiye Madenleri* (İstanbul 1931).

Reimann Reimann, O. "Inscriptions grecques provenant du receuil de Cyriaque d'Ancone," *BCH* 1 (1877) 81–88, 134–136, 286–294.

Richter Richter, G. M. A. *Catalogue of Greek Sculptures in the Metropolitan Museum of Art* (Cambridge, Mass. 1954).

Robert, *NIS* Robert, L. *Nouvelles Inscriptions de Sardes* Ier fascicule (Paris 1964).

Robert, *Villes*² Robert, L. *Villes de Asie Mineure*, 2nd rev. ed. (Paris 1962).

Robinson, *Agora* V Robinson, H. S. *The Athenian Agora* V, *The Pottery of the Roman Period: Chronology* (Princeton 1959).

Ryan Ryan, C. W. *A Guide to the Known Minerals of Turkey*. Mineral Research and Exploration Institute of Turkey (Ankara 1960).

Şahin Şahin, M. Ç. *Die Entwicklung der griechischen Monumentalaltäre* (Bonn 1972).

Sardis I (1922) Butler, H. C. *Sardis* I, *The Excavations*, Part 1: *1910–1914* (Leyden 1922).

Sardis II (1925) Butler, H. C. *Sardis* II, *Architecture*, Part 1: *The Temple of Artemis* (text and atlas of plates, Leyden 1925).

Sardis V (1924) Morey, C. R. *Sardis* V, *Roman and Christian Sculpture*, Part 1: *The Sarcophagus of Claudia Antonia Sabina* (Princeton 1924).

Sardis VI.1 (1916) Littmann, E. *Sardis* VI, *Lydian Inscriptions*, Part 1 (Ledyen 1916).

Sardis VI.2 (1924) Buckler, W. H. *Sardis* VI, *Lydian Inscriptions*, Part 2 (Leyden 1924).

Sardis VII (1932) Buckler, W. H. and Robinson, D. M. *Sardis* VII, *Greek and Latin Inscriptions*, Part 1 (Leyden 1932).

Sardis X (1926) Shear, T. L. *Sardis* X, *Terra-cottas*, Part 1: *Architectural Terra-cottas* (Cambridge, England 1926).

Sardis XI (1916) Bell, H. W. *Sardis* XI, *Coins*, Part 1: *1910–1914* (Leyden 1916).

Sardis XIII (1925) Curtis, C. D. *Sardis* XIII, *Jewelry and Gold Work*, Part 1: *1910–1914* (Rome 1925).

Sardis M1 (1971) Bates, G. E. *Byzantine Coins* (Cambridge, Mass. 1971). Archaeological Exploration of Sardis Monograph 1.

Sardis M2 (1972) Pedley, J. G. *Ancient Literary Sources on Sardis* (Cambridge, Mass. 1972). Archaeological Exploration of Sardis Monograph 2.

Sardis M3 (1975) Gusmani, R. *Neue epichorische Schriftzeugnisse aus Sardis (1958–1971)* (Cambridge, Mass. 1975). Archaeological Exploration of Sardis Monograph 3.

Saydamer Saydamer, M. "Turgutlu-Salihli arasındaki alüvyonların genel altın prospeksiyonu ile Sart çayı ve civarının altın bakımından detay etüdü hakkında rapor (Sart Çay)" (Report on gold prospecting of the alluvium between Turgutlu and Salihli with a detailed study of gold in the area around Sart Çay), Maden Tetkik ve Arama Enstitüsü (Ankara 1963).

Schäfer Schäfer, J. S. *Hellenistische Keramik aus Pergamon* (Berlin 1968).

Schede Schede, M. *Die Ruinen von Priene* (Berlin 1964).

Schleif Schleif, H. "Der grosse Altar der Hera von Samos," *AthMitt* 58 (1933) 174–210.

Schlikker Schlikker, F. W. "Der Schaubildentwurf im griechischen Tempelbau," *AA* 56 (1941) 748–765.

Schneider Schneider, A. M. *Die Landmauer von Konstantinopel* II (Berlin 1943).

Schneider, Karnapp Schneider, A. M. and Karnapp, W. "Die Stadtmauer von Iznik (Nicaea)" (Berlin 1938) = *Istanbuler Forschungen* 9.

Scranton Scranton, R. L. *Greek Walls* (Cambridge, Mass. 1941).

Shear, "Horse" Shear, T. L. "The Horse of Sardis," *ArtB* 10 (1928) 215–230.

Shear, "Lion" Shear, T. L. "The Lion Group at Sardis," *ArtB* 13 (1931) 127–137.

Shear, "Sixth Report" Shear, T. L. "Sixth Preliminary Report on the American Excavations at Sardes," *AJA* 26 (1922) 396–401.

Shear, "Staters" Shear, T. L. "A Hoard of Staters of Croesus at Sardes," *Numismatist* 35 (1922) 349–352.

Soc. Dilettanti Society of Dilettanti, *The Antiquities of Ionia* III (London 1840).

Täschner, *Osmanische Quellen* Täschner, Fr. *Das anatolische Wegenetz nach osmanischen Quellen* (Leipzig 1924–1936).

Täschner, *Wegenetz* Täschner, Fr. "Die Verkehrslage und das Wegenetz Anatoliens im Wandel der Zeiten," *Petermanns Mitteilungen* 73 (1926) Heft 9/10.

Tavernier Tavernier, Jean Baptiste. *The Six Voyages of John Baptista Tavernier, a Noble Man of France now living, through Turkey into Persia, and the East-Indies, finished in the year 1670* (London 1678).

TCAM de Bernardi Ferrero, D. *Theatri Classici in Asia Minore*, 3 vols. (Rome 1966–1970).

Texier Texier, C. "Asie Mineure, description graphique, historique et archéologique," *L'universe, histoire et description de tous les peuples* (Paris 1862).

Thompson, Wycherley, *Agora* XIV Thompson, H. A. and Wycherley, R. E. *The Athenian Agora* XIV, *The Agora of Athens: The History, Shape and Uses of an Ancient City Center* (Princeton 1972).

Tilia Tilia, A. B. "A Study on the Methods of Working and Restoring Stone and on the Parts left Unfinished in Achaemenian Architecture and Sculpture," *East and West* 18 (1968) 67–95.

Tölle   Tölle, R. "Uhren auf Samos," *Opus Nobile, Festschrift zum 60 Geburtstag von Ulf Jantzen* (Wiesbaden 1969) 164–171.

Türkdoğan   Türkdoğan, O.   *Salihli'de Türkistan Göçmenlerinin Yerleşmeleri* (Erzurum 1969).

Uluçay   Uluçay, M. Çağatay. *Saruhan Oğulları ve Eserlerine dair Vesikalar* (Istanbul 1940–1946).

Verzone   Verzone, P. "Le chiese di Hierapolis," *Cahiers Archéologiques* 8 (1956) 39–45.

Walter   Walter, O. "Antikenbericht aus Smyrna," *JOAI* 21–22 (1922–1924) cols. 223–260.

Ward-Perkins, "Aspendos"   Ward-Perkins, J. B. "The Aqueduct of Aspendos," *BSR* 23 (1955) 115–123.

Ward-Perkins, *Great Palace*   Ward-Perkins, J. B. "Notes on the Structure and Building Methods of Early Byzantine Architecture," in D. Talbot Rice, ed. *The Great Palace of the Byzantine Emperors* 2nd Report (Edinburgh 1958) 53–104.

Westermarck   Westermarck, U. *Das Bildnis des Philetairos von Pergamon: Corpus der Münzprägung= Stockholm Studies in Classical Archaeology* I (Stockholm 1961).

Wiegand, Schrader   Wiegand, T. and Schrader, H. *Priene, Ergebnisse der Ausgrabungen und Untersuchungen in den Jahren 1895–1898* (Berlin 1904).

Winter   Winter, F. E. *Greek Fortifications* (Toronto 1971).

Ziegenhaus, de Luca, *Pergamon* XI   Ziegenhaus, O. and de Luca, G. *Das Asklepieion* (Mit Beiträgen von Virginia Grace und Christoph Boehringer), Deutsches Archäologisches Institut. *Altertümer von Pergamon* XI, 1 (Berlin 1968).

CONCORDANCE OF FINDS

	Page	*Figure*
POTTERY		
Inventory Number		
P58.35:38	105	226
P58.36:39	105	227
P58.42:45	105	229
P58.60:64	106	230
P58.87:106	106	232
P58.93:104	106	233
P58.104:118	107	239
P58.110:124	106	234
P58.129:146	106	237
P58.150A:205	107	243
P58.152:209	107	238
P58.199:309	107	244
P58.200:310	107	242
P58.241:570	136	361
P58.245:558	136	
P58.301:571	142	
P58.340:629	136	
P58.344:631	142	381
P58.358:646	116	279
P58.359:647	116	
P58.361:624	142-143	383
P58.369:658	110	
P58.372:661	110	251
P58.388:676	111	255
P58.391:679	111	254
P58.405:681a	111	259
P58.406:582a	111	
P58.407:683	110	253
P58.409:685	110	252
P58.412:688	110	
P58.413:685a	111	260
P58.436:699	110	
P58.439:701	136	
P58.447:719	142	
P58.451:726	110	250
P58.474a:811	116	280
P58.484:786	127, 128	329
P58.486:788	127	
P58.500:834	116	278
P58.501:856	111	256
P58.503:860	111	
P58.546:918	113	
P58.549:927	113	270

	Page	*Figure*
POTTERY		
Inventory Number		
P58.550:928	113	
P58.552:931	115	
P58.663:1168	143	
P59.228:1586	145	
P59.232:1599	148	404, 405
P59.240:1609	145	393
P59.253:1630	145	394
P59.394:1919	136	360
P59.401:1940	44	29, 30
P59.404:1944	44	31
P59.423:1973	44	32, 33
P59.424:1974	44, 45	
P59.425:1975	44	34
P59.426:1976	44	35
P59.447:2022	44	36
P59.491:2075	44	37
P59.519:2125	136	364
P60.2:2233	142	376
P60.3:2234	142	377
P60.102:2370	81	149
P60.112:2380	81	150
P60.114:2382	81	151
P61.60:3256	81	
P67.145:7583	49	
P68.45:7660	112	261
P68.54:7673	112	
P68.55:7674	112	262
P68.187:7907	114	272
P69.12:7936	119-120	288
P69.13:7937	119	287
P69.25:7956	59	
P69.26:7957	59	
P69.28:7960	123	313
P69.44:7985	122	303
P69.47:7988	123	317
P69.48:7989	122	304
P69.53:8001	123	318
P69.54:8002	122	
P69.55:8003	123	314
P69.56:8004	123	310
P69.57:8005	123	311
P69.58:8006	122	308
P69.59:8007	123	

INDEX

ILLUSTRATIONS

The measure used in field shots is one meter divided into ten centimeter units. Scales used with objects are divided into one centimeter units. Scales on plans are in one meter units unless otherwise indicated. An explanation of grid and datum systems may be found on pages 7–12.

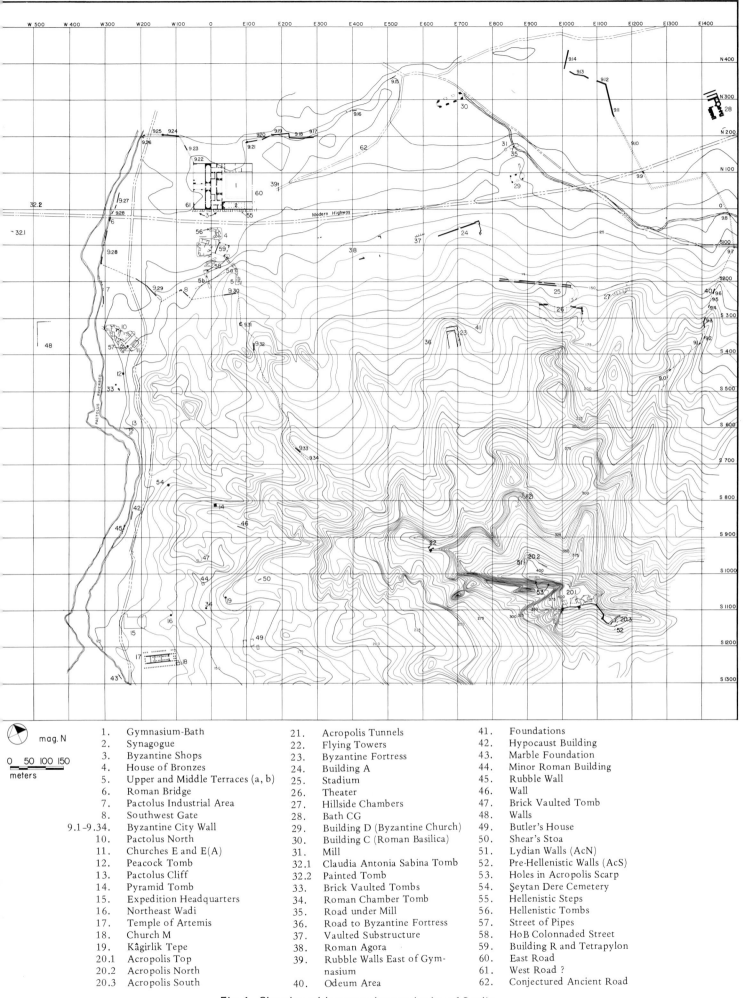

1.	Gymnasium-Bath	21.	Acropolis Tunnels	41.	Foundations
2.	Synagogue	22.	Flying Towers	42.	Hypocaust Building
3.	Byzantine Shops	23.	Byzantine Fortress	43.	Marble Foundation
4.	House of Bronzes	24.	Building A	44.	Minor Roman Building
5.	Upper and Middle Terraces (a, b)	25.	Stadium	45.	Rubble Wall
6.	Roman Bridge	26.	Theater	46.	Wall
7.	Pactolus Industrial Area	27.	Hillside Chambers	47.	Brick Vaulted Tomb
8.	Southwest Gate	28.	Bath CG	48.	Walls
9.1–9.34.	Byzantine City Wall	29.	Building D (Byzantine Church)	49.	Butler's House
10.	Pactolus North	30.	Building C (Roman Basilica)	50.	Shear's Stoa
11.	Churches E and E(A)	31.	Mill	51.	Lydian Walls (AcN)
12.	Peacock Tomb	32.1	Claudia Antonia Sabina Tomb	52.	Pre-Hellenistic Walls (AcS)
13.	Pactolus Cliff	32.2	Painted Tomb	53.	Holes in Acropolis Scarp
14.	Pyramid Tomb	33.	Brick Vaulted Tombs	54.	Şeytan Dere Cemetery
15.	Expedition Headquarters	34.	Roman Chamber Tomb	55.	Hellenistic Steps
16.	Northeast Wadi	35.	Road under Mill	56.	Hellenistic Tombs
17.	Temple of Artemis	36.	Road to Byzantine Fortress	57.	Street of Pipes
18.	Church M	37.	Vaulted Substructure	58.	HoB Colonnaded Street
19.	Kâgirlik Tepe	38.	Roman Agora	59.	Building R and Tetrapylon
20.1	Acropolis Top	39.	Rubble Walls East of Gymnasium	60.	East Road
20.2	Acropolis North			61.	West Road ?
20.3	Acropolis South	40.	Odeum Area	62.	Conjectured Ancient Road

mag. N

0   50 100 150
meters

Fig. 1   Site plan with excavations and ruins of Sardis.

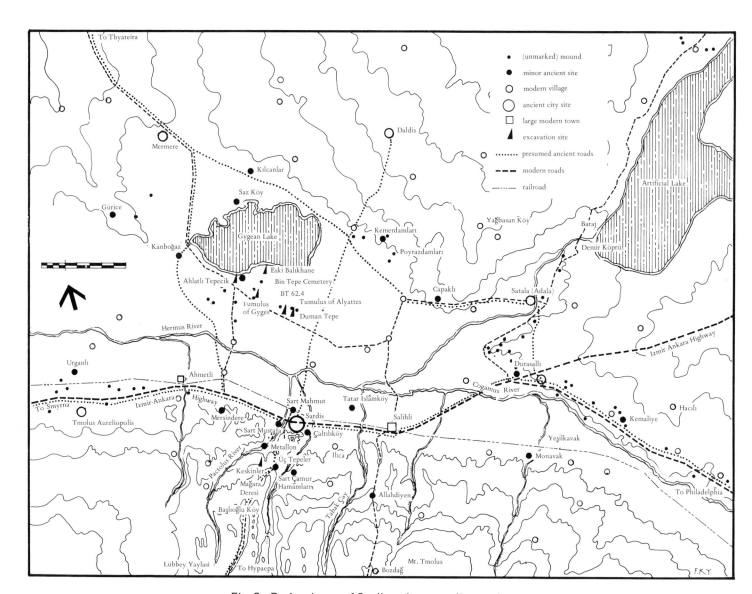

Fig. 2 Regional map of Sardis and surrounding territory.

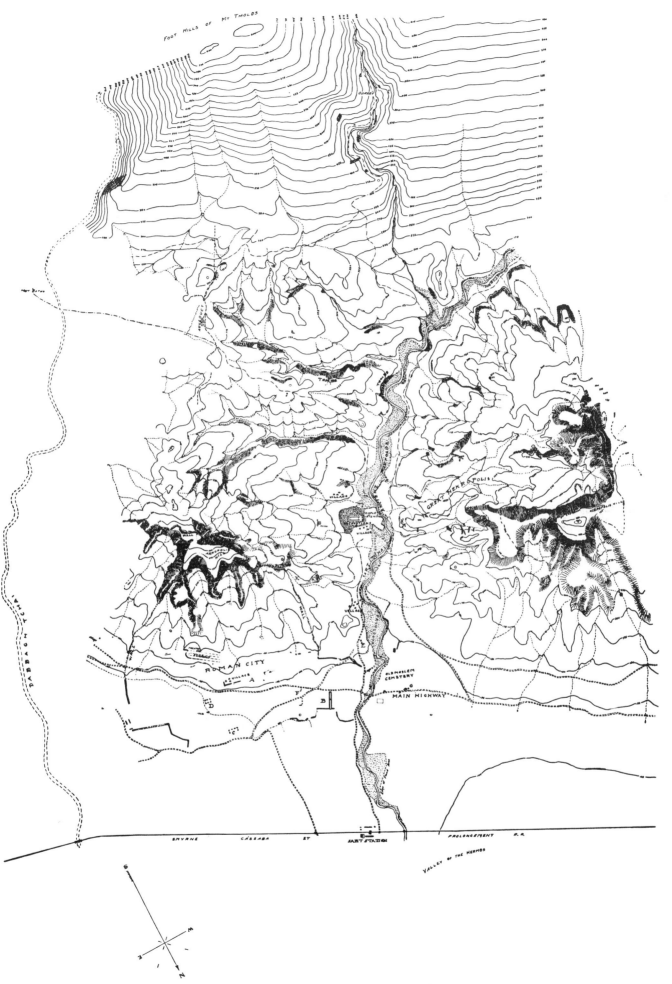

Fig. 3   Map of Sardis and environs. After *Sardis* I (1922) pl. I.

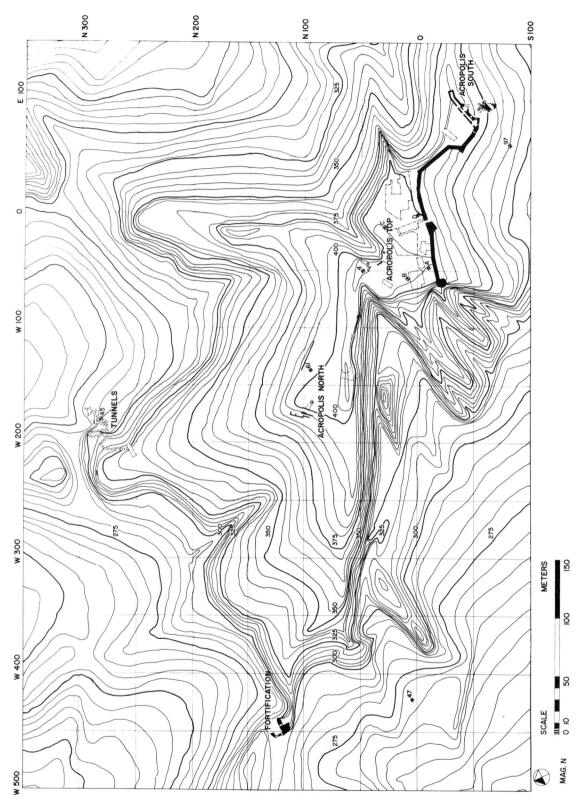

Fig. 4 Overall plan of Acropolis area.

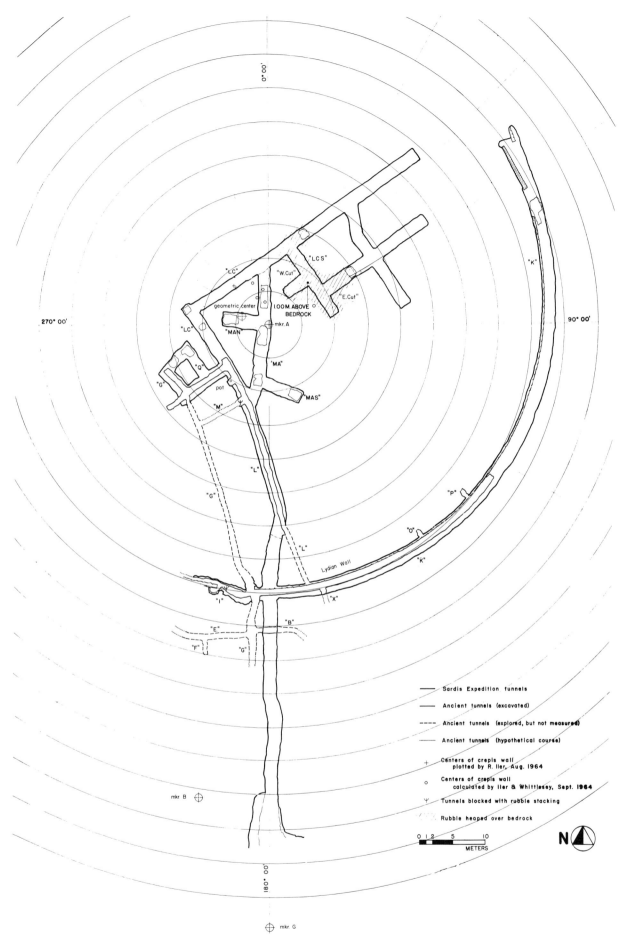

0° 00'

270° 00'

"LC"
"LCS"
"W.Cut"
"E.Cut"
"K"
geometric center
1.00 M. ABOVE BEDROCK
mkr. A
"LC"
"MAN"
"MA"
"Q"
"G"
"MAS"
pot
"M"
"L"
"G"
"L"
"P"
"O"
"K"
Lydian Wall
"I"
"X"
"B"
"E"
"F"
"G"

90° 00'

Sardis Expedition tunnels

Ancient tunnels (excavated)

Ancient tunnels (explored, but not measured)

Ancient tunnels (hypothetical course)

+ Centers of crepis wall
plotted by R. Iler, Aug. 1964

○ Centers of crepis wall
calculated by Iler & Whittlesey, Sept. 1964

Ψ Tunnels blocked with rubble stacking

Rubble heaped over bedrock

0 1 2   5   10
METERS

N

mkr B

180° 00'

mkr G

Fig. 5 Plan of tunnels at Karnıyarık Tepe.

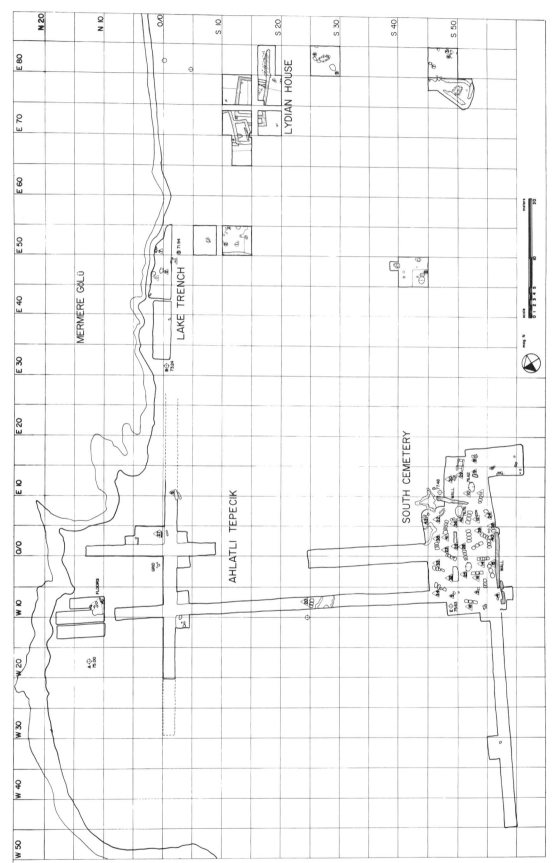

Fig. 6 Overall plan of excavations at Ahlatlı Tepecik.

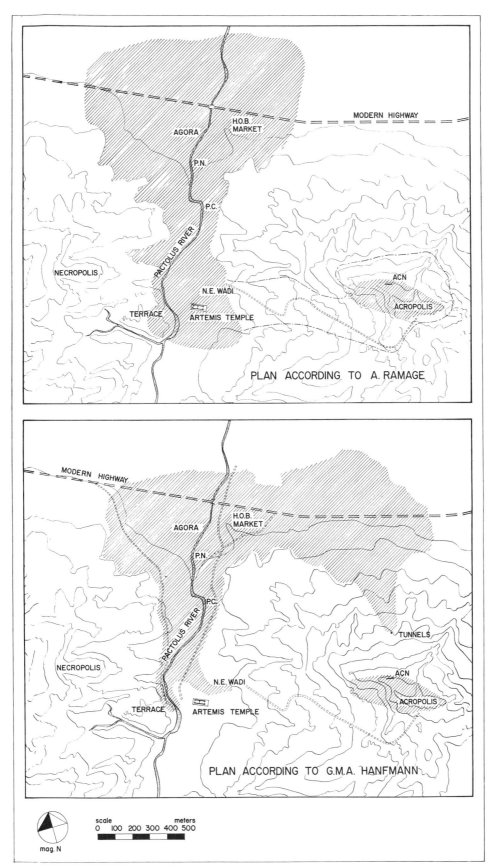

Fig. 7   Sardis, the Lydian city. Hypothetical plans according to A. Ramage and G. M. A. Hanfmann.

Fig. 8 Map of Anatolia and the Aegean.

Fig. 9 Fertile plain of Sardis under cultivation, looking N. Reconstruction of Gymnasium-Bath with Marble Court and Synagogue at upper center and Lydian Market area (HoB) opposite; village of Sart to left.

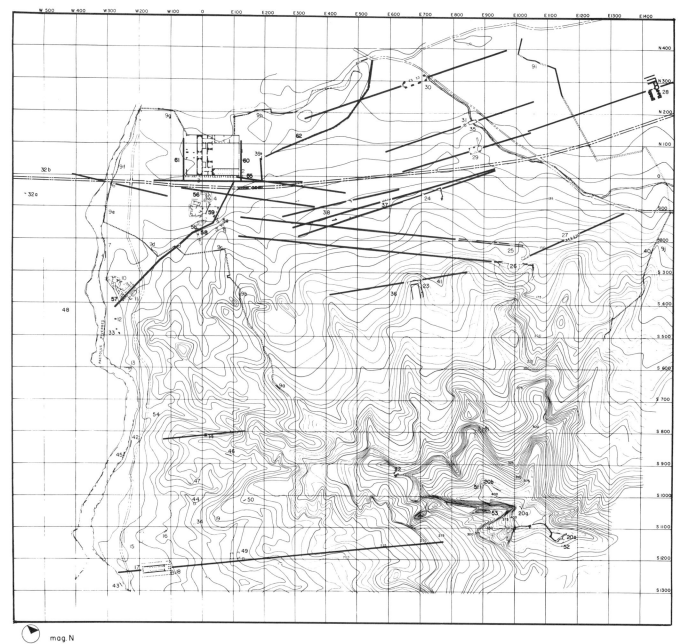

mag. N

0 50 100 150
meters

Fig. 10 Sketch plan of alignments of ancient structures.

1. Gymnasium-Bath	20c. Acropolis South	41. Foundations
2. Synagogue	21. Acropolis Tunnels	42. Hypocaust Building
3. Byzantine Shops	22. Flying Towers	43. Marble Foundation
4. House of Bronzes	23. Byzantine Fortress	44. Minor Roman Building
5. Upper Terrace	24. Building A	45. Rubble Wall
5a. Middle Terrace East	25. Stadium	46. Wall
5b. Middle Terrace West	26. Theater	47. Brick Vaulted Tomb
6. Roman Bridge	27. Hillside Chambers	48. Walls
7. Pactolus Industrial Area	28. Bath CG	49. Butler's House
8. Southwest Gate	29. Building D (Byzantine Church)	50. Shear's Stoa
9a–9j. Byzantine City Wall	30. Building C (Roman Basilica)	51. Lydian Walls (AcN)
10. Pactolus North	31. Mill	52. Pre-Hellenistic Walls (AcS)
11. Churches E and E(A)	32a. Claudia Antonia Sabina Tomb	53. Holes in Acropolis Scarp
12. Peacock Tomb	32b. Painted Tomb	54. Seytan Dere Cemetery
13. Pactolus Cliff	33. Brick Vaulted Tombs	55. Hellenistic Steps
14. Pyramid Tomb	34. Roman Chamber Tomb	56. Hellenistic Tombs
15. Expedition Headquarters	35. Road under Mill	57. Street of Pipes
16. Northeast Wadi	36. Road to Byzantine Fortress	58. HoB Colonnaded Street
17. Temple of Artemis	37. Vaulted Substructure	59. Building R and Tetrapylon
18. Church M	38. Roman Agora	60. East Road
19. Kâgirlik Tepe	39. Rubble Walls East of Gymnasium	61. West Road ?
20a. Acropolis Top	40. Odeum Area	62. Conjectured Ancient Road
20b. Acropolis North		

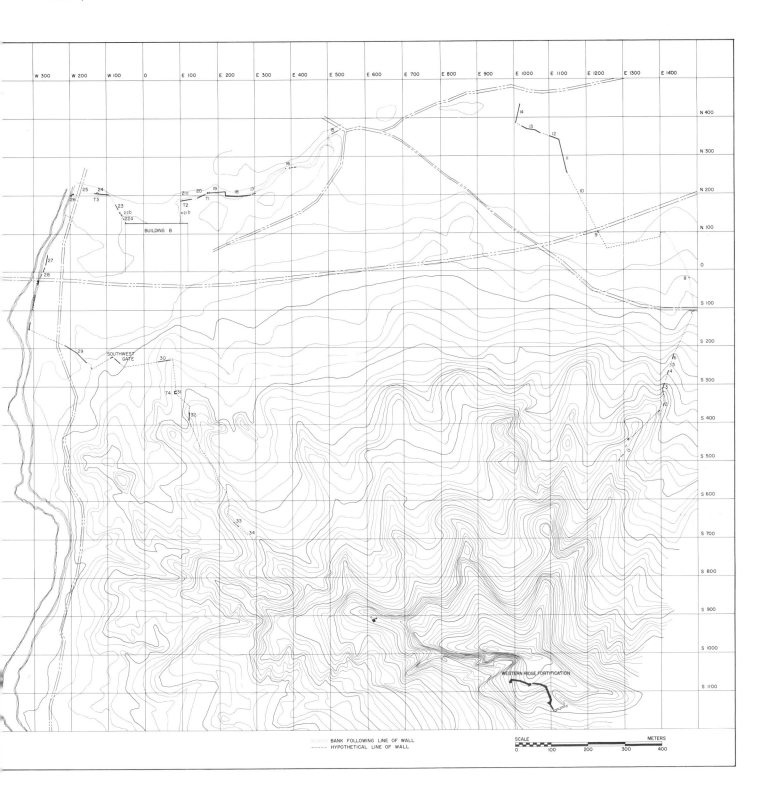

BANK FOLLOWING LINE OF WALL
----- HYPOTHETICAL LINE OF WALL

Fig. 11 Line of the City Wall.

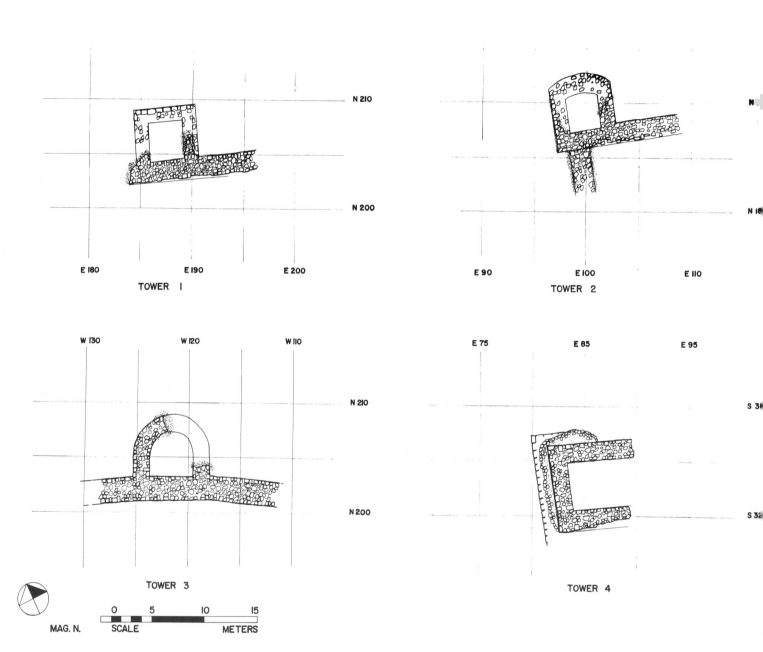

N 210

N 200

E 180   E 190   E 200

TOWER 1

N

N 1

E 90   E 100   E 110

TOWER 2

W 130   W 120   W 110

N 210

N 200

TOWER 3

E 75   E 85   E 95

S 3

S 32

TOWER 4

MAG. N.   SCALE   METERS

0   5   10   15

Fig. 12 Plans of towers.

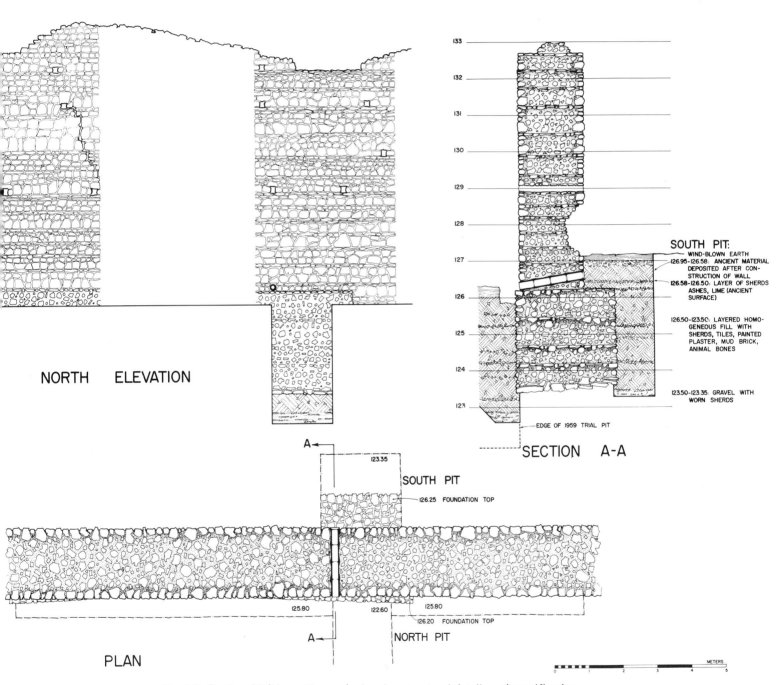

NORTH ELEVATION

SOUTH PIT:
- WIND-BLOWN EARTH
- 126.95-126.58: ANCIENT MATERIAL DEPOSITED AFTER CONSTRUCTION OF WALL
- 126.58-126.50: LAYER OF SHERDS ASHES, LIME (ANCIENT SURFACE)
- 126.50-123.50: LAYERED HOMOGENEOUS FILL WITH SHERDS, TILES, PAINTED PLASTER, MUD BRICK, ANIMAL BONES
- 123.50-123.35: GRAVEL WITH WORN SHERDS

EDGE OF 1959 TRIAL PIT

SECTION A-A

A

123.35

SOUTH PIT

126.25 FOUNDATION TOP

125.80   122.60   125.80

126.20 FOUNDATION TOP

A

NORTH PIT

PLAN

METERS
0 1 2 3 4 5

Fig. 13   Section 30 (Upper Terrace), showing structural details and stratification.

Fig. 14   Section 3.

Fig. 15   View of the "Saw."

Fig. 16   Section 0. Side view showing how conglomerate is cut back to serve as foundation.

Fig. 17 Section 17. Looking SE, showing break in wall.

Fig. 18 Section 18. Looking SW.

Fig. 19   Section 24.

Fig. 20   Section 24. Semicircular tower 3,
looking SE.

Fig. 21 Section 30 (Upper Terrace). Overall view of N side, looking S.

Fig. 22 Section 31. S side of tower 4, looking W to Sart Mustafa village.

Fig. 23 Tower 4. Close-up of sima with false lion head spout.

Fig. 24 The Western Ridge Fortification ("Flying Towers") on the Acropolis.

Fig. 25 N side of section 30 (Upper Terrace).

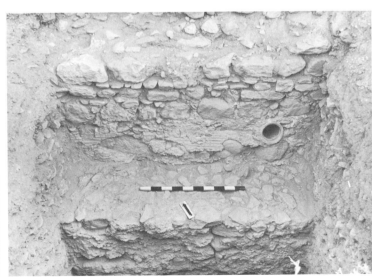

Fig. 26 Section 30 (Pit). Bench at top of foundation, looking N.

Fig. 27 Section 3. Top surface showing step
down, looking SSW.

Fig. 28 Section 31. West side of tower 4, looking E.

Finds from Upper Terrace Trenches:

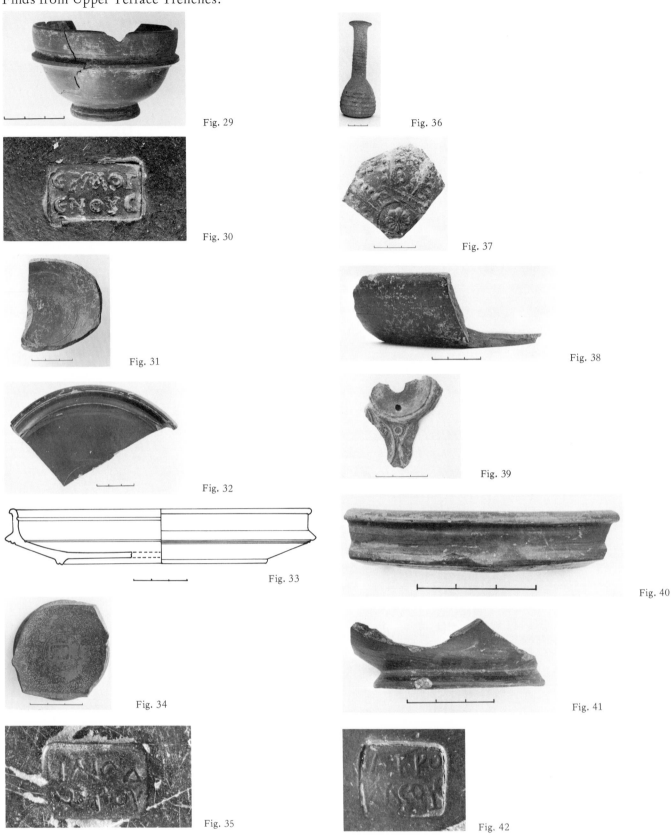

Fig. 29

Fig. 30

Fig. 31

Fig. 32

Fig. 33

Fig. 34

Fig. 35

Fig. 36

Fig. 37

Fig. 38

Fig. 39

Fig. 40

Fig. 41

Fig. 42

Fig. 29   Eastern sigillate B bowl   P59.401.

Fig. 30   Detail of potter's stamp, Fig. 29.

Fig. 31   Fragment of eastern sigillate B base   P59.404.

Fig. 32   Eastern sigillate B plate fragment   P59.423.

Fig. 33   Section-profile, Fig. 32.

Fig. 34   Fragment of eastern sigillate B base   P59.425.

Fig. 35   Detail of potter's stamp P59.426.

Fig. 36   Plain, red piriform unguentarium   P59.447.

Fig. 37   Hellenistic relief ware fragment   P59.491.

Fig. 38   Fragment of eastern sigillate B bowl   P71.18.

Fig. 39   Late Hellenistic lamp fragment   L71.2.

Fig. 40   Eastern sigillate B bowl fragment   P71.7.

Fig. 41   Eastern sigillate B bowl fragment   P71.17.

Fig. 42   Detail of potter's stamp, Fig. 41   IN71.12.

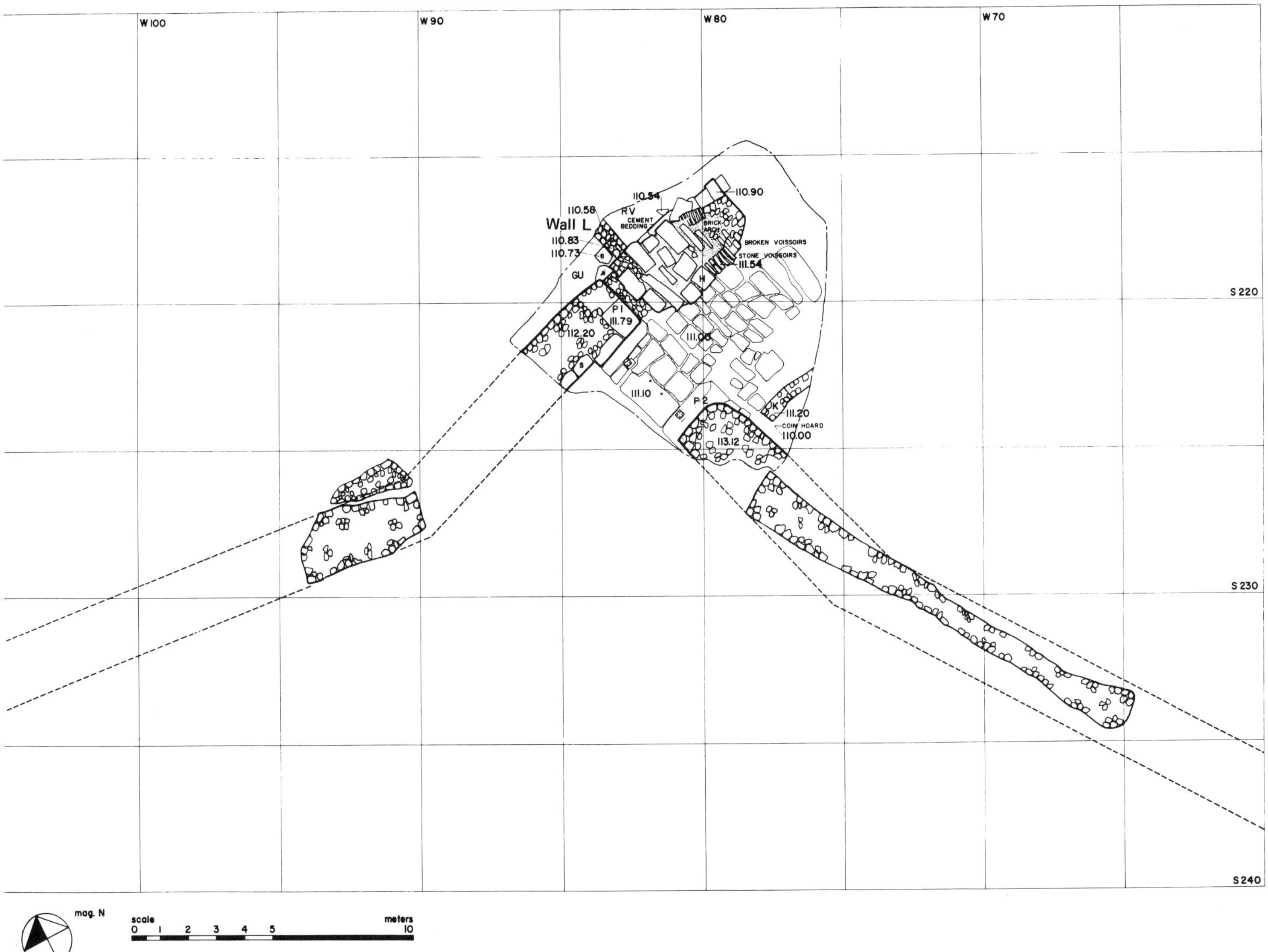

Fig. 43 Plan as excavated.

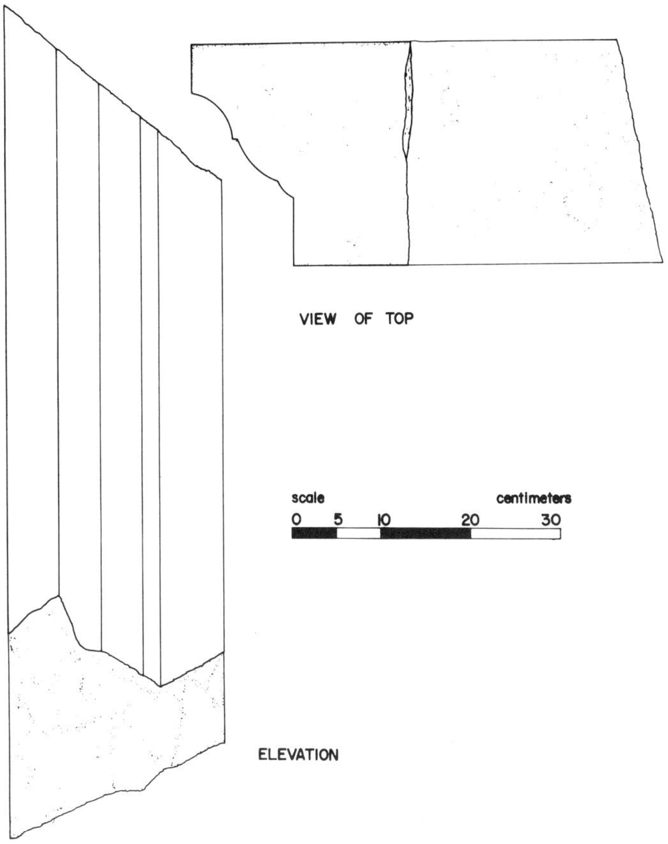

Fig. 44 Reused spoils and door jamb.

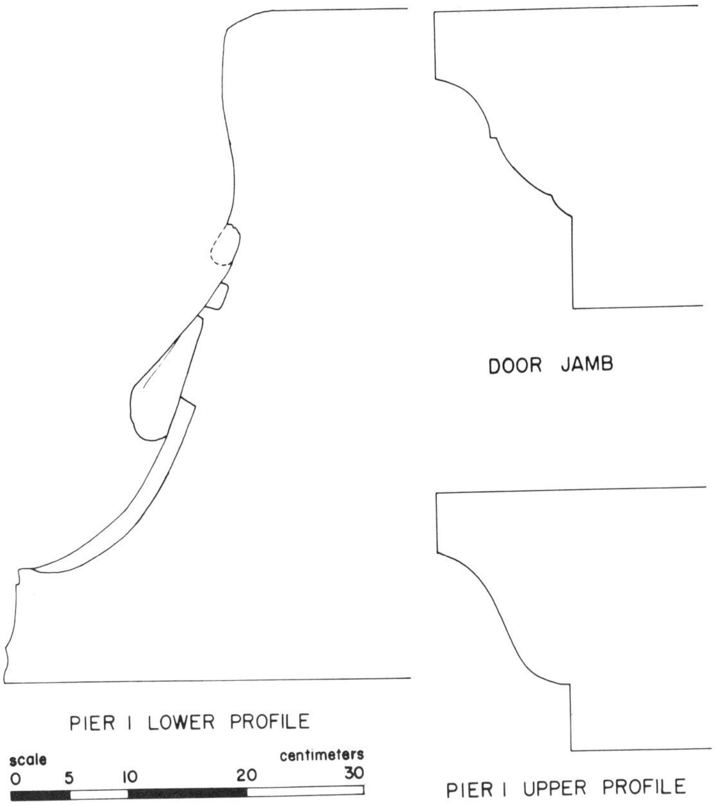

Fig. 45 Profiles of reused spoils.

The Southwest Gate

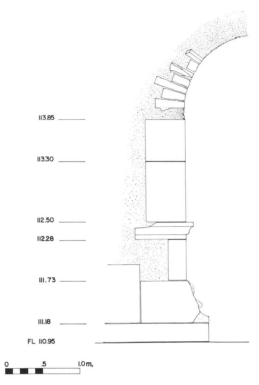

Fig. 46 Tentative reconstruction of pier 1 and side passage, looking NW.

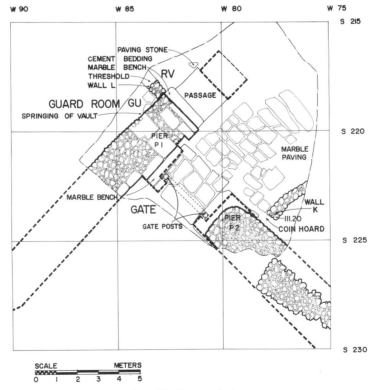

Fig. 47 Restored plan.

The Southwest Gate

Fig. 48   Aerial view.

Fig. 49   Marble pavement and shield relief (left center), looking W.

The Southwest Gate

Fig. 50   Cuttings for gateposts, looking N.

Fig. 52   Pilgrim flask, side 1
P70.33.

Fig. 53   Side 2, Fig. 52.

Fig. 51   Acanthus-cavetto marble block in pier 1.

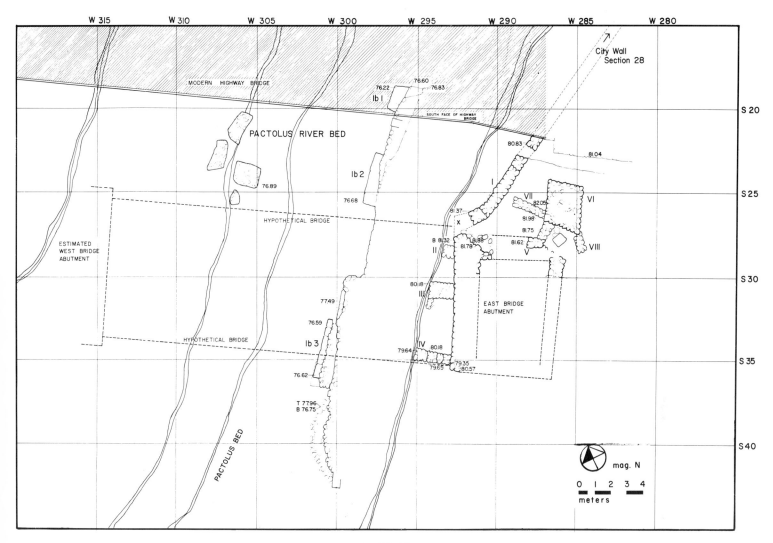

Fig. 54 Plan.

Fig. 55 View showing road, new bridge (foreground); walls I, V-VIII (left); cleavage x (center); E pier, walls BW II-IV (right).

Fig. 56 Section of wall south of bridge. From left: East Bridge Abutment and wall V on right; platform VI, wall VII pointing toward wall I.

Fig. 57 S face of S pier, looking NE; East Bridge Abutment with walls IV (with "window") and III in foreground.

The Pactolus Bridge

Fig. 58 Overall view from riverbed with wall *lb 3* with large spoil and E pier structures of ancient bridge in background.

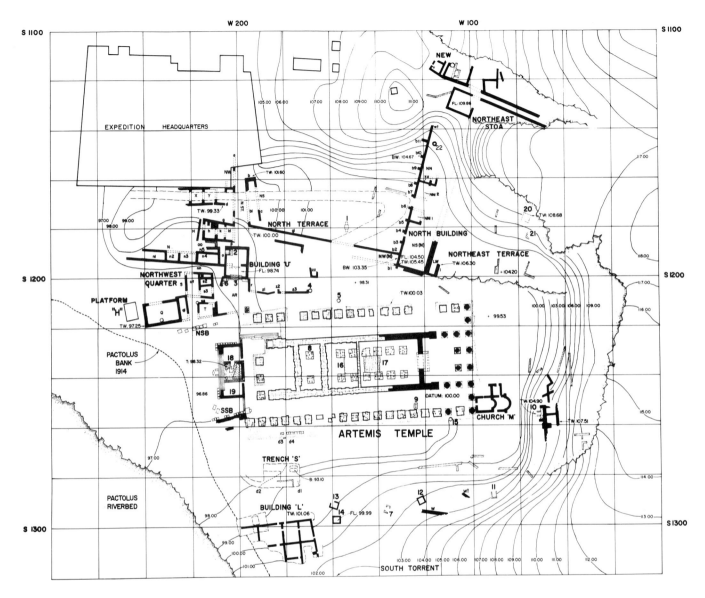

Fig. 59 Plan.

1.	Lydian Lion-Eagle Monument	16.	Concrete Base
2.	Vaulted Tomb	17.	Sandstone Base
3.	Marble Steps, Building U	18.	Building LA, Lydian Altar
4,5.	Terracotta Wells	19.	Perimeter Structure
6.	Stelai	20,21.	Bases
7.	Sarcophagus	22.	Well
8.	Mortgage Inscription on Wall		Hatched walls existed in 1914, since removed
9.	Two Small Columns		
10.	Exedra Monument		Levels based on datum 100.00
11–14.	Vaulted Tombs		(138.38 a.s.l.)
15.	Terracotta Well		

Fig. 60   View from across the Pactolus.

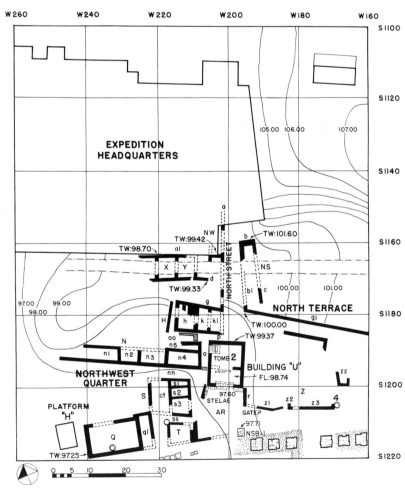

Fig. 61   Plan of Northwest Quarter.

Fig. 62   North Street, looking N. Unit NW on left, Unit NS on right.

Fig. 63   View of Building U with North Street in background. Looking N from Altar LA 1.

Fig. 64   North Building. Looking S along wall *wt*.

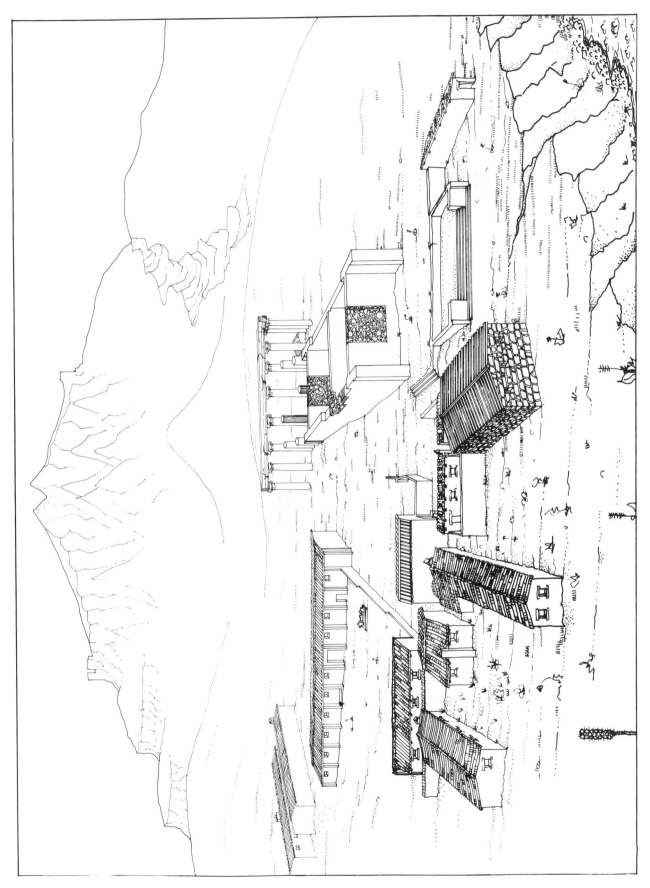

Fig. 65   Reconstruction of the Byzantine buildings.

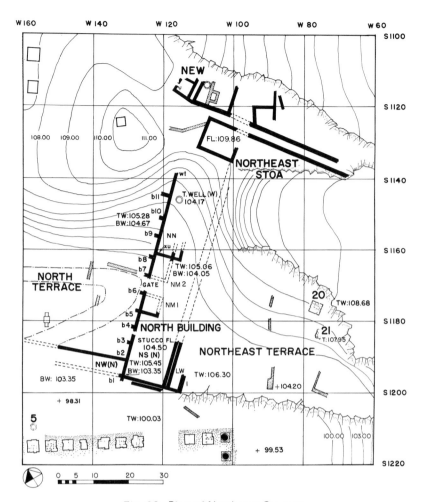

Fig. 66   Plan of Northeast Quarter.

Fig. 67   Unit N and NSB alignment, looking NE toward Building U, North and Northeast Terraces.

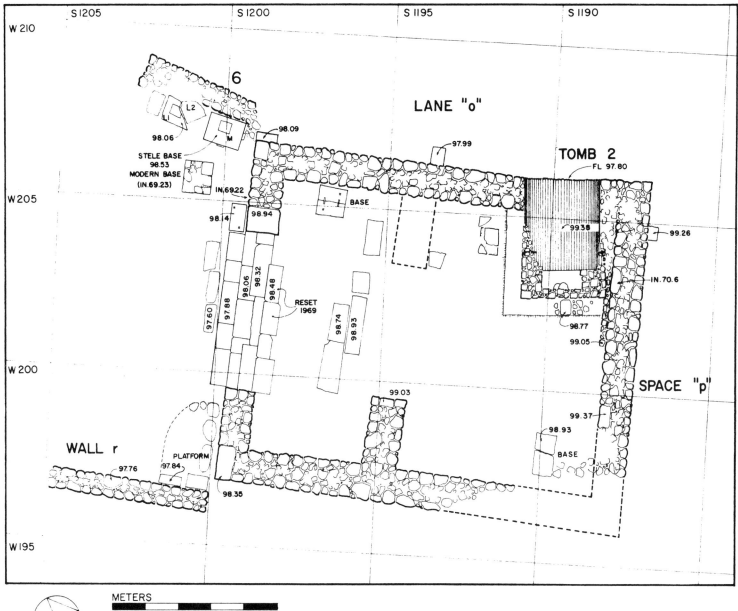

Fig. 68   Plan of condition in 1970.

Building U

Fig. 69   Axial view, looking N.

Fig. 70   Close-up of block from N wall with inscription   IN70.6.

Fig. 71   S wall with inscription   IN69.22.

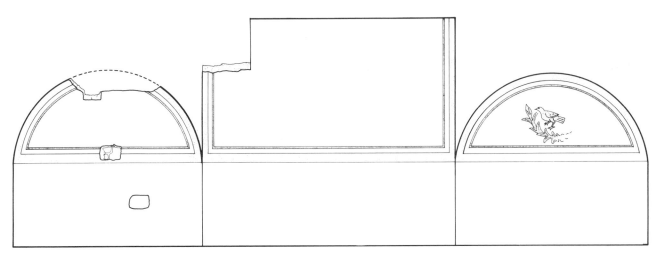

INTERIOR: PAINTING OF EAST, SOUTH, AND WEST WALLS

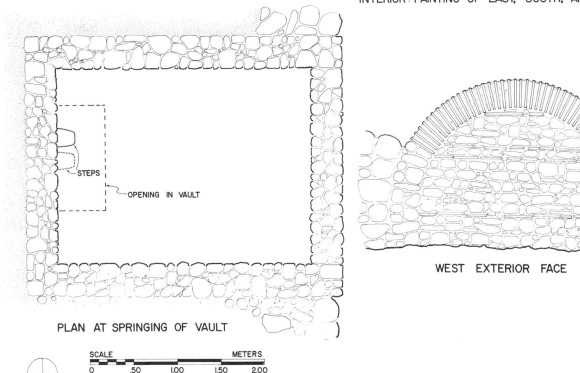

STEPS

OPENING IN VAULT

PLAN AT SPRINGING OF VAULT

WEST EXTERIOR FACE

SCALE   METERS
0   .50   1.00   1.50   2.00

Fig. 72   Tomb 2. Plan, interior reconstruction, exterior elevation.

Building U

Fig. 73   View of tomb 2, looking N.

Fig. 74   Tomb 2 interior.

Fig. 75   Timarchos stele on base No. 6, S of Building U

Fig. 76   Building Q, looking NE.

Fig. 77   North Terrace, Northeast Terrace, and North Building, looking NE to E.

North Building

Fig. 78   View including wall *wt* and Lion Monument base on North Terrace, looking SE.

Fig. 79   Buttresses along wall *wt,* "break" (center right), and "gate" (far left), looking NE.

North Building

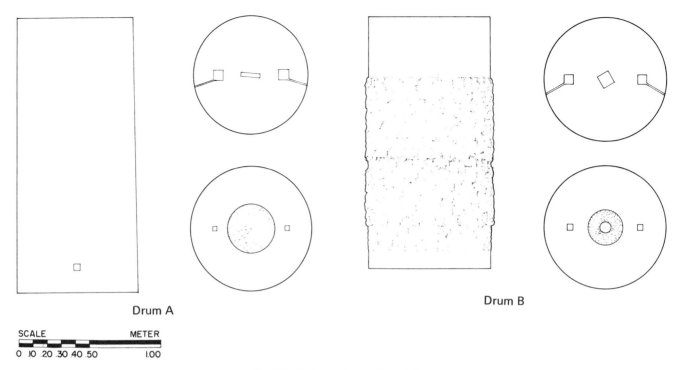

Drum A

Drum B

SCALE METER

0 .10 .20 .30 40 .50 1.00

Fig. 80 Column drums A and B.

Fig. 81 Underside of pediment.

PLAN OF BOTTOM

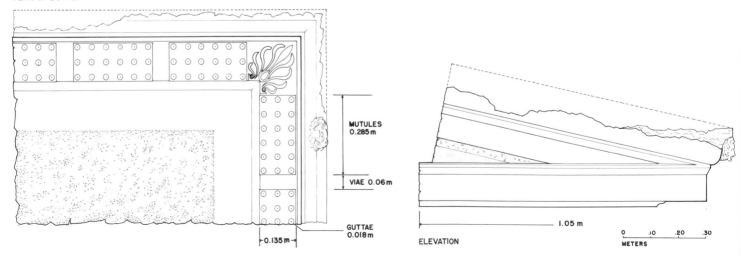

MUTULES
0.285 m

VIAE 0.06 m

GUTTAE
0.018 m

0.135 m

1.05 m

ELEVATION

0 .10 .20 .30

METERS

Fig. 82 Pediment fragment.

Fig. 83   North Building, looking W. Stucco on W wall of Unit NS.

Fig. 84   NE corner of Northeast Terrace, looking N. Stratification of gravel in scarp.

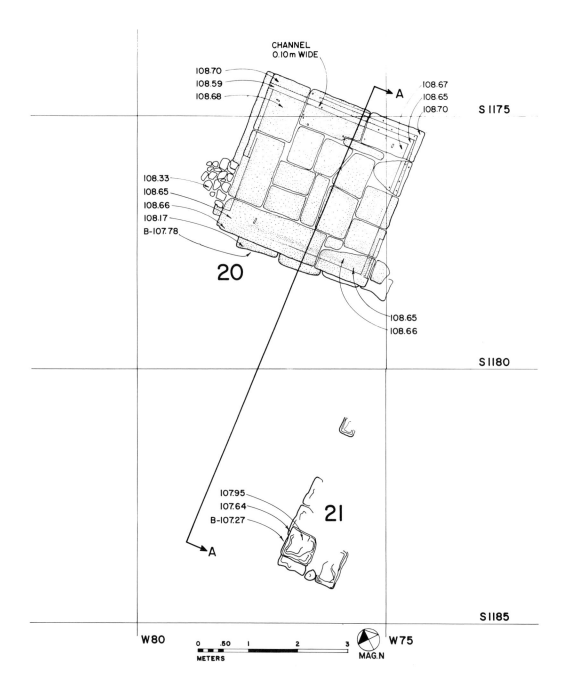

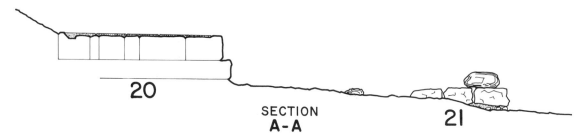

Fig. 85   Northeast Terrace. Plan and section of Monuments 20 and 21.

Fig. 86   Monuments 20 and 21, looking N.

Fig. 87   Top of Monument 20, looking S.

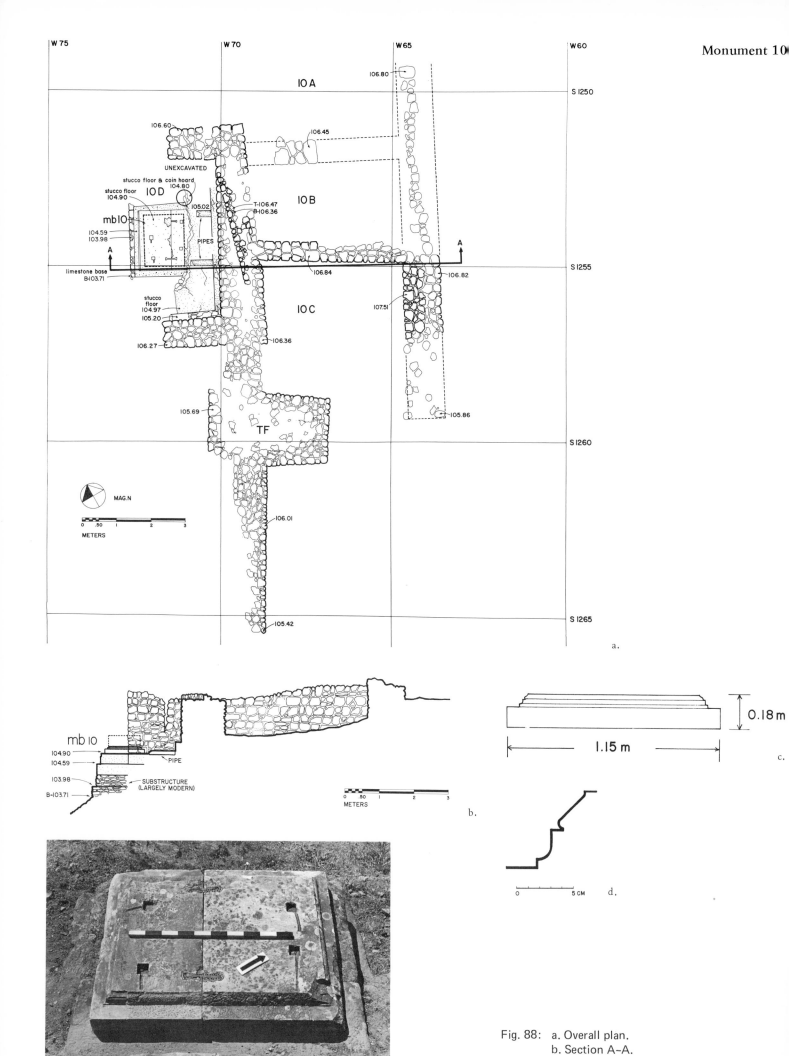

W 75 W 70 W 65 W 60

10 A

106.80

S 1250

106.60

106.45

UNEXCAVATED

stucco floor & coin hoard
104.80
stucco floor
104.90   10 D
105.02

mb 10

104.59
103.98

T-106.47
B-106.36

10 B

A

PIPES

A

limestone base
B-103.71

106.84

106.82

S 1255

stucco
floor
104.97
105.20

10 C

107.51

106.27

106.36

106.80

MAG. N

0 .50 1 2 3
METERS

105.69

TF

106.01

S 1260

105.86

S 1265

105.42

a.

mb 10

104.90
104.59

103.98

B-103.71

PIPE

SUBSTRUCTURE
(LARGELY MODERN)

0 .50 1 2 3
METERS

b.

0.18 m

1.15 m

c.

0   5 CM   d.

Fig. 88: a. Overall plan.
b. Section A–A.
c. Elevation of restored monument.
d. Profile of restored monument.
e. Restored monument, looking E.

e.

Monument 10

Fig. 89   Exedra 10 D and base, looking E.

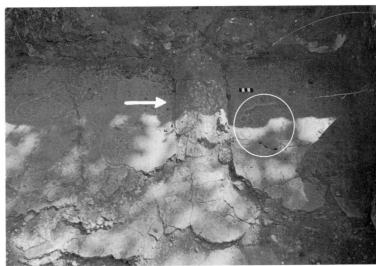

Fig. 90   Exedra 10 D, looking E. Pipe and stucco floors with footprints.

Fig. 91   Base profile, looking NE.

Fig. 92   Fragment of red, Hellenistic relief ware bowl   P69.94.

Fig. 93   Base block with cuttings.

Fig. 94   Base block with cuttings. Adjoins block, Fig. 93.

Fig. 95 South side of precinct. General view from Necropolis.

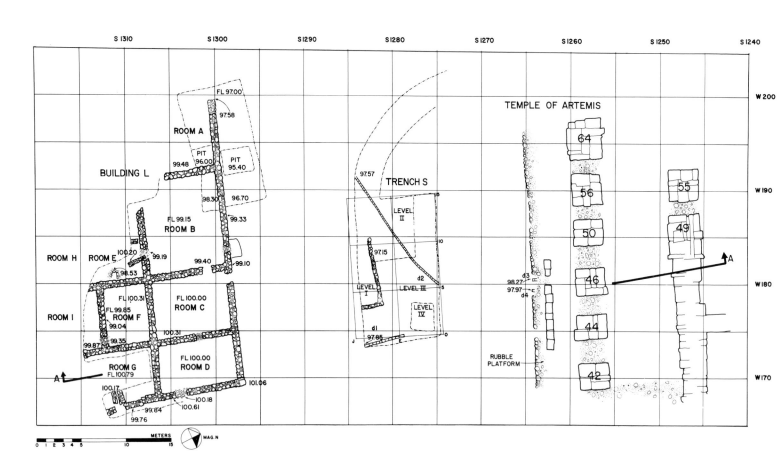

S 1310   S 1300   S 1290   S 1280   S 1270   S 1260   S 1250   S 1240

W 200

W 190

W 180

W 170

TEMPLE OF ARTEMIS

FL 97.00

97.58

ROOM A

PIT 96.00   PIT 95.40

99.48

98.30   96.70

FL 99.15

ROOM B

99.33

BUILDING L

99.19

ROOM H   ROOM E

100.20

98.53

99.40   99.10

FL 100.31

ROOM I

FL 99.85

ROOM F

99.04

FL 100.00

ROOM C

99.87   99.35

100.31

ROOM G

FL 100.79

FL 100.00

ROOM D

100.17

101.06

100.18

99.84   100.61

99.76

97.57

TRENCH S

LEVEL II

97.15

LEVEL I   LEVEL III

LEVEL IV

d1

97.85

97.72

RUBBLE PLATFORM

98.27

97.97

64

56

50

46

44

42

55

49

A

METERS
0 1 2 3 4 5   10   15   MAG. N

ROOM G   ROOM D   SECTION A-A

BUILDING L

97.72

96.20

95.50

93.10

TRENCH S

TEMPLE OF ARTEMIS

100.00

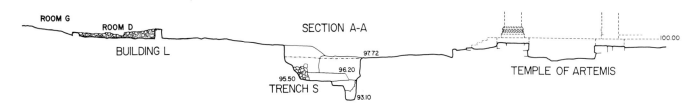

Fig. 96 Plan of Trench S and Building L in relation to SE corner of temple.

Fig. 97   Rubble platform along south side of temple, looking N.

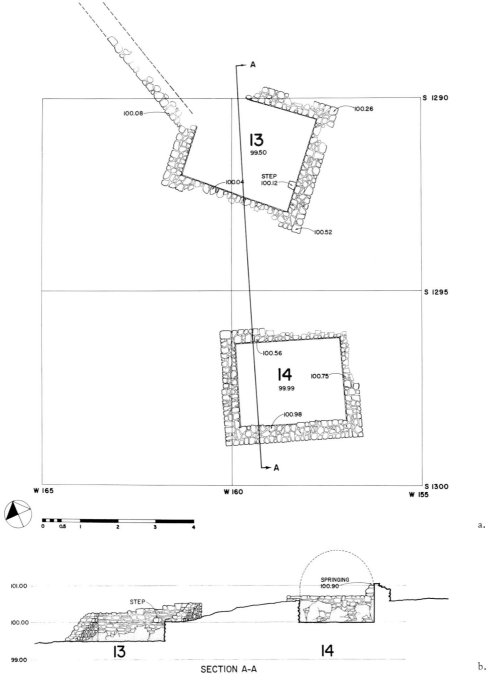

Fig. 98   Plan and section of Tombs 13 and 14.

Fig. 99 Tomb 13. View into tomb including wall, looking SE.

Fig. 100 Tomb 14. General view looking W with Building L in background.

Fig. 101 Lydian sarcophagus.

Fig. 102   Overall view of N stelai bases with Building Q, looking N.

Fig. 103   Overall view of LA with stelai bases 1-26 and N perimeter wall.

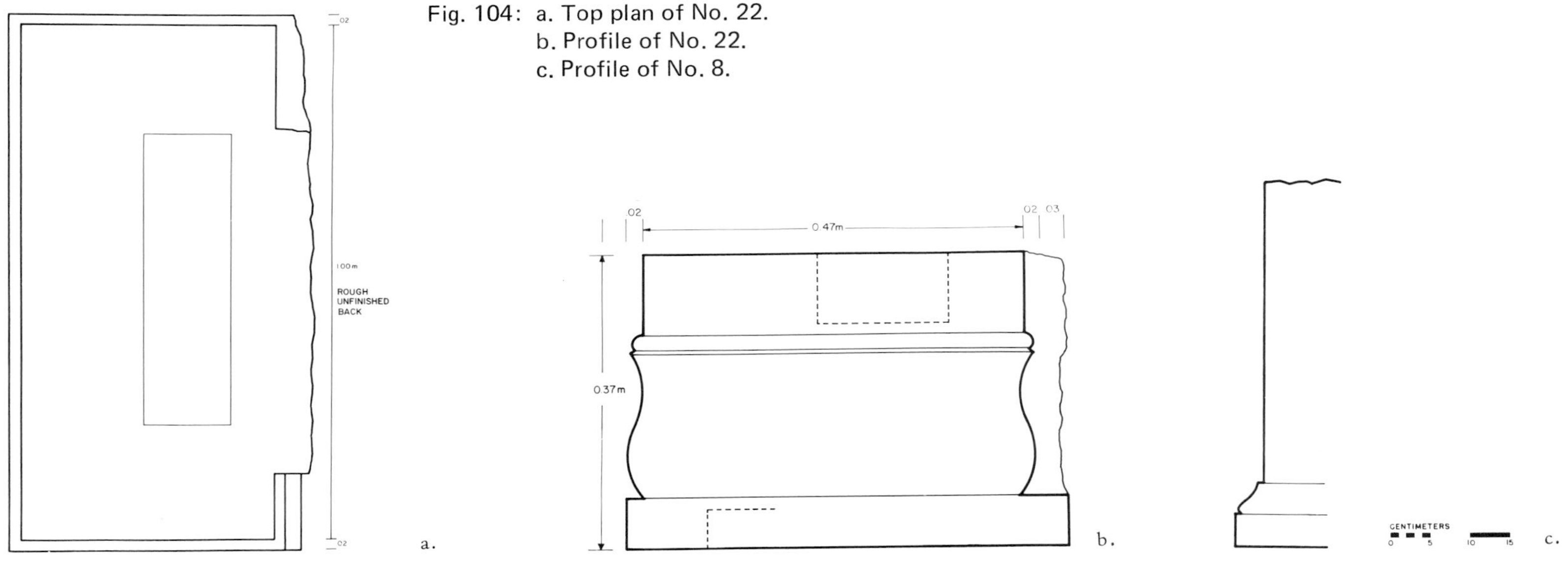

Stelai Bases

Fig. 104: a. Top plan of No. 22.
b. Profile of No. 22.
c. Profile of No. 8.

Fig. 106   Nos. 8–11A, looking E.

Fig. 105   Nos. 7–9A, looking NW.

Fig. 108　No. 22. Looking SE, showing cuttings.

Fig. 110　Nos. 25 and 26 after resetting, looking SE.

Fig. 107　Nos. 16–24. Along N perimeter wall of LA, looking S.

Fig. 109　No. 25 with inscription　IN69.25.

Stelai Bases

Fig. 111   No. 27, T 1 and T 2.

Fig. 112   Nos. 28-31. S end of W perimeter wall of LA, looking NE.

Fig. 113   Alignment of bases and *rb 1,* looking E.

Fig. 114   Nos. 34-44, looking SW.

Fig. 115   Roman coin of ca. A.D. 270-290   C70.3a.

Fig. 116   Reverse of coin, Fig. 115.

Fig. 117 Artemis Temple. Pier 64 with adjoining area, looking S and down.

Fig. 118 Stelai bases 36–39, looking SW.

Fig. 119 Stelai bases 40–42, looking S.

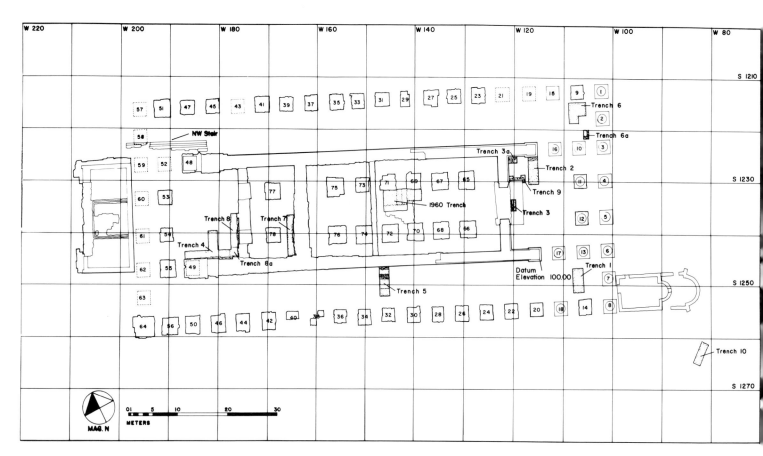

Fig. 120   Plan showing 1972 exploratory trenches and numbering of columns.

Fig. 121   Columns 11 and 12 on pedestals. After *Sardis* II (1925) ill. 38.

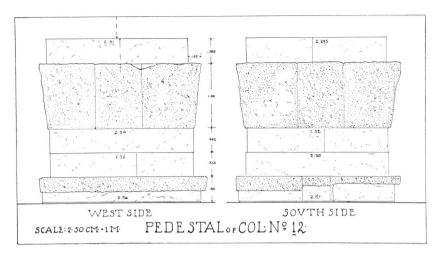

Fig. 122   Pedestal of column 12. After *Sardis* II (1925) ill. 39.

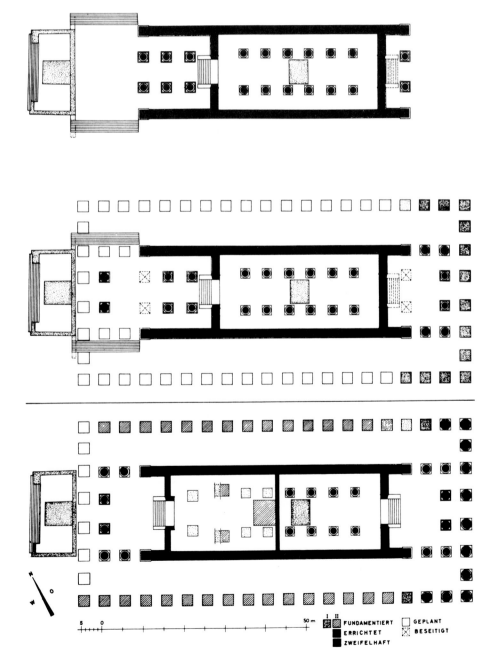

Fig. 123   Reconstructed plans of three building periods: ca. 300 B.C.; early second century; Roman. After Gruben, *AthMitt* 76 (1961) Taf. V.

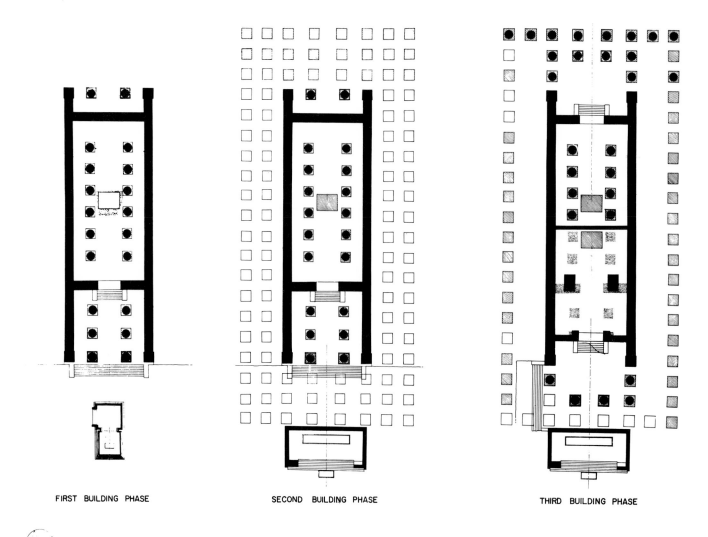

FIRST BUILDING PHASE   SECOND BUILDING PHASE   THIRD BUILDING PHASE

MAG. N.   SCALE   METERS   0   10   20

Fig. 124 Hypothetical reconstruction of plans of three building phases: archaic, Hellenistic, and Roman, by K. J. Frazer.

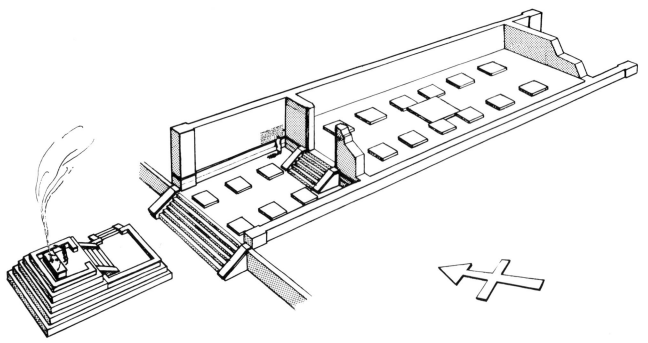

Fig. 125 Hypothetical perspective of archaic and first Hellenistic building phases by K. J. Frazer.

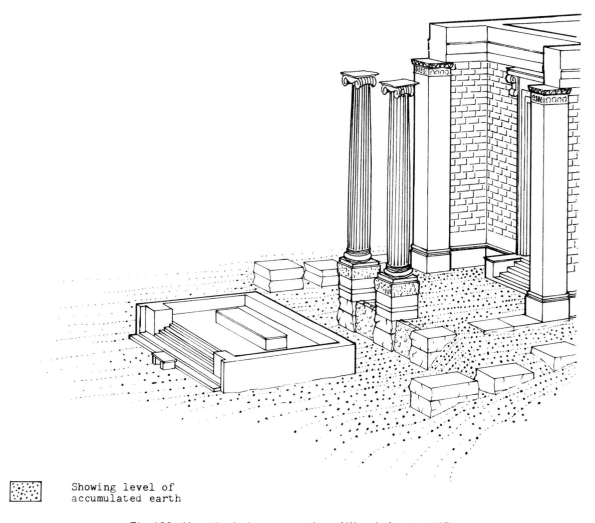

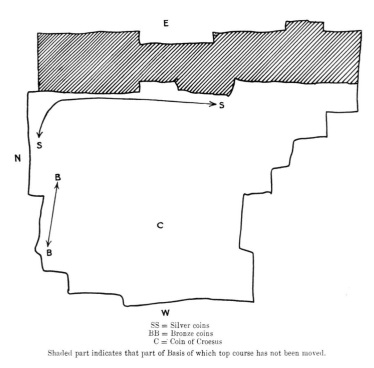

Showing level of
accumulated earth

Fig. 126 Hypothetical reconstruction of W end after A.D. 17.

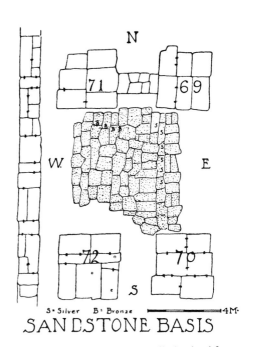

S = Silver   B = Bronze ▬▬▬▬▬▬4 M·

SANDSTONE BASIS

Fig. 127 Plan of east cella basis. After
Sardis I (1922) ill. 71.

SS = Silver coins
BB = Bronze coins
C = Coin of Croesus

Shaded part indicates that part of Basis of which top course has not been moved.

Fig. 128 Schematic plan of image base with findspots of coins. After
Sardis XI (1916) v.

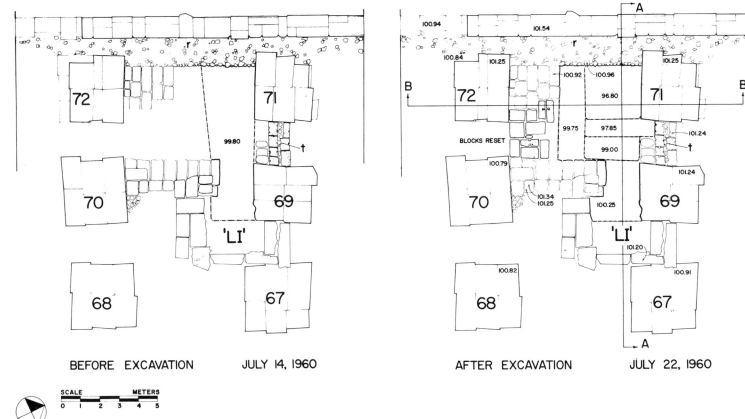

BEFORE EXCAVATION   JULY 14, 1960   AFTER EXCAVATION   JULY 22, 1960

SCALE   METERS
0   1   2   3   4   5

Fig. 129   Plan of east cella basis. Sounding, 1960.

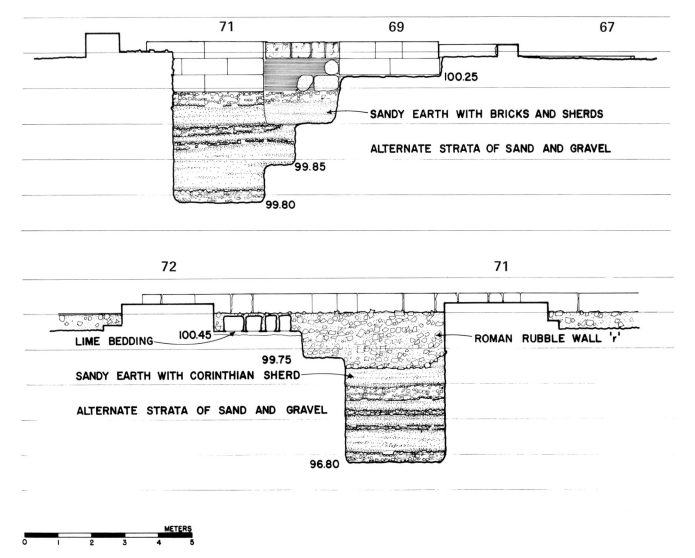

METERS
0   1   2   3   4   5

Fig. 130   East cella basis. Sections of sounding, 1960.

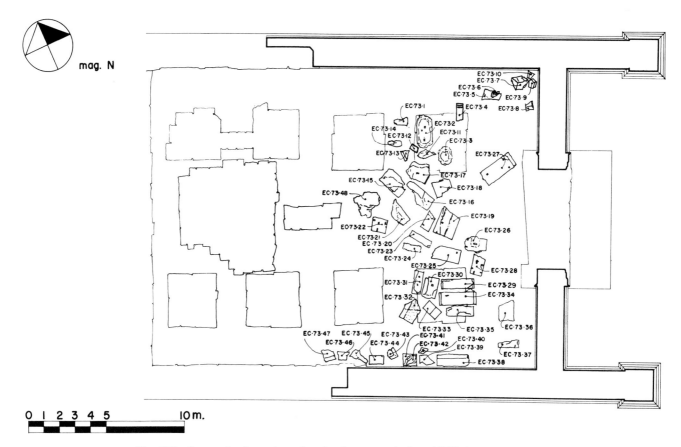

mag. N

0 1 2 3 4 5   10 m.

Fig. 131   East cella. Location of major fragments before 1973 cleanup.

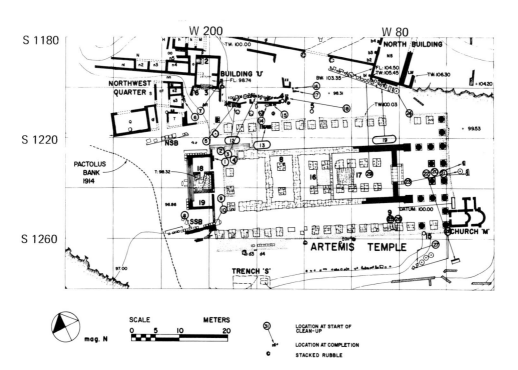

mag. N

SCALE   METERS
0   5   10   20

LOCATION AT START OF CLEAN-UP

LOCATION AT COMPLETION

STACKED RUBBLE

Fig. 132   Artemis Precinct. Location of major fragments after 1973 cleanup.

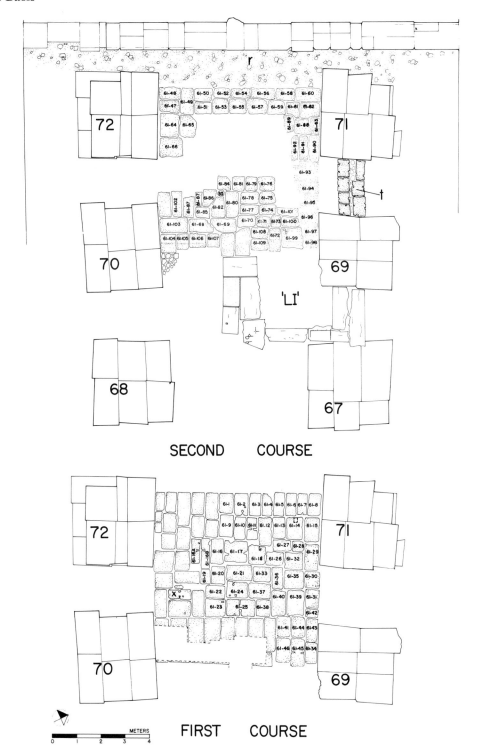

SECOND COURSE

FIRST COURSE

Fig. 133 Location of masonry blocks, 1961.

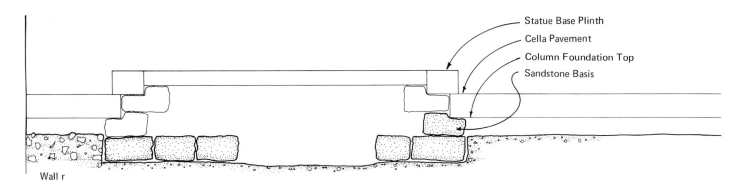

Statue Base Plinth

Cella Pavement

Column Foundation Top

Sandstone Basis

Wall r

Fig. 134 Reconstructed section.

Fig. 135 Overall view looking E.

Fig. 136 Stones showing cuttings, looking N.

Fig. 137 Stone 61.51, large trimming tool marks.

Fig. 138 Stone 61.51, lighter chisel marks.

Fig. 139 Stones showing clamp holes, trimming, and finishing, looking N.

The East Cella Basis

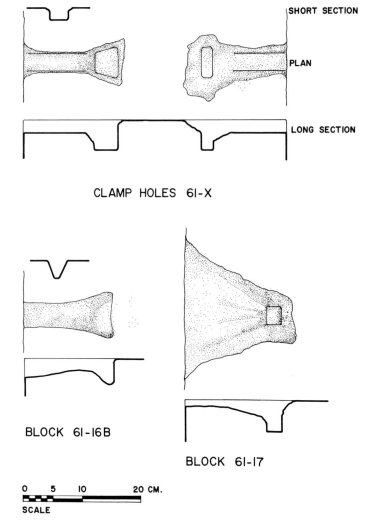

CLAMP HOLES 61-X

BLOCK 61-16B

BLOCK 61-17

0 5 10 20 CM.

SCALE

Fig. 140 Clamping details.

Fig. 141 Stone 61.16A and 61.16B seen from above, detail of clamp holes.

Fig. 142 Stone 61.11 seen from above, clamp holes.

Fig. 143   Cella cross wall with cemented rubble on either side, looking S.

Fig. 144   Overall view of cella looking W, showing edge of base.

Fig. 145   View looking W, showing stratified trench in east cella.

Fig. 146   Fragment of colossus of Antoninus Pius.   S61.27:15.

Fig. 147   Profile, Fig. 146.

Fig. 148   Fragment of colossal Zeus.   S61.27:14.

Fig. 149   Lydian black on red bowl rim sherd   P60.102.

Fig. 150   Lydian cup base P60.112.

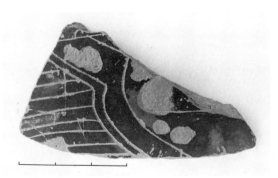

Fig. 151   "Corinthianizing" sherd   P60.114.

Fig. 152   Spindle whorl T60.6.

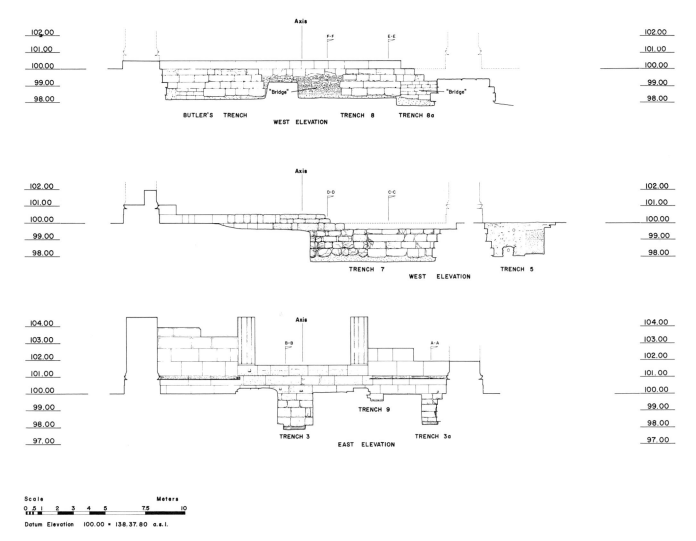

Fig. 153   Elevations of 1972 trenches.

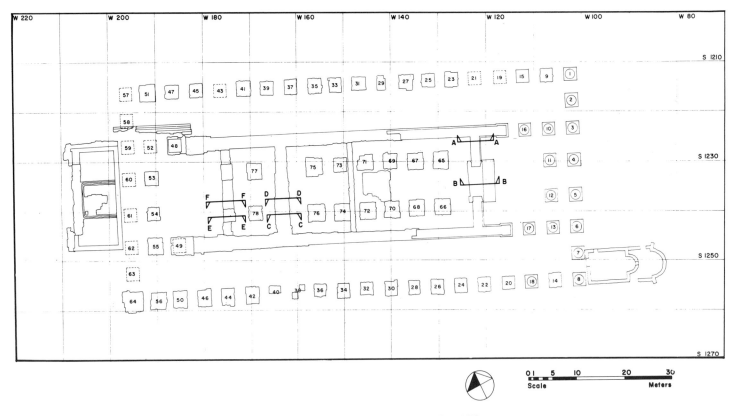

Fig. 154   Key plan to elevations, Fig. 153.

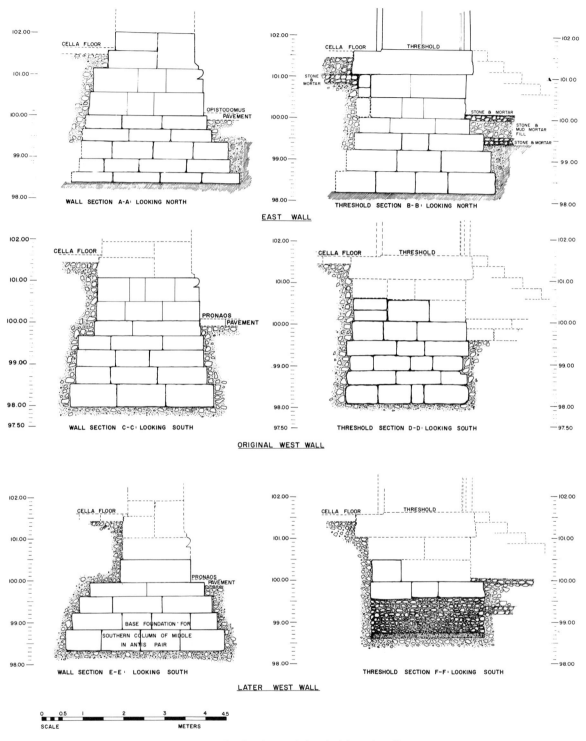

Fig. 155 Sections of thresholds and walls.

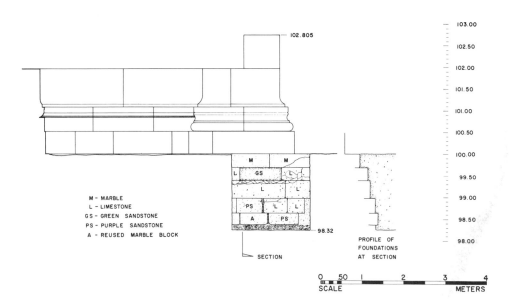

M – MARBLE
L – LIMESTONE
GS – GREEN SANDSTONE
PS – PURPLE SANDSTONE
A – REUSED MARBLE BLOCK

PROFILE OF
FOUNDATIONS
AT SECTION

SECTION

SCALE   METERS

Fig. 156   Trench 2 section.

Fig. 157   Trench 1, looking N.

Fig. 158 Trenches 2, 3a, and 9, looking NNW.

Trench 2

Fig. 159 Overall view looking N.

Fig. 160 Block with inscribed Κα.

Fig. 161 Detail of Fig. 160.

Capital "H"

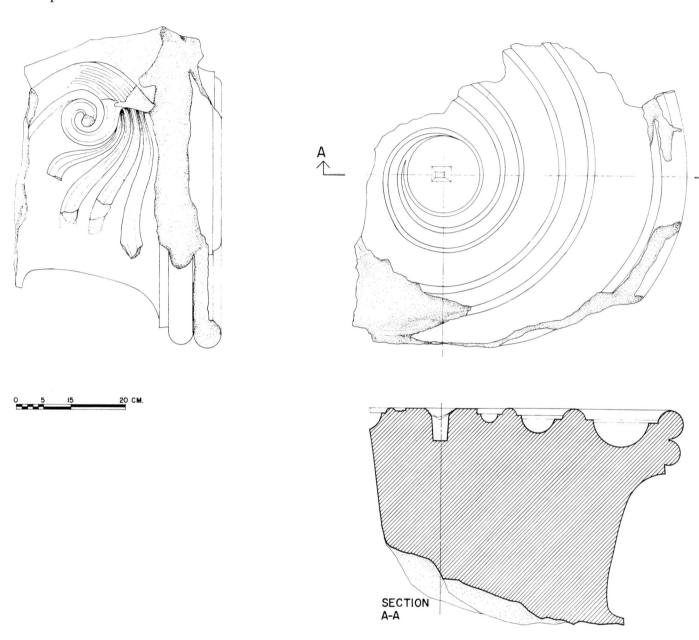

Fig. 162 Drawing of fragments.

SECTION
A-A

Fig. 163 Front view with volute.

Fig. 164 Back view with palmette.

Fig. 165   Trench 3. E door foundations, looking down and W.

Trench 3a

Fig. 166   S foundations of NE anta, looking N.

Fig. 167   Dressed stone in euthynteria course, looking NNE.

Fig. 168   Dressed stone in course below euthynteria, looking NNE.

Trench 5

Fig. 169   Overall view looking N.

Fig. 170   Early pipe exposed, looking down and E.

Fig. 171   Detail of pipe, Fig. 170, before removal, looking S and down.

Fig. 172   Trench 6, looking NE.

Fig. 173   Trench 7, looking NE.

Fig. 174   Trench 8, looking SE.

Fig. 175   Trench 9, looking S.

Fig. 176   Terracotta antefix from Trench 2   T72.1.

Fig. 177   Lead plumb bob from Trench 3
M72.1.

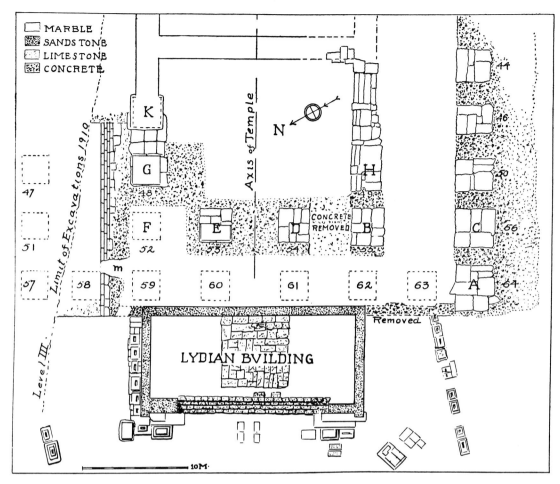

Fig. 178   Plan of "Lydian Building" and foundations. After *Sardis* II (1925) ill. 95.

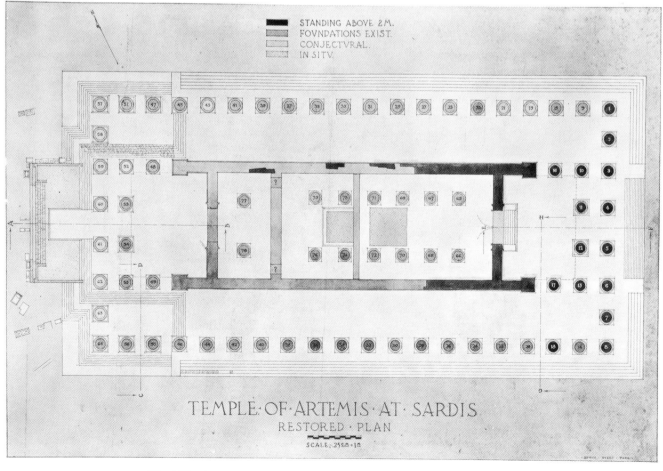

Fig. 179   Restored plan of Artemis Temple. After *Sardis* II (1925) pl. A.

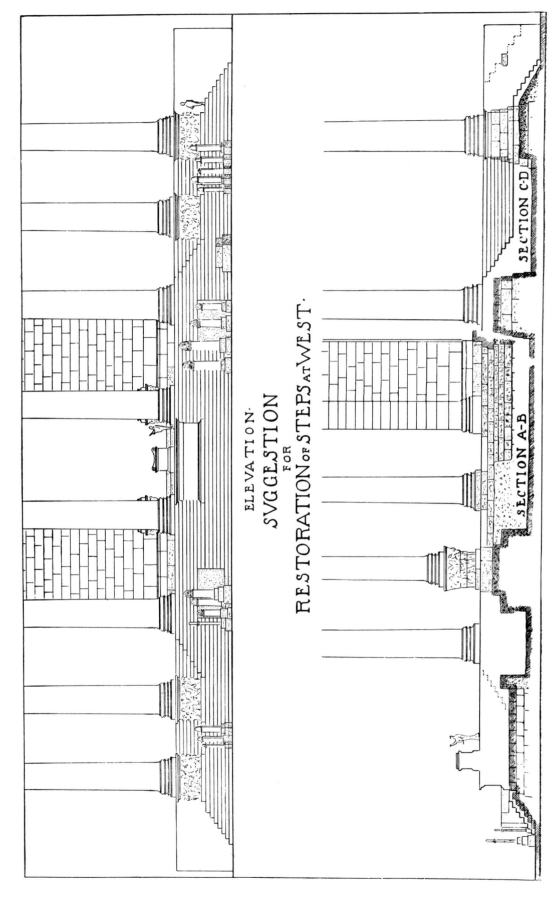

ELEVATION·
SVGGESTION
FOR
RESTORATION OF STEPS AT WEST·

SECTION C-D

SECTION A-B

Fig. 180 Elevation and section of W end of temple. After *Sardis* II (1925) ill. 97.

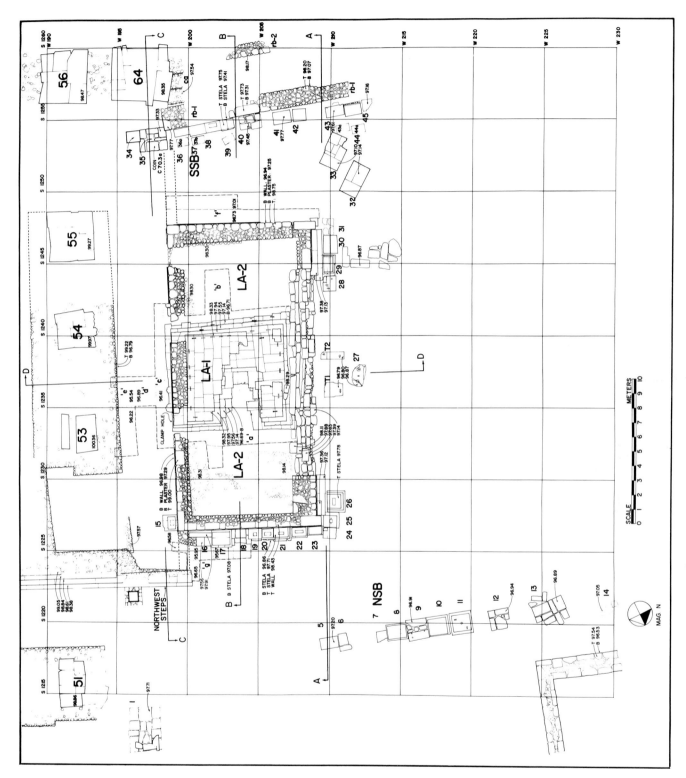

Fig. 181 Plan of the LA complex and adjacent monuments. Condition in 1970.

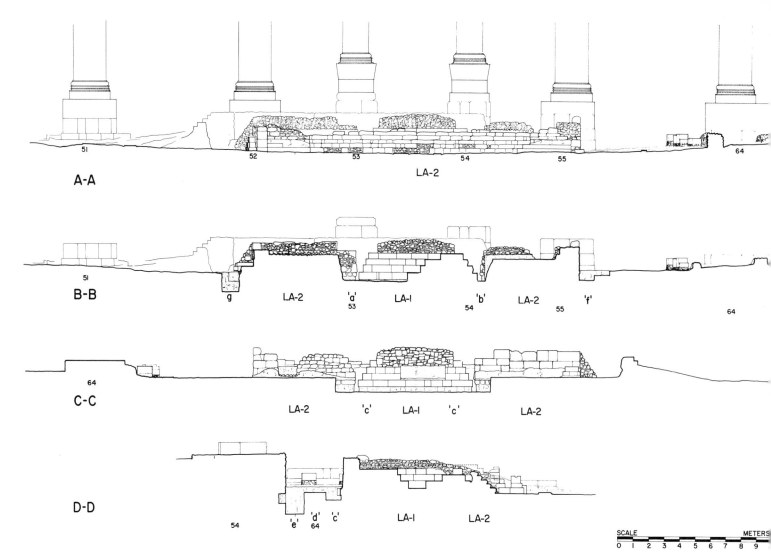

A-A

51 52 53 54 55 64

LA-2

B-B

51 g 53 54 55 64

LA-2 'a' LA-I 'b' LA-2 'f'

C-C

64

LA-2 'c' LA-I 'c' LA-2

D-D

54 'e' 'd' 'c' 64

LA-I LA-2

SCALE METERS
0 1 2 3 4 5 6 7 8 9

Fig. 182   Sections of LA and adjacent monuments. Condition in 1970.

Fig. 183   Overall view looking S.

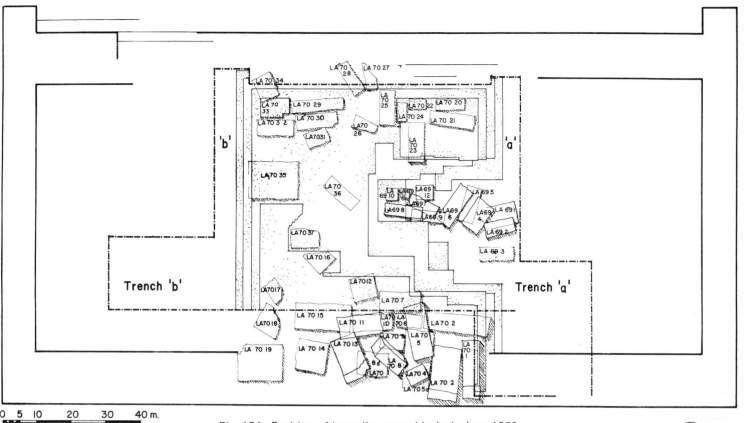

Fig. 184   Position of loose limestone blocks in June 1970.

SCALE
0 5 10   20   30   40 m.

Fig. 185   The W steps, looking N. Pavement block at upper right.

Fig. 186   Overall view looking WSW.

Fig. 187   E face of E perimeter wall, looking W.

Fig. 188   E face of E perimeter wall with projecting stone and coursing above.

Fig. 189   S breakthrough in E perimeter wall.

Fig. 190   E trench of E perimeter wall, looking WSW.

Fig. 191   S trench at S perimeter wall.

Fig. 192   Nozzle fragment of Lydian lamp
L69.10.

Fig. 193   Lydian red on white plate fragment with graffito   P69.77 (IN69.27).

Fig. 194   Lydian black on red ring foot
fragment   P69.79.

Fig. 195   Base of Lydian plain ware pot
P69.81.

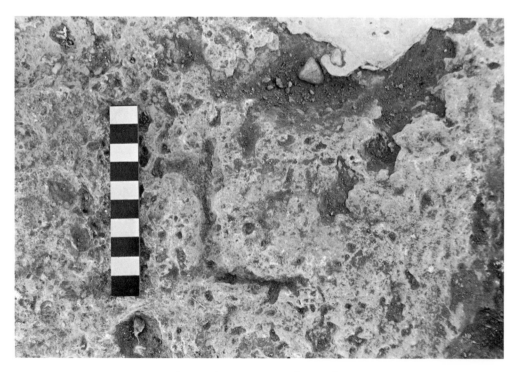

Fig. 196   Detail of setting mark.

Fig. 197   S breakthrough in E perimeter wall, looking NW.

Fig. 198   N breakthrough in E perimeter wall, looking W.

Fig. 199   E perimeter wall from above, projecting stone with groove.

Fig. 202 Close-up of S breakthrough in E perimeter wall, looking N.

Fig. 200 N breakthrough in E perimeter wall, looking SW.

Fig. 201 Platform showing wavy laying of stones, looking N.

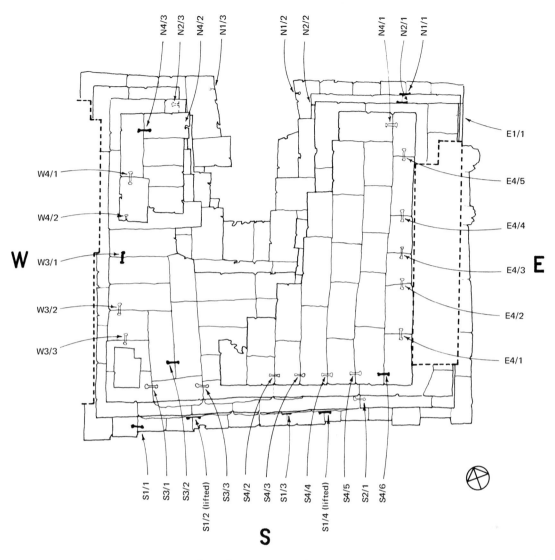

N

W

E

S

N4/3 N2/3 N4/2 N1/3   N1/2 N2/2   N4/1 N2/1 N1/1

E1/1

E4/5

E4/4

E4/3

E4/2

E4/1

W4/1

W4/2

W3/1

W3/2

W3/3

S1/1 S3/1 S3/2 S1/2 (lifted) S3/3 S4/2 S4/3 S1/3 S4/4 S1/4 (lifted) S4/5 S2/1 S4/6

Fig. 203   Plan of clamp designations.

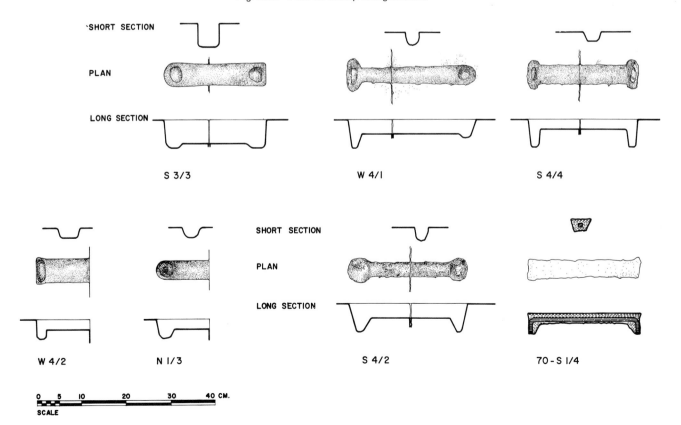

SHORT SECTION

PLAN

LONG SECTION

S 3/3

W 4/1

S 4/4

SHORT SECTION

PLAN

LONG SECTION

W 4/2

N 1/3

S 4/2

70-S 1/4

0   5   10   20   30   40 CM.

SCALE

Fig. 204   Clamping details

Fig. 205   Clamp *in situ.*

Fig. 206   Clamp at S steps of LA 1.

Fig. 207   Clamp hole.

Fig. 208   Marble fragment with egg and dart   S69.13.

Fig. 209   Marble fragment with lotus-palmette   S69.12.

Fig. 210   Archaic limestone fragment with egg and dart   AT/H 73.1.

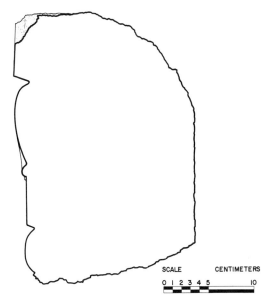

Fig. 211   Section, Fig. 210.

Fig. 213   NW corner of W side, looking SW.

Fig. 212   E perimeter wall, looking W.

Fig. 214   Section through plaster levels in E face, LA 2, detail looking N.

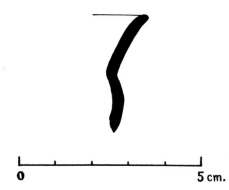

Fig. 215   Sherds from LA excavation.

Fig. 216   Profile of Achaemenid-Ionian bowl fragment, Fig. 215b.

Fig. 217   Ionian cup fragment   P70.29.

Fig. 218   Sherds associated with LA 2.

Fig. 219 Overall view of trench showing stratification and relation to temple.

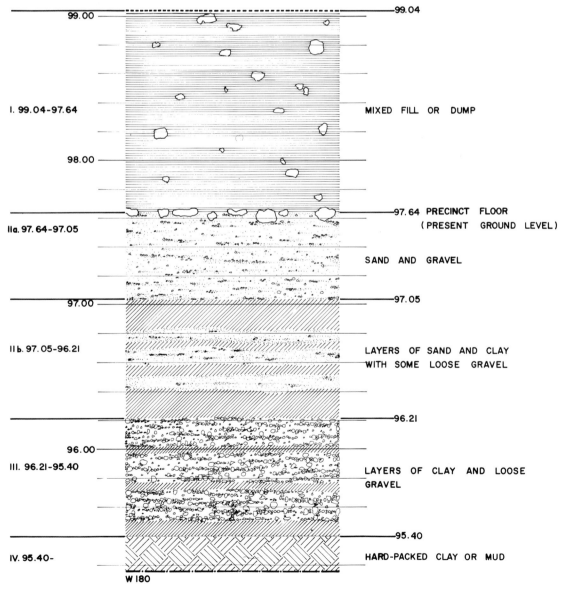

Fig. 220 Schematic section of N face.

Trench S

Level I

Fig. 221   Large Byzantine pipe in SE corner.

Fig. 222   Small Byzantine pipe.

Fig. 223   Detail of small Byzantine pipe showing joints.

Fig. 224

Fig. 225

Fig. 226

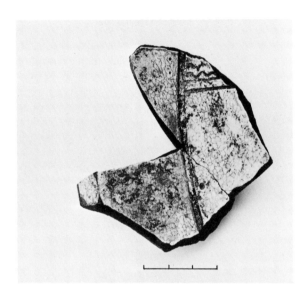

Fig. 227

Fig. 228

Fig. 229

Fig. 230

Level I Finds:

Fig. 224 Imitation of Roman coin ca. A.D. 270–295 C58.1.

Fig. 225 Reverse, Fig. 224.

Fig. 226 Ring foot of Middle Byzantine bowl P58.35.

Fig. 227 Fragments of Middle Byzantine bowl   P58.36.

Fig. 228 Black-glazed Hellenistic mastos   P58.1 and P58.56.

Fig. 229 Fragment of black-glazed skyphos rim   P58.42.

Fig. 230 Lydian bichrome fragment   P58.60.

Trench S

Fig. 231　Patch of stones in level IIA and small Byzantine pipe in level I.

Fig. 232

Fig. 233

Fig. 234

Fig. 235

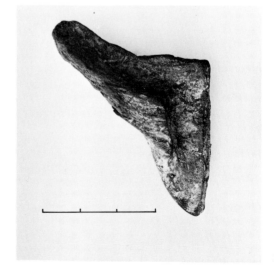

Fig. 236

Level IIA Finds:

Fig. 232　Fragment of Hellenistic relief ware
P58.87.

Fig. 233　Neck of Hellenistic black-glazed jug
P58.93.

Fig. 234　Shoulder fragment of jug with Lydian
graffito　　P58.110 (IN58.14).

Fig. 235　Nozzle and part of reservoir of Lydian lamp
L58.1.

Fig. 236　Nozzle fragment of Lydian lamp　　L58.2.

Trench S

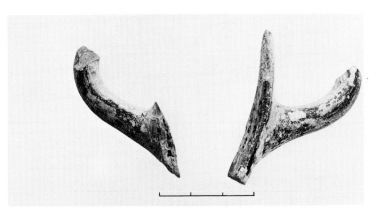

Fig. 237

Fig. 238

Fig. 239

Fig. 240

Fig. 241

Level IIB Finds:

Fig. 237　Fragments of Lydian cup handle　　P58.129.

Fig. 238　Protogeometric sherd　　P58.152.

Fig. 239　Ionian or Lydian Geometric cup fragment　　P58.104.

Fig. 240　Lydian lamp fragment　　L58.3.

Fig. 241　Stone sling bullet　　S58.1.

Trench S

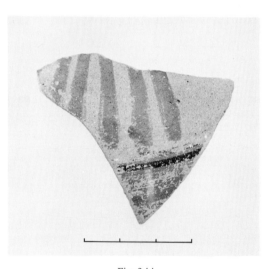

Fig. 242

Fig. 243

Fig. 244

Fig. 245

Level III Finds:

Fig. 242   Early Lydian sherd   P58.200.

Fig. 243   Fragment of Lydian juglet   P58.150A.

Fig. 244   Lydian vase fragment   P58.199.

Fig. 245   Lydian terracotta die   T58.5.

Fig. 246   Test pit showing level IV. Sterile clay in moist soil.

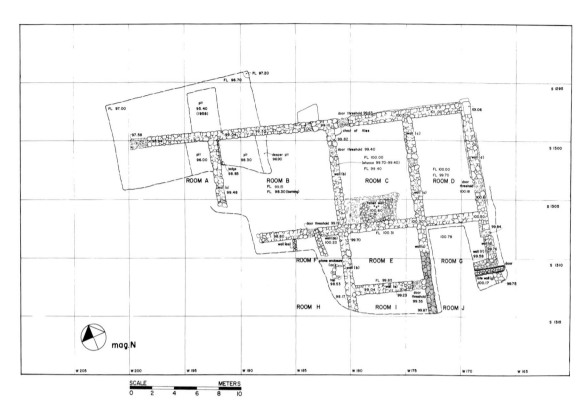

Fig. 247   Detailed plan.

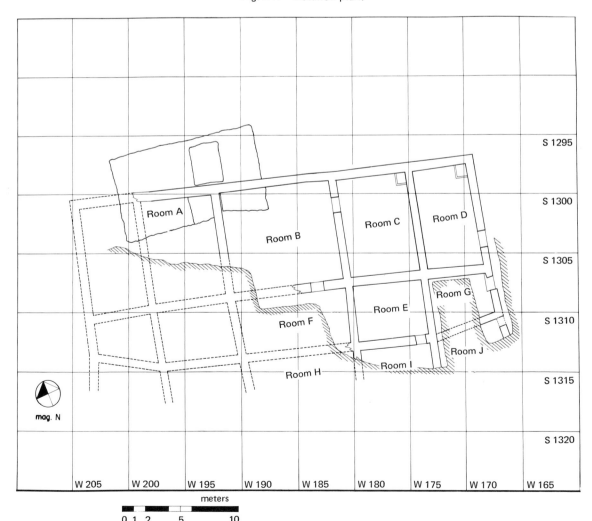

Fig. 248   Hypothetical restored plan.

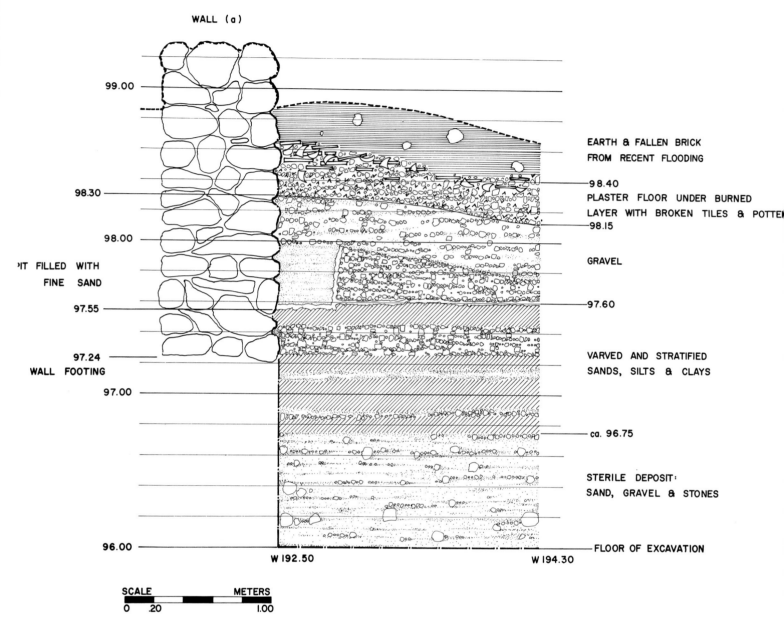

WALL (a)

99.00

98.30

98.00

PIT FILLED WITH
FINE SAND

97.55

97.24
WALL FOOTING

97.00

96.00

W 192.50   W 194.30

EARTH & FALLEN BRICK
FROM RECENT FLOODING

98.40
PLASTER FLOOR UNDER BURNED
LAYER WITH BROKEN TILES & POTTER
98.15

GRAVEL

97.60

VARVED AND STRATIFIED
SANDS, SILTS & CLAYS

ca. 96.75

STERILE DEPOSIT:
SAND, GRAVEL & STONES

FLOOR OF EXCAVATION

SCALE   METERS
0   .20   1.00

Fig. 249 Building L. Section of pit in Room A, S face.

Building L

Fig. 250

Fig. 251

Fig. 252

Fig. 253

Fig. 254

Fig. 255

Fig. 256

Room A Finds:

Fig. 250   Fragment of relief ware   P58.451.

Fig. 251   Fragment of kantharos handle, red on red-buff fabric   P58.372.

Fig. 252   Fragments of Hellenistic plate rim   P58.409.

Fig. 253   Fragment of Lydian Protogeometric red ware   P58.407.

Fig. 254   Foot and body fragments of Lydian bowl P58.391.

Fig. 255   Rim fragments of red Lydian crater   P58.388.

Fig. 256   Fragment of Lydian plate   P58.501.

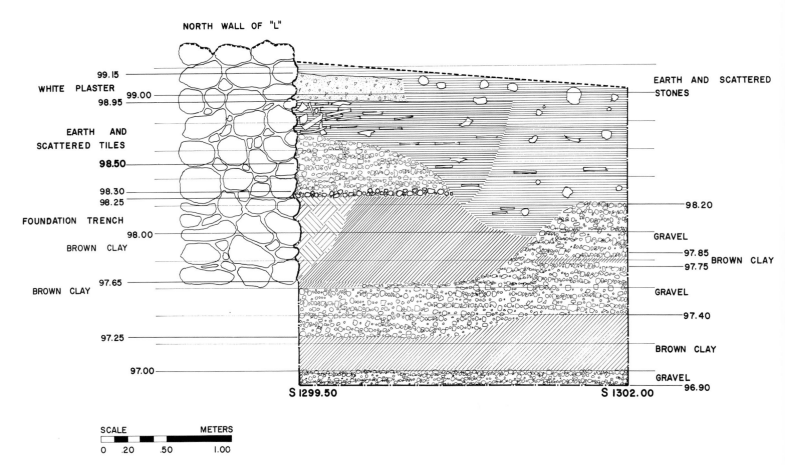

NORTH WALL OF "L"

99.15
WHITE PLASTER
99.00
98.95

EARTH AND
SCATTERED TILES
98.50

98.30
98.25

FOUNDATION TRENCH

98.00
BROWN CLAY

BROWN CLAY
97.65

97.25

97.00

S 1299.50

EARTH AND SCATTERED
STONES

98.20

GRAVEL
97.85
BROWN CLAY
97.75

GRAVEL

97.40

BROWN CLAY

GRAVEL
96.90

S 1302.00

SCALE   METERS
0   .20   .50   1.00

Fig. 257   Building L. Section of pit in Room B, N part of E face.

Building L

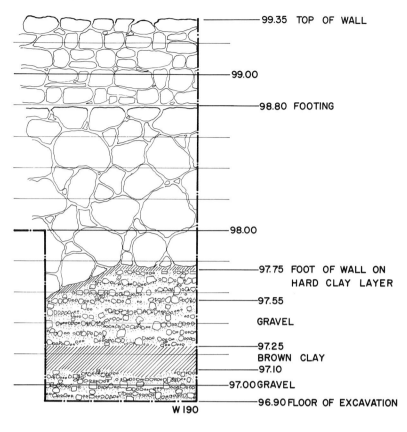

NORTH WALL OF "L"

99.35 TOP OF WALL

99.00

98.80 FOOTING

98.00

97.75 FOOT OF WALL ON
HARD CLAY LAYER

97.55

GRAVEL

97.25
BROWN CLAY
97.10

97.00 GRAVEL

96.90 FLOOR OF EXCAVATION

W 190

SCALE   METERS

0   .20   .50   1.00

Fig. 258 Section of pit in Room B, N face.

Fig. 259

Fig. 260

Fig. 261

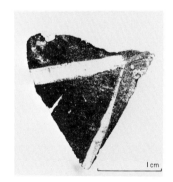

Fig. 262

Fig. 263

Room B Finds:

Fig. 259 Fragment of Attic Greek black-glazed cup P58.405.

Fig. 260 Byzantine bowl foot, interior   P58.413.

Fig. 261 Roman bowl fragment with inverted rim   P68.45.

Fig. 262 Base of Hellenistic omphalos bowl, exterior P68.55.

Fig. 263 Nozzle of Hellenistic lamp   L58.30.

Building L

Fig. 264 Room C. Patch of wall plaster over mortared rubble wall.

Fig. 265 Rooms F and E in foreground; B and C in background. Looking N.

Fig. 266   Room J in foreground; Rooms G and D in background. Looking N.

Fig. 267   Wall *c* of Room E at break, looking NE.

Fig. 268   Door between Rooms E and I (wall *e*).

Building L

Fig. 269   SE corner of Room G with walls *d, f,* and *g,* looking SE.

Fig. 270   Fragment of relief ware rim from Room C
P58.549.

Fig. 272   Black-gloss plate fragment from Room E
P68.187.

Figure 271   Lamp handle with
acanthus pattern from Room E
L68.20.

Building L

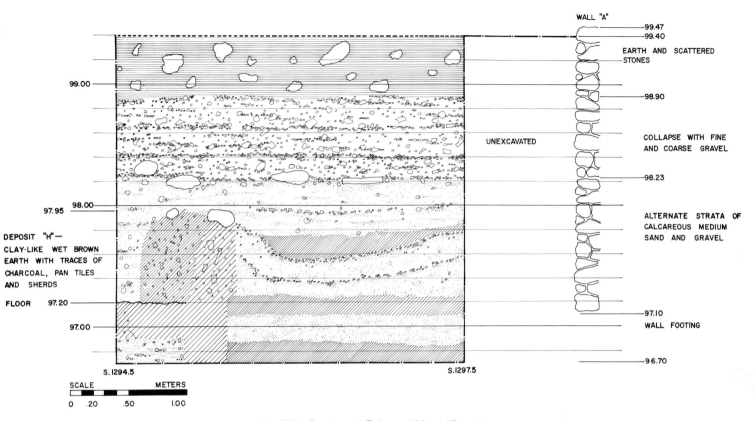

DEPOSIT "H" —
CLAY-LIKE WET BROWN
EARTH WITH TRACES OF
CHARCOAL, PAN TILES
AND SHERDS

FLOOR 97.20

WALL "A"

99.47
99.40

EARTH AND SCATTERED STONES

99.00

98.90

UNEXCAVATED

COLLAPSE WITH FINE AND COARSE GRAVEL

98.23

97.95 98.00

ALTERNATE STRATA OF CALCAREOUS MEDIUM SAND AND GRAVEL

97.00

97.10

WALL FOOTING

96.70

S.1294.5   S.1297.5

SCALE   METERS
0   .20   .50   1.00

Fig. 273   Section of E face of North Trench.

Fig. 274   North Trench. Showing deep pit, looking E.

Fig. 275 Top and collar fragment of "Ephesus" lamp from Room G   L58.53.

Fig. 276

Fig. 277

Fig. 278

Fig. 280

Fig. 279

b.   a.

Fig. 281

North Trench Finds:

Fig. 276   Lamp fragment   L58.5.

Fig. 277   Lamp fragment, rim and open reservoir
L58.31.

Fig. 278   Fragment of Lydian(?) jug   P58.500.

Fig. 279   Fragments of red relief ware   P58.358.

Fig. 280   Fragment of Greek black-glazed ware   P58.474a.

Fig. 281   Terracotta loom weights   T58.19 and T58.20.

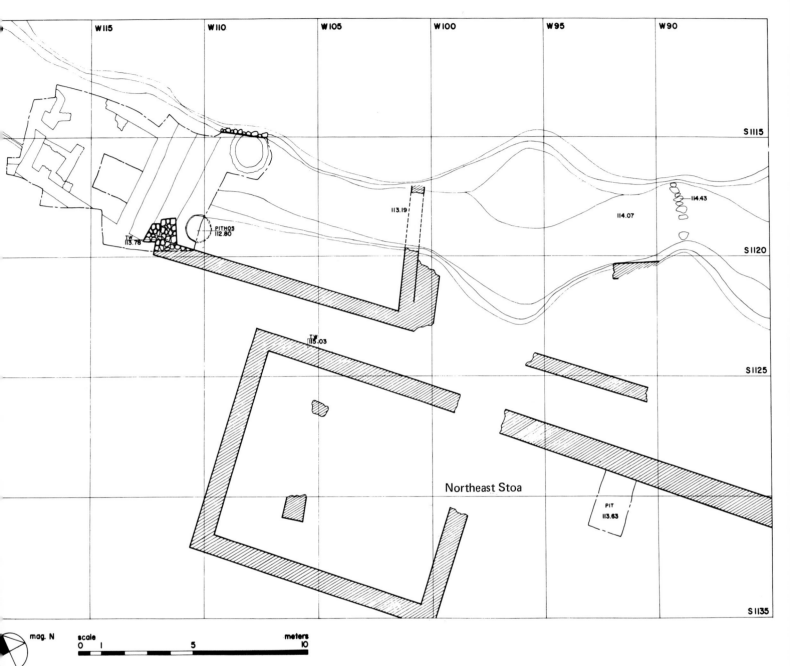

Fig. 282 Northeast Wadi, plan of excavated remains.

Northeast Wadi

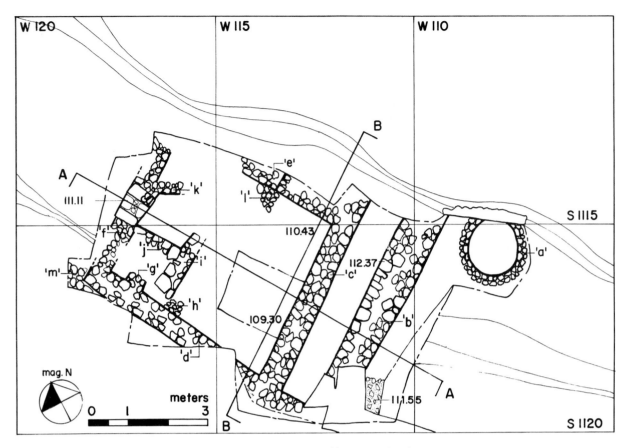

Fig. 283 Plan of pre-Hellenistic level.

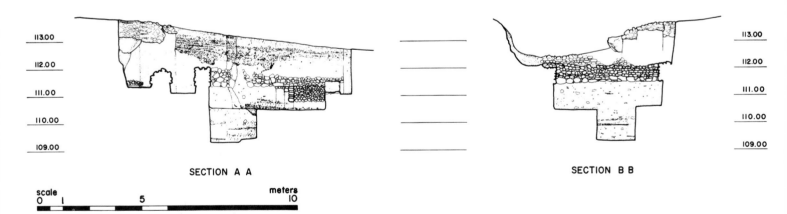

SECTION A A

SECTION B B

Fig. 284 Sectional-elevation.

Fig. 285   General view.

Fig. 286   Pithos *in situ.*

Fig. 287

Fig. 288

Northeast Wadi

Objects from Pithos, Fig. 286:

Fig. 287   Unguentarium with ring foot   P69.13.

Fig. 288   Dolphin vase attachment   P69.12.

Fig. 289   Terracotta bust of a woman   T69.3.

Fig. 290   Profile, Fig. 289.

Fig. 291   Terracotta head of a child   T69.4.

Fig. 289

Fig. 290

Fig. 291

Fig. 292   Butler's trench exposing NEW. After *Sardis* I (1922) ill. 169.

Northeast Wadi

Fig. 293   Circular wall *a,* looking NE.

Fig. 294   West end of trench, looking NW.

Northeast Wadi

Fig. 296   NW part of trench, doorway(?), looking NNE.

Fig. 295   Scarp of trench and S scarp of pit, looking SE.

Fig. 297   Underground storage unit, looking NW.

Northeast Wadi

Fig. 298   Doorway to underground storage unit, looking SE.

Fig. 299   View of Lydian pottery *in situ*.

Fig. 300   Wild Goat fragment *in situ*.

Fig. 301

Fig. 302

Fig. 303

Fig. 304

Fig. 305

Northeast Wadi

Pottery from Pre-Hellenistic Deposit:

Fig. 301 Shoulder fragment of "Rhodian" sub-Geometric oinochoe   P69.89a.

Fig. 302 Neck and body fragments of bichrome crater P69.90.

Fig. 303 Fragments of Orientalizing skyphos-bowl P69.44.

Fig. 304 Fragments of Orientalizing lebes   P69.48.

Fig. 305 Rim fragment of Orientalizing dish   P69.88.

Fig. 306 Northeast Wadi. Deposit of pottery *in situ* between walls *b* and *c.*

Fig. 307

Fig. 308

Fig. 309

Fig. 310

Fig. 311

Northeast Wadi

Pottery from Deposit, Fig. 306:

Fig. 307   Shoulder and body fragment of Orientalizing amphora   P69.71.

Fig. 308   Lydian round-mouth oinochoe   P69.58.

Fig. 309   Lydion   P69.82.

Fig. 310   Lydian column crater   P69.56.

Fig. 311   Lydian stand   P69.57.

Fig. 312   Lydian lamp with omphalos,
5th to 6th century B.C.   L69.7.

Northeast Wadi

Fig. 313   Shoulder and body
fragments of closed Orientalizing vessel   P69.28.

Fig. 314   Mid-body fragments of closed
Orientalizing vessel   P69.55.

Fig. 315   Mid-body fragments of closed Orientalizing
vessel   P69.73.

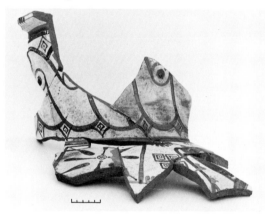

Fig. 316   Neck and shoulder fragments of large
Orientalizing amphora   P69.76A–K.

Fig. 317   Fragments of marbled
omphalos phiale   P69.47.

Fig. 318   Fragment of closed
Orientalizing vessel   P69.53.

Fig. 319   Bowl center fragment of
Chiot chalice   P69.84.

Fig. 320   General view of cemetery hill showing trench.

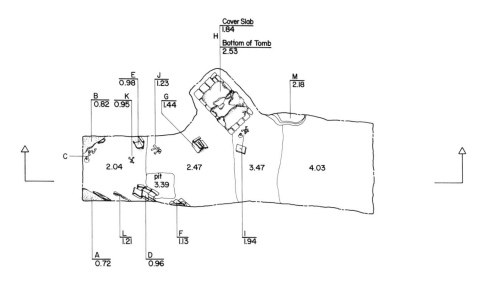

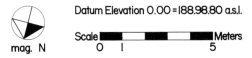

Datum Elevation 0.00 = 188.98.80 a.s.l.

Scale ▮▮▮▭▮▮▭▮▮ Meters
        0   1   5

mag. N

Fig. 321   Plan of cemetery.

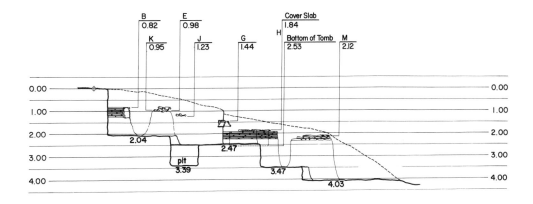

Datum Elevation 0.00=188.98.80 a.s.l.

Scale ▮▮▮▭▮▮▭▮▮ Meters
        0   1   5

Fig. 322   Sections of cemetery.

Kâgirlik Tepe

Fig. 323   Grave 58.B from NW.

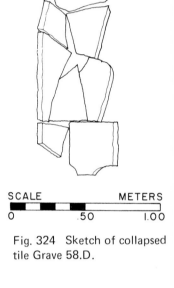

SCALE   METERS
0   .50   1.00

Fig. 324   Sketch of collapsed
tile Grave 58.D.

Fig. 325   Grave 58.H unopened with Grave 58.G to left.

Kâgirlik Tepe

Fig. 326   Grave 58.H opened, showing brick construction.

Fig. 327   Handle and rim fragment of lamp, 1st to 2nd century A.D.   L58.35.

Fig. 329   Fragment of Roman relief ware   P58.484.

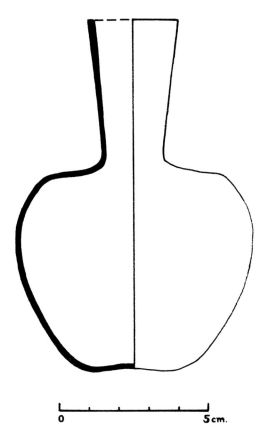

Fig. 328   Glass flask, 2nd to 3rd century A.D.   G58.14.

Fig. 330   Bronze finger ring   M58.58.

Fig. 331   General view.

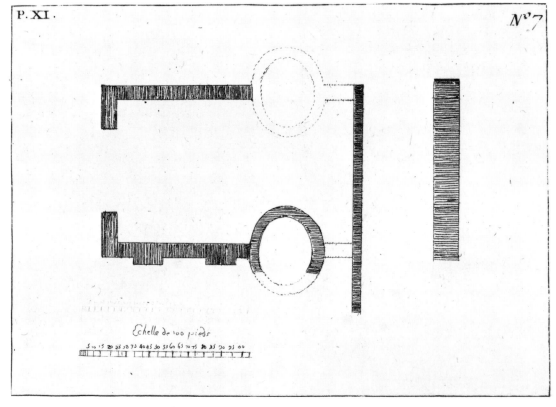

Fig. 332   Plan of CG. After Peyssonel, pl. XI.

Fig. 333 · View of CG in flood. After Le Bas, pl. 56–58.

Fig. 334   South face of CGE, showing piers and windows, looking N.

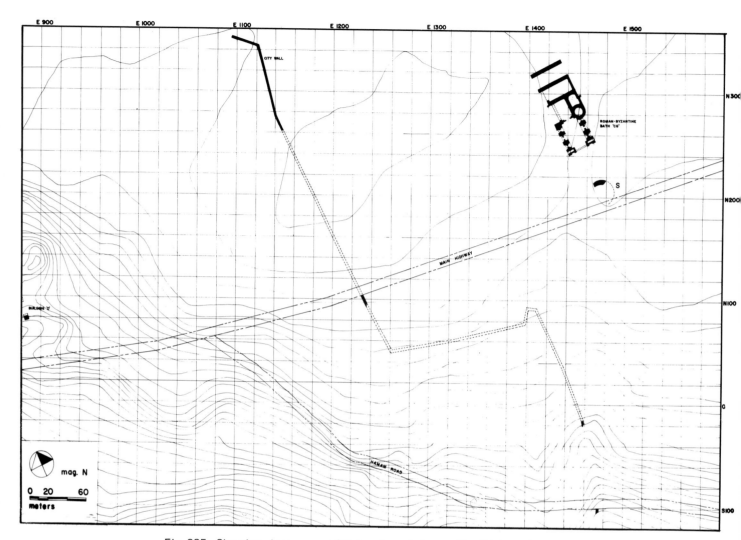

Fig. 335 Site plan. Area around CG showing relation to City Walls and main road.

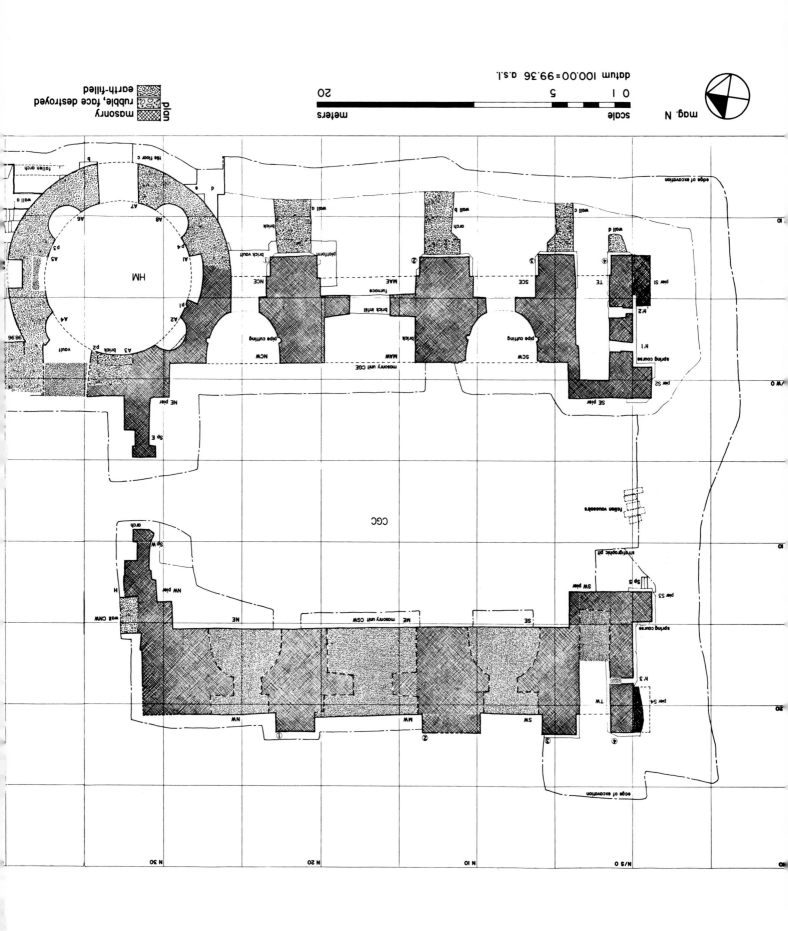

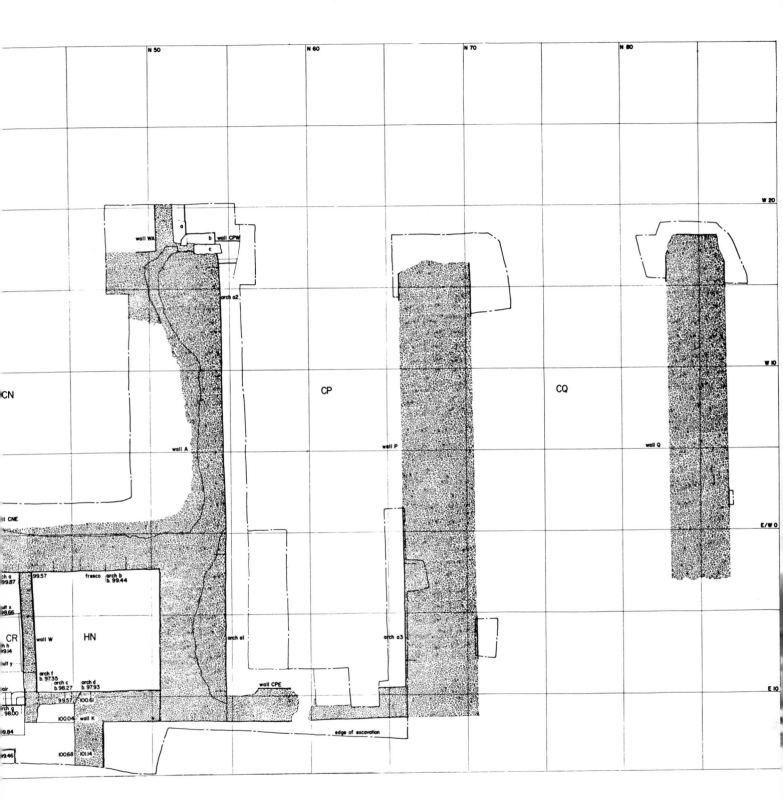

Fig. 336 General plan of excavated remains.

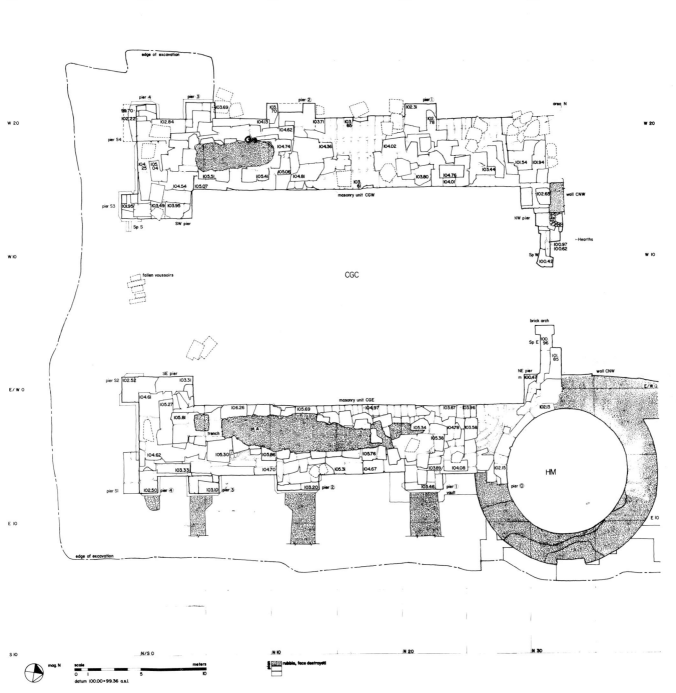

Fig. 337   Plan of top levels of Main Hall CGC.

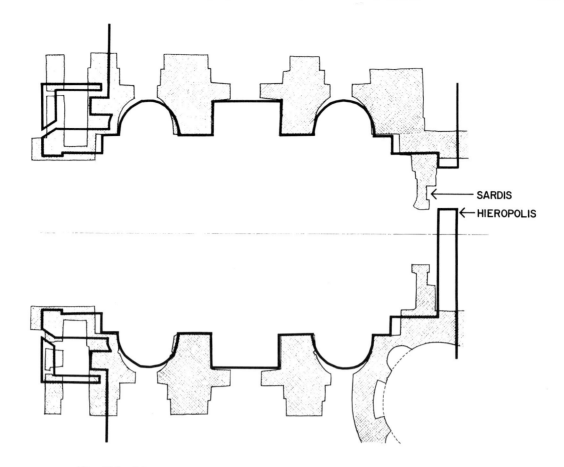

SARDIS

HIEROPOLIS

Fig. 338 CG and Hierapolis bath. Sketch plan showing comparative dimensions.

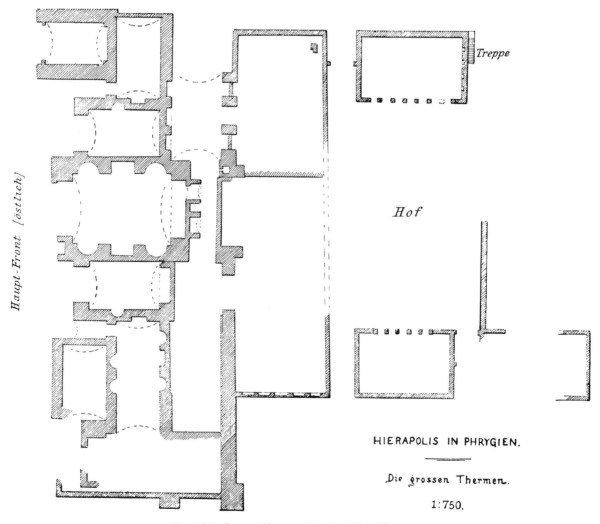

Haupt-Front. [östlich]

Treppe

Hof

HIERAPOLIS IN PHRYGIEN.

Die grossen Thermen.

1:750.

Fig. 339 Plan of Hierapolis bath. After Humann, 9.

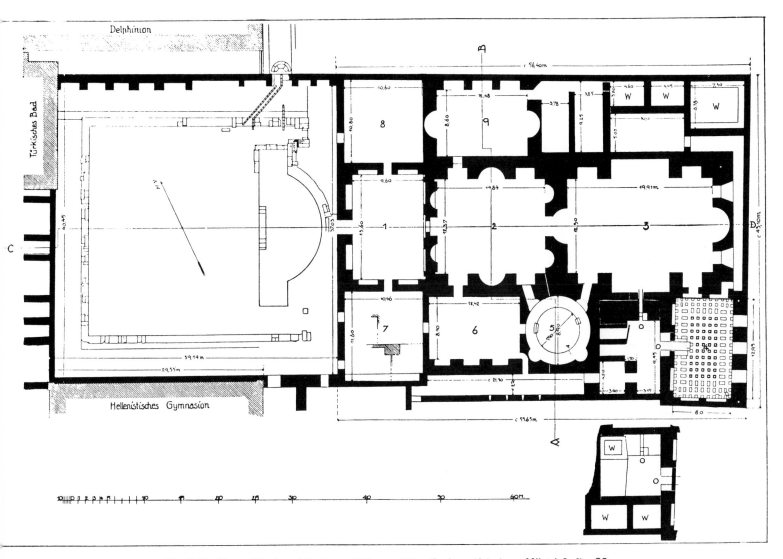

Fig. 340 Plan of Baths of Capito at Miletus. After Gerkan, Krischen, *Milet* I.9, fig. 29.

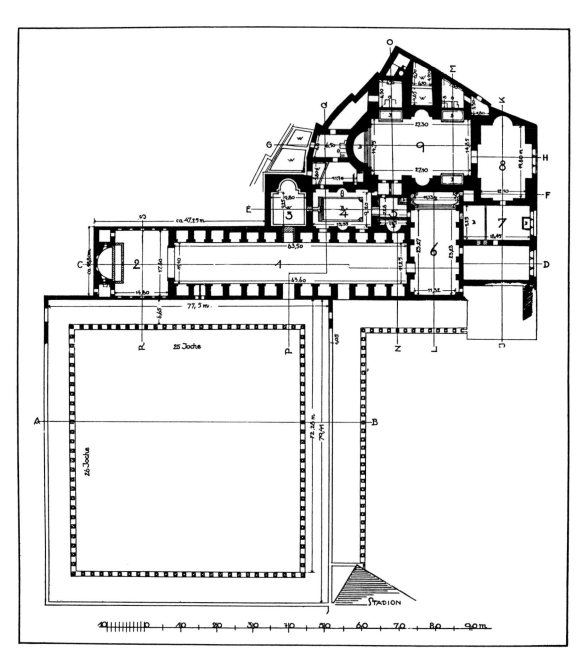

Fig. 341   Plan of Baths of Faustina at Miletus. After Gerkan, Krischen, *Milet* I.9, fig. 115.

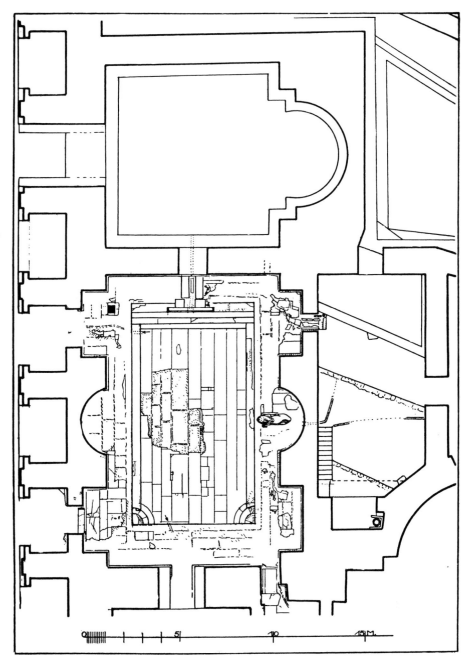

Fig. 342 Baths of Faustina at Miletus. Plan detail of frigidarium after Gerkan, Krischen, *Milet* I.9, fig. 85.

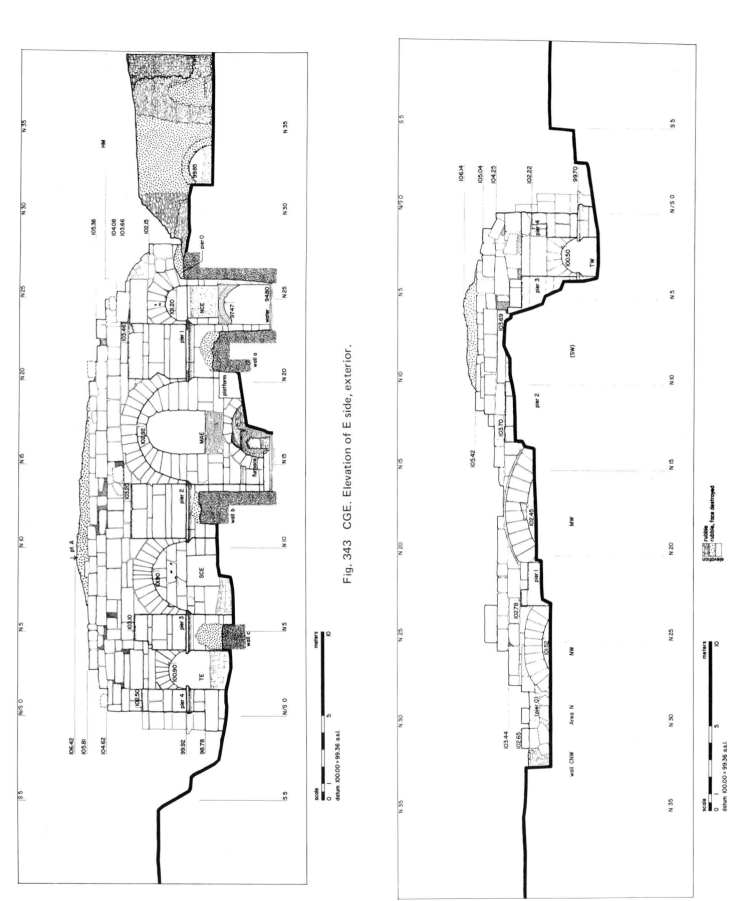

Fig. 343 CGE. Elevation of E side, exterior.

Fig. 344 CGW. Elevation of W side, exterior.

CGE

Fig. 345   General view of MAE, showing piers 1 and 2, rubble walls *a*, and *b*, and lower masonry arch.

Fig. 346   General view of NCE. Showing rubble wall *a*, outer S wall of HM, and lower brick arch.

Fig. 347   SW corner. Termination of string course profile.

Fig. 348   SE corner of CGW. Termination of string course profile
with screen wall SpS below.

Fig. 349   S end of CGC. Fallen voussoirs *in situ,* looking N.

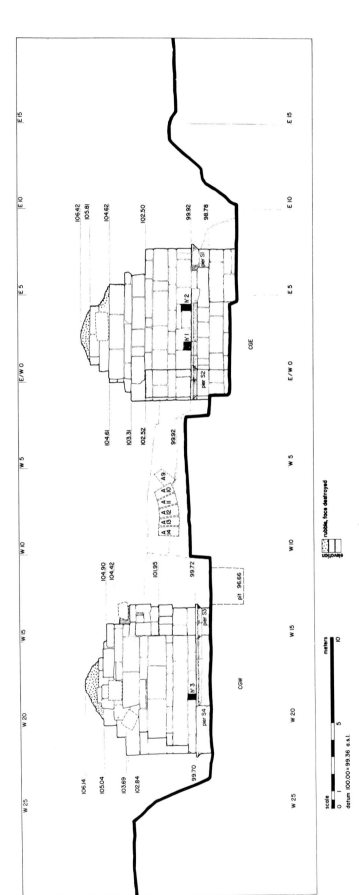

Fig. 350 S exterior elevation of CGC.

Fig. 351 Sections of niches, looking N.

CGE

Fig. 353 SCE, looking W.

Fig. 352 S side of rubble wall *b* showing "blind arch," looking N.

Bath CG

Fig. 355   Subfurnium area of MAE, looking SW.

Fig. 356   Detail of subfurnium area of MAE, looking N.

Fig. 357   Top of S end of CGE, showing rubble over masonry, looking S.

Fig. 358   Hierapolis baths. Wall of main hall showing springing of central vault and revetment pin holes.

Fig. 359 Bronze "plaques"   M59.56 and M59.57.

Fig. 362 Marble fragment with inscription   IN58.5

Fig. 360 Fragment of plain red ware lid   P58.394.

Fig. 363 Marble fragment with rosette   S58.27.

Fig. 361 Part of ring-foot bowl, Byzantine plain ware   P58.241.

Fig. 364 Red, ribbed jug   P59.519.

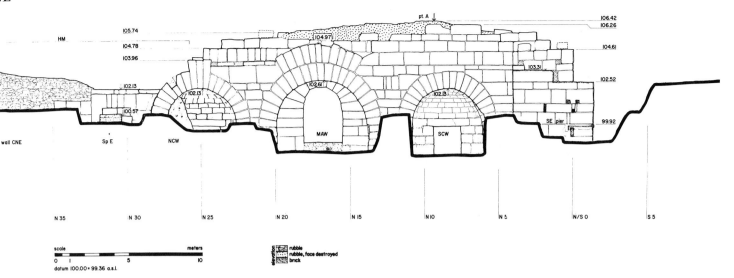

105.74 104.78 103.96 102.13 100.57 104.97 102.61 102.13 102.13 106.42 106.26 104.61 103.31 102.52 99.92

HM pt A

N 35   N 30   N 25   N 20   N 15   N 10   N 5   N/S 0   S 5

scale   meters
0 1   5   10
datum 100.00 = 99.36 a.s.l.

rubble
rubble, face destroyed
brick

Fig. 365   W elevation.

Fig. 366   SCW and wall above, showing revetment pin holes.

Fig. 367   MAW, looking E.

CGE

Fig. 368   W side, looking SE.

Fig. 369   S wall of SCW, showing patch of secondary brickwork (left of center), revetment pin holes (lower half), and drainpipe cutting (center).

Fig. 370   N side of MAW showing brickwork.

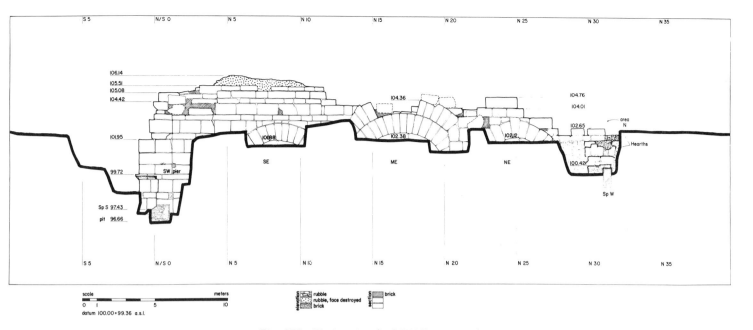

Fig. 371   W elevation (= CGW E elevation).

Fig. 372   Spurwall SpE, looking NE.

Fig. 373   Spurwall SpW, looking W.

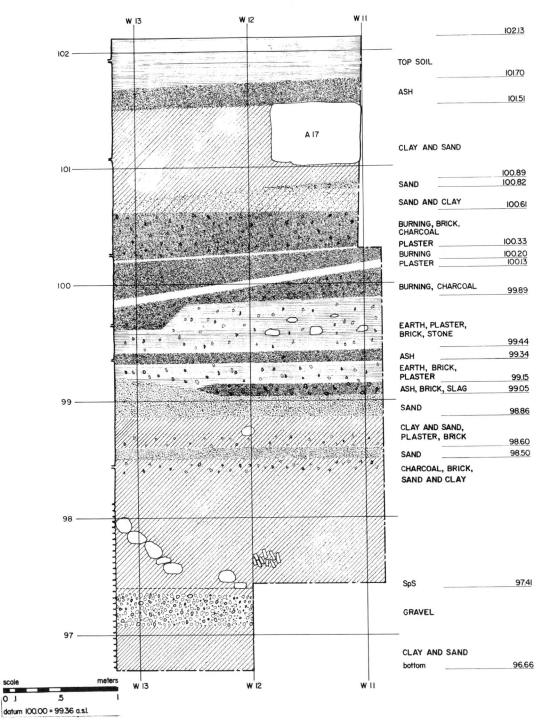

Fig. 374   CGW. Section of N face of stratigraphic pit at pier S 3.

Fig. 375 Hearth area of CGC.

Fig. 376

Fig. 379

Fig. 377

Fig. 380

Fig. 378

CGC Finds:

Fig. 376 Base of Middle Byzantine bowl, interior   P60.2.

Fig. 377 Fragment of Middle Byzantine bowl rim, interior   P60.3.

Fig. 378 Sculptured marble fragment   S58.3.

Fig. 379 Bronze "sacral instrument"   M60.4.

Fig. 380 Lead clamp anchor   M58.25.

Fig. 381

Fig. 382

SCW Finds:

Fig. 381 Middle Byzantine plate fragments, interior   P58.344.

Fig. 382 Iron knife   M58.22.

Fig. 383

Fig. 384

MAW Finds:

Fig. 383 Red ware fragments P58.361.

Fig. 384 Terracotta figurine of horseman   T58.25.

Fig. 385   SE outer side showing join with CGE, ashlar masonry and rubble.

Fig. 386   Top of masonry section.

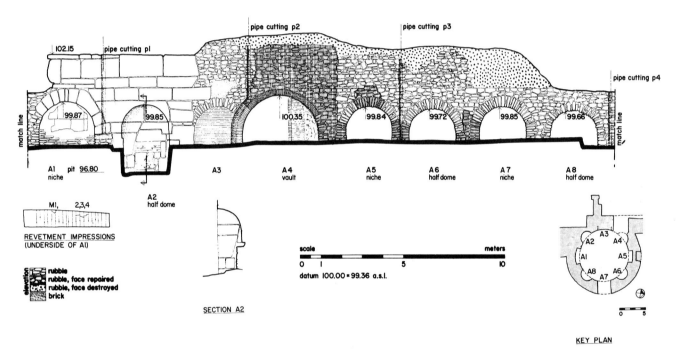

Fig. 387   HM. Interior elevation, details of revetment impressions, section of A 2.

Fig. 389 Fragments of revetment tiles *in situ* underside of A 1 on W.

Fig. 388 View of ashlar section showing pipe 1 between A 1 and A 2.

HM Finds:

Fig. 393   Red ware pine cone flask   P59.240.

Fig. 394   Fragment of Late Roman bowl with graffito   P59.253.

HM

Fig. 391   A 6, looking NE.

Fig. 392   Earlier voussoirs and later brickwork of A 3 exposed.

Fig. 395   Overall view of CR and HN, looking W.

Fig. 396   CR. N exterior wall of HM, showing springing of vault *y*, outer side of A 5, vault *x*, and wall W.

Fig. 396a   CR. Note brick arch set in A 5 (see arrow), removed in 1969.

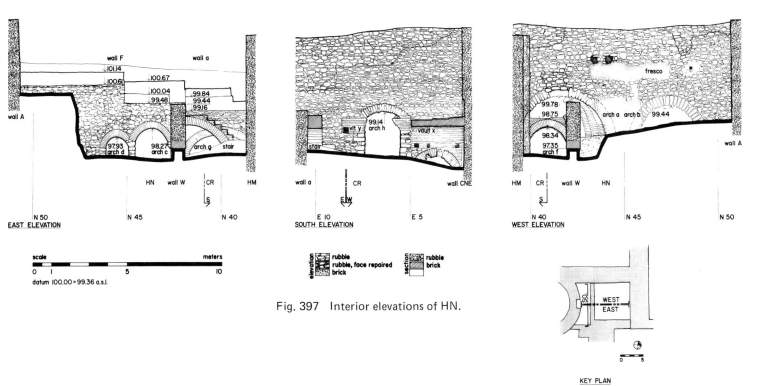

EAST ELEVATION

wall F — wall a

101.14
100.61
100.67
100.04
99.48
99.84
99.44
99.16

wall A

97.93 arch d 98.27 arch c arch g stair

HN   wall W   CR   HM   S

N 50   N 45   N 40

SOUTH ELEVATION

99.14 arch h vlt y vault x

stair

wall a   CR   E W   wall CNE

E 10   E 5

WEST ELEVATION

fresco

99.78 98.75 arch a arch b 99.44

98.34 97.35 arch f   wall A

HM   CR   wall W   HN   S

N 40   N 45   N 50

scale   meters
0 1   5   10
datum 100.00 = 99.36 a.s.l.

elevation: rubble / rubble, face repaired / brick
section: rubble / brick

Fig. 397   Interior elevations of HN.

KEY PLAN

WEST / EAST

0   5

Fig. 398   CR. Staircase St, arch *g* in wall *a*, wall W to left with arch *f* at bottom, looking E.

Fig. 399   CR. Detail of treads and lower landing of staircase St.

Fig. 400   Landings E of CR and HN, looking N.

Fig. 401   S, outer side of HM, looking N. Later brick and rubble
wall *d* extending eastward (to right).

Fig. 402　Wall CNE. Detail showing fresco traces *in situ* and two beam holes.

Fig. 403　Late Roman lamp
L60.47.

Fig. 404　Fragments of Middle Byzantine
bowl, exterior　　P59.232.

Fig. 405　Interior, Fig. 404.

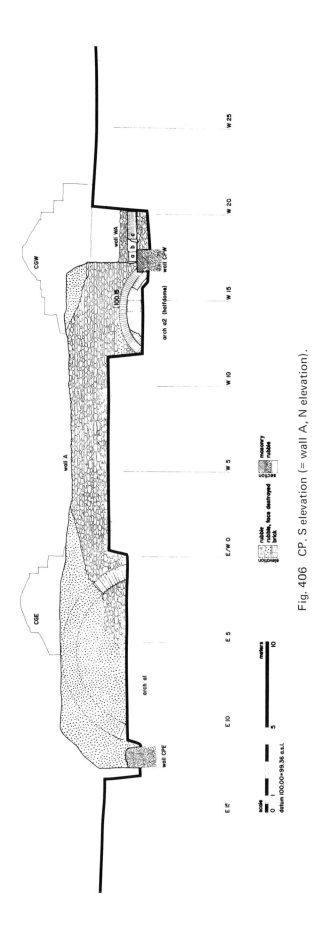

Fig. 406 CP. S elevation (= wall A, N elevation).

Fig. 407   CP. S side of wall P from above showing arch *a'3.*

Fig. 408   CQ. S face of wall Q at W end.

Fig. 409   Detail of block *b*.

Fig. 410   Half-dome under block *a* with marble slabs between.

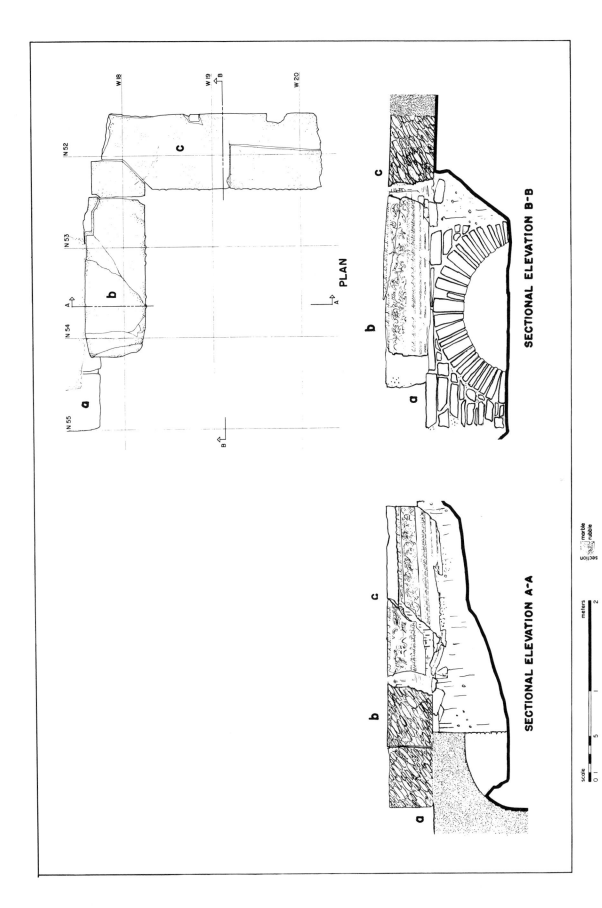

Fig. 411 Unit W of CP. Plan and sectional-elevations of marble blocks *a*, *b*, and *c*.

Fig. 412   Pier 2, looking N.

Fig. 413   N side of pier 1, showing bonding.

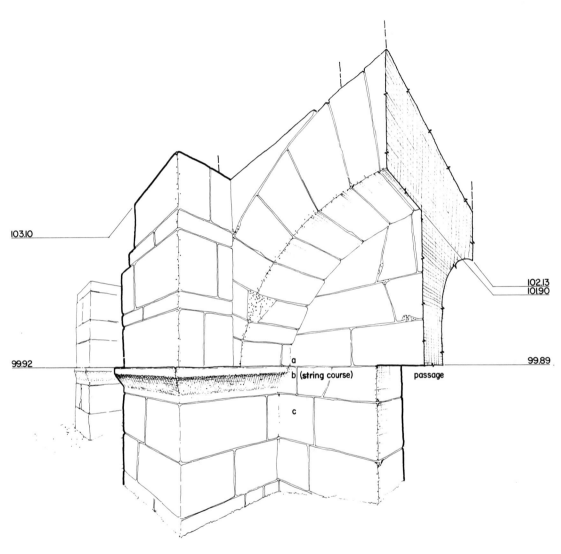

103.10

102.13
101.90

99.92

99.89

a

b (string course)

passage

c

datum 100.00=99.36 a.s.l.

Fig. 414   SCE. Detail of pier 3, showing bonding of stones *a, b,* and *c.*

CGE

Fig. 415 S side of pier 4, showing bonding.

Fig. 416 SE pier with large marble block just E of meter stick, looking E.

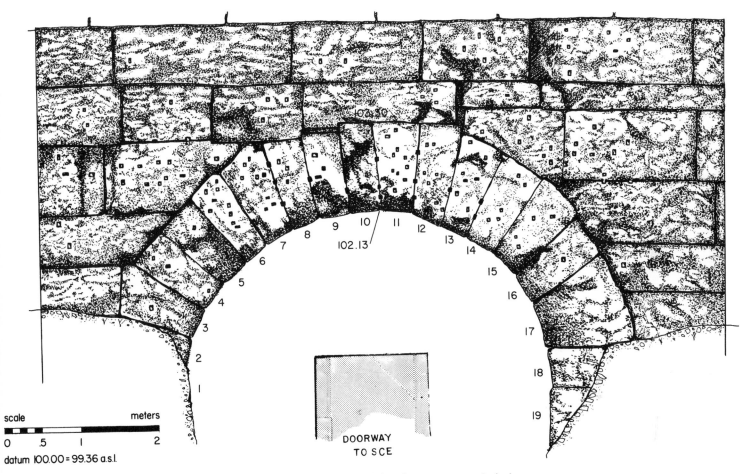

scale

meters

0   .5   1   2

datum 100.00 = 99.36 a.s.l.

Fig. 417   SCW. Elevation detail showing revetment pin holes.

Fig. 419 SCE. Detail showing lewis hole in stone above lintel.

Fig. 418 SCW. Detail of wedges in keystone.

Fig. 420 SCE/SCW N door jamb. Detail of tool marks of large point or punch.

Fig. 421 SCE. Marks of multiple claw chisel or hammer.

Fig. 422   N side of rubble wall *b.*

Fig. 423   HM. General view of A 1, looking S.

Fig. 424   HM. A 3 partly exposed showing joining of rubble and ashlar under grout above arch.

Fig. 425 TE. S side of interior, showing opening *h'2*.

Fig. 426 NCW. Exterior of dome, looking W.

Fig. 427 SCW. S side of interior showing details of holes.

Fig. 428   Reconstruction of CG wall painting by G. Bakir, 1959   WP60.1.

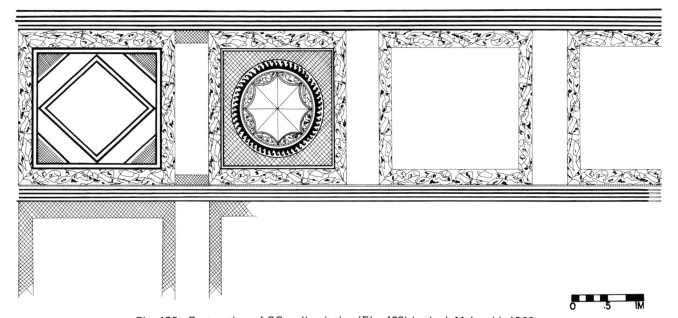

Fig. 429   Restoration of CG wall painting (Fig. 428) by L. J. Majewski, 1969.

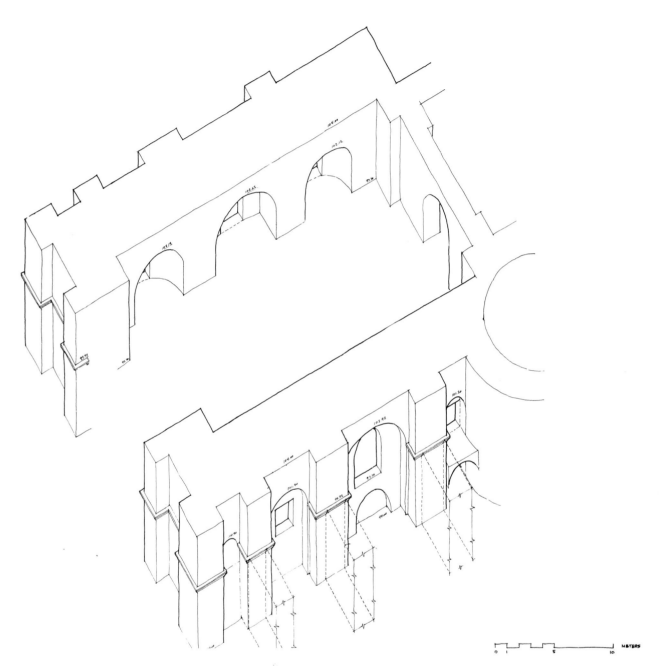

Fig. 430 Hypothetical reconstruction of Hall CGC.

Fig. 431   Corner of N face, looking SW.

Fig. 433   General view showing zigzag interior.

Fig. 432   Looking SW.

Wall S

Fig. 434   Grave 69.2 with two skeletons *in situ*.

Fig. 435   Grave 69.2 after excavation, showing tiles on bottom.

Fig. 436   IN69.14 *in situ*.